ENERGY FLASH

Simon Reynolds is the author of several highly acclaimed books about music, most recently *Rip It Up and Start Again: Postpunk 1978–84* and *Bring the Noise: 20 Years of Writing About Hip Rock and Hip Hop*. He is a freelance contributor to publications including the *New York Times*, the *Observer*, *Salon*, the *Guardian*, *Uncut*, and *The Wire*, and also operates the weblog Blissblog at http://blissout.blogspot.com. Born in London in 1963, he lives with his wife and two children in New York.

Energy Flash

A Journey Through Rave Music and Dance Culture

SIMON REYNOLDS

PICADOR

First published 1998 by Picador

This new edition published 2008 by Picador
an imprint of Pan Macmillan Ltd
Pan Macmillan, 20 New Wharf Road, London N1 9RR
Basingstoke and Oxford
Associated companies throughout the world
www.panmacmillan.com

ISBN 978-0-330-45420-9

A CIP catalogue record for this book is available from
the British Library.

Typeset by SetSystems Ltd, Saffron Walden, Essex
Printed and bound in Great Britain by
Mackays of Chatham plc, Chatham, Kent

to
joy

CONTENTS

For deleted scenes and further material related to *Energy Flash*, go to
http://energyflashbysimonreynolds.blogspot.com

List of Illustrations

Acknowledgements

Updated Edition

First up, thanks to Lee Brackstone for catalyzing the idea of *Energy Flash* Mark 2.

Thanks to my editor Richard Milner and to all at Picador, and to my agent Tony Peake.

The updated portions of *Energy Flash* 2008 draw on articles written between 1998 and the present. There are too many magazines and editors to mention, but in particular I would like to thank Heiko Hoffman at *Groove*, the *Wire* collective (Tony Herrington, Chris Bohn, Rob Young, Anne Hilde Neset), Chuck Eddy at *Village Voice*, and a series of music editors at *Spin* (Will Hermes, Sia Michel, Charles Aaron). 'Trance Mission' is partly based on a feature that appeared in *Spin* magazine, June 2000 and 'Two Steps Beyond' remixes material from features in *Spin* (November 2000) and *Vibe* (April 2001).

I'd also like to thank the inventors of Blogger for enabling me to waste thousands and thousands of hours of my life, in the process generating vast quantities of wordage and thoughtage on grime, micro-house, dubstep, and other facets of post-1998 dance culture, which have naturally fed into this updated *Energy Flash*. Seriously, though, Blogger – it's a wonderful thing, and it was both splendid and necessary to have an outlet while occupied with *Rip It Up and Start Again*.

An inventory of all the people I've had fruitful and fun conversations about dance music this past decade – in person and/or via email and/or through interblog debate – would make for a document running to several pages. But I must mention Paul Kennedy, Matthew 'Woebot' Ingram, Bat (a.k.a. Anindya Bhattacharyya), Luke 'Heronbone' Davis, Geeta Dayal, Michaelangelo Matos, Andy Battaglia, Tim Finney, Kevin Martin, Philip Sherburne, Simon 'Silverdollar' Hampson, Martin Clark, Mark 'K-Punk' Fisher, Tony Marcus, Nick 'Gutterbreakz' Edwards, Kode 9, Tobias Rapp, DJ Ripley and Kid Kameleon (big up ya chests for helping with the DJ chapter), Jess Harvell, Ronan Fitzgerald, DJ Clever, Derek Walmsley, Brendan M. Gillen. Many of these folk I've shared dance floors with. Thanks to all who turned me onto stuff through tips or acts of musical generosity. Extra-large big up to those who sent me pirate tapes from Blighty, *bless you all*, especially Bethan Cole, Burhan Tufail (RIP, miss you), Simon Silverdollar, Luke Heronbone . . .

And of course, it goes almost without saying, but I'll say it: love and thanks to my wife Joy Press, my boy Kieran and my little girl Tasmin.

Original Edition

Massive shout to Sam Batra for getting me into this raving caper in the first place; thanks for all the adventures. Big shouts to the rest of the Batra possee (Claire Brighton, Tom Vaughan, Glenda Richards) and other clubbing comrades (Susan Masters, Jane Lyons), not forgetting the original jungle-theory crew (Kodwo Eshun, Rupert Howe).

Thanks to the following for providing information/contracts/clippings, loaning/taping records or radio transmissions, general theory-stim, and diverse forms of assistance: Adrian Burns, Jill Mingo, Sarah Champion, Kodwo Eshun, Jim Tremayne @ *DJ Times*, Rupert Howe, Jones, David Pescovits, David J. Prince, Steve Redhead, Pat Blashill, Rick Salzer, Erik Davis, Chris Scott, Dave Howell, Stephanie Smiley @ Domestic, Burhan Tufail, Achim Szepanski, Daniel Gish, Sebastian Vaughan @ Network 23, Tom Vaughan, Mike Rubin, Bat (A. Bhattacharyya), Chris Sharp, Barney Hoskyns, Matt Worley, and Ian Gittins. Apologies to anyone I forgot.

Special thanks to my brother Jez Reynolds for the music-technology low-down and for taking us to Even Furthur, to my parents Sydney Reynolds and Jenny Reynolds for the cuttings supply, and to Louise Gray for the archival material.

Extra special thanks to my wife Joy Press for keeping my spirits up, cracking the whip, being the book's first reader, and generally acting as the serotinin in my life.

Gratuitous shout to Foul Play for making (and remixing) some of the rushiest records of all time. Condolences to FP's John Morrow concerning the tragid death of partner Steven Bradshaw in August 1997.

Thanks to those who granted interviews specifically for this book: Juan Atkins, Derrick May, Eddie 'Flashin'' Fowlkes, Kevin Saunderson,

Carl Craig, James Pennington, Mark Moore, Paul Oakenfold, Barry Ashworth, Louise Gray, Mr C, Jay Pender, Joe Wieczorek, Gavin Hills, Jack Barron, Helen Mead, Steve Beckett, Doug Baird of Spiral Tribe, Chantal Passamonte, Dego McFarlane, Marcus formerly of Don FM, Jeff Mills, Richie Hawtin, John Aquaviva, Wade Hampton, Frankie Bones, Heather Hart, Dennis 'the Menace' Catalfumo, DB, Scotto, Jody Radzik, Nick Philip, Malachy O'Brien, Scott and Robbie Hardkiss, Steve Levy, Todd C. Roberts, Les Borsai, Daven Michaels.

This book contains 'samples' from my journalistic output of the last ten years. Thanks to the following editors for giving me the space to explore ideas: Mark Sinker and Tony Herrington at *The Wire*, David Frankel and Jack Bankowsky at *Artforum*, Matthew Slotover at *Frieze*, Ann Powers and Eric Weisbard at *Village Voice*, Matthew Collin and Avril Mair at *iD*, Paul Lester at *Melody Maker*, Nick Terry at *The Lizard*, and Philip Watson at *GQ*. (Parts of Chapter 11: Marching Into Madness first appeared as 'Gabba Gabba Haze' in *GQ*, October 1996.)

Thanks to my agents Tony Peake and Ira Silverberg, and editors Michael Pietsch (USA) and Richard Milner (UK).

Author's Note

This expanded edition of *Energy Flash* does not contain the discography or bibliography in the original 1998 version. Partly this is for reasons of space, but also because during the ten years since the book came out, the unevenness of the original discography has become steadily more apparent, and the idea of rectifying that (let alone expanding it to cover the last decade) made me feel all weak at the knees. For those who feel the absence, go to http://energyflashdiscogbibliog.blogspot.com, where you will find the original discography and bibliography. The latter is enhanced with a further reading list, a selection of useful books and significant articles that have come out since *Energy Flash* was first published.

Preface to the Updated Edition

Every so often this past decade, someone has asked me what I'd do differently if I was writing *Energy Flash* now – what do I feel I missed? Is there anything I got wrong or where my ideas have turned 180 degrees? And usually I'll make some noises about maybe making the book a bit more comprehensive and impartial: having more on house as it diversified in the nineties, being less dismissive of trance and progressive. Or I'll say that I would maybe deal more with the prehistory of rave: the 'street sounds' culture of the UK in the eighties, electro and things like that; post-disco club styles; or the way industrial in America and Electronic Body Music in Europe fed into rave.

If I had actually done all this, *Energy Flash* would certainly be more even-handed and authoritative. It would probably be twice the size. But it would be half the book. Because what makes *Energy Flash* work is the partisan zeal burning through it, the unbalanced ardour for one particular sector of electronic dance culture: hardcore rave and all it spawned. This is what makes the book an authentic testament of obsession and belief. And if you think about it, that's how all true musical fandom manifests. In the abstract, I'm patriotic for dance culture as a whole; I'm on its side, every last bit of it. But in practice, there're certain zones that I really feel passionate about. And that's how it is with rock fans and hip-hop fans too. In certain contexts, rap or rock as a whole is the Cause, something you stand by. But once the focus shifts internal to the genre, your passion is focused around certain areas or artists. Other subgenres within the larger formation now become the enemy, because they are letting down the side; they don't live up to all that rock/rap/rave can be. Hence the oscillation within *Energy Flash* between bigging up the Rave-Dance-Electronic Project as a whole and championing particular strands of it, those genres I consider the forward sectors.

This tension between impartial and partial also comes about because I'm what social anthropologists call a 'participant observer'. My, cough, methodology is to get involved with the subjects of my research (dance subcultures) in their natural environment (clubs, raves), where I throw myself wholeheartedly into the rituals while standing slightly outside them. It's a tricky place to write from, and the result, in *Energy Flash*, is a constant shifting back and forth between calm 'omniscience' and enflamed monomania. But I wouldn't want to have one without the other. Neither an academic study nor a 'Generation E' memoir but some impossible mishmash of the two is the goal.

This updated and expanded incarnation of *Energy Flash* doesn't alter the main body of the book as published in 1998 (except for correcting a few errors) but adds four new chapters covering what happened in the last decade: the resurgence of trance, the 2step garage explosion, the retro-electro eighties revival, and – in a sweeping overview – the crisis and consolidation of dance culture that took place this decade and the emergence of noughties-defining genres like microhouse, breakcore, grime and dubstep. Restored to this edition is a chapter on DJing and remixing which originally appeared only in the American version of the book but is here updated to include developments since 1998. Finally, there's a megamix of my general and theoretical ideas about dance culture, woven partly from interviews given over the last ten years, and constructed as a dialogue with an imaginary interlocutor.

If the tone in the new material added to *Energy Flash* shifts discernibly towards the objective, it's still pretty clear what my bias is: each new development is ultimately measured against the early nineties surge-phase of rave. Over the years since *Energy Flash* came out, loads of people have contacted me because of the book, and I've noticed that people touched by the rave adventure seem to have a compulsion to narrativize their experiences, turn all that glorious disorder into a coherent story, their own journey through rave music and dance culture. So if at times my undying allegiance to hardcore seems to distort my perception, all I can say is: *This is my truth. Tell me yours.*

Simon Reynolds
May 2007

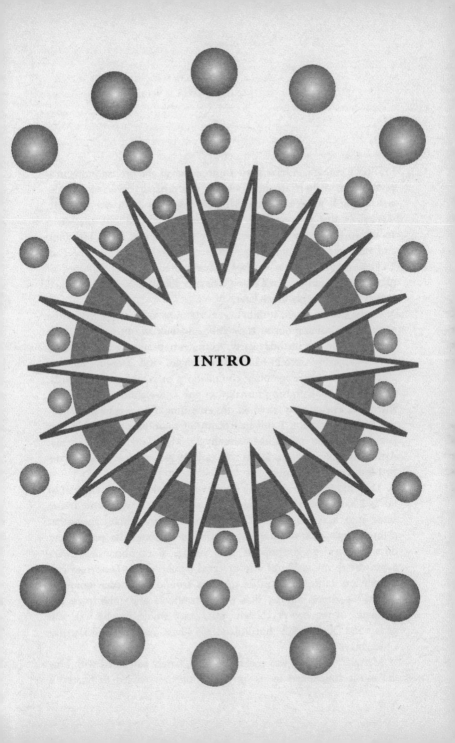

INTRO

I'm lucky enough to have gotten into music at the precise moment – punk's immediate aftermath – when it was generally believed that 'the way forward' for rock involved borrowing ideas from dance music. 'Lucky', in that I arrived too late to get brainwashed with the 'disco sucks' worldview. My first albums were all post-punk forays into funk and dub terrain: Public Image Limited's *Metal Box*, The Slits' *Cut*, Talking Heads' *Remain In Light*. Any mercifully brief fantasies of playing in a band involved being a bassist, like Jah Wobble; I learned to play air guitar only much later.

In the early eighties, it didn't seem aberrant to be as excited by the electro-funk coming out of New York on labels like Prelude, as I was by The Fall or The Birthday Party. As much time and money went into hunter-gathering second-hand disco singles and Donna Summer albums, as sixties garage-punk compilations or records by The Byrds. Starting out as a music journalist in the late eighties, most of my rhetorical energy was devoted to crusading for a resurgent neo-psychedelic rock. But I still had plenty of spare passion for hip hop and proto-house artists like Schoolly D, Mantronix, Public Enemy, Arthur Russell and Nitro Deluxe. In early 1988 I even wrote one of the first features on acid house.

That said, my take on dance music was fundamentally rockist, in so far as I had never really engaged with the milieu in which the music came into its own: clubs. This was perhaps forgivable, given that eighties 'style culture' dominated London clubland. Its posing and door policies, go-go imports and vintage funk obscurities, were anathema to my vision of a resurrected psychedelia, a Dionysian cult of oblivion. Little did I realize that just around the corner loomed a *psychedelic dance* culture; that the instruments and time-space co-ordinates of the neo-psychedelic resurgence would not be wah-wah pedals and Detroit 1969, but Roland 303's bass-machines and Detroit/Chicago 1987.

My take on dance was rockist because, barely aquainted with how the music functioned in its 'proper' context, I tended to fixate on singular artists. This is how rock critics still tend to engage with dance music: they look for the auteur–geniuses who seem most promising in terms of long-term, album-based careers. But dance scenes simply don't work like this: the 12-inch single is what counts, there's little brand loyalty to artists, and DJs are more of a focal point for fans than the faceless, anonymous producers. In the three years before I engaged with rave culture on its own terrain and terms, I accordingly celebrated groups like 808 State, The Orb, The Shamen, Ultramarine, on the grounds that they were making music that made sense at home and at album length. Today I cringe to remember that, reviewing the second Bomb The Bass LP, I proposed the term 'progressive dance' to describe this new breed of album-oriented artist. Cringe, because this divide between so-called 'progressive' electronica and mere 'rave fodder' has since become for me the very definition of 'getting it completely wrong'.

I finally got it 'right' in 1991, as one drop in the demographic deluge that was 1991–2's Second Wave of Rave, carried along by the tide of formerly indie-rock friends who'd turned on, tuned in and freaked out. It was some revelation to experience this music in its proper context – as a component in a system. It was an entirely different and un-rock way of using music: the anthemic track rather than the album, the total flow of the DJ's mix, the alternative media of pirate radio and specialist record stores, music as a synergistic partner with drugs, and the whole magic/tragic cycle of living for the weekend and paying for it with the midweek comedown. There was a liberating joy in surrendering to the radical anonymity of the music, in not caring about the names of tracks or artists. The 'meaning' of the music pertained to the macro level of the entire culture, and it was so much huger than the sum of its parts.

'What we must lose now is this insidious, corrosive knowingness, this need to collect and contain. We must open our brains that have been stopped and plugged with random information, and once again must our limbs carve in air the patterns of their desire – not the calibrated measures and slick syncopation of jazz-funk but a carnal music of total release. We must make of joy once more a crime against the state.' This single paragraph by NME writer Barney Hoskyns, written about The Birthday Party in 1981, changed all my ideas about music. It set me on a quest for the kind of Dionysian spirit that Hoskyns located in The Birthday Party. As a fan I found it in Hendrix and The Stooges, as a critic in bands like The Young Gods, Pixies, My

Bloody Valentine, to name just a few. But apart from the odd bare-chested maniac or bloody-shirted mosher, I'd never witnessed the kind of physical abandon imagined by Hoskyns on any mass level.

The last place I'd expected to find a modern Dionysian tumult was in the cool-crippled context of dance music. But that's what I saw in 1991 at Progeny, one of a series of DJ-and-multi-band extravaganzas organized by The Shamen. The latter were pretty good, and Orbital's live improvisation around their spine-tingling classic 'Chime' was thrilling. But what really blew my mind were the DJs whipping up a *Sturm und Drang* with the *Carmina-Burana*-gone-Cubist bombast of hardcore techno, the light-beams intersecting to conjure frescoes in the air, and, above all, the crowd: nubile boys, stripped to the waist and iridescent with sweat, bobbing and weaving as though practising some arcane martial art; blissed girls, eyes closed, carving strange hieroglyphic patterns in the air. This was the Dionysian paroxysm programmed and looped for eternity.

My second, fatally addictive rave-alation occurred a few months later at a quadruple bill of top 1991 rave acts – N-Joi, K-Klass, Bassheads and M-People. This time, fully E'd up, I finally grasped in a visceral sense why the music was made the way it was: how certain tingly textures goosepimpled your skin and particular oscillator-riffs triggered the E-rush, the way the gaseous diva vocals mirrored your own gushing emotions. Finally, I understood ecstasy as a *sonic* science. And it became even more crystal clear that the audience was the star: that bloke over there doing fishy-finger-dancing was as much a part of the entertainment, the tableau, as the DJs or bands. Dance-moves spread through the crowd like superfast viruses. I was instantly entrained in a new kind of dancing – tics and spasms, twitches and jerks, the agitation of bodies broken down into separate components, then re-integrated at the level of the dancefloor *as a whole*. Each sub-individual part (a limb, a hand cocked like a pistol) was a cog in a collective 'desiring machine', interlocking with the sound-system's bass-throbs and sequencer-riffs. Unity and self-expression fused in a forcefield of pulsating, undulating euphoria.

Getting into the raving aspect of house and techno somewhat late had a peculiar effect: I found myself, as fan and critic, on the wrong side of the tracks. In class and age terms (as a middle-class 28-year-old), I should logically have gravitated towards 'progressive house' and 'intelligent techno', then being vaunted as the only alternative to the

degenerate excesses of hardcore rave. But, partly because I was a
neophyte still in the honeymoon phase of raving, and partly because of
a bias towards extremity in music, I found myself drawn ever deeper
into hardcore. Confronted by the condescension of the cognoscenti, I
developed my own counter-prejudice, which informs this entire book:
the conviction that hardcore scenes in dance culture are the real
creative motor of the music, and that self-proclaimed progressive
initiatives usually involve a backing away from the edge, a reversion to
more traditional ideas of 'musicality'. *Hardcore* is that nexus where a
number of attitudes and energies mesh: druggy hedonism, an instinc-
tively avant-garde surrender to the 'will' of technology, a 'fuck art, let's
dance' DJ-oriented funktionalism, a smidgeon of underclass rage.
Hardcore refers to different sounds in different countries and at
different times, but the word generally guarantees a stance of subcultural intransigence, a refusal to be co-opted or cop out.

In London circa 1991–2, hardcore referred to ultra-fast, breakbeat-
driven drug-noise, and it was abhorred by all right-thinking techno
hipsters. To me it was patently the most exhilaratingly strange and
deranged music of the nineties, a mad end-of-millennium channelling
of the spirit of punk (in the sixties garage and seventies Stooges/Pistols
senses) into the body of hip hop (breakbeats and bass). There's been
no small glee, let me tell you, in watching hardcore evolve into jungle
and drum and bass, and thereby win universal acclaim as the leading
edge of contemporary music.

But the experience of being in the 'wrong' place at the right time
has instilled a useful Pavlovian response: whenever I hear the word
'hardcore' (or synonyms like 'dark', 'ruffneck', 'cheesy') used to malign
a scene or sound, my ears prick up. Conversely, terms like 'progressive'
or 'intelligent' trigger the alarm bells: when an underground scene
starts talking this talk, it's usually a sign that it's gearing up to play the
media game as a prequel to buying into the trad music industry
structure of auteur-stars, concept albums and long-term careers. Above
all, it's a sign of impending musical debility, creeping self-importance
and the haemorrhaging away of fun. Hardcore scenes are strongest
when they remain remote from all of that, and instead thrive as
anonymous collectives, subcultural machines in which ideas circulate
back and forth between DJs and producers, and the genre evolves
incrementally, week by week.

What I'm proposing in this book is that music shaped by and for drug experiences (even *bad* drug experiences) can go further out precisely because it's not made with enduring 'art' status or avant-garde cachet as a goal. Hardcore rave's dancefloor functionalism and druggy hedonism make it more wildly warped than the output of most self-conscious experimentalists. In *Energy Flash*, I trace a continuum of hardcore that runs from the most machinic forms of house (jack tracks and acid tracks) through British and European rave styles like bleep-and-bass, breakbeat house, Belgian hardcore, jungle, gabba, big beat and speed garage. A lot of exquisite music was made outside this continuum, and is covered in this book. But I still believe that the essence of rave resides with 'hardcore pressure': the rave audience's demand for a soundtrack to going mental and getting fucked up.

This begs the question of whether the meaning of rave music is reducible to drugs, or even a single drug, Ecstasy. Does this music only make sense when the listener is under the influence? I don't believe that for a second; some of the most tripped-out dance music has been made by straight-edge types who rarely if ever touch an illegal substance (4 Hero, Dave Clarke and Josh Wink being only three of the most famous abstainers). At the same time, rave culture as a whole is barely conceivable without drugs, or at least without drug metaphors: by itself, the music *drugs* the listener.

Rave is more than music + drugs; it's a matrix of lifestyle, ritualized behaviour and beliefs. To the participant, it feels like a religion; from the standpoint of the mainstream observer, it looks more like a sinister cult. I think again of that declaration: 'we must make of joy a crime against the state'. In 1992, two aspects of underground rave that particularly thrilled and enthralled my imagination were literally crimes against the state: pirate radio, and the resurgence of illegal raves instigated by renegade sound-systems like Spiral Tribe.

What the London pirate stations and the free parties conjured up was the sense of rave as a vision quest. Both transformed mundane Britain, its dreary metropolitan thoroughfares and placid country lanes, into a cartography of adventure and forbidden pleasures. A huge part of the excitement of the rave lifestyle is the nocturnal itineraries that connect favourite clubs. Anyone who's ever been involved in rave has their own enchanted pathways: for my gang, one was the pilgrimage between two profane shrines, Labrynth and Trade. It was a journey between worlds – Labrynth's ultra-violet catacombs thronged with working-class East End teenagers, Trade's gay pleasuredome in the centre of London – but both, in their different ways, were *hardcore*. It's in these clubs that I experienced raving in its purest and most deranged form; blissfully ignorant of the DJs' identities or the tracks' names, lost in music, out-of-time.

These kind of experiences, shared by millions, can't really be documented, although the post-Irvine Welsh mania for 'rave fiction' has made an attempt. Most of this writing consists of thinly disguised drug memoirs, and as everybody knows, other people's drug anecdotes are as boring as their dreams. So how do you write the history of a culture that is fundamentally amnesiac and non-verbal? Unlike rock music, rave isn't oriented around lyrics; for the critic, this requires a shift of emphasis, so that you no longer ask what the music 'means' but how it *works*. What is the affective charge of a certain kind of bass sound, or particular rhythm? Rave music represents a fundamental break with rock, or at least the dominant English Lit and social realist paradigms of rock criticism, which focus on songs and storytelling. Where rock relates an experience (autobiographical or imaginary), rave *constructs* an experience. Bypassing interpretation, the listener is hurled into a vortex of heightened sensations, abstract emotions and artificial energies.

For some, this makes the idea of 'rave culture' a contradiction in terms. One might define 'culture' as something that tells you where you came from and where you're going, something that nourishes the spirit, imparts life-wisdom, and generally makes life habitable. Rave provokes the question: is it possible to base a culture around sensations rather than truths, fascination rather than meaning?

For all my believer's ardour, there's a thread of doubt running through this book. As an adult with Left-liberal allegiances, I worry sometimes whether recreational drug use is any kind of adequate basis for a culture, let alone a counterculture. Is rave simply about the dissipation of utopian energies into the void, or does the idealism it catalyses spill over into and transform ordinary life? Can the oceanic, 'only connect!' feelings experienced on the dancefloor be integrated into everyday struggles to be 'better at being human'? Learning to 'lose your self' can be an enlightenment, but it can also be strangely selfish: a greed for intense, ravishing experiences.

Dance culture has long been home to two radically opposed versions of what rave is 'all about'. On one side, the transcendentalist, neo-psychedelic discourse of higher planes of consciousness and oceanic merger with Humanity/Gaia/the Cosmos. On the other, Ecstasy and rave music slot into an emergent 'rush culture' of teenage kicks and cheap thrills: video-games; skateboarding, snow-boarding, bunjee jumping and other 'extreme sports'; blockbuster movies whose narratives are merely flimsy frameworks for the display of spectacular special effects.

For all my reservations about the spiritually corrupting and politically retreatist ramifications of rave culture, my own experience is different. Even as I cherish its power to empty my head, I've found this 'mindless' music endlessly thought-provoking. And despite its ostensibly escapist nature, rave has actually politicized me, made me think harder about questions of class, race, gender, technology. Mostly devoid of lyrics and almost never overtly political, rave music – like dub reggae and hip hop – uses sound and rhythm to construct psychic landscapes of exile and utopia. One of this book's themes is the utopian/dystopian dialectic running through Ecstasy culture, the way the hunger for heaven-on-earth almost always leads on to a 'darkside' phase of drug excess and paranoia.

Energy Flash strives to combine the thoughtless immediacy of my experiences in the thick of the scene, with the 'thinking around the subject' that ensued after the heat of the moment. As a history, it's an attempt to chronicle how this extraordinary culture coalesced into being, and to track how those strands have subsequently unravelled to form the current post-rave diaspora. But pulsing inside the text, its *raison d'être*, is the incandescent memory of amnesiac moments, dance-floor frenzies that propelled me outside time and history. *Bliss on.*

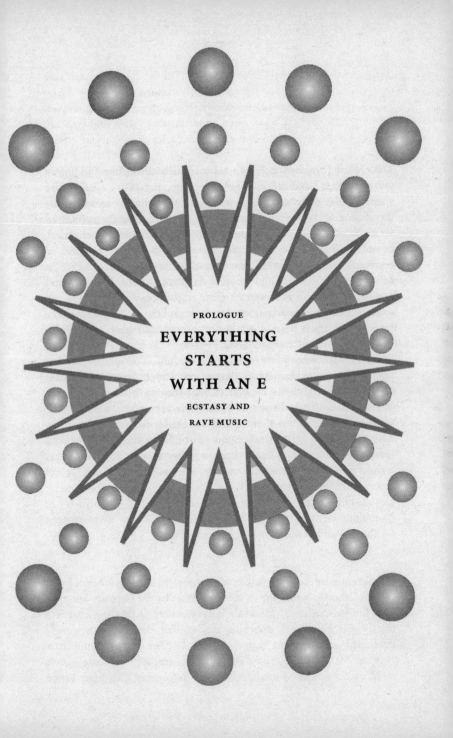

PROLOGUE

EVERYTHING STARTS WITH AN E

ECSTASY AND
RAVE MUSIC

The Oxford Dictionary defines ecstasy as 'an overwhelming feeling of joy or rapture,' and 'an emotional or religious frenzy or trance-like state.' In the early eighties, ecstasy acquired another meaning: the illegal drug MDMA, whose range of effects spans all of the definitions above. A 'psychedelic amphetamine', MDMA is a remarkable chemical, combining the sensory intensification and auditory enhancement of marijuana and low-dose LSD, the sleep-defying, energy-boosting effects of speed, and the uninhibited conviviality of alcohol. If that wasn't enough, MDMA offers unique effects of empathy and insight.

Depending on expectations and context, the Ecstasy experience ranges from open-hearted *tête-à-tête* through collective euphoria to full-blown mystical rapture. Used in therapy, Ecstasy can facilitate a profound experience of interpersonal communication and self-discovery. In the rave environment, Ecstasy acts as both party-igniting fun-fuel *non pareil* and the catalyst for ego-melting mass communion. What all these different uses of MDMA have in common is *ekstasis*: the Greek etymological root of ecstasy, its literal meaning is 'standing outside oneself'. MDMA takes you out of yourself and into blissful merger with something larger than the paltry, isolate 'I', whether that trans-individual is the couple-in-love, or the dancing crowd, or the cosmos. MDMA is the 'we' drug. It's no coincidence that Ecstasy escalated into a pop cultural phenomemon at the end of the go-for-it, go-it-alone eighties (the real Me Decade). For Ecstasy is the remedy for the alienation caused by an atomized society.

*

MDMA (methylenedioxymethamphetamine) was first synthesized and patented shortly before the First World War, by the German company Merck. One version of MDMA's history maintains that the drug was briefly prescribed as a slimming aid, another that it was originally developed as an appetite suppressant for German troops. If the latter is true, MDMA's aggression-diminishing, empathy-inducing effects would have quickly disqualified its use in combat situations. When it was used in the early nineties in experimental therapy sessions for traumatized Nicuaragran soldiers, 75 per cent of the subjects expressed a desire for peace and an end to war, with several talking of loving everyone, including the enemy. And in the 1950s, American military researchers experimented with MDMA's potential as a dis-orientation-drug, something that would psychologically disarm enemy troops.

The modern story of MDMA begins with its rediscovery in the early 1960s by Alexander Shulgin, widely regarded as 'the stepfather of Ecstasy'. Shulgin was then a biochemist working for Dow Chemicals and pursuing an interest in psychedelics on the sly. Later in the decade, he opened his own government-approved laboratory in San Francisco dedicated to the synthesis of new psycho-active substances, all of which he tested on himself and his wife/co-researcher, Ann. Shulgin soon became a prime mover in America's network of neuro-consciousness explorers. By 1976, the first reports on MDMA's therapeutic potential were appearing in medical journals. In the late seventies and early eighties, MDMA – then nicknamed Adam, because of the way it facilitated a sort of Edenic rebirth of the trusting and innocent 'inner child' – spread throughout a looseknit circuit of therapists in America. Used in marriage therapy and psychoanalysis, the drug proved highly beneficial. Advocates claimed that a five hour MDMA trip could help the patient work through emotional blockages that would otherwise have taken five months of weekly sessions.

Similar arguments had been made in favour of LSD, although the accent was on acid as a tool of spiritual discovery. Just like the 'serious' psychonauts of the sixties, Adam's evangelists hoped to restrict the use of the drug to clinically supervised sessions, while gradually campaigning for MDMA's medical legitimacy. But the more 'frivolous' potential of MDMA – its euphoria-inducing effects – couldn't be kept secret for long. By the early eighties, there was a fully fledged Ecstasy scene in Dallas and Austin nightclubs, and X (US slang for MDMA) was becoming an increasingly popular 'legal high' throughout America.

Inevitably the authorities clamped down. On 1 July 1985, MDMA was banned for one year. The DEA ignored the judge's recommendation that the drug be put in Schedule 3 and instead put it in its most dangerous category, Schedule 1; this outlaw status was sealed by the Federal Court of Appeals in 1988. In the UK, Ecstasy was already a Class A illegal drug alongside heroin and cocaine; this was because the

Misuse of Drugs Act 1971 (Modification) Order of 1977 applied to the whole family of chemicals to which MDMA belonged.

MDMA's therapeutic supporters protest that drug-war paranoia outlawed a miracle-drug with myriad benign applications. But the truth is that even before its illegalization, Ecstasy had already slipped decisively out of the custodianship of psychotherapy. Instead of being used as Shulgin and his allies had envisioned – in bonding sessions between couples, as a tool of personal discovery – Ecstasy proved to have other, infinitely more alluring applications. When large numbers of people took Ecstasy together, the drug catalysed a strange and wondrous atmosphere of *collective intimacy*, an electric sense of connection between complete strangers. Even more significantly, MDMA turned out to have a uniquely synergistic/synaesthetic interaction with music, especially uptempo, repetitive, electronic dance music.

All Loved-Up

In a quite literal sense, MDMA is an E-lectrifying experience, charging up the fantastically complex computer that is the human brain. The drug's effect on brain chemistry is to dramatically increase the availability of dopamine and serotonin, neurotransmitters which conduct electrical impulses between brain cells (aka neurons). Excess dopamine stimulates locomotor activity, revs up the metabolism and creates euphoria; serotonin usually regulates mood and well-being, but in excess it intensifies sensory stimuli and makes perceptions more vivid, sometimes to the point of hallucination.

Although MDMA floods the nervous system with dopamine (like speed) and serotonin (like LSD), it's more than just a 'psychedelic amphetamine'; when profit-minded dealers try to make pseudo-E cocktails out of speed and acid, their dodgy wares lack MDMA's famous 'warm glow'. Trying to convey this special attribute of MDMA, the drug's early therapeutic supporters coined new pharmaceutical classifications like *empathogen* (a feeling enhancer) and *entactogen* (literally 'touching within'; a substance that puts you in touch with others and yourself). Ecstasy has been hailed as 'penicillin for the psyche', as 'a stabilizer' rather than an upper, and as 'artificial sanity' that temporarily quietens the neurotic self, freeing the individual from anxiety and fear.

The Ecstasy trip divides into three distinct phases. Depending on the emptiness of your stomach, it takes approximately an hour to 'come up': the senses light up, you start 'rushing', and for a short while the experience can be overwhelming, with dizziness and mild nausea. Then there's the plateau stage, which lasts about four hours, followed by a long, gentle comedown, and an afterglow phase which can last well into the next day.

What you experience during the plateau phase is highly dependent on 'set and setting' (the early LSD evangelists' term for the mindset of the drug taker and the context in which the drug is taken). In a one-on-one session (lovers, close friends, analyst-and-analysand), the emphasis is on the breaking down of emotional defences, heart-to-heart intimacy, the freeflow of verbal and tactile affection. The first time I took Ecstasy was in a romantic, private context. The experience was so intense, so special, that I felt it would be sacrilegious to repeat it lest it become routinized, and it was over two years before I did it again.

At a rave, the emotional outpouring and huggy demonstrativeness is still a huge part of the MDMA experience (which is why ravers use the term 'loved-up'), but the intimacy is dispersed into a generalized bonhomie: you bond with the gang you came with, but also people you've never met. Anyone who's been to a rave knows the electric thrill of catching a stranger's eye, making contact through the shared glee of knowing that you're both buzzing off the same drug-music synergy. Part of what makes the classic rave experience so rewarding and so addictive are the 'superficial' but touching rituals of sharing water, shaking hands, having someone a tad worse for wear lean on you as if you were bosom buddies.

The blitz of noise and lights at a rave tilts the MDMA experience towards the drug's purely sensuous and sensational effects. With its mildly trippy, pre-hallucinogenic feel, Ecstasy makes colours, sounds, smells, tastes and tactile sensations more vivid (a classic indication that you've 'come up' is that chewing gum suddenly tastes horribly artificial). The experience combines clarity and a limpid, soft-focus radiance. Ecstasy also has a particular physical sensation that's hard to describe: an oozy yearn, a bliss-ache, a trembley effervesence that makes you feel like you've got champagne for blood.

All music sounds better on E – crisper and more distinct, but also engulfing in its immediacy. House and techno sound especially fabulous.

The music's emphasis on texture and timbre enhances the drug's mildly synaesthetic effects, so that sounds seem to caress the listener's skin. You feel like you're dancing inside the music; sound becomes a fluid medium in which you're immersed. Rave music's hypnotic beats and sequenced loops also make it perfectly suited to interact with another attribute of Ecstasy; recent research suggests that the drug stimulates the brain's 1b receptor, which encourages repetitive behaviour. Organized around the absence of crescendo or narrative progression, rave music instils a pleasurable tension, a rapt suspension that fits perfectly with the sustained pre-orgasmic plateau of the MDMA high.

These Ecstasy-enhancing aspects latent in house and techno were unintended by their original creators, and were only discovered accidentally by the first people who mixed the music and the drug. But over the years, rave music has gradually evolved into a self-conscious science of intensifying MDMA's sensations. House and techno producers have developed a drug-determined repertoire of effects, textures and riffs that are expressly designed to trigger the tingly rushes that traverse the Ecstatic body. Processes like EQing, filtering, pannning, phasing and the Aphex Aural Exciter are used to tweak the frequencies, harmonics and stereo-imaging of different sounds, making them leap out of the mix with an eerie three-dimensionality or glisten with a hallucinatory vividness. Today's house track is a forever-fluctuating, fractal mosaic of glow-pulses and flicker-riffs, a teasing tapestry whose different strands take turns to move in and out of the sonic spotlight. Experienced under the influence of MDMA, the effect is synaesthetic – like tremulous fingertips tantalizing the back of your neck, or like the simultaneously aural/tactile equivalent of a shimmer. In a sense, Ecstasy turns the entire body-surface into an ear, a ultra-sensitized membrane that responds to certain frequencies. Which is why the more funktionalist, drug-determined forms of rave music are arguably only really 'understood' (in a physical, non-intellectual sense) by the drugged, and are only really 'audible' on a big club sound-system that realizes the sensurround, immersive potential of the tracks.

Beyond its musical applications, Ecstasy is above all a *social* drug. It's rarely used by a solitary individual, because the feelings it unleashes have nowhere to go. (A friend of mine, bored, once took some left-over E at home on his own, and spent the night kissing the walls and hugging himself.) In the rave context, Ecstasy's urge-to-merge can spill over into an oceanic mysticism. Rave theorists talk of tribal consciousness, 'morphic resonance', an empathy that shades into the telepathic. Writing about his memories of London's most hedonistically crazed gay club, Trade, Richard Smith came up with the brilliant phrase 'a . . . communism of the emotions'. The closest I've had to a mystical experience occurred, funnily enough, at Trade. Borne aloft in the cradling rush of sound, swirled up and away into a cloud of unknowing, for the first time I truly *grasped* what it was to be 'lost in music'. There's a whole hour for which I can't account.

That night, I was on MDA, the more hallucinogenic parent drug of MDMA. With real Ecstasy, the psychedelic component of the experience is gentler, taking the form not of perceptual distortion but of a numinous glow. There's a sense of hyper-real immediacy, cleansed perceptions, the recovery of a child-like amazement at the here-and-now. This feeling of gnosis – being in the *know*, living in the *now* – can launch some Ecstasy-initiates on a journey of spiritual discovery beyond recreational drug use. Others return again and again to MDMA's enchantments, only to discover that the 'magic pill' has a dark side.

Ecstasy on Trial

In neurochemistry, there's no such thing as a free lunch; MDMA comes with a plethora of costs and catches. Most of MDMA's physical side-effects are merely irritating: dry mouth, jittery nerves, slight nausea (usually during the rush phase, then wearing off quickly). Most notable of all is jaw-tension, which results in 'bruxism' (teeth-grinding) or, with excessive intake, face-pulling. Ravers deal with this by furiously chewing gum or sucking on dummies. Although in the short-term Ecstasy has the opposite of a hangover (a delicious afterglow that lasts into the next day), the major repercussion of doing the drug is the comedown a few days later. Symptoms can include fatigue, emotional burn-out, irritability, and moodswings between elation and desolation that are comparable to heartbreak.

Dopamine (the speedy component of the experience) is more rapidly replaced in the brain than serotonin (the loved-up part). It takes about a week for serotonin levels to normalize. Taking Ecstasy is like going on an emotional spree, spending your happiness in advance. With irregular use, such extravagance isn't a problem. But with sustained and excessive use, the brain's serotonin levels become seriously depleted, so that it takes around six weeks' abstinence from MDMA to restore normal levels.

If you take E every day, within a few days the blissful, empathetic, serotonin glow wears off, leaving only the speedy, dopamine buzz; this in-built diminishing returns syndrome is one reason why MDMA isn't considered physically addictive. The honeymoon period with Ecstasy that most ravers enjoy can, however, create an emotional addiction, in so far as normal life seems dreary compared to the loved-up abandon of the weekend. This is when Ecstasy's potential for abuse enters the picture. Because the original blissed-out intensity of the early experiences never really returns, users are tempted to increase the dose, which only increases the speediness and amplifies the unpleasant side-effects. Serious hedonists get locked into a punishing cycle of weekend excess followed by the inevitable brutal midweek crash. As well as compulsive bingeing on E, many get drawn into compensatory poly-drug use – taking other substances to mimic the effects originally achieved by MDMA alone. Alongside the physical attrition wreaked by such a lifestyle – weight-loss, frequent illness caused by sleep-deprivation in tandem with the virus-fostering nature of hot, sweaty clubs – the long-term abuse of Ecstasy can also result in psychological damage: anxiety disorders, panic attacks, paranoia and depression.

Although MDMA may actually be far more dangerous for its psychological side-effects (some experts worry about a generation that will grow up to face higher rates of depression and suicide), the case against Ecstasy has mostly been pursued in terms of its physical risks. There is some evidence that Ecstasy affects the axons (containers in the brain that hold serotonin), but since no deleterious effects have been detected in long-term users' behaviour or neurology, talk of 'brain damage' is premature. The truth is that most problems associated with Ecstasy seem to be caused by the *way* it is used. The psychological costs stem from recklessly excessive, long-term intake; the physical dangers are almost all related to its usage in the rave context, where over-exertion and dehydration can lead to heatstroke.

Even without physical activity, Ecstasy raises your body temperature; dehydration and non-stop dancing can push it as high as 108° F, at which point the blood forms clots. Because this uses up the clotting agent – normally at work sealing the myriad miniscule abrasions that occur inside the body – the result can be internal bleeding, followed by collapse. The solution is to drink plenty of fluids (safe-raving counsellors recommend a pint an hour), and take regular chill-out breaks. But the problem is that MDMA affects the subjective awareness of body-temperature: those in danger often feel like they're cool. Cash-restricted ravers would often rather spend their money on the 'essentials' (more drugs) than outrageously overpriced soft drinks. Club owners have been known to turn off the cold-water taps, in order to increase bar takings. Such cynical practices have declined, as more clubs adopt the harm-reduction policies devised by safe-raving pressure groups. Ravers also know more about how to take care of themselves. But a little bit of education can also be dangerous. Take the case of Britain's most famous Ecstasy fatality, Leah Betts, who died in 1995 at her own eighteenth birthday party. Feeling unwell, and having heard that water was the remedy, she appears to have drunk too much too rapidly; the inquest revealed that she died by drowning. The problem was that the drink-lots-of-fluids advice applies only to intense aerobic activity, and wasn't appropriate in her circumstances. MDMA also seems to have affected her body's capacity to process the liquid.

Although there have been a few cases of people dying after taking just one pill because of a statistically remote allergic reaction, most Ecstasy-related fatalities have involved bingeing, over-exertion and mixing of drugs (sometimes the more toxic amphetamine; sometimes alcohol, which dehydrates the body). Because of all these co-factors, it's hard to ascertain exactly how dangerous MDMA is. Ecstasy apologists often compare the chemical favourably with other drugs, legal and illegal. In the UK there are around 100,000 deaths per year from tobacco-related illnesses, 30–40,000 from alcohol-related illnesses and accidents, and 500 from paracetamol. On average, heroin and solvent abuse each claim about 150 lives per annum, while amphetamine's death-toll is about 25. In the first ten years of British rave, Ecstasy has been implicated in approximately 60 deaths: an average of six per year. Given the vast number people taking the drug during those eight years (conservative estimates put it at half a million per weekend in Britain), Ecstasy appears to be relatively safe – at least compared with such socially sanctioned leisure activities as mountaineering, skiing and motorbiking. Statistically, you're more at risk driving to the rave than being on E at the rave. Driving home under the influence is another matter altogether, given E's deleterious effect on co-ordination and reaction-time.

As with liquor in America in the twenties, prohibition has created a climate in which Ecstasy is more hazardous than it might be if the substance was legal. Prohibition actually made drinkers get drunker (black market moonshine often had a dangerously high alcohol content), and it created a climate of lawlessness. Similarly, because the overwhelming majority of early experiences with Ecstasy are so reward-ing, punters become curious about other banned substances, and get drawn into the culture of polydrug usage. MDMA's positive aura has rubbed off on other, far less deserving chemicals. This is the flaw in a drug policy that conflates all 'drugs' as a single demon, and fails to distinguish between different levels of risk and reward.

From the consumer's point of view, the worst thing about illegali-zation is that you don't know what you're buying. The illegal drug market in Britain has given rise to an ever-expanding range of brands of Ecstasy, distinguished by their colouring or by tiny pictograms stamped into the tablet, and varying widely in content: Brands like Doves, New Yorkers, California Sunrises, M&Ms, Dennis the Menaces, Rhubarb & Custards, Snowballs, Burgers, Flatliners, Shamrocks, Swans, Swallows, Turbos, Phase Fours, Big Brown Ones, Refreshers, Love-hearts, White Calis, Riddlers, Elephants, *ad infinitum* (and in some cases, *ad nauseam*). Ravers become connoisseurs of their differering effects and how they interact with each other or with other drugs.

Although the purity of Ecstasy fluctuates, the general rule today appears to be that you have about a 10 per cent chance of buying a total dud (usually containing decongestants, antihistamines or harmless inert substances) and about a 66 per cent likelihood of getting a variable dose of pure MDMA. The slack is taken up by pills that contain MDMA-related substances (MDA, MDEA), or amphetamine, or cocktails of drugs designed to simulate MDMA's effects (e.g. amphetamine + LSD). Instead of making ravers more cautious, the uncertainty of supply seems to have the opposite effect. Ravers eagerly assume that they've been sold an inferior product, and take more pills to compensate; hence the perennial mantra 'E's are shit these days, you have to take five of them to get a buzz'. Often the 'weakness' of any given Ecstasy pill is caused by the serotonin-depletion effect; the bliss-deficit is in the raver's brain, not the tablet. If E was legally available in doses of guaranteed purity and fixed levels of MDMA content, it would be easier for users to monitor their intake, to realize when they're overdoing it.

Excessive, routinized use combines with Ecstasy's diminishing-returns syndrome to form a vicious circle, a negative synergy. The individual's experience of Ecstasy is degraded; on the collective level, Ecstasy scenes lose their idyllic lustre and become a soul-destroying grind. This utopian/dystopian dialectic intrinsic to rave culture demands the coining of some new quasi-pharmacological terms: *vitalyst* ('vitalize' + 'catalyst') and *obliviate* (oblivion + opiate). These terms describe drug *experiences*, rather than intrinsic and immutable properties of the drugs themselves; the same drug, abused, can cross the line between positive and negative. Ecstasy starts out as a 'vitalyst': you feel more alive, more sensitized, more *human*; on the macro-level, rave scenes in their early days buzz with creativity and we're-gonna-change-the-world idealism. But with regular, rampant use, Ecstasy can become just another 'obliviate', like alcohol and narcotics: something that numbs the soul and transforms rave scenes into retreats from reality. This utopian/dystopian shift from 'paradise-regained' to 'pleasure-prison' is a recurring narrative experienced by successive Ecstasy generations all across the world. For seemingly programmed into the chemical structure of MDMA is the instruction: *use me, don't abuse me.*

ONE

A TALE OF
THREE CITIES

DETROIT TECHNO,
CHICAGO HOUSE
AND NEW YORK
GARAGE

'Kraftwerk was always very culty, but it was very Detroit too because of the industry in Detroit, and because of the mentality. That music automatically appeals to the people like a tribal calling . . . It sounded like somebody making music with hammers and nails.'

– Derrick May, 1992

To promote Kraftwerk's 1991 remixed 'greatest hits' compilation, *The Mix*, the group's American label Elektra came up with an amusing advert: the famous one-and-only photo of blues pioneer Robert Johnson, but with his suit filled by a robot's body. The visual pun was witty and eyecatching, but most importantly, it was *accurate*. Just as Johnson was the godfather of rock's gritty authenticity and wracked catharsis, Kraftwerk invented the pristine, post-human pop phuture we now inhabit. The story of techno begins not in early eighties Detroit, as is so often claimed, but in early seventies Dusseldorf, where Kraftwerk built their KlingKlang sound-factory and churned out pioneering synth-and-drum-machine tracks like 'Autobahn', 'Trans-Europe Express' and 'The Man-Machine'.

In one of those weird pop-historical loops, Kraftwerk were themselves influenced by Detroit – by the adrenalinized insurgency of the MC5 and The Stooges (whose noise, Iggy Pop has said, was partly inspired by the pounding clangour of the Motor City's auto factories). Like the other Krautrock bands – Can, Faust, Neu! – Kraftwerk were also inspired by the mantric minimalism and non-R & B rhythms of the Velvet Underground (whose John Cale produced the first Stooges album). Replacing guitars and drums with synthesizer pulses and programmed beats, Kraftwerk sublimated the Velvets' white light/white heat speed-rush into the cruise-control serenity of *motorik*, a metronomic, regular-as-carburettor rhythm that was at once post-rock and proto-techno. 'Autobahn' – a 24-minute hymn to the exhilaration of gliding down the freeway that sounded like a cyborg Beach Boys – was (in abbreviated form) a chart smash throughout the world in 1975.

Two years later on the *Trans-Europe Express* album, the title track – all indefatigable girder-beats and arching, Doppler Effect synths – segues into 'Metal On Metal', a funky iron foundry that sounded like a Luigi Russolo Art of Noises megamix for a Futurist discotheque.

'They were so stiff, they were funky,' techno pioneer Carl Craig has said of Kraftwerk. This paradox – which effectively translates as 'they were so white, they were black' – is as close as anyone has got to explaining the mystery of why Kraftwerk's music (and above all 'Trans-Europe Express', their most dispassionately metronomic and Teutonic track) had such a massive impact on black American youth. In New York, Kraftwerk almost single-handedly sired the electro movement. Africa Bambaataa and Soulsonic Force's 1982 smash 'Planet Rock' stole its doomy melody from 'Trans-Europe' and its beatbox rhythm from Kraftwerk's 1981 track 'Numbers'.

But while the body-popping, electric boogaloo era passed quickly (with New York hip hop pursuing a grittier, Seventies funk direction), Kraftwerk had a more enduring impact in Detroit, where the band's music plugged into the Europhile tastes of arty, middle-class blacks. From Cybotron's 1982 'Cosmic Cars' to Carl Craig's 1995 'Autobahn' homage *Landcruising*, Detroit techno still fits Derrick May's famous description: 'like George Clinton and Kraftwerk stuck in an elevator with nothing but a sequencer to keep them occupied.'

The Techno Rebels

'When I first heard synthesizers dropped on records it was great . . . like UFOs landing on records, so I got one,' Juan Atkins has said. 'It wasn't any one particular group that turned me on to synthesizers. But "Flashlight" [Parliament's Number One R & B hit from early 1978] was the first record I heard where maybe 75 per cent of the production was electronic – the bassline was electronic, and it was mostly synthesizers.'

Atkins was then a sixteen-year-old living in Belleville, a small town thirty miles from Detroit, and playing bass, drums and 'a little bit of lead guitar' in various garage funk bands. Three years earlier, he had befriended two kids in the year below him at junior high school: Derrick May and Kevin Saunderson. 'In Belleville,' remembers Saunderson, 'it was pretty racial still at that time, 'cos it was a decent area. You had to have a little bit of money, the houses were off lakes, and there wasn't a lot of black people there. So we three kind of gelled right away.'

Atkins became May's musical mentor, hipping him to all kinds of weird shit, from Parliament-Funkadelic to Kraftwerk. Says May, 'I'm telling you, man: Juan was the most important person in my life, other than my mother. If it wasn't for Juan I would never have heard any of this shit, I don't know where I'd be if it wasn't for him.'

Although the music they were into was all dancefloor oriented, the Belleville Three brought an art-rock seriousness to bear on what rock fans then dissed as mere 'disco'.

'For us, it was always a dedication,' says May. 'We use to sit back and philosophize on what these people thought about when they made their music, and how they felt the next phase of the music would go. And you know, half the shit we thought about the artist never even fucking thought about! ... Because Belleville was a rural town, we perceived the music a little bit different than you would if you encountered it in nightclubs or through watching other people dance. We'd sit back with the lights off and listen to records by Kraftwerk and Funkadelic and Parliament and Bootsy and Yellow Magic Orchestra, and try to actually understand what they were thinking about when they made it. We never just took it as entertainment, we took it as a serious philosophy.'

Through Atkins, May and Saunderson were exposed to all manner of post-Kraftwerk European electropop (Gary Numan, Giorgio Moroder's $E = MC^2$), alongside quirky American New Wave like the B52's. Why did this cold, funkless European music strike a chord with black youth from Detroit and Chicago? Atkins attributes it to 'something about industry and the Midwest. When you read the history books of America, they tell you that when the UAW – the United Auto Workers – formed, this was the first time that white people and black people came together on an equal footing, fighting for the same thing: better wages, better working conditions.'

Atkins, May and Saunderson belonged to a new generation of Detroit area black youth who grew up accustomed to affluence. 'My grandfather worked at Ford for twenty years, he was like a career auto worker,' says Atkins. 'A lot of the kids and the grand-kids that came up after this integration, they got used to a better way of living. It's funny that Detroit is now one of the most depressed cities in America, but it's still the city that has the most affluent blacks in the country. If you had a job at the plant at this time, you were making bucks. And it wasn't like the white guy standing next to you is getting five or ten dollars an hour more than you. Everybody was equal. So what happened is that you've got this environment with these kids that come up somewhat snobby, 'cos hey, their parents are making money working at Ford or General Motors or Chrysler, been elevated to a foreman, or even elevated to get a white collar job.' The Europhilia of these middle-class black youths, says Atkins, was part of their attempt 'to distance themselves from the kids that were coming up in the projects, in the ghetto.'

Eddie Fowlkes – soon to become the fourth member of the Belleville clique, despite being from a rougher area of Detroit – remembers that kids from the posher West Side of Detroit 'were more into slick clothes and cars, 'cos the West Side kids had more money than the kids on the East Side. They had more opportunity to travel, get books, and get things. They were into stuff like Cartier and all the shit they read about in GQ. So you had black kids on the West Side dressing like GQ, and it all kind of snowballed into a scene, a culture.' According to Jeff Mills – a ruling DJ–producer in the nineties, but then in his last year of high school – American Gigolo was a hugely influential movie on these Euro-fashion-obsessed black youth, just for the chic lifestyle of Richard Gere's lead character, his massive wardrobe of scores of shirts and shoes.

One expression of this upwardly mobile subculture was clubs and dance music. But these weren't nightclubs but high-school social clubs with names like Snobs, Brats, Ciabattino, Rafael, Charivari; the latter was named after a New York clothing store, and made what some claim is the first Detroit techno track, 'Sharevari' (released in 1981 and credited to A Number of Names). These clubs would hire spaces and throw parties. 'They were obsessed with being GQ down, and with Italian "progressive" music – Italian disco, basically,' says Carl Craig, another early acolyte of May and Atkins. Dubbed 'progressive' because their music stemmed from Giorgio Moroder's synth-and-drum-machine-based Eurodisco, rather than the symphonic Philly sound, Italian artists like Alexander Robotnik, Klein and MBO and Capricorn filled the gap left by the death of disco in America. On the Detroit dance party circuit, you would also hear electro-funk from New York labels like West End and Prelude , artists like Sharon Redd, Taana Gardner, the Peech Boys and Was (Not Was); English New Romantic and European synth-pop artists like Visage, Yello, Telex, Yazoo, Ultravox; and American New Wave from The B52's, Devo and Talking Heads. 'Man, I don't know if this could happen nowhere else in the country but Detroit,' laughs Atkins. 'Can you imagine three or four hundred black kids dancing to "Rock Lobster"? That shit actually happened in Detroit!'

Another factor that shaped Detroit youth's Europhile tastes was the influential radio DJ Charles Johnson, 'the Electrifyin' Mojo', whose show 'The Midnight Funk Association' aired every night on WGPR (the first black FM station in the city) through the late seventies and early eighties. Alongside P-Funk and synth-driven tracks by Prince like 'Controversy', Mojo would play Kraftwerk's 'Tour De France' and other Euro electro-pop. Every night, Mojo would do his Mothership spiel, encouraging listeners to flash their headlights or bedroom lamp so that the intergalactic craft would know where to touchdown. 'He had the most magnanimous voice you ever heard,' remembers Derrick May. 'This guy would just overpower you with his imagination. You became entranced by the radio. Which is something I have not heard since, and will probably never hear again.'

Around 1980, Atkins and May started making tentative steps towards becoming DJs themselves. 'Juan and I started messing around with our idea of doing our own personal remixes, as a joke, using a pause button, tape deck, and a basic turntable. Just taking a record and pausing it up, doing edits with the pause button. We got damn good at it. That led to constant experimentation, constantly freaking out, trying all kinds of crazy shit. And Juan thought, "Damn, man, let's go to the next level, let's start up our own DJ company." We found a guy who owned a music studio, a sort of rental place, hiring out gear. And he was nice enough to give us a room in back and set up a pair of turntables and speakers, and let us just have hours. Didn't charge us a dime! In that room, Juan would teach me how to mix. I remember the two records I learned how to mix with: David Bowie's "Fashion", and Edwin Birdsong's "Rapper Dapper Snapper". I had to mix those records for weeks, with Juan, like, in my ass, every time I fucked up!'

Calling themselves Deep Space Soundworks, Atkins and May played their first DJ engagement in 1981, at a party thrown by a friend of Derrick's, as warm-up for Detroit's most famous DJ, Ken Collier. 'It was *packed*, but nobody was dancing,' remembers May. 'We were spinning 45s [7-inches] and we didn't even have slipmatts on the turntable. Collier took over, and man, the dancefloor filled in 2.2

seconds. It was the most embarrassing, humbling experience of our lives!'

In the early eighties, Detroit had a huge circuit of parties, and the competition amongst the forty or fifty DJs in town was fierce. Every weekend, there were several parties, often organized around concepts (forinstance,everyonewearingthesamecolour).

'Everywhere you went you had to be on your shit, because Detroit crowds were so particular, and if you really weren't throwing down or you had a fucked-up mix, people would look at you and just walk off the dancefloor. And that's how we developed our skills, 'cos we had no room for error. These people wouldn't accept it. In Detroit, a party was the main event. People would go out and get new clothes for this shit.' May and Atkins applied the same kind of theoretical intensity to the art of mixing and set-building that they'd once invested in listening to records. 'We built a philosophy behind spinning records. We'd sit and think what the guy who made the record was thinking about, and find a record that would fit with it, so that the people on the dancefloor would comprehend the concept. When I think about all the brainpower that went into it! We'd sit up the whole night before the party, think about what we'd play the following night, the people who'd be at the party,theconceptoftheclientele.Itwasinsane!'

Eventually Deep Space got into throwing their own parties. 'We'd rent, like, a pub, and turn the pub into a club,' remembers Eddie Fowlkes, by then a member of the DJ team. 'The first place we threw a party was, I think, Roskos, which was like a pinball joint. What you tried to do is bring the people into a different place, where they couldn't even imagine somebody having a party. And when we started doing that, everybody in Detroit started doing offbeat shit. It was like "damn, I used to eat lunch here with my Mom and now I'm partying here!"'

Eventually, the social club party scene got so successful that the GQ kids found that an undesirable element began to turn up: the very ghetto youth from the projects that they'd put so much energy into defining themselves against. That was when the clubs started putting the phrase 'no jits' on the flyers: 'jit' being short for 'jitterbug', Detroit slangforruffianorgangsta.

'They would put "no jits allowed"', says May, 'but how you gonna tell some 250 pound ruffneck, standing about six foot four, "you're not coming to my party" – when you're some little five foot two pretty boy? I don't think so! He's coming in! It was a *hope* that they wouldn't come! It was to make them feel unwanted. And that was when the scene started to self-destruct. West Side kids and the whole élite high school scene, the elitist people that lived in certain areas, they just wanted to keep this shit to themselves. Then other people said "I like that too, I wanna come" and those elitists decided they didn't want 'em there, and that was wrong. It was the beginning of the end. That's when the guns started popping up at the parties, and fights started happening. By '86, it was over.'

Prior to forming Deep Space, Juan Atkins had already started making music as one half of Cybotron. Studying music and media courses at Washtenaw Community College in Ypsilanti, Michigan, he befriended a fellow student called Rick Davis. Quite a bit older than Atkins, Davis was an eccentric figure with a past: in 1968, he'd been shipped out to Vietnam just in time to experience the Tet offensive.

'Once you got to know Rick, he was like a big teddy bear,' remembers Atkins. 'But if you didn't know him, he could come off somewhat foreboding. Rick was a Viet vet. He was *there*, man – in the jungle. He told me stories where he's been in situations where he saw his best mate get ate by a tiger, or where he was going through the bush, shots rang out, and everybody in the platoon got wiped out but him. That's got to do something to you, mentally.' Davis and Atkins discovered they had interests in common – science fiction, futurologists like Alvin Toffler, and electronic music. Prior to Cybotron, Davis had done experimental tracks on his own, like 'The Methane Sea'. But like a lot of Viet vets, Davis also had a heavy acid rock background; he was a huge fan of Hendrix.

Although both Atkins and Davis shared instrumental duties and contributed lyrics and concepts, Atkins' focus was on 'putting the records together', making Cybotron music work as dance tracks. Davis handled a lot of the 'philosophical aspects' of what was a highly conceptual project. He'd cobbled together a strange personal creed out of Alvin Toffler's *The Third Wave* and Zohar, the 'Bible' of classical Jewish Kabbalah. The gist of it was that, through 'interfacing the spirituality of human beings into the cybernetic matrix', you could transform yourself into an supra-humanentity.

In line with Zoharian numerology, Davis changed his name to 3070; when a third member, guitarist John Howesley joined Cybotron, he was designated John 5. Atkins and Davis devised their own technospeak dictionary, The Grid. 'This was a time when the video-game phenom-enon was coming in,' remembers Atkins. 'We used a lot of video terms to refer to real-life situations. We conceived of the streets or the environment as being like the Game Grid. And Cybotron was con-sidered a "super-sprite". Certain images in a video programme are referred to as "sprites", and a super sprite had certain powers on the game-gridthataregularspritedidn'thave.'

Independently influenced by the same Euro sounds, Cybotron's cold, synth-dominated sound and drum-machine rhythms paralleled the electro then emerging from New York. Their first single, 'Alleys Of Your Mind' – released on their own Deep Space label – was playlisted by the Electrifyin' Mojo in 1981 and became a big local hit, selling around 15,000 copies in Detroit alone. The next two singles, 'Cosmic Cars' and 'Clear' did even better, resulting in Cybotron being signed by the Berkeley, California label Fantasy, who released the *Clear* album.

In Detroit, everybody assumed Cybotron were white guys from Europe. And indeed, apart from a subliminal funk pulsing amidst the crisp-and-dry programmed beats, there was scant evidence to hint otherwise. Davis' vocals had the Angloid/android neurosis of a John Foxx or Gary Numan, making Cybotron the missing link between the New Romantics and William Gibson's *Neuromancer*. But for all their futuristic *mise-en-scène*, the vision underlying Cybotron songs was Detroit-specific, capturing a city in transition: from industrial boom-town to post-Fordist wasteland, from US capital of auto manufacturing to US capital of homicide. Following the late sixties and early seventies syndrome of 'white flight' to the suburbs, the decline of the auto industry, and the de-gentrification of once securely middle-class black districts,Detroit'scitycentrehadbecomeaghost-town.

With its dominant mood of paranoia and desolation ('I wish I could escape from this crazy place', as Davis sang it in 'Cosmic Cars'), Cybotron's tech-*noir* should have been the soundtrack to *Robocop*, the dystopian sci-fi movie set in a Detroit of the near-future. Songs like 'Alleys of Your Mind' and 'Techno City' were 'just social commentary, more or less,' says Atkins, citing 'thought-control' and the 'double-edged sword' of technology as Cybotron's major preoccupations. Lyrics like 'enter the program / technofy your mind' and 'don't you let them robotize your behind' – from the gloom-funk epic 'Enter' – testify to an ambivalent investment in technology. As Atkins puts it, 'With technology, there's a lot of good things, but by the same token, it enablesthepowersthatbetohavemorecontrol.'

'Techno City' was inspired by Fritz Lang's vision in *Metropolis* of a future megalopolis divided into privileged sectors high up in the sky and subterranean prole zones. According to Davis, Techno City was equivalent to Detroit's Woodward Avenue ghetto; the dream of its denizens was to work their way up to the cybodrome, where the artists and intellectuals lived. Again, these utopian/dystopian fantasies were just a thinly veiled allegory of the unofficial apartheid taking shape in urban America, with the emergence of privately policed fortress communitiesandtownship-likeethnicghettos.

Perhaps the most extreme expression of Cybotron's ambivalent attitude to the future – half-anticipation, half-dread – was 'R9', a track inspired by a chapter in the Bible's Book of Revelation. 'What you have on the record is the War of Armageddon,' laughs Atkins. But despite the track's jagged gouts of dissonance, hideously warped textures, and background screams for 'Help!' this is no nightmare vision of the future, says Atkins. 'For the people who don't have anything, any kind of change is good. There's two ways of looking at it.' The fevered apocalyptic imagery climaxed in 'Vision', with Davis whispering about a 'vast celestial wasteland', then whimpering 'I need something to believein'.

OfftoBattle

After 'Vision' was recorded, Cybotron split. Davis – 'the Jimi Hendrix of the synthesizer', according to Atkins – wanted to go in a rock direction. 'I felt that we had built up a strong following on records like "Alleys", "Cosmic Cars" and "Clear",' says Atkins. 'Why would you come with a rock 'n' roll record, when you had all the black radio programmersalloverthecountryeatingoutofyourhand?'

Atkins started working on his own material using the name Model 500. Setting up his own label Metroplex, he put out 'No UFOs'; the sound, Motor City *motorik*, was harder and faster than Cybotron, streamlined and austere, with ciphered vocals demoted low in the mix. Then Eddie Fowlkes – now calling himself Eddie 'Flashin'' Fowlkes – decided he wanted to make a record too; his 'Goodbye Kiss' was the secondMetroplexrelease.

Suddenly, the other members of the Deep Space clique wanted to get in on the action. Up to this point, Derrick May had conceived of himself as primarily a DJ; he'd had some success outside Deep Space, spinning at Liedernacht, a club located in the ballroom at the Leland House Hotel, and DJ-ing on the radio. His first recording effort, 'Let's Go' – effectively a collaboration with Atkins – was Metroplex's third release on Metroplex. Finally, Kevin Saunderson joined the fray with 'Triangle of Love', recorded under the name Kreem.

Although the clique was tight, pooling its limited equipment and helping out on each others records, there was friction. Soon, each member of the Belleville Three was running his own record label. May's Transmat began as a sub-label imprint of Metroplex.

'If you notice the catalogue numbers on Transmat releases, they're all MS,' says Atkins. 'That stands for Metroplex Subsidiary ... The kind of guy Derrick is, if his records had been released on Metroplex, me and him would probably not be friends today. Because Derrick would have tried to tell me how to run the company.' Saunderson, meanwhile, started his own label KMS, which stood for Kevin Maurice Saunderson. 'I was working a security job at a hospital and running my business from telephone booths and hospital phones.' Eventually, all three labels settled in close vicinity to each other in Detroit's Eastern Market district.

With their cottage industry independence and their futuristic sound achieved using low-level technology, the Belleville Three fit the model of 'the Techno Rebels' proposed by Alvin Toffler in his *The Third Wave*. Rejecting Luddite strategies, these renegades embraced technology as a means of empowerment and resistance against the very corporate plutocracy that invented and mass-produced these new machines. And so Juan Atkins described himself as 'a warrior for the technological revolution'. But songs like 'Off To Battle' and 'Interfearance' were aimed as much at rival cottage-industrialists as at the larger powers. ' "Off To Battle",' says Atkins, was addressed to 'a lot of new, amateur electronic artists ... It was a battle cry to 'keep the standards high.'

Where Model 500 records were tough, glacial and a little eerie, Derrick May's music – as Mayday and Rythim Is Rythim – added a plangent, heart-tugging poignancy to the distinctively crisp and dry minimalism of the Detroit sound. On tracks like the elegantly elegaic 'It Is What It Is', he pioneered the use of quasi-symphonic string sounds. In one case, they were genuinely symphonic: 'Strings of Life' was based on samples gleaned from the Detroit Symphony Orchestra. May reworked these orchestral stabs into a sort of cyber-Salsa groove. His own phrase was '23rd-Century ballroom music'.

Atkins and May both attribute the dreaminess of Detroit techno to the desolation of the city, which May describes in terms of a sort of sensory-cultural deprivation. 'It's the emptiness in the city that puts the wholeness in the music. It's like a blind person can smell and touch and can sense things that a person with eyes would never notice. And I tend to think a lot of us here in Detroit have been blind: blinded by what was happening around us. And we sort of took those other senses and enhanced them, and that's how the music developed.' Hence the oddly indefinable emotions in May's tracks like 'Nude Photo' and 'Beyond The Dance', the weird mix of euphoria and anxiety.

Having grown up in New York until he moved to the Detroit area in his early teens, Kevin Saunderson was the most disco-influenced of the Belleville Three. His tracks – released under a plethora of aliases, including Reese, Reese and Santonio, Inter City, Keynotes, and E-Dancer – had titles as baldly self-descriptive as the music was stripped down and coldly compulsive: 'The Sound', 'How To Play Our Music', 'Forcefield', 'Rock To The Beat', 'Bassline', 'Funky, Funk, Funk', 'Let's, Let's, Let's Dance'. Of the three, Saunderson had the sharpest commercial instincts, and the greatest commercial success. But he also produced the darkest avant-funk of the early Detroit era, with Reese's 'Just Want Another Chance'.

Recorded in 1986, the track was inspired by Manhattan's celebrated proto-house club Paradise Garage, which Saunderson would visit when he returned to New York to see his older brothers. 'I used to imagine what kind of sound I would like to have coming out of a system like that,' he remembers, referring to the infamously low-end intensive, tectonic plate-shaking sound-system. 'It made me vibe that kind of vibe.' Over a baleful black-hole bassline running at about half the speed of the drum program, Saunderson intones the gutteral monologue of some kind of stalker or love-addict. 'I just vibed that, started thinking about this cat in a relationship, how this person was deep with this other person, really wanted to be with them, and kind of screwed up.' The 'Reese bass' has since been resurrected and mutated by a number of artists in the nineties, most notably by darkside jungle producers Trace and Ed Rush.

Displaying the kind of canny, market-conscious versatility that would characterize his whole career, Kevin Saunderson could also turn out tracks as light and upful as Inner City's 'Big Fun' and 'Good Life' – to date, Detroit techno's biggest hits. 'Big Fun' was spawned almost accidentally out of the collaborative symbiosis that characterized Detroit's incestuous and interdependent scene. James Pennington – soon to release tracks for Transmat under the name Suburban Knight – made a bassline round at Kevin's apartment, left it on tape, and went to work. 'Kevin said, "Let me use this, man," ' remembers Eddie Fowlkes, 'James said, "Okay, just put my name on it." Next thing you know, you got Inner City.' With Art Forest co-writing, Chicago-based diva Paris Grey singing the melody, and Juan Atkins mixing the track down, the result was 'Big Fun'.

'It was real tight,' reminisces Fowlkes fondly of this golden age of Detroit. 'Everyone was helping each other out, there was no egos, and nobody could compete with Juan because he had already done stuff [as Cybotron] and knew where he wanted to go. We were just like kids following the Pied Piper.'

The Detroit-Chicago Alliance

Detroit techno came to the world's attention indirectly, as an adjunct to Chicago's house scene. When British A & R scouts came to Chicago to investigate house in 1986–7, they discovered that many of the top-selling tracks were actually from Detroit. 'We would sell ten to fifteen thousand records in Chicago alone,' says Juan Atkins. 'We were selling more records in Chicago than even Chicago artists. We kind of went hand in hand with the house movement. To a certain degree, I think we helped *start* that thing. 'Cos we were the first ones making records. Jesse Saunders came out with that record ["On and On"] maybe two or three weeks after we had "No UFOs" out, and he was the first guy in Chicago who was making tracks.'

'Chicago was one of a couple of cities in America where disco never died,' Atkins continues. 'The DJs kept playing it on radio and the clubs. And since there were no new disco records coming through they were looking to fill the gap with whatever they could find.' This meant Euro synth-pop, Italian 'progressive' and, eventually, the early Detroit tracks. The Belleville Three quickly got to know everybody in the Chicago scene. And they started to make the four hour drive to Chicago every weekend to hear the Hot Mix Five – Farley Jackmaster Funk, Steve Silk Hurley, Ralphi Rosario, Mickey Oliver, and Kenny Jammin' Jason – spin on local radio station WBMX. 'It seemed like they had mixes going on all day on the radio,' remembers Kevin Saunderson. 'Me and Derrick would drive to Chicago every weekend just to hear the mix shows and be a part of the scene, see what's going on and get new records. It was an inspiration for us. Especially once we started making records, you couldn't keep us out of Chicago.'

Bar the odd session that May would do for Electrifyin' Mojo, you couldn't hear mixing on the radio in Detroit. Despite its Europhile tendencies, Detroit was always more of a funk city than a disco town. This difference came through in the music: the rhythm programming in Detroit techno was more syncopated, had more of a groove to it. House had a metronomic, four-to-the-floor beat, what Eddie Fowlkes calls 'a straight straight foot' – a reference to 'Farley's Foot', the mechanical kick drum that Chicago DJs like Farley 'Jackmaster' Funk and Frankie Knuckles would superimpose over their disco mixes. Chicago house tended to feature diva vocals, disco-style; Detroit tracks were almost always instrumentals. The final big difference was that Detroit techno, while arty and upwardly mobile, was a straight black scene. Chicago house was a gay black scene.

Disco's Revenge

'Disco music is a disease. I call it Disco Dystrophy. The people victimized by this killer disease walk around like zombies. We must do everything possible to stop the spread of this plague.'

–DJ Steve Dahl, 1979

'I don't know that I have any objection to dancing, I just don't do it. Sort of like sucking other men's dicks. I don't feel that there is anything wrong with it, but it doesn't appeal to me.'

–Chicago rocker and technophobe Steve Albini,
speaking in Reactor #8.0, 1993

Sucking, of course, was always the accusation levelled at disco. At the height of 'disco sucks' fever in 1979, Chicago's Comiskey Park baseball stadium was the site for a 'Disco Demolition Derby', which was organized by Detroit DJ Steve Dahl, and took place halfway through a double-header between the Chicago White Sox and the Detroit Tigers. But when the 100,000 plus records were dynamited, discophobic mobs rampaged on to the field; the rioting, post-explosion debris and damage to the pitch resulted in the game being forfeited to the Tigers.

The 'Disco Sucks' phenomenon recalls the Nazi book burnings, or the exhibitions of Degenerate Art. Modern day spectacles of *kulturkampf* like Comiskey were impelled by a similar disgust: the belief that disco was rootless, inauthentic, decadent, a betrayal of the virile principles of the true American *volk* music, rock 'n' roll. Hence T-Shirts like 'Death Before Disco', hence organizations like DREAD (Detroit Rockers Engaged In The Abolition of Disco) and Dahl's own 'Insane Coho Lips Antidisco Army'.

Discophobia wasn't just limited to white rockers, though; many blacks despised it as a soul-less, mechanistic travesty of da funk. And so the sleeve of Funkadelic's 1979 album *Uncle Jam Wants You* bore the slogan 'it's the rescue dance music "from the blahs" band'. Funkateer critic Greg Tate coined the term 'DisCOINTELPRO' – a pun on the FBI's campaign to infiltrate black radical organizations like the Panthers – to denigrate disco as 'a form of record industry sabotage . . . [which] destroyed the self-supporting black band movement out of which P-Funk . . . grew.' In 1987, Public Enemy's Chuck D articulated hip hop's antipathy to house, disco's descendant, telling me: 'it's sophisticated, anti-black, anti-feel, the most ARTIFICIAL shit I ever heard. It represents the gay scene, it's separating blacks from their past and their culture, it's upwardly mobile.'

Chicago house music was born of a double exclusion, then: not just black, but gay and black. Its refusal, its cultural dissidence, took the form of embracing a music that the majority culture deemed dead and buried. House didn't just resurrect disco, it mutated the form, intensifying the very aspects of the music that most offended white rockers and black funkateers: the machinic repetition, the synthetic and electronic textures, the rootlessness, the 'depraved' hypersexuality and 'decadent' druggy hedonism. Stylistically, house assembled itself from disregarded and degraded pop-culture detritus that the mainstream considered passé, disposable, un-American: the proto-disco of the Salsoul and Philadelphia International labels, English synthpop, and Moroder's Eurodisco.

If Dusseldorf was the ultimate source for Detroit techno, you could perhaps argue that the prehistory of house begins in Munich. Here it was that Giorgio Moroder invented Eurodisco. Setting up Say Yes Productions with British guitarist Pete Bellote, Moroder recruited Donna Summer, then singing in rock musicals like *Hair* and *Godspell*, and transformed her into a disco ice queen. Moroder can claim three innovations that laid the foundations for house. First, the dramatically extended megamix: 1975's seventeen minute long orgasmotronic epic 'Love To Love You Baby'. Second, the four-to-the-floor disco pulse rhythm: Moroder used a drum machine to simplify funk rhythms to make it easier for whites to dance. Third, and perhaps most crucial, was Moroder's creation of purely electronic dance music. One of his earliest songs – 'Son of My Father', a 1972 UK Number One for Chicory Tip – was one of the very first synth-pop hits. But it was Donna Summer's 1977 global smash 'I Feel Love' that was the real revolution. Constructed almost entirely out of synthesized sounds, 'I Feel Love' had no verse or chorus laid out in advance; Summer improvised her gaseous, eroto-mystic vocals over Moroder and Bellote's grid-like juggernaut of percussive pulses and clockwork clicks. The result, at once pornotopian and curiously unbodied, was acid house and trance techno *avant la lettre*.

In the absence of fresh disco product, Chicago DJs had to rework the existing material into new shapes. House – a term that originally referred to the kind of music you'd hear at The Warehouse, a gay nightclub in Chicago – was born not as a distinct genre but as an approach to making 'dead' music come alive, by cut 'n' mix, segue, montage, and other DJ tricks. Just as the term disco derived from the discotheque (a place where you heard recorded music, not live performances), so house began as a disc-jockey culture. In fact, it was an imported DJ culture, transplanted from New York by Frankie Knuckles, who DJ-ed at The Warehouse from 1979 until 1983.

Born in 1955, Knuckles grew up in the South Bronx. At Nicky Siano's underground dance club, The Gallery, Knuckles helped out by, amongst other things, spiking the punch with LSD and even going so far as to inject the drug into the free fruit. In the early seventies, Knuckles DJ-ed for several years – alongside another future 'deep house' legend, Larry Levan – at The Continental Baths, a gay 'pleasure palace', and then at SoHo. Levan was originally the first choice of the

Chicago entrepreneurs who set up The Warehouse. But Levan decided to stay on in New York at SoHo, so it was Knuckles who moved to Chicago in early 1977 to take up the DJ spot. A three storey, former factory in West Central Chicago, The Warehouse drew around two thousand mostly gay and black hedonists to dance from midnight Saturday to midday Sunday. The four dollar admission was low, there was free juice and water, and the atmosphere on the middle storey dancefloor was intense. It was here that Knuckles began to experiment with editing disco breaks on a reel-to-reel tape recorder, reworking and recombining the raw material – Philadelphia International classics, underground club hits on the Salsoul label by the likes of Loleatta Holloway and First Choice, Moroder-beat – that would soon evolve intohouse.

In 1983, The Warehouse's promoters doubled the entrance fee, prompting Knuckles to quit and set up his own Friday night club, The Power Plant. The Warehouse retaliated by opening another Saturday club, The Music Box, based around a young kid from California called Ron Hardy. Playing in a rawer style than Knuckles, Hardy created an even more intense and disorientating atmosphere; using two copies of the same record, he'd stretch a track out into a Tantric eternity, teasing the audience by frustrating their anticipation of the breakdown. Unlike the Detroit scene, where drug-taking was unusual, Chicago house went hand in hand with stimulants and hallucinogens. People smoked pot, sniffed poppers (also known as 'rush'), and snorted cocaine. Acid was popular, because it was cheap, long-lasting and the blotters were easily concealed on your person. And some clubbers smoked 'happy sticks', reefers dipped in angel dust (the deranging hallucinogen PCP). At the rougher and more hardcore hedonist Music Box, where it got so hot people tore their shirts off, the vibe was accordingly somewhat dark; Hardy eventually became a drug addict, anddiedin1993.

With other regular parties emerging like The Loft, The Playground, and East Hollywood, competition between DJs grew fierce. To get an edge over their rivals, DJs would devise more complicated mixing tricks and employ special effects, like Frankie Knuckles' steam loco-motive sound. Both Farley and Knuckles started to use a live drum machine to bolster their mixes and make the experience more hypnotic; Knuckles is said to have bought his Roland 909 beat-box from Derrick

May. The stomping four-to-the-floor kick-drum would become the defining mark of house music. Other elements – hissing hi-hat patterns, synthetic hand-claps, synth-vamps, chiming bass-loops, drum rolls that pushed the track to the next plateau of pre-orgasmic intensity – emerged when Chicagoans started making records to slake the DJs insatiable demand for fresh material. Called 'tracks', as opposed to songs, because they consisted of little more than a drum track, this proto-house music was initially played by DJs on reel-to-reel tape and cassette.

Although many have claimed the title of 'first house track', most agree that the first vinyl release was Jesse Saunders' and Vince Lawrence's 'On and On' (a raw, ultra-minimal version of the Salsoul classic by First Choice), which the duo put out in 1983 on their own Jes Say label. Saunders and Lawrence approached Larry Sherman, a local entrepreneur who had bought out Chicago's only record pressing plant, and asked him to press up 500 12 inches for them on trust. They promised to return within twenty minutes and pay him $4 per disc. Not only did they come back and pay him in full, they also asked him to press another thousand copies.

Stunned by the demand for this new music in Chicago, Sherman started the Trax label, and débuted with another Jesse Saunders track, 'Wanna Dance', released under the name Le Noiz. Sherman's role in the genesis of house is much disputed. Some regard him as a visionary entrepreneur who fostered the scene and provided work for the musicians in the day to day operations of Trax. Others accuse Sherman of pursuing short-term profit and neglecting the long-term career prospects of his artists, thereby contributing to the premature demise of the Chicago scene in the late eighties.

In the mid-eighties, though, Trax and Chicago's other leading house label DJ International played a major role not just in developing a local market for house tracks, but in getting the records distributed to other cities in America and to Europe. It was a DJ International track – Farley 'Jackmaster' Funk and Jesse Saunders's 'Love Can't Turn Around', a cover of an Isaac Hayes song – that became the first international house hit, making the UK Top Ten in September 1986. Propelled by a bassline made out of what sounds like a sampled tuba motif and by almost boogie-woogie piano vamps, 'Love Can't Turn Around' features the fabulously overwrought histrionics of Darryl Pandy, whose hyper-melismatic vocals are the missing link between gospel and gender-bending male-diva Sylvester, the disco star responsiblefor'YouMakeMeFeel(MightyReal)'.

Other hits followed in early 1987: 'Jack The Groove' by Raze (actually from Washington DC) got to Number Twenty in the UK, and Steve Silk Hurley's 'Jack Your Body' was a Number One smash in January. But by the middle of that year, house seemed to be petering out like any other clubland fad. The self-reflexive song-titles, which usually involved the words 'house' and 'jack' (the Chicago style of palsied dancing), seemed to place house firmly in the pop tradition of dance crazes like the Twist and the Mashed Potato, novelties with inbuilt obsolescence. House's depthless doggerel (funktional catchphrases like 'work your body', 'move your body', 'let's rock') and sonic gimmicks (the stutter effect often put on vocals) were impressively post-human and depersonalized, but quickly became irritating. At the time, I remember commenting in a singles review column that house had proved itself a lame duck; compared with hip hop, there didn't seem much of a future for it. I was dead wrong, of course, as wrong as a boy can be, for what we'd heard so far was only the tip of the iceberg. Asforhousehavingmuchofafuture. . .house*was*thefuture.

NewJackCity

'Love Can't Turn Around' and 'Jack Your Body', early house's two biggest hits, each represented a different side of house: songs versus tracks, a R & B derived tradition of soul-full expression versus depersonalized functionalism. From my point of view, it's the 'tracks' that ultimately proved to be the most interesting side of house culture. The songful style of 'deep' house rapidly collapsed into an affirmation of traditional musicianly values and uplifting humanist sentiments. But 'jack tracks', and the 'acid tracks' that followed them, honed in on a different potential latent within disco: jettisoning all the residues of soul and humanity, this was machine-music without apology, machine-made music that turned you into a machine. Its mind-nullifying repetitionofferedliberationthroughtrance-dance.

In many ways, house seemed like a flashblack to the white avant-funk and experimental electronic music of the early eighties, when post-punks in England and New York turned to black dance styles as the way forward. Generally, with the exception of Talking Heads and

PiL, avant-funk never had much impact in its own day. But, in a sort of every dog will have its day syndrome, many of the avant-funksters enjoyed substantial success when they reinvented themselves as key members of the first wave of British homegrown house. A Certain Ratio's Simon Topping teamed up with another Mancunian avant-disco veteran, Quando Quango's Mike Pickering, to record the Brithouse favourite 'Carino' as T. Coy; Pickering went on to lead the hugely popular but more songful M. People. Cabaret Voltaire's Richard Kirk reappeared as Sweet Exorcist, 400 Blow's Tony Thorpe purveyed UK acid house as Moody Boys, Biting Tongues' Graham Massey becamethemusicalbrainsbehind808State.

Perhaps the most prophetic of the early eighties avant-funk outfits was Dusseldorf's D. A. F., who began as an experimental industrial unit, then stripped down their chaotic sound to a harsh, homo-erotic avant-disco influenced by the New Savagery ideas of artist Joseph Beuys. On their three albums for Virgin, *Alles Ist Gut*, *Gold Und Liebe* and *Fur Immer*, the inelastic synth-pulses and frigid frenzy of the beats are uncannily pre-emptive of acid house. D. A. F. were stripped down lyrically as well as musically. Tracks like 'Mein Hertz Macht Bum (My Heart Goes Boom)' and 'Absolute Bodycontrol' offered sexmusic shorn of romantic mystique and rendered in clinical, cardiovascular language, while 'Der Mussolini' (chorus: 'dance der Mussolini ... dance der Adolf Hitler') put a twisted spin on the standard avant-funk obsession withcontrol.

D. A. F. and their offshoot group Liaisons Dangereuses actually had some currency in the early Chicago scene. Their sinewy sound embodied an idea – the dancefloor as a gymnasium of desire, liberation achieved through submission to a regime of strenuous bliss – that was a latent content of gay disco's erotics. As Walter Hughes notes, songs like Village People's 'Y. M. C. A.' and 'In The Navy' used 'the language of recruitment and evangelism' to bring out the homo-erotics of discipline, while the lyrics of disco songs often represented love in the imagery of 'enslavement, insanity, or addiction, a disease or a police state'.

As house music evolved, this idea – freedom achieved by abandoning subjectivity and self-will, the ecstasy of being en*thrall*ed by the beat – became more explicit. Gradually, the hyper-sexual imagery was supplanted by a post-sexual delirium, reflected in the Chicago dancing style known as 'jacking'. In disco, dance had gradually shed its role as courtship ritual and opened up into what Hughes calls 'increasingly unpaired, unchoreographed' freestyle. Jacking took this to the next stage, replacing pelvic-thrust and booty-shake with a whole-body frenzyofpolymorphouslyperverseticsandconvulsivepogo-ing.

Etymologically, 'jack' seems to be a corruption of 'jerk', but also may have some link to 'jacking off'. The house dancefloor suggests the circle jerk, a spectacle of collective auto-eroticism, sterile *jouissance*. 'Jacking' also makes me think of jacking into an electrical circuit. Plugged into the sound-system, the jacker looks a bit like a robot with epilepsy (itself an electrical disorder of the nervous system). In jack tracks like Fast Eddie Smith's 'Jack To The Sound' and Secret Secret's 'We Come To Jack', lyrics are restricted to terse commands and work-that-body exhortations. Eventually, acid house bypassed verbals altogether and proceeded to what felt like direct possession of your nervoussystemviathebass-biologyinterface.

Robotnik vacancy, voodoo delirium, whirling dervishes, zombiedom, marionettes, slaves-to-the-rhythm: the metaphors that house music and 'jacking' irresistibly invite all contain the notion of becoming less-than-human. Other aspects of the music exacerbate the sense of attenuated self-hood. With a few exceptions, house singers tend to be ciphers, their vocals merely plastic material to be manipulated by the producer. In early house, the vocals were often garbled, sped-up and slowed down, pulverized into syllable or phoneme-size particles, and above all subjected to the ubiquitous, humiliating stutter-effect, whereby a phrase was transformed on the sampling keyboard into a staccato riff. Ralphi Rosario's classic 'You Used To Hold Me' divides into two distinct halves. At first, diva Xavier Gold is in the spotlight, putting in a sterling performance as the cynically materialistic and vengeful lover. Then Rosario takes control, vivisecting Gold's vocal so that stray vowels and sibilants bounce like jumping beans over the groove, and transforming one syllable of passion into a spasmic Morse coderiff.

House makes the producer the star, not the singer. It's the culmi-nation of an unwritten (because unwriteable) history of black dance pop, a history determined not by sacred cow auteurs but by producers, session musicians and engineers – backroom boys. House music takes this depersonalization further: it gets rid of human musicians (the house band that gave Motown or Stax or Studio One its distinctive sound), leaving just the producer and his machines. Operating as a cottage factory churning out a high turnover of tracks, the house producer replaces the artist's signature with the industrialist's trademark. Closer to an architect or draughtsman, the house auteur is absent from his own creation; house tracks are less like artworks, in the expressive sense, than vehicles, rhythmic engines that take the dancer on a ride.

As well as being post-biographical, house is post-geographical pop. If Chicago is the origin, it's because it happens to be a junction point in the international trade routes of disco. Breaking with the traditional horticultural language we use to describe the evolution of pop – cross-pollination, hybridization – house's 'roots' lie in deracination. The music sounds inorganic: machines talking to each other, in an un-real acoustic space. When sounds from real-world acoustic sources enter house's pleasuredome, they tend to be processed and disembodied – as with the distortion and manipulation inflicted upon the human voice, evacuating its soul and reducing it to a shallow *effect*.

But this is only one side of house culture: the machine-music side that evolved from jack tracks to acid house, music that's all surface and post-human intensity. Just as important was the humanist, uplifting strain of 'deep house' that affiliated itself to the R & B tradition: songs like Sterling Void's 'It's All Right', Joe Smooth's 'Promised Land' and his album *Rejoice*. Combining Philly's silky symphonic strings and mellifluous vocals with gospel's imagery of salvation and succour, this strain of house was sufficiently worthy and wholesome to win over English soul boys such as Paul Weller and his fanboy clone Doctor Robert (formerly of The Blow Monkeys). Weller actually covered 'Promised Land' in early 1989.

In house, there's a divide between finding yourself (through becoming a member of the house) and losing yourself (in solipsistic hallucinatory bliss). The split in house between finding an identity/expressing your self and losing self/losing control could be mapped on to the tension in gay culture between the politics of pride, unity and collective resilience, and the more hardcore 'erotic politics' of impersonal sexual encounters, 'deviant' practices and drugs. House offered a sense of communion and community to those who might have been alienated from organized religion because of their sexuality. And so Frankie Knuckles described The Warehouse as a 'church for people who have fallen from grace', while another house pioneer, Marshall Jefferson, likened house to 'old time religion in the way that people just get happy and screamin''. Male divas like Daryl Pandy and Robert Owens hadtrainedinchurchchoirs.

In 'deep house', the inspirational lyrics often echo the civil rights movement of the sixties, conflating the quest for black civic dignity with the struggle for gay pride. Joe Smooth's 'Promised Land' and Db's 'I Have A Dream' both explicitly evoke Martin Luther King; the first promises 'brothers, sisters, one day we'll be free', the latter dreams of 'one house nation under a groove'. The Children's 'Freedom' is a fraught plea for tolerance and fraternity. The spoken-word monologue beseeches 'don't oppress me' and 'don't judge me', and asks, bewildered and vulnerable: 'can't you accept me for what I am?' The name 'The Children' comes from Chicago house slang: to be a 'child' was to be gay, a member of house's surrogate family. 'Step-child' was the term forastraightpersonacceptedbygays.

In other house tracks, religious and sexual rapture are fused in a kind of Gnostic eroto-mysticism. Jamie Principle's 'Baby Wants To Ride' begins with a prayer from Principle, and then the Voice of God declaring that it's time to relate 'the Revelation of my Second Coming'. But the 'coming' is revealed to be decidedly profane: an encounter with a dominatrix, who strips him and makes him beg on bended knees, then rides him through a porno-copia of sexual positions. Principle revels in the passivity of being a plaything, a (sexual) object, feyly gasping: 'She took me ... She made me scream.' A Prince obsessed androgyne, Principle – née Byron Walton – told *Melody Maker*: 'Men always want their women to scream when they're having sex. But the men aren't meant to scream or wouldn't admit to doing it. But I can't accept that male role. If a woman makes a man scream, I think that's just as important, just as much a success. If I want to scream, I scream.' Not content with blasphemously conflating SM with the Book of Revelation, 'Baby Wants To Ride' adds politics to the liberation theology: Principle exhorts the South African government to set his people free, disses AmeriKKKa as a 'bullshit land', and complains it'shardtoride'whenyou'relivinginafascistdream'.

In Fingers Inc's 'Distant Planet', this longing for sanctuary from racial and sexual oppression takes the form of cosmic mysticism, *à la* Sun Ra. The distant planet is a place 'where anyone can walk without fear'; if you're treated like an alien, you wanna go where the alien feels at home. Eerie and trepidatious, the track has a mood of desolate utopianism. The musical brains behind Fingers Inc, Larry Heard, is an interestingly conflicted house auteur. With its nimble-fingered fluency and over-melismatic Robert Owens vocals, most Fingers Inc output reflects Heard's background as a jazz/R & B drummer and keyboardist reared on fusion and progressive rock (George Duke, Mahavishnu Orchestra, Return to Forever, Genesis, Rick Wakeman). Songs like 'Mysteries Of Love', 'Another Side' and 'A Path' are the electro-blues of a seeker. Heard declared: 'Jack means nothing to me'. But ironically, his most thrilling music took the form of the brutally dehumanized and machinic tracks – 'Amnesia (Unknown Mix)' and 'Washing Machine' – he released under the alias Mr Fingers. 'Washing Machine' – an interminable brain-wash cycle of burbling bass-loops and jarringly off-kilter hi-hats – is a mantra for a state of mindlessness.

Everybody Needs *a 303*

The machinic, trance-inducing side of house exemplified by 'Washing Machine' took another turn in 1987, when jack tracks evolved into 'acid tracks': a style defined by a mindwarping bass sound that originated from a specific piece of equipment, the Roland TB 303 Bassline. The Roland 303 was originally put on the market in 1983 as a bass-line synthesizer designed to partner the Roland 606 drum machine, and targeted at guitarists who wanted basslines to jam off. It was singularly unsuited for this purpose, and by 1985 Roland ceased manufacturing the machine. But a few Italian disco producers discovered the 303's potential for weird Moroder-esque sounds: Alexander Robotnik's 'Les Problemes D'Amour', released in 1983, was a huge 'progressive' hit in Chicago, selling around twelve thousand import copies. A few years later, house producers, already enamoured of Roland drum machines and synths, started messing around with the 303, discovering applications that the manufacturers had never imagined.

The 303 is a slim silver box with a one-octave keyboard (but four-octave range), plus six knobs which control parameters like 'decay', 'accent', 'resonance', 'tuning', 'envelope modulation', and 'cut off frequency'. Having programmed a bass-riff on the keyboard, you tweak the knobs to modulate the pitch, accent, 'slide', and other parameters of each individual note in the bassline. The result is bass patterns that are as complex and trippy as a computer fractal, riddled with wriggly nuancesandglissandi,curlicuesandwhorls.

In early 1988, Farley 'Jackmaster' Funk told me the 303 was 'an obsolete, old-fashioned piece of technology that no one had ever thought of using that way before'. At the time, this reminded me of the then indie-rock vogue for the cheesily overstated effects of late sixties and early seventies guitar pedals. As Dinosaur Jr's J. Mascis put it, these quaint effects units appealed because they provided 'harsh-eties rather than subleties'. Similarly, the 303 and similar analogue synthesizers were rediscovered by house artists because their gauchely moderne sounds, once laughable, suddenly seemed otherworldly and futuristic again. They were also cheap, as musicians and recording studios sold themtomakespaceforthenewdigitalsynthsandsamplers.

The first Chicago 303 track, Phuture's 'Acid Tracks', was released in 1987 but recorded a couple of years earlier. DJ Pierre, Spanky and Herb Jackson were messing around with a 303, hoping to get a conventional bassline for a Spanky rhythm track. 'The acid squiggle was there to start with,' Pierre has said. 'The machine already had that crazy acid sound in it that you were supposed to erase and put your own in, because it was just some MIDI gerbil. But we liked it.' Marshall Jefferson, who produced the track, confirmed the accidental origins of this revolutionary house genre, telling David Toop: ' "Acid Tracks" wasn't pre-programmed, man ... DJ Pierre, he was over and he was just messing with this thing and he came up with that pattern, man ... So we were listening to it, getting drunk man. "Hey, this is kinda hot, man.Thisisagreatmood,man.Let'sputitout.Whatthefuck?" '

Eleven minutes and seventeen seconds long, 'Acid Tracks' is just a drum track and endless variations on that bass-sound: somewhere between a faecal squelch and a neurotic whinny, between the bubbling of volcanic mud and the primordial low-end drone of a didgeridoo. The 303 bassline is a paradox: it's an amnesiac hook, totally compelling as you listen, but hard to memorize or reproduce after the event, either as pattern or timbre. Its effect is mental dislocation; after the mania for acid tunes went into overdrive, Marshall Jefferson complained that artists weren't using the 303 to create moods but for 'disrupting thoughtpatterns'.

Having recorded the session, Pierre, Jefferson and Co gave a tape to

Ron Hardy. The track became such a sensation at The Music Box that it was known as Ron Hardy's Acid Trax, a reference to the rumour that the club's intense, flipped out vibe was caused by the promoters' putting LSD in the water supply. Subsequently, acid producers have striven to distance the music from hallucinogenics. In early 1988, Tyree told me, 'It has nothing to do with drugs, it's just a name that fits because the music's crazy, it's weird and wired. But it affects you like a drug, it takes you over. People go into a trance, they just lose it! It makes everything seem so fast, it's like an upper.' Another story circulating by mid-1988, and probably intended as a whitewash, was that 'acid' came from 'acid burn', Chicago slang for ripping somebody off, and specifically, for sampling somebody else's sound. But since sampling didn'tplayamajorroleinacidhouse,thiswasneverreallyplausible.

Wary of seeming to condone drug use, Phuture liked to point to the anti-cocaine song on the flipside of 'Acid Tracks'. In some ways even more eerily brilliant than 'Acid Tracks', 'Your Only Friend' personifies the drug as a robot-voiced Slavemaster, who introduces himself at the start with the words – 'This is Cocaine speaking' – then proceeds to relate just how far he'll debase you: 'I'll make you lie for me / I'll make you die for me / In the end, I'll be your only friend.' In the background, ectoplasmic wisps of hideously fey, enfeebled falsetto moan and whimper wordlessly, representing the addict languishing in the throes ofwithdrawal.

'Your Only Friend' is one of a number of tracks of this era that have the disorientation and sinister, fixated quality of acid house, without actually employing a Roland 303. The It's 'Donnie', a collaboration between Larry Heard and vocalist Harry Dennis, is the fever-dream of a love-junkie; Dennis's stuttering vocals sound like he's wracked by spasms and deep-body shudders. The lyrics present a fantastically melodramatic scenario of abandonment and betrayal, a girl called Donnie having run off with another man despite all the diamond rings, furs and Cadillacs he showered upon her; 'I can't quite understand', gibbers the singer, disorientated by his dejection. By the end, Dennis is commiserating with a double-tracked doppelganger of himself, who's even more aggrieved: 'She ain't even given me a chance to give her what I *wanted* to give her.' Then there was Sleezy D's 'I've Lost Control', whose creator Marshall Jefferson has said he was trying to achieve a mood similar to old Black Sabbath or Led Zeppelin records. Consisting of nothing but simmering percussion, stray smears of flanged sound, and deranged screams, groans and madman's laughter from the reverberant recesses of the mix-scape, 'I've Lost Control' does indeed sound a bit like the famous 'ambient' mid-section of 'Whole Lotta Love', where Robert Plant writhes in orgasmic agony. And the metallic, man-machine vocal, impassively intoning 'I'm losing it . . . I've lost it', also recalls Sabbath's 'Iron Man'. The Sleezy D persona sounds like his subjectivity is literally disintegrating in the acid maelstrom.

'I've Lost Control' and 'Donnie' got carried along by the *après* Phuture deluge of 303-based acid tracks: Laurent X's 'Machines', Armando's 'Land of Confusion', Mike Dunn's 'Magic Feet', Bam Bam's 'Where's Your Child?', Fast Eddie's 'Acid Thunder', and scores more. Adonis and The Endless Poker's 'Poke It' features a series of terse injunctions – 'poke it', 'house you', 'work' – so distorted they sound likeadogbarking,whichareoffsetbyrealcaninewoofs.

Ironically, it was the genre's pioneer, DJ Pierre who – after recording a few more acid anthems like Pierre's Pfantasy Club's 'Dream Girl' and 'Fantasy Girl' – was one of the first to abandon the sound. Explaining his shift away from 'tracks' to songs, he said 'It's kinda soul-less . . . There's no emotion that goes with it apart from jumping up and down and making you want to dance.' In fact there *is* an emotion to acid house, it's just that it's one that seems to stem from some infra-human domain – the passion of sub-atomic particles, the siren-song of entropy, an'Om'emanatingfromthebellyofMotherEarth.

Although the acid fad petered out by 1989, the Roland 303 has endured, securing a permanent place in the arsenal of house and techno producers, and enjoying periodic revivals. In some ways, it's like the wah-wah guitar: instantly recognizable, yet capable of infinite variationsandadaptations,andforeverdriftinginandoutoffashion.

ParadiseLost

By 1988, house music was having a massive impact in Britain and Europe, but Chicago itself was in decline. The previous year, the authorities had begun to crack down on the house scene, with the police banning after-hours parties and witholding late-night licences from clubs. WBMX went off the air in 1988, and sales of house records slowed, eventually dwindling down to an average of 1500 copies, a mere tenth of sales at Chicago's peak. Many of the scene's prime movers became inactive, disillusioned by bad deals. Others spent most of their time in Europe, where financial prospects were better. Some left town for good. Frankie Knuckles moved back to New York. And DJ Pierre moved to New Jersey in 1990, and became a major exponent ofNewYork'ssong-orienteddeephousesound,'garage'.

Garage's roots go back to New York's early seventies disco underground. Mostly gay black and gay Hispanic, this scene was characterized by a bacchanalian fervour fuelled by acid, amphetamine and the Ecstasy-like downer Quaalude. It was in this milieu – clubs like The Gallery, Salvation, Sanctuary, The Loft, The Ginza, and DJs like Francis Grosso, David Rodriguez, Steve D'Aquisto, Michael Cappello, David Mancuso – that Frankie Knuckles and his colleague Larry Levan learned the art of mixing. Garage is named in homage to the DJ-ing sensibility and sensurround ambience Levan developed at his legendary club The Paradise Garage, but as a style, it only really took shape after theclubshutitsdoorsinlate1987.

The Paradise Garage opened in January 1977, and was named after its location: an indoor parking lot in SoHo. Like Chicago's Warehouse, the Saturday night clientele was gay (the club's Friday night was mixed straight and gay). Philly and Salsoul were the soundtrack, with the songs gospel-derived exhortations to freedom and fraternity creating a sort of pleasure-principled religious atmosphere. John Iozia described the Garage as both pagan ('an anthropologist's wet dream ... tribal and totally anti-Western') and ecclesiastical (the dancefloor was a fervent congregation of 'space-age Baptists'). Just as regulars used to call The Gallery 'Saturday Mass', and Salvation was styled as a cathedral, so Garage veterans regarded the club as 'their church'. The young Larry had in fact been an altar boy at an Episcopalian Church, while the Bozak DJ-mixer he used at the Garage was modelled on an audio-mixer that the manufacturer had originally developed for church sound-systems.

Levan was one of the very first examples of the DJ-as-shaman, a techno-mystic who developed a science of total sound in order to create spiritual experiences for his followers. Working in tandem with engineer Richard Long, he custom-built the Garage's sound-system, developing his own speakers and a special low-end intensive sub-woofer known as Larry's Horn. Later, during his all-night DJ-ing stints he would progressively upgrade the cartridges on his three turntables, so that the sensory experience would peak around 5 a.m. And during the week, he would spend hours adjusting the positioning of speakers and making sure the sensurround sound was physically overwhelming yet crystal clear. Garage veterans testify that the sheer sonic impact of the system seemed to wreak sub-molecular changes in your body.

Alongside pioneering the DJ-as-shaman's 'technologies of ectsasy', Levan was also an early DJ–producer. He remixed classics like Taana Gardner's 'Heartbeat' and Class Action's 'Weekend', and co-founded The Peech Boys with synth-player Michael deBenedictus and singer Bernard Fowler. The band's ambient-tinged post-disco epics like 'Don't Make Me Wait' and 'Life Is Something Special' are notable for their cavernous reverberance and dub-deep bass. Peech Boys were on the cutting edge of the early eighties New York electro-funk sound, alongside acts like D-Train, Vicky D, Rocker's Revenge, Frances Joli and Sharon Redd, labels like West End and Prelude, and producers such as Arthur Baker, John Robie, Francois Kevorkian, and John 'Jellybean' Benitez.

Another figure who played a key role in building a bridge between electro-funk and garage was Arthur Russell. An avant-garde composer and cellist who once drummed for Laurie Anderson and nearly became a member of Talking Heads, Russell experienced an epiphany at Siano's Gallery, where he was struck by the parallels between disco repetition and the New York downtown minimalism of Philip Glass et al, and was overwhelmed by the immersive quality of music transmitted over a gigantic sound-system. Thereafter his career straddled two sides of New York's downtown: avant-garde minimalism and disco-funk. Russell's 1980 Loose Joints track 'Is It All Over My Face' was a Paradise Garage favourite. In 1982, he co-founded the Sleeping Bag label with Will Socolov, and released the surrealistic and dub-spacious 'Go Bang #5' as Dinosaur L. Infatuated with the ocean (he sometimes used the tag Killer Whale as a writing credit, and as Indian Ocean, he released brilliant proto-house tracks like 'Schoolbells' and 'Treehouse'), Russell was obsessed with echo. His major complaint about most dancefloor fodder was its 'dryness' (its lack of reverb), and he recorded an album of cello-and-slurred-vocal ballads called *The World of Echo*. But his all-time masterpiece of oceanic mysticism was the polyrhythmically perverse 'Let's Go Swimming'.

If one word could sum up the garage aesthetic, it's 'deep'; hence tracks like Hardrive's 'Deep Inside', and band names like Deep Dish.

'Deep' captures the most progressive aspect of garage (its immersive, dub-inflected production) but also its traditionalism (its fetish for songs and classy diva vocals, its allegiance to soul and R & B, its aura of adult-oriented maturity). Of all the post-house, post-techno styles, garage places the most premium on conventional notions of musicality. Garage has little truck with the rhetoric of futurism; samplers and synthesizers are used for economic reasons, as a way of emulating the opulent production values and sumptuous orchestral arrangements of Philly, Salsoul and classic disco.

After the Garage's demise in late 1987 and Larry Levan's decline into drug abuse and ill-health, the spirit of garage was preserved at clubs like The Sound Factory, Better Days and Zanzibar, by DJs like Junior Vasquez, Bruce Forrest, Tee Scott, and Tony Humphries. In the nineties, DJ–producers like Vasquez, Masters At Work, Roger Sanchez, David Morales, Benji Candelario, Danny Tenaglia, Erick Morillo and Armand Van Helden kept the flame alive. In Britain, garage thrived as a kind of back-to-basics scene for sophisticates who'd either outgrown rave or had always recoiled aghast from its juvenile rowdyism. In South London, the Ministry of Sound modelled itself on the Paradise Garage, creating an ambience of upwardly mobile exclusivity and priding itself on having the best sound-system in the world (a claim that has not gone undisputed).

In the late eighties, the two labels that did most to define the nascent garage sound were Nu Groove and Strictly Rhythm. Started in August 1988 by Frank and Karen Mendez (respectively an ex-DJ and a music researcher on radio station Hot 103), Nu Groove's slinky, jazz-inflected house was infused with a subtle artiness and an absurdist sense of humour, reflected in the band names and song titles: NY Housin' Authority's 'The Projects' and its sequel 'The Apartments', Lake Eerie's 'Sex 4 Daze'. Many important New York house producers recorded for Nu Groove: Lenny Dee and Victor Simonelli (as Critical Rhythm), Joey Beltram (as Code 6 and Lost Entity), Ronnie and Rheji Burrell, Kenny Gonzalez.

Strictly Rhythm was where DJ Pierre ended up working as an A & R director and developed his 'fractal' Wild Pitch production style – based around tweaking EQ levels, using filtering effects and constantly adjusting levels in the mix – as heard on classics like Photon Inc's 'Generate Power' and Phuture's 'Rise From Your Grave'. With its sultry percussion, skipping, syncopated snares and surging, butt-coercive basslines, the Strictly Rhythm sound – as shaped by producers like Roger Sanchez and Kenny 'Dope' Gonzalez & 'Little' Louie Vega – was more hard driving and feverish than Nu Groove's (whose tracks were often so refined sounding they verged on *pent*-house muzak). Early Strictly Rhythm is also notable for the brimming, aqueous production on tracks like House 2 House's 'Hypnotize Me (Trance Mix)', all gulf-stream currents of blood-temperature synth and bubble trails of mermaid-diva vocal. The atmosphere on 'Hypnotize Me' and similar tracks like After Hours' 'Waterfalls (3 a.m. Mix)' is condensation-stippled post-coital languor, a balmy plateau of serene sensuality. Combined with the humidity of a club environment, the effect is subaquaticorintra-uterine.

Working together as Masters At Work and Sole Fusion, and separately under a plethora of pseudonyms, Kenny 'Dope' Gonzalez and 'Little' Louie Vega went on to become probably the most famous of the New York house production teams. The Masters of Work name was a gift from Todd Terry, who'd used it for his early tracks 'Alright Alright' and 'Dum Dum Cry'. Terry is most famous for developing a strain of New York 'hard house' that was far tougher and rawer than garage. Instead of symphonic disco, this sound was rooted in electro, old skool hip hop and the brash, crashing electro-funk style known as LatinFreestyle.

Alongside Terry, the pioneers of this New York hardcore house style were Nitro Deluxe. Their 1987 track 'This Brutal House' had a huge impact in Britain, and eventually made the Top Thirty in early 1988 as a remix, 'Let's Get Brutal'. Glassy and glacial, 'This Brutal House' is the missing link between the mid-eighties New York electro of Man Parrish and the early nineties British rave style 'bleep-and-bass'. The track is a vast drumscape of seething Latin percussion and distant snare-crashes on the horizon of the mix, underpinned by sub-bass that has the floor juddering impact of dub reggae. The only element that connects 'This Brutal House' to the sounds coming out of Chicago is the eerie vocal effects: a human cry is played on the sampling keyboard like a jittery trumpet ostinato, then arpeggiated into what sounds like Tweety Bird singing scat. Nitro Deluxe's follow-up 'On A Mission' is even more despotic in its vivisection of the human voice. The 'Say Your Love' mix puts the word 'say' through a digital mangler, shattering it into a pandemonium of pitch-bent whimpers, hiccups, bleats and oinks; the 'Closet Mission' mix multitracks and varispeeds the syllable into a cyclonic swirl of phoneme-particles that sounds like an aviary on fire, then rapid-fires a stream of 94 r.p.m. micro-syllables like electrons fromacathoderaytube.

Todd Terry's own style was a bridge between the cut-up collage tracks of Mantronix and the sample-heavy house soon to emerge from Britain. Terry is a no-nonsense, whack-'em-out, I-wanna-get-paid-in-full kind of guy; he's described himself as 'more of a trackmaster ... I'm not a writer of songs, they're too much trouble. Plus you make twice the money off of tracks, [because] they're quicker.' Lacking both the artistic pretensions of the Detroit aesthetes and the soul-affiliated spirituality of the deep house and garage producers, Terry has proved that mercenary motives can result in great popular art like Royal House's 'Can You Party' and 'Party People', Orange Lemon's 'Dreams of Santa Anna', Black Riot's 'A Day In The Life' and CLS's 'Can You FeelIt?'

Terry's roots in hip hop block parties come through in early tracks like Black Riot's 'A Day In The Life' and the pre-Vega/Gonzalez Masters At Work outings 'Dum Dum Cry' and 'Alright Alright': the sound is all jagged edits and stabs, scratch FX, toytown melody-riffs, sampler-vocal riffs *à la* The Art of Noise, blaring bursts of abstract sound, depth-charge bass and breakbeats. That rough-and-ready, thrown-together quality also characterizes Royal House's 'Can You Party', a UK Number Fourteen hit in October 1988. With its 'Can you feel it?' invocations, sirens, and bursts of mob uproar (cunningly designed to trigger a feedback loop of excitement in the crowd), 'Can You Party' anticipates the rabble-rousing hardcore rave anthems of the early nineties. Basically a rewrite of 'Can You Party', 'Party People' intensifies the palsied atmosphere until the very air seems to be trembling with some intangible fever. The track turns around a Morse Code riff seemingly made out of heavily reverbed piano or audience hubbub, a riff that seems to possess your nervous system like digital epilepsy, inducing strangely geometric convulsions. Like much of Terry's work, the track is jarring because it's like a series of crescendos and detonations, a frenzy of context-less intensities without rhyme or reason.

With their jagged edges and lo-fi grit, Terry's cut-and-paste tracks were a world away from garage's polished production and smooth plateaux of pleasure. On the Royal House album, Terry used funky breakbeats and jittery electro beat-box rhythms as well as house's four-to-the-floor kick drum. Terry's sound was hip house, a hybrid sub-genre that was simultaneously being reached by Chicago producers Tyree and DJ Fast Eddie. Tyree told me in early 1988 that he was already working on a fusion of house and rap: 'At my parties, I mix house tracks with hip hop records on 45 r.p.m. – it makes LL Cool J sound like a chipmunk!' In early 1989, the first recorded examples of this hybrid came through. Some tracks simply layered rather feeble rapping over a house track. Others, like Fast Eddie's 'Hip House' and 'Yo Yo get Funky', combined house rhythms and 303 acid-pulses with James Brown samples, sound effects, and breakbeats. Perhaps the best of the bunch was Tyree's 'Hardcore Hip House', with its weird blend of funky drummer shuffle beats, house piano vamps, and Tyree rapping about how 'hip house is soon to be / the giant in the industry'. It wasn't, but the hybrid sound and the chant 'I'm comin' hardcore' were prophetic of the breakbeat house/hardcore sound that would become the staple of the British rave scene in the early nineties.

By 1989, then, Black America had generated four distinct and fully-formed genres of electronic dance music: Detroit techno; the deep house/garage sound of Chicago and New York; acid house and minimal jack tracks; breakbeat-and-sample based hip house. Transplanted to the other side of the Atlantic, each of these sounds would mutate – beyond all recognition, and *through* a kind of creative misrecognition on the part of the British and Europeans.

TWO

LIVING
A DREAM

ACID HOUSE AND
UK RAVE,
1988–89

In 1987, London clubland was as crippled by cool as ever. The Soho craze for rare groove (early seventies, sub-James Brown funk) represented the fag-end of eighties style culture, what with its elitist obscurantism (rare groove DJs covered up the labels with Tipp-Ex to prevent their rivals identifying the tracks) and its deference to a bygone, outdated notion of 'blackness'.

House music seemed to be a fad that had been and gone, at least as far as London clubland was concerned. 'House never kicked off the way we thought,' remembers Mark Moore, one of the few DJs who played Chicago and Detroit tracks. 'I remember spinning Derrick May's "Strings of Life" at the Mud Club and clearing the entire floor.' House did have a toe-hold in the gay scene, at clubs like Jungle and Pyramid, where Moore spun alongside other house crusaders like Colin Faver and Eddie Richards. But most gay clubbers still preferred Eurobeat and Hi-NRG, says Moore, and reckoned the arty Pyramid crowd were 'weirdos'.

Ironically, straight audiences regarded house suspiciously as 'queers' music'. The only straight club that regularly played it was Delirium, run by Noel and Maurice Watson and modelled on New York's Paradise Garage. But most of the club's following were rare groove and hip hop kids who, according to Moore, 'hated it when it went into house. They had to have a cage built around the DJ box so they wouldn't get bottled by hip hop kids when they played house! The Watson brothers made a brave effort to make it kick off, but it just didn't happen.'

At the end of 1987, however, there were signs of life in the vogue for DJ-records – breakbeat-and-sample collages that eschewed rapping in favour of absurdist sound-bites and, tempo-wise, were closer to house than hip hop. Enabled by the arrival of cheap samplers like the Casio SK1, and usually recorded for next to nothing, these DJ records stormed the pop charts, starting with M/A/R/R/S's Number One smash 'Pump Up The Volume' in late 1987 and continuing into early 1988 with Bomb The Bass's Number Two hit 'Beat Dis' and S'Express's Number One hit 'Theme from S'Express'.

S'Express was Mark Moore, and 'Theme' was a kind of reward from Rhythm King Records for the DJs unofficial A & R work for the label, which brought them successful club acts like Renegade Soundwave, The Beatmasters and The Cookie Crew. With its campy 'I've got the hots for you' hook and 'suck me off' samples courtesy of performance artist Karen Finley, 'Theme' was the vinyl expression of Moore's irreverent and eclectic DJ sensibility. Although it was closer to a kitschadelic, postmodern update of disco than the Chicago sound, 'Theme' was received as one of the first British house records. More importantly, the track's tacky euphoria chimed in with the anti-cool ethos of the new 'Balearic' clubs like Shoom and The Project.

'Balearic' referred to the DJ-ing approach of Alfredo Fiorillo, a former journalist who'd fled the fascist rigours of his native Argentina for the laid back bohemian idyll of Ibiza. 'Balearic' didn't refer to a style of music but to a revolt against style codes and the very tyranny of tastefulness then strangling London club culture. DJ Alfredo's long sets at Amnesia – which, like most Ibizan nightclubs, had no roof, so you danced under the stars – encompassed the indie hypno-grooves of The Woodentops, the mystic rock of U2 and The Waterboys, early house, Europop, plus oddities from the likes of Peter Gabriel and Thrashing Doves.

'It was just the best of all kinds of music, and really refreshing, 'cos in London you were just hearing the same old sound,' remembers Paul Oakenfold. In the mid-eighties, Oakenfold was involved in London's hip hop scene as a DJ, club promoter and agent for Profile and Def Jam acts like Run DMC and the Beastie Boys. He first went out to Ibiza in 1985, where he discovered that the real action resided not in the touristic San Antonio, where British beer boys ran rampant, but in the more upmarket Ibiza Town on the other side of the island. Inspired by clubs like Amnesia, Pasha and Ku, Oakenfold and his mate Trevor Fung tried in late 1985 to start a Balearic-style club in South London, named The Funhouse after John 'Jellybean' Benitez's New York nightspot. 'It was exactly the same as what we did in '87 , but we done it in '85 and it didn't work. People couldn't understand the concept of playing all kinds of music together . . . It was something that we tried six months and lost a lot of money, so we just shelved it.'

The other element absent in 1985 was Ecstasy – which was readily available in Ibiza and helped open up minds to diverse, 'uncool' sounds. The turning point came in the summer of 1987. Oakenfold hired a villa in Ibiza and brought over a bunch of DJ friends to celebrate his twenty-sixth birthday: 'I invited Danny Rampling, Johnny Walker and Nicky Holloway, and all three came over and experienced what I'd been through' – the magic of dancing all night on Ecstasy.

By this point, hundreds of British youth had heard about the scene in Ibiza Town. Kids like Barry Ashworth, a nineteen-year-old plasterer from the Streatham area. 'We was in Majorca, still on that suburban thug-like thing, and then we left Majorca, about fourteen of us, 'cos we'd ended up in the biggest bar fight you'd ever seen. We had to leave the island, so we headed straight off to Ibiza. There was a handful of mates I'd been to school with who were already there and plotted up, already into it.' The bloke who gave Ashworth his first E was a tough character, a former boxing champion – 'but here he was on mescalin for three days at Amnesia – with all these goats in pens on the edge of the dancefloor, pissing and shitting everywhere . . . I flew back after a couple of weeks, then went back there literally every month for the rest of the season.' Back in England, Ashworth got involved in putting on parties like Deja Vu, Monkey Drum and Naked Lunch; that summer in Ibiza, he says, set the framework 'for the next seven years'.

When Oakenfold returned to London, he and Ian St Paul reactivated the 'Balearic' concept they'd put on the shelf back in 1985 after the failure of The Funhouse. At Streatham's Project Club, where he'd been DJ-ing on Fridays, he persuaded the owner to let him start an illegal after-hours event. When the regular night's crowd had been turfed out at 2 a.m., the exit door would be opened to admit about 150 Ibiza veterans. Oakenfold flew in Alfredo to play and 'invited all the main heads, the key people in London, from fashion to film to music to clubland'. What these prime movers encountered was a complete subcultural package of slang, behaviour and clothing, that had hatched during the summer in Ibiza. The look was a weird mix of Mediterranean beach bum, hippy and football casual – baggy trousers and T-shirts, paisley bandanas, dungarees, ponchos, Converse Allstars baseball boots – loose-fitting, because the Ecstasy and non-stop trance dancing made you sweat buckets. 'Baggy trousers, baggy top, trainers – it wasn't what you wore, it was your attitude that got you in the club. London clubs had always been about people drinking, trying to chat up girls, looking good but not dancing. All of a sudden we completely changed that around – you'd come down and you'd dance for six hours. The idea was "if you're not into dancing, then don't come down"'.

The Project all-nighters got so popular – 'We had seven hundred trying to get in, it just got out of hand, we couldn't keep it quiet anymore' – that the club was soon raided by the police. So St Paul and Oakenfold started The Future, a Thursday night event at The Sanctuary, around the back of the huge gay club Heaven. Future was members only; the card bore the commandment 'dance you fuckers!' On his first visit to Future, says Mark Moore, 'I remember thinking "This is it, this is the crowd for this kind of music." It was exactly the same mix – early house, plus all that indie stuff – I'd been playing to the gay crowd, except this was a straight crowd.' He took Philip Salon, doyen of eighties 'style culture' and the impresario behind The Mud Club, down to Future. 'I told him, "This *is* the future, this is what it's going to be like," and he was saying "No, no, they're all suburban *norms*." And I'm like, "Yeah, but this music and this energy, this is the next thing that's gonna happen, I'm telling you."'

Around this time – November 1987 – Danny Rampling and his wife Jenni started Shoom, a tiny club located in a Southwark gym called the Fitness Centre, just a few hundred yards south of the Thames. Although Danny supplied the club's musical vision (pure Balearic), the powerhouse behind Shoom is generally reputed to be Jenni Rampling. A formidable figure who'd previously been the manageress of the Bond Street branch of the shoe shop Pied À Terre, Jenni maintained the club's membership scheme and newsletter, kept the press at arm's length and controlled the door with a ruthlessness that became infamous.

'We used to say that Jenni had the Battle of Britain spirit,' recalls Mark Moore, 'There was this kind of naïve pioneering spirit.'

'The Ramplings were a very ordinary, upwardly mobile working class couple from Bermondsey,' remembers journalist Louise Gray, an early Shoom convert. 'Suddenly they were thrown into this fantastically trendy set where they had luminaries pounding on their doors, and they were being taken up by people like Fat Tony and Boy George – very queeny, nightlife sophisticates.'

The first time Gray actually managed to get inside Shoom, 'we arrived terribly early, about 10.30, and we couldn't really figure out what the fuss was about. There was about twenty people, dancing wildly. I was sitting talking, and then this girl just appeared absolutely out of nowhere, plonked herself down on my knee, grabbed the corners of my mouth and pulled them up into a smile. She said 'Be Happy!' and then jumped off. I was completely nonplussed – I'd never experienced behaviour like that, and thought it quite crazed.'

Suddenly the club filled up very fast – not just with people, but with 'peasouper, strawberry-flavoured smoke, lit only by strobes. If you went on to the dancefloor, you could only see a few inches ahead. It was just exciting, there was a real contact high. I didn't have any drugs that night, but that was when I realized that drugs had something to do with it.' Drugs had everything to do with it: the name 'Shoom' was freshly-coined slang for rushing, for the surging, heart-in-mouth sensation of coming up on Ecstasy. The imagery on the flyers, membership cards and newsletters was blatantly druggy: pills with Smiley faces on them, exhortations to 'Get Right On One, Matey!!!'

Unlike your typical West End club, the Shoom scene was not about being seen, but about losing it – your cool, your self-consciousness, your *self*. Quoting T. S. Eliot, Gray describes the fruit-flavoured smoke as 'the fog that both connects and separates. You'd have these faces looming at you out of the fog. It was like a sea of connected alienation.'

Says Mark Moore: 'Often it was so chaotic, you couldn't really see in front of you, you couldn't really talk to anyone. So a lot of the time you just spent on your own dancing ... You'd have people in their own world, doing that mad trance dancing, oblivious to everything else. But then you also had blokes coming up who were, like, "yeah, all right mate!! Smile! Smile!" And hugging you.'

Coming from the arty end of the gay scene, Moore was used to this kind of demonstrativeness. But at Shoom he encountered 'this whole new mentality ... It was all these suburbanites who – without wishing to sound élitist – it was as if they'd taken this Ecstasy and they were releasing themselves, *for the first time*. It was like they'd suddenly been let out of this box they'd been kept inside and they were just beginning to come to terms with the idea that, y'know, "I'm a man but I can hug my mate," stuff like that.' Gay behavioural codes and modes of expressivity were entering the body-consciousness of straight working-class boys, via Ecstasy.

Oriented around communal frenzy rather than posing, Shoom was the chrysalis for rave culture, in so far as *the rave* in its pure populist form is the antithesis of *the club*. At the same time, Shoom *was* a club, more so than most Soho nightspots in fact, because it had a membership scheme. And Jenni Rampling's door policy was as strict as Studio

54; as word of Shoom spread and people flocked down to find out what the fuss was all about, she rapidly acquired a reputation for being a 'queen bitch' who'd turn away people who only weeks earlier had managed to get in. 'Saturday night at the Fitness Centre, and by eleven o'clock, a hundred people or more would just be absolutely ramming to get in,' remembers Louise Gray. 'It was a monumentally difficult door to run . . . She'd see the people she wanted to get in and they'd be virtually dragged through the crowd, like through a bush backwards.'

The Shoom ethos was love-and-peace-and-unity, universal tolerance and we-are-all-the-same. It was supposed to be the death-knell of clubland's snobbish exclusivity, but there was an essential contradiction in the way that the Shoom experience was restricted only to the original clique and their guests, plus a few minor celebrities like Patsy Kensit and Paul Rutherford of Frankie Goes To Hollywood. As one of the many 'blanked' by Jenni, I can well remember the feeling of disillusion: don't believe the hype, it's just like any old West End nightclub.

Then again, Shoom's close-knit, we-are-family atmosphere depended on keeping at bay the influx of intrigued neophytes, not to mention the hooligan element. 'They really pushed that whole love-and-happiness-and-bonding thing, really believed in it,' says Moore. 'People slagged Jenni off . . . but I admire her for doing what she thought was right. It's fine to be all lovey-dovey, but there are certain people who you don't want in your club, 'cos you won't be able to achieve that vibe.'

Those who did belong were treated to ice pops, fruit, badges and other giveaways. 'One time Mark Moore and I decided to nip out and get a coffee and a bagel in Brick Lane,' remembers Gray. 'Jenni gave us fifty quid to buy around 500 bagels. We got there at about 4 a.m. and said "please can we have 500 bagels." They thought we were mad! They filled up these binliners and we carried them back to Shoom, and the Ramplings went round handing out bagels.' Members also received the Shoom newsletter, with the text typed in capitals and many headlines hand-drawn. Inside were sketchy record reviews and crudely drawn cartoons (like The Smileys, a stickman-and-woman who strolled around London spreading love-peace-warmth vibes), plus testimonials from Shoomers: 'Let your pure inner self manifest and only then will you be shooming!' 'I Felt As If I Was Living A Dream.'

Revolution in Progress

The democratic promise of the Balearic ethos could not be kept the preserve of the chosen few for long. In the spring of 1988, Oakenfold took it to the next level when he launched Spectrum as a Monday night club in the 2000 capacity Heaven, round the corner from where The Future had taken place. 'Everyone said to us, you can't do a club on a Monday. But we did a deal with Heaven so that as long as we broke even, it was okay. After two weeks, we owed twelve grand. The third week, they were all set to close us down, but we broke even. And from then on, it just got bigger and bigger.'

Spectrum's subtitle was 'Theatre of Madness', and this was no idle boast. 'I was quite shocked, almost appalled, actually,' remembers Nick Philip, a hip hop fan who was intrigued enough to check out Spectrum at its height. 'Just the hedonism, and how out of line everyone was getting. Back in the late eighties, the club scene was quite uptight, you had to wear exactly the right clothes to get in, and you might see the odd person there who was really out of it, but it was not the general rule. But at Spectrum, everyone looked like they were from fucking Mars. Drenched in sweat, wearing baggy shit, and all just looking at the DJ with their arms in the air, like it was some really weird religious ceremony. I was quite freaked out by it.'

The atmosphere was even more deranged at The Trip, a club started by Nicky Holloway in June 1988. Instead of the laid-back, sunkissed Balearic vibe, the music was full-on acid house. The location – The Astoria, in the heart of London's West End – signalled the scene's emergence into the full glare of public consciousness. When The Trip closed at 3 a.m., the punters would pour out into Charing Cross Road, stopping the traffic and partying in the street. 'Then the police would come,' remembers Mark Moore, 'and the sirens would get turned on. Everyone would crowd around the police van and chant "acieed!"' – the war cry of 1988 – '"and dance to the siren". The police didn't know what to make of it, it was like, "what the fuck is going on?!?"' Then everyone would troop en masse to the municipal multi-storey car park near the YMCA in Bedford Street, where they'd dance around their vehicles to house music pumping out of the car stereos.

Because of Britain's antiquated club licensing laws, the night's mayhem ended prematurely. One result was the chill-out scene. 'The chill out was good, 'cos that's when you'd invite complete strangers back to your place and that's when you'd make new friends,' remembers Moore. If you wanted to carry on dancing through the night, you had to turn to the illegal warehouse parties or after-hours, unlicensed clubs like the legendary RIP at Clink Street.

RIP was the brainchild of creative-and-romantic partners Paul Stone and Lu Vukovic. He had been involved in organizing dub reggae parties in Portsmouth; she was an idealistic former anarcho-punk. Stone recruited the DJ team of Kid Batchelor, 'Evil' Eddie Richards and Mr C, who had been running Fantasy, one of the first straight house clubs in London. The first RIP party took place in April 1988 at a tiny underground location in Eversholt Street, Euston. A couple of months later, RIP started up again at Clink Street, a dingy building in South East London that had once been a jail.

'It was used as an illegal drinking den before we got our hands on it,' says Mr C, later to become a pop star as the rapper in The Shamen. 'And there was a recording studio in there, which we used as the DJ booth.' In one room, Eddie Richards and Kid Batchelor played; in the other Mr C spun, followed by the Shock Sound System, another bunch of early house supporters who included future Brit-house luminary Ashley Beedle. 'We started off RIP every Saturday night, and within a month it was choc-a-bloc. Then we started the Friday night as well, which was called A Transmission – for Acid Transmission. Then we did Zoo on Sundays, so we'd have all weekend at it.' The parties would go until nine or ten in the morning.

Many people thought RIP was an acronym for Rave In Peace. It actually stood for 'Revolution In Progress'. The phrase captures the near-militant underground attitude of the music policy and the slightly sinister atmosphere of the club, a world away from the teddy bears and ice lollies of Shoom. 'If Shoom was "underground" and "edgy", Clink Street was dark as fuck, sound-in-Hell!' laughs Mr C. 'It was pretty heavy in there – there was a lot of soccer thugs, and villains. Saying that, next to them was some of the most beautiful people you ever saw in your life. All types of people from all walks of life just came together to get completely nutted. It was complete madness.

'We never had any trouble. But people were completely up for it. Everybody was on something. And back then, it wasn't just about E. LSD was just as popular. It was an equal mix, and a lot of people taking E and acid together as a synergy thing, what used to be called "candy flips".' The music was tripped-out, too, a long way from Balearic. 'Unless Colin Faver was playing Shoom, it was generally namby pamby sort of stuff, lightweight gear,' sneers Mr C. 'Clink Street was about the intense, underground side of house.'

That said, many people frequented both clubs, especially since they were less than a mile apart in South East London. 'Clink St is within spitting distance of Shoom,' remembers Louise Gray. 'To get there you'd have to go through the fruit and vegetable market. All the costermongers would be there in the small hours, taking in the cabbage supplies from all over rural England, and suddenly they'd be confronted by this army of psychedelic kids in their cut-off T-shirts and cut-off jeans, marching through the market to Clink Street. It must have been an incredibly bizarre sight!'

Absolute Beginners

Ecstasy had been available in London since the early eighties, but the supply was highly restricted. You had to know someone who brought it over from America, where it was legal until 1985. There was something of an Ecstasy scene at Taboo, Leigh Bowery's club for fashion freaks, but nobody had discovered its application as a trance-dance drug. Instead, small groups of friends were using it for private bonding sessions.

In 1988, Ecstasy became much easier to get hold of, though it was still rather pricey at around £20 a tab. In the spring of that year, Louise Gray had her first Ecstasy experience at a Hedonism warehouse party in West London. 'I remember at one point feeling immensely hot and claustrophobic, having to go outside and lie down, and thinking that I might throw up. People figured out pretty soon that Ecstasy did something to your stomach, during the initial rush. Some people had to shoot off immediately to the loo, 'cos they were going to get the runs; others were sick. After Hedonism, I remember being put in a taxi by my friend, and lying on the floor of this cab at five in the morning, telling this cabbie my life story!'

Nobody really knew much about Ecstasy, about how it worked or what was the best way to take it. People quickly worked out that alcohol dulled the E buzz; at Shoom, Lucozade became the beverage of choice, partly because it replenished energy and partly because it was the only drink available at the Fitness Centre. Myths sprang up around the new drug, like the notion that Vitamin C killed the buzz, which ruled out orange juice. There was also considerable confusion over Ecstasy's legal status, and nobody knew if it was an addictive substance or not. The other big Ecstasy myth concerned the drug's aphrodisiac powers. 'All these strange reports were coming through that it turned you into a sex fiend,' says Gray. 'But if anything it was the complete opposite. Very little sex happened that year. People were very cuddly, and that was very nice: you could be cuddled by complete strangers in a very non-threatening way, 'cos you knew nothing was going to happen. If you got upset about something, this crowd of strangers' hands would descend on you. It was touchy feely, an amorphous sensuality – but it wasn't a *sexuality*.

'That's one of the reasons the Ecstasy scene was so docile – the libido had actually been sublimated into a completely different form. People weren't going out to pull. You might meet someone there who was nice and then you'd see them and then sex would happen at some other stage. I think that was one of the reasons why you could have such an extraordinary mix of people – male gays, but also working-class boys who hadn't had any contact with the trendy culture, and maybe in another life they might have gone queer-bashing or Paki-bashing. Suddenly they were thrown into this environment where everyone was kissy-kissy, but it didn't matter, they weren't threatened in any way.'

Love Thugs

Thanks to Ecstasy, all the class and race and sex-preference barriers were getting fluxed up; all sorts of people who might never have exchanged words or glances were being swirled together in a promiscuous chaos. One of the most striking changes was the way that the territorial rivalry between areas of London – largely expressed through supporting different football teams – was dissipated. Almost overnight, the Stanley-knife wielding trouble-maker had metamorphosized into the 'love thug', or as Brit-rapper Gary Clail later put it, 'the emotional hooligan'.

'You were getting a lot of the football firms down at Spectrum and The Trip,' says Moore. 'The bouncers were quite close to the street and they kept saying "It's gonna kick off in here," 'cos of there being rival firms in the same club. But they were all on E so they were just hugging each other, they couldn't be bothered to fight.'

Before the summer of 1988, a typical night out for your average working-class lad consisted of 'getting drunk, chatting up a bird, or having a fight with another area,' claims Barry Ashworth. 'Leading up to that time, it was a pretty violent period in football. And then thoughout the country everybody started necking pills, and then people started going to the terraces necked up too.'

This interface between football fanaticism, with its ritualized inebriation and hand-to-hand combat, and acid house, with its anti-alcohol bias and hippy-dippy pacifism, seems on the surface an extremely unlikely upshot. Actually, there are quite a few parallels between football and raving. In the eighties, with mass unemployment and Thatcher's defeat of the unions, the football match and the warehouse party offered rare opportunities for the working class to experience a sense of collective identity: to belong to a 'we' rather than an atomized, impotent 'I'.

In *Among The Thugs*, Bill Buford argues that the spatial organization of the football stadium – fans are shunted like cattle down narrow dark passages into packed 'pens' – is almost deliberately designed to generate a herd-mentality. Crammed tightly into intimate physical contact with strangers, the spectators gradually lose any sense of separate self-hood and instead melt into crowd-consciousness. As the match proceeds, the game's rhythms of tension and release traverse the crowd-body in the form of shared, physically felt sensations: catching your breath in anticipation of a goal, then exploding in euphoria or (rather more often) sighing in anti-climax. On the rare occasion of a goal being scored, total strangers often embrace each other.

The experience of going to The Trip and Spectrum, or even better to the bigger-scale warehouse parties like Apocalypse Now, was not dissimilar to a football match: collective fervour, bodies pressed together, the liberation of losing yourself in the crowd. The big difference is that football is a remarkably inefficient 'desiring machine' compared with the acid party, where the DJ offers an endless sequence of crescendos. Given the tendency of the football match to result in a no-score or low-scoring draw, there is far more scope for frustration rather than relief.

Like a sort of avant-garde of football fandom, the thugs evolved ways of intensifying the game's sensations of tribal unity. In Buford's account, by the mid-eighties football hooliganism was a neo-pagan cult of sacrificial violence, complete with shamanic warrior-priests (called 'generals'), tribal markings (team or star player tattoos, instead of cabbalistic symbols) and rituals of self-intoxication. Like Viking berserkers, hooligans use alcohol, chanting, and sprinting *en masse*, to generate a mob-will. The result is a collective adrenalin-surge that propels them over the brink between normality and running amok. Buford describes his own experience of participating in one street battle as a Dionysian transport: time slows down, perceptions become ultra-vivid, there's an access to 'an experience of absolute completeness'. The thugs themselves talk of these exalted moments using the language of drugs ('the crack, the buzz, and the fix') or spirituality ('it's a religion, really').

In 1988–9, soccer hooligans discovered that E offered an even better buzz than the adrenalin-and-endorphin rush of hand-to-hand combat, and they temporarily gave up their carefully strategized confrontations. Instead of gouging each other in the face with broken glasses, supporters of rival teams fraternized in pubs after the match, scored drugs off each other, and trooped off to raves. Irvine Welsh's novel *Marabou Stork Nightmares* tells the story of a thug who is transformed into a New Man thanks to E and rave. But, as Welsh has pointed out, when the MDMA-buzz inevitably faded in the early nineties, many hooligans reverted to their old, tried-and-true techniques of getting a rush.

Mantra for a State of Mind

Back in 1988, the Love Thug was a crucial element in the myth-in-progress that was popularly dubbed 'The Second Summer Of Love': the heartless hoolie turned loved-up nutter was proof that Ecstasy really was a wonder drug, the agent of a spiritual and social revolution.

Flooded with idealism and will-to-belief, some members of the first Ecstasy generation were latching on to ideas about spirituality and the New Age, struggling to articulate the overwhelming Ecstasy-induced feelings coursing through their nervous systems. 'A lot of people were born again,' marvels Mark Moore. 'They gave up their relatively normal lives, 'cos they thought "Why am I doing this shitty job?" You got all these people suddenly deciding to go off and travel. People I'd known for years were suddenly dressing all ethnic and getting spiritual. The whole New Age thing surged forward.'

For most, the back-to-the-sixties/dawning of the Age of Aquarius imagery was tongue-in-cheek, a figleaf for pure hedonism. But many felt utterly transformed. 'I remember getting prophet books myself, the Bhagavad-Gita,' says Ashworth. 'All kinds of things that I certainly wouldn't have bothered with, coming from my kind of background. Growing up in that background, nobody can quite express themselves: a man was a man, nobody actually *speaks*. The way you communicated was literally by your force, by acting macho. And all of sudden, you started saying things to people that you would never ever have said . . . "I *loooove* you!"' MDMA was a miracle cure for the English disease of emotional constipation, reserve, inhibition. And it wasn't just about telling your friends you loved them, it was about telling people who *weren't* your friends you loved them!

Because of Ecstasy and the mingling and fraternization it incited, the living death of the eighties – characterized by social atomization and the Thatcher inculcated work ethic – seemed to be coming to an abrupt end. 'Everyone was vitalized,' says Gray. And yet, for all the self-conscious counterculture echoes, acid house was a curiously apolitical phenomenon, at least in the sense of activism and protest. While the tenor of the peace-and-unity rhetoric ran against the Thatcherite grain, in other respects – the rampant hedonism, the fact that Ecstasy was priced out of the range of the unemployed – acid house's pleasure-principled euphoria was very much a product of the eighties: a kind of *spiritual materialism*, a greed for intense experiences. As far as the sterner pop-culture critics were concerned, acieed was escapism, pure and simple: Stewart Cosgrove argued in *New Statesman and Society* that acid house's 'pleasures come not from resistance but from surrender.' A year later, Tim London of the politicized dance-pop band Soho railed: 'Summer of Love? What a load of old bollocks. Summer of Having a Good Time, more like! Just like kids have always done, since the days of *Saturday Night Fever*. All this bollocks about the E culture, it's just people projecting their ideas on to something that's always been there: mindless hedonism.'

Acid house's biggest impact was in the domain of leisure; it caused a shift from alcohol to Ecstasy-and-soft-drinks, created a mass recreational drug culture, and stoked a craving for all-night-dancing that would rub up against the antedeluvian club licensing laws. The energy liberated by Ecstasy felt revolutionary, but it wasn't directed against the social 'stasis quo'. Acieed was more like a secession from normality, a subculture based around what Antonio Melechi characterizes as a kind of *collective disappearance.* 'One of the things I found exhilarating at that point,' confirms Louise Gray, 'was the idea that there was this whole society of people who lived at night and slept during the day. This carnival idea of turning the ordinary world completely on its head. Like slipping into a parallel universe, almost.' London was transformed into a magical city, transected by new pathways and highly charged itineraries. 'During the day, Charing Cross and The Strand and the journey to South London would mean one thing – I might go to the bank or Sainsbury's – but once the sun went down, it was a *route*, stretching from Heaven to Shoom to Clink Street.'

By autumn 1988, it was possible to virtually live in this parallel universe, full time. There was a party every night. Fridays, there was The Mud Club and then A Transmission at Clink Street. Saturdays, the raver faced a dilemma – Shoom or The Trip – followed by RIP at Clink Street right through til dawn. Sunday night offered the mellow, coming-down-from-the-night-before vibe of Confusion, Nicky Harwood's club in Soho. Monday was Spectrum; Tuesday, you could go to the gay club Daisy Chain, at The Fridge in Brixton. Wednesday, the Pyramid at Heaven; Thursday, a new Heaven night called Rage. If this regime of bliss wasn't enough, there was a host of other acid nights around town like Babylon, Love, Loud Noise, Enter the Dragon, Elysium and even the tacky old Camden Palace; at the weekends, there were also the one-off warehouse parties. Back then, remembers Barry Ashworth, 'You was *arseholed* four, five nights a week.'

Keep Taking the Tabloids

Alongside the reinvocations of late sixties psychedelia, the acid-house revellers often compared the feeling in the summer of 1988 to punk rock – the same explosion of suppressed energies, the same overnight Year Zero transformation of tastes and values. All that was missing was the mass media's discovery of the new subculture, and the inevitable 'moral panic' over what the kids of today were up to.

When the newspapers finally discovered the acid-house explosion, their coverage was initially quite positive. The *Sun* described the scene as 'cool and groovy', printed a guide to the slang, and even ran a special offer for Smiley T-shirts, priced at a very reasonable £5.50. But a few weeks later, the tabloid abruptly changed its tune with a story entitled 'Evil Of Ecstasy'. Readers were warned that MDMA could cause heart attacks and brain damage, and (incorrectly) that the drug was often cut with rat poison, heroin and embalming fluid. The *Sun*'s resident doctor, Vernon Coleman, spared no efforts in his attempt to deter Britain's 'pill potty' youth, conjuring up the prospect of horrendous hallucinations lasting up to twelve hours, panic attacks and flashbacks, and the probability of being sexually assaulted while under the influence.

In the following weeks, the *Sun* ran further exposés like 'Acid House Horror', prompting its tabloid rival the *Mirror* to pitch in with '£12 Trip To An Evil Night of Ecstasy'. As the newspapers engaged in a contest to see who could come up with the most luridly distorted reportage, acieed's 'folk devil' revealed itself not to be the poor deluded youth themselves (as was the case with the mods, punk rockers, skinheads and football casuals) but the sinister figures behind the parties and the pill pushing: the 'Acid House baron', a mercenary Pied Piper figure luring the children of England into a world of bad trips and orgiastic delirium.

The Ecstasy-related death of twenty-one-year-old Janet Mayes on 28 October provided the tabloids with the 'killer drug' angle they'd been waiting for. On 2 November, the *Sun*'s front page pointed the finger at a jailbird/boxer turned bouncer who, it was alleged, was the 'Mr Big Of Acid Parties'. Inside, the paper announced that it was withdrawing its Smiley T-shirt offer, and offering instead free 'Say No To Drugs' badges, with a frowning Smiley. A cartoon, 'Trip To Hell', depicted a devil-in-disguise handing out pills like candy and ushering kids into the 'Acid House'; in the next frame, the welcome mat turns into a trapdoor, dropping the youths into the flames of Hades.

Chiming in with the grand tradition of yellow-press scare stories about cocaine and 'reefer madness', the tabloids were obsessed with Ecstasy's utterly mythical aphrodisiac powers. Readers were warned that they might end up in bed with ugly people, or find themselves in a writhing tangle with several nude strangers; an Ecstasy-dabbler testified that he kept getting slapped for stroking people's faces, then found his girlfriend caressing a strange man's chest. At one acid club, the *Sun*'s reporter hallucinated 'OUTRAGEOUS sex romps taking place on a special stage in front of the dancefloor'.

The fact that the new music was called 'acid house' led to some confusion on the newspapers' part about exactly which demon drug they were decrying. 'The screaming teenager jerked like a demented doll as the LSD he swallowed an hour earlier took its terrible toll,' declared one *Sun* report. 'The boy ... had become sucked into the hellish nightmare engulfing thousands of youngsters as the Acid House scourge sweeps Britain ... Callous organizers and drug dealers simply looked on and LAUGHED ... DJs encouraged the frenzied crowd with chants of "Are you on one? Let's go MENTAL, let's go FATAL."'

Inflamed by the tabloids, the backlash began in earnest. Radio One DJ Peter Powell described acid house as 'the closest thing to mass zombiedom'; Sir Ralph Halpern banned Smiley T-shirts from 650 branches of his Top Shop and Top Man retail chain; pop stars – including a few veterans of early Shoom – reeled out the platitudes about how you didn't need to take drugs to have a good time, kids, honest. And the police began to crack down on warehouse parties, raiding events by Kaleidoscope and Brainstorm, and using frogmen to assault a pleasure boat rave in Greenwich. Police attempted to blockade the entrance at another massive party in Greenwich but after nego-tiations, the party went ahead. The *Sun* reported the Guy Fawkes all-nighter as 'Acid Raid Cops Flee 3000 At Party: Drug Pushers Carry On', describing how the police, fearing a riot, left the 'freaked out' youngsters to carry on 'raving it up at the sex-and-drugs orgy'; *News of the World* upped the ante with the headline 'CRAZED ACID MOB ATTACK POLICE'.

Après Nous, le Deluge

All the scaremongering tabloid coverage, plus TV reports like *News At Ten*'s exposé of an Apocalypse Now warehouse party, did not have the intended effect of discouraging the youth of Britain. If anything, 'it just helped it grow even bigger,' says Mark Moore. 'It was like what Bill Grundy did for the Sex Pistols.' The result was an influx of younger kids and suburbanites into the scene.

Despite their populist rhetoric and antagonism towards traditional clubland élitism, the original Balearic scenesters were horrified by the arrival of the great unwashed and unhip. Oakenfold blames the tabloids: 'They ruined it for us. Before, it was responsible people [taking drugs]. It wasn't silly. It got silly when they made it commercial. And that's when it got worrying 'cos you had young kids doing drugs 'cos they were told by the press that that was what everyone was doing. They felt that was what they had to do, to be a part of it. Drugs became mainstream, and everyone became sheep. Our club was about individuals, characters. But it got watered down and it became horrible drugs, horrible people.'

The backlash against the johnny-come-lately acieed freaks was led by Boy's Own, a clique of Balearic DJs and tastemakers – Terry Farley, Andy Weatherall, Cymon Eckel and Steve Mayes – who threw private parties under the railway arches near London Bridge, and put out the *Boy's Own* fanzine, an irregular and irreverent publication dedicated to documenting the minutiae of music, clothes and football. *Boy's Own* coined the famous slogan 'better dead than acid ted'. The 'acid ted' was the timewarp kid who wasn't hip enough to change with the times. The idea was that the neophyte ravers in bandanas and day-glo T-shirts, shouting 'acieed!' and dancing on the tables at Camden Palace, were the equivalent of the 40-year-old teddy boys with rockabilly quiffs, drainpipes and brothel creepers that you used to see in the High Street.

The *Boy's Own* aesthetic was an update of sixties mod: the same homosocial obsessions with the sharpest clothes, the obscurest import dance singles from Black America, and the pills that allowed you to skip sleep and spend the weekend dancing. In the sixties, the dapper mods were at war with the scruffy rockers, greasy-haired bikers who were descended from the fifties' teddy boys. Journalist Gavin Hills says of the eighties football 'casual' milieu that spawned *Boy's Own*, 'they were the equivalent of the mods – into music, a bit of football, a bit of violence. It was about a different kind of cool – "suss", about being "sussed", not being a *knob*. Knowing how to behave in certain ways, and a certain language, a way of talking.' This mod versus rockers, Balearic versus 'acid ted' antagonism was grounded in an enduring class divide that runs through British pop history: an upper working-class superiority complex vis-à-vis the undiscriminating unskilled proles.

As well as a class struggle, the backlash against 'acid teds' was generational: the fatigued cynicism of veterans suddenly surrounded by johnny-come-latelys in the first flush of E'd up enthusiasm. 'Even at that stage,' says Hills of late 1988, 'people were saying "E's aren't as good as they were." People like Terry Farley were complaining "clubs are just full of kids now". All the clichés that you've heard every year since were uttered at that time!' But, as even *Boy's Own* fan Barry Ashworth admits, 'All the things that the acid teds did, the Boy's Own types would have been doing themselves a few months before.'

All of a sudden acid house was declared passé; Chicago deep house and New Jersey garage was the in thing. Not only acieed music, but the whole 'mental' attitude that the 'acid teds' had embraced and exaggerated was deemed unseemly. One Shoom newsletter beseeched the laddish element 'please, don't take your shirts off'; Ashworth remembers having to go round his own club 'saying "put your top back on, man!"' Louise Gray admits 'We *were* rather snotty about the teenagers who were suddenly coming through, swallowing handfuls of pills and going round gurning.' As well as 'acid ted', another derogatory term used by Shoomers for the new arrivals was 'lilac camels' – lilac was a popular colour for sneakers, while 'camel' referred to the way these E'd up kids would masticate gum frenetically and loll their tongues out of their mouths.

By late 1988, there was a return to style, a reaction against the 'day-glo warriors' who had turned the Balearic hooligan-meets-hippy anti-style into a uniform. 'I remember the first Brainstorm party in autumn '88,' says Mr C, 'thinking, "There's no acid teds in here, I can see hardly any day-glo." Everyone was dressed up in their really good gear. The whole dress thing seemed to step up after that summer of '88; people started to get a grip.'

Despite the Summer of Love-and-Unity rhetoric that everyone paid lipservice to, less than a year into its existence the scene had begun to stratify. On one side, there was the original Balearic crowd, with their intimate clubs and mellow eclecticism; on the other, the hardcore acieed freaks swarming to warehouse parties whose flyers promised 'no balearic, just pure psycho-delic shit'. Up to a point, the Balearic backlash against the alleged 'herd mentality' of the acid teds was understandable: if the clubs that had once been full of familiar Faces (in the mod sense of the word) were suddenly mobbed with rowdy strangers, inevitably these people appeared faceless, de-individuated, sheep-like. But it was also a response to a power shift: the Balearics' 'subcultural capital' (to use the theorist Sarah Thornton's formulation) had suddenly gone public. The ensemble of sounds, gestures, rites and apparel that they had invented had become common currency, tarnished and tawdry. Panicked, the Balearics began the retreat from the populist premises that had originally defined their revolt against West End clubland, a retreat that would eventually lead them back to door policies, expensive designer clothes, and cocaine rather than Ecstasy.

Mental Mental Radio Rental

By the end of 1988, the scene had also lost some of its innocence – ironically, because of the influx of fresh-faced teenagers who were taking psychoactive substances they weren't emotionally mature enough to handle. 'The original people who got into acid house were largely an older crowd,' says Louise Gray. 'Mid-twenties onwards, people who'd had a history of experimenting with drugs ... I remember being at Confusion and there was this sixteen-year-old girl from Upminster who'd taken acid, and her friends had left her, and she was completely cabbaged, very disorientated and upset.'

That said, many of the more experienced, original scenesters were also in a bad way. 'You'd see people who were completely abusing it,' remembers Mr C. 'Seven or eight pills on a Friday, ten pills on a Saturday, and half a dozen on a Sunday.' Amazingly, given the lack of knowledge about the drug and the need to avoid dehydration, there were almost no E deaths in 1988; physical damage was limited to weight loss and the continual mild flu that for many people lasted the whole summer. Most of the casualties in 1988 were *mindwrecks*. As their tolerance to Ecstasy built up and their intake rose, some were experiencing the typical symptoms of long-term and excessive drug use: moodswings, paranoia, feeling uncanny. 'There were people that were having nightmares, and completely shot nervous systems,' says Mr C. A few suffered mental breakdowns.

'At the Mud Club one Friday, this girl came up and she was so off it that she was incapable of any rational conversation,' remembers Gray. 'She just sang this little refrain "Spectrum! Monday! On One, All day!" – 'cos it was the Bank Holiday coming and Spectrum was having an all-dayer.' This girl – a well-known figure on the scene – was eventually 'found wandering around the streets where she lived in her night-dress and ended up being put in a mental ward'. Says Mark

Moore, 'She shivers now when you mention house music, she says "It was never me, I was never there." She's into acid jazz now.'

Others just didn't want to stop, despite the early warning signs around them. 'That initial phase of taking Ecstasy, the pleasure of it is so unexpected, you just keep doing it,' says Jack Barron, a rock journalist swept up in acid-house fever. His love affair with the drug reached a climax when he 'took thirty-eight E's in a week ... I was completely convinced that there was this parallel universe which came to us in our dreams, and in which we all flew around ... The separation between dream time and day time ... well, there *wasn't* any. I wouldn't particularly recommend it.' Amazingly, he didn't crash for good after this seven nights of madness, but 'just kept going'.

Motor City Madness

Despite all the freefloating idealism and energy triggered by Ecstasy, a surprisingly small amount of artistic expression survives the era. Apart from *Boy's Own*, there was next to no fanzine documentation of the scene as it happened. People were simply too busy having fun. But it was a creative period, says Gray, 'as far as short-term things went – design, T-shirts, flyers. The Olympics happened in 1988, and within *hours* of Ben Johnson being disqualified for drug use, there was a T-shirt with Ben Johnson going across the finishing line and the legend "Get Right On One, Matey!" Which we all thought was terribly witty!'

Home-grown house took a while to come through, too. The early British stabs at this Black American music were imitative, and often quite poor imitations. D-Mob's 'We Call It Acieeed' got to Number Three in November 1988, and was something like the acid house counterpart of Bill Haley's 'Rock Around The Clock': self-reflexive title, a thin-sounding pastiche of the real underground black music. It didn't even feature a proper Roland 303, and worse, came with a rap that disingenuously claimed that 'acid' wasn't about a drug. The other early homegrown acid smash – 'Acid Man' by Jolly Roger (DJ Eddie Richards in disguise) – was a bit better, featuring genuine 303 squelch-a-rama and a prim matronly voice that commands, 'Stop that infernal racket, I mean NOW!' Better still, Humanoid's 'Stakker Humanoid' – Number Seventeen in December 1988 – was a terrific surge of acieed-meets-techno, as lithe and deadly as a bionic cheetah.

As a British pop cultural explosion, acid house was unique in so far as it was based almost entirely around non-indigenous music. During 1988–9, the scene had three years' worth of American house and techno classics to draw on, as well as all the new tracks streaming out of Chicago, New York and Detroit each week. Faced with this deluge of music made by Black American artists, it took UK producers a while to find their own distinctively British voice.

In its dependence on imports, acid house strongly resembled Northern Soul, the strange seventies cult based around sixties sub-Motown dance singles from the Detroit area. Baby Ford – buddy of Mark Moore and a then rising British house producer with near-hits like 'Oochy Koochy' – made this parallel in his album track 'Poem For Wigan'. A homage to Northern Soul's mecca the Wigan Casino, the song starts with a sample from a documentary on the early seventies scene: 'To get enjoyment during their teens and twenties, they have to build, more or less, an alternative society, just to enjoy themselves, because they can't within the normal channels . . . If you go to Wigan on Saturday night . . . people think we're crazy.' Like acid house, Northern Soul was all about uptempo Black American music and popping pills so you could dance till dawn; it revolved around name DJs, obscure tracks, and long-distance journeys to clubs that were worshipped as temples. In both cases, the raw material of a Black American music was transformed into a way of life, through a form of creative mis-recognition.

It was a Northern Soul connection that led to the domestic release of Detroit techno in Britain. Dance music entrepreneur Neil Rushton had been a 'Northern Soul freak, into Motown'. Intrigued by the Detroit tracks simply because of where they came from, he contacted the Belleville Three and licensed their tracks for UK release through his label Kool Kat (soon renamed Network). Rushton then sold the idea of doing a Detroit compilation to Virgin subsidiary Ten Records. Detroit's music had hitherto reached British ears as a subset of Chicago house; Rushton and the Belleville Three decided to fasten on the word 'techno' – a term that had been bandied around but never stressed – in order to define Detroit as a distinct genre. The single from the compilation – Kevin Saunderson's Inner City track 'Big Fun' – was a huge hit; the follow-up, the glassy shimmer-funk of 'Good Life', was even bigger. Worldwide, both tracks sold over two million. While Saunderson and singer Paris Grey were being treated like stars, Juan

Atkins's Model 500 tracks and Derrick May's 'Strings of Life' and 'Nude Photo' ruled the underground.

For the Belleville Three, it was something of a revelation to be embraced by the white European audience. 'You gotta remember, we were brought up with this racial conflict thing, instilled in us since babies,' says Atkins, describing Detroit's unofficial apartheid of different neighbourhoods, different schools, different radio stations. 'If you're a kid in Detroit, [you might] never even have to *see* a white person, unless they're on TV. The closest association I had with people outside my race was when I started travelling to Europe. The first time I went to the UK, man, I played for *five thousand white kids*. It really expanded my horizons.'

The revelation was tempered by certain reservations about how these crazy white kids had taken techno and made it a component of a totally different subculture. There was virtually no drug element to the Detroit party circuit. For the DJ–philosopher Derrick May, in particular, the deranged and debauched atmosphere of the British scene was a world away from his vision of the ideal techno audience of urbane aesthetes. Compare the druggy names of British clubs and warehouse parties (Brainstorm, Trip City, Hedonism) with the sober, lofty-sounding moniker of the Detroit club where May was then realizing his vision: The Detroit Musical Institution. (That was the original name: this legendary club has since come to be remembered as the Music Institute, while at the time its patrons called it the 'Tute). By the early nineties, May's distaste for Brit-rave excesses had hardened into bitter contempt: 'I don't even like to use the word "techno" because it's been bastardized and prostituted in every form you can possibly imagine . . . To me, the form and philosophy of it is nothing to do with what we originally intended it to be.'

May's resentment is shared by Eddie Fowlkes, who talks of 'cultural rape' and titled an album *Black Technosoul* to stress the R & B roots that nourish Detroit's music, and that European rave progressively severed. 'Techno was a *musical* thing,' he says. 'There wasn't no *culture* – no whistles, no E's or throwing parties at old warehouses. A warehouse party in Detroit – it was swept clean, painted, mirrors on the wall, a nice sound-system. It wasn't dirty and raunchy.'

Although Fowlkes means to indict, this comment could equally serve as a tribute to the British youth who took this imported music and built a *culture* around it, an entire apparatus of clothes and rituals, dance-moves and drug-lore. Eventually the cultural framework they built actually changed the music itself, mutated and mutilated the sacred Detroit blueprint, adding new inputs and intensifying certain elements that enhanced the drug sensations. And these transformations would be spawned above all in the 'dirty, raunchy' milieu of warehouse parties, and the massive one-off raves and rave-style clubs that followed in their wake.

Warehousing Benefits

Warehouse parties went back to the late seventies, to the reggae 'blues', shebeens and illegal after-hours drinking dens. In the eighties, the scene stretched from funk, soul and hip hop parties like The Dirtbox and Westworld, to the legendary events thrown in abandoned British Rail depots and derelict schools by The Mutoid Waste Company, an anarcho-punk collective who lived in caravans and constructed post-apocalyptic sculptures out of scrap machinery and salvage from skips. Some of the most mainstream house DJs of the nineties – Jeremy Healey, Judge Jules – cut their teeth at warehouse events like The Circus and Family Funktion.

Acid house mania incited an explosion of warehouse parties, as ravers looked to circumvent the restricted opening hours of licensed clubs. Alongside their regular weekend parties at Clink Street, the RIP crew went peripatetic in late 1988, organizing a series of Brainstorm events. 'Snap the padlocks with bolt cutters and kick off the door, on the day,' remembers Mr C of these one-night squat parties. Film studios and disused industrial hangars were typical locations. There was also a spate of riverboat parties, often kicking off in the Docklands area of East London. 'Just get on a boat and everybody cane it,' says Gavin Hills. Drifting down the Thames, 'you're not gonna get raided'.

According to Hills, these riverboat raves were controlled by the ICF, one of a number of football firms turned criminal syndicates, who'd realized just how much money they could earn through sinking their claws into the warehouse scene – not just from admissions, but from monopolizing the drug supply. While the firms were sometimes directly involved in parties from the ground up, often they would latch on to successful party organizers who'd already built up a following, then apply the pressure.

One East End party promoter who narrowly escaped the hoodlums' clutches was Joe Wieczorek, the Dickensian figure behind Labrynth, the world's longest running rave-club. Born in 1957, the son of a Polish-Jewish Auschwitz survivor, Wieczorek had a background in doing security for rock bands; at one point, he was employed as a double for his 'spitting image', Les McKeown of The Bay City Rollers. An 'avid Spurs fan', Wieczorek also had links to the football hooligan scene; in the mid-eighties, he'd run an East End pub called The Pickle House, which became a meeting point for Tottenham Hotspur fans when they had matches with Millwall or West Ham (the team supported by the ICF).

Wieczorek retired from the publican game, heartily sick of alcohol culture and the East End hard-man ethos that accompanied it. All this made him ripe for conversion to acid house; he was highly impressed when he ran into a former football enemy, a Millwall man, loved-up on E at a warehouse do near Kingsland Road. 'The last time me and him met, he was sticking a great big blade in me back.' As he got more involved in the scene, he found that a remarkable number of the people involved in parties were former football hooligans. 'Quite a few of the DJs at the time, were ex-football-oriented, as well. And that amazed me – of all the sets of people to bump into after I've turned me back on it! The first time I saw all that West Ham lot doing security on doors, I thought "how did you lot get involved in *this*?"' Later, he discovered that the football firm/rave organizer crossover was a nationwide phenomenon: for instance, the people behind the pirate radio station Dream FM in Leeds were 'that old Service Crew lot'.

From late 1988 on, warehouse parties were rife throughout the East End, partly because it was where a lot of the 'acid ted' newcomers came from, and partly because of the abundance of derelict, disused buildings. Wieczorek decided to have a crack at it himself. Advertised with hand-drawn flyers photocopied by his partner Sue Barnes on the sly at her workplace, the first Labrynth was at Vale Road, Manor House, in mid-October 1988.

The more cunning warehouse promoters had become adept at fooling the police into accepting that events were legit and fully licensed; they would brandish falsified leases and paperwork. Wieczorek made an appointment with Bethnal Green firestation, to discuss safety at rave events. 'The guy left us in his office for five minutes, and all I did was pick up a piece of headed notepaper, folded it up and put it in me pocket.' Brian Semmens, one of the Labrynth crew, used his computer skills to forge 'a fire certificate'; no such thing existed, but it looked official, and it worked. At one party, 'The chief constable at Tottingham and Haringay actually came and shook my hand and said "This is an extremely well run event." The moment they saw the certificate, and the odd fire extinguisher, they were just not interested in stopping it.'

After this, there was no stopping Wieczorek and Co, and they launched themselves on an astounding run of weekly parties, pulling off around 120 illegal warehouse events at some 47 different venues. Sites were easy to find. 'I used to go out in the daytime, with wirecutters, piece of plastic, whatever ... Half of them, you don't have to break into, you just open them ... Always disused, always not taking anyone's bread-and-butter.' By this point, the Old Bill had cottoned on to the fire certificate and fake lease ruses, and thwarted about nine parties. 'The feeling after you've spent eight hours clearing up a warehouse ... Moving the boxes, filling in the holes, sorting out the toilets, decorating it, putting in the sound-system, lights and laser. And then Plod comes along and goes "caught ya!" That feeling was like, you're so close but you're so far.' Since the average event cost a couple of grand to set up, the arrival of the police was a financial calamity as well; after one period of heavy police pressure, the Labrynth crew came close to giving up. 'Another two weeks and we'd have had to move somewhere else, we'd have owed so much money to too many people.'

Like other rising 1989 promoters, Labrynth stuck with the previous year's 'Second Summer of Love' spirit, even as the original Balearic crew were reneging on its promises of unity and universal brotherhood. A picture of a mustachioed and mystic-looking George Harrison with an eye in his palm became the Labrynth logo. Grainy black-and-white snapshots of the crowd appeared on the flyers for their 'Every Picture Tells A Story' events, spelling out the fact that the audience was the star; the E was circled, a heavy hint that 'only the happiest of people need apply' (the Labrynth motto).

All through 1989, Labrynth was the number two East End party organization, after Genesis. The other prime mover was the pirate radio station Centre Force, which ran a club called Echoes and was reputed to have shady connections with the ICF. Then RIP started doing regular nights at a literally subterranean venue called The Dungeons: a labyrinth of tunnels connected to a pub and a courtyard.

Despite the competition, Genesis maintained their reputation for throwing the most impressive parties in East London; Wieczorek reckons they would have grown into major legitimate promoters. But they threw in the towel, he believes, because of the very gangster pressure that Labrynth managed to sidestep. 'The very people you'd grown up with and trusted and respected, who'd perhaps been your elders on the manor, these were the very people who were taking your bread and butter. Who could you turn to? The only way out was to slip out of it by using your head.' Wieczorek says he can remember 'the actual conversation where I was told that they' – a syndicate of former ICF football thugs – 'were taking over the warehouse party scene. It seemed like they did what they wanted where they wanted. Every other manor, their firms or what-have-you's, didn't count.'

After attempting to sweet-talk Labrynth into their fold, the gangsters attempted a hostile takeover, using threats and intimidation. Barnes was 'pulled up when she was out shopping. [They] turned up at my house and one of 'em pulled out a shooter.' The pressure reached an ugly climax at a Labrynth party in Silvertown on 29 April 1989: Joe's birthday, and nearly his death day. Early in the night, Wieczorek spotted some dodgy characters he remembered from Canning Town days. He bundled Barnes out of the building and into their van, telling her to go and give out flyers in Old Street. As he was returning to the party, his mobile phone rang. It was Evenson Allen from the DJ-MC team Ratpack, in tears, screaming 'What's happening, man? Who are these people?' A gang of thugs had rushed the dancefloor wielding machetes, and attacking 'every black geezer in there', to make it look like a racial bias attack. Wieczorek believes it was a reprisal for his having refused a protection arrangement in which he would have had to hire security men 'at 185 pound a man per night, and we had to have ten men, *all that cack*.' One Labrynth associate lost an eye; Wieczorek believes, 'If I had been there, I'd have been dead.'

This and other incidents convinced Wieczorek and Barnes there was too much aggro in the illegal party game. It was time to go legitimate. Further incentive came from the police, who had formed a special 'acid squad' to wipe out the warehouse scene, and later unsuccessfully prosecuted the pirate station Centre Force for running a drug-peddling ring. One of the acid squad, claims Wieczorek, 'came to see me and said: "If you don't stop doing warehouse parties, we're going to put you in prison or find a way to sort you out."' Not long afterwards,

Labrynth took up residency at Dalston's Four Aces club, a suitably labyrinthine warren of corridors and caverns, where it remained until it moved to bigger premises next door in 1997.

Into Orbit

The involvement of the criminal football gangs in the warehouse scene was a sign of the times. The characters who took acid house to the next stage – massive raves in aircraft hangars, grain silos and open fields, mostly at sites near the M25 orbital motorway that encircled London – weren't subcultural movers and shakers; they were underworld figures or entrepreneurs not averse to breaking a few laws. Unlike the original Balearic and acieed figures – DJs and scenemakers – the new breed of promoters weren't motivated by musical concerns. They might have developed a taste for E, might even have genuinely gotten into the music and the vibe, but the impetus to make the events bigger and more spectacular was primarily profit-driven. Transforming an underground scene into a mass movement had the happy combined effect of amplifying the atmosphere of loved-up communion while raking in the tax-free income.

The spirit underlying this next phase of the acid house revolution was anarcho-capitalist. If the Summer of Love rhetoric ran against the Thatcherite grain (the Prime Minister had infamously proclaimed 'there is no such thing as society, just collections of individuals'), the people behind the emergent organizations like Sunrise, Energy, World Dance and Biology were generally loadsamoney types whose audacity was utterly in tune with the quick-killing spirit that fuelled the late eighties economic boom. Sunrise's Tony Colston-Hayter turned Tory ideology against Tory family values, protesting 'Surely this ridiculous 3 a.m. curfew on dancing is an anachronism in today's enterprise culture?' His associates at Sunrise included former football casual Dave Roberts and Paul Staines, a Libertarian Conservative whose day job was acting as an assistant to rabid freemarket ideologue and Thatcher-adviser David Hart.

Unlike the Oakenfolds and Ramplings, these new promoters tended not to have any background in club promotion. Colston-Hayter's CV included setting up his own game machine companies while still a schoolboy, and stints as a professional black-jack gambler. World

Dance's Jay Pender was a foreign exchange broker. 'I realized rave was a sort of "power to the people" thing, where you could just *do it* if you had some contacts and the bottle,' he says. Attending the Sunrise 2000 party at an equestrian centre in Iver Heath, Buckinghamshire, Pender's money-making instincts were piqued by the number of people milling about outside asking for spare tickets. After having a blinding time at the rave, he went home and 'phoned an old colleague in the city. I said, "Have you seen the papers?" He said, "What do you mean?" I said, "All these warehouse parties." I told him I wanted to put together the biggest rave yet, and what I needed was a green field site on the M25. He phoned me back in half an hour with a location. I visited it the next day, and it was perfect. We put the whole thing together, but this first site fell through the day before the rave. We hadn't applied for permission, but we argued with the police that we didn't *need* any, because it wasn't a public event. You had to be a member to get in. Of course, to become a member, all you had to do was fill in your address and give us fifteen pounds – so it was a bit of a wobble!'

The rave-as-private-party concept was Colston-Hayter's idea; in true Thatcherite spirit, he had found a loophole in the law. (Also in that fuck-society spirit, Sunrise's profits would be siphoned to an offshore tax-haven.) Colston-Hayter's other great stratagem was using the British Telecom Voice Bank system as a method for outwitting the police. Flyers advertised only a phone number, not an address. The Voice Bank allowed for a series of rendezvous locations to be updated remotely via mobile phone; party-goers would drive to these meeting-points and be told where to go next. The convoy would descend upon the site, presenting the police with a de facto rave that couldn't be dispersed for fear of a riot. Only then would the exact location be posted on the answering machine.

Hitherto, warehouse parties had mostly drawn in the region of three or four thousand; the orbital rave dramatically upped the ante, as organizers competed to throw the biggest and most dazzling events. On 24 June 1989, Sunrise established a new record with its 11,000 strong 'Midsummer Night's Dream' event at an aircraft hangar in White Waltham, Berkshire. They also attracted the attention of the tabloids, who had forgotten all about the Acid House barons. The *Sun*'s front-page story painted a lurid picture of 'thrill-seeking young-sters in a dance frenzy', complete with absurd details like 'ecstasy wrappers' strewn on the floor afterwards. Home Secretary Douglas

Hurd promised to draft legislation to 'stop the menace of acid parties'. In response, a news-sheet distributed outside London clubs declared 'House parties will rock all summer and the Old Bill, the establishment and the gutter press can go fuck themselves.' The stage was set for a summer of fun and trouble.

For many, 1989 was the year it really kicked off. The combined thrills of cocking a snook at the police and experiencing the sheer scale of the raves was addictive. The magical routes that had traversed and transformed London the previous summer were now shifted outside the city limits, into the semi-rural Home Counties. '1989 was the real explosion,' says Gavin Hills. 'The raves were very special. In some respects it was still underground, still something of a special club, even though it was a mass movement. It was Us against Them. Going out and trying to get past roadblocks, having a laugh. It was an adventure.'

Attending a huge Energy rave in April 1989, says Jack Barron, 'had just as profound an effect on me as any of the early clubs. More so, in fact, 'cos you've suddenly got a sense that *this thing is spreading*.' For Barron's friend, journalist Helen Mead, dancing with ten thousand people 'on Ecstasy' was 'completely fucking mindblowing compared with doing it in Shoom with two hundred people ... And I never remember any sense of worry at those big events. You'd maybe gone with five people, and you'd be in these absolutely massive places, and you'd always be wandering off – whether it was 'cos you'd had your eyes closed and then found you'd danced half a mile away, or going to the loo, navigating your way through these huge places, absolutely off your tits. But I never remember feeling lost, or stuck anywhere, or not knowing where I was going.'

For Brooklyn DJ Frankie Bones, accustomed only to clubs with a few hundred capacity, the sheer size of the orbital events blew him away. After making his UK debut at 6 a.m. in front of 25,000 people at an Energy mega-rave, he wrote the track 'Energy Dawn' as a tribute, telling *iD*: 'England is fantasy land.' For the rest of the summer, he became a regular on the British rave circuit, spending two weeks in New York then two weeks in the UK. 'It happened so big and so fast that nobody knew what it was right away, everything *was* peace, love and unity,' he says now. 'The M25, that was a sick time ... You could basically go on the M25 and find raves back in '89, there'd be carloads of people driving around.' For many, the build-up to the rave, and the aftermath, was just as exciting as the event itself. Motorway service stations became the scene for impromptu parties; like the post-Trip car park scene in the summer of 1988, people would be dancing around their car stereos. For a couple of months, there were mass post-rave chill-out sessions on Clapham Common in South London.

As the big promoters competed to lure the punters, flyers were emblazoned with increasingly extravagant and highly technical claims about the raves' spectacular sound-systems and lights: 80 K pro-quadrophonic sound, turbo bass, water-cooled four-colour lasers, golden scans, terrastrobes, arc lines, varilights, robozaps, *ad absurdum*. According to Joe Wieczorek, these boasts were 'nine out of ten, total crap. Space filler. *Fanny*. For a long time, one of the things that let this whole scene down, was if you didn't have and you couldn't afford, you put down that you did.' A lot of the fancy-sounding verbiage was actually made up. As well as brain-frazzling sound-and-visuals, the raves promised side-shows and added attractions, like fairground rides, gyroscopes, fireworks and the soon-to-be-infamous 'bouncy castle'.

If the original Balearic crowd had been dismayed by the acid teds, the orbital raves were even more repugnant. Shoom had organized a few excursions to the countryside: at one, Down On The Farm, the local fire brigade were hired to come down at the height of the party and pump foam into the dancefloor, turning it into a giant bubblebath. Boy's Own also ventured outside London in August 1989, throwing a lakeside party at East Grinstead, complete with a pantomime cow. But with only 800 people in attendance, this was far from the mega-raves, which were now closer to stadium rock concerts than warehouse jams.

In 1988, the word 'rave' was in common parlance, but only as a verb, e.g. 'I'm going raving at this warehouse party.' A year later, 'rave' had become a noun, while 'raver', for many, was a derogatory stereotype, an insult. Where 'raving' came from Black British dance culture and ultimately from Jamaica, 'raver' plugged into a different etymology. The *Daily Mail* used it to describe the boorish antics of trad jazz fans at the Beaulieu Jazz Festival in 1961; a few years later, a TV documentary employed the word to evoke the hysterical nymphomania of teengirl fans and groupies. There had also been an 'All Night Rave' at the Roundhouse in October 1966, a psychotropic spectacular featuring Pink Floyd and The Soft Machine.

With its multiple connotations – delirium, madness, frenzied behaviour, extreme enthusiasm, the Black British idea of letting off steam at the weekend – 'raving' perfectly described the out-of-control dancing of the acid scene in 1988. But by 1989, the Balearic crowd had coined the derogatory term 'cheesy quaver'; the ravers' rowdy rituals of abandon and joyous uniformity of attire now signified a 'herd mentality', something that clubbers defined themselves against. For Shoomers, orbital raves were 'mass, teenage . . . One didn't do it,' says Louise Gray. 'Sod the fields, the outdoor bollocks!' is how Mr C encapsulates the RIP posse's attitude. 'We'd always been into doing it in the city, as far into the centre of the city as we could possibly have. Because it's urban, it's for Londoners . . . and we don't like sheep!'

Mr C DJ-ed at a few Sunrise, Biology and Energy events, but 'wasn't generally impressed. It was bit too impersonal.' The competition between rave organizations for star line-ups meant that 'you'd get twelve DJs playing in twelve hours, and each DJ would only get an hour. In an hour, you're only going to fit in ten or fifteen records, and you're gonna play the biggest fifteen records in your box – in order to make the people scream the loudest. So it was no longer about how psychedelic and challenging the music was, it was about how big and loud it was.'

Where a club DJ might play a two or three hour set, taking you on a journey through peaks and troughs, the structure of raves was transforming the music and the scene, orienting it around anthems – instantaneous, high-impact, sensation oriented. In a break with the DJ-dominated club ethos, you were starting to get live rave performers: there was a craze for keyboard whizzkids like Adamski, Guru Josh and Mr Monday. 'Adamski was a bone of contention, whether he was any good or not,' remembers Gavin Hills. *Boy's Own* spoofed Adamski's album *LIVEANDIRECT* – a live house album for Christ's sake, how rock 'n' roll – as *LIVEANDIRE*. The Balearic backlash intensified, taking the form of a return not just to clubs, but to clubland in its pre-acieed form: dressing flash, 'quality sounds for quality people'. The vogue for deep house and New Jersey garage – Turntable Orchestra, Blaze, Phase II, Adeva – strengthened.

Paul Oakenfold, meanwhile, was beginning his transition into the West End, doing 'real trendy parties'. In years to come, he would defy the rave-driven trend towards harder-and-faster extremes and push a downtempo sound – a mix of dubby tracks by Massive Attack and On U Sound, plus the new indie-dance crossover stuff emerging out of Manchester. The culmination of this anti-rave stance was Oakenfold's ludicrous 98 b.p.m. movement (the idea being that the tempo of dance music should never rise into three figures).

Musically, there was still some crossover between the Balearic scene and the rave circuit: tracks like Nightwriters's 'Let The Music Use You', Lil Louis's orgasmotronic epic 'French Kiss', Ce Ce Rogers's 'Someday' and 10 City's 'Devotion' were anthems on both sides of the divide. But by late summer, the ruling sound at the big raves was the almost preposterously uplifting Italo-house sound – all oscillating piano vamps and shrieking disco divas – that had been hatched in Adriatic resorts like Rimini and Riccioni. Starlight's 'Numero Uno' and Black Box's 'Ride On Time' were the big chart hits. When 'Ride On Time' – whose vocal was pilfered wholesale from Loleatta Holloway's 'Love Sensation' – annexed the Number One spot for six whole weeks in September 1989, it felt like a victory for the rave nation, the climax of the *second* Second Summer Of Love.

Raving Mad

By this point, though, the orbital rave scene was beginning to unravel. The police's Pay Party Unit had built up a massive computer database on the major rave organizers; they were setting up phone taps, eavesdropping on pirate radio, and deploying helicopters. Out in the country lanes, the police were playing cat and mouse with the convoys of ravers, and twisting the arms of landowners to renege on the deals they'd struck with the likes of Sunrise and Energy. The ravers were beginning to get disenchanted: not only were there more and more rip-off events with shitty sound-systems, no-show DJs and none of the advertised facilities, but there was a good chance the raves wouldn't happen at all.

'Biology was the one that was a disaster,' recalls Helen Mead, referring to a hubris-foredoomed megarave in the Guildford area in October 1989. 'It was supposed to be the first million pound party. I just remember driving around all night 'cos they had to change the site three times.' The strategy of the Pay Party Unit was attrition: wear down the spirits of the ravers, make them so sick of the wild goose chases and the bitter anti-climactic disappointment when an event was quashed, that they'd return to the guaranteed pleasures of licensed clubs. As well as the dangers of inadequate fire-and-safety precautions and the debauchery of mass teenage drug consumption, the police were concerned by the fact that major criminal organizations were muscling in on the orbital scene, trafficking in drugs and attempting to extort their slice of the massive takings.

'Rave' also carries a faint connotation of 'rage'. The ravers weren't going to let go of their good thing without a fight. 'I remember one event, down near Watford,' says Gavin Hills. 'We knew that the rave was on, but the police had sealed it off. Bouncers started beating up the police, and everybody charged in. I remember getting chased by all these police through these fields, and I jumped in the air, 'cos there was this barbed wire fence coming, ripped my baggy trousers, sliced my legs, and ended face up in the mud. But everybody cheered 'cos I'd got into the field.'

There was an attempt to take the resistance into the political arena. With the tabloids stoking public concern, Graham Bright, Conservative MP for Luton South, drafted a private member's bill to increase the penalties for unlicensed parties. Faced with the prospect of £20,000 fines and six month prison sentences, Tony Colston-Hayter and his libertarian sidekick Paul Staines attended the Conservative Party's annual conference in November, where they announced the formation of the Freedom To Party campaign. Although all the leading rave promoters were involved, the movement petered out after a few not-very-well attended rallies – seemingly yet more proof of the apolitical, unmotivated character of the Ecstasy generation.

With the big rave almost extinct – at least in the South of England – and Graham Bright's Entertainments (Increased Penalties) Bill heading inexorably towards its passage into law ('defending raves is like defending leprosy at the moment', commented Staines at the time), the general feeling was that it was all over, for good. Exacerbating the sense of brutal comedown was a sudden drought of Ecstasy; anecdotal evidence suggests that at the end of 1989, the drug supply dried up for about eight months. 'Clubs were empty in early 1990,' Hills recalls. 'Around the summer of 1990, pills started appearing again. Then you had proper techno, and most people got into rave in 1991. The gap between those two things is entirely chemical based.'

The living dream of rave was too alluring to fade away, even after the setback of the Bright Bill. Rave resurged, but with a different inflection. Local authorities began to adopt a more liberal approach to giving out permits to commercial rave promoters. Licensing hours were finally liberalized (although regional variations remained), allowing for the growth of rave-style clubs where you could party til 6 a.m., 8 a.m., sometimes even noon the next day. Spreading to every provincial corner of the UK, rave culture became a highly organized leisure system, and an enormously lucrative economic infrastructure. Still underground, in terms of its atmosphere, it was at the same time the norm: what Everykid did, every weekend.

THREE

TWENTY-
FOUR-HOUR
PARTY PEOPLE

MADCHESTER, POSITIVITY
AND THE RAVE 'N' ROLL
CROSSOVER

'The black kids always had something going, '89 was the year the white kids woke up.'

— Ian Brown, singer of The Stone Roses

'Whitey could dance, with a pill in him.'

— Mani, bassist of The Stone Roses

Manchester has long been Britain's number two Pop City after London. But in the post-punk era the city's musical output tended to be synonomous with the un-pop hue of grey: Buzzcocks's melodic but monochrome punk ditties, The Fall's baleful intransigence, Joy Division's angst-rock, New Order's doubt-wracked disco. Dedicated to their own out-of-time, sixties notion of pop, The Smiths defined themselves against contemporary, dance-oriented chart fodder. 'Panic' was an anthem for disenfranchised discophobes, Morrissey railing 'burn down the disco / hang the blessed DJ'. The crime? Playing mere good-times music that said 'nothing', lyrically, about real life.

Disco and DJ culture had the last laugh, however. Thanks to house clubs like The Haçienda, Thunderdome and Konspiracy, Manchester transformed itself into 'Madchester', the mecca for 24-Hour Party People and smiley-faced ravers from across Northern England and the Midlands. By 1989, the famously grey and overcast city had gone day-glo; Morrissey-style miserabilism was replaced by glad-all-over extroversion, nourished by a diet of 'disco biscuits' (Ecstasy).

With its combination of bohemia (a large population of college and art students, and the biggest gay community outside London) and demographic reach (around fifteen million people live within a couple of hours drive of the city centre), Manchester was well-placed to become the focus of a pop cultural explosion. Manchester's ghetto district, Moss Side, is a major drug distribution junction for the North West of England. House – which was played as early as 1986 on local station Piccadilly Radio by DJ Stu Allen – chimed in with a longstanding regional preference for uptempo dance music, as seen in the seventies with the amphetamine-driven Northern Soul scene.

The Haçienda was founded and funded by New Order and the boss of their record label Factory, Anthony H. Wilson: a sort of Northern equivalent to punk svengali Malcolm McLaren, and fuelled by a similarly potent mix of neo-situationist pranksterism and bottom-line interest in generating cash from chaos. The nightclub's name was inspired by the situationists' utopian slogan 'The Haçienda Must Be Built'. Converted from a yachting warehouse showroom, the Haçienda was initially industrial and dystopian in ambience. The atmosphere perked up when DJs like Martin Prendergast and Mike Pickering started to add house to the mix. Pickering, an ex-Northern Soul fan and member of Factory avant-funk band Quando Quango, had experienced the fervent vibe at The Paradise Garage, thanks to Quando's popularity in New York.

In July 1988, The Haçienda started a Wednesday night event called Hot with a Balearic feel. On the first night, there was a swimming pool and sun lamps; punters danced in beach wear. Then, with Pickering and new DJ Graeme Park on the decks, Friday's long-established Nude became the mental night. As the fervour for acid house swelled, weekday nights at The Haçienda followed, with names like Void and Hallucienda. Rival clubs like Thunderdome and Konspiracy opened, attracting a rougher audience from the more working class North Manchester. Here the soundtrack was harder: 'like punk, almost ... real Acid stormtrooper stuff,' according to Martin Price from local house crew 808 State. For serious edge-walkers, there was also The Kitchen in Hulme, a sinkhole of urban deprivation. An illegal squat-club in a derelict housing estate, The Kitchen was a murky, multi-tiered warren of rooms, created by knocking through the walls between flats. 'Dodgy,' is how Helen Mead describes it. 'It was gangsters, drugs and guns ... You'd hear about rapes going on there, stuff like that.'

Throughout the North West of England, clubs sprang up that modelled themselves on the Madchester vibe. Blackpool had Frenzy, Stoke-on-Trent had Delight, and Liverpool stepped into the fray when its own Haçienda-scale mega-club, the 2400 capacity Quadrant Park, went house in early 1990. In October that year, 'Quaddie' opened Britain's first weekly legal all-nighter, called The Pavilion and located in the basement below the main club. And as with the London house scene, the demand for raves spilled out into the countryside of

Lancashire and Cheshire, in the form of illegal parties like Joy, Live The Dream and Blastoff, often held in abandoned mills. With its industrial estates, Blackburn became a hotbed for warehouse parties; at its peak, ten thousand kids arrived in cars every weekend, in search of the rave. 24-Hour party people who didn't want to stop after the 2 a.m. shutdown at licensed clubs also held impromptu parties in the car parks at Knutsford and Charnock Richard motorway service stations.

Acieed Casuals

'Nowadays it's just the normal Joe comin' in and doing his thing, all the ponceyness has gone.'

– Paris Angels

With the right sound and the right drug in place, all that was needed was a fashion look, and some local heroes. The pop media came up with the term 'scallydelia' to designate both a laddish breed of Mancunian band – Happy Mondays, The Stone Roses, Inspiral Carpets, Northside and Paris Angels – and the style of clothes they sported. It was actually something of a misnomer, since the 'scally' (short for scallywag) was strictly speaking a Liverpudlian archetype. The Mancunian counterpart was the Perry boy, named after their Fred Perry shirts. The Scally/Perry look began on football terraces as early as 1984, when 'casuals' – hooligans into expensive designer-label fashion and vicious confrontations with followers of rival teams – started to wear flared jeans and jumbo cords. Mancunian clothing emporiums like Joe Bloggs started making 24-inch flares and their even more voluminous denim counterpart, 'parallels'. By 1989, the scallydelic wardrobe encompassed anything baggy (hooded tops, long-sleeved shirts, old cricket hats) and brightly hued (pastel or lilac coloured Kickers and Wallabees, psychotropic patterns). This penchant for flower-power garishness reflected the scally's twin tastes for Pink Floyd-style acid rock and acid house; loose-fitting clothes were better for dancing, gaudy colours looked good when you were tripping. These 'acieed casuals' stopped wearing T-shirts with ostentatious designer-logos in favour of ones emblazoned with Madchester-patriot slogans like 'And On The Sixth Day God Created Manchester', 'Woodstock '69, Manchester '89', 'This Is Not Manchester This Is A Trip', or band T-shirts like the Inspiral Carpets' infamous 'Cool As Fuck' series.

Thanks to the benign influence of E and 'draw' (marijuana), the 1989–90 football season became what academic Steve Redhead called 'the Winter of Love', celebrated in chants like 'Oh! we're all blissed up and we're gonna win the cup.' Violence on the terraces dropped dramatically, with many fans taking E during matches to heighten the homosocial camaraderie and rowdy sentimentality. That summer New Order sneaked the cheeky line 'E is for England' into their World Cup song 'World In Motion' (their first Number One hit, in tandem with the England football squad).

There are other connections between football and pop music. Both are traditional escape routes for glory-hungry working-class jack-the-lads, and both offer possibilities for male bonding through shared passion for something 'objective' (and therefore legitimate). Football and rock also enable the cultivation of connoisseurship: facts, figures, changing line-ups, discographies. One medium for all this partisanship and pride-in-knowledge is the fanzine. Inevitably, 'zines emerged that combined both masculine passions. The first and most famous of the soccer–music 'zines was Liverpool's *The End*, which was founded in the early eighties and co-edited by Peter Hooton of The Farm, a band that scored Top Ten hits in the early nineties ('Groovy Train', 'All Together Now') when it added a house undercarriage to its sixties-influenced guitarpop. *The End* was a big influence on the cockney neo-mods behind *Boy's Own*.

Sixties Mod went from being based around import records to being focused around figurehead bands like The Who and The Small Faces. In Madchester, there soon emerged a similar demand for bands to follow. Ecstasy had catalysed an invincible feeling of change-is-gonna-come positivity, which was seemingly substantiated by events across the world like the downfall of Communism in Eastern Europe. Surfing these energy-currents of idealism and expectation, bands like The Stone Roses and Happy Mondays gave the new mood a focus, and to varying degrees articulated the Madchester attitude.

'We're Thatcher's children.' So Shaun Ryder, the Happy Mondays 'singer', was wont to claim. The Conservative leader's assault on the welfare system and the unions was intended to train the working class in the bourgeois virtues of providence, initiative, investment, belt-tightening and holding out for the long term dividend. But a significant segment of working class youth in Britain responded to the challenge of 'enterprise culture' in a hand-to-mouth, here-and-now way; not by becoming opportunity-conscious but criminal-minded. The result was not so much a black economy as a blag economy, where survival depended on having an eye for the quick killing and being a fast talker.

Eager to participate in the late eighties Thatcherite boom but excluded by mass unemployment, these kids resorted to all manner of shady money-making schemes: bootlegging (fake designer clothes, bootlegged records and computer games), organizing illegal warehouse parties and raves, drug dealing, petty theft, and fraud of all kinds (benefit fraud, credit-card fraud). Others claimed social security while raking in cash-in-hand doing short-term, no-security work. It was from this lumpen-proletarian milieu that the Happy Mondays emerged. The truth was that the band and its ilk were Thatcher's *illegitimate* children: an unintended outcome, and operating on the wrong side of the law.

By 1989, the Happy Mondays had already released two albums on Factory, *Squirrel and G-Man Twenty Four Hour Party People Plastic Face Carnt Smile (White Out)* and *Bummed*. Although rough-and-ragged, the Mondays sound – a cross between The Fall and fatback funk – fit fairly well into the Factory tradition of arty, angsty white dance. *Squirrel* was produced by ex-Velvet John Cale, *Bummed* by Martin Hannett, who had shrouded Joy Division and A Certain Ratio in the mausoleum-reverberant Factory sound.

There was, however, a distinctively druggy aura to the Mondays' woozy thug-funk. *Bummed* was recorded under the influence of Ecstasy, the band practically shoving it down Hannett's throat. Shaun Ryder's gargoyle voice leered out of the mix like a goblin, and his words resembled dosser-talk: querulously urgent but impenetrable, spittle-flecked discharge from scrambled synapses. Stealing its hook from The Beatles' 'Ticket To Ride' 'Lazy-Itis' proposed a dole-age revision of psychedelia: 'I think I did the right thing / In slippin' away.' Absenting themselves from productivity, from the obligation to make something of themselves, Ryder and Co just *drifted*: wasted youth who whiled away the days shooting rats with air rifles, going on trips to Europe to find flash clothes, and *tripping*, period. A haphazard accretion of hallucinactory images and crooked insights. Ryder's lyrics were like a guttersnipe version of cut-up: phrases that lodged in his head while stoned in front of the TV, the drivel of acid-casualty mates.

Where The Fall's Mark E. Smith penned oblique observations of Northern underclass grotesquerie, Shaun Ryder's drivel was more like the id of the lumpen-proletariat speaking its bloody mind aloud.

By 1989, the Mondays had picked up a following of Ecstasy-guzzling love thugs. 'Everyone in the place was on E and it made us look better and sound better,' Ryder told *iD* some time later. 'I know they were all on E because we used to go out in the audience selling E like T-shirts.' If the 'brains' behind the Mondays was Ryder, in many ways the focal point and font of the group's anti-charisma was Bez (Mark Berry). The son of a Detective Inspector, Bez played Vicious to Ryder's Rotten. Strictly speaking, his contribution to the group was negligible (on the third album his credit reads 'Bez: Bez'!). Onstage, he shook maracas and danced, a listless, moronic traipse that resembled a peasant crushing grapes. Bez's real function was to incarnate the band's debauched spirit, like a Keith Richards relieved of all instrumental duties. He was the subject in an experiment designed to determine just how far hedonism could be taken. As Ryder put it, 'It was thru Bez with E ... just "get 'em down yer throat, son! Move! Go on! Throw 'em down yer neck!" ... That's how we really got to see how E can get you, like, right out there. You've just got to pelt it down yer.' One journalist told me Bez confessed that he actually preferred lager to Ecstasy; when asked why he took so much E, Bez replied, dourly – 'It's me job.' Whatever the truth, for the fans Bez became both a role model and their stand-in representative: the ultimate chancer, proof that any one of them could have been up there if they'd lucked out, enjoying all the drugs and ardent groupies.

After a failed attempt at scoring a hit with a Paul Oakenfold house remix of the brilliant *Bummed* track 'Wrote For Luck', Happy Mondays finally got to Number Nineteen in December 1989 with the 'Madchester Rave On' EP. The lead song, 'Hallelujah', was a twisted stab at a Christmas single. A queasy merger of rock riffs and studio-programmed beats, 'Hallelujah' has Ryder jeeringly defining himself as an Anti-Saviour – 'ain't here to save ya / just here to spike and play some games'. 'Rave On' is even more a case of organized confusion. An oozy, ectoplasmic mess of mis-treated vocals, effects-wracked guitars, and background hubbub, the track wavers and ripples as if filtered through Bez's E-addled ears. It's like a sonic equivalent to the seeing-double effects and after-image light-streaks in the brilliant video for 'Wrote For Luck' (filmed at Legends, where Paul Oakenfold held a Manchester branch of Spectrum). Sounding at his most bleary and smeary, Ryder hollers a party-til-we-drop rallying cry in the chorus 'need a massive boogie till we all pack out'.

Although they most resembled an English answer to the Butthole Surfers, Happy Mondays were celebrated by the music press as a sort of Acieed Pogues gatecrashing *Top of the Pops*. (Funnily enough, the Pogues' dentally challenged singer Shane McGowan had gotten into rave music in a big way, and around this time was attempting, unsuccessfully, to persuade his colleagues to record a twenty minute acid track entitled 'You've Got To Connect Yourself'). The other big music press analogy was the Sex Pistols: the Mondays were acclaimed as the first, truly working-class band to emerge since punk, 'real kids' in possession of the truth that's 'only known by guttersnipes' (as fake-proles The Clash had it).

The Stone Roses – in the Top Ten at the same time as the Mondays with their breakthrough single 'Fool's Gold' – were far closer to 1977 punk, or at least the John Lydon version of it: working class, self-educated, slightly arty, politically-aware, and angry, whereas the Mondays were lumpen-prole oiks on the prowl and on the make. Sonically, the Roses sounded a bit like Pistols if Beatles-fan Glen Matlock had managed to prevail over the use of minor chords. But beneath the Byrdsy chimes and Hendrixy flourishes of their self-titled debut album lurked class-war lyrics that were anything but hippy-dippy. The cuddly-sounding 'Bye Bye Badman' was targeted at a riot policeman: 'I'm throwing stones at you, man', singer Ian Brown cooed like he was whispering sweet-nothings. They even had their own equivalent to 'God Save The Queen' in 'Elizabeth, My Dear'. 'We're all anti-royalist, anti-patriarch,' Brown told me. ''Cos it's 1989. Time to get real. When the ravens leave the Tower, England shall fall, they say. We want to be there shooting the ravens.'

Crucially, the band – Brown, guitarist John Squire, drummer Reni and bassist Mani – exuded the right Manchester attitude, alternately lippy and laidback. 'We hate tense people,' Squire told me. 'The tense people are the ones who are only interested in making money and who ruin things for everybody else,' he explained, before defining his political ideals with an almost Lennonesque flair for contradiction: 'Everybody should be a millionaire, everybody on the planet.'

'Madchester' replaced the workaholic materialism of the eighties with a new spirit, encoded in the slang buzzword 'baggy': loose-fitting clothes, a loose-minded, take-it-as-it-comes optimism, a loose-limbed dance beat descended from James Brown's 'Funky Drummer'. But if there was one factor that sealed the Roses' bond with their following, it was the band's cockiness, proclaimed in anthems like 'I Wanna Be Adored' and 'I Am The Resurrection', and choruses like 'the past is yours / the future's mine': a self-confidence that fit the turn-of-decade positivity like a glove, and briefly resurrected a heretical notion – that being young could be *fun*.

In 1989, The Stone Roses spoke often of their boredom with eighties rock, and claimed that they only listened to seventies funk and house music. 'I don't think it's unusual for our fans to be into dance music,' Brown said. 'Those dividing lines aren't there any more. When you go to warehouse parties they play acid house and house beats, but they put Hendrix and the Beatles over the top. They've even started to use our stuff.' And he put a political spin on rave. 'That's the thing about 1989. You see eleven thousand people dancing at a warehouse and really it's basically that people are realizing that this is a cruel world and you've got to find people with similar attitudes and watch each others' backs.'

With its fatback shuffle-drums simulating the hypno-groove aesthetic of club music, its bubbling B-line and chickenscratch wah-wah guitar, 'Fool's Gold' was the Roses' first nod towards rave. Lurking low in the mix, Ian Brown whispered another baleful lyric of obscure emnity – 'I'm standing alone ... I'm seeing you sinking' – doubtless aimed at the 'tense twats' of Thatcherite spiv culture.

There's a theory that people fall in love when they're ripe, and project their latent amorousness on to the least unsuitable candidate to come along. In Manchester, E seems to have facilitated the bonding process. 'We knew in early '89 when we did gigs, you could just feel people *willing* you to go for it,' Brown recollected six years later. This local hero status went nationwide by the end of 1989, as the Roses took on the mantle of the Great White Hope, plugging into Brit-rock's perennial, in-built demand for a four-man trad-guitar combo that Means Something, *à la* The Jam and The Smiths.

After the triumph of 'Fool's Gold', 1990 saw the Roses struggling to articulate the perilously vague creed of 'positivity' that Manchester represented. Having already broken with the mould of the traditional rock gig by organizing quasi-raves at Alexandra Palace and Blackpool Empress Ballroom (at which they replaced support bands with DJs like

Paul Oakenfold), they convened a 28,000-strong outdoor festival at Spike Island on 27 May 1990. But the pressure was getting to them. Manchester was now big news, and at the press conference the day before the festival, the Roses's laconic, sullen demeanour enraged the representatives of the world media. When *Spin*'s Frank Owen, a Moss Side expatriate, protested that the band were treating the journalists like 'fucking bullshit!' Brown responded: 'Sort your head out, man.' A fight broke out between Owen and a Roses partisan in the audience, and the press conference ended in uproar. Spike Island itself was botched by bad organization and poor sound. Ian Brown came onstage shouting 'Time! Time! Time! The time is now.' But the Roses' next single, 'One Love' – an insipid retread of 'Fool's Gold' – failed to sustain the sense of momentum or define what was at stake.

In April, Happy Mondays threw their own pseudo-rave equivalent of Spike Island, with a gig at Wembley Arena timed to coincide with the band's and Madchester's biggest hit yet, 'Step On' – a stomping, vaguely house-ified version of Johnny Kongos's 1971 boogie smash 'He's Gonna Step On You Again' – which stalled at Number Five. When Shaun Ryder lurched onstage, he greeted the throng of monged-out fans with the cryptic query 'where's me pickled herrings?' By this point, the Mondays' 'significance' had come to reside in precisely this kind of bathos. Music press mascots on account of their debauched exploits, the Mondays were esteemed merely for unprepossessing details: Shaun's refusal to trim his untamed nose hairs and bum fluff, Bez's glazed and gaunt vacancy. Somewhere along the line, the Mondays seemed to have degenerated from the radically mindblowing to the merely mindless – a massive levelling down of consciousness, a bovine pleasure.

With Tony Wilson hyping the Mondays as the new Sex Pistols, the next step in the Great Rave 'n' Roll Swindle was the conquest of America. Earlier in the year, he'd told *The Face* that he wouldn't be bothered if any one of the Mondays died of pharmaceutical excess: 'listen, [Joy Division's] Ian Curtis dying on me was the greatest thing that's happened to my life. Death sells!' But such McLarenesque cynicism didn't play so well in the USA. That summer, at the 1990 New Music Seminar in New York, Tony Wilson chaired a panel provocatively titled 'Wake Up America, You're Dead'. Here he expounded a potted history of the last three years of UK pop – Ibiza, Ecstasy, acieed, Madchester – and prophesized that the British groups would export back to White America the black dance music they'd ignored, just as the Stones and Beatles had done in the sixties.

But what offended the audience of industry insiders wasn't the way Wilson poured scorn on the US record biz for ignoring the revolutionary black music on its own doorstep, but his gleeful revelation that the Mondays were drug dealers, and the appearance of comedian Keith Allen in the guise of a Dr Feelgood who boasted of having 'thousands' of E tablets 'in my hotel'. The joke fell on stony-faced ground, largely because 'drug pusher' had a different connotation in an America beset with gang-related bloodshed. In Britain, the image of the Ecstasy dealer as a harmless minor villain was soon to change; Wilson's wind-up ricochetted back to haunt him when drug gangs started to bring guns into The Haçienda later that year.

Trip City

'Detroit and Chicago have been to us and other current groups, what Memphis and Chicago were to the Stones and the other white R & B groups of the sixties. Acid house was the first time I got excited about music that was happening in my lifetime.'
— Tim Burgess, singer of The Charlatans

The flaw in Burgess's theory was that apart from the Mondays and the Roses, all the other North West of England bands sounded less like modern *equivalents* of the mod bands, and more like straightforward sixties beat revivalists. There was only the most tenuous relationship to modern dance music, and an alarming degree of attention to period detail. The Charlatans had the 'baggy', shuffle-funk beat, all right, but were morbidly obsessed with the milky, Ovalteeny tones of the Hammond organ (their keyboard player admired Jon Lord of Deep Purple). Inspiral Carpets exhumed the tinpot Farfisa organ, nasal harmonies and gormless page-boy haircuts of '96 Tears'-style garage punkadelia. Candy Flip – named after the slang term for an E and LSD cocktail – scored a Top Five hit with their 'baggy' version of 'Strawberry Fields'. Other 'scene' bands – The High, Ocean Colour Scene, The La's, Mock Turtles – were even more hopelessly classicist.

If Manchester had really eclipsed London as the rave capital of the UK, where – you might have been forgiven for asking – the fook were the proper Mancunian house artists?! In truth, there were only two contenders – 808 State and A Guy Called Gerald. Of Caribbean parentage, Gerald Simpson had grown up on a mixture of electro (Afrika Bambaataa, Mantronix), synth pop (Yellow Magic Orchestra, Numan, Visage), art-rock (Peter Gabriel, Bowie) and jazz-fusion (Herbie Hancock, Chick Corea, Miles Davis). In the late eighties, Simpson hooked up with Graham Massey (a refugee from the avant-funk unit Biting Tongues) in a Brit-rap collective called The Hit Squad. The group practised in the basement of Manchester's leading import-dance-and-indiepop record store, Eastern Bloc, which was co-owned by Martin Price. With Price supplying 'concepts and images', Massey and Simpson then formed an acid-house outfit which evolved into 808 State, named after the famous Roland 808 drum-machine so beloved by B-boys.

After working on New Build, an album of acid jams, Simpson quarrelled with the rest of the group over money and went solo as A Guy Called Gerald – but not before contributing heavily to a track called 'Pacific State'. The next thing he knew, his erstwhile partners had recruited two teenage DJs, Andy Barker and Darren Partington aka The Spinmasters (famous for their sets at The Thunderdome and on Manchester radio), and 'Pacific State' was in the Top Ten. Rubbing shoulders with 'Fool's Gold' and 'Rave On', 'Pacific' was the third Madchester chart smash in the closing months of 1989. Simpson tried to get an injunction against the record, eventually settling for royalties and a publishing credit. But he could take solace from the fact that he'd beaten 808 to the punch with 'Voodoo Ray', a Number Twelve hit in July 1989 and the first truly great British house anthem.

With its undulant groove and dense percussive foliage (Gerald was trying to get 'a sort of samba vibe, I was listening to a lot of Latin stuff'), its glassy, gem-faceted bass-pulse and tropical bird synth-chatter, 'Voodoo Ray' looks ahead to the polyrhythmic luxuriance of Gerald's mid-nineties forays into jungle, as do the tremulous whimpers and giggles of the blissed-out female vocal. The main hook – a siren-like voice chanting 'Oooh oo-oooh / Aaaah – aa-hahah, yeaahh' – was offset by a sinister male voice intoning 'voodoo ray': a mysterious phrase that suggests a shamanic figure or voudun priest, or possibly a mind-controlling beam. In fact, it was a happy accident: originally, 'it was meant to be "Voodoo Rage", but I didn't have enough memory in the sampler so I had to chop the G off!' says Gerald. 'I had this idea of people locking into a beat, this picture of a voodoo ceremony. But instead of it being really aggressive, it ended up something really mysterious – sort of sucking you in.'

Gerald followed 'Voodoo Ray' with 'FX', a track written for the soundtrack to *Trip City* (based on Trevor Miller's experimental novel set in a near-future club scene where everyone is addicted to a hallucinogen called FX), and then, in early 1990, with his major label debut *Automannik*. But the deal with CBS quickly turned sour: the company wanted 'ten more versions of "Voodoo Ray",' and Gerald's tougher-sounding, conceptual album *High Life Low Profile* was never released. Disillusioned, Gerald disappeared into the rave underground, resurfacing in the mid-nineties as one of the most experimental producers in the jungle scene.

808 State fared somewhat better with major-label affiliate ZTT, maintaining a presence in the singles chart while prospering as an album-oriented act. With its cheesy, mellow-yellow saxophone and sampled bird-song, 'Pacific State' caught the crest of the vogue for Ambient or New Age house: 'coming down music, a sound for when the sun's coming up and the trip's near its end,' as Martin Price put it. The original idea behind 'Pacific', though, was an attempt at a modern equivalent of fifties 'exotica'; Graham Massey was a big fan of Martin Denny, whose tiki music (quasi-Polynesian mood-music for suburban cocktail parties) often featured tropical bird-calls.

On the album *90*, 'Sunrise' was a far superior take on the same idea; tendrils of flute, mist-swirls of spectral sample-texture, and lambent synth-horizons conjure up a Polynesian dawnscape. On this track and the earlier 'State Ritual' (which sounded like aborigines trying to make acid house using flutes and wooden-gourds), 808 State are denizens of the 'Fourth World' (Jon Hassell's term for a future fusion that melded Western hi-tech and traditional ethnic musics, as sketched on albums like *Dream Theory In Malaya* and *Aka-Darbari-Java/Magic Realism*). Later in 1990, 808 actually remixed 'Voiceprint', from Hassell's hip-hop influenced album *City: Works of Fiction*, adapting it for the contemporary house dancefloor. Primarily a Miles-influenced trumpeter, Hassell was a veteran of the early seventies jazz-fusion era. 808 State gave props to Weather Report and Herbie Hancock, fusioneer graduates of Miles's late sixties and early seventies ensembles. Darren spoke of 'trying to create that big band image, that big sound onstage, but all we've got is just a few boxes. We want it so that from every corner of those speakers something's coming out. Those bands were doing it then, and we're doing it now.'

On their next album *Ex-El*, 808 State plunged even deeper into the realm of nineties fusion, revealing its pleasures and pitfalls. Tracks like 'San Fransisco' and 'Lambrusco Cowboy' offer a pan-global fantasia of reeling vistas and undulating impressionism. 'Qmart' is like a helicopter's eye view of the savannah, with herds of antelope and wildebeest scattering hither and thither like shoals of tropical fish. Despite its Nubian/Egyptological title, 'Nephatiti' is urban to the core, a perfect in-car soundtrack; like the opening sequence of underpasses and flyovers in Tarkovksy's *Solaris*, it makes you feel like a corpuscle in the city's bloodstream. But elsewhere, there's a tendency towards fusion's cardinal sins: sterile, showboating monumentalism, florid detail verging on the rococo.

Although *Ex-El* featured cameos from New Order's Bernard Sumner and Bjork, for the most part 808 State's music was faceless, text-free, *profoundly superficial*. But belying their image as knob-twiddling technicians with nothing to say, 808 State in person were mouthy, vociferous, and in Martin Price's case, almost pathologically opinionated. They had bags of personality – it just wasn't a particularly agreeable personality. The first time I interviewed Price and Massey, circa *90*, the duo were quick to define 808 State against the Cabaret Voltaire/A Certain Ratio/On U Sound tradition of avant-funk, despite Massey's own background in that scene. Arguing that rave music had outflanked the egghead experimentalists, Massey declared: 'Mainstream clubs are just so out there and futuristic in comparison. You get beer boys and Sharons 'n' Tracies dancing to the weirdest crap going, at places like The Thunderdome, and they don't know what's hit 'em. Yer average Joe Bloggs is dancing to stuff that's basically avant-garde.'

Seven months later, in the summer of 1990, Price railed against indie-rock/rave crossover bands like The Beloved, The Shamen and Primal Scream. 'You've got totally non-credible acts cashing in on the sort of music 808 State have been doing for years.' Deriding indie-rock as 'peer group stuff . . . just another stupid way to get girlfriends by going round with a big question mark over your head,' he ranted: 'Now they've discovered that the better peer group is in the dance field and they want to change their whole fucking lives. But they don't do it bravely, and say "All right, I made a mistake, I'm now totally into dance." They stay stuck between two stools.'

'Fucking Norman Cook on *The Late Show* saying "It's like punk rock,"' frothed Price, referring to former Housemartins' bassist Norman Cook, who'd recently got to Number One with his dubby-dance combo Beats International. 'If somebody says [techno]'s like punk to my face, I'll fucking smash 'em in the teeth. It's nothing to do with punk. Nobody wants to see a load of idiots torturing themselves on stage with guitars any more. This is about machines, punk was about arm power. The muscles and sinews in dance music are when you're sweating your bollocks off on the dancefloor.'

White Punks on E

Although the equation of homespun house and punk rock *was* a little simplistic, the UK dance scene in 1990 was packed with old punks who'd traded in their guitars for the new technology: The Orb's Alex Paterson, Bobby Gillespie of Primal Scream, Bill Drummond and Jimmy Cauty of the KLF. Even former PiL bassist Jah Wobble returned from the wilderness, playing on tracks by Primal Scream and The Orb, and peddling, via his ethnodelic ensemble Invaders Of The Heart, a distinctly New Agey creed of 'healing rhythms', 'redemptive chants' and ego-melting 'energy flows'.

Punk's negativism was really a poisoned Romantic utopianism. In the late eighties, that curdled idealism – blocked by the societal impasses and cultural dead-ends of the seventies – flowed free, thanks to Ecstasy and the feel-good factor engendered by the economic boom. Prefigured in Prince's prattle about a New Power Generation, in Soul II Soul's community-conscious funky-dredd anthems 'Back To Life' and 'Get A Life', and the 'hippy-hop' of De La Soul and other Native Tongue rap groups like Jungle Brothers and A Tribe Called Quest, positivity emerged as *the* pop ideology of the new decade. Drawing on diverse sources – American discourses of self-realization and interpersonal therapy, New Age notions of healing music and 'abundance conscious-ness', sixties flower power, deep house's gospel exhortations – positivity heralded the dawn of a nineties zeitgeist that emphasized caring and sharing, a return to quality of life over standard of living, and green eco-consciousness. The anti-social egotism of the eighties, exemplified in pop terms by rap and Madonna, was eclipsed by a shift from 'I' to 'we', from materialism to idealism, from attitude to platitude.

Needless to say, the loved-up rave scene was a fertile climate for the proliferation of New Agey ideas. Between 1988 and 1990, there was a subtle modulation – from music to lose yourself in (acieed) to music to find yourself in (ambient house). Alongside 808's 'Pacific State', there was S'Express's 'Mantra For A State of Mind' (described by Mark Moore as 'music to cleanse your mind'), Innocence's 'Natural Thing', The Grid's 'Floatation', The Beloved's 'The Sun Rising', The KLF's *Chill Out* and The Orb's 'A Huge Evergrowing Pulsating Brain That Rules From the Centre of The Ultraworld'. This brief fad for dub-tempo house and beat-free chill-out music was accompanied by talk of giving up synthetics like MDMA in favour of 'organic highs': gurano, psychoactive cocktails, and 'brain machine' goggles whose flickering light-patterns induced mildly trippy trance states. On the fashion front, ravers started dressing all in white, signalling their newborn purity of soul. Oh, it was easy (and highly enjoyable, let me tell you!) to mock the nebulous naïvety of the positivity prophets. But clearly, the feeling of 'something in the air' stemmed from a genuine and deep-seated, if poorly grounded, idealism and hunger for change.

Not all of the positivity-punks were old: Adamski, rave's first pin-up, was only eleven when he formed a punk rock band called The Stupid Babies in 1979. A big Malcolm McLaren fan, Adam Tinley pursued his passion for chaos in the confrontational Diskort Datkord (who often performed in the nude). After doing disco/noise versions of X-Ray Spex's 'Identity' and Bowie's 'Rebel Rebel', Adamski became a big draw on the rave scene during the brief vogue for live perform-ances by keyboard whizzkids, and scored a hit with 'NRG'.

'I liked the energy and the visual side of punk, but it was all just saying "no, no, no, no," whereas now everybody's saying "yes, yes, yes,"' Adamski told me in 1990. 'I much prefer the positivity thing we have now.' Ironically, he'd just scored his biggest hit with the gloomy and harrowed 'Killer', an awesome slice of techno-blues that cracked apart the jollity of *Top of the Pops* with its grievous ache of loss and longing. Sung and co-written by Black British singer Seal, 'Killer' was rave's very own 'What's Goin' On', and in the summer of 1990 it annexed the Number One spot for nearly a month. The futuristic frigidity of its sound and the sci-fi imagery of the video (Adamski as a 'nineties alchemist' messing about in the laboratory) made me imagine Adamski as a Gary Numan for the twenty-first century: a nubile, Aryan *petit prince*, alone in the world with only his techno toys for company.

Unfortunately Adamski blew it by following 'Killer' with 'The Space Jungle' (a throwaway cover version of Presley's 'All Shook Up') and the pitiful album *Doctor Adamski's Musical Pharmacy*, whose only faintly redeeming moment was the ultra-*naif* alphabet-song 'Everything Is Fine', which began 'A is for adrenalin, amnesia and anything else that makes life easier' and got worse.

If Adamski degenerated into rave's very own Captain Sensible, The KLF were much closer to his original reinvocation of the spirit of Malcolm McLaren. Back in the 1987–8 era of sample-based DJ tracks, KLF-ers Bill Drummond and Jimmy Cauty had formed a hip hop outfit called The Justified Ancients of Mu Mu. Borrowed from Robert Anton Wilson's *Illuminatus!*, this was the name of an imaginary anarcho-mystic organization said to have been fighting Authority since the dawn of History; Mu means 'chaos'. Their first effort, 'All You Need Is Love', pirated hefty chunks of the Beatles and the MC5, and the album *1987: What The Fuck Is Going On?* had to be withdrawn after Abba, one of numerous sample victims, threatened legal action. As The Timelords the duo scored a Number One hit with 'Doctorin' The Tardis', cobbled together out of the *Dr Who* theme and Gary Glitter's 'Rock 'n' Roll, Part Two'. They then wrote a book about the experience, *The Manual: How To Have A Number One The Easy Way*.

Growing sick of their reputation as sub-McLaren pop pranksters, and convinced that 'irony and reference points are the dark destroyers of great music', the pair – now named The KLF – decided rave was the way forward. 'In all of us there's a need for communal otherness,' said Drummond. 'When you're at a rave and there's thirty thousand of you in a field and a record comes on and you all love the record together, that's a religious feeling.' Dedicating themselves to a sound they called 'stadium house', The KLF recorded thrilling pop-techno stampedes like 'What Time Is Love', '3 AM Eternal' and 'Last Train to Trance-Central', scoring four Top Five hits and a Number One between late 1990 and early 1992. Despite its populist appeal, The KLF's output was still infused with their mystic, punks-on-E spirit of 'zenarchy'. In the video for '3 AM Eternal', The KLF are garbed in ceremonial robes and move in formation as though enacting a religious ceremony, while *The White Room* album featured songs like 'Church Of The KLF'. And in 1991, the band held a pagan rave to celebrate 'The Rites of Mu' on the Hebridean island of Jura, burning a sixty foot high Wicker Man and forcing the assembled journalists and media folk to chant and cavort in white robes.

While The KLF ultimately had too much of a sense of irony to really go the nouveau hippy route, other converts to rave were enthused with a born-again fervour. The Beloved were New Order clones until singer Jon Marsh experienced life-changing rave-alations at Shoom and Spectrum. 'The whole of 1988 from March onwards is a complete blur,' he told *iD*. 'An orgy of parties.' Shoom appears to have made mush of his brain, judging by the lyrics of 'Up Up and Away' on their breakthrough album *Happiness*: 'Hello New day ... Give the world a message and the word is YES.' To be fair, their first hit 'The Sun Rising' was a rare shock of the sublime in the charts, with its beatific backwards guitar and madrigal vocals (sampled from *A Feather on the Breath of God: Sequences and Hymns by the Abbess Hildegard of Bingen*). But the follow-up, 'Hello' was a lazy list-song that juxtaposed Jean-Paul Sartre with crap comedians Cannon and Ball, a 'Reasons To Be Cheerful, Part Three' for the MDMA generation.

Then there was The Shamen, whose singer–guitarist Colin Angus hailed New Age as 'the first modern Western spiritual movement' and explained his self-invented 'visualization technique' for making wishes come true: 'It's hard work, you have to be positive and motivated nonstop.' His partner Mr C added: 'It's not about willing something to happen. It's about *knowing* it's going to happen.' The Shamen made a conscious decision to cut themselves off from all sources of negativity in the outside world, like newspapers or TV, and devote themselves to sustaining their own spiritually uplifting, parallel universe of pleasure.

The Shamen began in the mid-eighties as a retro-psychedelic band, complete with phased-and-flanged guitars, Op Art back projections, and melodies that recalled The Electric Prunes' 'I Had Too Much To Dream Last Night'. Already interested in hallucinogenic altered states, Angus and co-founder Will Sinnot were among the first indie rockers to be drawn into rave culture. Where bands like Primal Scream and Happy Mondays depended on the dancefloor savvy of DJ–producers like Andy Weatherall or Paul Oakenfold to overhaul their basically traditional rock songs, Colin Angus painstakingly taught himself to program sampling and sequencer technology. By 1989, they had broken with the mould of the rock gig and were throwing mini-raves under the name Synergy (later Progeny), combining live techno bands and

DJs, stunning light-shows and video-projections, and an array of sideshows ranging from 'chill-out' rooms to for-hire virtual reality equipment. Angus's dream was for The Shamen to become a sort of twenty-first century Grateful Dead, creating a forum for communal freak-outs outside the musical mainstream.

After an awkward transitional phase in which they combined anti-Amerikan agit-prop lyrics with trance-dance rhythms, The Shamen shifted to full-on positivity on their breakthrough album *En-Tact* (the name came from 'entactogen', the pharmacologist's neologism for Ecstasy). Tracks like 'Move Any Mountain' and 'Human NRG' are affirmation therapy with a beat. Despite the fatuously uplifting sentiments, though, the electronic textures of 'Possible Worlds' and 'Omega Amigo' brim so rapturously, you gladly succumb to the utopianism of the text.

The KLF may have joked about 'The Church of the KLF', but The Shamen actually had a distinctly high-minded attitude to getting high; Colin Angus, with his fastidious, desiccated manner, has something of the aura of a Presbyterian preacher. In a UK rave scene organized around 'getting off your tits' and 'losing the plot', the band talked earnestly of 'a spiritual revolution'. Angus praised psychedelic-plant prophet Terence McKenna for his 'very rational and lucid ideas about how there's been longstanding human tradition of using psychedelic drugs.' The Shamen then turned the bearded sage into an unlikely pop star when they included snatches of his pro-hallucinogen sermonizing on their Top Twenty hit 'Re: Evolution'.

White punk-on-E usually equalled *nouveau hippy*. Other dance-rock crossover bands offered a decidedly less pious and more delinquent take on rave 'n' roll. Touted as London's answer to Happy Mondays, Flowered Up were inner-city kids from the Regent's Park Estate; their name was a metaphor for youthful idealism struggling up through the cracked paving stones of the urban wasteland. The band had its very own Bez in Barry Mooncult, whose job was to cavort onstage dressed as a giant flower. Like Shaun Ryder, frontman Liam sang about the seamy side of Ecstasy culture in a gutteral working-class accent. 'It's On' expressed the elation of pulling off 'the biggest deal of your life'; 'Phobia' evoked the nocturnal paranoia caused by taking one E too many; the Top Twenty hit 'Weekender' was a heavy-riffing epic about the punishing syndrome of living for the weekend's big blow-out, with Liam warning the party-hard hedonist not to get burned out, and samples from *Quadrophenia* underlining the rave-as-mod analogy.

Flowered Up also threw wild parties, like their infamous three day squat-rave at a luxurious mansion block in Blackheath, which climaxed with the place being trashed (despite the fact that the owner was reputedly a hoodlum involved with gambling). 'I remember sitting by this Victorian indoor swimming pool talking to some guy,' says Jack Barron. 'Suddenly this chair flew through the window section between the lounge and the kitchen, followed by a *person*.' On a similar sixties-into-nineties mod tip as Flowered Up, EMF were a gang of West Country reprobates (the name stood for Ecstasy Motherfuckers) who'd started out throwing micro-raves in the Forest of Dean; their irresistibly swaggering 'Unbelievable' got to Number Three in the winter of 1990.

Of all the post-Manchester crossover bands, Primal Scream were most successful in merging rock's Romanticism and rave's drug-tech futurism. Like fellow Scots The Shamen, Primal Scream began in the early eighties as psychedelic resurrectionists attempting to distil the child-man innocence out of The Byrds, Love and the softer Velvet Underground. By 1988, the Scream's testicles dropped catastrophically, and they veered off in an unconvincing blues direction, complete with raunchy on-the-road excess. During 1989, the band and other people from their label, Creation, started going to acid-house parties. 'Contemporary rock ceased to excite us,' singer and spiritual leader Bobby Gillespie said later. 'At raves, the music was better, the people were better, the girls were better, and the drugs were better.'

The first recorded evidence of these realigned allegiances emerged when Primal Scream asked their DJ friend Andrew Weatherall of the Boy's Own posse to remix the Stonesy 'I'm Losing More Than I'll Ever Have'. Using rhythm guitar, piano vamps, horn stabs, and other elements from the original, Weatherall built a new track over a chunky-funky, mid-tempo Soul II Soul style rhythmic undercarriage. Samples of Peter Fonda from Roger Corman's bikersploitation movie *The Wild Angels* – "We wanna be *free*. We wanna get *loaded* and have a good time!" – gave the song its new title: 'Loaded'. At once sepia-tinted retro and state-of-art – imagine a dub version of 'Sympathy For The Devil' – 'Loaded' got to Number Sixteen in early 1990, selling over a hundred thousand copies.

For the follow-up 'Come Together', Primal Scream recruited both Weatherall and Boy's Own's Terry Farley. The Farley mix puts looped breakbeats under the band's Byrdsy twelve-string song; Gillespie celebrates rave-as-the-Swinging-sixties-all-over-again, breathlessly panting 'kiss me . . . trip me / ride me to the stars / ohhh, it's all too much'. But the Weatherall version dispenses with the group's playing entirely, and adds churchy organs and a gospel choir, thereby transforming a sex-and-drugs ballad into a redemption anthem of spiritual unity. Samples of Jessie Jackson proclaiming 'it's a new day . . . together we have power' plugged into a different aspect of the sixties, the Civil Rights struggle. 'I see the song as a modern day "Street Fighting Man",' the inveterate rock-scholar Gillespie told me. 'It's certainly not a statement of vapid New Age optimism. I see Weatherall's version as being tragic, like "If only the world could be as one . . . but I know it never will be."'

Watching Weatherall at work taught Primal Scream all about 'rhythm and space . . . the sampler gave us a whole new palette of colours . . . a whole new world of psychedelic possibilities.' The result was the band's masterpiece, 'Higher Than The Sun'. Here the band, in tandem with Weatherall and The Orb's Alex Paterson, brilliantly merged two different traditions of psychedelic experience, acid rock and acid house. Shades of Primal Scream's rock classicist past (Brian Wilson, Love's *Forever Changes*) mingled and melded with influences from dub, techno, Tim Buckley and Sun Ra. Never one for hiding his own light under a bushel, Gillespie described 'Higher Than The Sun' as the most important record since 'Anarchy In The UK'. Certainly the lyric (about being your own god) recalled the solipsistic sovereignty of 'Anarchy In The UK' (albeit fuelled by Ecstasy rather than amphetamine), but what Gillespie really meant was that 'Higher' was a rock-historical 'cut-off record – it makes everybody else look ancient'.

While The Orb's version was great, it was the two Weatherall mixes – 'American Spring' and 'Dub Symphony' – that were truly mindblowing. The former pivoted around an exquisite harspischord motif like a scattered handful of stardust. 'Dub Symphony' began with Gillespie's effete, bliss-stricken gasp 'I – I – I – I – I – I'm-I'm higher than the su-uh-uhn', looped into a swoon of endless, unendurable rapture, over dub-detonating reports of snare-drum. Then Jah Wobble's bass takes the song deeper in and further out, as spooky synth sounds beseech like interstellar sirens luring the starsailor to shipwreck in the asteroid belt.

With its are-you-experienced / you-don't-live-today lyrics ('Hallucinogens can open me or untie me / I drift in inner space, free of time ... I've glimpsed, I have tasted / Fantastical places'), its cosmic narcissism and ravished, bliss-enfeebled vocals, 'Higher Than The Sun' is a blatant drug hymn. Gillespie preferred to see it as 'a spiritual song, me disconnecting myself from everything, but being totally in touch with myself ... I'm sure that when astronauts are up in space, they must get the impulse to just disconnect themselves from the ship and drift off into space and never come back.'

After 'Higher' and its sequel 'Don't Fight It, Feel It' – pumping, drug-buzzy techno for which Gillespie ceded the mic' to Brit-diva Denise Johnson – Primal Scream released the long-awaited *Screamadelica*. But when they toured the album in the last months of 1991, Primal Scream rediscovered their rock 'n' roll hearts. Drifting away from the dancefloor and Ecstasy culture, they devolved towards raunchy rock 'n' soul and harder drugs, signalled by the *Dixie-Narco* EP.

Through 1992–3, murky reports came through of the band's apparent attempt to replay the misadventures of the Stones at their most wrecked and reckless in the early seventies. What had been so great about Primal Scream circa 'Higher' was the interface they'd forged between rock history and the dance present. When the band returned in 1994 with *Give Out But Don't Give Up* – recorded with 'legendary' Rod Stewart/Cream/Aretha Franklin producer Tom Dowd and the 'legendary' Muscle Shoals rhythm section – it became horribly apparent that the Primals had removed the dance present, leaving just the rock history. Some wondered if *Screamadelica* all came down to the mixing-board genius of Andy Weatherall. But the symbiosis/synergy cuts both ways: the truth is, *sans* Scream, Weatherall never did anything half as good in his Sabres of Paradise guise.

After the Luv Has Gone

'Y'know, two years ago, I'd've said legalize E ... But now ... I don't know, like. 'Cos E ... it can make ya nice and mellow but it's also capable of doin' proper naughty things to you as well ... E can get you into big fookin' bother ... Fuck, if we legalized E, man, we'd probably have a race of fuckin' mutants on our 'ands!'
                              – Shaun Ryder, talking to *The Face*'s Nick Kent, 1990

Hailed by the music press as the album of 1991 and winner of the prestigious music-industry Mercury Prize, *Screamadelica* was the high-point of the rock/rave crossover era initiated by the Manchester bands. But by then, Madchester was already in its twilight. As early as July 1990, when the Roses' 'One Love' failed to make Number One, you could sense that the moment had peaked. Frustrated by an invidious contract with their label Silvertone, the Roses went to court only to find themselves in legal limbo, unable to record or release a note. The case dragged on until May 1991, when the Roses were freed and immediately signed to Geffen in a huge deal. But Silvertone appealed the verdict, paralysing the band for another year.

While the Roses were tangled in litigation, Manchester's funtopia turned to nightmare. In any drug-based pop scene, there comes a point when the collective trip turns bad, when the rush gives way to the CRASH. Trying to reach a higher high, 'too many people take one too many,' as Ian Brown put it. Drugs get adulterated as dealers try to maximize profit margins. The clientele turns to scuzzier substances, either to sustain the buzz (freebasing coke, injecting speed) or cushion the come down (heroin).

Once, remembers Brown, there was 'a feeling of community strength' in Manchester, '[you'd come] out of a club at the end of the night feeling like you were going to change the world. Then guns come in, and heroin starts being put in Ecstasy. It took a lot of the love vibe out.' Drugs meant money; money meant warfare for market control between rival drug gangs from Cheetham Hill, Moss Side and Salford. The Roses actually saw one Mancunian gang-leader get shot at a reggae concert in mid-1990. But it was a series of violent incidents at Thunderdome and The Haçienda that most publicly announced the souring of the Madchester dream. 'Before The Haçienda got gun-detectors on the door, you'd see sixteen-year-old baby-gangsters standing at the bar with a gun in a holster, right in view.'

Bad memories of this dark period inspired 'Begging You', the most thrilling track on the Stone Roses 1995 *long*-time-a-comin' follow-up album *Second Coming*. A hyperkinetic rock–techno fusion of ballistic blues-riffs and looped beats, '"Begging You",' explained Brown, 'is like when you're sat in a club and everything's beautiful and you're E'd up, and you've got some voice going in your ear saying how they can get you a gun or an ounce of this-or-that.' With its churning centrifugal groove and almighty turbine-roar guitar, the song sounds exactly like the panic rush of an E'd up raver wondering how and why the rave-dream's dying all around him. Right to the end, the Roses got their impetus from rave culture – it's just that with this song, the energy was dystopian rather than utopian.

There had been intimations of doom as early as 14 July 1989, when sixteen-year-old Claire Leighton collapsed at The Haçienda and later died, reportedly from an allergic reaction to E. In early 1990, new national legislation came into force in the Manchester area, making club licences easier to revoke; the local police force had already set up Operation Clubwatch to monitor the drug trafficking in The Haçienda and other Mancunian rave clubs. In December of 1990, Konspiracy lost its licence. Always a seedy, nefarious place, the club had rapidly become over-run by the drug gangs, who hawked their wares brazenly on the dancefloor and stairways, and intimidated the staff, demanding huge amounts of free liquor and brutalizing anyone who obstructed them. As well as the usual gunplay and fights between rival gangsters, innocents got caught in the fray: one student was stabbed.

Facing the same fate as Konspiracy, The Haçienda hired a top barrister and managed to get a licence hearing delayed until early in 1991, giving them time to clean up the club and install a £10,000 security system that included metal detectors and video surveillance cameras. Inevitably, this ruined The Haçienda's atmosphere and led to declining attendance, but it did mean that at the start of 1991 the club was given a six-month reprieve by the licensing authority. But a month later, The Haçienda closed voluntarily, after an incident in which hoodlums threatened a door manager with a hand-gun.

When the club reopened in May that year, attendance was poor, and violent incidents continued to sour the atmosphere, like the time a Salford gang sneaked into The Haçienda and stabbed several bouncers as a reprisal for being barred entrance. By this point, the city's media image had decisively deteriorated from 'Madchester' to 'Gunchester'; there'd been scores of shootings in Manchester's ghetto zones, including one in which a twelve-year-old boy was shot through the eye. In February, Cheetham Hill gangleader 'White Tony' Johnson was killed with a bullet through the mouth and his sidekick 'Black Tony' was wounded. That month, Robert Parsonage, a student, died of internal bleeding after taking five Ecstasy tablets and collapsing at a party in Stalybridge. There were similar problems throughout the North West; Quadrant Park's famed all-nighter The Pavilion closed voluntarily, following incidents of stabbing and robbery, and another Ecstasy death. The free party scene had disintegrated thanks to the police crackdown. When a series of illegal parties in Cheshire woodland were stopped by the authorities in early 1991, desperate ravers ventured even further afield, into the wildernesses of the Lake District and Wales.

The latter was where some of the Stone Roses had relocated. Manny, so long the 'rogue Rose', moved to a small village in South Wales. 'Heroin and methadone, fourteen deaths in a year for me, and that's fucking outrageous,' he said circa *Second Coming*. 'Kids I'd known since I was seven. I've seen people I've never ever thought would take the drug, *fucked*. Me, I'll turn my back on them people, however much it hurts me. That's why I moved out of Manchester, I don't wanna be near it.'

Hardcore hedonists even before rave, Happy Mondays stuck with it to the bitter end. Released late in 1990, the hit album *Pills 'N' Thrills and Bellyaches* was a summation of the Madchester era. With its glossy, neat-and-tidy Paul Oakenfold production, the album's contents were tame compared with the dishevelled *Rave On* EP. But there were three Mondays classics. 'Loose Fit', slow-burning funk with a shimmering Beatlesy guitar-motif, was Ryder's manifesto of baggy bad taste and spiritual laissez-faire: 'Doesn't have to be legit / 'S gotta be a loose fit.' Starting with the sound of a charter plane taking off, 'Holiday' showed that the Mondays' version of 'politics of Ecstasy' had nothing to do with the Tim Leary/Terence McKenna style 'spiritual hedonism' of The Shamen, but was rather modelled on the boorishly orgiastic antics of British youth in Mediterranean sunspots. 'Holiday' segued into the guitar-solo epic 'Harmony', a debauched and delirious parody of the Pepsi Cola vision of world unity, with Ryder hollering 'what we need is a big big cooking pot' in which to cook up a broth of 'every wonderful beautiful drug . . . we got.'

Happy Mondays' pipe-dream of taking a permanent vacation became hellish reality, when the band attempted to record their fourth album in Barbados. Progress on the record was agonizingly slow: Bez trashed several jeeps and broke his arm, while Ryder, fresh from quitting a long-standing heroin habit, succumbed to the cheapness of drugs in the Caribbean, and got into crack cocaine. In the drug dens where he spent most of his days acquiring a thirty to fifty-rock *per diem* crack habit, the hyped-up natives played dancehall reggae records at an insane 78 r.p.m.; sadly, none of that mania and derangement made it into the Mondays' new music. Despite the gimme-gimme-gimme, 'more E, Vicar?' attitude of the title *Yes Please!* the music was enfeebled by its drugginess rather than galvanized. At best, it recalled the oceanic funk of late Can or John Martyn's *One World*, at worst, the Island Records jet-set funk-muzak of Steve Winwood.

Costing over a quarter of a million pounds, *Yes Please!* put Factory out of business, disappointed the fans, and was promptly followed by the band's break-up. But amazingly, Ryder and Bez got their second chance at the big time after hooking up with a Mancunian rapper called Kermit to form Black Grape. At 1996's Tribal Gathering mega-rave, the band were greeted as heroic survivors when they headlined the main tent. Despite the rockier sound and ostensibly abstemious title of Black Grape's *It's Great When You're Straight ... Yeah*, Shaun and Bez were still every raver's favourite drug-fiends.

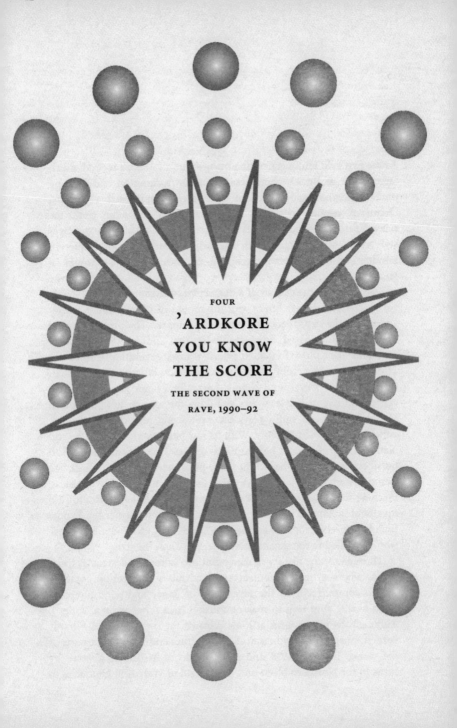

FOUR

'ARDKORE
YOU KNOW
THE SCORE

THE SECOND WAVE OF
RAVE, 1990–92

As the first acid house generation burned out, by 1990, a second, much larger wave of British youth was tuning in, turning on and freaking out. Although illegal raves had been largely suppressed, a thriving circuit of commercial raves had emerged; at the same time, the relaxation of licensing laws allowed for the growth of all-night rave-style clubs. Rave spread from the original metropolitan cliques in London and Manchester to become a nationwide suburban/provincial leisure culture.

1990 also saw the genesis of a distinctively British rave sound, 'hardcore', which decisively broke with the mould of Detroit and Chicago, and ended the dependence on American imports. The proliferation of cheap computer-based home-studio set-ups and sampler/sequencer programs like Cubase fomented a do-it-yourself revolution reminiscent of punk, and was accompanied by an explosion of independent labels. By 1991 this underground sound – actually a confederacy of hybrid genres and regional styles – was assaulting the mainstream pop charts. Despite next-to-no radio play, the rave scene hurled anthem after anthem into the Top Twenty. With its raw phuturism, coded lingo and blatant drug references, hardcore was as shocking and alien(ating) to outsiders as punk had been. But many punk veterans, now in their late twenties and early thirties, decried the new music as a soul-less, machine-made noise devoid of poetry; mere apolitical escapism for E'd up zombies. Zapped by a new generation gap, these former rebels now found themselves fogies who just didn't get what was going on. Those who did rallied to the slogan, 'hardcore, you *know* the score'.

Throughout the history of dance culture, 'hardcore' designates those scenes where druggy hedonism and underclass desperation combine with a commitment to the physicality of dance and a no-nonsense funktionalist approach to making music ('tracks' rather than 'songs'). Although the intransigent attitude remains the same, musically 'hardcore' means different things at different times and in different parts of the world. Between 1990 and 1993, hardcore in Britain referred by turns to the Northern bleep-and-bass sound of Warp and Unique 3, to the hip-house and ragga-techno sounds of the Shut Up And Dance label, to the anthemic pop-rave of acts like N-Joi and Shades of Rhythm, to Belgian and German brutalist tekno, and, finally, to the breakbeat-driven furore of hardcore jungle.

Weirdly, British hardcore was simultaneously 'blacker' and 'whiter' than the original Chicago and Detroit music. Because of unbreachable racial divisions, the idea of 'hip-house' never really took off in America. But in the more integrated UK hip hop and house music were part of the same continuum of imported 'street beats'; Jamaican sound-system culture had long established roots. Influenced by reggae and hip hop, hardcore producers intensified the sub-bass frequencies, used looped breakbeats to funk up house's four-to-the-floor machine-beat, and embraced sampling with deranged glee. But as well as gritty, B-boy funk, British hardcore also brought a white rock *attack* to the Detroit blueprint. Following the lead of the bombastic Belgians and Germans, UK producers deployed riff-like 'stabs' and bursts of blaring noise.

Detroit had never been a rave scene, never been about drugs; techno had begun as a Europhile fantasy of elegance and refinement. So you can imagine the originators' horror when real Europeans transformed techno into a vulgar uproar for E'd up mobs: anthemic, cheesily sentimental, unabashedly drug-crazed. The British and their allies on the Continent shed the pall of cool that restrained Detroit, and raised the music's temperature to a swelter. No wonder anti-hardcore hipsters and Detroit-nostalgics always complained about 'sweaty ravers'.

During those three years, 1990–92, the British hardcore scene wasn't so much a melting pot as a *mental pot*; an alembic, heated by the flames of drug abuse, that generated new sonic amalgams with every season. All hail the 'alchemical generation', to twist Irvine Welsh's famous phrase: half a million British kids who boldly sacrificed their brain-cells to spawn some of the maddest music this planet has ever heard.

Low Frequency Oscillations

For all the music's futurism, hardcore was organized around two almost touchingly quaint models: the cottage industry and the local community. Artists – usually DJs with first-hand experience of how to work a crowd's bass-biology reflexes – made their tracks on home-studio set-ups or at cheap local studios, then pressed up anywhere from five hundred to a few thousand white label 12-inch singles and sold them direct to specialist dance shops.

Steve Beckett, co-founder of Sheffield's Warp label, remembers a golden age when the word 'white label' was like a magic password. 'I'd be driving to shops like Selectadisc in Nottingham and Derby, and you'd say "white label" and they'd be like "right! come in!" They'd take fifty off you for five quid each, no problem. It was a real special thing then, because hardly anybody was doing it. Dance music was all imports, then people in Britain starting doing it for themselves, and then their tracks started to get better than the tunes from America.'

Warp was a classic example of an enduring hardcore archetype: it was both a label and a specialist record store, and had close ties to the crucial Sheffield clubs like Jive Turkey, Cuba and Occasions. Other examples include Bradford's Unique 3, who DJ-ed at the The Soundyard and started their own label Chill, and Romford's Suburban Base, which grew out of owner Dan Donelly's Boogie Times shop. In the typically incestuous scenario, the DJs work in the shop, spin at the club and make tracks for the label. The shop enables the music-makers to keep in touch with the punters and to service DJs; the club provides opportunities to test out new tracks on the dancefloor, then return to the studio to make adjustments. Hardcore rave was fuelled by the same vital blend of commerce and aesthetics as the Jamaican record business, with its cowboy labels, self-cobbled studios, and sound-system parties.

If one record can be said to have trailblazed the floorquaking sub-bass style of Northern house, it's Unique 3's 1989 track '7 A.M.', the flipside of their debut single 'The Theme'. Cold and cavernous, '7 A.M.' has only one hook: an ultra-minimal percussive/melodic motif which sounds like it's played on a glockenspiel built from icicles and stalactites. Beneath this shockingly empty soundspace throbs the subliminal pressure of the solar-plexus-pummelling bass. The Bradford boys' next release, the Top Thirty cracking 'Weight For the Bass', was even more spartan than '7 A.M.'. The 'Original Soundyard Dubplate Mix' recalls Nitro Deluxe's brutal house or Mantronix's neo-electro, but with a Jamaican twist. Over the heart-palpitating B-line, which jabs and judders in sync with the cardiac-arrythmia inducing pattern of the programmed drums, there's a plangent, ultra-trebley piano vamp in the Italo-house style. 'Weight' conjures the unlikely vision of dreadlocked roots rockers on E and rude-boys swapping their guns for fluorescent light-sticks.

According to Steve Beckett, this new Yorkshire house sound actually did come out of Jamaica, via North England reggae sound-systems: 'people like Ital Rockers in Leeds who didn't get as much recognition, but who were doing the *mental*-est records ever. They'd cut just twenty or thirty tracks on acetate, and have sound-systems parties underneath this hotel. No lights, 200 people, and they'd play reggae, then hip hop, then these bleep-and-bass tunes. And they'd be toasting on top of it.'

For Beckett and partner Rob Mitchell, 'The Theme' was the impetus to start their own label from the upstairs room of a shared house, using £2,000 and money from the Enterprise Allowance scheme. Having tried and failed to sign Unique 3, Warp debuted with a track by Sheffield boys Robert Gordon, Shaun Maher and Winston Hazell, aka Forgemasters. The tune's title, 'Track With No Name', stridently affirmed the house scene's radical anonymity (another crucial element of the hardcore ethos). And the band's name, borrowed from the big local steelworks Forgemasters, chimed in with a lineage of constructivist dance music that ran back through Die Krupps' metal-bashing disco tracks 'Steelworks Symphony' and 'Wahre Arbeit, Wahre Lohn', through Heaven 17's 'Crushed By The Wheels of Industry', all the way to Kraftwerk, whose name is German for power plant.

Sheffield is famous for its stainless steel and its hardline socialist, Red Flag waving Labour council. In pop terms, Sheffield also evokes the word 'industrial': the bleak avant-funk of Cabaret Voltaire, Clock DVA and Chakk, the shiny, spotless synth-pop of The Human League. Not only did these early eighties bands inaugurate a Sheffield tradition of experimenting with synthesizers, drum machines and tape-loops, they also established a local infrastructure of cheap and cheerful recording studios, like Cabaret Voltaire's Western Works, and Chakk's Fon. Built using the massive advance from Chakk's ill-starred major label deal, Fon spawned Krush's early Brit-house smash 'House Arrest', a Number Three hit at the end of 1987; Forgemasters' Rob Gordon was a member of the Fon Force production squad.

Another resource from Sheffield's industrial past that lent itself to the Northern house explosion was a plethora of ideal venues for illegal parties – warehouses in the city's non-residential, industrial zones. (Later, when the police started to crack down, promoters used quarries outside the city limits.) 'You'd have, like, a thousand people in a warehouse,' remembers Beckett. 'There'd be metal gangways around the side of the walls with people hanging off them. Complete mayhem! It was more like a festival than a party. Always just a few lights, or complete darkness, so you were just dancing in the dark.'

'It had a real blues feel to it,' he continues, referring not to rhythm-and-blues but to illegal reggae parties. 'There was quite a criminal element involved: just a couple of people on the door, no proper security. The reason they were doing it was to make a quick profit. That was what the early rave scene was all about, but somehow it didn't have the commercial feel of the big raves later on. That's what gave the scene an edge – it felt like everybody was doing something dodgy and illegal. Which they were!'

The post-punk industrial outfits had a penchant for using 'non-musical' noises, *à la* fifties *musique concrète*. The Warp artists' version of this was to use a non-musical function inside samplers and synthesizers: the sine-wave test-tones provided so that the frequencies can be set on the recording heads, prior to laying a track down on a master-tape. 'In a sampler, you'll just have a tone-generator,' explains Beckett. 'It's not supposed to be for making music, just for testing the equipment. You've got a treble-tone, a mid-tone and a bass-tone, which people used to get the biggest bass possible. Then they'd overlay different bass-sounds, so there might be three or four basslines in one track.'

This sine-wave sub-bass can be heard on the third Warp release, 'Testone' by Sweet Exorcist (Cabaret Voltaire's Richard Kirk and DJ Parrot). Closer to electro than house music, the dehydrated drum machine beats and pocket-calculator blip-melody recall Kraftwerk's 'Tour De France' and Man Parrish's 'Hip Hop Be Bop (Don't Stop)'. What drove the Ecstasy-sensitized crowds wild, though, was the bowel-tremor undertow of low-end frequencies, impacting you like an iceberg (90 per cent of the devastation takes place below the threshold of perception).

Test-tones were just one strand in what rapidly evolved into a science of bass. Another Warp act LFO – it stood for Low Frequency Oscillation – would create a bass sound, record it on to cassette with the recording levels right up in the red zone, sample that deliberately distorted sound, and repeat the process: all in search of the heaviest, hurtful-est bass sound. 'A lot of it was in the cut,' says Beckett, referring to cutting the lacquer, which is the first stage in the process of pressing vinyl. 'You've got filters on your cutting heads. Basically, it was about taking off all the filters and all the compression, and just pushing the levels up as far as you could. The engineer, this guy Kevin, would be sitting there watching the temperature gauge go right up, 'cos your cutting heads get really hot if you haven't got the filters on. He'd be sweating, saying "you're gonna fuckin' destroy, me, ya bastards", 'cos if the heads blew he'd get sacked. But he loved it really. He used to know what we wanted 'cos he'd worked with the On U Sound dub reggae people.'

People called the Northern style of house 'bleep-and-bass' or just 'bleep' (the latter referring to the Kraftwerk/electro-style one-finger synth-motifs). But it was the bass pressure that really counted. 'I don't remember us ever talking about bleeps,' says Beckett, 'But there was definitely loads of detailed conversations about how you could get the bass heavier, how Kevin cut it. It became a competition. There was this Wednesday nightclub at Kiki's, where there was a separate bar made of glass, and the track "LFO" was actually shaking the bar. That was when we knew we'd got it right.' With Warp's second release, Nightmares On Wax's 'Dextrous', Beckett says 'we had to put out the Quiet Bass Mix, 'cos we couldn't physically cut the Loud Bass Mix'.

Nightmares On Wax, the Leeds-based black/white duo of Kevin Harper and George Evelyn, also recorded the all-time Warp classic 'Aftermath'. Over a baleful B-line, a distraught diva intones 'there's something going round inside my head / I think it's something I feel / It's something unreal.' Echo effects send the last word reeling, like a ghostly/ghastly apparition inside the sensorium of a tripped-out raver; the diva's voice is phased and reversed in a jagged-timelapse effect; a noise-loop of eerie metallic scraping sounds like the onset of migraine. With its ecstasy-is-agony disorientation, 'Aftermath' is a premonition of the 'darkside' gloom that would descend upon hardcore three years later, as ravers succumbed to the paranoiac effects of long-term, excessive drug abuse. Of all the bleep-and-bass tracks, 'Aftermath' has had the most enduring influence, both directly (it's been sampled many times by jungle artists, most notably on the 1994 Renegade track 'Something I Feel') and indirectly. Coco Steel and Lovebomb's 1992 Warp release 'Feel It' – bleep-and-bass's twilight anthem – is an unofficial sequel to 'Aftermath': there's the same hair-raising, stalking vibe and twitchy, staccato feel, but the diva's distress is replaced by curt dominatrix injunctions to 'fee-eee-eee-eel it'.

'Aftermath' peaked at Number Thirty-eight in the UK Chart in the autumn of 1990; a few months earlier, Warp had scored two simultaneous Top Twenty hits with LFO's ultra-minimal, robot-voiced 'LFO' and Tricky Disco's chirpy, cartoon-tekno outing 'Tricky Disco'. LFO were Mark Bell and Gez Varley, two teenagers from Leeds. In just a few weeks, the duo went from giving local DJs tracks on cassette to selling 130,000 singles and refusing invitations to appear on *Top of the Pops*. Having scored three national hits and a bunch of club smashes with tracks by Sweet Exorcist, Tuff Little Unit, The Step and Tomas, Warp found itself at the end of the year in the unlikely position of commanding nearly 2 per cent of Britain's record sales for 1990. But they were also facing bankruptcy, having signed a bad distribution deal with the dance indie label Rhythm King.

LFO saved the label by recording the highly successful long-player *Frequencies* – not just the definitive bleep-and-bass record, but one of the dozen or so truly great *albums* the electronic dance genre has yet produced. The LFO sound consisted of creaky sonorities like fatigued metal buckling or stressed machinery having a nervous breakdown, and wonderfully sticky, Velcro-like synth-textures that tug at your skin-surface and get your goosepimples rippling in formation. Above, or *beneath* all, they used a myriad shades of bass: SUB-sub-bass, trowel-in-your-ear-hole-bass, enema-bass, internal-injuries-bass. Samples of house-diva Liz Torres bring an abstract urgency to the dislocated groove and glistening, globular bass-tones of 'You Have To Understand'. On 'El Ef Oh', the title's phonemes are drastically filtered to sound like death-rattle gasps or purple gas seeping from a zombie's mouth, while the percussion crackles like jabs from an electric cattle prod. 'Mentok 1' is a weird surge of oozy, spongy texture-goo. 'Think A Moment' is a Cubist catacomb of wheezing synths, gluey bass, corrugated noises, and glum refrains reminiscent of David Bowie and Brian Eno's lugubrious *Low* instrumentals. 'Groovy Distortion' chugs and puffs like a steam engine on a gradient, with textured percussion that sounds like a cat coughing up a hairball.

A precise and rigorous grid of pulses and tics, LFO's sound owed far more to electro than to house or techno. Indeed, Varley and Bell had originally met as members of rival crews at a 1984 breakdancing contest. Strangely, no figures from old skool hip hop feature in the roll-call of illustrious forefathers on 'What Is House', the title track of LFO's brilliant late 1991 EP – instead, it's acid house gods Phuture, Mr Fingers and Adonis, and Euro-synth pioneers Tangerine Dream and

Kraftwerk who get props from a slurred, distorted voice oddly reminiscent of Mark E. Smith. And then LFO promptly disappeared, emitting not a bleep or a clonk until late 1994's 'Tied Up' and the patchy 1996 album *Advance*.

Attempting to convey the generation gap created by the bleep-and-bass invasion of the British pop charts, a colleague of mine once likened LFO and their ilk to fifties rockabilly. Rock 'n' roll and bleep-and-bass both seemed like alien musics that came out of nowhere; both flouted then accepted pop notions of melody and meaningfulness, and offensively asserted the priority of rhythm and the backbeat. Other commentators cited the twangy guitar instrumentals of the early sixties as a precedent: The Shadows, Duane Eddy, The Tornadoes' 'Telstar', all of which fascinated teenagers with their gimmicky futurism and otherworldly sheen.

Outside the Warp fraternity, there was a legion of independently released bleep-and-bass classics: Ability II's 'Pressure', F-X-U's 'The Chase', Hi-Ryze's 'Ride The Rhythm', Autonation's 'Crosswires', Ubik's 'System Overload' EP. Even Detroit-aligned Network got on the case, putting out Forgemasters' awesomely inorganic 'Stress' (sounds so shiny, sibilant and serrated they seem to lacerate the ear-drum), along with insidiously catchy yet utterly unmelodic tracks by Rhythmatic like 'Frequency' and 'Take Me Back'. And 808 State dropped the ambient house swirl in favour of synth-fart brutalism on hits like 'In Yer Face' and 'Cubik'.

Greatest of the non-Warp outfits, and one of the few to survive the bleep-and-bass era, was Orbital (aka Paul and Phil Hartnoll). Knocked out in their attic studio at the brothers' home in Sevenoaks, a London commuter belt town, Orbital's debut 'Chime' cost virtually nothing to make but got to Number Seventeen in the UK charts. Appearing on *Top of the Pops* in the spring of 1990, Orbital infuriated the producers and confirmed all the Luddites' fears about techno knob-twiddlers' non-musicianship: the brothers simply pressed a button (all it took to trigger the track) and stood there listlessly, not even pretending to mime.

The British 'Strings of Life', 'Chime' sounds at once urgent and serene, capturing the classic Ecstasy sensation of sublime suspension, of being stuck on an endless pre-orgasmic plateau. 'Chime' pivots around a tintinnabulating, crystalline sequence of notes that hop and skip down the octave like a shiver shimmying down your spine. This motif is one of the first instances of what would become a defining hardcore device, the melody-riff: a hook that is as percussive as it's melodious. Then a Roland 303 enters, jabbering like a bunch of funky gibbons, while a second sub-bassline quakes beneath it at half-tempo. At the breakdown, muzak-strings (sweeping, beatific) clash with staccato string-stabs (impatient, neurotic), then the melody-riff cascades in again like a downpour of diamonds and pearls. And your goosepimples run riot.

To this day, 'Chime' is a rave anthem, guaranteed to trigger uproar; the Hartnolls claim that various elements of the track have reappeared as samples in some fifty other tracks. But Orbital themselves quickly distanced themselves from hardcore rave, preferring to weave celestial techno-symphonies like 'Belfast', a soaring lament for the strife-torn city. Pivoting around the same eight-note sequence of psalmic female vocal – sampled from *A Feather on the Breath of God: Sequences and Hymns by the Abbess Hildegard of Bingen* – stolen by The Beloved for 'The Sun Rising', 'Belfast' always make me think of Wim Wenders's *Wings of Desire*, with its guardian angels who invisibly bring succour to the anguished.

Dance Before the Police Come

In 1990, long before rave culture fragmented into sub-scenes and the semantics went haywire, there were really only two words for the music – house and techno – and even these tended to be interchangeable. House could range from soulful and songful ('deep' or 'garage') to track-oriented ('hardcore house'). The latter term was vague enough to encompass a multitude of styles that were united less by sound than by context and effect: they all incited frenzy at big raves.

Just as the subliminal influence of the UK's reggae and hip hop scenes shaped a distinctive Northern style of hardcore, similar factors spawned a quite different sound in the South. There was the same emphasis on sub-bass pressure, but instead of the Warp-style bands' programmed drum machine rhythms, the South of England producers sampled and looped breakbeats. The break is the percussion-only section of a funk or disco track. House producers got these breakbeats second-hand from hip hop records, or from album compilations of the most highly sought after breaks. American producers like Todd Terry,

Fast Eddie and Tyree, and Brooklyn's Lenny Dee and Frankie Bones had already experimented with the idea, but it was in the UK that 'breakbeat house' caught on like wildfire. Partly, it was because looping breaks lent itself to the anyone-can-do-it aspect of the hardcore home-studio boom. It's easier for novices to get a good groove going by using samples of real-time drumming, than by painstakingly programming a rhythm track on a drum machine. And it's cheaper too, since the basic set-up to make tracks is turntables, a sampler and a sequencer program, with no need for drum machines or synthesizers. But breaks also appealed to a multiracial, London and surrounding counties population who'd grown up on Black American imports like jazz-funk, hip hop and rare groove. With their raw, 'live' feel, breakbeats added extra grit and oomph to house's clinical rhythms.

Although artists like Demon Boyz, Rebel MC, and Blapps Posse/Dynamic Guvnors all played a part in forging the UK hip-house hybrid, the key figures in the rise of breakbeat house were PJ and Smiley, two black British youths from Stoke Newington in North East London. Using the name Shut Up And Dance, they operated as a band, a production team and a label. In the mid-eighties, they'd started out on the sound-system Heatwave, where they took Def Jam tracks and sped the breaks up from 100 b.p.m. to 130 b.p.m., then chanted MC-style over the top. They also put out a few Brit-rap tracks as Private Party, including 'My Tennants', an Anglicized rebuke to Run DMC's sponsorship-rap 'My Adidas'. Like Warp, they began Shut Up and Dance in 1989 as a white label operation, selling tracks direct to dance stores from their car boot, and servicing the burgeoning pirate-radio stations. The duo's pro-pirate stance – 'once a station goes legal it's shit,' they declared to *Melody Maker* – was given anthem-form in a track by SUAD act Rum and Black, '**** The Legal Stations': a grainy slice of breakbeat-and-bass minimalism pivoting around a soundbite that complains 'turn off that muthafuckin' radio' and a looped squeal of guitar-feedback sampled from Prince's 'Let's Go Crazy'.

Based on the flagrant theft of highly recognizable chunks from main-stream pop records by the likes of Suzanne Vega and The Eurythmics, SUAD cut-and-paste tracks seemed like sonic documents of hardcore rave's black economy: uncleared samples, dodgy warehouse raves, pirate radio, drug dealing, bootleg tracks and no-permission, no-royalty mix-tapes. It sounded like fast money music, the perfect soundtrack for an underground/underworld geared to the blag and the scam.

But Shut Up and Dance saw themselves as young black entrepreneurs engaged in bettering themselves *and* giving back something to their disenfranchised community. They had a conscience: at heart, they were disenchanted hip hoppers, inspired by Public Enemy's righteous politics but bored by their increasingly staid production. 'We're not a rave group, we're a fast hip hop group,' they told *Melody Maker*. 'We've moved hip hop on in a way that people like Public Enemy haven't dared to.' On tracks like 'Rest In Peace (Rap Will Never)' and 'Here Comes A Different Type Of Rap Track Not The Usual 4 Bar Loop Crap', they pledged allegiance to rap even as they berated it for its sonic stasis quo.

But SUAD's early output didn't galvanize the moribund Britrap scene. Instead their tracks found favour with the hardcore house audience, despite the fact that SUAD specialized in a kind of social realism that foregrounded not just the grim realities that rave aimed to evade, but many of the squalid, exploitative aspects of the rave scene itself. Alongside anti-racism polemic ('White White World'), urban vigilante rage ('This Town Needs A Sheriff') and survivalist determination ('Derek Went Mad', with its ghostly sample of a fragile male voice whispering 'but I'll return a stronger man'), there were tracks like '£10 To Get In', a jibe at rip-off raves. The remix sequel '£20 To Get In' begins with a white cockney punter ringing up a phone-line for instructions on how to get to a warehouse party, only to be horrified by the extortionate entrance fee. 'I thought it was £10!!'. 'No, mate,' says the black promoter in a deadpan, take-it-or-leave-it voice, 'it's 'ad a remix.'

Shut Up And Dance were at pains to distance themselves from drug culture. They bemoaned London's escalating crack problem on their Top Fifty hit 'Autobiography of a Crackhead' and its flipside 'The Green Man', a stirring, string-swept instrumental named after a Hackney pub notorious for its open drug-dealing. And their biggest hit, 'Raving I'm Raving', targeted Ecstasy. If you actually listen to the lyrics, 'Raving' isn't a celebratory anthem but a withering probe into the void at the heart of the rave dream. The track is based almost entirely on Marc Cohn's AOR ballad hit single of late 1991, 'Walking In Memphis'. Retaining the song's heartbusting piano chords but tweaking the words slightly, PJ and Smiley created a raver's anthem with a booby-trap lyric. 'Bought myself a first-class ticket,' gushes singer Peter Bouncer, referring to a tab of Ecstasy, before rapturously evoking his touchdown in a loved-up wonderland. 'Everybody was happy / Ecstasy shining down on me . . . I'm raving I'm raving / But do I really feel the way I feel?' At this fissure of doubt, a foreboding bassline kicks in, followed by a loop of anguished female vocal.

For most of the 50,000 ravers who bought the track, 'Raving I'm Raving' was doubtless received as an irony-free affirmation of the rave dream-state, a glorious hymn to MDMA. Going straight into the national pop chart at Number Two on its first week of release, the booby-trap concealed in 'Raving I'm Raving' promptly blew up in PJ and Smiley's face. Within two weeks of its release, the track had to be withdrawn after protests from Marc Cohn and his record company. Cohn insisted that no more pressings be made and all profits be donated to charity. SUAD went into liquidation, with PJ and Smiley railing against an alleged record industry conspiracy to put young black entrepreneurs out of business. When they returned to the fray in 1994 – bitter, battle-scarred and desperately plugging their 'Phuck the Biz' EP – SUAD were still harping on the same theme, telling all who would listen that SUAD could have been another Motown.

With their looped-breaks-and-uncleared-samples aesthetic, their roots in hip hop and reggae's sound-system culture, their ambivalence about Ecstasy, and their street survivalist politics (on the cover of their debut album, *Dance Before The Police Come!*, they struck kung fu poses, barechested, oiled and musclebound), Shut Up And Dance laid the groundwork for jungle, the subculture that would evolve out of breakbeat hardcore. Other acts on SUAD anticipated crucial strands of the jungalistic sound-spectrum. Rum and Black's 'Bogeyman', with its scared-out-of-her-wits woman's whimper of 'oh no, don't go in there' and distorted blurts of jazz trumpet, was 1993-style darkside hardcore *avant la lettre*. On tracks like 'Illegal Gunshot', 'Hooligan 69', 'Spliffhead', 'Wipe The Needle', and the awesome 'Mixed Truth', The Ragga Twins mashed up ruff B-boy breaks, uproarious dancehall reggae chatter and Euro-techno terror-riffs with results that uncannily prophesized the ragga-influenced jungle sound of 1994. And the bittersweet breakbeat-driven torch songs of sultry chanteuse Nicolette on *Now Is Early* looked ahead to the jazz-tinged directions that jungle would explore in 1995–6. All in all, Shut Up And Dance left a major legacy.

Mentasm Madness

'I'm sure the constant exposure to amplifiers and electric guitars . . .
has altered my body chemistry . . . It is the proximity of the electric
hum in the background and just the tremendous feeling of buoyancy
and power . . . I was really determined to use the noises on myself,
as if I were a scientist experimenting on himself, like Dr Jekyll . . .'
                    – Iggy Pop, anticipating hardcore in his memoir *I Need More*

Across the English Channel, another version of hardcore was hatching:
hard as fuck, whiter-than-white, based around riffs rather than bleeps
and distorted noise rather than clean lines. Believe it or not, for about
eighteen months *Belgium* ruled the world of techno. Groups as
geographically distant as Detroit's Underground Resistance and Dollis
Hill's Manix paid tribute to the mysterious Lowlands nation: UR put
out the 'Belgian Resistance' single, Manix recorded the track 'Never
Been To Belgium'.

The seeds of the new sound, however, germinated somewhere
between Belgium and Brooklyn, New York, where DJ–producers like
Lenny Dee, Mundo Muzique and Joey Beltram were pushing rave
music in a harder and faster direction. Beltram revolutionized techno
twice before he reached the age of twenty-one. First, with 1990's
'Energy Flash', which gets my vote as the greatest techno track of all
time. With its radioactive bass-glow and pulsing loop-riff, 'Energy
Flash' sucks you into a miasmic maelstrom like nothing since the first
acid house tracks. An insinuating whisper murmurs 'acid, ecstasy', like
a dealer in the murk, or the voice-of-craving inside an addict's head.
The track really does sound like the speedfreak's drug 'flash', like being
plugged into an electric mains (no wonder amphetamine-*aficionados*
talk of being 'wired').

Years later, I realized 'Energy Flash' thrills me for exactly the same
reasons as Stooges songs like 'Loose' and 'Raw Power'. Proto-punk and
hardcore techno are both an intransitive surge of object-less aggression:
'raw power got no place to go . . . it don't wanna know', as Iggy sang.
Instead of being a form of self-expression, this is music as *forcefield*,
in which the individual is suspended and subjective consciousness is
wiped clean away. The title of Beltram's second genre-revolutionizing
classic, 1991's 'Mentasm', could be a synonym for another Iggy trope:

the 'O-mind', a paradoxical state of hyper-alert oblivion in which self-aggrandizement and self-annihilation fuse. Produced in collaboration with Mundo Muzique and released under the name Second Phase, 'Mentasm' was even more influential than 'Energy Flash'. The monstrous 'mentasm' sound – a swarming killer-bee drone derived from the Roland Juno Alpha synthesizer, a writhing, seething cyclone-hiss that sends ripples of shivery, shuddery rapture over your entire body-surface – spread through rave culture like a virus, infecting everyone from the Belgian, Dutch and German hardcore crews to British breakbeat artists like 4 Hero, Doc Scott and Rufige Cru. The 'mentasm stab' – which took the sound and gave it a convulsive riff-pattern – was hardcore's great unifier, guaranteed to activate your E-rush.

The 'Mentasm' noise has a similar manic-yet-dirge-like quality to the down-tuned guitar sound used by Black Sabbath and their doom-metal ilk. That's no coincidence: Beltram was consciously aiming to recreate the vibe of Sabbath and Led Zeppelin. 'I like evil, dark-sounding music and I guess it's because I grew up listening to heavy metal,' he told *Melody Maker*. 'I like the mood it creates. It's very psychedelic, but not in the bell-bottom, flower power way.' On the Beltram/Program 2 collaboration 'The Omen (Psycho Mix)', he actually sampled Robert Plant's languishing screams and orgasmic whimpers from the weird 'ambient' mid-section of 'Whole Lotta Love'.

Beltram has said that 'Energy Flash' and 'Mentasm' were deliberate attempts to 'make the music go faster, 'cos as a DJ I like to play records faster'. Techno responded to his challenge, much to the consternation of Detroit purists. Initially, Beltram found his greatest reception in Belgium. Speaking to *iD* in 1991, he enthused: 'The Belgians were the first people who could relate to me. Belgium was very, very advanced.' Indeed, the first real Euro-hardcore track, Rhythm Device's 'Acid Rock', saw producer Frank De Wulf independently hit upon the same techno-as-heavy-metal idea as Beltram: the track imitated Deep Purple's monster-riffing dirge 'Smoke On the Water'.

Belgium's pop music inferiority-complex had ended at the end of the eighties with the New Beat craze, which stormed the country's pop charts and briefly looked like it was gonna be Britain's Next Big Thing after acid house. 'Before New Beat, there was no chance for Belgians to break records into our own chart, it was totally dominated by Anglo-American music,' said Renaat Van DePapeliere of R & S, the label that released 'Mentasm' and 'Energy Flash'. New Beat began when DJs started to spin gay Hi-NRG records at 33 r.p.m. rather than the correct 45 r.p.m., creating an eerie, viscous, trance-dance groove. At the height of the craze, Renaat recalled, the Ghent club Boccaccio 'was like a temple. Everyone was dressed in black and white, dancing this weird, robotic dance.' Groups like Lords of Acid and A Split Second started to make records with the same uncanny, slow-mo feel.

As the nineties progressed, the b.p.m. returned to normal, then accelerated, as DJs started playing techno with their turntables set to +8. A native hardcore was born, with labels like Hithouse, Big Time International, Who's That Beat, Beat Box and Music Man, and groups like Set Up System, Cubic 22, T99, 80 Aum, Incubus, Holy Noise and Meng Syndicate. All peddled a distinctively Belgian brand of industrial-tinged techno where melody was displaced by noise. Set Up System's 'Fairy Dust' (the title probably refers to amphetamine) featured a fingernails-on-a-blackboard scree-riff that sounded like a brain-eraser wiping the slate of consciousness clean. On T99's 'Anasthasia', the 'Mentasm' stab mutated into what some called the 'Belgian hoover' effect: bombastic blasts of ungodly dissonance that sounded like *Carmina Burana* sung by a choir of satan-worshipping cyborgs.

As Belgian hardcore swamped Europe, dominating the underground rave circuit and penetrating the pop charts, the techno cognoscenti blanched in horror at the new style's brutalism. With its corrugated, rock-like riffs and stomping beats, tracks like Cubic 22's 'Night In Motion' seemed to sever house's familial ties to disco and black R & B. Belgian and German hardcore was heavily influenced by the late eighties school of Electronic Body Music (EBM), with its stiff, regimented rhythms and aerobic triumphalism. EBM bands like Front 242 flirted with Constructivist and fascist imagery in songs like 'Masterhit', and something of that musclebound, man-of-steel aura carried through to Euro-hardcore. LA Style's massive hit 'James Brown Is Dead' seemed like a gloating celebration of hardcore's Teutonic funklessness; the track's *Sturm und Drang* fanfares and cavernous production (geared for massive raves in industrial hangars) imparted an unnervingly Nuremberg-like vibe.

Many anti-hardcore hipsters attributed the new style's megalomaniacal aggression and high tempo to a decline in the quality of Ecstasy, which they believed was heavily cut with amphetamine. House's trippy vibe had degenerated into a manic *power*-trippiness. Hence Ravesignal's

'Mindwar' and 'Horsepower', the awesome creations of R & S producer CJ Bolland. With its Doppler-effect speed-rush and revving-engine pulse-rhythms, 'Horsepower' is Giorgio Moroder's Eurodisco souped up on steroids and testosterone. Imagine 'I Feel Love' if Giorgio had made it with Arnold Schwarzenegger in mind, not Donna Summer. In the film *Pumping Iron*, Arnie talked about how the feeling of flexing his muscles was akin to orgasm, 'so I'm coming all the time'; the parallels between this and the 'arrested orgasm' sensation created by Ecstasy and amphetamine are striking.

That's very much the vibe exuded by Human Resource's Euro-hardcore classic 'Dominator', on which the rapper's boasts of ruffer-than-ruff invincibility climax with the Lacanian epiphany: 'In other words, sucker, there is no Other / I wanna kiss myself.' Taking the mentasmic drone to its nether limit, 'Dominator' is simultaneously sluggish and palsied; you feel like your nerve-endings have gone dead, but beneath the armature of numbed flesh, your heart's beating furiously. And this was a pretty accurate reflection of the insensate, punch-drunk state many hardcore ravers were in by the end of the night, after necking several pills of dubious composition, topped off by a gram of sulphate and a couple of acid blotters.

Midway through 'Dominator', a startlingly realistic alarm-bell lets rip, cueing the Pavlovian response to flee. Hardcore was full of similar sound-effects – sirens, church bells – that created a sense of emergency and insurgency. This was the *panic-rush*, as celebrated in tracks like Praga Khan's 'Rave Alarm', HHFD's 'Start The Panic', John +Julie's 'Red Alert' and Force Mass Motion's 'Feel The Panic'; an edgy, jittery exhilaration caused by the metabolic acceleration and paranoiac side-effects of doing too much Ecstasy and amphetamine. The original Greek panic, the 'panic fear' of the horned god Pan, was a transport of ecstasy-beyond-terror. Activating the brain's 'flight-or-fight' response speed floods the body with the adrenalin-like neurotransmitter norephinephrine. In a panic state, perceptions are heightened, sense-impressions are more vivid, because you're on red alert. As with a soldier in a combat situation, such a drastic intensification of the immediate present can be a Dionysian thrill. But the side effects of too much speed (hypertension, paranoia, heart arrythmia) are unpleasant, while the attrition wreaked by long-term abuse leads to a kind of physical and spiritual battle-fatigue. By late 1991, you could see the walking wounded on the dancefloor.

For veteran ravers who remembered happier days, the experience now offered by British hardcore clubs like Wasp Factory, Crazy Club, Eclipse, In-Ter-Dance and Storm seemed closer to an assault course than a fun night out. European raving was, if anything, even more of an endurance test. Renaat Van DePapeliere raved about a club in Cologne where temperatures would reach tropical levels and DJs wore oxygen masks. Berlin had The Bunker (a warren of pitch-black and strobe-strafed catacombs), E-Werk (a disused electrical power-plant), and, most famously Tresor – once the vaulted subterranean safe of a 1920s department store, now a sweat-bath, sardine-crammed with ravers garbed in paramilitary camouflage gear (a fashion started by hardcore warrior DJ Tanith). East Berlin, with its deserted Communist Party premises and derelict warehouses, was infested with illegal parties. Frankfurt, meanwhile, had the Omen and Dorian Gray clubs, and had spawned a distinctive German hardcore sound via labels like PCP (Planet Core Productions) and Force Inc.

I never made it to any of these heavenly hell-holes of Euro-hardcore, but I caught something of the vibe at a regular Saturday night event in Central London called the Breakfast Club. Run by an organization with the vividly evocative name Slime Time (and whose slogan was: 'fuck off nutty tunes for fuck off nutty ravers'), the Breakfast Club began at 5 a.m. and went on until 11 a.m. Sunday. The atmosphere on the floor was somewhere between a National Front rally and a soccer match. The music was an ambush of sound and fury, cyber-Wagner fanfares, subsonic bass-quake and blaring samples. Juddering, staccato rhythms enforced a new kind of dancing, all twitches and jerks, like disciplined epilepsy. Close-cropped boys danced like they were shadow boxing; some moulded their hands into the shape of cocked pistols and let rip. No wonder the other big hardcore club in the centre of London was called *Rage*.

The buzzwords of the era were revealing. Pleasure was expressed in a masochist slang of catatonia and brain-damage: on a good night, you'd get 'faced' (off your face), 'sledgied' (into a coma), 'cabbaged' or 'monged' (turned into a vegetable). Good tracks were 'mental', 'kickin'', 'bangin'', 'nosebleed' or 'bone' (as in boneheaded). Every European hardcore scene had its own variations: the Belgians called the music 'skizzo' (schizophrenic), the Germans used the term 'bretter' (as a noun, it means means 'hard board', as a verb 'to beat'). The weekender side of rave had always fitted neatly into the traditional working class 'culture of consolation'; with hardcore, it had now evolved into a culture of concussion, a regime of punishing bliss 'strictly for the headstrong'.

Hipsters grumbled about 'cheesy quavers' and 'E-monsters' losing it to 140 b.p.m. 'nuttercore'. And the nutter stereotype really did exist: teenage boys with sunken cheeks, pursed lips and massively dilated pupils, T-shirts tied round their waist to reveal gaunt adolescent physiques emaciated further by excessive Ecstasy intake. In a 1991 research paper, 'Raving and Dance Drugs: House Music Clubs and Parties in North-West England', Dr Russell Newcombe noted the emergence of the 'nutter' as a minority within the rave scene. Dedicated to getting severely 'cabbaged', these headstrong youth resorted to 'stacking': taking from three to six tablets per session, and sometimes between ten and twenty E's over the course of a three day weekend. These kids quickly became locked into a cycle of overdoing it, then paying for it with a grievous mid-week comedown; this savage depression could only be overcome by the thought that Friday would soon roll around, presenting the opportunity to do it all again. Unwilling to face the Saturday morning crash, these kids would pop more pills in order to stay awake right through till Sunday. Lacking the patience to wait the hour it takes to 'come up' on E, they'd eagerly assume that they'd bought a dud pill, and take another: an unbeatable recipe for disaster. Some would grind up two or three E's and snort them because nasal ingestion was a faster-acting method of administration.

As manufacturers responded to the massive escalation in the demand for Ecstasy caused by this Second Wave of Rave, police seizures of MDMA and other synthetic drugs rose dramatically. In 1990, the London Metroplitan seized 5500 kilos; in 1991, the figure was more than 66,000 kilos. Reflecting both increased numbers of people using Ecstasy and the rise of a reckless, nihilistic attitude to drug intake, the number of MDMA-related deaths began to escalate. From 1989–90, there were only two or three deaths linked to MDMA; in the second half of 1991, there were five. During the 1988–90 period, Guy's Hospital in London reported an average of fifteen cases per month of adverse reactions due to Ecstasy; by 1991, they were receiving between thirty or forty distressed ravers per month, suffering effects like paranoia, racing heartbeat and the sometimes fatal condition of heatstroke.

Metal Machine Music

Hardcore crusaders like Renaat of R & S celebrated the way that techno had resurrected the generation gap, supplanting punk as the noise that parents, older brothers, and squares in general, just couldn't accept as music. But hardcore also created a generation gap *within* rave culture, as acid house veterans and hipster élitists decried the new brutalism as a barbaric travesty of the original vision of Detroit and Chicago.

British house producer Joey Negro lambasted hardcore not as punk rock but as equivalent to the Johnny-come-lately, lumpen-prole version of punk called Oi! Speaking to *DJ*, he described the Belgian style of techno as 'young people's fuck-off music. Latterday Sham 69, Angelic Upstarts or the UK Subs.' A more common analogy was with heavy metal. In the same magazine, Claire Morgan Jones argued that rave, 'the late twentieth-century reworking of sixties style peace, love and understanding' had degenerated into 'a knee-jerk club ritual many have started to call "the new heavy metal".' Noting the submerged homo-eroticism of working-class lads stripped to the waist and sniffing amyl nitrate like gay clubbers, she complained that, in the evolution of house into hardcore, 'all the curve and swing [has] been squeezed out . . . all it seems to be about is boys, bass and bother'.

When they started out, Warp Records and its artists all used the word 'hardcore' to situate themselves within rave culture; Steve Beckett declared in late 1989 that 'we're totally committed to [releasing] uncompromising, hardcore tracks'. But by 1991, Warp and its roster were at some pains to distance themselves from what they felt was a commercialized and conformist rave scene. Although Nightmares On Wax had been enthusiastic in 1990 about the 'big bass sound' of Belgium and Italy, the following year the duo were complaining about 'heavy metal house' and 'soppy and poppy' bubblegum rave played at 'tacky Sharon and Tracey clubs'. NOW's debut album *A Word Of Science* largely abandoned bleeps and clonks in favour of mellow 'smoker's delight' grooves influenced by seventies funk.

Former punks with a highly developed political consciousness, Orbital were as offended by the social implications of hardcore's 'nutter' mentality, as by its lumpen sound. 'It's like a science fiction film,' Paul Hartnoll told me in 1992. 'You've got everybody going out on a Friday or a Saturday, or both, taking their so-called E's' – an allusion to the common belief that most Ecstasy pills really consisted of amphetamine and valium – 'and they carry on through Sunday having a mad time, and by Monday they're deadbeat zombies. For the rest of the week, they're "yes sir, no sir," and then by Thursday they're waiting for the weekend again. It just subdues them. The drugs wear you down so you're ready to accept the drudgery of working life.'

Another standard accusation was that hardcore was 'just' drug-noise that was unlistenable if you weren't off your face. Even CJ Bolland complained that 'people have gotten so into the drugs that the music is made to cause a reaction on that drug. If you hear it when you're straight, it won't do anything for you. Most new tunes aren't tunes any more, just a very hard kick drum and a very mad sound.' Eventually Bolland's label, R & S, backed away from hardcore's bacchanalian bombast: Renaat started an ambient sub-label called Apollo. This was a nice, classically-informed touch, since Apollo is the polar opposite of Dionysus (the god of frenzy, intoxication, oblivion) and 'Appollonian' was Nietzsche's term for contemplative, pastoral, dream-like art.

While Warp and other bleep-and-bass pioneers turned their backs on hardcore, a new breed of British indie label emerged to cater to the headstrong. 'Hard as fuck! It's the rock of the future,' enthused Caspar Pound, twenty-one-year-old boss of Rising High. Speaking to *iD* in early 1992, he rebutted his interviewer's suggestion that hardcore was mere aural thuggery for 'rave bootboys', retorting: 'It's ridiculous, these are people who in the 1960s were scared of rock 'n' roll and said it was the devil's music ... The best thing about hardcore is all the soul's been taken out. We've had 200 years of human element in music and it's about time for a change.' He singled out the German scene for praise: 'It's stronger, it's darker, it's scarier ... I don't like going to a club and seeing 600 people waving their arms about with smiling faces. I like to see 600 people in a dark, hot place; it isn't about happiness, it's more aggressive, more intense.'

Alongside labels like Kickin', Vinyl Solution, Rabbit City and Edge, Rising High took their cue from the Belgians and created a British Brutalist sound. Like the sixties architectural style of the same name, it was all grim slabs of grey noise, harsh angularity, and a doom-laden, dystopian vibe. Recording as Industrial High and The Hypnotist, Pound specialized in Nietzschean grandiosity (tracks like 'God of the Universe', 'A Modern Prometheus') and rabble-rousing anthems ('Hardcore You Know the Score' and 'Night of the Living E-heads', which rallied a legion of zombie-warriors with the battle cry 'Hardkore will never die!'). Of all the Rising High affiliated artists, the most important was probably the duo of Lee Newman and Michael Wells, who released a torrent of rave anthems via a plethora of pseudonyms and labels: Tricky Disco, John + Julie, GTO, Signs of Chaos, Force Mass Motion, Church of Ecstasy and Technohead. Wells and Newman's pinnacle was their John + Julie track 'Circles (Vicious Mix)'. Starting with a madly gyrating carousel-melody and a dervish-diva vocal that goes 'round and round / turning around', 'Circles' lets rip a sub-bass riff, or *rift*, to make the Warp posse weep: a faecal, flatulent eruption of low-end frequencies, a sound like concrete liquefying.

Kickin' Records went even further towards fulfilling Pound's vision of hardcore as 'the rock of the future'. From the headbanging riffs to the imagery of madness, mass rally and Satanism (Messiah's 'You're Going Insane' and '20,000 Hardcore Members', The Scientist's 'The Exorcist'), Kickin' really were 'heavy metal house'. Wishdokta's 'Evil Surrounds Us' actually sampled Axl Rose's gloating screech – 'D'ya know where you are?!?' – from Guns N' Roses' 'Welcome to the Jungle', while Messiah were eventually signed by Rick Rubin's hard rock label, American.

The hardcore as 'new heavy metal' analogy had some validity. Sonically, the Belgian and British brutalists restored the mid-frequency sounds that dance music had dropped in order to boost the bass; the exact same mid-frequencies supplied by distorted electric guitars. 'Historically it has been perhaps the bass that people danced to,' said German DJ Westbam in 1992. 'But at the moment it is the mid-frequencies that people scream along to . . . In techno music these have been turned up more and more . . . they are also the most aggressive sounds, the ones that penetrate the most and make you numb . . .'

There were rock historical parallels too. In the late sixties and early seventies, British groups bastardized the blues, and their American imitators bastardized their bastardizations, and somewhere in all this, heavy metal was spawned. In the late eighties, black producers from Chicago and Detroit took Teutonic electronic music and turned it into acid house and techno; in the early nineties, Belgian and British youth took these elegant, Europhile sounds and spawned a mutant form – hardcore. The insults hurled at hardcore by 1988–9 nostalgics bore a striking similarity to the language with which aghast counter-cultural veterans greeted stadium rock: bombastic, proto-fascist, a degraded

version of a noble tradition. Just as blues-bore purists had harked back
to Cream while recoiling from Sabbath and Zep, so too did Detroit
connoisseurs pine for Derrick May while flinching at the post-Beltram
barbarians. By early 1992, the hipsters were busily erecting bulwarks of
'good taste' against the hooligan hordes. Some, in an unfortunate echo
of prog rock, rallied to the banner of 'progressive house' (labels like
Guerrilla and Hard Hands, artists like Leftfield and Spooky); others
began to talk of 'intelligent techno' (B12, The Black Dog, Future Sound
of London).

What the anti-hardcore contingent missed was the crucial historical
lesson to be gleaned from the 'new heavy metal' analogy: no one today
listens to the purist blues boom or progressive rock bands of the early
seventies. The much despised Sabbath, though, have achieved immortality as one of the most crucial sources for alternative music in the
eighties and nineties, worshipped by everybody from Black Flag and
the Butthole Surfers to the Seattle grungsters Nirvana and Sound-
garden. 'Maturity' was always only one way forward for the music of
the post-acieed/Detroit diaspora. Just as heavy metal distilled blues
rock, hardcore took the essence of acid and techno (mind-evacuating
repetition, stroboscopic synths, bass-quake frequencies) and coarsened
and intensified it. Bad drugs (barbiturates like Mandrax and Quaalude
for metalheads in the seventies, dodgy Ecstasy for hardcore ravers)
helped these kids focus on and exacerbate that essence. For people
who'd grown up on club culture, with its ethos of cool and discrimination, hardcore was a horror-story. But for rock-reared ears like mine,
hardcore's sonic extremism and insurrectionary fervour was thrilling.

Around the time of the anti-hardcore backlash, some ravers began
to deliberately mispell and mispronounce the word as 'ardkore –
matching the uncouth, rabble-rousing snarl with which slogans like
''Ardkore, you know the score' were chanted, intensifying the delinquent, underclass associations of the sound, and turning the supposedly
uneducated taste of the nutty raver into a badge of pride. But the mis-
spelt 'ardkore also served to emphasize the fact that this was a distinct
and brand-new genre of music, not a bastardized offshoot. Far from
hurtling down a dead end of noise and velocity (as the techno purists
alleged), hardcore rave by early 1992 had smashed right on through,
and was mutating into a barely imaginable new form of music light-
years beyond Detroit. And at the core of that future-sound wasn't
bleeps or mentasm-riffs, but breakbeats and samples.

Monsters of Rave

While 'ardkore ruled the underground, Britain had already developed a rave overground that fulfilled The KLF's fantasy of 'stadium house'. Between 1990 and 1992, a circuit of commercial mega-raves evolved: Amnesia, Raindance, Kaos, Mayhem, Eclipse, World Dance, Heaven on Earth, World Party, Helter Skelter, Elevation, Fantazia, Dreamscape, Vision, and many more. These massive events drew crowds ranging from 10–25,000 plus to dance all night inside giant hangars or under circus-size tents in the open countryside. Flyers promised a no-expense-spared spectacle ('intelligent lighting', four-colour lasers, strobe flowers, sky-trackers, data-flash grids, 'fully themed' stage sets), side-shows (bouncy castles, funfairs, bungee-jumping, fortune-tellers, face-painting), food and merchandise vendors, and above all massive volume (100 K sound-systems with 'bone-shaking bass'). In order to get a licence from the local authorities, they absurdly and disingen-uously forbade 'illegal substances', promised stringent searches, and 'firm but friendly security'. The two-hour queue, the humiliating body-frisk, and the surly bouncer, all became part and parcel of the rave experience.

At these multi-arena events, the line-up included not just the big name DJs – Top Buzz, Fabio and Grooverider, Carl Cox, Ratpack, Ellis Dee, Slipmatt – but also artist PAs. These *bands* – N-Joi, Bizarre Inc, The Prodigy, Shades of Rhythm – had sets choc-a-bloc with crowd-pleasing anthems, and they put on a show, of sorts (usually it meant a couple of anorexic girl-dancers in Lycra, and an MC hollering himself hoarse). But crucially, for the first time there was a visual referent for the music, it wasn't just 'faceless techno bollocks'.

As rave became big business, the rave transformed itself from a lawless zone into a highly organized space programmed for your pleasure. And rave culture itself became highly ritualized. There was a uniform – floppy chapeaux, hoods, woolly hats, white gloves, gas-masks; loose-fitting or stretchy clothes (baggy jeans and T-shirts for boys, Lycra for girls), along with accessories like whistles, air-horns, and fluorescent glow-sticks. Hardcore youth evolved a choreography of geometric dance-moves and developed a drug lore of Ecstasy-enhancing tricks. Ravers smeared their naked torsos with Vicks VapoRub or sniffed on inhalers; the menthol fumes allegedly increased the buzz and brought on a rush. Herbal ointments and panaceas like Olbas Oil and Dr Bach's Remedy enjoyed a vogue. Completing the subcultural package, there was an amiable repertoire of loved-up bonhomie: shaking hands and even hugging total strangers, cadging a sip of Evian water or Coke, enquiring 'All right, mate?' or 'Where you from, what you on?'

On the mega-rave circuit, a pop hardcore sound gradually emerged, fusing the piano vamps and shrieking divas of 1989-era Italo house with Belgian hardcore's monster-riffs and Shut Up And Dance style breakbeats and rumblin' bass. In 1991, this sound stormed the UK charts. For every major-label distributed crossover act like Shades of Rhythm and N-Joi, there were a dozen underground outfits who operated on shoe-string indie labels but nonetheless shared the same sound (affirmative, anthemic) and the same ambition (to make the charts). Some, like Congress's '40 Miles', cracked the Top Twenty; many got within spitting distance (Manix's 'Oblivion' EP, Rhythm Section's 'Midsummer Madness' EP); most remained underground anthems.

Backed by the demographic heft of the 'ardkore nation, the most popular live PA acts – Shades of Rhythm, N-Joi and Bizarre Inc – scored the biggest hits. Peterborough's Shades of Rhythm – a DJ crew who'd started out throwing illegal parties in the summer of 1989 – debuted impressively with the sinister, twitchy double A-side 'Homicide'/'Exorcist', but were rapidly reduced to glossy rave-fodder like 'Sweet Sensation', 'The Sound of Eden' and 'Extacy' (a big hit in November '91). Essex's N-Joi made the Top Thirty earlier that year with 'Adrenalin', a track that begins with the sound of crowd uproar; played live, it triggered a feedback loop, as the raving massive respond to what they believe is their own excitement. Tracks like 'Mindflux' and 'Anthem' (Number Eight in April 1991) and the 'live techno' EP 'Live In Manchester' were populist rave at its most functional, all chugging, fartacious B-lines, whistle sounds and crowd-rousing appeals.

After a year of sustained presence on the charts (some twenty-two Top Forty hits, ten of them in the Top Ten), the British rave explosion peaked in the last months of 1991. In November and December 1991, the Top Twenty was inundated with a series of anthems – covering the full spectrum from glossy pop-rave to Belgian brutalism to the emergent underground sound of breakbeat 'ardkore – by Moby, Altern

8, Bassheads, Bizarre Inc, Shades of Rhythm, SL2, Human Resource, Digital Orgasm, K-Klass, 2 Unlimited, and Shaft. On the outskirts of the Top Forty, tracks by Manix, T99, the Hypnotist, Quadrophonia, Ravesignal, A Split Second, Congress and UHF exacerbated the sense of a barbarian horde waiting to overrun the pop citadel. In terms of hit rate, this 'golden age of hardcore' compares with the punk/New Wave period of the late seventies. The record industry responded with a flood of cash-in TV-advertised compilations like *Hardcore Uproar*, *Steamin'* and *Kaos Theory* with words like 'slammin" and 'bangin" liberally scattered on the sleeves. As with punk, fogies (in this case, punk veterans) responded to two or three hardcore tunes on each week's *Top of the Pops* with the hardy perennial: 'But it's just not music!' The producers of *Top of the Pops* evidently concurred with the Luddites, or so some people alleged. For it was around this time that the programme's rules about miming to a backing tape were replaced by a new format geared around 'live vocals', a change deliberately designed, it was darkly hinted, to make techno bands look bad.

Hardcore's assault on the pop mainstream continued with slightly less intensity right through to the summer of 1992. Every month, the rave audience hurled an anthem or two up into the higher reaches of the chart. The Prodigy's 'Everybody In The Place' reached Number Two in January, and was kept from the top spot only by the re-release of Queen's 'Bohemian Rhapsody'. SL2's proto-jungle smash 'On A Ragga Tip' got to Number Two, as did Shut Up and Dance's 'Raving I'm Raving'. Hits of varying sizes were scored by Kicks Like A Mule, Isotonik, Seduction, Urban Shakedown, Messiah, Utah Saints, Toxic 2, Praga Khan, Liquid, Skin Up, and Altern 8.

Altern 8 were something like the Slade of techno. Both bands had a penchant for deliberately misspelling their song-titles. In Slade's case, this was to accentuate their hooligan image ('Cum On Feel the Noize', 'Mama Weer All Crazee Now' et al), whereas Altern 8 merely sustained the visual pun of their name with track titles like 'Activ-8', 'Hypnotic St-8', 'Brutal-8-E', 'E-Vapor-8', *ad nauseam*. Like Slade, they had a wacky look (chemical warfare protection suits, yellow dust-masks and gas-masks, which cleverly managed to turn techno's 'faceless anonymity' into a marketable image), and like Slade, their rabble-rousing sound was a hit with the kids but despised by the crits.

Based in Stafford, Mark Archer and Chris Peat started out as Nexus 21, using a typical home-studio that cost around £1,500 to make

Detroit influenced techno for Network. When they shifted their sound to boombastic bass, gimmicky samples and looped breaks, Archer and Peat invented Altern 8 as a jokey alter-ego, in order to keep Nexus 21's reputation clean of hardcore's taint. A Top Three hit in November 1991, 'Activ-8' featured a sample of their label boss's five-year-old daughter (aka MC Crazy Claire) saying 'nice one, top one, get sorted' – a blatant reference to getting E'd up that completely bypassed the BBC censors. Appearing on *Top of the Pops*, Altern 8 got the cameraman to zoom in on the jar of Vicks VapoRub they'd put on top of their sampler: the nudge-nudge, wink-wink equivalent of flaunting a bong or coke spoon on prime time TV. 'E-Vapor-8' cheekily compacted two drug references into a single word.

By their own admission, Altern 8 were 'a cheapskate KLF'. The tabloids lapped up their scams and larks, like their plan to drop 'Brand E' Christmas puddings from a hot-air balloon as alms for the poor of Stafford. Chris Peat stood for Parliament on the 'Hardcore – U Know the Score' ticket; his manifesto called for compulsory raves for all mankind and proposed that teachers should use megaphones during lessons. Their early tracks 'Infiltrate 202' and 'Frequency' were crudely exciting, in a lumpen, lowest-common-denominator way. But by the time their debut album/greatest-hits-package *Full On: Mask Hysteria* came out in the last months of 1992, Altern 8 were already forgotten, like so many teenybopper bands before them.

If Altern 8 were like Slade (who had a run of huge hits, but have left barely a singe mark on rock's official history), The Prodigy were more like The Sweet or T. Rex. Prodigy 1991 chart smashes 'Charly' and 'Everybody In The Place' are all teenage rampage and sublimely vacant insurgency. Not only have these popkore classics – universally scorned by hipsters at the time – aged extremely well, but the band went on to enjoy an illustrious future as a sort of cyber-rock band, beloved by studenty music-press readers as well as ravers.

Based in Braintree, Essex, The Prodigy was basically Liam Howlett, a twenty-year-old whizzkid producer blessed with a flair for melody (thanks to classical training in piano) and breakbeat-manipulation skills acquired from his days as a British B-boy. Right from the start, however, The Prodigy was presented as a *band*: on album sleeves, during live performances, and in the videos, the visual slack was taken up by Howlett's three buddies Leeroy, Maxim Reality and Keith Flint, whose job it was to leap about and yell stuff at the audience. It was the music that counted, though, and this was classic pop juvenilia, kiddy-kartoon zany-mania dedicated to sheer sensation and mindless kicks. Howlett's forte was dynamics, bridge, breakdowns, the kinaesthetics of tension and release. Years later, Flint described The Prodigy as 'buzz music'. This was music whose only subject was its own sensations; hence self-reflexive titles like 'Hyperspeed', 'Wind It Up', 'Everybody In The Place (Fairground Mix)', 'Full Throttle', 'G-Force'.

Following three Top Five hits in a little over a year, The Prodigy's late 1992 debut album *Experience* was everything that Altern 8's *Full On: Mask Hysteria* failed to be: a commercial success, and an album you could listen to all the way through (as opposed to a patchy collection of the hits-so-far). Yet there was no whiff of compromise: *Experience* offered an only slightly more polished and hookful version of the breakbeat madness percolating in the rave underground. 'Ruff In The Jungle Bizness' namechecked the emergent sub-genre of 'jungalistic 'ardkore', while 'Fire' buried a sniggery E reference deep in the mix: a sample of an uncouth youth blurting 'and you're *rushing*!!!!'

Despite their exhilarating merger of underground energy and pop appeal, The Prodigy were regarded as hopelessly uncool by tastemakers. Leading dance monthly *Mixmag* accused Liam and Co of destroying the rave scene (which the club oriented *Mixmag* disdained anyway) with its late 1991 hit single 'Charly'. Based around samples taken from a public safety commercial of a cartoon cat's miaow and a little boy's voice going 'Charly says, "always tell your mummy before you go off somewhere"', this fabulous track inspired the craze for 'toytown tekno': a spate of tracks that sampled kid's TV themes and combined nostalgic infantilism with cheesy drug innuendos. An early imitator was Shaft's 'Roobarb and Custard', based on the seventies animation series of the same name; 'rhubarb and custard' just happened to be a pink-and-yellow brand of E. But the fad really escalated in July 1992. Urban Hype's 'A Trip to Trumpton' (featuring the famous 'Pugh, Pugh, Barney McGrew, Cuthbert, Dibble and Grubb' sample from a 'Watch With Mother' sixties TV programme) got to Number Six, while Smart E's 'Sesame's Treet' (schoolkids chorusing the 'Sesame's Street' theme, dodgy E-as-candy puns) reached Number 2. By this point, many within the hardcore underground shared *Mixmag*'s disgust, and the leading labels and producers began to push the music in an anti-commercial direction.

So maybe The Prodigy *did* kill rave. Certainly, 'Trumpton' and

'Sesame's' were the last hardcore hits. In August 1992, Acen's brilliant 'Trip II The Moon' peaked at Number Thirty-eight, while 2 Bad Mice's 'Hold It Down/Waremouse' stumbled just outside the Top Forty. It would be two years before hardcore's next real hit, when the re-released 'Let Me Be Your Fantasy' by Baby D, would be carried all the way to Number One by a powerful current of rave nostalgia. In the meantime, The Shamen's own Number One 'Ebeneezer Goode' confirmed the sense that rave had turned into a joke. A giant piss-take, the song anthropomorphized Ecstasy as a Dickensian scoundrel who always livens up the party. Despite a chorus of ''eezer Goode, 'eezer Good' that sounded suspiciously like advocacy ('E's are good'), and a cheeky reference to 'Vera's' (rhyming slang for 'skins' or rolling papers, via WW2 singer Vera Lynn), the Shamen disingenuously insisted that the song wasn't about drugs at all. What else could they say?

Speed Freaks

'Too much speed is comparable to too much light ... we see nothing.'

– Paul Virilio, *Pure War*

During rave's 1991–2 crossover chart explosion, a new form of hardcore was hatching in the underground. Based around hectic breakbeats, dub-reggae bass and sped-up vocal samples, the new style was a hyperkinetic update of the Shut Up And Dance sound, but with a drug-crazed delirium and polyrhythmic density that SUAD never approached.

Urban Shakedown's 'Some Justice', a Top Thirty hit in June 1992, is a classic example: chopped-up, ricochetting breaks, a seismic undertow of sinewave bass, and a monster-riff pulsating in a Morse Code pattern. In 1992, it seemed like there were thousands of underground anthems based around the Morse Code oscillator-riff: DJs Unite's 'DJs Unite', Kaotic Chemistry's 'Space Cakes', Weekend Rush's 'Desire', Timelapse's 'Sued For A Sample', Sonz of A Loop Da Loop Era's 'Peace and Loveism', to name but a handful. Fusing the staccato aggression of the mentasm stab and the tremulous euphoria of the octave-skipping piano-vamp, the oscillator-riff literally electrifies the listener. Plugged into the music's alternating current of E-lectricity, you feel like you're being shocked alive. As 1992 progressed, the Morse Code riff got ever more jittery and convulsive, matching the spastic intricacy of the semaphore patterns carved in the air by speedfreak ravers.

'Ardkore's oscillator-riff is like the aural equivalent of the strobe's stop-gap photography effect. Both zap the raver with a series of ultra-intense NOW!s. A staple of the rave lightshow, the strobe's flicker can trigger epileptic fits in the susceptible. In fact, the 'disturbed electrical rhythms' and 'clouded consciousness' that characterize epilepsy could be a description of 'ardkore itself! Just before an attack, epileptics are said to feel 'a special state of happiness, a juvenile exhilaration' – which sounds just like the MDMA experience. 'Sublime' wrote Dostoevsky, a sufferer. 'For that moment you'd give your whole life . . . At that moment I understood the meaning of that singular expression: there will no longer be time.' This is the feeling The KLF captured with the title '3 AM Eternal'. Indeed the Greeks regarded epilepsy as a sacred malady.

But two terms related to epilepsy are probably closer to rave's essence. The first is 'nympholepsy': an ecstastic frenzy caused by desire of the unattainable. The second is 'picnolepsy', theorist Paul Virilio's term for frequent, incredibly brief ruptures in consciousness, a series of micro-orgasms or 'tiny deaths' (as opposed to the 'little death' caused by a *grand mal* seizure). Speed – in the vehicular sense – is the central concept of Virilio's thought. But you could just as easily read 'speed' in his books like *The Aesthetics of Disappearance* as referring both to amphetamine and to 'ardkore's ever-escalating tempos.

In 1992, 'ardkore was just one strand of a picnoleptic 'rush culture' based around the cult of velocity, ranging from Playstation video-games (another hi-tech leisure device known to trigger epileptic attacks) to the nefarious pastime of 'joyriding'. The latter was the cause of much public concern in the early nineties; teenage tearaways from lawless council estates had taken to stealing cars and, within a few hours, burning out the engines by subjecting them to violent accelera-tion, U-turns and other forms of stunt-driving. If neighbours com-plained about the noise and the danger, they risked getting beaten up. The 'enterprise culture' variant on the joyride was ram-raiding: driving the hijacked car through a shop's plate-glass window and looting the premises. Joyriding, Nintendo, roller-coasters, bungee jumping, 'ardkore, amphetamine: these hyper-hyper activities all offer a peculiar sexless exhilaration, masculine but distinctly prepubescent.

Speed kills, said the hippies. On the back-cover of 4 Hero's late 1991 EP 'The Headhunter', there's a cartoon, drawn by the band's Dego McFarlane, that testifies to an anxiety about ''ardkore's ever-escalating beats-per-minute. Three mysterious cloaked figures stare aghast at a gang of grotesquely misshapen mutants: 4 Hero themselves, it transpires. 'Oh my God!' says the first stranger. 'What happened to them?' The second figure explains: 'In their race to fuse hip hop and house . . . they obviously overlooked the consequences and side effects of their experiments.' The third stranger elaborates: '. . . in the hunt for diverse head banger beats, they must have reached 135 b.p.m.s and at that stage their physical structure becomes misshappen, unnatural deformities occur.' Several years later, McFarlane explained to me that 4 Hero felt a real ambivalence about where the cult of velocity was taking them. 'We started off at about 120 b.p.m. and around "Headhunter" it was getting towards 140 b.p.m. Going to that speed was causing deformations in the music.' The cartoon was a self-mocking scenario of 4 Hero as 'B-movie scientists . . . The experiments get out of hand, he does some shit, takes the serum or whatever, and messes himself up . . . Even ourselves, we were saying "Bloody hell, it's getting fast." And a lot of people were like "It's too fast, it's the wrong speed." '

This was the main complaint of the anti-hardcore contingent: the music was too fast to dance to, it just didn't make sense. At the end of 1991, the average rave tune was around 125 b.p.m.; by the last months of 1992, it was reaching speeds of 150 b.p.m. plus. DJs were crankin' tunes up to +8 using the pitch-adjust control on their turntables; serious speedfreaks went further, doctoring the variable resistor inside the Technics decks which controls the pitch-adjust, thereby enabling the turntable to go to +20 or higher. 'Ardkore was hurtling into the unknown, going faster than anyone had ever gone before, and all because of the malign drug/tech logic of amphetamine and speed-cut E. Using his alter-ego Tek 9, Dego McFarlane released 'You Got To Slow Down', a sort of speeding ticket to a scene that was seriously overdoing the stimulants, the song pivoting around a soul-diva sample that leaps up the octaves until it's a helium-shrill shriek. This 'repulsive distortion' (to quote the 'Headhunter' cartoon) mirrored the soul-warping effects of amphetamine and too many E's.

Such sped-up 'squeaky vocals' were one of the defining character-
istics of 1992 'ardkore. In order to get their vocal samples to run in
synch with the 140 b.p.m. breakbeats, producers started to play the
soundbites on a higher octave on their sampling keyboards; this
compressed the timespan of the vocal snatch so that it slotted into the
frenetic rhythm, but it had the side effect of creating the 'cartoon
chipmunk' voices that were such an insurmountable irritation-factor
for outsiders. Speed grievously unbalanced rave music's frequency-
spectrum; the mid-range dropped right out, leaving just bowel-quaking
bass and ultra-shrill treble. The female vocals – sampled from ethereal
vocalists like Kate Bush, Liz Frazer, Stevie Nicks, Tasmin Archer, or
soul-diva acappellas from classic house tracks – were high-pitched
anyway. Modulated on the keyboard, looped into inhuman swoon-
machines, these particles of passion hurtled beyond the syntax of desire
into a realm of abstract urgency, closer to fireworks than 'soul'.
Moulded like plasma, they became a barrage of intensities without
pretext or context, shudders and shivers that were not so much
inhuman as infra-human: elf-chatter, astral babytalk, Martian doowop.
And these swoony helium-vocals were a huge hit with the punters; not
only did they mirror the drugged intensities pulsing inside the raver's
body, they actively triggered and amplified the E-rush.

Inadvertantly avant-garde, the chipmunk voices sounded *hysterical*,
in both the medical (over-excited emotions, uncontrollable impulses)
and humorous senses of the word. They brought a cartoony absurdism
to techno, puncturing the pompous piety of the Detroit purists. Those
who complained that 'ardkore wasn't 'proper techno' had a point;
while the purists followed Detroit in fixating on the supposedly more
'musical' synthesizer, 'ardkore was sampladelic music, based around a
collage mess-thetic. You could see the joins, which was so much more
postmodern and exciting. Your typical 'ardkore track was a mish-mash
of incongruous textures (spooky ectoplasm rubbing up against gimmicky cartoon gibberish) and incompatible moods (mystic, manic,
macabre). By 1992, hardcore was a bizarre composite of rush-activating
elements – Beltram stabs, Italo-piano riffs, breakbeats, melodramatic
strings, sped-up ultra-melismatic vocals and dub bass. These stylistic
fragments shared only one thing: welded together, they enhanced the
senti-MENTAL sensation of buzzing on speed-cut Ecstasy, its oxymoronic blend of aggression and open-hearted tenderness. Fusing the urge
to surge and the urge to merge, 'ardkore created a raging oceanic feeling.

'Ardkore's vulgar approach to sampling always makes me think of cargo cults: hallucinating the sublime and otherworldly in all manner of pop-cultural jetsam. I'm thinking of tracks like NRG's 'I Need Your Lovin'', which made the hardest of hearts melt to that hideously soppy Korgis' ballad 'Everybody's Got To Learn Sometimes', or the Payback track that transformed the *EastEnders* theme into a John Cage urban-gamelan percussion piece, or DJ Seduction's 'Sub Dub', which sampled folk-rock maiden Maddy Prior's dulcet-toned reverie of walking through 'rushes and through briars' to a field where 'lambs do sport and play'. When it came to making music, 'ardkore youth seemed to have no preconceptions and no discrimination (in the sense of prejudice as much as discernment). If a noise or riff could be made to work in a track, they'd nick it. Listening to the latest torrent of white-labels on the pirate stations, I'd imagine these hyped-up teenagers rifling through their elder brothers' or parents' record collection looking for nifty samples.

'Ardkore was *avant-lumpen*: the subculture's general impulse towards druggy disorientation required that initially recognizable soundbites be distorted, debased, rendered alien. The sampler worked as an estrangement device, a deracination machine, producing sonorities whose physical origin was increasingly impossible to trace. But unlike the traditional conception of an avant-garde, with its heroic auteurs and lonely pioneers striding out into the unknown, 'ardkore's creativity operated on the collective, macro-level of the entire genre: a syndrome Brian Eno calls 'scenius', as opposed to 'genius'. When anyone came up with a new idea, it was instantly ripped off a hundred times. Inspired errors and random fucking about produced new riffs and noises, 'mutations' that entered the dancefloor eco-system and were then inscribed in the music's DNA-code.

At the time, 'ardkore really did seem like some monstrous, amorphous creature, sucking in sound and regurgitating great vomit-gusts of anonymous, white-label brilliance. Looking back now, it's possible to map out a cartography of creativity, trace the trajectories of key producers and identify the house style of crucial labels. Some of these prime movers – fledgling labels like Moving Shadow, Suburban Base, Reinforced, Ram, Formation, and producers like Rob Playford (Kaotic Chemistry/2 Bad Mice), DJ SS, Andy C (Desired State/Origin Unknown), Goldie (Rufige Cru), DJ Hype, Krome and Time, Hyper-On Experience – went on to become recognized and respected auteur-figures in the jungle scene. But many more fell by the wayside or drifted off into other genres when the hardcore boom went bust: labels like Ibiza, Third Party, Big City, outfits like Bodysnatch, Sub Love, Sudden Def, DJ Trax, Criminal Minds, Citadel of Kaos, Holy Ghost Inc, Satin Storm, Mixrace, Phantasy and Gemini.

Of all these, the mysterious trio Noise Factory warrant a special mention, if only for their by-name-by-nature approach to churning out tracks: in a little over a year, their production-line spat out around a dozen underground anthems on almost as many EPs, all released via Ibiza and Third Party. Tracks like 'My Mind', 'Futoroid', 'Breakage #4', 'Survival' and 'Straight From the Bedroom' were haywire contraptions of jittery breaks, mad noises, and grainy, low-resolution samples: ruff-cut patches of orchestral arrangement, dislocated shrieks of ambiguously pitched diva-bliss, plaintive roots reggae incantations and dancehall ragga chants.

The music on Third Party, Ibiza and Big City mirrored the subcultural underside of the commercial pop-rave explosion in 1992: a black economy of rip-off raves, dodgy drugs, desperate pleasures and bad attitudes (muggings at raves, bouncers who frisked you for illegal substances then re-sold them inside the venue). Ibiza's first release, the 'Happy Hour EP', featured Low Noise Block's 'Rave In A Bedroom', which sampled Rik from *The Young Ones*' incredulous complaint – 'five pounds to get into my own bedroom! What've you done, turned it into a roller-disco?!?' Kicks Like A Mule's Top Ten hit 'The Bouncer', with its tersely intransigent bouncer samples of 'not tonight, you're not coming in', provoked Bodysnatch's answer record 'Revenge Of The Punter': a litany of murderous malevolence ('now you're taking liberties', 'step to this, if you wanna be *done*') synched up to fitful death-funk rhythms. Noise Factory's 'The Fire' twisted Stevie Nicks's mystical FM-rock classic 'Sara' into the plaint of a neophyte raver whose insides are ablaze with the scalding bliss of unusually pure E: 'Wait a minute, baby, stay with me a while / Said you'd give me light, but you never told me 'bout the fire.'

This new London-based version of 'ardkore was like a reprise of Shut Up And Dance's urban realism, but stripped of overt politics or any shred of 'change will come' hope. It was music for ravers who knew the rave dream was a lie, but carried on taking the bad medicine. 'I bring you the future, the future, the future', stammered the vocal-riff on Noise Factory's 'Breakage #4', and this was no idle boast. Ibiza's record sleeves bore the prophetic word – JUNGLIZM.

White Label Fever

Something tells me that British hardcore's golden age circa 1991–2 will one day be remembered as fondly as the American garage punk of the mid-sixties. The parallels are striking. Both genres were the domain of untrained teenagers fixated on gimmicky sonic effects: wah-wah and fuzz-tone with garage, swarming sampler-noises with 'ardkore. Both were oriented around the riff: in the sixties, there were a million variations on 'Train Kept A Rollin'' or 'You Really Got Me', in the early nineties, a myriad takes on the 'Mentasm' stab or on the Morse Code riff first heard on Landlord's 'I Like It' and Todd Terry's CLS classic 'Can You Feel It'. The drugs and drug-vibe were similar too: a heady blend of euphoria, aggression and tripped-out disorientation.

Sixties punk was a do-it-yourself movement of bored kids getting together to jam in the garage, just as their nineties 'ardkore equivalents gathered round the Amiga or Atari computer in a bedroom. Released on indie labels, their rough-and-ready lo-fi recordings might become regional hits, then – if they were really lucky – go nationwide. *Billboard* smashes like Count Five's 'Psychotic Reactions' and The Seeds' 'Pushing Too Hard' seemed to come out of nowhere, just like Urban Shakedown's 'Some Justice' and SL2's 'On A Ragga Tip'. And in both eras, for every hit there were a hundred obscure one-off bursts of inspiration.

The biggest parallel between 'ardkore and the 'punkadelic' music of 1965–7 is that both were utterly despised by hipsters at the time. Just as hippy snobs worshipped Cream and sneered at the garage bands for their lack of musicianship, the techno connoisseurs rallied to the art-wank of Future Sound Of London while dismissing 'ardkore for its low production values. Years later, garage punk was rehabilitated through the fanatical advocacy of writers like Lester Bangs and musicians like Lenny Kaye. After Kaye's celebrated *Nuggets* anthology of lost one-hit wonders, there followed a deluge of compilation series – the most famous being *Pebbles*, *Mindrocker* and *Back From The Grave* – dedicated to plucking from History's dustbin all the one-miss blunders from American garageland. Already, there are signs that a similar rehabilitation process is underway with 'ardkore: there's a collector's market for the original 12-inch singles, and a few 1991–2 compilations have become available. Who knows, a future form of techno may reinvoke the ideas and attitude of 'ardkore, in the same way that the punks of 1976 staged a partial return to the stark riffs and dynamic minimalism of sixties mod and garage punk. 'Ardkore was partly determined by the limited computer memory and 'sample-time' producers had at their disposal. But constraints can be energizing: today's better-endowed producers often seem to drown in the mire of options, creating hopelessly cluttered and over-nuanced music.

Juvenile Dementia

In every pop era, there are those hipsters who are seeking some kind of art status for the music they love. And in every era, 'valid' art-music is defined against 'mindless trash', which may be too polished and commercial, or too raw and anti-musical, but either way is deemed immature and lacking in depth. For sure, 'ardkore was one-dimensional music. But for my money, 'ardkore commands that dimension with a single-minded intensity that is as close to the primal essence of rock 'n' roll as you can get. What's the essence? Not sex or drugs or dance, but any or all of these in so far as they're about *intensity*, a heightened sense of *here-and-now*.

To live in the now, without memory or future-anxiety, is literally child-ish. For those with an investment in techno's maturation as an art form, one of the most offensive aspects of 'ardkore was its regressive streak. Hits like 'Sesame's Treet' were only the tip of the infantilistic iceberg: there was Bolt's 'Horsepower', based around the wonderfully stirring theme music from the kids' TV series *Black Beauty*, and Major Malfunction's 'Ice Cream Van', with its music-box chimes and little girl singing 'we all scream for ice cream'. The greatest Ibiza track of all, Bad Girl's 'Bad Girl', features a sped-up she-sprite sing-songing a playground paean to ''erb an' weed, weed an' ganja, ganja an' weed, an' 'erb an' marijuana', her prepubescent voice lurking amidst a grotto of globular bass-goo. 2 Bad Mice's 'Drumscare' starts with a looped entreaty – 'E-wanna-E-wanna-E-wanna-E-wanna-E' – that sounds like a spoilt child demanding sweeties. It's surely no coincidence that many of the brands of Ecstasy at this time played on this regressive craving for oral gratification, taking their names from bygone seventies candy (love hearts, refreshers), or school dinner desserts (rhubarb-and-custards).

Citing the childhood game of spinning round and round to induce 'a dizziness that reduced [the] environment to a sort of luminous chaos', Virilio reminds us that 'child-society frequently utilizes turnings, spinning around, disequilibrium. It looks for sensations of vertigo and disorder as sources of pleasure.' This idea of dervish-whirling your way into blissful disorientation permeated 'ardkore in the form of dozens of samples that refer to spinning round, like Noise Factory's 'My Mind': 'spinning round, you're dancing like a hurricane / round and round, we search for love in a world gone insane'. And every big commercial rave had funfair attractions like whirligigs and bouncy castles.

Alongside its juvenile craving for thrills and spills, the other threatening aspect of 'ardkore was its naked drugginess. This was emblazoned in sniggery double-entendres like Skin Up's 'Ivory', with its 'give us an E please, Bob' sample from *Blockbuster*, a TV game-show based around spelling out words, or Lenny D Ice's 'We Are I.E.', which sampled an African chant and turned it into an affirmation of collective identity through MDMA. But the drugginess is also brazenly apparent in the *sound* of 'ardkore, the way the music seemed to bypass the aesthetic faculties and take effect by direct neurological interface. Critics who liked to deal with rock as a surrogate form of literature were the most perturbed by this anti-humanist noise. But dance cognoscenti looking to establish techno's status as a 'progressive' artform were also embarrassed. Just as it seemed possible to make the case that electronic music could be more than a soundtrack to drugging and dancing, along came 'ardkore: not so much music as a science of inducing and enhancing the E-rush. Could you even listen to this music 'on the natural', enjoy it in an un-altered state? Well, I did and do, all the time. But whether I'd *feel it*, viscerally understand it, if my nervous system hadn't been reprogrammed by MDMA, is another matter. Perhaps you only need to do it once, to get sens-E-tized, and then the music will induce memory-rushes and body-flashbacks.

Rage to Live

For many, 'ardkore was a depressing manifestation of rave culture's nihilistic escapism, scantily garbed in the gladrags of a vague and poorly grounded idealism. What interests me about hardcore was the way it simultaneously affirmed rave's utopianism yet hinted at the illusory nature of this heaven-on-earth, which can only be sustained by artificial energy and capsules of synthetic happiness. Tracks like Rhythm Section's 'Dreamworld' and Desired State's 'This Is A Dream' conjure up a poignant vision of paradise even as they remind the listener of its vaporous and transitory unreality.

'Ardkore was really just the latest twist on the traditional contours of working-class leisure, the latest variant on the sulphate-fuelled 48-hour weekend of mod and Northern Soul lore. There's an even earlier precedent: the *Tanzwuth* (dance-mania) or St Vitus Dance, in which medieval youth *jigged* their way out of their constrictions to the raucous soundtrack provided by itinerant minstrels. Helped along by fasting, sleep-deprivation and binging on wine, these proto-ravers would get swept up in 'fits of wild dancing, leaping, hopping and clapping that ended in syncope [mass fainting]', according to an essay in *The New England Journal of Medicine* which sought a precedent for outbreaks at rock concerts of hyperventilation, palpitations and mass swooning. 'Syncope' shares etymological roots with syncopation, the defining rhythmic quality of the 'ardkore breakbeat. Just like raves, *Tanzwuth* carnivals were feared by the authorities as 'demoniacal festivals for the rude multitudes', despite the fact that they probably served an ultimately conservative function by dissipating the tensions and frustrations created by the hierarchical, regimented nature of medieval society.

In 1992, a slice of rap circulated through 'ardkore's sample gene-pool: 'can't beat the system / go with the flow'. On one level, it was just a boast about how much damage the sound-system can inflict. But perhaps there's a submerged and enduring political resonance in there too: amidst the socio-economic deterioration of a Britain well into its second decade of one party Tory rule, where alternatives seemed unimaginable, horizons grew ever narrower, and there was no constructive outlet for anger or idealism, what else was left but to zone out, go with the flow, *disappear*? In their quest to reach escape velocity, 'ardkore youth ended up in the speed-trap: a dead-end zone where going nowhere fast becomes a kind of hyperkinetic stasis, strung out between spasm and entropy.

Yet there's an inchoate fury in 'ardkore, a protean rage, that still feels affirmative to me rather than nihilistic; an urge for total release from constraints, a lust for explosive exhilaration, that incites me like virtually no other music. 'Ardkore seethes with a RAGE TO LIVE, to cram all the intensity absent from a week of drudgery into a few hours of fervour. 'Ardkore frenzy was where the somnambulist youth of Britain snapped out of the living death of the nineties, and grasped a few moments of fugitive bliss. As the chorus of Xenophobia's 'Rush In The House' put it, 'E come alive E come alive E come alive'. 'Ardkore's speedfreaks were literally *rushing* away from their problems, and who could really blame them?

FIVE

FIGHT FOR
YOUR RIGHT
TO PARTY

SPIRAL TRIBE AND THE

CRUSTY-RAVER

MOVEMENT

It's 11 p.m. on a Saturday night, 23 May 1992. We're cruising along a country lane somewhere in the English West Country, when the abnormally – one might even say *suspiciously* – heavy traffic comes to a halt. Someone up ahead has stopped to take a leak. Suddenly, from almost every car, boys emerge to follow suit. It's an image I'll never forget: irradiated in the gleam of a hundred headlights, innumerable arcs of urine spraying into the hedgerow, as far as the eye can see.

An hour earlier we'd been hurtling down the motorway, *en route* to my first Spiral Tribe outdoor rave. The Spirals are part of the cross-over between the rave scene and the 'crusty' subculture – crusties being squat-dwelling anarcho-hippy-punk types named after their matted dreadlocks and post-apocalyptic garb. At the bottom of the crusty spectrum are destitute idlers who panhandle for a living; at the top end are more enterprising types who organize illegal parties, deal drugs, or make and sell artifacts and clothes.

My friends have Tribal connections, and one of the clan's DJs has cadged a ride. He tells us about 'doets', a new drug in circulation, which he says is a super-potent cocktail of speed, LSD, E and ketamine that propels the user on a thirty hour trip with '*amazing* visuals, man!' Then he plays a tape of Spiral Tribe's debut EP. The killer track, 'Doet', is a juggernaut of noise kickstarted by a nursery rhyme – 'If you're at a rave and you can't score an E / you must be / buzzin'' / on acid' – and the rabble-rousing exhortation 'Rush your fucking bollocks off!!!' This is Spiral Tribe's slogan of the summer. The insolent, uncouth voice on 'Doet' belong to MC Scallywag, whose mischievous rewrite of The Kinks' 'You Really Got Me' ('Ectsasy, it's really got me now . . . got me so I don't know what I'm doing') is the hook in Xenophobia's 'Rush In The House', another of that summer's 'ardkore anthems.

Gradually, we realize we are no longer alone; our car has become part of a convoy, and the breathless anticipation, the sense of strength-in-numbers grows until almost unbearable, as does the fear that the police will thwart the rave. Our destination is Castlemorton Common in Worcestershire, not far from the border with Wales. This year it is the site for the Avon Free Festival, one of the dozen or more summer festivals attended by 'New Age travellers' – basically nomadic crusties.

Travelling as a lifestyle began in the early seventies, as convoys of hippies spent the summer wandering from site to site on the free festival circuit, which included the Rainbow Festival, Cantlin Stone, Ribblehead, Inglestone Common, Rough Tor, Magic Mushroom, and Cinsbury Ring Free. Gradually, these raggle-taggle remnants of the original counter-culture built up a neo-medieval economy based around crafts, alternative medicine and entertainment: jugglers, acrobats, healers, food vendors, candle makers, clothes sellers, tattooists, piercers, jewellers, and drug pedlars. The New Age traveller first burst into public consciousness as a modern 'folk-devil' in June 1985, thanks to The Battle of the Beanfield. Police diverted the Convoy *en route* to the Stonehenge Free Festival (the traditional site for Summer Solstice celebrations) and went on the rampage, trashing vehicles and clubbing men and women alike. The then Home Secretary Douglas Hurd referred to the travellers as 'medieval brigands', while Prime Minister Margaret Thatcher declared 'I am only too pleased to make life as difficult as possible for these hippy convoys.' Despite persecution from the authorities, the travelling movement not only survived, it grew. As squatting became a less viable option and the government mounted a clampdown on welfare claimants, many urban crusties tired of the squalor of settled life and took to the roving lifestyle. By the end of the eighties, some estimates put the number of travellers at 40,000.

At the 1990 Glastonbury rock festival, crusties and hippies danced to house and techno sound-systems like Club Dog and Tonka, while outside the festival bounds, there was confrontation as travellers (who'd hitherto been let in for free) railed against the high ticket price and demanded a free camp site. 1990 also saw ravers – sick of commercialized, rip-off raves – turning up at the free festivals, where techno was gradually eclipsing the hippies' previous staple (cosmic trance-rock of the Hawkwind/Here and Now/Magic Mushroom Band stripe). Sound-system collectives, like Nottingham's DiY, formed and started to throw free parties at abandoned airfields or on hilltops, drawing a mixed crowd of urban ravers and crusty road-warriors.

Spiral Tribe started hooking up with the travellers in the summer of 1991, and rapidly became prime movers on the scene, luring thousands of urban ravers to party at disused airfields and abandoned quarries; often, the events coincided with traditional free festivals. Gradually, the Spirals – alongside similar sound-system outfits like Bedlam, Circus Warp, Techno Travellers, Armageddon, Adrenalin, and Circus Normal – fermented a peculiar symbiosis between the straight rave scene and the anarcho-hippy nomads; the 'ardkore weekenders brought an infusion of money generated by working in the straight world, the travellers provided an environment for freaking out. There were tensions, initially: some older travellers, used to folk and acid rock, disliked the harsh new techno soundtrack. Inevitably, there was mutual suspicion based on differences of lifestyles, look and outlook: the travellers with their dreadlocks and shaved patches of scalp, hessian jackets, camouflage fatigues, DM boots and ring-piercings galore; the fashion-conscious middle-class ravers; the baggy-trouser-and-T-shirted 'ardkore proles. But as they discovered common ground in drugs, dance and the desire to have a wild time dirt-cheap, travellers and ravers formed what cultural critic Lawrence Grossberg calls an 'affective alliance': the affect, in this instance, being an exhilarating feeling of freedom, combined with the belief that freedom ain't really free if you have to pay for it.

Little do we know it as we wind along the West Country lanes, but Castlemorton is set to be the high-water mark and absolute climax of this crusty-raver alliance. Previous Spiral-instigated parties have drawn crowds in the region of five or six thousand. But arriving at the darkened Common, it quickly becomes apparent that the event has escalated beyond all expectations. Thanks to Bank Holiday Monday's prolongation of the weekend, and exceptionally fine weather, Castlemorton is well on its way to becoming the biggest illegal rave in history. Estimates vary from twenty thousand to forty thousand present.

Our first surprise is the absence of largescale police presence. We encounter only a pair of genial constables who direct us to a safer parking space, lest 'all your paint gets scraped off by one of the big buses'. The midsummer night scene is somewhere between a medieval encampment and a Third World shanty town. The lanes are choked with caravans, buses, ex-military transports, gaudily painted horse-drawn vehicles, and hundreds of cars (in the near pitch black, I keep gouging my hips on jutting wing-mirrors). The fields are jammed with a higgledy-piggledy throng of tents, pavilions, and eerie-looking fluorescent sculptures (the work of Sam Hegarty, resident artist for the Circus Irritant sound-system).

The Third World/medieval vibe is exacerbated by the bazaar atmosphere. Pedlars hawk their illicit wares, hollering 'get your acid!'

or 'hash cookies for sale', propositioning us with wraps of speed, magic mushroom pies and innumerable brands of Ecstasy. The most medieval aspect of all, we discover later, is the total absence of sanitation. Venturing out on to the camp's perimeter, we quickly learn to tread gingerly, in order to avoid the excrement amid the bracken, and the toilet paper hanging from gorse bushes. A big placard commands 'Bury Your Shit', but unlike the seasoned travellers, urban ravers haven't come armed with spades.

After stumbling through the choc-a-bloc murk for what feels like a small eternity, we finally make it to Spiral Tribe's own enclosure, a Wild West style wagon circle of vans and trucks circumscribing a grassy dancefloor. While the event is free, in accordance with the Spiral credo 'no money, no ego', ravers are invited to give donations in order to keep 'the gennies' (electricity generators) running. Inside the circle, the scene is like a pagan gathering. With their amazing, undulating dance moves, it seems like the crowd has evolved into a single, pulsating organism. Faces are contorted by expressions midway between orgasm and sobbing. 'Lost the plot, we've lost the plot,' hollers one MC, 'Off my fuckin' tree.' It's time for us to get 'on the vibe', as the Spirals put it, and we quickly score some Tangerine Sunsets at £15 a shot, sold out of the back of a van.

Later, another Spiral MC, crop-headed Simone, hollers 'Let's lose it, together,' then chants the chorus of another track from the forthcoming Spiral Tribe EP, which quotes the lament of a nineteenth-century American Indian chieftain. 'I am a savage, and I can't understand / How the beauty of the Earth can be sold back to man,' toasts Simone. Dancing with the stars overhead, it's hard not to succumb to the back-to-Nature romanticism. It's all part of Spiral Tribe's eco-mystical creed, which is crystallized in the buzzword 'terra-technic': using technology to unlock the primal energy of Mother Earth. (It's also a pun on the Technics SL1200 Mk2 turntable favoured by DJs.) Tonight, the subsonic bass-throb of their sound-system certainly feels like it's forging a connection between my bowels and the Earth's core. Years later, Spiral DJ Aztek described the terra-technic rush in *Eternity* magazine: 'the sensation is like being earthed and receiving some sort of energy signal'. (Of course, this might have something to do with his professed intake of around eight or nine Ecstasy tablets per weekend, at that time!)

Around 4.30 a.m., the grey pre-dawn light uncovers a scene weirdly poised between idyllic and apocalyptic. The breathtaking Malvern

Hills, shrouded with mist, are a sight for sore eyes. But at the Malverns' feet, the festival site is an eyesore. Shagged-out dancers huddle around small bonfires to ward off the clammy, creeping damp. Undernourished travellers' dogs roam freely. Bedraggled figures wander around scavenging for cigarette butts to make joints; others panhandle for money to buy more E.

The consensus is that the Tangerine Sunsets are a disappointment. But a spare Rhubarb and Custard left-over from a previous rave is shared, and that's all it takes to push us over the edge. On my weakened, sleep-deprived system and empty stomach, the effect is almost instantaneous: I've got that walking-on-air, helium-for-blood feeling. Even though the music sounds harsh and distorted because it's overdriven at top volume through an inadequate PA, I'm swept up in a frenzy of belligerent euphoria. A friend tells me later I've actually been growling!

One image sums up Castlemorton for me. A beautiful, androgynous girl – short black bob, virulent red lipstick, Ray-Ban sunglasses, burgundy short-sleeve top – is dancing on top of a van. Her fingers stab and slice, carving cryptograms in the dawn air, and her mouth is puckered in a pout of indescribable, sublime impudence. She's totally, fiercely *on the vibe*, living in the moment, loving it.

By ten in the morning, the sun's breaking through, the temperature's rising, and our rush has dwindled to a buzzy lassitude. We sprawl on the grass. A photographer friend-of-a-friend, supposedly here to document history-in-the-making, has been dozing for five hours; he wakes, mutters 'Wicked sleep!' and we piss ourselves laughing. All around, the exposed flesh of slumped, catatonic bodies is visibly blistering in the baking heat. A couple of well-trained four-year-old crusty-kids are wandering around selling outrageously overpriced packets of Rizla rolling papers to desperate ravers, and Spiral personnel are collecting the first night's rubbish in binliners. Overhead a police helicopter patrols intermittently (later, a crusty will fire a flare-gun at it, much to the public's outrage). By noon, shattered, we decide it's time to go home. Bidding farewells, we wend our way through the revellers and wreckage. On the long journey home, my friend keeps falling asleep at the wheel.

During the next five days of its existence, Castlemorton inspires questions in Parliament, makes the front page of every newspaper, and incites nationwide panic about the possibility that the next destination on the crusty itinerary is your very own neighbourhood. Tabloids like the *Sun* stoke public fear and resentment of 'the scum army' of dole-scrounging soap-dodgers having fun on your tax money. In the quality newspapers, commentators line up to fulminate against the malodorous anarcho-mystics. Novelist Anthony Burgess (mis)informs his *Evening Standard* readers that New Age travellers like to listen to New Age music, and decries the outdoor rave phenomenon as 'the megacrowd, reducing the individual intelligence to that of an amoeba . . . dehumanization purchased in the name of freedom.'

Back at Castlemorton itself, local residents complain of fences being torn up for firewood, of dogs savaging sheep and chickens being released from coops, of finding syringes in the hedgerows, of catching crusties defecating in their back gardens or trying to sell acid to their kids. Above all, they whine about the incessant barrage of techno, which sends them 'all funny'. 'There's something hypnotic about the continuous pounding beat of the music, and it's driving people living in the front line into a frenzy,' one 42-year-old villager tells a newspaper. Lambasting the West Mercia police for its failure to thwart the rave and its kid-glove handling of the party-goers, local farmers form a vigilante militia. The police, for their part, claim they wanted to avoid a repeat of the Battle of the Beanfield.

On the last day, after inexplicably hanging around rather than attempting to sneak a getaway, thirteen members of the Tribe are arrested, and several sound-systems are impounded. Police forces across rural Britain start collaborating in Operation Snapshot: the creation of a massive database with names of ringleaders and licence numbers of travellers' and ravers' vehicles. An intensive campaign of surveillance and intelligence work is mounted to ensure that any future Castlemortons are nipped in the bud. And the Conservative government begins to hatch the ultimate death-blow to the free party scene: the Criminal Justice and Public Order Act.

Terra-Technic Terrorists

'Let us admit that we have attended parties where for one brief night a republic of gratified desires was attained. Shall we not confess that the politics of that night have more reality and force for us than

those, of say, the entire US government? Some of the "parties" we've
mentioned lasted for two or three years.'
> – Hakim Bey, 'The Temporary Autonomous Zone'

I first met Spiral Tribe a few months prior to Castlemorton, at a 'legit'
club called the Soundshaft with which the Tribe had some vague
connection. Within minutes, I'm informed that I'm already part of the
cosmic 'spiral'. Synchronicity is at work: my T-shirt, of sampler-
wielding cyber-punks The Young Gods, happens to have a luminous
spiral in the middle. What's more, there are pictures of bees on the
sleeves, which echo a recent Spiral Tribe rave at a farm, where a hive
was knocked over, unleashing a vast cloud of bees. (Nobody got stung.)
Even more synchronistically, the farm was in Hertfordshire, a county
with which the Tribe claim a 'special connection', and where I just so
happen to have spent my childhood. The Tribe grin like maniacs, each
coincidence confirming their mystical worldview.

The next night, I attend my first Spiral Tribe party, at a dilapidated
squatters' house in North East London. Five years earlier, an equivalent
squat party's soundtrack would have been dub reggae or hippy music
like Gong. But tonight, a thick, tactile web of techno-voodoo rhythms
writhes through the murk. Gyrating light-beams glance off walls
mottled with dry rot and mildew, illuminating cryptic Spiral Tribe
insignia, and refracting through the curlicues of ganja smoke. Downstairs in the makeshift chill-out room, assorted Spiral folk huddle by
a gas fire, rolling spliffs. Some snort ketamine, an anaesthetic drug
suddenly in favour with the hardcore psychedelic contingent within
rave culture. Slang terms for ketamine are 'baby food' (users sink into
a blissful, infantile inertia) and 'God' (some users are engulfed in a
heavenly radiance, and, if religious, become convinced they've met
their Maker) .

A week after the squat-party, I get the chance to interrogate Spiral
Tribe in the aftermath of another event, this time at a derelict pub.
Upstairs, survivors lie slumped and glazed on soiled mattresses. On the
wall, someone has aerosol-sprayed a pentagram with the number
twenty-three in one corner. The uncanny power and alleged omnipres-
ence of the number twenty-three is one of a motley array of mystical
beliefs to which the Spirals subscribe. It's the sum of paired chromo-
somes in a DNA helix. All Spiral Tribe information phone lines contain

the number. And Castlemorton kicked off on 23 May. 'Twenty-three is gonna slap you in the face, freak you out, it'll really start to make you doubt your security in what you know,' the Tribe's spokesman Mark Harrison warns me, promising that I'll start seeing the number all over the place. (I don't.)

Expounding his anarcho-mystic creed, Mark has the visionary gleam of a prophet in his eyes. After half an hour of his breathless, punctuation-free discourse, I'm mesmerized. I begin to see why he has such a hold over his disciples – and that's what they are, for all the party line of no hierarchy. At one point, a Tribesman describes Mark as the Second Coming, only to be swiftly silenced by a reproving glance from the guru himself. Yet despite the cultic, almost Manson-like aura, a surprising amount of what Mark and his acolytes say makes sense.

'We keep everything illegal because it's only outside the law that there's any real life to be had. The real energy in rave culture comes from illegal dance parties, pirate radio, and white label 12 inches that bypass the record industry altogether. Rave is about people creating their own reality. At our parties, you step into the circle and enter ritual space, Spiral Tribe reality. Last summer, we did a party that went on for fourteen days non-stop,' he boasts, referring to The White Goddess Festival at Camelford in Cornwall, which lasted from 22 August to 4 September 1991. 'It's a myth that you need to sleep. Stay awake and you begin to discover the real edges of reality. You stop believing in anything that anyone told you was true, all the false reality that was hammered into you from birth.'

'In the old days, rock bands had to go to record companies and sign their souls away just to be able to put out a record,' says saucer-eyed Seb, the former music student largely responsible for Spiral Tribe's own mindwarping, mutant techno. 'But now cheap technology means anyone can do it. Just compare the music released on white labels with the stuff released by major companies – you can taste the freedom. Rock 'n' roll had that freedom once, very briefly, before it was turned into a commodity.' Seb refuses to be credited on the Tribe's EPs. 'If money is your God, we're the Antichrist,' he enthuses, 'The record industry turns energy into money, into dead metal. We want to release the trapped energy. All the money we make goes back into the music.'

Although Spiral Tribe recognize that for a lot of hardcore fans, raving is just the latest twist on the working-class 'living for the weekend' ethos, they claim that people often come to their parties and see the light. 'Sometimes, people come to our parties and say "Fuck it, I'm not going to work tomorrow." Next thing, they've sold the house, bought a vehicle, and they're sorted.' 'Sorted', in Spiral Tribe parlance, means more than just fixed up with E, it means attuned to a new reality, 'spiral reality'. 'Ask any of us the time and we say "spiral time."' Sure enough, Seb's watch is resolutely stopped at the wrong time.

Like a lot of millenarian groups, Spiral Tribe combine paranoid conspiracy theories (the Masons, the Illuminati, et al) with fantasies about returning to a lost paradise. 'If you compare techno with music from primitive or non-Western cultures,' says Seb, 'you'll find that those musics, like techno, are based on harmony and rhythm, not melody. That's what's amazing about the house revolution, everyone was waiting for it, and nobody had done it – stripped it all down to the percussive, even the vocals. It's all voodoo pulses, from Africa. If you look at what happened with *The Rite of Spring* by Stravinsky, he got rid of melody, he entered harmony and rhythm, and he had a riot at the first concert. With our music and our parties, we're not trying to get into the future, we're trying to get back to where we were before Western Civilization fucked it all up.'

In many respects, Spiral Tribe and the entire free-party movement constitute an uncanny fulfilment of the prophecies of Hakim Bey. In his visionary tracts, 'Chaos: The Broadsheets of Ontological Anarchism' (1985) and 'The Temporary Autonomous Zone' (1990), Bey called for the rebirth of a new 'festal culture' based around the 'jubilee concept' and 'spiritual hedonism'. His notion of 'a psychic paleolithism based on High-Tech' fits the Spirals' back-to-Nature, terra-technic shtick like a glove. Similarly, the Spiral's tribal disorganization corresponds to Bey's exaltation of 'clans ... secret or initiatic societies ... "children's republics," and so on,' as opposed to the claustrophobia of the nuclear family. Later that summer, all Spiral members shave their hair off to symbolize their group-mind.

On a more general level, the illegal free rave, with its lack of entrance fee or security, is a perfect real-world example of the 'temporary autonomous zone', aka the TAZ. For Bey, the TAZ is an advance glimpse of utopia, 'a microcosm of that "anarchist dream" of a free culture', but its success depends on its very impermanence. 'The "nomadic war machine" conquers without being noticed', filling 'cracks and vacancies' left by the State, then scattering in order to re-group and attack elsewhere. 'Cracks and vacancies' sounds very like the abandoned air bases (like Smeatharpe in Devon), industrial warehouses and derelict government buildings that Spiral Tribe and other sound-systems take over for a few days, before moving on. Less literally, the free festival circuit answers Bey's call for 'the construction of shifting "autonomous zones" within an invisible nomadic network'. Rave culture as a whole arguably fulfils his 'spiritual project: the creation or discovery of pilgrimages in which the concept "shrine" has been replaced ... by the concept "peak experience"'; 'a peak experi-ence' that must be 'on the social as well as individual scale'.

Bummer in the City

When I interview Spiral Tribe they are already promising that 1992 will be 'the maddest summer since 1989', a non-stop conflagration of illegal raves and altercations with the authorities. The ignition point is set to be 'Sound System City', a massive convocation of ravers celebrating the Summer Solstice on 21 June, at a site as near as possible to Stonehenge as the police's four-mile exclusion zone will allow.

In the event, the subcultural energies fermented by the Tribe slip out of their control: the 'maddest summer' peaks too early, at Castlemorton. And Spiral Tribe take all the credit and all the blame. On one hand, thirteen members are charged with a variety of offences including causing a public nuisance contrary to common law. (Skilled propagandists, the Spirals twist the phrase into 'public new-sense'.) But on the other hand, all the music rags and national newspapers want to talk to them, and they get signed to dance label Big Life, whose owner Jaz Summers is convinced that this crusty-raver malarkey is the next punk rock, with Spiral Tribe as its Sex Pistols.

With corporate money at their disposal, the Tribe hire a massive articulated lorry and a 23 K sound-system for their next and most daring confrontation with the authorities. Given the exclusion zone around Stonehenge, they decide to up the stakes and hold the Summer Solstice mega-rave right in the heart of the capital. Sound System City will be built at Mudchute Farm – a public park, in the East London area known as the Isle of Dogs, that's rumoured to be situated above a ley-line. The rave will be illluminated by the flashing light on top of the ill-fated Canary Wharf tower. Part of the unsuccessful Docklands development scheme, and built to be Britain's new financial centre, Canary Wharf is a symbol of Tory hubris, of late eighties 'boom' economics gone bust. But Sound System City itself becomes a symbol of Spiral Tribe's own hubris: it's the first and biggest in a series of defeats that results in the 'maddest summer' petering out ignominiously.

11.45 p.m., Saturday, 21 June: my posse arrive too early. There's only one other car in the vicinity, its back seat crammed to the roof with bottles of Evian: obviously the owners are budding entrepreneurs looking to slake ravers' thirst. We drift across the eerily calm and deserted field, and run into a reconnaisance team from the Tribe on the other side, busy working out how to break the lock on the gate and drive their monstertruck on to Mudchute Farm. Brusquely, they order us to disappear, lest local residents get suspicious. We retreat to a friend's house for an hour, then set out again. By this point, the major access roads into the Isle of Dogs are blocked by police, who are turning back anybody who doesn't live in the area. Hundreds of frustrated ravers mill about on the pavement, trying to muster enough courage to rush the barricades. The rave has kicked off, we learn; over a thousand people are already in the area, partying their socks off, but nobody else can get through to Mudchute.

There's one faint hope: the two main roads are sealed, but there's a pedestrian-only tunnel under the Thames that connects the Docklands area to Greenwich and the rest of South East London. We hightail it across the river, but we're too late: the boys in blue have cordoned off the entrance. 'Rush 'em,' says a crustie, sniggering at the druggy double-entendre, but nobody does. The muffled thud-thud-boom of the Spiral's distant sound-system taunts and tantalizes us. Spirits flagging, we cross the Thames again and navigate a circuitous route through the backstreets of North East London in an attempt to work our way down to the Isle of Dogs, all the while cursing the poor strategic aforethought of the Spirals in choosing a site accessible via only two main roads, both of which are easily blocked. Around daybreak, we get within a half-mile of Mudchute. Looking at the map, we realize it might be possible to cross the Docklands Light Railway and get to the rave. Just as we're looking for an egress, a private security firm van drives up. Defeated, we beat a retreat. Later, we learn that the police easily dispersed the rave around 3.30 a.m., with no arrests; some hardcore Spiral-types have headed north to a free party in Leicestershire.

Other abortive raves follow throughout the summer of 1992; the police intelligence network is too efficient, local farmers spread manure on their fields, and the desperately unhappy travellers are shunted back and forth across county lines. One Spiral rave in Surrey, supposedly on private land and at the owner's invitation, sounds like a good bet, but the local police quash it anyway. The result is a glum convoy of some fifty cars, which – prevented from reaching any of the back-up sites – winds up on a picturesque stone quay facing the English Channel. The sense of anti-climax is crushing, and as we drive back to London, I resolve never to go on another Spiral rave. Amazingly, my friend sets out again at 8 a.m. when she learns that the Spirals have finally pulled off a free party after all, only to find a gaggle of red-eyed crusties crashed out on a beach around a pathetic Tandy hi-fi system.

Actually, I do attend one more Spiral party, in the winter of 1992. The location is a derelict Inland Revenue depot in a grim area of North West London. This is the anti-Castlemorton, totally devoid of midsummer-night's-dreaminess. The dancehall is basically an industrial hangar, just like at a big commercial rave, but with no facilities whatsoever: nowhere to sit, nothing to drink, no toilet (people piss on the wooden floorboards in an adjoining room), barely any lights. Five months after Castlemorton, the music seems to have gotten harsher and more punitive; one Spiral-affiliated outfit plays a set of undanceably fast, stiffly regimented, metallic beats, which sounds like ball-bearings rattling around in a concrete pipe. As the matt-grey mid-winter dawn filters weak and sickly through the skylight, exposing some seriously haggard E-casualties around us, the consensus is: this is the end of an era.

Criminal Injustice

With the Castlemorton trial looming over their heads, Spiral Tribe maintained a high media profile for a while, putting out a series of EPs like 'Breach The Peace' and 'Forward The Revolution'. Stymied in Britain on the free-party front, another faction of the Tribe – who bitterly disapproved of the record deal with Big Life – moved to the Continent, where the police tended to be more tolerant. Like other traveller sound-systems, the Spirals roamed throughout the EC, bringing the 'teknival' – as they now called it – to Italy, Austria, the Czech Republic, Hungary and France. Here, the Tribe catalysed a Gallic free-party scene into being, and scored their greatest triumph in August 1995 when they instigated a twelve day *rave gratuite* on an Atlantic beach near Bayonne; because the site was owned by the military, the local police were powerless to intervene. In Bologna, where squat-culture and anarchism have deep roots, the Spirals hooked up with fellow exiles the Mutoid Waste Company to throw *techno fiestas*. And in Berlin, they acquired a Mig fighter plane and other ex-Soviet military hardware – heavy (literally) symbols of the Spirals' 'nomadic war machine' approach to throwing raves, but also useful ammunition in their long term strategy of making the parties more visually 'competitive'.

Seb and other music-making Spirals eventually settled in Paris, where they founded the Network 23 label and churned out trippy, high-velocity tracks somewhere between gabba and acid house. After struggling to operate their own totally independent pan-European distribution network, Network 23 eventually signed a distribution deal – an ideological lapse which incensed Mark. By this point, the guru had officially left the Tribe and was running his own Stormcore company, selling clothes and records. Unwilling to go on the road in Europe, others in the Spiral milieu succumbed to drug abuse, becoming serious psychonauts (in the Tribal worldview, LSD and ketamine had long been regarded as altogether more hardcore than 'fluffy' Ecstasy), junkies, crackheads, or just members of 'the Brew Crew'.

After spending nearly two years and several million pounds on the trial, the Malvern authorities had failed to convict any of the Spirals. Meanwhile, the Conservative government had devised a whole bunch of new laws to ensure that an event of Castlemorton's scale would never be repeated. These were presented to Parliament in the summer of 1994 as Part 5 of the Criminal Justice and Public Order Bill. Alongside a host of pernicious extensions of police powers (the removal of the right to silence, arbitrary stop-and-search powers), Part 5 targeted squatters, travellers, illegal raves and free festivals.

Defining a rave as a mere one hundred people playing amplified music 'characterized by the emission of a succession of repetitive beats', the Bill gave local police forces the discretionary power to harass gatherings as small as ten. If an officer 'reasonably believes' the ten are setting up a rave, or merely waiting for one to start, he can order them to disperse; failure to comply is a crime punishable by a three month prison sentence or a £2,500 fine. Moreover, the police are granted the power to stop anyone who comes within a one mile radius of this potential rave and order them to proceed no further. Other provisions practically illegalize squatting, travelling, and 'aggravated trespass', a new offence aimed to thwart fox-hunt saboteurs and 'eco-warrior' activists (crustie types who defend nature spots from motorway construction, by living in the trees or even tunnels they dig under the site).

A desperate attempt by a decrepit government to toughen up its image, the Criminal Justice Bill appealed to the most mean-spirited, intolerant side of the British mentality, a sort of internal xenophobia towards those who look and live differently. Underneath the bigotry lurked an undercurrent of resentment felt by many law-abiding, norm-obeying types *vis-à-vis* those who repudiate suburban slow-death and choose instead the open road. The fact that these anarcho-mystic drop-outs had chosen to reject society, rather than simply been ejected from it like your regular ne'er do well, simply added insult to injury.

Few people sympathized with the squatters and travellers, and fewer were prepared to defend them. With the Labour opposition in the House of Commons avoiding the issue for fear of appearing soft on crime, it fell to civil-liberties pressure-groups like Liberty, and to the ravers, travellers and squatters themselves to fight back with counter-propaganda and protest marches. On 1 May 1994, a fifteen thousand strong march, organized by SQUASH (Squatters Action for Secure Homes) and the Advance Party (a nationwide alliance of sound-systems), converged on Trafalgar Square. Despite chants like 'Kill the Bill' (a provocative pun linking the proposed laws and the Metropolitan Police, popularly known as 'the Old Bill') and the odd scuffle between coppers and drunken crusties, the event passed without incident. Bigger protests in July and October that year did result in some minor public disorder – clashes in Hyde Park and Park Lane, vandalism in Oxford Street – but nothing on the scale of the anti-Poll Tax riots of 1990.

There were protest records, too: an EP called 'Repetitive Beats' by Retribution (a gaggle of dancefloor luminaries including members of The Drum Club, System 7 and Fun-Da-Mental), and Autechre's 'Anti' EP, whose lead track 'Flutter' was programmed to have deliberately fitful rhythms, in order to bypass the CJB's clause about 'the emission of a succession of repetitive beats'. (The record label advised DJs, however, to have 'a lawyer and a musicologist present at all times to confirm the non-repetitive nature of the music in the event of police harassment'.) Both records testified to a widespread misapprehension amongst ravers that techno itself was about to be made illegal in all circumstances, not just at unlicensed parties. In a similar vein of pot-addled paranoia and delusory self-aggrandizement ('Our music is a threat to the powers-that-be!!'), conspiracy-theorists alleged that Part 5 of the CJB was the government's payback to the major brewers for their handsome contributions to the Conservative Party coffers; it was an attempt to kill Ecstasy culture (where alcohol is deemed passé) and to arrest the decline in pub profits by literally driving the youth back to drink.

But all the campaigning, protest records, consciousness-raising and Big-Brother-Is-Coming scaremongering was to no avail. On 3 November 1994, The Criminal Justice and Public Order Act was passed into law, and the crusty-raver 'teknival' scene quailed in anticipation of the clampdown.

Part-Time Crusties

And yet the scene didn't die. One segment went further underground, throwing smaller, less spectacularly annoying parties, with the tacit tolerance of the police. And another faction of the scene went overground, in the form of licensed 'festi-clubs' like Whirl-Y-Gig, Club Dog and Sativa. Of these, Club Dog was the most significant, creating a milieu in which the original free-party revellers mingled with part-time crusties, non-aligned trance fans and recent converts from rock to techno. Taking place every Friday at the Sir George Robey in Finsbury Park, Club Dog had actually been a focus for London's hippy/punk proto-crustie scene (what organizer Bob Dog called 'Warriors of the New Age') as far back as 1988. For the first four years of its existence, the staples of the Dog's soundtrack were acid rock, world music and dub reggae of the On U Sound stripe (Dub Syndicate, Suns of Arqua). Reflecting the impact of electronic music on the free festival scene, Club Dog gradually began to incorporate 'live techno' sets from bands like Orbital, Eat Static (the trance alter-ego of fusionoid festival faves Ozric Tentacles), Banco de Gaia, System 7 (featuring kosmik-rock guitar virtuoso Steve Hillage) and Psykick Warriors ov Gaia.

Next came the massively successful monthly Megadog events, whose rock gig meets rave meets festival vibe offered punters a paying-but-cheap legal alternative to the outlawed free parties, and a haven for the embattled crusty counter-culture. Megadog then went on tour in the form of Midi Circus (named after the MIDI technology that allows samplers and sequencers to be synched up with live playing and non-digital instruments). The Planet Dog label followed, catering to a distinct crusty-techno sound that had emerged: bands like Optic Eye, Children of the Bong, Wizards of Twiddly, Tribal Drift, Zuvuya, Loop Guru and Transglobal Underground. Despite the use of 'ethnodelic' flavourings (didgeridoo-pulsations, world-music samples), crusty-tekno is ultra-Caucasian, often recalling those original trance-rock-turned-synth-pioneers Tangerine Dream.

Coalescing at roughly the same time as the Megadog scene, Goa Trance was another compromised consolation for the utopian longings blocked by the Criminal Justice Act. The scene is named after a style of techno associated with Goa, an area on the South West Coast of India that's about twice the size of London. Goa was a Portuguese colony right up until 1961, but almost as soon as India seized the territory back, another wave of European invaders arrived: hippies in search of a drug paradise, where you could live like a king for a few dollars a day and hashish was cheaper than cornflakes.

By the late eighties, Goa had evolved into a *dance*-and-drug paradise. I first heard about Goa's all-night freak-outs in the jungle and on the beaches from a friend's brother in 1988. He told me that while the drug-in-vogue was LSD, the music wasn't acid house yet but Euro-beat, electro-pop and gay Hi-NRG – Front 242, Skinny Puppy, Yello, the vocal-free dub mixes of tracks by New Order and Pet Shop Boys. With a glazed, flashback-look in his eyes, he told me of going to an 'anti-rave' thrown by some acid-fried psycho on a sloping promontory of granite, where the beats were hard as hell and a huge crack running down the middle of the rock made utterly real the possibility that you might 'lose it' on the dancefloor, *forever*. He told me of drug lords flying in from their offshore island havens, disembarking the helicopter with their coked-out supermodel-skinny girlfriends, haughty in the *haute*-est Euro *couture*. 'You gotta go there,' he urged breathlessly. 'It's the end of the journey, man. Apocalypse Now.'

In the nineties, acid house and trance techno conquered Goa's party scene, and the region quickly became commercialized and swamped by raver-tourists looking not for transcendental experience but for another Ibiza. Aghast, the serious 'heads' and spiritual seekers moved on, abandoning Goa's most famous beaches – Anjuna, Vagator and Arambol – for more remote locations in India, or fleeing to Thailand (where the raves are called 'frenzies'). At the same time, the Goa 'vibe' was filtering back to Europe (literally, when DJ–producer Sven Vath used a portable DAT-recorder to sample jungle atmospheres for his *Accident in Paradise* album) as a specific post-rave *sound*.

Just as the Balearic craze during the first explosion of UK rave was an attempt to continue the fun had by British ravers in Ibiza after the holiday's end, Goa Trance is a homage to a place that seems like heaven-on-earth, even to those who've never been. Goa has become a floating signifier for taking a permanent vacation from ordinary life. Non-coincidentally, Ibiza and Goa were both havens for hippies in the sixties. Even as Goa was being despoiled by tourism, it was circulating – as a viral, 'virtual' presence – across the Western world. From London to Tel Aviv, Goa trance clubs offer a microcosmic version of the real thing.

In 1996, Goa Trance exploded into media consciousness, with the rise of parties like Return to the Source, Spacehopper, Herbal Tea Party, labels like Dragonfly, Flying Rhino, TIP, Blue Room Released, and bands like Man With No Name, Mandra Gora, Earth Nation, Hallucinogen, Green Nuns of the Revolution, Moonweed, Prana. As with the real Goa, the scene's drug of choice is acid far more than Ecstasy, and the LSD is supposed to be unusually pure and strong. Appropriately, the decor at Goa Trance events is psychotropic (lots of fluorescent, reflective and phosphorescent material), and the music is ornate and cinematic, full of arpeggiated synth-refrains and mandala-swirls of sound. Imagine New Age music with a metronomic pulse-beat; Giorgio Moroder's Eurodisco infused with Eastern-promise and oriented around transcendental surge rather than Donna Summer-style pornotopian rapture. Speaking to *DJ* magazine, trance decktician Goa Gil talked of giving 'youth in Babylon' (the capitalist, consumerist West) 'a higher transmission'; of dance as 'an active meditation'. For all its cult of the mystic Orient, Goa Trance is sonically whiter-than-white. All the creativity is in the top level (melody and filigree), with not a lot going on in the rhythm section.

The Goa Trance scene is a sort of deodorized, upmarket version of crusty-tekno, without the ragged-trousered poverty-chic. But both Megadog teknival culture and Goa Trance have a similar function. They are an inner-city surrogate for the pre-Criminal Justice Act festivals and free parties, attempts to resurrect a lost golden age on much reduced premises.

Guerrilla Parties

The golden age may be long gone, but free parties continue to take place on a much smaller scale, often in desolate, unlovely inner-city locations as opposed to the pastoral heart of England. Sound-systems like Disorganization, Liberator, Chiba City Sound, Silverfish, Jiba, Immersion, Virus, Desert Storm, UNSound-systems, Vox Populi and Turbo Unit persevere despite police harassment.

Perhaps the most persistent sound-system collective, and certainly the most persecuted, is Luton's Exodus. One member was unjustly tried for murder (and cleared), while in 1993 the arrest of Exodus leaders in order to thwart a planned rave provoked a three thousand strong protest outside the police station. The fervent support for Exodus stems as much from their community activism as their parties in abandoned farms and quarries. They established a squatter's commune called HAZ manor in a derelict old people's home, while their long-standing Ark project involves the creation of a community centre/party-space for local youth. Short for Housing Action Zone, HAZ is a nod to Hakim Bey's TAZ. The name Exodus itself is a homage to Bob Marley that reactivates the punk dream of a 'white ethnicity' equivalent to Rastafarianism: British bohemians as a lost tribe of internal exiles, stranded in a Babylon that's burning with boredom. 'Babylon' may not be a paranoid figment of the ganja-addled imagination. The anti-Exodus campaign of harassment seems to stem from the malign influence of the Freemasons and the brewing industry on the local Conservative Party, from whose ranks emerged Luton MP Graham Bright, the man behind the 1990 Parliamentary legislation targeted at orbital raves.

The new breed of post-CJA sound-systems follow the precept 'small-is-beautiful'. By carefully choosing isolated locations and restricting the size of events by keeping them word-of-mouth, collectives like Smoke-screen, Krunch, Quadrant and Elemental can pull off micro-raves in the countryside, simply because it's too much trouble for local police to break up the party once it's running. Keeping a low profile may not result in mythic confrontations with Babylon, à la Spiral Tribe, but it's a sound long-term strategy, ensuring the survival of a free-party scene that provides the only alternative to the increasingly costly and commercialized clubbing mainstream.

The one attempt in recent years to score a Castlemorton-scale triumph ended in humiliating disarray. In the summer of 1995, less than a year after the passage of the Criminal Justice and Public Order Act, a group called United Systems attempted to stage the biggest free rave since Castlemorton. A breakaway offshoot from the Advance Party, United Systems believe not in campaigning but in direct action to contest the CJA: 'Only free parties can save free parties.'

The mega-rave was named Mother, at once an echo of the terra-technic, Gaian mysticism of the Spirals and a declaration of overween-ing ambition (as in 'the mother of all parties'). The site was a failed theme-park called Corby Wonderworld in Northamptonshire, with a parallel party at Smeatharpe Airfield in Devon. But details of the rave leaked out on to the Internet, and both mega-raves were met with roadblocks and policemen wielding Section 60 of the CJA to turn away ravers. At Corby, three members of the Black Moon sound-system were arrested, with the police using their CJA powers for the first time; the perpetrators were eventually fined, and their equipment was impounded. Mini-raves did take place, however, at Sleaford, on the beach at Steart, and at a site in Grafham Waters, Cambridge, where Anglia Water let the travellers stay for a night.

Defeated but defiant, United Systems declared: 'We are unbloodied, unbowed, undaunted and remain totally commited to our cause. They may have nailed the Mother but she had babies throughout the country that weekend. We live and learn and there's always a next time – we're not going to go away.' Later that year, they started the legitimate club DMZ in the heart of London, in order to a build a 'fighting fund' to defend the eight United Systems members on trial for Mother. The location was the Soundshaft (the club where I first met Spiral Tribe) and the soundtrack was hardest-core gabba: martial music for tekno troopers, the militant sound of post-CJA rage. 'It's people beating back, 'cos they've been beaten just for having a good time,' DMZ organizer Nick told me. From the guerrilla lingo of their flyers and communiqués to the camouflage decor of the club, DMZ's stance was 'All about preparedness. DMZ stands for Demilitarized Zone. And that implies the rest of the world is a war zone, right?'

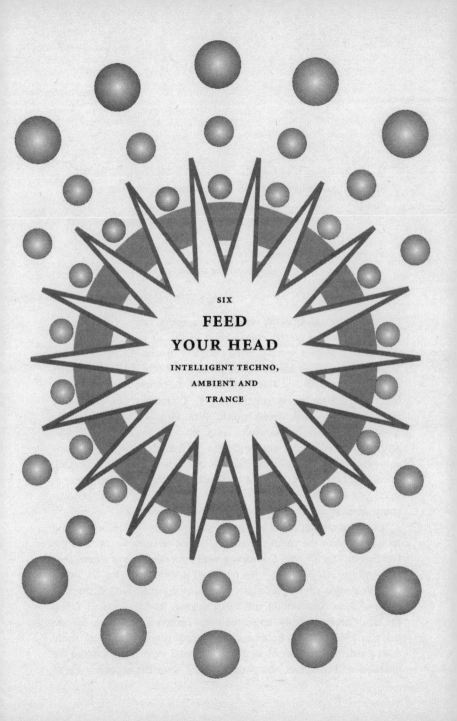

SIX

**FEED
YOUR HEAD**

INTELLIGENT TECHNO,
AMBIENT AND
TRANCE

'Are you sitting comfortably? Artificial Intelligence is for long journeys, quiet nights and club drowsy dawns. Listen with an open mind.'

    – sleevenote on Warp's *Artificial Intelligence* compilation, 1992

'No breakbeats, no Lycra.'

    – typical slogan for an 'intelligent techno' club, 1992

On the cover of *Artificial Intelligence*, a robot reclines in a comfy armchair, blowing perfect smoke rings in the air and chilling to the atmospheric sounds wafting from a sleek hi-fi unit. In his left hand, there's a fat spliff; at his feet, what looks like a can of Sapporo. Joint-making materials – Silk Cut, extra-long Rizla papers – are strewn on top of an album sleeve on the carpet. Two other LPs are clearly recognizable as classic 'head' music, Pink Floyd's *Dark Side of The Moon* and Kraftwerk's *Autobahn*. With no little wit, *Artificial Intelligence*'s cover tableau of domestic bliss-out heralds the birth of a new *post-rave* genre, which Warp Records christened 'electronic listening music'. Other names followed – armchair techno, ambient techno, intelligent techno, electronica – but all described the same phenomenon: *dance music for the sedentary and stay-at-home*.

The most striking thing about the gatefold sleeve (a deliberate prog rock echo) isn't the robot's sweatless, supine serenity so much as the fact that he's *on his own*. Coinciding with the emergence of a new 'chill out' culture, *Artificial Intelligence* offered a soundtrack for the raved out, for people who'd either given up on, or grown out of, the rave myth of mass communion and social mixing. And the reason? When the myth became reality, when the plebs turned up en masse for the party in 1991–2, 'rave' became a dirty word; Ecstasy was passé, more than a little undignified. Musically, battle lines were drawn around the question of breakbeats and samples: they were the stylistic core of 'ardkore, but for the post-rave refugees, they signified techno's corruption and commercialization.

Warp's baldly descriptive term 'electronic listening music' was rapidly displaced by a more loaded epithet, 'intelligent techno'. Beneath the rhetoric lurked the perennial bourgeois-bohemian impulse to delineate a firm border between the discerning few and the undiscriminating mass. Hence the not uncommon 1992 slogan for 'intelligent' or 'pure techno' clubs: the promise 'no breakbeats, no lycra'. On the surface, 'no breakbeats' merely indicated that a particular sound – the breakbeat-driven hardcore that dominated the big raves and pop charts alike – wasn't on the menu. But by implication, it proposed the purging of the black, hip-hop influence that had 'polluted' the Detroit-descended genealogy of pure techno. 'Lycra' was blatant snobbery: a reference to the clingy, sweat-absorbent clothing in which raver-girls shook their funky stuff, this was code language that summoned the folk-myth image of the 'techno Tracey' (the working-class latecomer who wants to join the scene but doesn't really get it). In just four words, 'no breakbeats, no lyrca' conflated racism, classism and sexism into a rallying cry for a mostly male connoiseur élite, self-appointed custodians of the techno canon.

Part of this return to the 'original principles' of Detroit and Chicago involved shunning the sampler in favour of analogue synthesizers, including the Roland 303 'acieed' bass-machine. Analogue sound was often characterized as 'warmer' than digital; the 'hands on' nature of these early synths, with their knobs, dials and filters, was also felt to be more 'musical'. When intelligent techno artists did resort to sampling, their use was governed by an ethos of masking and warping sources, in explicit opposition to the recognizable quotes and lifts that characterized 'ardkore's cut-up approach.

For all its rhetoric of 'progression', intelligent techno involved a full-scale retreat from the most radically posthuman and hedonistically funktional aspects of rave music towards more traditional ideas about creativity, namely the auteur theory of the solitary genius who humanizes technology rather than subordinates himself to the drug-tech interface. There was even a resurgence of rock notions like the 'concept album' and 'live musicianship', with bands like Underworld and Orbital developing new forms of onstage improvisation based around the live mixing of sequenced, pre-recorded parts.

Perhaps you can detect my reservations about these developments.

None of the above means to argue that electronic listening music wasn't a necessary initiative: the white-label hardcore boom had saturated the dance scene with derivative, poorly produced tracks composed of Nth-generation samples, and there was a gap crying out to be filled by contemplative, home-compatible music. Nor is it to deny the fact that a lot of truly beautiful and innovative music was made under the 'intelligent' banner. But because it was founded on exclusions (musical and social), electronic listening music ultimately paved the way for its own dead-end redundancy. What started as a fresh, innovative idea – techno liberated from the demands of the dancefloor – quickly turned into a new form of myopic orthodoxy. The root of the problem was the retreat from dance itself: resurrecting progressive rock's elevation of head over body, melodic complexity over rhythmic compulsion, the new home-listening electronica set itself on a course that led to New Age.

Furniture Music

For Warp, 'electronic listening music' was simultaneously an aesthetic initiative and a business strategy. Aiming to evade the fate that befell most independent dance labels – getting burned out by the high-turnover of dancefloor trends – Warp decided to take measures to foster brand and band loyalty. 'We'd seen from running the shop how dance labels had about a year of being on top,' says Steve Beckett. 'We were determined that wasn't gonna happen to us. The only way to avoid it was to get more artist-oriented and album-oriented'.

At hardcore's height in early 1992, remembers Beckett, 'you started to hear tracks by B12 and Plaid and Speedy J that just didn't fit into any category, B-sides and last tracks on EPs. We realized that they weren't meant for 12 inches, it was just that this was the only outlet for that kind of music. We realized you could make a really good album out of it. You could sit down and listen to it like you would a Kraftwerk or Pink Floyd album. That's why we put those sleeves on the cover of *Artificial Intelligence* – to get it into people's heads that you weren't *supposed* to dance to it!'

By early 1992, there was a demand, among worn-out veteran ravers, for music to accompany and enhance the comedown phase after clubbing 'n' raving. 'That's still the highpoint of most people's nights,' argues Beckett. 'That's when you start hearing the really interesting, mindblowing stuff. If you're coming down off [drugs], you can get really lost in your own thoughts and concentrate on the music, pay more attention to detail ... From our point of view, it also felt like a lot of the dance music around had gotten really throwaway, just white labels from people jumping on the bandwagon to make a quick five hundred or thousand quid out of it. It felt like somebody should start paying attention to the production and the artwork – the whole way the music was presented.'

Responding to *Artificial Intelligence* and similar compilations like *The Philosophy of Sound and Machine*, the music press and style magazines began to run pieces spotlighting an international network of anti-rave 'dissidents': artists like The Black Dog, B12, Kirk DeGiorgio and Mixmaster Morris, labels like Infonet, Irdial, Rephlex, Tresor, Beyond, Porky's Productions, Time. Speaking to *iD*, crusading ambient DJ Mixmaster Morris articulated the common sentiment that Detroit's original spirit had been obliterated by a welter of ultra-thrash drug-noise: '... Detroit techno was much more ambient than it was hardcore ... It had such lightness of touch, it was *radically* beautiful. In the rave scene now, everyone demands instant gratification, a cliché every four bars.' In *Lime Lizard*, Porky's Dave Brennand railed against the loved-up cheesy sentimentalism of hardcore, boasting that he had 'no interest in doing anything that has one ounce of mozzarella ...'

Although Beckett claims the title *Artificial Intelligence* was 'a tongue in cheek reference to the idea that this music is totally made by computers, you just press a button and a tune comes out,' the word 'intelligent' rapidly took on a dubious life of its own. Many shared the attitude of Mixmaster Morris, who in 1994 defined 'intelligent techno' as 'the opposite of stupid hardcore', and declared that 'techno got boring when hardcore took all the weirdness and creativity and innovation out of Acid House ...' Morris's slogan 'I Think Therefore I Ambient' recast progressive rock's neo-Cartesian split between head and body as the struggle between atmospheric mindfood (ambient) versus thoughtless rhythmic compulsion (hardcore). By 1993, with 'progressive house' and 'trance' set in place as dancefloor-friendly adjuncts to electronic listening music, a firm line had been drawn. On one side, still raving after all these sneers, was the moronic inferno of hardcore, with its heedless (head-less?) hedonism; on the other, the post-rave cognoscenti, with their intimate clubs and chill-out zones.

Listening to *Artificial Intelligence* now, it's hard to imagine why the album had such an impact. Speedy J's 'De-Orbit' and the two tracks by Musicology (alter-ego of Detroit-pietists B12) constituted little more than test-card muzak. *Electro-Soma*, B12's debut long-player that followed as part of Warp's Artificial Intelligence series of single-artist albums, took its name from soma: the Prozac-like tranquillizer in Aldous Huxley's *Brave New World*, which was derived from an Ancient Indian intoxicating plant juice venerated as a drink of immortality by Vedic worshippers. *Electro-Soma*'s effect is more akin to a queasy docility, like being forcibly anaesthetized with Glade air-freshener. *Artificial Intelligence* did however showcase material from three outfits destined to become major players in the realm of electronica: Autechre, The Black Dog and The Aphex Twin.

Autechre – the Manchester based duo of Sean Booth and Rob Brown – followed a typical trajectory for English techno boffins. Having grown up on electro, graffiti, and Mantronix, they were dislodged from their B-boy path by the phuture shock of acid house. Profiling the duo for *The Lizard*, writer Peter McIntyre identified a sort of constructivist/Cubist aesthetic running through Autechre's output, which he connected with Brown's studies in architectural design. 'We're big fans of geometry in both design and sound,' the duo confirmed. 'There's nothing better than tight geometry.' On albums like *Incunabula*, *Amber* and *Tri Repetae*, and EPs like *Garbage* and *Anvil Vapre*, they constructed unlovely but queerly compelling sound-sculptures: abstruse and angular concatenations of sonic glyphs, blocs of distortion and mutilated sample-tones, with occasional light relief in the form of pretty pulse-scapes of chime-colour like 'Yulquen'.

Comparisons with Leger and Mondrian aside, Autechre's music is most redolent of wildstyle graffiti, where typography is convoluted and abstracted to the point of illegibility. The graf parallel fits because their music is basically avant-garde electro: Man Parrish meets Pierre Henry, or The Art of Noise meets Luigi Russolo's 'The Art Of Noises'. The cryptographic opacity carried through to the song-titles: 'c/pach', 'gnit', 'rsdio', 'second scepe', 'vletrmx21'. Although *Artificial Intelligence*'s sleevenotes had insisted that the new electronica 'cannot be described as soulless or machine made', what's most interesting about Autechre's work is the absence of heart and humanity, the way that the listener's impulse to forge an emotional connection simply ricochets off the impenetrable, gnomic surfaces of their sound. At times you can't help wonder if the 'aut' in their name stands for autism: listening, the mind's eye conjures up a vision of two small boys surrounded by tekno toys, lost in their own little pre-verbal world of chromatics and texture and contour.

The Black Dog – the trio of Ed Handley, Andy Turner and Ken Downie – were almost as hermetic as Autechre, but more committed to traditional art notions of 'expression'. They once defined their project as the quest for 'a computer soul', while Ken Downie told *Eternity* that The Black Dog started in order to fill 'a hole in music. Acid house had been "squashed" by the police and rinky-dinky Italian house music was getting played everywhere. Emotion had left via the window.'

The musical emotions in The Black Dog (and alter-egos Plaid and Balil) aren't the straightforward, run-of-the-mill, everyday sort, but rather more elusive: subtle, indefinable shades of mood, ambiguous and evanescent feelings for which even an oxymoron like 'bittersweet' seems rather crude. Eschewing live appearance and seldom doing interviews, The Black Dog nonetheless created a cult aura around their often hard-to-find discography. One of their chosen mediums was cyberspace: long before the current craze for techno web-sites, The Black Dog established a computer bulletin board called Black Dog Towers. Visitors could gawp at artwork and learn more about the Dog's interest in arcane knowledges, such as paganism, out-of-body experiences, UFOs, Kabbalah, and 'aeonics' (mass shifts in consciousness). Ken Downie – the principal eso-terrorist in the band – has described himself as a magician. One of The Black Dog's earliest tracks, 'Virtual (Gods in Space)', features a sample – 'make the events occur that you want to occur' – which gives a magickal spin to the punk DIY ethos.

Although far from the euphoric fervour of rave, The Black Dog's early 1990–92 material is remarkably similar to the breakbeat hardcore of the day. Like Hyper-On Experience, DJ Trax et al, the mode of construction is basically the Mantronix collage aesthetic updated for the rave era: incongruous samples + looped breakbeats + oscillator riffs. But the mood of 'Seers + Sale', 'Apt', 'Chiba' and 'Age Of Slack' is quirky Dada absurdism rather than Loony Toons zany. The crisp, echoed breakbeat and keyboard vamp on 'Seers + Sale' recalls 2 Bad Mice classics like 'Waremouse', except that the riff sounds like it's played on a church organ, so the effect is eldritch rather than E-lated.

On 1991's 'Chiba', the Morse Code riff has a glancing lightness of inflection that anticipates the Detroit-breakbeat of Innerzone Orchestra's 'Bug In The Bassbin'.

Carl Craig, the producer behind Innerzone Orchestra, clearly recognized The Black Dog as kindred spirits in sonic watercolours; in 1992 his Planet E label released their classic Balil track 'Nort Route'. Strangely redolent of the early eighties – the Sinophile phunk of Sylvian and Sakomoto's 'Bamboo Music', the phuturistic panache of Thomas Leer – 'Nort Route' daubs synth-goo into an exquisite calligraphic melody-shape over an off-kilter breakbeat. The track trembles and brims with a peculiar emotion, a euphoric melancholy that David Toop came closest to capturing with his phrase 'nostalgia for the future'. What The Black Dog/Balil/Plaid tracks most resembled was a sort of digital update of fifties exotica. But instead of imitating remote alien cultures, as the original exotica did, it was like The Black Dog were somehow giving us advance glimpses of the hybrid musics of the next millennium: the Hispanic-Polynesian dance crazes of the Pacific Rim, or music for discotheques and wine bars in Chiba City and The Sprawl (the megalopolises in William Gibson's *Neuromancer* and *Count Zero*). While some of the Dog's later work – on albums like *Bytes*, *Parallel*, *The Temple of Transparent Balls* and *Spanners* – crosses the thin line between mood-music and muzak, it's still marked by a rhythmic inventiveness that's unusual in the electronic listening field. With its percussive density and discombobulated time signatures, The Black Dog's music often feels like it's designed for the asymmetrical dancing of creatures with an *odd* number of limbs – not bipeds, but quintupeds or nonopeds.

Surfing on Sinewaves

If anyone substantiated Warp's concept of electronic listening music, it was Richard James, aka Aphex Twin. On *Artificial Intelligence*, he appeared as The Dice Man, just one of a bewildering plethora of pseudonyms – AFX, Caustic Window, Soit P. P., Bluecalx, Polygon Window and Powerpill. Despite this penchant for alter-egos and a professed indifference to publicity, Richard James has been by far the most successful of the new breed of 'armchair techno' auteurs at cultivating a cult of personality. He's fostered this by painting a picture of an extremely abnormal childhood in the remote coastal county of Cornwall.

James's avant-garde impulses emerged almost as soon as he was potty-trained. As a small child he messed about on the family piano, exploring different tuning scales and hitting the strings inside instead of the keys. 'I used to play *with* the piano, rather than play tunes on the keyboard,' he told me. These infantile experiments uncannily parallel the 'prepared piano' techniques devised by John Cage and other twentieth-century composers. Many years later his infamous DJ performances – he'd place the stylus on sandpapers instead of vinyl and modulate the hellaciously abrasive din using a graphics equalizer – echoed Cage's 'Cartridge Music' piece, in which the turntable's stylus cartridge was rubbed against inappropriate objects and surfaces.

Like Cage and other avant-classical composers, James's interest has always been sound-in-itself, or as he puts it with characteristic down-to-earthiness: 'I've always been into banging things and making weird noises.' *Musique concrète* style tape manipulation was swiftly followed by teenage forays into Stockhausen-esque electro-acoustic experiments. 'I bought a synth when I was twelve, thought it was a load of shit, took it apart and started pissing about with it. I learned about electronics in school until I was quite competent and could build my own circuits from scratch. I started modifying analogue synths and junk that I'd bought, and got addicted to making noises.' This obsession with generating a repertoire of unique timbres eventually led James to study electronics at Kingston University.

The geographical/cultural remoteness of Cornwall is another crucial element in the mythos of Aphex as isolated child prodigy. James claims that when he first heard acid and techno, he was astounded because he'd quite independently been making similar sounds for years. James immediately threw himself into purchasing every techno record he could lay his hands on, and he started DJ-ing at clubs and beach-raves. Finally his mates persuaded him to put out his own tracks, which he'd been giving them on cassette for years.

James immediately won acclaim with the cosmic-jacuzzi swirl of 'Analogue Bubblebath', the title track of his 1991 debut EP. With its fluttery, diaphanous riff-pattern and hazy-yet-crystalline production, 'Bubblebath' announced a new softcore direction in techno – medita-tional, melodically-intricate and ambient-tinged. But the EP also revealed that James was no slouch when it came to industrial-strength hardcore. The chemical-formula title and astringent sound of 'Isoprophlex' suggests a nasty corrosive fluid, the kind whose container carries warnings like 'avoid inhalation' and 'irrigate the eye area immediately, then seek medical help'. James's next track, 'Didgeridoo', impacted the hardcore dancefloor in a big way. Inspired by hearing traveller-minstrels playing the didgeridoo at festival-raves in Cornwall, the track is by far the best of a 1992 techno mini-genre based around the strange similarity between the Australian aboriginal pipe and the acieed bass-squelch of the Roland 303. But it doesn't actually feature a didgeridoo; eschewing samples, James laboured for three days to concoct an electronic simulacrum of the primordial drone.

'Analogue Bubblebath' and 'Didgeridoo' mark out the poles of the Aphex sound-spectrum: synth-siphoned balm for the soul versus clangorously percussive noise. James's debut album, *Selected Ambient Works, 85–92* is tilted towards softcore. The opening track 'Xtal' is a shimmer of tremulously translucent synths, hissy hi-hat and muffled bass; a girl softly intones a daydreamy, 'la-la-la' melody, her slightly off-key voice seemingly diffracted by the gossamer haze of sound. The nine minutes long mood-piece 'Tha' is twilight-after-rain melancholia worthy of the Eno-collaboration instrumentals on Bowie's *Low*. Over a pensive bassline and water-drip percussion, a mist of susurrating sound drifts like the chinese-whispery hubbub of a railway station concourse or an abbey's cloisters. The voices are so reverb-atomized you catch only the outline of words before they crumble like chalk-dust and disperse.

Fusing narcosis and speed-rush, 'Pulsewidth' is ambient techno, literally; everything's soft-focus, the aural equivalent of vaseline-on-the-lens, yet the fluorescent bass-pulse is irresistibly dynamic, propelling you towards a breathtaking breakdown before surging off again. The sensation is like 'swimming through cotton wool' (Graham Greene's description of a botched suicide attempt when he took deadly nightshade and tried to drown himself in the school pool). 'Heliosphan' is impossibly stirring and stately, its cupola-high synth-cadence and wistful melody offset by impish twirls of nonchantly jazzy keyboards. Imagine the theme music for a fifties government film about Britain's new garden cities: serene, symmetrical, euphonious, evoking the socially engineered perfection of a post-war New Order.

Selected Ambient Works climaxes with 'We Are the Music Makers'. The track makes you wait and wait through long stretches of just beats and bass-fuzz, teasing you with intermittent flickers of twinkly synth in the cornermost crevice of the soundscape. Then there's a one-note dapple of reverb-hazy piano, like green-tinted sunlight peeking through a woodland canopy and caressing your half-closed eyelids, before the melody finally blossoms in full spangly-tingly glory.

Almost as striking as the music on *Selected* was the second half of the title: *85–92*. This was Richard James highlighting the fact that most of the record was culled from the backlogged output of his teenage years. In interviews, he talked about how he'd amassed a personal archive of around a thousand tracks, enough for a hundred albums. In truth, James had no real notion of how much music he'd made in the previous eight years; he had lost track of his tracks. 'Every time I go back to Cornwall,' he told me, 'my friends play me tapes of tunes I gave 'em, stuff I haven't heard for years. In their cars I'll find cassettes of material that I haven't even got copies of. Lots of them sound like the tape is just about to wear out, like it'll break if you play it one more time . . . See, once it's recorded, I lose all interest in it.'

More tantalizing glimpses into James's trove of unreleased material came with the two albums that followed swiftly on the heels of *Selected*: Polygon Window's *Surfing On Sine Waves* and AFX's *Analogue Bubble-bath 3*. If tracks like 'If It Really Is Me' verged on a sort of astral muzak, most of *Surfing* was harder and darker than its ambient predecessor. The stand-out track, 'Quoth' features no melody, no synths, no bass even, just frenzied metallic percussion. It makes me think of Alfred Bester's science fiction classic *Tiger, Tiger*, where the anti-hero Gulliver Foyle encounters a *Lord of the Flies* community of asteroid-belt castaways, who've built themselves a planetoid out of space junk; 'Quoth' could be the savage pounding of tribal rhythms against the hulls of shipwrecked spacecraft.

Clad only in bubblewrap and devoid of track information, *Analogue Bubblebath 3* also cleaved to the industrial end of the Aphex sound-spectrum. Most of the thirteen tracks are undanceably angular anti-grooves, adorned with blurts of noise and interlaced with the occasional ribbon of minimal melody. One track sounds like a gamelan symphony for glass and rubber percussion; another begins with the sound of a vacuum cleaner, before letting rip with an out-of-tune pianola-like oscillator-riff, conjuring the image of a rave in a cavern beneath the crater-pocked lunar surface of Ganymede. Like the hair-raisingly forbidding 'Hedphelym' on *Selected Ambient Works*, track eleven is like stumbling upon a pagan shrine on an alien world. But there's two lapses back into the outright beauty of *Selected Ambient Works*. Track four has a forlorn, Satiesque melody floating at quarter-tempo over an incongruously strident, unrelenting beat. And track eight is kosmik *kinder-muzik*, a sublime confection of music-box melody and thunderous dub that always makes me think of an ice-cream van doing the rounds on The Clangers' planet.

Fostering his crackpot genius image, Richard James claimed he could survive on a mere two or three hours of sleep a night. 'When I was little I decided sleep was a waste of your life. If you lived to a hundred but you didn't sleep, it'd be like living to two hundred. Originally, it wasn't for more time to make music, I just thought sleep was a bit of a con. I'd always been able get away with four hours a night, but I tried to narrow it down to two. It gets very strange when I don't sleep for a long while, 'cos it's not that I'm actually that good at staying awake. I can only do it if I'm making music. But it's fucking excellent, not sleeping, it's sort of nice and not-nice at the same time. Your minds starts getting scatty, like you're senile. You do unpredictable things, like making tea but pouring it in a cereal bowl instead of a cup.'

I reckon sleep-deprivation has a lot to do with the eerie, spaced-out aura of James's music. Some neurologists believe humans have an innate need to dream. Which is why you feel 'unreal' when you've stayed up all night or are jetlagged: the brain is trying to dream while you're still conscious. Aphex Twin music appears to be created in a mind-state that's constantly flitting between 'hypnagogic' and 'hypnopompic'. Hypnagogic is the half-awake phase just before you drop off in bed at night, when the mind's eye fills with hyper-real imagery (but not the surreal visions you get in the classic R.E.M. dream-state). Hypnapompic is that early morning sensation of dis-reality gestured at in My Bloody Valentine's lyric 'when you're awake you're still in a dream'. James often makes tunes in a somnambulistic trance. 'When I'm in the studio my eyes get tired from looking at monitors and sometimes I'll finish a track with my eyes shut. I know where all the dials are, and so I can do a track by touch.'

Turn On, Tune In, Drop Off

Released at the end of 1992, *Selected Ambient Works* coincided not just with the electronic listening boom but with a resurgence of interest in 'chill-out' music as a supplement or sequel to the rave. The idea had been first mooted in 1989 in the form of a short-lived fad for 'ambient house'. At Land of Oz, Paul Oakenfold's acid house night at Heaven, there was a VIP area called The White Room. Here Dr. Alex Paterson – soon to be the mainman in The Orb – provided soul-soothing succour for the acieed-frazzled by spinning records by Brian Eno, Pink Floyd, The Eagles, War, 10cc and Mike Oldfield, all at very low volume and accompanied by multi-screen video projections. Hippy-rock guru Steve Hillage is said to have dropped by one night, only to hear Paterson playing *Rainbow Dome Musick*, an album Hillage had composed for the New Age-y Festival for Mind-Body-Spirit in 1979.

In 1989–90, the Spacetime parties were also taking place at Cable Street in the East End of London. Specifically designed to encourage people to talk rather than dance, the events were organized by Jonah Sharp and featured live music by Mixmaster Morris. Meanwhile, in his magazine *Evolution* (originally *Encyclopaedia Psychedelica*), counterculture vet Fraser Clark was evangelizing his vision of rave as the expression of a new Gaia-worshipping eco-consciousness. Clark coined the term 'zippie' to describe a new kind of hippy who rejected sixties' Luddite pastoralism and embraced the cyberdelic, mind-expanding potential of technology.

There was music too, dubbed New Age house or ambient house: Sueno Latino's 'Sueno Latino' (a dance version of acid-rocker Manuel Gottsching's proto-techno masterpiece *E2–E4*), 808 State's 'Pacific State', The Grid's 'Floatation', Quadrophenia's 'Paradise', Audio One's 'Journeys Into Rhythm', Innocence's 'Natural Thing' (featuring a sample from Pink Floyd's 'Shine On You Crazy Diamond'). Most of this stuff was pretty tepid: slow-mo house grooves overlaid with bird-song samples, serendipitous piano chords, mawkish woodwind solos, plangent acoustic guitars, and breathy female vocals whispering New Age positivity poesy. Two records stood out from the dross: The KLF's *Chill Out* album and The Orb's 'A Huge Ever Growing Pulsating Brain That Rules From the Centre of the Ultraworld'.

Although it initially seemed like it was going to be just another cheap joke from prankster duo Bill Drummond and Jimmy Cauty, The KLF's *Chill Out* turned out to be an atmospheric trans-American travelogue woven out of samples from sound effects records and MOR songs like Elvis Presley's 'In The Ghetto', Acker Bilk's 'Stranger On The Shore' and Fleetwood Mac's 'Albatross'. The sleeve spoofed Pink Floyd's *Atom Heart Mother* (with grazing sheep replacing the Floyd's ruminating cow), and a sticker on the front hinted 'File Under Ambient'. The Orb's 'A Huge Ever Growing Pulsating Brain' came emblazoned with the slogan 'Ambient House For The E Generation'. Twenty-four minutes long, the track is a shimmerscape of sound effects (crowing roosters, church bells, splashing pebbles), angelic close harmony singing, the helium-high croon of Minnie Ripperton's 'Loving You', and a synth-pulse as radiant as a nimbus (the luminous vapour that surrounds God). The net effect is sheer nirvana or near-death experience, like your cerebral cortex is being flooded with pain-and-doubt killing endorphins.

Like The KLF, The Orb consisted of punk rock veterans: Alex Paterson had been a roadie and drum technician for Killing Joke, and sometimes sang Sex Pistols encores when the band toured. Through the Killing Joke connection, he got an A & R job at their label E. G., home to ambient pioneers Brian Eno and Harold Budd. After appearing uncredited on The KLF's *Chill Out* and *Space* albums, Paterson collaborated with Jimmy Cauty on 'A Huge Ever Growing Brain'. Teaming up with engineer Kris Weston, aka Thrash, Paterson then transformed The Orb into a real band.

'A Huge Ever Growing Brain' was released in December 1989. When The Orb's debut album *Adventures Beyond The Ultraworld* finally materialized in the spring of 1991, it seemed monumentally tardy: the *magnum* (and I mean whopping – it was a 110 minute long dubble-elpee) *opus* of a clubland fad long past its sell-by date. In fact, *Adventures* was the harbinger of an imminent deluge of dub-flavoured ambient techno. Following *Chill Out*'s Pink Floyd homage, the sleeve depicted Battersea Power Station, previously seen on the cover of *Animals*; inside, there was a track entitled 'Back Side Of The Moon'. These nudge-nudge wink-wink acknowledgements of the Floyd connection seemed designed to pre-empt the carping complaints of punk veterans: THIS is what Sid Vicious died for?

But for all the protective irony and the contemporary house beats, there was no mistaking the fact that *Adventures* was the unabashed return of cosmic rock. Titles like 'Earth (Gaia)' and 'Little Fluffy Clouds' (with its samples of Rickie Lee Jones's blissful reveries of the Arizona skyline of her childhood) harked back to the cosmic pastoralism and nostalgia for lost innocence that characterized late sixties outfits like The Incredible String Band. The quirked-out humour and daft sound effects recalled seventies space-rockers Hawkwind and Gong; Steve Hillage, a Gong veteran, actually shared production duties on 'Supernova At The End Of The Universe' and 'Back Side Of The Moon'. On 'Supernova', braided wisps of evanescent sound – distant cloudbreak, radio murmurings, cascades of stardust, silvered shivers of harp – were draped incongruously over a kickin' beat. 'Back Side' featured crackly samples of astronauts talking about Tranquility Base, the landing site on the Moon's Sea of Tranquility. With its beatific, beat-free lassitude and zero-gravity suspension, *Adventures* was like a cut-price aural surrogate for the flotation tank, then in vogue with stressed out yuppies. The Orb's music lowered your metabolic rate to the level of a particularly well-adjusted and 'centred' sea anemone.

'I've been waiting for music like this all my life', ran a sample in 'Back Side'. Immodest, maybe, but it was no idle boast: thousands apparently *had* been waiting, and next summer, the band's follow-up, *u. f. orb*, went straight into the British Album Charts at Number One. It was preceded by a single, 'Blue Room', which got to Number Eight in the hit parade, despite being just under forty minutes long and featuring only one real hook: 'ah wah wah a wah wah', the wordless siren-song of reggae vocalist Aisha, the protégé of UK dub wizard the Mad Professor. Paterson and Thrash appeared on *Top of the Pops*, but instead of miming with instruments, they played a *Star Trek*-style 3D chess-set in front of back-projected film of aquabatic dolphins. Named after the room at the Wright Patterson airforce base where the remains of crash-landed aliens are allegedly kept by the US government, 'Blue Room' alternates between ambience (synth-motes like spangly space debris) and aquafunk (an undulant, slow-mo groove that feels like skanking underwater). With Steve Hillage's cirrus-streaks of heavily sustained guitar offset by Jah Wobble's thunderquake bass, 'Blue Room' was an astonishing reconciliation of hippy and post-punk; imagine Public Image Ltd if Johnny Rotten had never famously scrawled 'I Hate' in felt-pen over his Pink Floyd T-shirt.

On *u. f. orb* itself, 'Towers of Dub' began with a Victor Lewis-Smith phone prank. The posh-voiced comedian calls London Weekend

Television and, pretending to be Marcus Garvey, asks if Haile Selassie is waiting in reception: 'He's a, erm, black gentleman.' After the hapless receptionist has shouted out for the long-dead Abyssinian monarch and Rastafarian Messiah, Lewis-Smith asks him to pass on the message that 'I'll meet him at Babylon an' ting.' Combining and conflating the studio-as-instrument effects of several forms of 'head' music – acid rock, dub reggae, ambient – The Orb offered a musiquarium of sound that seemed to have migrated from an alternative pop universe: one where Pink Floyd, Brian Eno and King Tubby got together to form a seventies supergroup bringing 'cosmic ambient dub' to the stadium circuit.

By this point, The Orb *had* built up a formidable reputation as a live band. After 'Blue Room', they scored another big hit with 'Assassin', an uncharacteristically uptempo onslaught of tribal house rhythms and quicksilver, scimitar-flashing riffs. The best of the five mixes was recorded live at the 1992 Glastonbury Festival. The following year saw *Live 93*, a double-CD/quadruple-LP that recalled The Grateful Dead in the way that The Orb improvised wildly around a core of pre-recorded sequences. Catching the Orb tour when it reached New York's Roseland Theater in the autumn of 1993, I did spot straggly-bearded Deadhead types headnodding in the audience alongside the sixteen-year-old ravers. And I was struck by how everything about The Orb – from the cloud-castle immensity of the sound to the ama-a-a-a-zing visuals – was spectacular but impersonal. The band themselves figured as 'specks on their own landscape' (as David Stubbs said of the German neo-psychedelic group Faust). Throughout the show, Paterson and Thrash remained shrouded, bobble-hatted figures lurking behind their banks of gear, technicians in the stereo-laboratory as opposed to stars. Like a planetarium or a piece of majestic architecture, The Orb's music seemed to invite awe rather than involvement. And yet the grandiosity was veined with Monty Pythonesque daftness and post-punk irony, prompting me to wonder: can you really kiss the sky with your tongue-in-cheek?

Lie Down and Be Counted

The immediate effect of The Orb's success was to spawn a plague of ambient dub, aka digi-dub. While the fad generated a handful of genuinely sublime moments – Higher Intelligence Agency's 'Ketamine

Entity', Original Rockers 'The Underwater World of Jah Cousteau' – the trouble with the genre was that it was one of those hybrids, like jazz-funk and funk-metal, that only *seem* like a good idea. Too often, instead of Harold Budd meets Prince Far I, the results were more like Vangelis teaming up with Adrian Sherwood on an off-night: celestial synth-vapour (ambient) + meaninglessly overdone echo FX and stereophonic tomfoolery (dub).

The original roots music of seventies Jamaica had a spiritual halo, a halcyon haze, that the British digi-dub outfits tried and failed to recover; smoking vast quantities of weed wasn't enough. Partly this was because producers like Tubby, Lee Perry and Keith Hudson used lo-fi technology: self-cobbled effects, four-track recording (which meant that several instrumental parts had to be compressed on to one track, thereby creating classic dub's blissful blurriness). And partly it was because the Jamaican dubmeisters combined flesh-and-blood musicians with studio wizardry to achieve an uncanny fusion of presence and absence, funky feel and disembodied drift. The high-definition gloss and inelastic, sequenced rhythms of digital dub can't compare with the earthy-but-otherwordly vibe the Jamaicans got by taking a supple, interactive rhythm section and feeding it through the hall-of-mirrors vortex of the mixing desk. The analogue echo and reverb units cobbled together by the original Jamaican dub producers created a smudgy reverberance that feels closer to real-world acoustics. So instead of roots reggae's sacrosanct expanse, most ambient dub evoked only the virtual, geometrically plotted space of MIDI hardware: the music smelled sterile, not ambrosial.

The difference between classic dub and digital dub is like that between a stained-glass window and a computer graphic. This ecclesiastical analogy is appropriate in so far as the mystical aura of echo and reverberance is a thread connecting most twentieth-century musics that aspire to Timelessness: psychedelia, dub reggae, ambient, and the New Age sub-genre of 'resonant music' (recorded in temples, cathedrals and giant cisterns). As R. Murray Shafer points out in *The Soundscape*, Gothic and Norman churches were deliberately designed to swaddle the worshipper in 'a non-localizable sound-bath' of low-and-medium frequency echoes. And our prehistoric ancestors enacted rites in caves and grottoes chosen for their unusual acoustics.

The question remains: why do echo and reverb evoke the Timeless? I'd argue that, by simulating the way sound-waves behave underwater, the effects in dub and ambient hark back to our personal prehistory in the amniotic sea of the womb. It's not for nothing that studio engineers talk of a recording being 'dry' when it's devoid of reverb. The foetus can't hear until the twenty-fourth week of pregnancy, but after that it reacts to external sounds and bonds with the mother's voice, which must reach its ears blurred and refracted through the fleshly prism of her body. With its submarine sonar FX and numinous reverberance, dub reggae reinvokes the blurry sonic intimacy of womb-time, the lost paradise before individuation and anxiety. This might also account for why dub foregrounds the bass (its frequencies are less localizable, more immersive and engulfing) and why dub reggae runs at tempos – around 70–75 b.p.m. – that approximate the baby's heartbeat in the womb.

Ambient music is like the amnion, the delicate membrane surrounding the foetus in the womb. Even after birth, sound (alongside touch and smell) has primacy over vision, because the infant's eyesight takes some time to develop. Guy Rosalato writes of how the infant is swaddled in a 'sonorous envelope'; the mother's pre-verbal utterances are sonic caresses that constitute a 'pleasurable milieu which surround, sustains and cherishes'. Music, he argues, 'finds its roots and its nostalgia in [this] original atmosphere, which might be called a sonorous womb, a murmuring house – or music of the spheres.' Hence the Gaia/Earth Mother and heavenly imagery that pervades ambient; the music's angelic harmonies and kindly serenity all reinvoke Julia Kristeva's 'archaic ... englobing mother with no frustation, no separation...'

In *Civilisation and Its Discontents*, Freud wrote of a long-lost selfless self, the phase of primary narcissism in which the infant does not distinguish between itself, the mother and the world. 'Originally the ego includes everything ... the ego-feeling we are aware of now is ... only a shrunken vestige of a far more extensive feeling – a feeling which embraced the universe and expressed an inseparable connection of the ego with the external world.' Both dub and ambient attempt a magical return to this diffuse but majestic self-without-contours, the 'royal we' of the infant/mother symbiosis, or the lost kingdom of the womb. In Rastafarian reggae, though, this lost god-self is identified with Jah, a righteous *paternal* principle; nostalgia becomes anticipation, the dream of returning to the promised land, Zion. By comparison, ambient music – like its ancestor, psychedelia – tends to be feminine-identified, expressing its homesick longings through imagery of pastoral tranquility, oceanic bliss, childhood, and the celestial. Where roots reggae is spiritually militant, ambient music is an aural pacifier.

This is why the ambient boom of 1992–3 was regarded by many outside the dance scene as a cop out. Equating contemplation with complacency, *nouveau* punks like Manic Street Preachers and These Animal Men lambasted ambient-heads as *nouveau* hippies. For their part, the ambient producers were disarmingly frank about the apolitical nature of their bohemia. Alex Paterson declared: 'Our music doesn't reflect the times, it ignores them ... Society today is so suppressed, you can only make music that is escapist.' And Mixmaster Morris – like Paterson, a thirtysomething ex-punk – campaigned for the ambient cause under the slogan 'It's Time To Lie Down and Be Counted'.

Morris's 1992 debut as The Irresistible Force, *Flying High*, starts with samples from a meditation training album: a kindly, calming male voice advises you to relax your muscles so that they become your cushion, listen to all the sounds that surround you, and concentrate solely on the one that you find most pleasant. The album runs the gamut of ambient's sonic and metaphorical tropes: wispy curlicues of crybaby guitar, simulated and sampled bird-tweets, tremolo synth-ripples, wooshing ascents, spangly texture-swathes and one-note, single-phoneme pulses *à la* Laurie Anderson's 'O Superman'. On 'Sky High', what sounds like a scuba-diving barbershop quartet implores 'let's touch the sky'; 'Symphony In E' samples fifties comic actress Joyce Grenfell in schoolmistress mode, her strawberries-and-cream voice instructing her dance class of little girls to do free-expression.

One of the first and best albums produced during the second-wave of nineties chill-out culture, *Flying High* reminds me less of the Eno/Harold Budd/Laraji tradition of ambient minimalism, than of Space-men 3's 1989 classic *Playing With Fire*, the album on which the band abandoned Stooges/Velvet Underground mantra-rock for an Elysian tranquillity redolent of early Kraftwerk. Like Spacemen 3's music, *Flying High* is based around heavily processed verging on denatured sounds, mesmerizing loop-patterns, stereophonic effects, and drones. The similarity is less surprising when you consider that Spacemen 3 and The Irresistible Force share influences in Kraftwerk, Suicide and Laurie Anderson, while Morris would doubtless concur with the Spacemen's slogan 'taking drugs to make music to take drugs to'.

As part of his crusade for floaty soft-core, Mixmaster Morris DJ-ed at the first Telepathic Fish, an 'ambient tea party' organized by DJ/

design collective Open Mind. Kevin Foakes, Chantal Passamonte, David Vallade and Mario Tracey-Ageura formed Open Mind in the summer of 1992, after becoming disillusioned with rave culture's 'harder, faster' ethos. The first Telepathic Fish took place in the foursome's South East London house (Morris spun in the kitchen), but was such an unexpected success – five hundred people, queues round the block – that Open Mind had to locate subsequent tea parties in squatted venues, which they decorated and filled with mattresses. 'Basically, what we're trying to create at our events is a massive bedroom,' Foakes told me in 1993. 'After raves we used to chill out in each others' bedrooms. Now we've turned the bedroom into a party.'

Ravers had been chilling out informally since the early days of rave, inventing their own rituals to enhance the post-E afterglow and cushion the come-down. 'People are doing this at home all round the country,' said Passamonte. 'But we decided to do it for several hundred people, not just ten.' After a year of serious raving, the friends 'realized that what we *really* enjoyed was that thing of everyone coming back *after* the party. That's when you could really talk to people, and play mellower music. It's chatty, there's loads of people coming down from drugs, you get to hang out more and meet people.' And so they decided to dispense with the sweaty, expensive part of the night out and go straight to the 'good bit'. The same bright idea had occurred to other outfits across the country: Sonora in Glasgow, Oscillate in Birmingham, Zero Gravity in London. Together, they constitued the Second Coming of Chill Out.

In October 1993, the fifth Telepathic Fish took place at Cooltan, an art-space/gallery/dancehall set up by squatters in an abandoned unemployment benefit office on Brixton's Coldharbour Lane, where Prime Minister John Major had once signed on. (The name Cooltan came from the original location, a disused suntan lotion factory fifty yards down the street from where I lived in Brixton.) Mentally creased and physically crumpled after a night's raving, my friends and I found Telepathic Fish Number 5 the perfect place for 'getting your head together'. In stark contrast to the stress-makingly staccato (strobes, cut-up beats) assault of your average 'ardkore rave, Telepathic Fish was a wombadelic sound-and-light bath. The DJs massaged our ears with a seamless mix of mostly beat-and-vocal free atmospherics (ranging from the latest CDs from ambient techno labels like Fax and Recycle Or Die, to Gothic art-rock like Dead Can Dance and Main's experimental dronescapes), which they maintained at just the right volume for conversation. The lights, oil projections, and 'deep-sea decor' soothed eyes sore from the previous night's brain-blitz. There were tea and cakes and wholesome refreshments available at reasonable prices. Nothing really *happened* – a few punters did a bit of floaty dancing, most just got recumbent on the grubby mattresses and spliffed up – but it was a lovely way to spend a Sunday.

'Traditional clubs just don't work for us,' Chantal Passamonte had told me a few weeks earlier. 'Most promoters are interested in people getting overheated so they buy overpriced drinks.' Eventually, it got too hard to find venues that would accept the concept of cheap admission and low takings at the bar, and Open Mind chose the path of least resistance: doing mini-Fishes as chill-out side-rooms at one-off raves and regular events like Megatripolis. Eventually the tea-party concept was 'borrowed' by The Big Chill, whose Sunday ambient-extravaganzas initially took place in a North London church. By 1995, chill-out culture had evolved into what some called 'freestyle' or 'eclectro'. The headnodding, pot-smoking anti-dance stance endured, but the soundtrack was more beats-oriented: you were more likely to hear trip hop, weird electronica, nouveau electro, mellow jungle, even E-Z listening and soundtrack music, than you were ambient.

Underlying the 'ardkore/ambient split is a perennial class-based divide in British pop culture. It recalls the difference between the sixties mods (insomniac speedfreak urbanites who worked 9–5 jobs all week then danced all weekend) and the hippies (with their cult of indolence, marijuana and sleep). Where 'ardkore's buzzphrases often mimic the language of graft and toil ('get busy', 'work it up', ''ardkore pressure'), the ambient scene staged a quiet revolt against the 'work hard, play harder' mentality, where you're a slave to the rush hour then rush your nut off at the weekend. 'People who can afford to pay fifteen quid for a rave have all this aggression to get out of their systems from working all week,' Kevin Foakes said. 'The crowd that comes to our tea parties is more laid-back and bohemian.'

Chill-out zones and ambient parties resemble R. Murray Shafer's pipe-dream of 'the soniferous garden': acoustically designed bowers where the city-dwellers can go to have their ears cleansed of 'noise pollution', where you can get your soul's pH balance restored. 'Our parties are as close to getting it together in the country as you can get in London,' said Passamonte. With its samples of bird-song and trickling water, ambient techno is a digital update of nineteenth-century programme music – the pastoral symphony that imitates Nature, as with the aqua-mysticism and forest idylls of Claude Debussy works like *La mer, Jardins sous la pluie* and *Prelude a l'après-midi d'un faune.*

Perhaps the first and best stab at that seeming contradiction-in-terms, pastoral techno, was Ultramarine's *Every Man and Woman is a Star,* first released in 1991. The album is loosely conceptual, offering a soundtrack to an imaginary canoe journey across America; the duo, Ian Cooper and Paul Hammond, went so far as to thank Birkenstock Sandals and Perception Kayaks in the sleeve notes. There's also a fictitious anecdote about enjoying the hog-roast and moonshine hospitality of Dewey and Cassie, original back-to-Nature hippies still living off the land in Sweetleaf Country, Arkansas. Dewey waxes philosophical, telling them: 'There is music for the body and there is music for the mind. Music for the body picks you off the floor and hurls you into physical activity. Music for the mind floats you gently downstream, through pleasurable twists and turns, ups and downs, rapids and calm waters ... And sometimes there is music for the body *and* for the mind.' In a 1993 interview, though, Ultramarine seemed to align themselves with the mind: Hammond told me, 'We don't go clubbing. We like techno because of the minimalism and the starkness of its structure. The fact that you can dance to it is irrelevant to us.'

On *Every Man and Woman,* Ultramarine seamlessly mesh acoustic instruments (cascades of twelve-string guitar, dolorous violin), real-world samples (owl-hoots, babbling brooks) and synthetic sounds like Roland 303 basslines and programmed beats. The results are like acid house suffused with the folky-jazzy ambience of Roy Harper, John Martyn and the Canterbury scene (The Soft Machine, Robert Wyatt, Kevin Ayers). 'Weird Gear' is actually based around an Ayers lyric, while 'Lights In My Brain' samples a strung-out, unhinged Wyatt incantation and weaves it into an eerie acieed-jazz groovescape. (On 1993's *United Kingdoms,* the duo went one better and actually got Wyatt to sing the traditional folk-songs 'Happy Land' and 'Song of The Lower Classes', and to blow scat-bubbles over the bucolic whimsy of 'The Badger' and 'Dizzy Fox').

Every Man is all sun-ripened, meandering lassitude and undulant dub-sway tempos. 'Honey' captures a halcyon 'moment in love' and loops it for eternity; long-lost AOR singer Judy Tzuke murmurs 'need you tonight' (sampled from her 1979 one-hit wonder 'Stay With Me Til Dawn'), a flute flickers and darts like a kingfisher and a violin tugs at the heart-strings. My affection for this gorgeous song was only slightly diminished when I discovered that the wistful acoustic-guitar and bass riff that constitutes the groove is actually sampled from 'Muskrat Love' by dismal soft-rock band America – yet more evidence of Ultramarine's seventies rehabilitation project, which extended to The Eagles, Joni Mitchell and Mike Oldfield's *Hergest Ridge*.

'Skyclad' is another *Every Man* highpoint: over jazz-funk slap bass, synth-blips reel and twinkle like a clear night-sky, inducing a sublime sensation of 'intimate immensity', of being swathed in the Milky Way. 'We *are* a bit mystical,' Ian Cooper admitted, 'but not in a way we could define. It's more like we're into the heights that can be attained through simple pleasures, such as listening to music or looking at a particular landscape that means something to you.' *Every Man* is littered with samples testifying to this creed of mystical materialism and spiritual hedonism. 'Weird Gear' has Kevin Ayers declaring 'everyone is high until something makes them blue', while 'Stella' pivots around a woman explaining how dance helped her to shed cumbersome mental baggage and live in the fullness of the here-and-now by finding 'that emptiness where I can begin again'.

Like the early nineties positivity bands, the new chill-out music often verged on New Age affirmation therapy. (In fact, the samples in 'Stella' come from a Channel Four programme on New Age culture.) One of the most popular and prolific providers for chill-out DJs, Pete Namlook, had actually started out in the New Age band Romantic Warrior. Through his Frankfurt label Fax, Namlook churned out CDs – solo and in collaboration with the likes of Mixmaster Morris, Dr Atmo and Richie Hawtin – at the rate of two a week. All lambent horizons of celestial synth, psalmic melodies and wordless seraphim-on-high harmonies, 1993 albums like *Silence* and *Air* transformed your living room into a sacro-sanctuary of sensuously spiritual sound. At his best, Namlook's project resembled a digital update of 'chamber jazz' label ECM and their quest for 'the most beautiful sound next to silence'. But after a while the hushed solemnity of tracks like 'Spiritual Invocation' and 'Sweet Angels' starts to feel as piously protracted as a church service, and the 'welcome to the temple of sound, please take off your dancing shoes' vibe gives you itchy feet. And just as New Age labels like Windham Hill imitated ECM's distinctive cathedral-high production and cover images of barren tundra, desolate seascapes et al, similarly *après* Namlook came *le deluge* of pseudo-spiritual sopors passing themselves off as ambient techno.

Ambient Fear

Just as chill-out music was getting too flotation-tank comfy, Aphex Twin returned to the fray in early 1994 and took the concept of ambient techno on a sharp bend to the sinister. Breaking with the then dominant notion of the ambient album as a capsule of pastoral tranquillity, *Selected Ambient Works Volume II* returned to Brian Eno's original neutral definition in the sleevenotes of *On Land*, where he envisioned ambience simply as 'environmental music'.

Probably the best of Eno's ambient series, certainly the most uncanny, *On Land* involved aural recreations of childhood memories of specific places. Richard James turned to dreamscapes for inspiration. Around 70 per cent of *Selected Ambient Works Volume II* (a triple LP/double CD which James originally planned as a *quintuple* album) was created using self-taught 'lucid dreaming' techniques. 'I've been able to control my dreams since I was a kid,' James boasted. 'Just before I started work on the album I tried experimenting with the idea of dreaming about recording tracks. The main problem is remembering what I've dreamt about. Melodies are easy, but the actual sounds can be a little more difficult. Sometimes I sleep in the studio so that I can start work as soon as I wake up and there's less of chance of forgetting anything.'

James's haunting forays into dreamspace bore little resemblance to the hackneyed halcyon imagery purveyed by most ambient techno. Instead of songs, *Volume II* confronted the listener with apparitions, miasmas of ear-confounding ectoplasm that wove an appalling enchantment. Instead of titles, tracks were identified by pictograms: photographs of fabrics, metal surfaces, detritus, and so forth. The music itself was just as cryptic in its material-ist focus on timbre and texture. Track no. 1/Disc no. 1 is a *trompe l'oreille* lattice of glassy chimes and single phonemes of female vocal, which are looped, echoed and braided. The effect is as disorientating as it is graceful, like an acrobat gyrating in a zero-gravity hall-of-mirrors. Instead of ambient techno's fatuous gestures at the cosmic, James seems to focus on the microcosmos: *Volume II* is full of compositions that instil an odd mixture of awe and dread, as though you're peering through a microscope at the impossibly alien yet horribly intimate processes – cell-division, the DNA helix – that constitute our biological reality.

With dance beats rarer than hen's teeth, *Volume II* makes its predecessor seem almost boppy. James foregoes techno's kinetic imperatives for a petrified and petrifying beauty: a good subtitle for the album would be 'The Secret Life of Minerals'. Melody is mostly shunned in favour of percussive/harmonic chimes and amorphous drones. On Track no. 4/Disc no. 1, a featureless edifice of dread gradually takes shape amidst a pall of mist; Track no. 10/Disc no. 1 has the deadly opalescent allure of the glow-worm's web, down whose hollow filaments the luminous larvae glide towards their fatal trysts with trapped insects. There are only a handful of lapses into straightforward beauty. Track no. 3/Disc no. 1 recalls the devotional music of minimalist neo-classical composers like Arvo Part: its restrained grandeur creates a paradoxical effect, a sort of thunderous hush. Track no. 7/Disc no. 1 makes me think of Holst's 'Neptune, the Mystic' from *The Planets*, evoking the same image of a skater gliding over a lake of frozen methane. And Track no. 8/Disc no. 2 is like 'tomorrow's nostalgia today', a Hovis Ad for the mid-twenty-first century: 'Eee, it were grand back in t'1990s.'

Most of *Volume II* has more in common with the techniques of late twentieth-century avant-classical composers like Ligeti, Berio, Xenakis and Stockhausen. James talked of devising his own tunings and scales, of exploring the 'infinite number of notes between C and C sharp' and getting down 'to ultra-pure frequencies and sine waves'. Needless to say, many of his fans were alienated by these subdued and sombre sound-paintings. As audacious and magnificent as the album is, it simply isn't as hospitable a record as its predecessor. *Selected Ambient Works 85–92* infuses everyday life with a perpetual first flush of spring; I for one had listened to that album twice a day for several months.

But Aphex Twin's shift towards ambient *noir* did win him admirers in the hermetic realm of isolationist music, a loose confederation of experimental outfits like Thomas Koner and :zoviet*france, and lapsed rockers like Main, who'd abandoned riffs and rhythm in favour of drones and dirgescapes. Echoing Main's Robert Hampson, Richard James enthused to *The Face* about hanging out in power stations: 'If you just stand in the middle of a really massive one, you get a really

weird presence and you've got that hum ... That's totally dreamlike
for me ... just like a right strange dimension.'

Texturology

Selected Ambient Works Volume II represented a particularly focused
and uncompromising investigation of an area that had rapidly become
the defining obsession of electronic listening music: sound-in-itself.
Sometimes these were 'found sounds' from the environment, or
drastically processed samples from records, TV and other media. And
sometimes they were timbres immanent within antiquated analogue
synthesizers. Synaesthesia – the confusion of the senses – was a
common aesthetic goal, with producers striving to generate timbres
and textures so tantalizing you want to touch or taste them. Hence
Beaumont Hannant's series of 'Tastes and Textures' EPs and album
Texturology.

Some of the best of the new breed of texturologists were Aphex
Twin associates: Mike Paradinas of μ-Ziq released his early records
through Richard James's label Rephlex, Luke Vibert of Wagon Christ
was a friend from Cornwall, and Tom Middleton of Global Communi-
cations/Reload had once been the *other* Twin, having worked on the
Analogue Bubblebath EP. For the Reload album *A Collection of Short
Stories*, he and partner Mark Pritchard visited factories with a DAT
recorder in hand, sampling real-world sonorities and then transforming
them into percussion. Middleton told *The Wire*: 'It's all about science
... the science of manipulating eclectic sounds, recycling sounds and
bringing them up to date, or taking them into the future.'

Where the Reload material has the industrial-tinge of Aphex Twin's
harsher side, Global Communication is more about 'soul-nutrifying
sounds'. In the sleeve-notes of the debut Global album *76:14*, the duo
invites listeners to send in 'paintings, photographs, poetry, sculpture,
recipes and aromas', while in *Urb* magazine Middleton urged: 'You
have five senses – don't forget them. The world out there is a wealth of
colors, sounds, things to eat, things to smell.' In addition to this
interest in the synaesthetic and the sensuous, Middleton and Pritchard
set great store in sensitivity. *76:14* is suffused with a dewey-eyed
idealism and emotionalism that at times verges on the frankly moist.
But this impulse to tug at the heart-strings did produce one all-time

ambient techno classic in the nearly fifteen minute long 'Ob-Selon Mi-Nos'. The track is based around a tick-tocking grandfather clock, heartquakes of slow-mo bass, angelic sighs, and a plangent chime-melody as idyllic and iridescent as dewdrops on a cobweb. The soundscape is so smudged with reverb it's like you're hearing it through ears blurry with tears. Which is possibly how the track was recorded: inspired by Middleton's first funeral, 'Ob-Selon' was a learning exercise in grief. 'I'd never been to a funeral, and I didn't know how to react, so I held back emotion,' he told *Alternative Press*. 'This [track] was an outlet of what I was feeling.'

Texturology alone does not make for music (or at least music that appeals to more than a handful of stern vanguardists). What is required is a mode of organizing disparate textures and timbres into an attractive or compelling arrangement. One model of the textured groovescape was seventies fusion: players like Joe Zawinul and Herbie Hancock had been early synthesizer pioneers. Global Communication named one EP 'Maiden Voyage' in tribute to Hancock, while the best tracks on Bandulu's *Guidance* sounded like jazz-techno, as if Zawinul had somehow ended up band-leader of Tangerine Dream instead of Weather Report. The supple rhythms and musky, aromatic synth-swirls of 'Tribal Reign' open up your senses like a night in a rainforest; the cloud-nebula whorls and fractal eddies of tone-colour are like Time-Lapse photography of the Milky Way, with each of the sixteen frames per second capturing a millennium.

Minimalist and systems-music composers like Steve Reich, Terry Riley, Philip Glass and Michael Nyman offered another prototype for electronica: the 'cellular' construction of complex tapestries of sound by the repetition and interweaving of simple melodic units. On Orbital's second, eponymous album, 'Halcyon + On + On' takes the wordless, 'la di da la di dee' vocal hook from Opus III's New Age House anthem 'It's A Fine Day', and modulates it on the sampling keyboard – reversing and chopping it up, then resequencing it into a series of overlapping and intertwined loops. Singer Kirsty Hawkshaw's tremulous euphoria is swollen into the full-blown mystic bliss of Saint Theresa; her gasps and exhalations interlace to form a nine-minute locked groove of almost unendurable rapture. The sound of a cup of joy overflowing, 'Halcyon + On + On' would seem to be an obvious Ecstasy anthem, but in fact it was inspired by the Valium-like chemical Halcion, and was far from a celebration. The Hartnolls' mother had taken the tranquillizer for several years, and suffered from its manifold side-effects.

In 'Halcyon', it's the combination of *texture* (the breathy 'grain' and seraphic glow of Kirsty's voice) and *textile* (the intricate warp-and-weft of melody and harmony Orbital achieve by multitracking fragments of the original Opus III chorus) that's so breathtaking. Without patterning-skills or a gift for groove, though, texturology is just as capable as any musical methodology of propelling its practioners on a voyage to the innermost reaches of their own arseholes. If any proof is needed, just listen to the work, and words, of The Future Sound Of London.

From their immodest moniker to their fervent anti-dance stance, FSOL represent the unsightly flowering of 'the new progressive rock' always latent within the concept of electronic listening music. Okay, credit where credit's due: in their early incarnation as Humanoid, Brian Dougans and Gary Cobain created a propulsive slice of UK acieed-tekno with 1989's 'Stakker Humanoid'. And their other chart smash, FSOL's 'Papua New Guinea' was a sumptuous, gorgeously emotional rave anthem; it sampled the sublime aria-like tones of mystic-diva Lisa Gerrard from Dead Can Dance, and even used a breakbeat. But when they turned their backs on the dancefloor ('I see the term "dance" as really restrictive for us,' sniffed Dougans) and dedicated themselves to concept albums, FSOL's pop instincts withered.

In 1994, they released their second album, *Lifeforms*, a double-CD *magnum opus*. It's a Daliesque frightmare of liquifacient forms, a pseudo-organic sample-scape congested with scrofulous sound-tendrils and slithery slime-shapes. *Lifeforms* is texturology run rife: holed up in their studio, venturing out only to forage for found sounds, Dougans and Cobain bring out all the masturbatory connotations of that techno stereotype 'the knob-twiddler'. Each sampled source is treated, tinted and morphed until every last drop of 'vibe' or 'aura' is wrung out of it; the duo appear to have forgotten that the real art of sound-painting is knowing when to stop adding another layer or nuance. Like the computer-manipulated photo-montages on the sleeve and the globular shapes in FSOL videos, the music on *Lifeforms* combines the glossy garishness of hyper-realist painting with the varicose convolutions of Rococo.

With it vague conceptual nature and over-ornamented monumentalism, *Lifeforms* is digital progressive rock. Robert Fripp contributed 'guitar textures' for 'Flak'; in an alarming echo of ELP and Deep Purple recording with symphony orchestras, Dougans and Cobain even attempted to do a classically scored version of 'Eggshell'. FSOL had merely translated the prog ethos of ostentatious virtuosity into sampladelic terms: their great bugbear was recognizability in sampling. When *The Wire* played the duo 'mystery tracks' as a spur to aesthetic debate, FSOL poured scorn on a 1992 'ardkore anthem by Sonz of A Loop Da Loop Era. 'Deplorable era and a blind time,' declared Cobain. 'Anyone who managed to keep their head in that era and not do that sort of thing has benefited. I'm coming round to the [idea] that being obvious can be really beautiful if you do it well. But that's a kind of obviousness I hate.' Strangely, while Sonz tracks are fondly regarded as rave classics and producer Danny Breaks is a highly respected drum and bass *auteur*, nobody – not even the reviewers who hailed FSOL as sound-sculptors *non-pareil* – has much to say about *Lifeforms* these days. It's ELP and King Crimson all over again.

Metronomic Underground

One evening in mid-1992, I checked out Knowledge, a 'proper techno' night run by DJs Colin Faver and Colin Dale at London's SW1 club. I was immediately struck by the ascetic decor and the curiously sober frenzy of the mostly white-male audience (many sporting the shaven-haired 'Slaphead' look of the classic techno purist). Of course, nary a breakbeat was heard all night. (Lycra? Forget it.) Speaking to *iD*, Colin Dale explained the anti-hardcore agenda: 'That's why we started Knowledge – to show there was better music than the breakbeat stuff around.'

At Knowledge and similar clubs like Eurobeat 2000, Lost, Final Frontier, The Orbit, Pure and Deep Space the sounds you heard – purist techno, *nouveau* acid and hard trance from labels like Canada's +8, Holland's Djax-Up, Germany's Tresor and Labworks – were dancefloor-oriented, body-coercive cousins of armchair techno. Despite its fierce physicality, these styles shared the same cerebral cast: the boy's own aura of anal-retentive expertise, the vague, ill-defined conviction that something radical was at stake in this music. This was rave music purged of cheesy ravey-ness (the breakbeat, the sample, the riff-stab, the anthemic chorus, the E'd up sentimentality) and retooled for a student sensibility, that perennial class base for the 'progressive' since the late sixties.

Although the new purists paid lipservice to techno's Black American origins, their sound was starkly European, stripped of Detroit's jazzy inflections and Chicago's gay disco sensuality. Instead the whitest, most Kraftwerk-derived aspects of Detroit techno were layered on top of the least funky element in Chicago house, the four-to-the-floor kick-drum. By the end of 1992, this whiter-than-white sound had evolved into Teutonic trance, a hybrid of Tangerine Dream's cosmic rock and Giorgio Moroder's Eurodisco, as purveyed by labels like MFS and Harthouse, artists like The Source, Hardfloor, Oliver Lieb, Age of Love, Cosmic Baby and Speedy J.

Where ambient techno is soundscape painting for immobile contemplation, trance is cinematic and kinetic; producers often describe their music in terms of 'taking the listener on a journey'. Trance is *trippy*, in both the LSD and *motorik* senses of the word, evoking the frictionless trajectories of video-games, virtual reality or the 'console cowboys' hurtling through cyberspace in *Neuromancer*. Along with its cyberdelic futurism, trance also has a mystical streak, expressed in hippy-dippy titles like Paul Van Dyk's 'Visions Of Shiva' and Trance Induction's 'New Age Heartcore'. 'Trance' evokes whirling dervishes, voodoo dancers, and other ritualized techniques for reaching altered states via hyperventilation, dizziness and exhaustion.

Harking back to the 'purity' of the pre-rave era, trance revived the acid house sound of 1987–8. Presaged by late 1991 tracks like Mundo Muzique's 'Acid Pandemonium', the Roland 303 resurgence really exploded a year later with Hardfloor's 'Hardtrance Acperience', which sold 30,000 in Britain alone. Where the original Chicago acid was ultra-minimalist, the new acieeed was maximalist: 'Hardtrance' assembles itself according to an additive logic, gradually layering up at least three 303 bass-pulses (writhing like sex-crazed pythons), Moroder-style Doppler effects, sequencer-riffs, and tier upon tier of percussion. A terrific tension is built up, but there's no release, no climax.

At its coldly compulsive best – Arpeggiators' 'Freedom of Expression', Trope's 'Amphetamine', Commander Tom's 'Are Am Eye' and 'Dark Eyes' – trance exhilarates. But for me, it's the form of techno that's most thoroughly in thrall to the sequencer's precision-locked logic; tracks are grids rather than grooves. With its programmed drum machine beats and punctual pulses, trance resembles an orchestra of metronomes, all subordinate to the timekeeping of that tyrannical conductor, the kick-drum. This predictability is what allows the mind to disengage and 'trance out'.

Inside every trance producer is a prog-rocker struggling to get out and express himself, worse luck. Take Jam and Spoon. Their brilliant early track 'Stella' was part of the R & S label's flight from Dionysian rave towards Appollonian soft-core. There's literally no hard core to this track, just a muffled kick-drum, cirrus-swirls of angel's breath, and a feathery, one-chord pulse-riff that ascends from higher plane to higher plane. 'Stella' appeared on a 1992 EP titled 'Tales From a Danceographic Ocean' EP – a tongue-in-cheek nod to Yes's *Tales From Topographic Oceans*, prog rock's noodly nadir. Or perhaps it was simple homage, since Jam and Spoon's debut album was in effect a *quadruple*: two simultaneously released CDs, *Triptomatic Fairy Tales 2001* and *2002*, both crammed with kitschadelic sounds and song titles like 'Zen Flash Zen Bones' and 'Who Opened The Door To Nowhere'.

And then there's Sven Vath – co-founder of Harthouse and its sister label Eye Q, legendary DJ at the Omen in Frankfurt. In the sleevenotes to 1993's *Accident In Paradise*, Vath cites his ancestral spirits as Eno, Ryuichi Sakamoto, Harold Budd and Holger Czukay, but also, more tellingly, Peter Gabriel, Vangelis, Andreas Vollenweider and Mozart. With its didgeridoos, mystic-Orient melodies and DAT-recorded aural snapshots from Nepal and Goa, *Accident In Paradise* is a deodorized ethno-techno travelogue. But in true prog-rock fashion, the album is really steeped in nineteenth-century Euro-classical music; all arpeggiated synth-wank and piano trills as frou-frou as Enya, while 'Coda' features a harpsichord, for fuck's sake! The critics loved it (at last! a techno album that 'works as a whole' and sounds good on your domestic hi-fi), but even they had no stomach for Vath's next concept album atrocity *The Harlequin, The Dancer and The Robot*.

Food For Thought

'More participatory musics are more rhythmically complex (and harmonically simple); more contemplative musics are rhythmically simple (and more harmonically complex).'

– Simon Frith on the difference between African based and
European based musics, *Performing Rites*

The struggle between intelligent techno and hardcore was a bitter contest, waged across class and generational lines, to decide who 'owned' electronic dance music and what direction it should pursue. This was a schism between non-stop ecstatic dancing and sedate(d) contemplation, between the 12-inch and the album, between the demands of the audience and the prerogatives of the auteur. Neither side of this perennial divide had a monopoly on creativity; the electronic listening music initiative produced some beautiful and innovative sounds. But it's always struck me as odd that so many people involved in dance music seem to regard the physical response as somehow 'lesser'. The result was a glut of melodious, middlebrow 'mindfood' – music hedged on one side by its disdain for the functionalism of 'rave fodder', and on the other by its reluctance to really explore the extremities of mindfuck texturology. By 1995, these soi-disant experimentalists could only rescue themselves from the disembodied anaemia of 'intelligence' by rediscovering the breakbeat. Irony of ironies, they had to relearn the score from the hardcore.

SEVEN

SLIPPING
INTO
DARKNESS

THE UK RAVE DREAM
TURNS TO NIGHTMARE,
1992–93

There seems to be a moment, intrinsic to any drug culture, when the scene crosses over into 'the dark side'. It happened in San Francisco in the late sixties, when heroin, methamphetamine and the terrifyingly intense hallucinogen STP killed Haight Ashbury's love and peace vibe. In Ecstasy subcultures too, there tends to be a point where the MDMA honeymoon phase comes to an abrupt end; again and again, from Manchester in 1990 to Los Angeles in 1993, the descent into darkness occurs.

What makes British hardcore unique is the way the same shift from utopian to dystopian was reflected in the *music*. By late 1992, the happy rave tunes of 1990–91 were being eclipsed by a style called 'dark side' or 'dark-core'; hardcore became haunted by a collective apprehension that 'we've gone too far'. Thematically and sonically, darkside tracks mirrored the long-terms costs of sustained Ecstasy, marijuana and amphetamine use: side-effects such as depression, paranoia, dissociation, audio-hallucinations and creepy sensations of the uncanny.

The titles and sampled soundbites of this era immediately indicate that something is awry in the house of hardcore. There was imagery of brain damage (Bizzy B's 'Total Amnesia', 4 Hero's 'Mind Loss (A State of Amnesia)') and disorientation (2 Bad Mice's 'Mass Confusion', Satin Storm's 'Think I'm Going Out Of My Head'). There were tracks about death, like Ed Rush's 'Bludclot Artattack', with its 'you've got a ticket to hell' sample, and Origin Unknown's 'Valley Of the Shadows', which pivoted around an unnerving soundbite from a BBC documentary about near-death experiences: 'felt that I was in a long dark tunnel'. And then there were self-reflexive dark tracks that enshrouded the dancefloor in twilight-zone malaise, like Metalheads' 'Sinister' and Bay-B-Kane's 'Hello Darkness' (the title phrase came from a cheeky but thoroughly creepy sample from Simon and Garfunkel's 'The Sound of Silence'). Another major darkside trope was the idea of drug intensities as a sinister power source, a malign forcefield in which the raver is suspended and entrapped: DJ Crystl's 'Warpdrive', 4 Hero's 'The Power', and DJ Hype's 'Weird Energy'.

Perhaps most perturbing of all was an entire mini-genre of panic-attack songs – Remarc's 'Ricky', Johnny Jungle's 'Johnny', Subnation's 'Scottie' – all of which were based around a sample of someone shouting out a name, as a cry for help or in sheer horror. 'Scottie' is the real chiller-killer, both for its superbly rhythmic use of *Evil Dead* soundbites and for the way it dramatizes a psychological struggle between hysteria and resilience: the track oscillates giddily between the whimpered 'I don't wanna die' and the scared-but-determined 'we're not gonna die, we're gonna get out of here'. With its horror movie dialogue ('is there a way around the bridge?') doubling up as a musical reference ('bridges' being the percussion-only James Brown-style breakdowns out of which the track is entirely composed), 'Scottie' is horribly claustrophobic.

The stark 'n' severe drum and bass minimalism of 'Scottie' was just one of darkside's sonic strategies. Using effects like timestretching, pitchshifting and reversing, the darkside producers gave their break-beats a brittle, metallic sound, like scuttling claws; they layered beats to form a dense mesh of convoluted, convulsive polyrhythm, inducing a febrile feel of in-the-pocket funk and out-of-body delirium. 'Ard-kore's anthemic choruses and sentimental melodies were stripped away, in favour of gloomy, slimy-sounding electronic textures. Vocal samples were sped-up, slowed-down, reversed and 'ghosted', resulting in grotesque hall-of-mirrors distortions of 'the human'. Sounds swooped and receded within the stereo-field, creating a hair-raising atmosphere of apprehension and persecution; sustained drones and background hums induced tension.

All these sound-warping effects literalize the old 'ardkore imagery of 'madness' and 'going mental'. According to Achim Szepanski, whose Frankfurt label Mille Plateaux attempted a German take on dark-core breakbeat in 1992, these techniques of 'schizophonia' (the splitting of sounds from their physical, real-time source) take the listener into the heart of schizophrenic experience. 'Echo effects allow sound hallucinations to occur ... forms of perception develop that, strangely, one had previously attributed to lunatics or schizophrenics.' Harking back to the heavily treated timbres in fifties *musique concrète* and post-punk industrial music, darkside's repertoire of noises – 'screaming, chirping, creaking, hissing', as Szepanski put it – *sound like going insane*. Darkside also imitated or sampled the dissonant motifs developed by horror-movie and thriller soundtrack composers to evoke derangement, foreboding and trauma. (Indeed, Hollywood soundtrack and incidental music is one of the few areas in pop culture where the ideas of avant-garde twentieth-century classical music – serialism, electro-acoustic, *concrète* – have filtered into mass consciousness).

Exuding bad-trippy dread and twitchy, jittery paranoia, dark-core seemed to reflect a sort of collective come-down after the E-fuelled high of 1991–2. Alienated, ravers deserted in droves to the milder climes of happy house and mellow garage. But a substantial segment of the rave audience mobilized between 1990–92 followed through hardcore's drug-tech logic all the way into the unknown, the twilight-zone. Forming a sort of avant-garde within Britain's recreational drug culture, these were ravers who had perversely come to enjoy bad trips and weird vibes. Why? Perhaps because, rather than readjust to normality, it seemed preferable to stick with rave's 'living dream' even when it had turned to living nightmare. Perhaps because any kind of intensity is better than feeling numb.

Chaotic Chemistry

From my double vantage point as fan and critic, participant and observer, darkside was a pivotal and revelatory moment: the life-affirming, celebratory aspects of rave were turned inside out, the smiley-face torn off to reveal the true nihilism of any drug-based culture. Amidst all the positivity and idealism, that nihilism was always lurking, waiting to be hatched. When rave's 'desiring machine' is really crankin', when you're one of its cogs (locked into the pirate-radio signal or plugged into the sound-system), there's no feeling like it. Trouble is, the machine is demanding: it exacts a heavy toll on its human software. Artificial energy is required to bring the nervous system up to speed; the human frame was not built to withstand the attrition of sensations. Rave's regime of bliss wears out the machine's flesh-and-blood components, both physically (hot and sweaty, raves are incubators of viruses) and mentally (post-rave comedown, mid-week emotional fragility, and in the long run, burn-out and melan-cholia). By late 1992, hardcore rave resembled a machine-gone-mad.

Deleuze and Guattari warn that drug use can turn 'fascist' or 'suicidal', that the body-without-organs (the Ecstatic body) can become a 'black hole', voided and numb. In the beginning, Ecstasy makes you feel angelic; ultimately, it can turn you into a demon. Gradually, the experience of raving itself changes; single-minded fervour turns to tunnel-vision fixation. Getting high degenerates into getting out of it. Suddenly the clubs are full of dead souls, zombie-eyed and prematurely haggard. Instead of outstretched arms and all-embracing extroversion, there's grimly fixated vacancy, automaton body-moves, autistic self-absorption. What started off as life-affirming fun begins to smack of desperation. The folkloric drug tales get grimmer and grimmer: someone who threw up and then picked the half-digested pills out of the puke and gulped them down again, rumours of kids using syringes to shoot speed in the toilets. One night in 1993 at Labrynth stands out for me as the point at which I realized the scene had turned squalid. Outside, in the Labrynth's hitherto sacred grove of a garden, two teenage girls hold on to their friend as she retches – too many pills on an empty stomach. Gloating, demonic laughter floats across from a murky corner. Back inside the club's fluorescent catacombs, a seriously fucked-up guy, sweaty and shaking, cadges a cigarette off me, and says, so earnest it's scary, 'You just saved my life, mate.'

What I remember most of all is the number of ravers whose smiles had been replaced by sour, cheated expressions – they hadn't come up on their E's, probably because they'd over-indulged so heavily the past few years that the old buzz just couldn't be recovered. That moment of disenchantment is captured in Hyper-On Experience's 1993 anthem 'Lords of the Null Lines', a Gothic symphony of hiccuping, skittery rhythms and something-wicked-this-way-comes strings. 'There's a void where there should be ecstasy' laments the sampled diva. The line could refer to the desperation of a raver who suspects he's swallowed a dud or 'snidey' E, but it could equally describe the hollow numbness of veteran ravers whose brains have been emptied of serotonin, the 'joy-juice' which Ecstasy releases in a gush-and-rush of euphoria. Having caned E so hard for so long, these ravers find their pleasure-centre synapses are firing blanks.

Dark-core reflected the complicated pharmacological reality of the rave scene in 1992 and 1993; a chaos of amateur, untutored neuro-chemistry and unreliable medicine combined to form an unbeatable recipe for psychic malaise. First, ravers experienced a temporary dip in the quality of Ecstasy. With rave peaking commercially in 1992, dealers looked to exploit the influx of gullible, undiscriminating punters, and maximized their profits by cutting MDMA with cheaper drugs: primarily amphetamine and LSD, but also tranquillizers or inert substances.

The market was flooded with 'cocktail' pills that combined speed and acid in a crude attempt to approximate the Ecstasy feeling. This deterioration in the rave-drug's purity didn't last, but it birthed an enduring myth that 'Ecstasy isn't as good as it used to be', which in turn provided ravers with an excuse to take more pills to get the same effect. The unreliability of the drug – the fact that the raver stood a good chance of getting a dud – did not inspire caution or utter disillusionment, as you might expect, but a spirit of recklessness: take more rather than less, take another if the first one doesn't come on strong and fast enough.

This headstrong heedlessness was particularly risky given another pharmacological trend at work in this period: the selling of Ecstasy that contained MDA rather than MDMA. MDA is the chemical parent of MDMA and MDEA ('Eve'). Widely available in 1992 in the form of Snowball and White Caps, and apparently originating from government-controlled factories in Latvia, MDA offers an altogether fiercer, more deranging experience than Ecstasy, devoid of MDMA's empathic warmth. MDA's effects are closer to LSD's hallucinatory disorientation; it lasts much longer than proper Ecstasy, around eight to twelve hours; the comedown is harsher. MDA is also more toxic than MDMA: Snowballs often contained a high concentration of MDA, around 177 mgs, so that three pills would bring the raver within range of a fatal dose. At the very least, it would almost guarantee a psychedelic freak-out or an autistic veg-out. And yet, by 1992, three pills was by no mean an abnormal number to take during a session. While some blamed snowballs for 'killing the scene', mistakenly believing them to be cut with heroin, others actively sought out and savoured MDA's manic sensations.

The other syndrome at work in the darkside era was simple excess. By 1992, many hardcore 'veterans', who'd gotten into raving only a few years earlier and were often still in their teens, had increased their intake to three, four, five, or more pills per session. They were locked into a cycle of going raving once or twice a week, weekend after weekend. It was at this point that Ecstasy's serotonin-depletion effect came into play. Even if you take pure MDMA each and every time, the drug's blissful effects fade fast, leaving only a jittery, amphetamine-like rush. In hardcore, this speedfreak effect was made worse as ravers necked more pills in a futile and misguided attempt to recover the long-lost bliss of yore. The physical side-effects – hypertension, racing heart – got worse, and so did the darkside paranoia. Amphetamine and Ecstasy both flood the nervous system with dopamine, and 'dopamine over-activity' has been linked to such symptoms of schizophrenia as auditory hallucinations and delusional beliefs.

All of these syndromes (fake Ecstasy 'cocktails', MDA masquerading as MDMA, the diminishing returns of long-term use) were exacerbated because the norm among ravers is 'polydrug use'. Ecstasy is commonly taken with other illicit substances – amphetamine, LSD, cannabis, 'poppers' (legal inhalants like propyl, butyl or isobutyl nitrite), the barbiturate-like sleeping pill Temazepam – each with their own risks, side-effects and nasty adulterants. Recent research shows that nearly 80 per cent of British ravers take amphetamine as a booster to accompany their E; serious nutters chase down their E's with diverse configurations of speed, LSD and Temazepam. Nearly everybody smokes marijuana, which has its own effects of paranoia and perceptual distortion (especially potent with super-breeds of weed such as 'skunk'). The results of all this amateur pharmacology range from added fun to greater disorientation, increased toxicity, and more punishing come-downs. MDMA can be the classic gateway to a veritable drug super-market, in so far as uncertainty of supply can lead punters to experiment with other substances as an alternative route to the high.

By 1992, the hardcore raver was a veritable connoisseur of poisons, skilled at mix 'n' matching drugs to modify their own neurochemistry and achieve the precise degree of oblivion desired. This 'street knowl-edge' often expressed itself in the imagery of science: Bizzy B's 'Ecstasy Is A Science', the band Kaotic Chemistry. The latter's self-titled debut includes tracks like 'Five In One Night', 'Strip Search' and 'The Comedown', while the sleeve mischievously depicts the ingredients for an average night of Dionysian mayhem. On the front, a hand simul-taneously holds a spliff and chops out a line of speed with a credit card; on the back, the table is strewn with a dozen or more white pills. Kaotic Chemistry's 'LSD' EP continues the polydrug excess theme with 'Space Cakes', 'LSD', 'Drum Trip II' and 'Illegal Subs' (a later remix EP adds 'Vitamin K', named after a slang term for ketamine). The title 'Illegal Subs' is a nudge-nudge, wink-wink pun, referring both to illicit substances and to sub-bass levels so harmful they should be outlawed. The song itself is a sort of tribute to the 'ardkore nation, sampling a

Nation of Islam orator who hails her African-American audience as 'the people of chemistry ... of physics ... of music ... of civilization ... of rhythm'.

Some theorists of addiction argue that for certain borderline individuals, neurotic or emotionally damaged, taking drugs is a form of self-medication. This idea of 'healing toxins' is another theme running through hardcore, from Doc Scott's 'Surgery' and 'NHS' EPs, through Praga Khan's 'Injected With A Poison', to the Prodigy's 'Poison', with its chant 'I've got the poison / I've got the remedy'. Renegade physicians raiding the pharmacopoeia, hardcore ravers embarked upon a massive, uncontrolled psycho-social experiment, whose unconscious goal was perhaps to heal themselves, damaged products of a sick society. Grasping greedily for utopia *right here, right now*, they hurtled instead into a dystopian future.

Drowning in Love

In the utterly blissed hardcore of early 1992, you can hear darkness shadowing the swoony delirium. Take one of the scene's most success-ful labels, Production House. There's an aura of dangerously over-whelming bliss to tracks like Acen's 'Trip To the Moon Part One', with its fizzy electronics and portentous orchestral fanfares (sampled from John Barry's 'Space March' from the soundtrack to *You Only Live Twice*). What sounds like a classic E-rush exultation – 'I can't believe these feelings!!!' – could easily be an expression of distrust, a distraught intimation of unreality.

Lurking within the effervescent 'hyper-ness' of Production House tracks like DMS's 'Love Overdose' and 'Mindwreck' is a kind of death-wish. Appropriately enough, Acen's other big smash of 1992, 'Close Your Eyes', samples Jim Morrison, the original death-obsessed Diony-sian rock star. Mystic incantations from The Doors' epic 'Celebration of the Lizard' – 'forget your name ... go insane' – are sped up into a hilarious but eerie Munchkin squeak. 'The Darkside' remix of 'Close Your Eyes' adds the line 'forget the world, forget the people', fed through a hall-of-mirrors echo effect to conjure a bedlam of Morrison-ghosts. Two other samples – 'I think I'm gonna' and 'OVERDOSE!' – are concatenated to spell out the flirting-with-the-void vibe.

Even Baby D's 'Let Me Be Your Fantasy' – Production House's

biggest smash, eventually making Number One in the Pop Charts when rereleased in 1994 – is veined with ambivalence. With its grand piano trills and bittersweet tenderness, 'Fantasy' is that seemingly impossible entity, a rave ballad. Its creator, Dyce, has described the track as a love song to the hardcore scene, to the spirit of loved-up-ness itself. Listen to the lyrics, and it becomes clear that the siren-like figure is actually Ecstasy 'herself' serenading the listener: 'I'll take you up to the highest high ... Come and feel my energy ... Come take a trip to my wonderland ... I've got what it takes to make you mine.'

'Fantasy''s manoeuvre – personifying MDMA as the seductive chanteuse Baby D – was a singular masterstroke. More common was the hardcore track that took the needy beseeching of the sampled soul-diva and separated it from its original flesh-and-blood referent, in order to create a *love song to the drug*. Foul Play's 'Finest Illusion', a near-symphonic rush of pizzicato riffs and swoony cascades, is a classic example: if 'you're the finest I've ever known' doesn't refer to a particularly pure batch of MDMA, why else did the band title the track 'Finest Illusion'?

Recording as 4 Horsemen of the Apocalypse, Foul Play took this idea all the way into the twilight-zone with 'Drowning In Her'. The track has all the languishing langour and desolate dejection of a torch song; its tremulous textures and dolorous, dislocated feel conjure a mood of paralysis and enervation. Blurry with reverb, the sampled vocal hook sounds like 'drowning in love' but is actually 'drowning in her': *jouissance* is associated with an alluring but ultimately asphyxiating femininity. Mid-track, there's a sample of a single word, the horror-struck cry 'how??!?' This is taken from the spoken-word intro of 4 Hero's 1990 classic 'Mr Kirk's Nightmare' – itself sampled from Think's 1971 hit 'Once You Understand', a cautionary tale about the generation gap – in which a policeman comes to a father's house to tell him that his seventeen-year-old son Robert is dead. 'Dead!!?! How??!?' whimpers the aghast Mr Kirk, 'He died of an overdose,' says the officer. A classic example of rave music intertextuality, the sampled 'how' in 'Drowning In Her' triggers memories of 'Mr Kirk's Nighmare', of all the rumours and scare stories surrounding Ecstasy. It reminds the raver that each time they take a tablet of dubious origin they are dicing with death; that to dance with Ecstasy is to embrace a *femme fatale*.

You Got Me Burnin' Up

If anyone can claim to have invented dark-core, it's 4 Hero. Two years after 'Mr Kirk's Nightmare', the band returned to the subject of Ecstasy fatalities with 1992's sick-joke concept EP, 'Where's The Boy'. The funereal-black sleeve depicts a coffin with a question mark on it: the tomb of the unknown raver. The four tracks on 'Where's The Boy' trace out the theme of death by heatstroke, which in 1992 was first entering public consciousness as the explanation for a spate of E-related deaths. 'Burning' and 'Cooking Up Yah Brain' sound literally delirious. The sample-textures seem to ripple like a heat-haze of vapourized sweat, making me think of the *Guardian*'s description of one particular Ecstasy fatality caused by dehydration and overheating: after taking three E's, a teenager 'boiled alive in his own blood'. 'Time To Get Ill' samples the Beastie Boys to make a deadly pun that conflates 'ill' in the hip hop sense with the internal bleeding and major organ failure associated with severe heatstroke. The track sounds literally nauseous, all vomitous gurglings and migraine-like squeals. Finally, 'Where's The Boy (Trial By Ecstasy)' reinvokes 'Mr Kirk's Nightmare', with its dialogue between a policeman ('You killed the boy, you didn't just dream it?') and a middle-aged man ('yes!')

4 Hero and other artists on their label, Reinforced – Rufige Cru, Doc Scott, Nebula II – pioneered the *sound* of darkness too: metallic beats, murky modulated-bass, hideously warped vocals, ectoplasmic smears of sample-texture.

Holed up in Reinforced's HQ–studio, a claustrophobic loft in Dollis Hill, 4 Hero and Rufige's Cru's Goldie embarked on marathons of sampladelic research. 'I remember one session ... which lasted over three days,' Goldie told *The Mix*'s Tim Barr in 1996. 'We'd come up with mad ideas and then try to create them ... We were sampling from ourselves, and then resampling, twisting sounds around and pushing them into all sorts of places.' The resulting audio-grotesquerie, collected on fifteen DAT cassettes, offered a vast palette of sinister textures and mindbending effects for Reinforced artists to draw upon. As Goldie put it, 'we kind of wrote the manual over those three days'.

Perhaps the most crucial component of Reinforced's sonic arsenal was their mutant versions of the searing, snaking terror-riffs originally invented by Joey 'Mentasm' Beltram and the Belgians. The Beltram/

Belgian sound, says 4 Hero's Dego McFarlane, 'was like the punk rock of techno ... Back in '92, at clubs like AWOL, it was near enough slam-dancing and shit, people got very rowdy in those days.' Reinforced's roster took the 'mentasm stab' to new intensities of death-ray malignancy. On Nasty Habits' 'Here Comes The Drumz', the riff morphs like the 'liquid metal' plasma-flesh of the robo-assassin in *Terminator 2*.

The sound of dark-core is febrile, but it's a cold fever. Take Rufige Cru tracks like 'Darkrider' and 'Jim Skreech': the staccato string-stabs, scuttling breaks and shivery textures always make me think of 'crank bugs', the speedfreak delusion that insects are crawling under your skin. These tracks are so riddled, so infested with fidgety nuance and frenetic detail, there's never any point of repose or release: during the breakdown in 'Darkrider', midget-riffs keep revving away, like they're straining at the leash, impatient for the beat to kick in again. So much unrest is programmed into dark era Reinforced tracks, you can't just trance out, as with house or techno; you're always on edge.

After the 'Darkrider' EP, Rufige Cru's Goldie adopted the Metal-heads moniker and released 'Terminator', a track whose anti-natural-istic rhythms constituted a landmark in the evolution of breakbeat hardcore into a *rhythmic psychedelia*. Using pitch-shifting so that at the breakdowns the pitch of the drums veers vertiginously upwards, Goldie created a jagged time-lapse effect: the drums seem to speed up yet simultaneously stay in tempo. 'Terminator' sounds as predatorial and remorseless as its movie namesake, the killing man-machine played by Arnold Schwarzenegger. Sent back through time as the ambassador of the sentient War-Machine of the future, the Terminator is the incar-nation of will-to-death. In a similarly dystopian cyberpunk vein, Nebula II breakbeat-techno classics 'Peacemaker' and 'X-Plore H-Core' sound as a coldhearted, inorganic and implacable as a *Robocop*-style cyborg suppressing some twenty-first century inner-city insurrection; synths sting like tear-gas, riffs jab and jolt like electric cattle-prods, android vocals admonish and castigate.

Journey from the Light

Nasty Habits' 'Here Comes The Drumz' is the sound of inner-city turmoil; the track samples a snatch of Public Enemy rabble-rousing, with Chuck D declaiming the title phrase stagefront and Flavor Flav barging in to blurt 'Confusion!!' Produced by Doc Scott and released by Reinforced in late 1992, 'Drumz' is widely regarded as *the* dark track, the death-knell for happy-rave. What's striking about 'Drumz' is how murky and muddy it sounds. It's like all the treble frequencies have been stripped away, leaving just low-end turbulence: roiling drums, bass-pressure and ominous industrial drones.

Dance music theorist Will Straw argues that high-end sounds (strings, pianos, female voices) are coded as 'feminine', while low-end frequencies (drums and bass) are coded as 'masculine'. Purging hardcore's sped-up, Minnie Mouse vocals and melodramatic strings (the feminine/gay, pop/disco elements that made hardcore full of *jouissance*), darkside producers like Scott created masculinist/minimal-ist drum and bass, the stark sound of compulsion for compulsion's sake. This was a connoisseur's sound: 'It was mostly DJs who were into dark,' remembers Slipmatt, a populist DJ associated with the happier kind of hardcore, 'all I heard from [the punters] was moans.' Dark-core's creators were motivated by a conscious drive to take hardcore back underground, by removing all the uplifting elements of commer-cial crossover rave. Disgusted by 1992's chart-topping spate of squeaky-voiced, 'toytown techno', the scene's inner circle decided to alienate all the 'lightweights' and see who was really down with the programme.

That, says Dego McFarlane, was the meaning behind 4 Hero's 'Journey From the Light' EP; time to move out of the commercial limelight, away from 'all the happy stuff'. On this EP, all the effects formerly used to create a heavenly aura in hardcore are subtly tweaked, bent to the sinister. On 'The Elements', an angel-choir of varispeeded divas shriek in agony, like they're been demoted or downsized to hell; a door opens with an ominous creak, then slams; there's a sample from Don McLean's 'American Pie' – 'this'll be the day that I die' – sped up to sound horribly fey and enfeebled. 'The Power' teems with ghost-shivers and maggoty, squirmy sounds. 'In the Shadow (Sundown)' features mentasmic riffs so astringent and abrasive, you feel like your cranium is being scoured out, every last sentient speck of grey matter expunged.

Later in 1993, 4 Hero's 'Golden Age' EP and its attendant 'Golden Age Remixes' cloaked darker-than-thou themes with a new soft-core sensuality, at once mellow and morbid. 'Better Place Becomes Reality' jibes against rave's pleasuredome of illusions (amazingly, 4 Hero are all straight-edge non-drug users), with its soundbite of a girl complaining 'we need some *reality* reality, not this artificial reality'. A worm-holey miasma of stereo-panning and disorientating backwards sounds, 'Students of the Future (Nostradamus: The Revelation – Rufige Cru Mix)' pivots around the sample: 'Nostradamus tells us the world will finally come to an end'. The Nostradamus obsession is part of 4 Hero's interest in prophecy, futurology, science fiction and the loopier end of speculative science writing (books like *Wrinkles In Time* and *Fingerprints of the Gods*). Hip hop and rave culture (4 Hero are children of both) are rife with millenarianism, a feeling that history is accelerating towards some kind of culmination, whether it's a consummation devoutly to be anticipated or conflagration desperately to be dreaded. 'A lot of things point to it,' says McFarlane. 'If you've got any common sense, you look through history: the Dinosaurs came and went . . . How long is it until something like that happens? I'm not saying the world will just blow up like that, but something will happen. The whole human race will die.'

Voodoo Magic

'In delusional insanity . . . we may have a diabolical mysticism, a sort of religious mysticism turned upside down. The same sense of ineffable importance in the smallest events, the same texts and words coming with new meanings, the same voices and visions and leadings and missions, the same controlling by extraneous powers; only this time the emotion is pessimistic: instead of consolations we have desolations; the meanings are dreadful; and the powers are enemies to life'

– William James, *The Varieties of Religious Experience*

Drugs loosen the tyrannical grip of the ego, but they also let loose all the predatorial phantoms and noxious paranoia of the id. So in darkside, there was a strong vein of superstition, surfacing in titles like Doc Scott's 'Dark Angel', Nebula II's 'Seance', Rufige Cru's 'Ghosts of My Life' and Megadrive's 'Demon' (with its 'fury of a demon possessed me' sample). Sometimes the imagery was directly drawn from horror-movies, sometimes it was inspired by the residues of a Christian upbringing or by amateur forays into cosmology, angelology and mysticism. But often the pagan, animist imagery simply seems to have seeped up from the collective unconscious, the Dark Ages that we all carry around in our souls.

Boogie Times Tribe's 'The Dark Stranger' is a classic example of the Hollywood horror-movie influence on darkside. Samples from a documentary on the making of the Francis Ford Coppola film *Bram Stoker's Dracula* – Anthony Hopkins pontificating about 'the dark side of all human nature', Gary Oldman muttering about the shadowy intruder 'who comes for you in the night' – are juxtaposed with the acid-house era wail 'girl, I'm starting to lose it'. Where the original version of 'The Dark Stranger' verges on corn with its over-use of these soundbites and its hammy-horror soundtrack motifs, the Q-Bass Remix makes the music itself carry the full burden of dread. The remix starts with a hideously voluptuous slow-mo intro of slimy, shuddery sounds, like a chill running up a spine. Then the baleful bass and off-kilter beat kick in: the bass oozing and quaking like death-knell dub, the rhythm dominated by a deeply unsettling, hyper-syncopated hi-hat, like a heart skipping a beat then pounding triple time. Such cardiac arrythmia is a symptom of amphetamine overdose.

The parallels between sampladelia and magic have not been lost on its exponents. With his contraptions and arcane, self-invented terminology, the hardcore producer lies somewhere between the mad scientist and the sorcerer with his potions, alembics and spells. Goldie has said that 'rufige' was his term for pop-cultural detritus ('I was using fourth or fifth generation samples, just trash sound'), sonic scum that could nonetheless undergo alchemical transformation in the sampladelic crucible. The DJ too is often regarded as a shaman or dark magus. Rufige Cru's 'Darkrider' is a tribute to Grooverider, worshipped to this day as a 'god' for his playing at the legendary dark-core club Rage. Consciously or not, the metaphor of the DJ as 'rider' echoes the voodoo notion that the trance-dancer is being 'ridden' by the gods, the *loa*. Grooverider's role is equivalent to the *hungan* or high priest, whose drumming propels the voodoo acolytes into a frenzied state of oblivion. If this seems far-fetched, consider that in Haitian *voudun*, possession by the spirits occurs during the *cassée*, or dissonant percussive break. Dark-core is composed entirely of continuously looped breakbeats; in a sense, the whole music consists of *cassées*.

Darkside's voodoo-imagery – 4 Hero's 'Make Yah See Spiders On The Wall (Voodoo Beats)', Hyper-On Experience's 'Lords Of The Null

Lines' with its 'fucking voodoo magic' sample from *Predator 2* – was just the latest efflorescence of a metaphor with a long history in house music, from A Guy Called Gerald's 'Voodoo Ray' to D.H.S.'s 'Holo-Voodoo'. This trope of being bewitched, turned into a *zombi*, pervaded acid house and jack tracks – from Phuture's 'Your Only Friend' (which personified Cocaine as a robot-voiced slave-master) to Sleezy D's 'I've Lost Control', on which a dehumanized vocal ascends through panic ('I'm *losing* it') to fatalism ('I've lost it').

In the mid-nineties, Chicago house returned to the anti-melodic minimalism and slave-to-the-rhythm metaphors of the acieed era. Green Velvet released a series of brilliant 'dark' house tracks with Sleezy D-style spoken-voice monologues, 'I Want To Leave My Body', 'Conniption', 'Help Me', 'The Stalker (I'm Losing My Mind)' and 'Flash'. The latter pivots around a hilarious scenario that touched a nerve with rave kids in 1995. The voiceover escorts a gaggle of concerned parents through clubland, showing them what the 'naughty little kiddies' do for fun, like smoking joints or inhaling from big balloons of nitrous oxide ('laughing gas, but this is no laughing matter'). The 'Flash' of the chorus is the parents' cameras taking pictures of the miscreants in the murky club, but it sounds more like a drug 'flash': when the track lets rip a double-time battery of martial snares, it's like a heart going into spasm after too much amyl.

The truth is that there's always been a dark side to rave culture; almost from the beginning, the ecstatic experience of dance-and-drugs was shadowed by anxiety. 'Losing it' is a blissful release from the prisonhouse of identity, but there comes a point at which the relief of ceding self-consciousness/self-control bleeds into a fear of being *controlled* (by a demonic Other: the malign logic of the drug/tech interface). Again and again, the moment of endarkenment recurs in rave subcultures; the nihilism latent in its drug-fuelled utopianism is always lurking, waiting to be hatched.

Darkness Lingers

By the autumn of 1993, the pioneers of dark-core were moving on. 4 Hero began their journey back towards the light. Rufige Cru/Metal-heads' Goldie disparaged the horde of Reinforced copyists, explaining: '"Dark" came from the feeling of breakdown in society. It was winter, clubs were closing, the country was in decline. As an artist, I had to reflect it. But now all these kids have turned it into a joke, they think "dark" is about devil worship.'

Darkside paved the way for *both* the strands of breakbeat music that displaced it: the roisterous, ruffneck menace of jungle, and the densely-textured, ambient-tinged sound of drum and bass. With its premium on headfuck weirdness and disorientating effects, dark-core opened up a vital space for experimentation. In a way, 'dark', like the hip-hop term 'ill', is a sort of vernacular shorthand for 'avant-garde'. Many darkside tracks sounded like the improbable return of early eighties avant-funk: PiL's 'Death Disco', 23 Skidoo, Cabaret Voltaire, A Certain Ratio. Dark-core led directly to the artcore explosion of album artists like Goldie. At the same time, darkside's baleful minimalism was a prequel to jungle's gangsta militancy. Just like heavy metal kids signing up for Satan's army, or rappers flirting with psychosis (Cypress Hill's 'Insane In The Brain'), aligning yourself with 'the dark side' is a way of proclaiming yourself one bad muthafucker.

EIGHT

THE FUTURE
SOUND OF
DETROIT

UNDERGROUND
RESISTANCE, +8, AND
CARL CRAIG

The first wave of Detroit techno reached its peak in 1988–9. The city was pumping, thanks to clubs like The Shelter and the legendary Music Institute, where Derrick May, Kevin Saunderson, Chez Damier and D. Wynn spun. At the same time, the Detroit sound was hugely popular on the European rave scene, where 'Strings of Life' achieved anthemic status in 1989 (several years after it was recorded) and Inner City were veritable pop stars.

Then it all went wrong. In early 1990, the Music Institute closed; *Techno 2*, the patchy sequel to Virgin's Detroit techno compilation, was badly received; Kevin Saunderson pursued a misguided R & B direction on the second Inner City album. Juan Atkins, frustrated at Network (where the more commercial Inner City had priority), eventually took his album-oriented ambitions for Model 500 to the Belgian label R & S. Disillusioned by bad deals and the theft of keyboards and software by one of his protégés, Derrick May stopped making music altogether. To top it all, DJ-ing opportunities in Europe took the Belleville Three away from their hometown with increasing frequency, leaving something of a vacuum. Without the first-wave mentor figures to guide and push the scene, younger producers had to seize the initiative. In the vanguard of this 'Future Sound of Detroit' were two labels, two DJ–producer squads – Underground Resistance and +8.

Combat Dancin'

Where the Belleville Three had grown up on Kraftwerk and Parliament-Funkadelic, the new breed had eighties influences: electro, UK synth-pop, industrial and Electronic Body Music. The result was a harsh Detroit hardcore that paralleled the brutalism of rave music in Britain, Belgium, Holland and Germany. The string-swept romanticism of Rythim Is Rythim was displaced in favour of riffs, industrial textures and a dystopian bleakness.

Underground Resistance's attitude was *hardcore* in another respect: the music embodied a kind of abstract militancy. Presenting themselves as a sort of techno Public Enemy, Underground Resistance were dedicated to 'fighting the power' not just through rhetoric but through fostering their own autonomy. For several months before they released anything, Jeff Mills and Mike Banks planned and theorized their operation. 'Most of the conversations were structural – whether we should have employees, what type of rules if any the label would run by,' says Mills. 'We looked at what other people in Detroit had done and where we thought they'd made mistakes ... To make sure someone didn't come in and take advantage of us, we didn't do an exclusive distribution deal with one company. We contacted all the distributors ourselves, the retailers and DJs. We got engaged with what was really happening, without the middle man situation.'

Although Mills now insists that 'there was nothing political' about UR's anti-corporate DIY stance, Mike Banks would probably beg to disagree. I say probably because 'Mad Mike' – a self-described 'serious brother', famous for his refusal to be pimped or 'tap dance' on cue – declined to be interviewed, arguing that the history of Detroit techno should be written by a Detroit native, and someone black. Just as UR struggled to retain business autonomy, similarly Banks seems determined to keep control of Detroit's 'subcultural capital'.

Underground Resistance presented themselves as a paramilitary unit, sonic guerrillas engaged in a war with 'the programmers' (the mainstream entertainment industry). According to Mills, this imagery was in large part the result of Banks' 'affection for the military ... I think his brother and his father were career army.' As well as the obvious parallel with Public Enemy and their Security of the First World militia, Underground Resistance's 'bacdafucup' militancy also resembles the terrorist chic of Front 242, Belgian pioneers of Electronic Body Music. According to Mills, in the late eighties, Detroit 'went through a techno/industrial phase ... with bands like Nitzer Ebb, Front 242, Meat Beat Manifesto ...' The stiff, punish-your-body beats and caustic electronic textures of EBM were also a crucial influence on the Belgian hardcore techno sound of the early nineties, which probably explains why UR's early efforts sound so similar to those of Benelux acts like Meng Syndicate, 80 Aum and Incubus.

After debuting with a vocal house track featuring chanteuse Yolanda, Underground Resistance released the 'Sonic EP'. Tracks like

'Predator' and 'Elimination' resemble target-seeking missiles, remorseless and implacable killing machines. Etched into the vinyl at the record's centre are the first of a series of UR slogans: 'to advance sonic is the key', 'the needs of the many outweigh the needs of the few'. After the malignant-sounding 'Waveform EP' and 'Gamma-Ray', Underground Resistance upped the ante with a series of insurrectionary 1991 releases. On the label of the 'Riot EP', the 'I' in 'RIOT' is a drawing of a masked and sunglass-wearing UR trooper dressed in black, resembling a PLO hijacker. The music is a kind of sonic pun on the ambiguity of the word 'riot' – which can mean both unrestrained revelry or a mob uprising, just as 'rave' can mean both wild enthusiasm and maniacal rage. The title track pivots around the looped call-to-arms 'now is the time', background uproar that could be party-goers or a political rally, and a red-alert bleep like a B-movie computer set to self-destruct. 'Panic' features a Mayday-signal riff based on a pitchbent vocal sample that sounds like a mind-spasm, a twinge of trepidation, plus a rather weak rap that conjures a state of emergency and insurgency. 'Rage' is driven by a fuzz-blare riff that's like Deep Purple's 'Smoke On The Water' run backwards.

Etched into the outer rim of the 12-inch is the mysterious phrase: 'The Fire In Us All'. What Underground Resistance seem to herald on 'Riot' and its sister 12-inch 'Fuel For The Fire' is a kind of Dionysian politics, a cult of orgiastic, unconstructive anger. If this was techno's punk-rock, the parallels were less with the rabble-rousing but ultimately goodhearted Clash, and closer to the appetite-for-destruction throbbing inside Sex Pistols' songs like 'Anarchy In The UK', or indeed songs by Detroit's own proto-punk outfit, The Stooges, such as 'Search and Destroy' and 'Raw Power'. Paralleling Iggy Pop's obsessions with electricity and amplification, his dream of becoming the conduit for anti-social/inhuman energies that override all the system's circuit breakers, the label of 'Riot' declares: 'all energy arranged, produced and mixed by Underground Resistance'.

After 'Fuel For The Fire' (a 12-inch which formed a double-pack with 'Riot') UR released 'Sonic Destroyer' under the alter-ego X-I01. The flipside, 'G-Force', saw UR exploring the non-musical possibilities of vinyl as a medium. The tracks' grooves are strangely patterned, bunched together normally then separating out into spirals, so that the stylus moves across the record in alarming fast-slow lunges that parallel the jagged time-lapse effect of 'G-Force' (which *sounds* like tremendous pressures buckling and distorting the human frame). 'We thought that if we could physically alter how the record works, it kind of sends out a signal that things aren't always the way they're supposed to be, or they appear to be,' says Jeff Mills. 'That maybe you should pay more attention to what you're buying or what you're listening to.'

As well as triggering ideas and confounding expectations, these 'gimmicks' also made the records into fetish objects, and added to the mystique of the band, who were by now a cult in Europe. Indeed, the music Underground Resistance were making at their 1991–2 peak was very much in synch with the reigning Euro-hardcore sound. 'Sonic Destroyer' features a classic rave-style Morse Code oscillator-riff, plus gastro-enteric bass-blasts like someone voiding their bowels in panic. 'Fury' is similar to T99's 'Belgian hoover' classic 'Anasthasia', heavy me(n)tal techno with *Carmina Burana*-like choral stabs. The only difference is that the fuel for UR's (f)ire isn't amphetamine psychosis but their peculiar brand of non-specific belligerence (hence the vague album title *Revolution For Change*).

This early, bellicose phase of Underground Resistance peaked with the awesome 'Death Star', which sounds like a gigantic, demonic glitterball, flashing off death-rays in every direction, pulverizing planets and vaporizing interstellar armadas. This time the slogan carved into the vinyl is 'Unit Deathstar Mission – Eliminate Anti-Underground Forces', making explicit the *Star Wars*-derived allegory of UR as Jedi Knights resisting the Evil Empire of the music industry; UR as gnostic warrior-priests who can channel 'The Force' (as one of the B-side tracks is titled). Shortly after 'Death Star' came 'Message To the Majors', an even more blatant two-finger salute to the record companies then signing up techno acts in anticipation of rave's breakthrough in America.

In the summer of 1992, UR formed a sub-label called World Power Alliance and issued three one-sided singles, all pertaining to the Second World War. On the music-free side of each release was etched a lengthy and rather bombastic communiqué to the pan-global techno underground:

... The Alliance is dedicated to the Advancement of the Human Race by Way of Sonic Experimentation ... The W. P. A. was designed to bring the world's minds together to combat the mediocre audio and visual programming being fed to the inhabitants of Earth, this programming is stagnating the minds of the people building a wall between races and world peace. The Wall must be destroyed, and it will Fall . . . By using the untapped energy potential of sound, the W. P. A. will smash the wall much the same as certain frequencies shatter glass. Brothers of the underground, transmit your tones and frequencies from all locations of this world and wreak havoc on the programmers. THIS IS WAR! Long Live The Underground.

The idea for the World Power Alliance emerged after the three members of UR – Mills, Banks and Rob Noise (Robert Hood) – had travelled outside Detroit. 'We thought it would be interesting for each of us to devote a particular release to a particular country and their armed forces,' says Mills. That two of the three 'armed forces' chosen belonged to Axis, rather than Allied, powers, is striking proof of the curiously apolitical and disinterested admiration UR had for military qualities like discipline, ruthlessness, *realpolitik* and subterfuge. Banks' effort, 'Kamikaze', comes with label notes that extravagantly hail the death-bound Japanese divebombers: 'With dedication unmatched in history, young men sacrifice their lives for something they believe in. With bravery like that one can never be beaten.' The Jeff Mills' composition is named 'The Seawolf' after the German U-boats that preyed on Allied merchant ships, and, breaking with traditional naval chivalry, gave no warning before attacking. 'TERROR FROM BELOW' is etched in the vinyl; the track sounds like a stalking subaquatic hunter, with a Roland 303 pulse seeming to home in on its target like a periscope's cross-hairs. Last in the series was Hood's 'Belgian Resistance'. Probably a tribute to Benelux hardcore, its label notes offered a bizarre fantasy of an 'underground legion' of anti-Nazi Belgians 'breeding and waiting in the dark, battle scarred caverns, waiting for revenge', decades after German surrender.

Knight of the Hunter

Underground Resistance the label wasn't just an outlet for Banks', Mills' and Hood's collective output as UR. They also released tracks by other second-wave Detroit artists, such as Drexciya (the sub-oceanic science fiction of EPs like 'The Aquatic Invasion' and 'The Bubble Metropolis'), Scan 7 and Suburban Knight, aka James Pennington.

Born in 1965, Pennington was actually a first-wave Detroit techno producer; a room mate of Kevin Saunderson's, he'd contributed to Inner City's 'Big Fun', and his first two Suburban Knight singles came out on Derrick May's Transmat label. Recorded in the mid-eighties but released only in 1990, Pennington's second release via Transmat – 'The Art of Stalking' – launched him on an obsession that runs through all his Underground Resistance work: nocturnal predators.

A pioneering slice of Detroit darkside, 'The Art of Stalking' consists of little more than a high-pitched, pizzicato bassline and highly-strung drum-track. The track twitches with tiptoe-and-tenterhook trepidation, leaving it up to the listener whether to identify with the pursuer or the pursued. The inspiration came from Pennington's fondness for American TV's *Discovery* channel, and specifically a wildlife documentary about the plains of Africa which used night-vision camera to show 'the lions killing gazelle, tigers just walking stealthily through the jungle then disappearing in seconds.'

Named after the word for 'a creature who hunts by night', Pennington's debut for Underground Resistance was 'Nocturbulous Behaviour', a twilight-zone surge through dread-soaked streets. The credits read 'mixed by the Ultimate Survivor', making explicit the political subtext of Pennington's fascination with night-vision: social Darwinism, the dog-eat-dog struggle of post-Fordist Detroit, with its apartheid-style ghost-townships and affluent white suburbs. Specifically, Pennington was inspired by the way the bat evolved radar to achieve an evolutionary edge, a topic he returned to with 1996's 'Echo Location' (on the 'By Night' EP).

Another inspiration came from a German journalist who hailed Suburban Knight's music as 'an advancement of "metal tank"'. This imaginary genre – 'metal tank' – fired Pennington's imagination because he was already obsessed with Germany, partly because of Kraftwerk and partly because of his grandfather's Second World War stories. 'Just the coldness,' he free-associates, 'Grey. Harshness. I thought Germany was like how it's televisioned over here. A black-and-white country that's been bombed to hell. And then these guys [Kraftwerk] came out of the rubble and made this electronic shit. That fascinated me. All the stuff that my grandfather was telling me, and the music that we were listening to from overseas, really came together as one whole picture.'

Taking a tangent away from this Teutonic terrordome of the mind's eye, Pennington's next outing for UR was one disc of the 1994 double-pack 'Dark Energy', an explicitly Afro-centric statement. Bearing the slogan 'escape the chains on your music' and a black-edged silhouette of the Dark Continent, the label revealed that the tracks were recorded in the Black Planet Studios (a homage to Public Enemy's third album *Fear of a Black Planet*) and that 'Strike Leader James (Suburban Night) Pennington' was commander in chief of these 'sonic strikes against programming strongholds'.

On Pennington's disc, the phosphorescent-sounding 'Midnight Sunshine' was inspired by his grandpa's tales of anti-aircraft flares and by his own 'infatuation with Playstation flight-simulation games'. 'Mau Mau (The Spirit)' was a tribute to the tribal guerrillas who harried white settlers in fifties Kenya. Pennington explains that the track is about how the Mau Mau 'reigned over' the European colonists, despite the latter's technological superiority. With the Black Panthers' inspired 'Mind Of A Panther' completing the tryptych, 'Dark Energy' as a whole was about 'going back to my roots, man . . . my [curiosity about] never seeing my homeland. I can't say I come from Somali Land, I don't know. But I wanna get back there. It was great back in that day, with spears and shields, against the cannons and guns.' The EP was an attempt to draw spiritual sustenance from this mind's eye Motherland, in order to survive as an exile in AmeriKKKa. 'It's a struggle to find where our true roots are. We've still got brothers killing brothers. White on black killing. I just think it would be settled a lot more if you knew where you came from and all the things you'd been through as a people. Not just being a slave and colonialism. 'Cos that's all we know – we don't know any ethnic dishes. I think we'd be better as a people if we knew that, if I could honestly say to you, "I come from the Zulu tribe".'

Forbidding Planet

Underground Resistance's musical evolution chimes in with a dialectic that runs through 'serious' black pop, a tension between the militant tendency and the mystic impulse. On one hand, there's the lineage of consciousness-raising agit-prop and righteous rage: The Last Poets, Gil Scott Heron, Public Enemy, KRS1. On the other, there's the 'black science fiction' tradition of otherworldly dreamers and eso-terrorists: Sun Ra, Lee Perry, George Clinton, Earth Wind and Fire, A. R. Kane. With its outer-spatial imagery and utopian/dystopian futurism, most Detroit techno falls into the second camp: transcending terrestrial oppression by travelling 'strange celestial roads' of the imagination.

Of course, some artists shift back and forth across the militant/mystic divide; Underground Resistance are a prime example. 'Where does my fascination with space come from? From wanting to escape from here,' Mike Banks told *Jockey Slut* magazine in a rare interview. With the album *X-102 Discovers The Rings of Saturn* (1992), the trio left behind terrestrial alienation for alien realms. '*X-102* was the first release where it became non-territorial,' says Mills. 'It's a planet in the solar system, but it became non-mankind, it exceeded all those barriers and territories.' Underground Resistance seemed fascinated by Saturn's inhuman and inhospitable qualities, its hostility to life; the sleevenotes invite the listener to 'imagine being in an atmosphere where all your god given senses are extinct ... where your existence is but a mere fragment in a ring around a nucleus that glows like a ball of fire.' Where most techno evocations of outer space are idyllic verging on twee, *X-102* is harsh and bleak; tracks like 'Enceladus', 'Hyperion' and 'Titan' offer a kind of astral industrial music.

With tracks for each of Saturn's three rings and nine moons, and one for the planet surface itself, *X-102* was a concept album. The sleevenotes relate information on the composition and possible origins of Saturn's satellites and rings; on the vinyl version, the grooves are patterned to correspond to the relative width of the rings and the distances *inter alia*. For the next instalment in the series, X-103, Mills and Co turned from one Sun Ra obsession (Saturn) to another: Atlantis. The group spent over six months researching the X-103 project. 'We had to find out the theories and the facts of Atlantis ... the shape of the city, what was actually in the temples, and relating things like that to vinyl, how we make the label actually significant, the grooves of the record.' The inner sleeve depicts a city plan of Atlantis, with its tree-ring like districts orbiting the centre, its palaces, horse-racing stadium, gardens and gymnasia. Although both *Rings of Saturn* and *Atlantis* are brilliant albums, the conceptual overkill, with its odd echo of mid-seventies prog rock, was a worrying sign. It set the tone for Mills's solo career, in which – by his own admission – concepts took up more of his energy than making the actual music.

Razing the Speed Limit

Like Underground Resistance, +8 – the other prime mover in Detroit's second wave – gradually evolved from industrial-tinged hardcore to a trippy-but-minimal 'progressive' techno sound that increasingly came with high-falutin' concepts attached. The label was formed by Richie Hawtin and John Aquaviva shortly after the pair met at The Shelter, where the nineteen-year-old Hawtin was DJ-ing. Both lived across the border in Canada. Aquaviva was a successful local DJ in London, Ontario, while Hawtin lived in Windsor (the Canadian automotive capital directly adjacent to Detroit), where his British father was a robotic technician at General Motors. Hawtin grew up in an intensely electronic atmosphere, surrounded by computers and the electrical gizmos constructed by his dad, and was exposed from an early age to Hawtin Sr.'s collection of Kraftwerk, Tangerine Dream and other synth records. As a teenager, Hawtin got into Front 242-style Electronic Body Music, then discovered Detroit techno.

When the pair met in 1989, Aquaviva had been DJ-ing for some time using the moniker J. Aquaviva +8. The name combined a pun on Chicago 'jack' tracks with the idea of playing with the Technics pitch-adjust shifted to plus 8 for maximum velocity. 'At that time, as DJs we were all playing faster,' remembers Hawtin, 'When Jeff Mills played on the radio' – as the Wizard, Mills could be heard six nights a week on WJLB – 'everything was cranked up, and it was so intense and progressive. [In 1989–90] the whole vibe was "let's go! Screw what's going on today or yesterday, we're about what's going on *tomorrow*!"'

In this spirit, Hawtin and Aquaviva christened their label +8, and, for their second release, put out a white label that bore no artist or track information, just the slogan: 'The Future Sound of Detroit'. This forth-right proclamation – not just 'we have arrived', but the implication that the old guard were now history – got the fledgling label a lot of atten-tion, but also put quite a few backs up amongst the first-wave Detroit music-makers: who the fuck were these Caucasian Canuck upstarts? When the track became more widely available in late 1990, 'Technarchy' by Cybersonik (Hawtin, Aquaviva and their mate Dan Bell) became a huge anthem in the European rave scene. Its ponderous bumble-bee of a bass riff slotted perfectly next to the bruising bombast of Euro-hardcore, but there was also a unique +8 quality, a cold Midwestern trippiness.

Over the next eighteen months, +8 unleashed a series of progressively faster and fiercer tracks, partly fuelled by their friendly rivalry with Underground Resistance. 'Vortex' by Final Exposure (a collaboration between Hawtin and Joey Beltram and Mundo Muzique of Second Phase/'Mentasm' fame) is like being sucked up inside a cyclone composed of African killer-bees. Recording solo as F. U. S. E. (it stood for Futuristic Underground Subsonic Experiments), Hawtin revived the acid house Roland 303 sound on mantra-nomic monsters like 'Substance Abuse' and 'F. U.' The latter might be his all-time masterpiece: an audio-analogue of Vasarely's op art, 'F. U.' and its sequel 'F. U. 2' induce a dark exultation, a sense of locked-on-target propulsion.

+8's headlong escalation to harder-faster extremities peaked in early 1992 with Circuit Breaker's 'Overkill' / 'Frenz-E' and Cybersonik's 'Thrash'. The latter was intended almost as a piss-take on other rave producers who were equating intensity with hardness and velocity. 'It got to the point where we felt "wooah, time to put the brakes on!"' says Hawtin. He and Bell put out one final Cybersonik record at the start of 1993, 'Machine Gun' b/w 'Jackhammer', crediting its production to The White Noise Association. 'We don't even like that record, it was a statement [to the rest of the rave scene] – kind of, "we don't know what you guys are doing, but it's not what we're about".'

Like 'progressive'-minded producers across the globe, +8 were aghast at the drug-fuelled dynamic that was driving hardcore techno to new extremes of braindead brutalism. Despite having played no small role in this escalation, they were now recoiling from the remorseless acceleration of the tempo, the increasingly regimented and funkless nature of the rhythms. The music was changing not just because of Ecstasy and amphetamine abuse, but because of the context it was designed for – raves, not clubs. 'There was a revolution against clubs,' remembers Aquaviva, 'Kind of 'fuck this tired old shit, we're gonna do our own thing in a warehouse.' At one-off raves, promoters booked a lot of DJs, so that instead of one or two DJs playing all night for their regular crowd, it shifted to shorter sets.'

Rather than taking the audience on a journey with peaks and lows, the rave DJs played full-on non-stop for the whole of their hour on the decks – partly to avoid being blown away by the next DJs and partly to pander to the drug-fuelled requirements of the audience. 'Even though the DJs rose in stature, they were handcuffed in what they could do,' says Aquaviva. 'DJ-ing as an artform took a step back.' The music also got harder and faster because the warehouse raves were one-offs. 'Instead of going to a couple of clubs every week, the tendency was to save your pent-up energy for the one-off rave, go all out ... All these factors came together and made rave culture into a different animal from club culture – the raves were more like illegal rock 'n' roll concerts. It was fun at the time, but it got a little out of control.'

The turning point for Hawtin and Aquaviva came in early 1992 when they found themselves in a Rotterdam club called Parkzicht – the crucible for the Dutch ultra-hardcore sound called *gabba*. 'Gabba is Dutch for buddy,' says Aquaviva. 'A lot of the guys are dock workers, they're into harder music, so gabba is basically the sound of the buddies letting off steam.' At Parkzicht, the DJs and crowd were very partial to 'Thrash Beats', the stripped down version of Cybersonik's 'Thrash' – at 150 b.p.m., the fastest +8 release to date. Hawtin and Aquaviva noticed that the Rotterdam ruffneck audience were yelling along to the song. With slowly dawning horror, they realized that what sounded like a football chant was actually 'joden, joden' ('jews, jews'). In fact, it *was* a football chant, used by supporters of Rotterdam's team Feynoord against Amsterdam's Ajax (whose fans sometimes flew the Israeli flag at games, as a proud nod to the city's Jewish mercantile past). 'Our Dutch friends are, like, "no worries, it's just a football chant",' says Aquaviva. 'But I'm like, "fuck that, that's not who I am. I'm not a Nazi, I can make people rock without making them be hostile."'

From that point on, +8 changed tack. 'Intensity = good, hard = bad' was now the label's creed; bringing back the funk and the soul to electronic music was the quest. Aquaviva started the house-oriented sub-label Definitive, while Hawtin directed his energies towards the fusion of Detroit techno and Chicago acid via his new alter-ego Plastikman. 'It was always the one sound that didn't sound like anything you'd ever heard,' he says, trying to explain the Roland TB 303's magnetic appeal. Plastikman's 1993 debut album *Sheet One* was one long paean to the synergy of 303's and LSD. Tracks like 'Plasticine' offer a kind of monochrome, sensory-deprivation version of psychedelia. The cover – a simulation of a perforated sheet of acid blotters – is so convincing that a young man in Texas, pulled over for a traffic violation, was arrested when the cop saw the CD insert lying on his car seat. 'He was thrown in jail for a couple of days while the cops tested it,' says Hawtin, 'I felt sorry for the kid but I don't know if he was showing off to his friends, pretending he had acid. I know of other people who've sold the CD covers as real acid. There were people who ate the whole thing trying to get a buzz off it.'

Having helped kickstart gabba in Holland with 'Thrash Beats', +8 also contributed to the evolution of German trance. Hawtin's neo-acid direction was an important influence, but the real catalyst was the streamlined kineticism of +8 artist Speedy J, aka Dutch producer Jochem Paap. 'Along with other Detroit-sounding artists, we were some of the first people to go to Germany,' says Aquaviva. 'Towards the end of '91, we performed at Berlin Independence Days.' At this music festival, Speedy J played live, and 'blew us and all the Detroit guys away. And that spurred his track "Pullover" into the huge success that it was. Although he's Dutch, he's one of the foreigners who helped put the second wave of Detroit on the map. Speedy is as much Detroit and Chicago as anyone, and he took it to that other level, he set the tone in Europe. [The Germans] had their own scene, but we certainly gave them impetus [to become] one of the techno powerhouses.'

In the mid-nineties, Berlin became a haven for many Detroit producers. Blake Baxter and Jeff Mills moved there for some time; Juan Atkins and Eddie 'Flashin'' Fowlkes released tracks via the Berlin purist techno label Tresor, and collaborated with 3MB's Thomas Fehlmann and Moritz Von Oswald. Tresor subtitled their second compilation: *Berlin – Detroit: A Techno Alliance*. Underground Resistance were particularly influential on the Frankfurt labels Force Inc and PCP. Citing 'The Art of Stalking' as his favourite track of all time, PCP's The Mover offered a Teutonic take on Suburban Knight's creepy, crepuscular sound – tracks like 'Nightflight (Non-Stop To Kaos)', post-apocalyptic EPs like 'Frontal Sickness' and 'Final Sickness', and a 12 inch on R & S released under the very UR-like alter-ego Spiritual Combat. Meanwhile, Richie Hawtin and Speedy J's tracks for +8 influenced the 303-fired hardtrance of labels like Frankfurt's Harthouse and Berlin's MFS.

That said, +8 were eventually as perturbed by the evolution of trance as they were by Dutch gabba. 'At one hard party in Limburgh in '92, they had these Thorens turntables that could go to plus 25,' remembers Aquaviva. 'The DJ was playing this really heavy trance and the people were dancing like zombies, arms out and bouncing to the 160–180 b.p.m. rhythms. This freaked me out, I called it the Nazi waltz. Later I was DJ-ing, playing classic techno and house, and the DJ came up and said: "Can't you play anything the crowd likes, and that's y'know, faster?" I vowed never to play in Germany, and in fact it took me a year and half to play there again.'

Nonetheless, there did seem to be a striking affinity between the American Midwestern and German ideas of rave. There was an industrial influence, both environmental (in the Ruhr/General Motors sense) and musical (Electronic Body Music). There was even a weird racial link, in so far as Michigan, Minnesota, Illinois and other Midwestern states had a high proportion of German and Scandinavian settlers. 'I think the Midwest and Northern Europe have a lot of common bonds,' concurs Aquaviva. 'I DJ in the South of Europe a lot, and the Mediterranean people are much more laid back, so I play more groovier, house-ier music. Spain has very little in common with Detroit!'

As trance got more metronomic and monolithic, Richie Hawtin dedicated himself to bringing back 'the groove, the soulfulness' of the Roland 303 acid sound. 'To me the 303 always had this weird funkiness, I always found the 303 really *sexy*.' His response was a drastic drop in tempo on the second Plastikman album, 1994's *Muzik*, resulting in mid-tempo 303 ballads that took you on a pleasant stroll through the cosmos instead of breaking the speed limit on the Astrobahn. As a DJ, Hawtin was also bucking the trance-core trend for full-on velocity, by mixing in house and even garage tunes. 'That was during the years after the separation of [techno into different styles]. It was a depressing thing for a lot of us. I've always enjoyed playing longer sets. When I do them, I take things up-down, fast-slow, encompassing different kinds of music.'

This anti-rave philosophy informed +8's parties in the Midwest. 'It wasn't just about playing all new superhard stuff,' says Aquaviva, 'It was about two DJs playing the whole night, embracing the old principles of house, when there weren't enough records being made to play only one style all night.' Says Hawtin: 'We're not putting on raves, we're not putting on flashy coloured lightshows and your favourite ten DJs. It's me and John and one or two other people ... We create some kind of weird atmosphere in a room, put a great system in, and build an atmosphere for people to lose themselves into. Very minimal, stripped down, bare bones, but a lot of thought goes into it.' +8 did an event called Heaven and Hell, with 'a black room where it was just very intense, and a chill-out room which was all white – white mattresses, little children's bathing pools, bowls of fruit. It was like heaven, and it was to make people realize that this music isn't just about *losing it*.' Despite the LSD-blotter cover of *Sheet One*, +8 also began to distance themselves from hallucinogens, as they saw the drug abuse get out of hand on the American rave scene. 'People I know just went overboard with Ecstasy,' says Hawtin. 'So there's a little tag line on the second Plastikman album, that says "Just because you like chocolate cake, doesn't mean you eat it everyday." That was just a backhanded way of saying "'Cmon guys, figure it out, get a grip."'

We Are the Music Makers

Unlike Chicago acid house, Detroit techno was never a drug-oriented music. The word 'rave', with its connotations of frenzy and loss-of-control, had never been applicable to the elegant aestheticism of Derrick May and Co. By 1993, the more serious-minded producers in Britain and Europe were embarking on a return to Detroit principles, as a way of sidestepping what they perceived as the drug-determined dead ends of hardcore and hard trance. For guidance, they looked to three figures and three directions: the 'hi-tech jazz' being made by Mad Mike under the aegis of Underground Resistance and Red Planet, the austere minimalism of Jeff Mills, and the softcore romanticism of Carl Craig.

Born in 1969 and brought up in Detroit's middle-class West Side, Craig took Detroit's Europhile tendencies even further than his mentor Derrick May. As a sensitive teenager, he was into bands like The Cure, Bauhaus and The Smiths. 'I could relate to Morrissey, 'cos he sounded like somebody who never got any women,' he says. Alongside his diet of Anglo miserablism and avant-funk like Mark Stewart and Throbbing Gristle (he later named an EP 'Four Jazz Funk Greats' in homage to one of TG's albums), Craig shared the typical Motor City appetite for synth-driven dance music. He dug Prince, Kraftwerk and Italian 'progressive' disco. Falling under May's tutelage, he toured Europe as a member of Rythim Is Rythim, worked on the 1989 remix of 'Strings of Life', and in 1991 co-wrote the sublime 'Kao-Tic Harmony' (which was released as the flipside of Derrick May's only nineties release to date, 'Icon'). By this point, Craig was already making his own tracks and releasing them via his own labels RetroActive and Planet E, using a plethora of whimsical alter-egos: Psyche, BFC (it stood for Betty Ford Clinic), Piece, Six Nine, Shop, Innerzone Orchestra and Paperclip People.

Psyche's 'Elements' was the solitary highlight of *Techno 2*, the disappointing sequel to the Virgin compilation that had first put Detroit on the map. Reflective, in both the 'introspective' and 'opalescent' senses of the word, 'Elements' revealed Craig to be Detroit's most gifted miniaturist. With its open-hearted yearning and twinkling textures, 'Elements' conjured up the image of a lonely boy moping in a bedroom studio, where he combined his lo-tech palette of tone-colours and his teardrops to paint exquisite audio watercolours. There were shades of the electro-calligraphic brushwork of Thomas Leer, Japan and Sylvian/Sakomoto. This wasn't party-hard music, but the pensive frettings of one of life's wallflowers. Indeed, the low-key anxiety of 'Neurotic Behaviour' (from the first Psyche EP, released in 1990) was a world away from the psychotic tantrums of hardcore techno.

Taking the Detroit desolation of May's work towards an almost fey forlorn-ness, Craig became a role model for all those techno artists in Britain, like The Black Dog, who wanted to make album-length, home-oriented electronic mindfood. He became the producer's producer, worshipped for the texturological detail and nuance in his compositions. On BFC's 'Galaxy', the glowing synth-pulse really sounds like the spermazoic spangle of the Milky Way; on 'Evolution', the whispery treated breakbeat is a rustle that makes your brain itch, rather than your feet twitch. The guru of softcore, Craig's tracks generally elevate atmospherics over energy; his rhythms are relentlessly, restlessly intelligent, but rarely that dance-coercive; the rudimentary looped breakbeat on BFC's 'Please Stand By' is inspired by Shut Up And Dance, but it doesn't capture their 'ardkore fervour. Another Craig classic – Innerzone Orchestra's 1992 release 'Bug In The Bassbin' – has been hailed as a prototype for jungle. But the track's loping double-bassline and breakbeat shuffle, while engagingly off-kilter, is neither jungalistic nor particularly danceable.

Journalist Tony Marcus's verdict on the Six Nine track 'Desire' – closer to 'an emotion bomb than a dance record' – applies to most of Craig's work. As with the May/Craig collaboration 'Kao-Tic Harmony',

'Desire' features a keening synth melody that soars up and slides down the octave in fitful lurches; it feels like a kite, whose strings are attached to your heart, being tugged and buffeted by the wind. 1993's 'At Les' – released under Carl's own name – is even more moistly melancholy. The trickle-down synth-pattern sounds like a syncopated sob, like fat teardrops rolling down a cheek. Like a couple of other early Craig classics, the song reappeared on his 1997 album *More Songs About Food and Revolutionary Art*. The title is a high-minded sounding but vague call to arms. In the spirit of the first-wave Detroit aesthetes, this is a bourgois-bohemian crusade for refinement, taste, elegance. As Craig puts it in the sleevenotes, 'This is not a revolution against government. This is a revolution against ignorance.'

While Carl Craig became the touchstone for many British producers who wanted to make atmospheric home-listening electronica, those who remained committed to the dancefloor looked to Underground Resistance and its former members Jeff Mills and Robert Hood. With Mills and Hood departed, UR became a Mike Banks solo project in all but name. On the 'Galaxy 2 Galaxy' double-EP, Banks abandoned juggernaut industrialism for a rhapsodic fusion-tinged sound ('Hi-Tech Jazz', as the opening track put it), hints of which had been heard in earlier UR classics like 'Eye of the Storm' and 'Jupiter Jazz'. The warrior-priest iconography endured: the labels depicted Bruce Lee and Geronimo, the latter a nod to Banks' half Native American ancestry. But the music sounded pacific rather than militant – all fluttery arpeggiated twirls and nimble-fingered fluency. With the cosmic disco of 'Starsailing', UR seemed to have finally ascended into the mystic. Engraved into the run-out vinyl of the fourth side of the EP was a proclamation: 'Alpha / Omega – Final Transmission: I Found It / There Is Existence Other than Us / I Have Transformed. The Tones are the Keys To It All! I'll Be Back – Mad Mike.'

Any fears that Banks had swapped his rage for space-cadet serenity were partly assuaged by his series of Red Planet EPs. In Mars, the warlike planet, he found an image that perfectly reconciled the militant/ mystic dialectic. Although Jeff Mills now denies that there was ever any anger or politics involved in Underground Resistance, Banks – in his rare public utterances – has spoken out about the twin genocides in his family tree (his mother Blackfoot Indian, his father black) and how they fuel his struggle against the 'forktongue' propaganda of the 'programmers'. Like the Wu Tang Clan's use of rhymes as 'liquid

swords', Banks proposes resistance through tribal rhythms, through
the war dance. On the 'Red Planet VI' EP, the highpoint of the series,
'Ghostdancer' is named after the messianic religion that swept through
the reservation-trapped and defeat-traumatized Native American tribes
in the 1890s – the desperate belief that by dancing and chanting the
white invaders could be magicked out of existence and the dead
tribespeople brought back to life. Much of the time, however, the sleek
sheen of tracks like 'Skypainter' and 'Windwalker' summons up the
spirits of George Benson and Stanley Clarke rather than Crazy Horse
and Eldridge Cleaver.

Mills and Hood, meanwhile, were developing their enormously
influential brand of minimalist techno with the *Waveform Transmission*
album series. 1993's *Vol. 2* – recorded by Hood as The Vision –
proclaimed: 'This release is dedicated to the form of simplicity the
reasoning of vision.' Hood's 1994 double-pack 'Minimal Nation' and
Internal Empire album offered the aural equivalent of a bread-and-
water regime. Jeff Mills's output is at least energizing in its stark
ferocity. On *Waveform Transmission Vol. 1* and *Vol. 3*, four-on-the-
floor techno is taken as hard and fast as it can go without actually
turning into gabba. This is techno as monastic discipline, rigour as
mortification of the flesh. The spartan frenzy and flagellating pulses of
'The Hacker' and 'Wrath of The Punisher' are like a scourge for the
hedonistic excesses of rave. Chaste, chastening, a chastisement: Mills's
music brings a whole new spin to the drug slang 'getting caned'.

Mills's other big influence on Detroit purists is his conceptualism.
Waveform Transmission Vol. 3 came with lofty-sounding and frankly
pompous sleevenotes: 'As barriers fall around the world, the need to
understand others and the way they live, think and dream is a task that
is nearly impossible to imagine without theory and explanation. And
as we approach the next century with hope and prosperity, this need
soon becomes a necessity rather than a recreational urge.' For the
releases on his own Axis label, Mills's music became increasingly
concept-driven. 'Cycle 30', for instance, took the vinyl-innovations of
UR to the furthest degree: the release consisted of nine locked grooves,
five second riffs and beat-loops that were designed for DJs to use as
mixing material. 'Cycle 30' also referred to Mills's belief that 'roughly
every thirty years we seem to repeat ourselves in terms of music,
fashion, design ... In the sixties, there was this thirst for innovation
... If you go back [thirty years earlier] to the thirties, it's also a big

time of innovation: New York's World Fair, *Superman*, a lot of home appliances . . . the washing machine and all that crazy stuff, the toaster, the waffle iron.' Based on his belief in such dubious cycles, Mills argues that the era of minimal techno (allegedly an echo of sixties minimalist art) is about to give way to a form of abstract expressionist techno, with producers bringing more of their signature back into the music.

Keeping the Faith

Jeff Mills belongs to a tradition of black scholar-musicians and autodidacts: Sun Ra, Anthony Braxton, Derrick May, DJ Spooky. Instead of inspiring thoughtless, sweaty fun, Mills believes dance music should be the vehicle for lofty intellectualism and weighty-verging-on-ponderous concepts. 'Let me be very very clear,' he says, with the barest hint of annoyance. 'Underground Resistance wasn't militant, nor was it angry . . . I'm not angry now . . . The music that I make now has absolutely nothing to do with colour. It has nothing to do with man/woman, East/West, up/down, but more [to do with] "the mind". The mind has no colour . . . There's this perception that if you're black and you make music, then you must be angry. Or you must be "deep". Or you must be out to get money and women. Or you must be high when you made that record. It's one of the four. And the media does a really good job of staying within those four categories. But in these cases, it's neither of those.'

To which you might respond, what's left? If you remove race, class, gender, sexuality, the body and the craving for intoxication from the picture, what exactly remains to fuel the music? Just the 'pure' play of ideation. The result is music that appeals to a disinterested and disembodied consciousness. The formalism of minimal techno has some parallels with minimalism in the pictorial arts and in avant-classical composition; both have been critiqued as spiritualized evasions of political reality, as attempts to transcend the messy and profane realm of History and Materiality in the quest for the 'timeless' and territorially unbounded.

If the musical legacy of Derrick May and Jeff Mills is largely unimpeachable, the mentality they have fathered throughout the world of 'serious' techno is, I believe, a largely pernicious influence. This anti-Dionysian mindset favours elegance over energy, serenity over passion, restraint over abandon. It's a value system shared by Detroit purists both within the Motor City and across the globe. In Detroit itself, artists like Alan Oldham, Stacy Pullen/Silent Phase, Kenny Larkin, Dan Curtin, Claude Young, Jay Denham, Marc Kinchen, Terence Dixon and John Beltran, uphold the tradition. Many of these producers were corralled on to a 1996 double CD compiled by Eddie 'Flashin'' Fowlkes, which he titled *True People* as a stinging rebuke to the rest of the world for daring to tamper with the Detroit blueprint. Detroit is living in denial. Techno has long since slipped out of its custodianship, the evolution-through-mutation of music has thrown up such mongrels as bleep-and-bass, Belgian hardcore, jungle, trance and gabba, all of which owe as much to other cities (the Bronx; Kingston, Jamaica; Dusseldorf; Sheffield; London; Chicago) as they do to Detroit. The ancestral lineage of Detroit has been contaminated by 'alien' genes; the music's been 'bastardized'. But lest we forget, illegitimate heirs tend to lead more interesting lives.

If anything, the idea and ideal of 'Detroit' is even stronger outside the city, thanks to British Detroit-purists. Leading lights in the realm of neo-Detroit 'abstract dance' include the British labels Soma, Ferox, Ifach and Peacefrog, and producers like Peter Ford, Dave Angel, Neil Landstruum, Funk D'Void, Ian O'Brien (who titled a track 'Mad Mike Disease' as a nod to the endemic influence of the UR/Red Planet maestro), The Surgeon, Russ Gabriel, Luke Slater, Adam Beyer and Mark Broom (whose alter ego Midnight Funk Association is named after the Electrifyin' Mojo's legendary Detriot radio show). It is a world where people talk not of labels but 'imprints', and funk is spelt 'phunk' to give it an air of, er, phuturism.

One of the most vocal of the Detroit-acolytes is tech-jazz artist Kirk deGiorgio. From early efforts like 'Dance Intellect' to his late nineties As One output, deGiorgio has dedicated himself to the notion that Detroit techno is the successor to the synth-oriented jazz-funk of fusioneers like Herbie Hancock and George Duke. 'I never saw techno as anything else but a continuation of black music,' he told *Muzik* magazine in 1997. 'I didn't think of it as any new kind of music. It was just that the technology and the sounds were different.'

This neo-conservative attitude – the self-effacing notion that white musicians like deGiorgio himself have nothing to add to black music; the idea that music never really undergoes revolutions – reminds me of nothing so much as the British blues-bore purists of the late sixties and early seventies. Actually, given that Detroit techno was a response to European electro-pop, we should really reverse the analogy: Atkins, May and Saunderson are equivalent to Clapton, Beck and Page, virtuoso players worshipped for their purist fidelity to the original music (Kraftwerk for the Belleville Three, Muddy Waters for the ex-Yardbirds). The hip-hop influences (breakbeats and samples) that revolutionized British rave music are studiously shunned by the Detroit purists, who believe synthesizers are more 'musical' than computers. There is literally no *future* in this traditionalist approach; the notion that the music of Derrick May (or Carl Craig, or Jeff Mills) represents the Way, the Light and the Truth is no more helpful than the early seventies belief that 'Clapton Is God'.

This is not to say that Detroit techno has nothing more to offer electronic music. For instance, Kevin Saunderson (the most *im*purist of the Belleville Three – he even put out great hardcore tracks in 1992 like 'Uptempo' and 'Mental Techno', using the alter-ego Tronikhouse) has inspired some exciting records, like Dave Clarke's 'Red' series. In the wake of UR outfit Drexciya, the Detroit area has also seen an upsurge of electro-influenced music–artists like Ectomorph, Aux 88 and Dopplereffekt, labels like Interdimensional Transmissions and Direct Beat. Returning to Detroit techno's early eighties roots as a distant cousin of New York electro, these producers have thrillingly revived Kraftwerk's glacial Germanic geometry and rigid drum machine beats, but – breaking with Detroit's overly refined aura – they also add a booty-shaking boom influenced by Miami bass music's lewd low frequency oscillations.

Meanwhile, in Europe, the Tresor-affiliated labels Basic Channel and Chain Reaction have brilliantly pursued their vision of tech-house abstraction through a million shades of lustrous grey. But for the most part, European neo-Detroit techno-phunk is music that feels anal and inhibited, crippled by its fear of heterodoxy. Its 'radicalism' is defined by its refusals, by what it *denies itself* – overt tunefulness, explicit emotion, vulgar exuberance, breakbeats, intoxication. Detroit-purism was born of the impulse to de-crass-ify techno and restore it to its pre-rave sobriety and subtlety. A cruel irony, then, that Colin Faver's long-running 'Abstrakt Dance' show on KISS FM was terminated in the spring of 1997, in order to make room for happy hardcore, the cheesy-and-cheerful sound of rave fundamentalism at its most defiantly E'd up.

NINE

THIS SOUND
IS FOR THE
UNDERGROUND

PIRATE RADIO

'Well out of that now, into this – sounds of the Lucky Spin, believer! Along with the MC OC, along with the full studio crew. Lively business! Shout going out to Rattle, you know the koo. Cooked food, love it to the bone! To the marrow! Normality, believe! L-I-V-E and direct, to the koo. Are you ready, wind-your-waist crew? And those who's driving around Don-land North East South and West, *we've got you locked*!!! 10.57, get on the case, for the hardcore, hardcore bass. For ya face – 100 per cent bass! All right, red-eye crew, you know the koo. Going out to you, wind-your-waist crew . . . and all those who's *l-l-l-lickin'* *it* in Don-land in their cars, driving about Don-land, the Don-ites and Don-'eads. Do-it-like-this, jungalist! Believe me, 'ardkore's firing!'

– MC OC, Don FM, 1993

All through the nineties, London's 'ardkore and jungle pirate stations have disrupted the decorum of the FM airwaves with their vulgar fervour and rude-boy attitude. MCs surf the DJs' polyrhythmic pandemonium of breaks 'n' bass with a Dada-doggerel of druggy buzzwords, party-hard exhortations and renegade war-cries: sublime 'nonsense' that is purely invocatory, designed to bind its scattered addressees into a community, mobilize it into an army.

London's jungle pirates come and go, but at any time of year, you can scan the frequency spectrum at the weekend and find at least a dozen. There are many more illegal stations in the capital, and throughout Britain, representing other dance-genres neglected by mainstream radio: dancehall reggae, soul, house and garage, rap, and more. Some regard themselves as a providers of a community service, like North London reggae pirate Station FM, with its anti-drug messages and funki-dread positivity. And some are so well-organized and well-behaved they're like independent commercial radio stations that just haven't bothered to secure a licence, like Dream FM in Leeds, with its all-week-long transmissions and stringent rules about no swearing on air, no playing records with drug references.

My passion, though, is for the pirate stations that seem the most piratical, the stations for whom surviving outside the law is part of the thrill. And that means the jungle pirates. Actually, given that jungle stations like Kool got more 'professional' by the late nineties, it really means the unruly 'ardkore pirates of 1991–3: Touchdown, Defection, Rush, Format, Pulse, Eruption, Impact, Destiny, Function, and many more.

Out of a personal archive of hundreds of hours of taped transmissions, my favourite sequence is from a mid-week broadcast by a station called Lightning, seemingly hi-jacked for just one night by the FMB Crew (it stands for Fucking Mind Bending). After about an hour of rambling, nursery-rhyme banter, ranging from the sinister and scatological to the nonsensical and outright indecipherable, the duo suddenly get possessed by a kind of free-associational delirium. The soundtrack is a wondrously zany X Project track that warps choirboy Aled Jones's hit 'Walking In The Air' into a speedfreak anthem: 'we're walking in the air / while people down below are sleeping as we fly'.

MC no. 1: 'Biggin' up the Acting Hard Massive. Stiff as an 'ard on!
   Work it up! Working up the-rush-in-the-place!'
MC no. 2: 'And it's haitch with a hot.'
MC no. 1: 'Biggin' up the Hot Man, the Metal Man, hold it down.
   Cinders. You know the score . . . Cackooo Crew! Big it up, big it up,
   doing-the-do!'
MC no. 2: 'Havin' em in the loo, in the loo-'
MC no. 1: 'Hot hot-'
MC no. 2: 'Doing a lovely poo poo!'
MC no. 1: 'Buzzin' hard! Having a bubble, in the studio.'
MC no. 2: '*Trippin' out*! Phone us an ambulance. Phone don't work,
   give us bell – see if it works. Could save a life or two. Or three.
   Come on, rush with me!'
MC no. 1: 'Going out to Sammy in Stratford, you know the koo. The
   didgeridoo, the 'abadabadoo.'
MC no. 2 (increasingly deranged and demonic): 'Doing it doing it with
   the poo. Sounds of the big cack-ooo. Going out to the buzzin' 'ard
   crew. You know the koo, koo. Crispy like a crouton! Sounds of the
   'ot with an haitch. Getting hot in the place. Steamin'. Rollin'. You

know the koo. Flex tops are doing the do. Respect is due. To you and your crew.'

MC no. 1: 'Sounds of the South, man. Buzzin'.'

It loses something in transcription: the intonation, the grain of the voice, the instinctual syncopation and drugged slurriness. But I'm not taking the piss when I say that I rate this – and scores more snatches of phonetic poetry plucked from London's pirate airwaves – among my favourite 'cultural artefacts' of the twentieth century.

Fuck the Legal Stations

'The future does not exist for them.'

– Postmaster General Tony Benn, promising to outlaw
Britain's first wave of pirate radio stations, 1965.

Pirate radio gets its romantic name not just from its flagrant flouting of government restrictions on the airwaves, but from its early days in the sixties, when unlicensed stations broadcast from ships anchored at sea just outside British territorial waters, or from derelict Army and Navy forts on the Thames Estuary. By 1966, Radio London claimed over eight million listeners, and Radio Caroline over six million; pirate DJs were cult stars and stations had their own fan clubs. But this first golden age of pirate radio came to an abrupt end when Harold Wilson's Labour government instituted The Marine Broadcasting Offences Act in August 1967, making it unlawful to operate, finance, or aid in any way an unlicensed station. As a sop to public demand, the BBC launched its own national pop station, Radio One, and recruited many pirate DJs, such as Tony Blackburn, John Peel, Johnny Walker and Dave Lee Travis.

In the early eighties, pirate radio entered its second boom period, with the rise of black music stations like Horizon, JFM, Dread Broadcasting Corporation and LWR, specializing in the soul, reggae and funk that Radio One marginalized. But the nautical connotations of 'pirate' had faded; the new pirates broadcast not just from the mainland, but from tower blocks in the heart of the metropolis. As the government closed loopholes in the law and increased the penalties, the illegal stations grew ever more cunning in their struggle to outwit the anti-pirate agents of the Department of Trade and Industry (DTI). The invention of the microlink (a method of relaying the station's signal to a distant transmitter) made it harder for the DTI to trace and raid the illegal station's studio-HQ. The result was an explosion of piracy; by 1989–90, there were over 600 stations nationwide, and 60 in the London area alone. And by 1989, a new breed of rave pirates – Sunrise, Centre Force, Dance FM, Fantasy – had joined the ranks of established black dance stations like LWR and Kiss.

As in the sixties, the government responded with the double whammy of suppression and limited permission. In a weird echo of the pardons offered buccaneers and corsairs in the seventeenth century, pirate stations were offered an amnesty if they went off the air, and a chance to apply for one of the bonanza of licences being made available as part of the Conservative government's policy of 'freeing' the airwaves. LWR and Kiss closed down voluntarily, but only Kiss won a licence. The legitimization of Kiss FM, in combination with an ultra-tough Broadcasting Act in January 1990, reduced pirate activity to its lowest since 1967.

But in 1992, the London pirates resurged massively, as a crucial component of hardcore rave's underground infrastructure, alongside home-studio recording, indie labels, white label releases and specialist record stores. Abandoning the last vestiges of mainstream pop radio protocol, the new 'ardkore pirates sounded like 'raves on the air': rowdy, chaotic, with the DJ's voiceover replaced by a raucous rave-style MC (Master of Ceremonies), and with a strong emphasis on audience participation (enabled by the spread of the portable cellular phone, which made the studio location impossible to trace by the DTI). Despite the government's fresh package of draconian penalties (the threat of unlimited fines, prison sentences of up to two years, and the confiscation of all studio equipment – including the DJ's precious record collection), 1992–3 saw the biggest boom in the history of radio piracy. Undeterred, the pirate attitude was, in the words of a track by Rum and Black – '**** the Legal Stations'.

Renegade Soundwaves

Surviving as a pirate station in the nineties involves a mix of graft, skill and cunning similar to that possessed by their seafaring namesakes of the sixteenth and seventeenth centuries. Because it's easy for the DTI to track a transmission back to its source, pirate stations use a microwave transmitter to 'beam' their programmes from the studio to a remote transmitter, where it is then broadcast to the public. Because these 'micro-links' operate by a line-of-sight, directional beam, the DTI can trace the signal back to the pirate studio only once they've got to the top of the tower block and located the aerial transmitter. The smarter pirate stations attach a cut-out switch to the roof-top door, which cuts the power supply and breaks the link. This ensures that the DTI can't trace the beam from the top of the tower block back to the studio, and that all the pirate station loses in the raid is a transmitter worth a few hundred pounds. The pirate can then redirect its micro-link beam to a back-up transmitter on top of another building.

When the DTI comes down hard on a particular station, it can lose several transmitters each weekend. It's an expensive business, and the pirates that endure are those with a sound financial infrastructure. Revenue comes from advertising (mostly for raves and clubs, specialist record shops and compilation albums). The rest of the money comes from the DJs, who – in a testament to the idealism and love-not-money amateur ethos behind pirate radio – actually pay a small fee for the privilege of playing.

Right back to the sixties, pirate radio has been tarnished with a money-grubbing, criminal-minded reputation. In 1989, for instance, several Centre Force DJs were arrested for Ecstasy dealing, while accusations of gangster ties and coded, on-air drug transactions have often been levelled at the 'ardkore pirates. But for all their conspiratorial, clandestine aura, most pirates' criminal activities are limited to the struggle to protect the station and stay on the air. According to legend, one station – Rush FM – turned the upper storeys of an abandoned East London tower block into a fortress so impregnable that the DJs had to abseil up the side of the building to reach the studio. They sealed the normal entrance with concrete, through which they'd inserted metal scaffolding. They then pumped the scaffolding's metal tubing full of ammonia gas, and linked the scaffold to the electrical mains. When the local council turned up to break down the barricade, the man operating the pneumatic drill got electrocuted, the spark ignited the gas, and the concrete bulwark exploded, showering the workers with debris.

Such paranoid/paramilitary strategies are exceptional. But cut-off switches, booby traps and alarms are used to protect transmitters – not just from the DTI, but from other pirates who will steal the equipment if given the opportunity. Reflecting the dog-eat-dog nature of nineties lumpen-prole life, there appears to be scant solidarity between the pirates, little in the way of a fraternal feeling that they're all in the underground together. 'A transmitter rig is worth about £300,' says Marcus, a well-spoken eighteen-year-old formerly involved with legendary South London pirate Don FM. 'If you see one and take it, it's almost not seen as thieving. It's part of the game.'

But the main enemy is the DTI, whose official line (as one Trade and Technology Minister put it) is that 'These stations not only cause radio and TV interference for the ordinary listener, but can seriously endanger life by disrupting the radio communications of the emergency services and airport control towers.' In truth, most pirate transmissions are 'crystal-locked' to precise points on the FM frequency band, with no signal leakage. So why is the government dedicated to stamping out the pirates? Is it just the innate desire of state power to regulate all media? Or is there a fear of militant agit-prop being transmitted through the skies? Strangely, Britain has never seen much in the way of political 'free radio'. But an Italian 'free' station, Radio Alice, played a major role in catalysing the anarcho-syndicalist riots in Bologna in 1977; a 15,000 strong 'autonomist' uprising so politically threatening and culturally offensive to the establishment (left- *and* right-wing), that the Communist Mayor of Bologna invited the army to use armoured cars to suppress it. In America too, pirate radio is mostly politically motivated, not music-oriented.

If the concept of 'resistance' can be applied to British pirate radio, it's clearly on the level of symbolic warfare, that old cultural studies notion of 'resistance through rituals', as opposed to overt protest. If the pirates are subversive, it's because they hijack the mass media, the instrument of consensus, in order to articulate a minority consciousness that's local, tribal, and utterly opaque to non-initiates. Gilles Deleuze and Felix Guattari's concept of 'minor language' (versus 'major language') fits the way the pirates can seem to the outsider like mere sound and fury that signifies nothing, yet means everything to those who belong. It's no coincidence that two of the big catchphrases used by pirate MCs in 1991–3 were ''ardkore, you know the score' and 'you know the key' (the latter sometimes slurred and contorted into the even more cryptic 'you know the koo'). Which brings us to the MC, the figure who marshals and sustains the subculture's sense of itself as massive yet subterranean, a shared, secret underworld; the MC as master of 'ardkore's occult ceremonies, as *encryptor*.

You Know the Key

'A million sparks falling from the skyrockets of Rimbaud and Mowgli – slender terrorists whose gaudy bombs are compacted of polymorphous love and the precious shards of popular culture.'
    – Hakim Bey, seemingly prophesying the 'ardkore jungle pirates

The MC's job is a difficult one. He (almost never a 'she') must generate infinite variations on a very restricted repertoire of utterances: all-praise-the-DJ exhortations, druggy innuendos, exclamations of intense excitement, and testifications of inexhaustible faith in the entire subcultural project. By finding rhythmic and timbral twists to the restatement of these themes, the MC creates that intangible but crucial entity known as 'vibe'.

From relative unknowns like former Don FM stalwarts Rhyme Time and MC OC, to top-ranking junglist chatters like GQ, Navigator, Moose, Dett and Five-0, the mark of a superlative MC is a certain combination of timing and grain-of-the-voice. Where the hoarse, rabble-rousing 'ardkore MC of 1991 was like a cross between a cockney street-vendor and an aerobics-instructor, the jungle MCs that supplanted these white working-class nutters draw on techniques and flavours from rap, from the DJ talk-over of seventies' dub reggae, and from other Jamaican styles (toasting, dancehall chat).

My favourite era of pirate MC-ing, though, is the transitional phase of 1992–93, when the music was described as 'ardkore jungle or jungalistic 'ardkore. The patois-rich patter of this era of MC-ing was a genuine creole tongue, a delirious mix of ragga chat ('big it up!', 'brock out!', 'maximum boost', 'big up your chest'), E-monster drivel ('oh-my-gosh!', 'buzzin' 'ard'), American hip-hop slang ('madding up the place! blasting bizness!') and Oi!-like cockney yobbery ('luvvit to the bone, luvvit like cooked food!'). At the furthest extreme, the MC's druggy vocalese degenerated into non-verbal gibberish somewhere between Dadaist sound-poetry, speaking-in-tongues and early rap's 'human beatbox' trickery, e.g. Rhyme Time's vocal simulation of DJ techniques like scratching and the stuttering cut out effect caused by violent oscillation of the cross-fader or transformer.

MC patter has a high level of 'phatic' elements – utterances that establish an atmosphere of sociability rather than communicate information or ideas. In everyday life, 'phatic' designates the hello's and how-are-you's that grease the wheels of social intercourse, that initiate or conclude the conversation proper. But whereas in everyday life, phatic remarks are empty rituals, devoid of emotional weight or even truth-value (how often do you answer 'fine!' when you feel like crap?), in rave, these utterances are impossibly intensified with meaning and conviction.

MCs get round the semantic 'impoverishment' of pirate patter by utilizing an arsenal of non-verbal, incantatory techniques, bringing spoken language closer to the state of music: intonation, syncopation, alliteration, internal rhyme, slurring, rolling of 'r's, stuttering of consonants, twisting and stretching of vowels, comic accents, onomatopoeia. In pirate MC-ing, this excess of form over content, timbre over text, creates *jouissance*; for the listener, there's an intense, sensual thrill in hearing language being physically distended and distorted in the throat. Like babytalk, toddler-speak and lovers' sweet nothings, MC chanting is all assonance and echolalia, the voluptuousness and viciousness of primary oral/aggressive drives (twisted, extruded vowels/staccato, percussive consonants).

Pirate MC discourse isn't just demotic, at its best, it's *democratic* too, with a strong emphasis on audience participation. Witness the following Index FM phone-in session on Christmas Eve 1992.

> *MC no. 1:* 'Sounds of the Dominator, Index FM. And it's getting busy tonight, London. Rrrrrrush!!!
>   ''Ello mate?'
> *Caller no. 1:* (slurred, giggly, very out-of-it) ''Ello, London, I'd like to give a big shout out to the Car Park possee, yeah? First, there's my friend, my brother, Eli, then there's my friend over there called Anthony, and he's like, smasher, he's hard—'
> *MC no. 1:* 'Like you mate!'
> *Caller no. 1:* 'Innit, of course!'
> *MC no. 1:* 'You sound wrecked—'
> *Caller no. 1:* 'Yeah, I'm *totally* wrecked, mate—'
>   [UPROAR, chants of 'Oi, oi! Oi, oi!']

Caller no. 1: 'My bruvva my bruvva my bruvva my bruvva my
   bruvva—'

MC no. 1: 'Make some noise!'

Caller no. 1: 'Believe you me, mate, 'ardkore you know the score!'

MC no. 1: 'Respect, mate! 'Ardkore noise!'

Caller no. 1: 'Oi, can you gimme "Confusion", mate?'

MC no. 1: 'Go on mate!'

Caller no. 1: 'Gimme gimme gimme "Confusion"!'

MC no. 1: 'Yeah, we're looking for it, mate!'

Caller no. 1: '2 Bad Mice, 2 Bad Mice—'

MC no. 1: (getting emotional, close to tears) 'Last caller, we're gonna
   have to go. Respect going out to you, mate! Hold it down, last
   caller, *rude boy* FOR YEEEEAAARS! Believe me, send this one out
   to you, last caller! From the Dominator! Send this one out to you,
   mate. You're *a bad boy*, BELIEF!!! 90–3, the Index, comin' on
   strong, *belief!!!*'

MC no. 2: 'Don't forget, people – New Year's Eve, Index FM are going
   to be throwing a free rave in conjuction with UAC Promotions.
   Rrrrrave, rrrrrave!!!! Three mental floors of mayhem, lasers, lights,
   all the works – you know the score. Absolutely free, just for you. So
   keep it locked for more info.'

MC no. 1: (gasping feyly) '*Oh goshhhh*!!! Keep the pagers *rushing!*
   Come and *go.* OOOOOOH *goshhhhh!!* We're comin' on, we're
   comin on strong, *believe* . . . Deeper! Deeper into the groove—'

MC no. 2: 'Keep the calls rushhhhing!'

MC no. 1: 'Yeah, London Town, we've got another caller, wants to go
   live!'

Caller no. 2: (sounding rehearsed) 'Hi, I wanna big shout to all Gathall
   Crew, all Brockley crew, Pascal, Bassline, Smasher . . . We're in the
   house and we're rocking, *you be shocking*, for '92, mate!!'

MC no. 1: 'Believe it, mate!'

Caller no. 2: ''ARD-*KORE*, you *know* the score!!!'

MC no. 1: 'Where you coming from, mate?'

Caller no. 2: 'South London, mate . . . Brockley—'

MC no. 1: 'Wicked. Shout to the South London crew. Respect.'

Caller no. 2: 'Oi, can you play 2 Bad Mice, "Six Foot Under"?'

MC no. 1: 'Yeah mate, we'll dig that one out and stick it on, just for
   you.'

Caller no. 2: 'Nice one! Sweet as!'
MC no. 1: 'Index! Yeah, London, you're in tune to the live line, Index
  FM, *runnin' t'ings in London right 'bout now*. The one and only.'

Rapt then and now by this phone-in session and others like it, by the
listeners' fervent salutations and the MCs' invocations, I'm struck by
the crusading zeal and intransitive nature of their utterances: 'rushing!',
'buzzin' hard!', 'get busy!', 'come alive, London!', 'let's go!', 'time to
get hyper, helter-skelter!', 'hardcore's firing!', and, especially prominent
in the Index-at-Xmas session, the near-Gnostic exhortation 'belief!!'

Gnosis is the esoteric knowledge of spiritual truth that various pre-
Christian and early Christian cults believed could only be apprehended
directly by the initiate, a truth that cannot be mediated or explained in
words. In pirate discourse, 'the score' or 'the key' is code for the secret
knowledge to which only the hardcore, 'the headstrong people', are
privy. And this is *drug knowledge*, the physically felt intensities induced
by Ecstasy, amphetamine and the rest of the pharmacopoeia. The MC's
role, as encryptor, as master of the sacra-*mental* ceremonies, is to
ceaselessly reiterate that secret without ever translating it. The MC is a
potent inclusion/exclusion device; if you're not on the bus, if you're
not down with the programme, you'll never know what that idiot is
raving about.

The cold print of the Index-at-Xmas transcript can't convey the
electricity of everyone in the studio coming up on their E's at the same
time, by the NRG-currents pulsing down phone-lines and across the
cellular-phone ether from kids buzzing at home. Listening to pirate
phone-in sessions like this, I felt like there was a feedback loop of ever-
escalating exultation switching back and forth between the station and
the hardcore 'massive' at home. The whole subculture resembled a
giant mechanism designed to generate fervour without aim. 'Come
alive, London!', 'coming on strong': a power trip for the powerless, a
mass hallucination of in-the-place-to-be grandiosity. Bastard children
of Radio Alice, the pirates mobilize a goal-less, apolitical unity.
Massification, excitation and amplification: this alone is the pirates'
raison d'étre. A massive could be just two kids at home, huddled 'round
the radio, rolling spliffs and getting seriously 'red-eye'. By maintaining
lines of communication between all the micro-massives across the city,
the pirate station keeps alive the idea of the macro-massive as a virtual
presence, a latent potential, thereby shoring up the community's belief

in its own existence during the fallow, dead-time intervals before and after the rave.

Pirate Utopias

The rave and the pirate radio show (the 'rave on the air') are exemplary real-world manifestations of two influential theoretical models, Hakim Bey's 'temporary autonomous zone' (TAZ), and Deleuze and Guattari's 'desiring machine'. A decentred, non-hierarchical assemblage of people and technology, the desiring machine is characterized by flow-without-goal, expression-without-meaning. Powered by E-lectricity, the rave sound-system or pirate radio is a noise factory; the feedback-loop of the phone-in sessions makes me think of Hakim Bey's vision of the TAZ as a temporary 'power surge' against normality, as opposed to a doomed attempt at permanent revolution. A power surge is what it feels like – like being plugged into the National Grid. A great MC's effect has a literally electrifying effect on the listener; the audience is galvanized, shocked out of the living death of normality. 'Come alive, London!'

'Ardkore is where rave's anti-politics of rapture (techno as euphoria-generator without pretext or context) meets hip hop's cut 'n' mix. The combination of the DJ's inexhaustible, interminable meta-music flow and the MC's variations on a small set of themes, has the effect of abolishing narrative in favour of a thousand plateaus of crescendo, an endless successions of NOWs. Over and over, again and again, the DJ and the MC reaffirm 'we're here, we're now, this is the place to be, you and I are *we*'.

This radical immediacy fits Hakim Bey's anarcho-mystical creed of 'immediatism', so named to spell out its antagonism to all forms of mediated, spectacular, passivity-inducing leisure and culture. The rave is a machine for generating a series of heightened here-and-now's, a concatenated flow of sonic singularities and ultra-vivid tableaux. If the illegal rave comes closest to Bey's conception of the TAZ (which must always be a physical, tangible location), the pirate radio station works both as a 'virtual' TAZ-surrogate, and as an informational web that provides logistical support for the creation of future, geographically 'real' TAZs. Both these functions help to stoke the fires of anticipation and keep alive the dream that the TAZ will soon be reconstructed.

While pirates continue to provide ads and news about raves and clubs, this ancillary role of radio was most pronounced during 1991–2, when DJs like the Rough Crew provided ravers with phone-line numbers and travel directions concerning Spiral Tribe's free parties.

But perhaps what's most subversive about the pirates resides not in its advertising of illegal raves, or even in its own crimes of trespass on the airwaves, but in the way they transgress the principles of exhange-value, commodity-fetishism and personality-cult that govern the music industry. The pirates fill the air with an endless, anonymous flow (DJs and MCs almost never identify tracks or artists) of free music (you can tape all the new tunes, long before their official release). In *The Revolution of Everyday Life*, the Situationist Raoul Vaneigem argued that a new, utopian reality 'can only be based on the principle of the gift'. With their sacrificial expenditure of energy into the ether, their amateur pay-to-play ethos, the radio pirates have more than a whiff of the utopian about them. You can taste the freedom.

TEN

ROOTS
'N FUTURE

JUNGLE TAKES OVER
LONDON

Notting Hill Carnival, August 1993. Black sheep of the post-rave diaspora, jungle has been banished to a small public park called Horniman's Pleasance on the outskirts of the carnival zone. Adverts on pirate radio rave breathlessly about the park's 25,000 capacity, but the event doesn't quite live up to the hype. In fact, it's a dismal turn-out: around twenty-five people have shown up. A few try to dance, in a desultory fashion; most stand around looking confused. After half-an-hour, my posse's patience runs out, and we head back to the centre of the carnival, where the pumping house'n'garage systems have packed the side-streets off Portobello Road. A believer, I can't reconcile the awesome vitality of the music seething out of the pirate airwaves, with this seeming proof that jungle just ain't runnin'.

Notting Hill Carnival, August 1994. What a difference a year makes. This time, it seems like every other sound-system is blasting jungle, deafening and distorted through overdriven speakers. UK Apachi, man of the moment with his Top Forty cracking 'Original Nuttah' seems to be doing PAs at most of them; we see him perform at least three times. And wherever there's a jungle system, the streets are choked with a crush of mostly young black bodies. Trying to make your way into the crowd to get closer to the speakers is impossible; it's a battle even to stand your ground, let alone dance. And every so often, people start to scatter in a ripple effect – maybe because it looked like a fight was about to start, like someone had pulled a gun or a blade. Within seconds, people a few rows ahead have turned on their heels and are sprinting full-tilt straight at you, eyes wide with terror, and you're running too, to avoid a collision and whatever appalling incident has sparked the panic. Then almost instantly the fear dissipates, calm is restored, the MC offers some platitudes about peace and unity, and the sound-system detonates again. 1994, and jungle is *running 'tings in London town right 'bout now.*

*

'We like the speed of it, the barrage of stimuli. People often think of psychedelic experience in terms of slow-and-dreamy music, but rushed, garbled music like jungle is closer . . . It's part of the whole speeding-up process of Western society. And you can't have an escalated culture without more extremes of everything, positive and negative.'
– Kevin Shields, My Bloody Valentine

Out of the fluxed-up chaos of 'ardkore evolved an entirely new sound, a new subculture: jungle. Between 1992 and 1994, jungle shed the chrysalis of hardcore, and with it, every last vestige of the rave ethos. The only element of hardcore rave to survive was the sheer velocity of the music; it was as though Ecstasy culture had permanently hyped up the metabolism of a generation.

The speed aspect is crucial. Scene insiders offer platitudes like 'jungle is a feeling'. But if you need a definition, then the music's core is the accelerated, chopped-up breakbeat rhythms that create that feeling – what Bjork crystallized as 'fierce, fierce, fierce joy . . . sort of "I'm just too happy, I want to explode."' Happy isn't quite the word: jungle's militant euphoria is fuelled by the desperation of the early nineties. Composed literally out of fracture ('breaks'), jungle paints a sound-picture of social disintegration and instability. But the anxiety in the music is mastered and transformed into a kind of nonchalance; the disruptive breakbeats are looped into a rolling flow. In this way, jungle contains a non-verbal response to troubled times, a kind of warrior-stance. The resistance is in the rhythms. Jungle is the metabolic pulse of a body reprogrammed and rewired to cope with an era of unimaginably intense information overload. As such, its rhythmic innovations will pervade popular music well into the twenty-first century, as insidiously and insinuatingly as rock 'n' roll, funk and disco have done in the past.

Renegade Snares and Brutal Bass

'Percussion music is revolution.'
– John Cage, 1939

A breakbeat is the percussion-only section of a funk or disco track, the peak moment at which dancers cut loose and do their most impressive steps. In the mid-seventies Bronx, DJ Kool Herc invented the hip-hop technique of looping these breaks into a continuous, hypnotic groove, by using two turntables and two copies of the same record. By the mid-eighties, rap producers were using sampling and sequencing technology to loop beats with greater precision.

Prized for their gritty, live feel, breakbeats come from James Brown and his band the JB's, from the Meters, Kool and The Gang and the Jimmy Castor Bunch, from fusion artists like Bob James and Herbie Hancock, and from a legion of obscure funk and disco artists of the seventies. As hip-hop culture burgeoned in the early eighties, the choicest breakbeats – like 'Apache' by the Incredible Bongo Band – were collated on 'Breaks and Beats' compilations. The most famous break in all of jungle is 'Amen', a hard driving snare-and-cymbal sequence from 'Amen, My Brother' by the soul group The Winstons. Chopped up, processed through effects, resequenced, 'Amen' has been used in thousands of tracks, and is still being reworked. How would the drummer in the Winstons respond, if you told him that a stray moment of casual funkiness, thrown down in a studio in 1969, had gone on to underpin an entire genre of music? Close behind 'Amen', there's the classic break from Lyn Collins's 'Think', in which James Brown yells 'you're bad, sister' to Collins. Sped-up so that JB sounds like a funky elf with a chronic case of hiccups, 'Think' became a feverish, percussive tic almost as ubiquitous in jungle as 'Amen'.

In the early nineties, many house and techno producers had started to use breakbeats in tracks, either to add extra polyrhythmic 'feel' or simply because it was easier to loop and speed up a segment of 'real' drums than to program a drum machine. As breakbeat house and hardcore grew popular, this short-cut was transformed into a positive aesthetic by younger producers, many of whom had been original British B-boys. Living up to the root meaning of that term (the B refers to 'breaks'), producers like Gavin King of Urban Shakedown, DJ Hype, and Danny Breaks of Sonz of A Loop Da Loop Era layered multiple breakbeats to form an exhilarating bedlam of clashing and meshing polyrhythms.

This hyper-syncopated hardcore drew more Black British kids into rave culture, catalysing the feedback loop of black influence that resulted in jungle. But the breakbeat mess-thetic alienated as many as it seduced. While jungle, like most pop music, is in 4/4 time, it lacks the stomping, metronomic four-to-the-floor kick-drum that runs through techno, house and disco. Eurodisco pioneer Giorgio Moroder had deliberately simplified funk rhythms to make it easier for white dancers; the 'jungalistic hardcore' that emerged in 1992 reversed this process, and for many ravers, it was simply *too funky to dance to*. That year, Josh Lawford of *Ravescene* magazine prophesized that the break-beat was 'the death-knell of rave', and in a sense, he was correct. But it was more than just the disappearance of the four-to-the-floor kick that alienated ravers. Jungle's dense percussive web destabilizes the beat, traditionally the steady pulse of pop music. Breakbeats make the music feel treacherous. The in-built safety factor in most machine-made dance music, the predictability that allows the listener to trance out, was replaced by a palpable danger. Jungle makes you step in a different way, wary and *en garde*. It was this edginess that drove many ravers out of the hardcore scene and back to house.

Through 1993, these rhythmic innovations matured into a veritable *breakbeat science*. Sampled and fed into the computer, beats were chopped up, resequenced and processed with ever-increasing degrees of complexity. Effects like 'time-stretching/compression', pitchshifting, 'ghosting' and psychedelia-style reverse gave the percussion an eerie, chromatic quality that blurred the line between rhythm, melody and timbre. Separate drum 'hits' within a single breakbeat could be subjected to different degrees of echo and reverb, so that each percussive accent seems to occur in a different acoustic space. Eventually, producers started building their own breakbeats from scratch, using 'single shot' samples – isolated snare hits, hi-hat flutters, *et cetera*. The term 'breakbeat science' fits because the process of building up jungle rhythm tracks is incredibly time-consuming and tricky, involving a near-surgical precision. Like gene-splicing or designing a guided missile, the creative process isn't exactly fun; but the hope is that the end results will be spectacular, or devastating.

Breakbeat science transformed jungle into a *rhythmic psychedelia*. Unlike psychedelic rock of the sixties, which was 'head' music, jungle's disorientation is as much physical as mental. Triggering different muscular reflexes, jungle's multi-tiered polyrhythms are body-baffling and discombobulating, unless you fixate on and follow one strand of the groove. Lagging behind technology, the human body simply can't do full justice to the complex of rhythms. The ideal jungle dancer would be a cross between a virtuoso drummer (someone able to keep separate time with different limbs), a body-popping breakdancer, and a contortionist. Jungle demands extravagant, impossible, posthuman responses – it makes me wanna sprout extra limbs, rotate my upper torso in an 360 degree arc round my waist, morph into a springheeled panther, bounce off the ceiling, go all Tex Avery.

Alongside its kinaesthetic/psychedelic effects, jungle's radicalism resides in the way it upturns Western music's hierarchy of melody/harmony over rhythm/timbre. In jungle, the rhythm is the melody; the drum patterns are as hooky as the vocal samples or keyboard refrains. In Omni Trio's classic 'Renegade Snares', the snare tattoo is the mnemonic, even more than the three-note, one-finger piano motif. The original versions of 'Renegade' focus on a bustling, ants-in-your-pants snare-and-rimshot figure, like a cross between James Brown's 'Funky Drummer' and an Uzi fusillade. The subsequent remix and re-remix by Omni's allies Foul Play make the snares snake and flash across the stereofield like a streak of funky lightning. On all four versions, Omni and Foul Play make the drums sing inside your flesh.

This rhythm-as-melody aesthetic recalls West African music. It also parallels the preoccupations of avant-classical composers like John Cage and Steve Reich, who drew inspiration from the treasure-trove of chiming timbres generated by Indonesian gamelan percussion orchestras. Jungle fulfils the prophesy in Cage's 'Goal: New Music, New Dance' of a future form of electronic music made by and for dancers. 'What we can't do ourselves will be done by machines and electrical instruments which we will invent,' wrote Cage, seemingly predicting the sampler and sequencer.

Alongside breakbeat science, the other half of jungle's musical core is its radically mutational approach to bass. Until mid-1992, the bassline in hardcore generally followed the 140 b.p.m.; on tracks like Xenophobia's 'Rush In The House', the effect was as jittery as a shrew on the verge of a coronary, or, more to the point, a raver's heartbeat after necking three E's. Gradually, a slower bassline sound came in: at first, a seismic, sine-wave ooze of low-end frequencies; later a dub reggae bassline that ran at about 70 b.p.m. beneath the hectic breaks. The half-speed bassline transformed jungle into two-lane music, tempo-wise. Just as if you were driving on the motorway, you could enter in the slow lane, and groove to the skanking B-line, then shift to the fast lane when you felt like flailing to the drums.

As the beats grew ever more complicated, the bass took on a sophisticated melodic and textural role that broke with the metronomic, pulsating basslines in techno. Making a parallel with forties bebop, David Toop described this role: 'bass is returned to its function as a physically felt harmonic/rhythmic component rather than a stungun which punches home the chord changes'. *Physically felt* is the key phrase: jungle's sub-bass frequencies operate almost below the threshold of hearing, impacting the viscera like shockwaves from a bomb. 'Rumblizm' is how DJ Nicky Blackmarket designated jungle's low-end seismology. New effects and new kinds of riffs emerged every month: stabbing B-lines that updated the 'sonic boom' effect that rap producers had got from detuning the Roland 808 drum-machine; reversed B-lines emitting a sinister, radioactive glow, a sound dubbed 'dread bass' after the Dead Dred track which made it famous; shuddering tremolo effects like a spastic colon; metallic pings and sproings like syncopated robot farts. Just as they had meshed together multiple strands of percussion, producers eventually deployed two or more basslines simultaneously. In jungle, bass – hitherto dance music's reliable pulse – became a plasma-like substance forever morphing and mutating. Like the jittery breakbeats, this new *dangerbass* put you on edge – it felt like trying to dance over a minefield.

B-Boy Meets Rude Boy

How did this martial music emerge out of rave culture, with its lovedup, peacedelic spirit? Where did all the junglists come from, anyway? Some were original British B-boys who'd gotten swept up in the hardcore rave scene; others came from the reggae sound-system subculture of the eighties, whose music policy ran the spectrum of imported 'street sounds' from dub and dancehall to electro and rap.

Take the trajectory followed by Danny Breaks, the white whizzkid from Essex behind Sonz of A Loop Da Loop Era and later Droppin' Science. As a schoolboy, Danny was into electro, breakdancing and 'cutting up breaks on the turntables'. By the late eighties, Danny had decided that UK rap wasn't 'really runnin'. Even when the UK crews were rapping about everyday English life, 'it didn't come 'cross, 'cos so much of the flavour of rap is the American voice.' Rap also never developed the political role (what Chuck D called 'black folks' CNN') that it did in America, because, Danny argued, 'black and white are more integrated in Britain, at least amongst the young. There's outposts of racism like skinheads, but most of the youth don't care about your colour.' Because of this, British youth were always more interested in hip hop's sampladelic sorcery and breakbeat-manipulation, rather than the verbal, protest side of rap.

Like other 'ardkore junglists with roots in the electro/bodypopping/graffiti era – DJ Hype, Aphrodite, DJ Crystl, 4 Hero, Goldie, DJ SS – Danny's desire to 'do instrumental stuff with breaks and weird sounds' drew him gradually into the rave scene. When acid house hit in 1988, this first generation of British B-boys were swept up in rave fervour; acieed's phuturism eclipsed an American hip-hop sound already retreating to trad funk 'n' soul grooviness. This rave-revelation coincided, for many, with their final alienation from American rap, which had taken a turn towards the grimly serious – from the 'niggativity' of gangsta rappers like NWA and the Geto Boys, to the righteous 'edutainment' of KRS 1 and X-Clan.

Infiltrating the hardcore rave scene, these lapsed B-boys came up with their own hyperkinetic mutant of hip hop. Suppressing the storytelling and rhymin' skills side of rap, they reactivated a neglected legacy: the frigid futurism of electro, the cut 'n' mix collages and jarring edits of Davy DMX, Steinski and Mantronix. Sampladelia taken to the dizzy limit, 'ardkore was basically hip hop on E, rather than a debased form of techno (as its critics supposed). But consider the fact that MDMA is not exactly a B-boy drug (can you imagine a loved-up Chuck D?) and you'll have some idea of how strange a hip-hop mutant 'ardkore was. On tracks like Hyper-On Experience's 'Thunder Grip', like DJ Trax's 'Infinite Hype' and 'We Rock The Most', breakbeats swerve and skid like the automobiles in *Penelope Pitstop*; melody-shrapnel whizzes hither and thither; every cranny of the mix is infested with hiccupping vocal-shards and rap chants sped up to sound like pixies. The vibe is sheer Hanna-Barbera, but beneath the smiley-faced 'hyper-ness', the breaks and basslines are ruff B-boy bizness.

'Ardkore producers like Hype and 2 Bad Mice even revived scratching, an old skool technique which had virtually disappeared from US hip hop as it evolved from its DJ-and-MC-oriented street-party origins into a studio-based art geared around the producer and rapper-as-poet. Danny Breaks christened this 'ardkore sub-genre 'scratchadelic'; a classic example is 2 Bad Mice's remix of Blame's 'Music Takes You', where a squelchy scratch-riff slots right next to the Morse

Code keyboard-stab, piano-vamps and staccato blasts of hypergasmic diva (which sound like Minnie Mouse in the throes of coitus).

Although it started as a breakbeat-fuelled offshoot of techno, 'ardkore jungle had devolved by late 1992 into a speedfreak cousin of old skool hip hop. 'Ardkore was the messy birth-pangs of Britain's very own *equivalent* to (as opposed to *imitation* of) US hip hop: jungle. That said, you could equally make the case that jungle is a raved-up, digitized offshoot of Jamaican reggae. Musically, jungle's spatialized production, bassquake pressure and battery of extreme sonic effects, make it a sort of postmodern dub on steroids. As a subculture, jungle is riddled with Jamaican ideas – like 'dubplates' (exclusive tracks given to DJs far in advance of release), 'rewinds' (when the crowd exhorts the DJ to 'wheel and come again', or spin a track back to the start at high velocity, producing a violent screech by rubbing the stylus the wrong way). By the end of 1992, junglist MCs were adding patois buzzphrases from dancehall reggae – 'big it up!', 'brock out!', 'booy-acka!' – to their repertoire of ravey rallying cries and B-boy boasts, and exhorting the crowd to raise their lighters in the air (the ragga fan's traditional salute to the DJ). And by early 1994, the most popular jungle tracks were those based around vocal licks sampled from raggamuffin stars like Buju Banton, Cutty Ranks, Ninjaman and Spragga Benz, whose rasping, grainy voices and self-aggrandizing insolence fitted perfectly with the rough-cut rhythms.

Even the name 'jungle' comes from Jamaica (as does its more baldly descriptive synonym, 'drum and bass'). According to MC Navigator from London's ruling pirate station Kool FM, 'jungle' comes from 'junglist', and was first heard in 1991 as a sample used by Rebel MC, who pioneered British hip-house in the early nineties, then formed the proto-jungle label X Project. 'Rebel got this chant – "'alla the junglists'" – from a yard-tape,' Navigator told me, referring to the sound-system mix-tapes imported from Jamaica (Yard is the slang term for Kingston, and the root of 'yardie', a hustler or hoodlum). 'There's a place in Kingston called Arnette Gardens, and the people call it the Jungle. When you hear on a yard-tape the MC sending a big-up to "alla the junglists," they're calling out to a posse from Arnette. When Rebel sampled that, the people cottoned on, and soon they started to call the music "jungle".'

Africa Talks to You, the Concrete Jungle

'When I first heard jungle, it seemed full of possiblities in a way I hadn't encountered since hip hop. Hip hop's main influence on My Bloody Valentine was that it re-educated us about rhythm; now jungle's re-educating everyone again. I've been inspired by the way the rhythms shift and inverse on themselves, the way there'll be ten different beats at once, or effects like the beat's exploding. Someone wrote that black American music, being born of oppression, is downbeat, even when it's meant to be lifting your spirit, but that African music is always stepping off the ground. I think that's what jungle rhythms do . . .'

         – Kevin Shields, My Bloody Valentine, 1995

Actually, there's no real conflict between the jungle-as-twenty-first-century-hip-hop and jungle-as-cyber-dub theses. Jungle completes the circle in that it reconnects hip hop with one of its multiple sources: Jamaica. Like a high proportion of Bronx denizens, DJ Kool Herc was a Jamaican immigrant; as well as inventing breakbeat-science, Herc imported reggae's tradition of mega-bass sound-systems. Reconnecting the Bronx to Kingston, jungle is the latest and greatest of the 'post-slave', post-colonial hybrids hatched within what Paul Gilroy has dubbed 'the Black Atlantic'. Jungle is where all the different musics of the African-American/Afro-Caribbean diaspora (the scattering caused by slavery and forced migration) reconverge. In jungle, all the most African elements (polyrhythmic percussion, sub-aural bass frequencies, repetition) from funk, dub reggae, electro, rap, acieed and ragga, are welded together into the ultimate tribal trance-dance.

Beyond the idea of the entranced dancer being possessed by the spirits, 'voodoo' has another resonance with jungle, in so far as Haitian *voudun* is a hybrid culture, a mix 'n' blend of black and white. Like Cuban *santeria*, *voudun* is a syncretic religion combining elements of West African animism and Catholicism. Even more striking is the centrality of drums in *voudun* ceremonies and rites. Just as African drums were used as signals for slaves to escape or rebel in the Deep South, similarly *voudun* fuelled the revolt of the Haitian slaves, leading to the founding of the first black republic in the Western Hemisphere.

Of course, this isn't the reason London youth 'cottoned on', as Navigator put it, to the word 'jungle'. First and foremost, the term just seems to fit the music like a glove. When you're on the dancefloor, it feels like you're *inside a jungle* of seething polyrhythms, a sensation at once thrilling and scary. Then there's the 'urban jungle' metaphor, which runs through black pop history in a thread that connects The Wailers' 'Concrete Jungle' (1972) and Sly and the Family Stone's 'Africa Talks To You (The Asphalt Jungle)' (from 1971's *There's A Riot Goin' On*) to the prototypical documentary-realist rap, Grandmaster Flash and the Furious Five's 'The Message', whose chorus runs 'it's like a jungle sometimes / It makes me wonder / How I keep from going under.'

There's also the extensive, highly charged history in pop music of 'jungle rhythms', as object of both fear and desire. 'Jungle' reinvokes the anxieties of the white, elder generation confronted by the 'primitivistic' repetition and percussive stridency of fifties rock 'n' roll. Some of the more paranoid anti-rock evangelists hallucinated a Soviet Communist conspiracy to 'negrify' the youth, with Elvis the Pelvis as a Pied Piper leading the kids into the 'dark continent' of animalistic sexuality. Jungle returns to rock 'n' roll's original sin – the priorization of beat over melody – and drastically exacerbates it by stripping it down to just drum and bass.

Underlying the fear of 'the jungle beat', of course, was the fear of degradation through miscegenation, the loss of racial identity. In the nineties, such fears were no longer the preserve of white supremacists. The title of Spike Lee's anti-mixed marriage movie *Jungle Fever* comes from Nation of Islam supremo Louis Farrakhan, who uses it as a derogatory term for interracial relationships. In Britain, 'jungle fever' has sometimes been shouted as abuse by black youth at mixed-race couples.

The question of jungle's musical 'colour' bedevils outside commentators and scene insiders alike. Jungle is often hailed as the first significant and truly indigenous Black British music. This notion obscures the fact that alongside hip hop and reggae, the third crucial constituent of jungle is whiter-than-white: the brutal bombast of the Euro-hardcore sound spawned in Belgium and Brooklyn. But even if you concede jungle's musical 'blackness' as self-evident, this only makes it all the more striking that from Day One more than 50 per cent of the leading DJs and producers have been white. Some of the 'blackest' sounding, most hip-hop-and-ragga-influenced tracks come from pasty-faced producers like Andy C, Aphrodite, Dead Dred, and DJ Hype. An example of the havoc this can wreak even with scene insiders' preconceptions is the story of Goldie's first exposure to Doc Scott's music. 'I thought "this guy has got to be a nigger." When I found out it was a white guy with blue eyes it freaked me out.' Yet on other occasions, Goldie – himself half-English and half-Jamaican – has described Scott, his ally and mentor, as a true 'nigga'.

For the most part, junglists de-emphasize the word 'black' and stress 'British'; there's a weird patriotism, in part a pride-full response to years of having to look to Black America or Jamaica for beats, but also evidence that these second or third generation immigrants feel that the UK is their home. Even Nation of Islam influenced militants like Kemet Crew stress that jungle has always been a black-and-white scene, while Kool FM's credo is 'No matter your class, colour or creed, you're welcome in the house of jungle.' Far from being racist, as Shut Up and Dance once alleged, the term 'jungle' actually codifies the *multiracial* nature of the scene, as contrasted with the mostly white audience for trance techno and ambient. Jungle is a kick in the eye for both white-power organizations like the BNP and for black segregationists, because it shows that trans-racial alliances are possible. Not just because it makes 'blackness' seem cool to white kids, but because there's a genuine unity of experience shared by Britain's black and white underclass.

So when white producer DJ Hype samples a black orator who preaches 'we must unite on the basis of what we have in common', the common experience – inhabiting the same run-down tower-blocks and council estates, being harassed by the police, living for marijuana, breakbeats and b-b-b-bass – may be grim and impoverished, but it's 'real'. Even when they live in nowheresville suburbs like Hitchin and Romford rather than inner-city ghettos, junglists belong to a jilted generation who are bored and frustrated, and have little to live for but burning up dead time in a weekend's worth of 'jungle fever'. The true meaning of 'junglist' is defined not by race, but by class, in so far as all working-class urban youth are 'niggas' in the eyes of authority. Junglist youth constitute a kind of internal colony within the United Kingdom: a ghetto of labour surplus to the economy's requirements, of potential criminals under surveillance and guilty-until-proven-innocent as far as the Law is concerned.

Gangsta Rave

'A "nuttah" could be Bruce Lee beating five guys at once, or someone who fights for a just cause like Mandela or Malcolm X, or it could be a bad-boy who robs banks. It's just a word for someone who's a fighter.'

> – UK Apachi talking about the song 'Original Nuttah'

In many ways, jungle is outlaw music: the scene's three staples are pirate radio, drugs, and uncleared samples. From late 1992 onwards, the nascent jungle scene rapidly developed an overtly criminal-minded attitude. Tuning into the newer pirate stations like Don FM, you'd hear MCs sending out 'big shout''s to 'all the wrong 'uns', 'liberty-takers' and 'rude boys'. Listen closely to the MCs' cryptic patter, and you might easily assume that illicit transactions were being conducted in code.

The nefarious vibe filtered into the music too, in the form of samples of sirens and bloodcurdling gunshots, and soundbites from blaxploitation thrillers and gangsta movies. Shy FX's 'Original Nuttah' and 'Gangsta Kid' both hijacked Ray Liotta monologues from *Goodfellas*: 'as far back as I can remember I always wanted to be a gangsta'; 'Organized Crime' by Naz Aka Naz sampled the sombre theme from *The Godfather*. Gun-talk pervaded the music, with band names like Tek 9 and AK47, song titles like 'Hitman', 'Sound Murderer' and '28 Gun Bad Boy', and ragga-derived soundbites like the boast about carrying an 'oversize clip and carbine' in Conquering Lion's 'Code Red'. Most chilling of the lot had to be Family Of Intelligence's 'Champion of Champions': mid-track, the rhythm halts, and a gruff Yardie voice promises, in a grisly sing-song, to 'murder 'im, kill 'im . . . full 'im up of copper, full 'im up of lead / 'cos me bad boy vicious'.

Jungle's ghettocentric vibe reflected the state of the nation. The recession had hit Britain hard, inner-city youth were facing unemployment and a welfare system that had been systematically dismantled by the Conservative government during its fifteen years of one-party tyranny. 'American' problems like guns and crack were taking root. Desperate music for desperate times, jungle's two preoccupations were oblivion and crime. Inner-city kids wanted to get out of 'it' (dead-end post-Thatcherite reality) either by taking drugs or selling them. All this made the emergence of 'gangsta rave' – seemingly a contradiction in terms – a logical upshot of systemic failure.

As the music changed, so did the mood of the scene. In 1992, the received image of the 'ardkore raver was a sweaty, shirtless white teenager, grinning and gurning, reeking of Vicks and asking for a sip of your Evian. By 1994, the stereotypical junglist was a headnodding, stylishly dressed black twentysomething with hooded-eyes, holding a spliff in one hand and a bottle of champagne in the other. Out went all the trappings of rave – the woolly hats and baggy T-shirts, the white gloves and fluorescent glow-sticks. Despite the sauna-like humidity of clubs and raves like Telepathy, Innersense and Sunday Roast, junglists came encased in black flight-jackets (MA1, MA2, Puffa, etc.) For a while there was fashion amongst the more chic black junglists to carry handkerchiefs, in order to dab away every last drop of perspiration and preserve the aura of aloof coolness. Sweat symbolizes rowdy communion, everyone mucking in together, shedding inhibitions and self-consciousness. The new taboo on sweat signalled that the scene's emotional temperature had dropped. By 1993, eye contact was disappearing from the London hardcore scene; bonhomie gave way to a surly vigilance. Smiling (in black hip-hop culture, often considered a signifier of servility, a desire to please whitey) was replaced by the skrewface, a pinched sneer expressing disgust and derision.

What happened here? As hardcore evolved into jungle, it shed rave's emotional demonstrativeness and gestural abandon, which had originated in gay disco and entered white working-class body-consciousness via Ecstasy. In its place, a 'black' ethos of self-control and mask-like inscrutability was embraced by white and black alike. Paralleling and/ or catalysing this shift were changing patterns of drug use. 'Ardkore's nudge-nudge references to 'rushing', its sniggery E-based innuendos, were replaced by roots reggae soundbites about sensimilla, ganja and herb. There's a sense in which the disappearance of the Ecstasy vibe allowed young black Britons to enter the rave scene *en masse* and begin the transformation of hardcore into jungle. Ecstasy's effects of defenceless candour are probably too risky a cultural leap for the young black

▲ GET RIGHT ON ONE, MATEY: SPECTRUM HOSTS PAUL OAKENFOLD (LEFT) AND IAN ST PAUL (RIGHT) CHECK OUT THEIR FRIENDLY RIVALS SHOOM, APRIL 1988.
▼ LIVING THE DREAM: SHOOM DJ DANNY RAMPLING CONDUCTS HIS CONGREGATION, JULY 1988.

▲ SMILEY FACES: SPECTRUM REVELLERS OVERCOME BY BALEARIC BONHOMIE, JULY 1988.
▼ DANCING IN THE STREET: AFTER THE TRIP, ACIEED FIENDS CARRY ON RAVING IN TOTTENHAM COURT ROAD, SUMMER 1988.

▲ WE ARE E: RAVER SPORTING A CHEMICAL PROTECTION MASK, A POPULAR 'ARDKORE ACCOUTREMENT, AT THE ROLLER EXPRESS, EDMONTON, AUGUST 1992.

▼ BLOWING YOUR OWN TRUMPET: KIDS PARTICIPATE IN THE RAVE'S BLITZ OF SOUND-AND-VISUALS, USING WHISTLES, HORNS, GLOW-STICKS, MINI-LASERS, ETC.

▲ GETTING YOUR HEAD TOGETHER IN THE COUNTRY: BOY'S OWN OUTDOOR PARTY,
NEAR EAST GRINSTEAD, SURREY, AUGUST 1989.
▼ LICENSED TO CHILL: TRANCE HEADS AND HIPPY RAVERS RELAX IN THE
'TECHNO SILENCE SUITE' AT MEGATRIPOLIS, LONDON, 1993.

RAVE'N'ROLL SUICIDE: THE PRODIGY'S LIAM HOWLETT, STRICKEN BY GUILT FOLLOWING MEDIA ACCUSATIONS THAT THE BAND KILLED RAVE WITH 1991'S TOYTOWN TECHNO HIT, 'CHARLY'.

MYSTIC STEPPERS: ARTCORE JUNGLISTS 4 HERO.

▲ THE FAMOUS 'PEANUT PETE' DRUG EDUCATION COMICS: HERE ILLUSTRATING
THE DANGERS OF HEATSTROKE FROM E-FUELLED OVEREXERTION.
▼ TAKE A TRIP: FLYER FOR FURTHUR RAVE FESTIVAL IN WISCONSIN, APRIL/MAY 1994,
WITH HAIGHT-ASHBURY TYPOGRAPHY AND KEN KESEY'S ACID BUS PAYING HOMAGE
TO THE ORIGINAL PSYCHEDELIC COUNTERCULTURE.

▲ JUMP UP JUNGLE: DJ HYPE (RIGHT) AND PASCAL (LEFT) PLAY WITH THE
RUFFNECK JUNGLIST'S FAVOURITE LETHAL WEAPON.

▼ SMOOTH OPERATOR: AMBIENT JUNGLE PIONEER LTJ BUKEM DROPS IT
NEATLY AND DISCREETLY.

◄ DEAD DREAD:
JUNGLETTE WINDS HER WAIST
AT MOVEMENT CLUB,
LONDON 1997.

▼ GRIN AND BLARE IT:
RAVE SAVIOUR
NORMAN COOK
(AKA FATBOY SLIM)
CUTS UP ROUGH AT THE
BIG BEAT BOUTIQUE,
BRIGHTON, 1998.

male, who can't afford to jeopardize the psychic armour necessitated by the very different black experience of urban life.

As marijuana displaced the E, dancing lost its mania, became less ravey and out-of-control. The half-speed bassline gave dancers the option of grooving to the dub-sway bass rather than flailing to 160 b.p.m. breaks. At a rave in 1991–2, you'd see lots of open-body gestures; at climactic moments or cosmic interludes in the music, arms were held aloft, outstretched to the heavens in a universal gesture of mystic surrender. Jungle replaced this openness and vulnerability with more controlled movements, closer to shadow-boxing or martial arts. As the dancehall-reggae influence kicked in, ragga clothing and bodymoves infiltrated the scene. You saw girls in skin-tight hot pants, bustiers and micro-skirts, dropping to a panther-style half-crouch and flexing their abdomens with the kind of risqué, confrontational sexuality patented by ragga-star Patra. The effect – imagine a Zulu go-go girl – was sexy but menacing, seducing the male gaze only to stab it in the eye with every pelvic thrust.

Under Siege

Jungle's 'creole' culture could only have evolved in London. Paul Gilroy describes the city as 'an important junction point or crossroads on the webbed pathways of black Atlantic [political and cultural traffic]'. The assertion of African sonic priorities (polyrhythm, bass-frequencies) caused breakbeat-based hardcore to contract from a nationwide, chart-topping pop music into a regional underground, centred on London and its surrounding counties. This contraction was celebrated by such late 1992 tracks as Code 071's 'London Sumtin' Dis' and Bodysnatch's 'Just 4 U London'. Apart from the odd outpost in multiracial areas like the Midlands and Bristol, the rest of the country shunned jungle. From the rave-will-never-die movement called 'happy hardcore' to the club-based house mainstream, the four-to-the-floor kick drum ruled supreme everywhere but the capital.

As jungle bunkered down into a self-sufficient London underground, it developed something of a siege mentality and a sense of persecution. Following the spate of cutesy Prodigy-copyist hits in 1992 based on kids-TV theme tunes ('Trip To Trumpton', 'Sesame's Treet' et al), dance-mags like *Mixmag* had proclaimed the death of rave and cold-shouldered hardcore into a long phase of media black-out. During 1993, jungle sustained itself through its infrastructure of pirate radio small independent labels, dingy, off-the-beaten-track clubs and specialist record shops like Lucky Spin, Blackmarket, Unity and De Underground.

The result was a renegade underground economy that ran in the face of all the 'common sense' business notions adhered to by the music industry in the nineties. In defiance of the hegemony of the CD, jungle was oriented around vinyl. The 12-inch was an end-in-itself, not an advert for the album (which barely existed anyway). 12-inches were bought mostly by DJs, professional and aspiring; fans bought DJ mix-tapes, available at specialist stores, street markets or by mail order, rather than purchase the few shoddy compilations available. Cheaper still, they taped hours of cost-free cut 'n' mix off the pirate stations.

The mix-tape and the pirate radio bootleg were so popular because of jungle's other major break with record biz logic: at any given moment, a huge proportion of the music that's hot in the clubs cannot be purchased as commercially available vinyl. This is because of the thrall of the dubplate. Producers give influential DJs a pre-release version of a track on DAT, recorded straight from their home studio. The DJ presses up a metal acetate at his own expense (around £30), which lasts about 25 to 40 plays. The dub-plate is a Jamaican idea: seventies sound-systems pressed up their own tracks in order to outdo their rivals. Similarly, jungle's top DJs are desperate for exclusives to spin, and spend £200 plus a week on dubplates; these might be their own productions, or tracks by other artists who feel an affinity for the DJ's style. Dubplates are also a way of testing out a new track on a club sound-system, of seeing how the crowd respond and what scope there is for finetuning the record. This sounds 'democratic', but unfortunately the net effect of the dubplate system is that fans are tantalized for months (sometimes as long as a year!) until the track's official release, by which time DJs have stopped playing the tune; some dubplates never get issued at all. Mix-tapes are therefore the only way to get hold of the latest tunes.

Like hip hop, jungle's anti-corporate, pro-underground ideology was in no way proto-socialist. Rather, it concerned the struggle of smaller capitalist units (independent labels – often a crew of DJ/ producers surrounding an engineer with a home-studio set-up) to prevent their 'subcultural capital' (music) being co-opted by larger capitalist units (the mainstream record industry). What gave the junglistic producers/labels their edge was their ability to respond with greater speed and flexibility to the fluctuating demands of the dance-floor audience than the major labels ever could.

Situated in the fuzzy interzone between the criminal, the anarcho-capitalist and the anarcho-collectivist, jungle was by early 1994 firmly established as a self-sufficient economy, with no need of the outside world's support. So when the outside world started paying attention that summer, the junglist community didn't quite know how to respond. Having built up such an armature of wariness and suspicion, the scene was torn between its desire for recognition and paranoid fears of misrepresentation and co-optation.

One Sunday in June 1994, just as jungle was beginning to make the national newspapers, I went to a club called Thunder and Joy. At one point, I thought I heard the MC calling out to 'alla the journalists'. Of course, he really said 'junglists', but the aural hallucination was forgivable; only minutes earlier, he'd been railing against 'saboteurs and perpetrators'. It was the week that the media had gone jungle crazy, and on the pirates, MCs had been simmering with rage about one newspaper's gross misrepresentation of the scene.

A month later, and the pirate MCs were dissing *The Face* for printing General Levy's boast that 'I'm runnin' jungle'. An opportunist interloper from dancehall reggae, Levy provided the vocals to 'Incred-ible', a collaboration with jungle producer M-Beat; the track eventually became jungle's first (and so far only) Top Ten hit. In response to Levy's bragging, a cabal of top junglists banded together as The Committee with the intention of ensuring that jungle was covered 'correctly'. The first step taken by the Committee (aka the Council) was a boycott on 'Incredible', which rapidly escalated into further boycotts against DJs who carried on playing the track, promoters who booked Levy to perform PAs, DJs who continued to play for those promoters, and so on, *ad absurdum*. Legend has it that a posse was also sent out to corner Levy in a nightclub, where some kind of retribution was exacted. True or not, an abject apology from the General soon materialized in the Letters Page of *The Face*. And guess what? He blamed the media, claiming his quotes had been taken out of context.

For one brief moment, while the media spotlight focused on the scene and the record companies began to wave chequebooks, every junglist was united in hatred and resentment of General Levy. But almost immediately, jungle's musical tangle of roots and futurism (to misquote Phuture Assassins's classic 'Roots 'N Future') began to unravel. The scene began to be torn apart by its divided impulses: underground retrenchment versus crossover seduction, ghettocentricity versus gentrification.

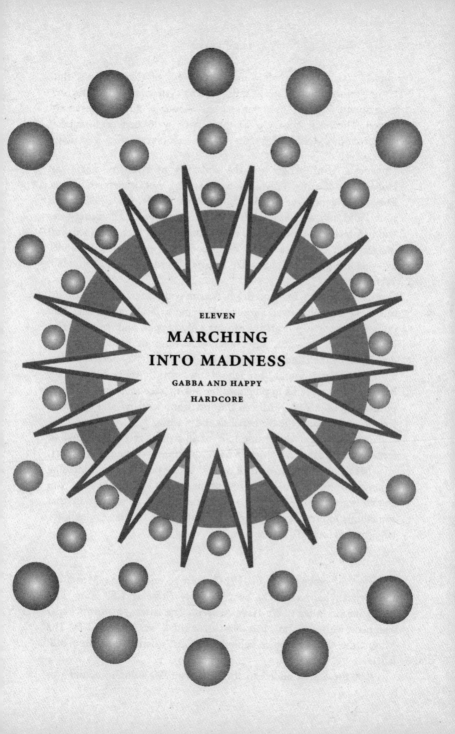

ELEVEN

MARCHING
INTO MADNESS

GABBA AND HAPPY

HARDCORE

Outside a grim hangar on the outskirts of Arnhem, north-east Holland, godfearing Calvinists are handing out leaflets to ravers. They're on a mission to save young souls. Inside, it's a hellzone of sound and fury, a Hieronymus Bosch horrorscape of grimacing faces and neo-medieval grotesquerie. Every other T-shirt is emblazoned with imagery that celebrates death, destruction and the dark side: skulls, axe-wielding goblins, slogans like 'Hades', 'Hard As Hell', 'Rotterdam Terror Corps'.

And the music? Imagine death-swarm synthesizers droning ominously like bombers over Dresden. Imagine a jackhammer beat that pounds as hard as a heart overdosing on adrenalin and steroids. This is gabba, the ultra-fast, super-aggressive form of hardcore techno developed by the Dutch in the early nineties, which has since spread as an underground sound throughout the world. Above all, gabba's berserker frenzy seems to plug into the Viking race-memory of ginger-pubed peoples across Northern Europe, from Scotland and Northern Ireland to Germany, the Netherlands and Austria.

For hipsters and 'discerning folk' of all stripes, gabba is a funkless, frenetic frightmare, the ultimate bastardization of techno. But experience has taught me that when all right-thinking people agree something is beyond the pale, utterly devoid of merit, that's precisely when you should start paying attention – for it's usually an indication that something interesting is going on. That's why I'm in Arnhem for Nightmare, Holland's ruffest rave.

*

The story of gabba begins in 1991–2, with Second Phase's 'Mentasm', the 'Belgian hoover' tracks by T99, Holy Noise and 80 Aum, and Mescalinum United's 'We Have Arrived'. The latter – a stormtrooper stampede with a blaring bass-blast of a riff – was produced by The Mover, the shadowy figure behind Frankfurt's darker-than-thou PCP label.

What the Dutch added to the 'Mentasm'/Mescalinum sound was

extra stomp: a distorted Roland 909 kick-drum, running at insanely
fast tempos ranging from 180 to 250 b.p.m. When gabba fans chant
'need a bass!', they're really talking about the trampoline-like boing of
the distorted kick-drum, the piledriving thud-thud-thud that kickstarts
the dance. Pure gabber is totally percussive/concussive. Every musical
element functions rhythmically, yet the rhythm is simplistic; we're
talking multiple tiers of four-to-the-floor, as opposed to polyrhythmic
interplay. The closer you listen, though, the more you appreciate the
degrees of invention within gabba's almost preposterously narrow sonic
and rhythmic spectrum. And the more you thrill to its visceral blast.

As well as a sound, gabba rapidly became a subculture. Pronounced
with a guttural, phlegm-rattling 'gah', gabba was originally Dutch
Yiddish for 'best mate'. But the word came to mean 'hooligan' or
'ruffneck' – 'a guy who is low-class, maybe jobless', says DJ–producer
Darkraver. Rotterdam's proletarian youth flipped the derogatory term
around, transforming it into a badge of pride. Regional antagonism
and underclass resentment fused in a fierce but tongue-in-cheek rivalry
with Amsterdam, R'dam's enemies both in football (Feynoord versus
Ajax) and in music (Amsterdam's tasteful house scene versus R'dam's
raucous hardcore). The very first gabba anthem, created by DJ Paul
Elstak, was Euromasters' 'Where The Fuck Is Amsterdam?'

Although gabba sounds like the most Aryan music this side of
death-metal, in some ways it is Holland's own equivalent to hip hop.
Many of the top producers – Elstak, Darkraver, Robert Meijer of High
Energy, Francois Prijt of Chosen Few – started as hip hop DJs. Gabba
tracks often use samples from the Def Jam rap/metal crossover era, like
Chuck D's boast/threat 'my Uzi weighs a ton'.

Mindwar

Gabba is music for the sensation-junkie, for kids reared on Nintendo,
Hellraiser, Manga comics, and Freddie Krueger. Raves like Nightmare
create a sensory overkill that blurs pleasuredome and terrordome,
using lasers, intelligent lighting, and mega-bass sound-systems to create
a hallucinogenic blitzkrieg of light and noise that recalls the nocturnal,
up-river battle scenes in *Apocalypse Now*. Gabba's militaristic imagery
– band names like Search and Destroy, Annihilator, Strontium 9000,
track titles like 'Iron Man', 'Dominator', 'The Endzone', 'Dark Knight',

compilations like *Battlegrounds* – recalls heavy metal's super-speedy, sadomasochistic sub-genres such as thrash, death-metal and grindcore.

How did gabba's militant sounds and aggressive attitudes emerge out of hardcore rave's smiley-faced benevolence and gloriously soppy sentimentality? Ecstasy is the androgynizing drug. But regular and excessive usage causes E to degenerate into little more than amphetamine – not chemically, but in terms of its psychological effect. Revving up motor-activity, amphetamine literally mechanizes and motorizes the human body, resulting in 'punding': compulsive, repetitive and stereotyped actions, nervous tics. Amphetamine is a cyborgizing drug: hence speedfreak slang like getting 'wired', 'crank', 'motorhead'.

Amphetamine also has historical connections with warfare, where its adrenalizing, insomniac and hyper-vigilant 'flight-or-fight' effects became extremely useful. Millions of pills were given to troops during the Second World War, to fight fatigue, boost morale and promote aggression. After the Second World War, speed was the drug-of-choice for veterans who couldn't adjust to civilian life (Hell's Angels, truckers), and for kids who were bored senseless (Mods got 'blocked' on purple hearts and black bombers before battling the Rockers on the beaches of Brighton). Today, the bosozoku – Japan's delinquent 'speed tribes' – fuse mod and rocker with their greaser image, their fondness for listening to cassettes of their turbo-charged bikes revving up and for getting wired on injectable methamphetamine.

As Ecstasy's androgynizing powers began to fade, so there was a gradual remasculation of rave culture, and a militarization of the music and imagery. In England, 'ardkore turned into jungle; in Scotland and Northern Europe, hardcore turned into gabba. In both cases, the tempo rose dramatically to match the overdriven metabolisms of a new generation of speedfreaks – in gabba's case, rising to 180, 200, 250, even 300 b.p.m.

All this goes some way towards explaining gabba's aura of mass rally and proto-fascistic brotherhood. With its sensations of velocity, fixation and aimless belligerence, gabba offers all the pleasures of war without the consequences; it's an intransitive war, a 'Mindwar' as one track by Annihilator puts it. Bruce Sterling coined the term 'military/entertainment complex' to describe the way that technological spin-offs from military research feed into the leisure industry, from video-games to virtual reality. These toys originated in the flight-simulator developed by the military to train jet-fighter pilots. Playstation games like *Mortal Kombat* and post-rave styles like jungle and gabba are to virtual reality what cocaine is to crack. By stoking an appetite for ever-escalating doses of hyper-stimulation, they recalibrate the nervous system in preparation for insertion into the virtual domain.

If the crack metaphor seems hyperbolic, consider the way that TV ads for video-games play on the addictive nature of velocity and violence, the two sensations they offer the player. One commercial shows a mother begging her sallow, red-eyed teenage son to 'please try to go outside today, honey'; with its murky gloom, and its fixated occupants, the living room suddenly takes on the atmosphere of a crackhouse. The game *Zoop* is advertised as 'America's largest killer . . . of time'. The commercial shows a boy doing cold-turkey in a padded cell, twitching and puking. Peering through the peephole, the doctor asks 'How long's he been playing?'; the nurse answers 'Seventeen straight days,' setting up an association with the speedfreak's sleep-defying 'run'. Here is Paul Virilio's 'becoming-speed' or cyber-theorist Arthur Kroker's 'speed-flesh': a sexless euphoria that bypasses the adolescent's hormonally-troubled body to recover the prepubescent boy's fantasy world of explosions and pyromania.

Bald Terror

Not only is gabba exactly the sort of music that really ought to be playing in the background of all those carnographic video-games, but at Nightmare, I realize that the bombardment of noise and light, the 200 b.p.m. tempos and air-scything lasers, are designed to make the gabba kid feel like he's actually *inside* a video-game. And like Nintendo, gabba is a mostly male subculture (an early classic of the genre was Sperminator's 'No Woman Allowed'!).

The classic gabba boy has a small, shaven head with bright pink ears sticking out from the skull, making him look like an alien. His pale, gaunt, speedfreak torso peeks out from an open 'Aussie', a gaudily patterned tracksuit top that looks like a tie-dye shell-suit, but which can cost up to £500. The classic gabba girl combines flaxen-haired Dutch cuteness with skinhead menace; a common look is a ponytail dangling over a shaved patch of scalp from the ears right round the back of the head. Some gabba boys go for a similar semi-Mohican effect, sporting Oriental-style topknots and pigtails.

As for the gabba dance, it's somewhere between the punk pogo and Morris dancing. At Nightmare, I marvel all night at the kids' incredibly intricate, absurdly fast footwork, which resembles kickboxing. How do they manage to keep their footing on the sweat and soft-drink soaked floor? Other gabbas prefer to simply rage hard, slicing and dicing the air, growling and grinding their teeth. But the vibe isn't intimidating, because these kids are self-absorbed almost to the point of autism, lost in music and mayhem. One guy, who's skip-gliding across the floor in a trance, collides with me and goes haywire like a spinning coin that's hit a chair leg.

The strange, almost fey grace of the gabba dance is all down to Ecstasy and amphetamine, which enable dancers to lock into the groove and keep up with gabba's insane tempo. Everywhere at Nightmare, I can see the symptoms of excessive intake of E's and whizz – the crazed, blazing impudence in the eyes, facial expressions contorted midway between snarl and smile, tongues jutting out of mouths, and grimacing caused by the jaw-tension that's a side effect of Ecstasy. One guy's pulling such monstrous, gargoyle faces, I can almost hear his jaw-bone cracking.

Sven, an amiable, cleancut fellow, chats me up. Like almost everyone in Holland he speaks fluent English, but he prefers to communicate by writing in my notepad. His friend Wimpi tries to participate, but is so cabbaged on E that he takes several minutes to work out which end of the pen is for writing, then gives up after scrawling an unreadable hieroglyph. Sven tells me he's very proud of gabba because it's a uniquely Dutch music. He says he likes 'relaxing gabba, the kind they're playing tonight'. This strike me as bizarre, considering that most people, most techno fans even, would be driven screaming out the door within minutes. And Sven admits that, 'No, the scene would not be the same without the drugs.'

In the spirit of the occasion, and in order to really *feel* the music, I score an E for twenty guilder (about £8), gulp it down and wait for the rush. Ecstasy makes you more vulnerable to the music; defences knocked down, you start to merge with the noise instead of resisting it. Above all, E brings your metabolism up to speed, makes your insides buzz as fiercely as the swarming killer-bee riffs. Swept up in gabba's cyclone of velocity and victim-less ultraviolence, I feel like

I'm inside a forcefield, my flesh seared and irradiated with demonic energy.

*

Gabba has a terrible reputation. For some, it's 'kill your mother' music, nasty noise for trainee psychopaths. For others, it's 'Nazi techno'. When the scene first emerged, many were quick to equate the gabbas' cropped hair with white-power skinheads, a connection helped by the Feynoord supporters' unfortunate habit of hurling anti-Semitic chants at their Ajax opponents (a reference to Amsterdam's historical role as a Jewish merchant centre). In October 1997, the *Daily Star* somewhat belatedly discovered England's tiny gabba scene. Grossly exaggerating the threat it posed to British youth, it published an exposé bearing headlines and captions like 'Bop Till You Drop . . . *Dead*', 'Nazi Gabba Hell', and 'Jack Boots and Birds: Nazis have adopted sick Gabber'.

Gabba's aggression does seem to hold an attraction for the extreme right; I've heard stories of Austrian neo-fascists doing drill to gabba's regimented rhythms, of jackbooted and swastika-adorned thugs at Italian hardcore events. To counter this, Netherlands labels often print slogans like 'United Gabbers Against Racism and Fascism' or 'Hardcore Against Hate and Violence' on their record sleeves, while Dutch fans call themselves 'bald gabbas' to distinguish themselves from white-power skinheads.

Most of the time, though, gabba ignites a firestorm of belligerence with no specific target. Despite an emotional spectrum ranging from hostility to paranoia (song titles like 'I'm the Fuck You Man', 'Mad As Hell', 'I'll Show You My Gun'), there's rarely any tension or fights at Dutch or Scottish raves. Instead, gabba kids direct their aggression at their own bodies, punishing their nervous systems with noise and drugs. In the early days of gabba, the big buzzword was 'hakke' – pronouced 'hack-uh', it sounds like 'hardcore' but means to strike someone with an axe. Echoing British rave slang like 'sledgehammered' and 'caned', 'hakke' captures the concussive nature of gabba's quest for oblivion.

What redeems gabba is its playful sense of humour. The logo of the K. N. O. R. label is a horned demon in nappies, while Babyboom's mascot is a nappy-clad infant giving you the finger: both images nicely blend rave's regression with heavy metal's puerility. Funniest of all are the series of T-shirts put out by the Forz label: a teddy bear with a sub-machine gun, a teddy wielding the sort of Christmas pudding bomb clutched by nineteenth-century anarchists, and most tasteless of the lot, one where Teddy's blown his head clean off with a pistol. Stuffing, rather than blood, is spattered on the floor, while the slogan reads 'Game Over'.

As well as Nintendo, gabba always makes me think of Bill Buford's book on football hooliganism, *Among the Thugs*, and specifically that moment he describes when the mob becomes conscious of its collective power, and wills itself over the brink between normality and running amok. Gabba is arrested at just that brink of adrenalinized pandemonium. The missing link between thrash metal and gay Hi-NRG disco, gabba is the ultimate masculinist music. A transsexual once said that when she started taking testosterone, 'it felt like mainlining rock 'n' roll'. Suffice to say that if she'd doubled the dose, the sensation would be like gabba.

The ugly side of the music's sado-masochismo is audible later on at Nightmare when technical difficulties led to the bizarre spectacle of Gabba Unplugged. As technicians fiddle beneath the DJ's decks, the burglar-masked MC leads the crowd in a chant: 'Happy / Is For Homos'. This is a reference to the poppy, sentimental strain of 'happy gabba' or 'fun-core' which has recently taken the Dutch charts by storm, and even scored a Top Ten smash in Britain with Technohead's irresistibly zany pro-marijuana anthem 'I Wanna Be A Hippy'. The chant also seems like a diss to a DJ who performed earlier tonight, Paul Elstak – the Rotterdam producer who invented gabba but who has recently disgusted the scene's diehards by going cheesy and chuneful with hits like 'Rainbow in the Sky' and 'Life Is Like A Dance'.

Backstage, Elstak shrugs off the anti-happy backlash, which has resulted in answer songs like 'Paul Elstak, We Love You No More' (a dig at his soppy chart smash 'Luv U More'). The way he explains it, gabba had to mellow out at some point. 'By 1994, the music was too hard, too fast. Fewer girls were dancing, and we lost the party atmosphere. And kids were taking too many drugs to keep up with the speed.' Elstak and producers like Darkraver and Gizmo picked up on the lighter, less frenetic hardcore sound invented by Scottish producer Scott Brown, and kickstarted the happy-gabba explosion.

'Happy' was also a bid for respectability, after drug-related deaths had thrown the scene into disrepute. In Rotterdam, says Elstak, 'one party was cancelled 'cos the authorities saw the flyer for the event and it was very aggressive, lots of blood and guts'. One reason Nightmare has gone on the road to towns like Arnhem is that raves are being refused licences in Rotterdam at the moment. And then there's the Church, whose animosity is directed not just at gabba but all forms of rave music. According to Technohead's Michael Wells, the Church 'feels threatened because it used to be where people turned for meaning and a sense of belonging'. For European youth, rave has usurped that role.

Bounce to the Beat

'I lost my religion the day I discovered raving.' So says Chris, a nineteen-year-old lapsed Catholic and confirmed hardcore disciple. We're hanging out in the chill-out zone of Rezerection, Scotland's biggest rave, and – chiming in with the Christian theme – it's 3 a.m. on Easter Sunday morning.

Chris, his fair hair cropped in the Caesar-cut that UK hardcore boys favour, tells me that rave is 'a way of life, a culture'. It's a way-of-life that demands sacrifices; when he was working, he spent £3,000 in one year on tickets, drugs, transport, and now that he's on the dole, events like Rez require weeks of planning and scrimping. And drugs are an inseparable part of that way of life. 'They help you forget all your problems for one night,' says Chris. I'm told that some of the kids at Rez take an E every hour, sometimes as many as twelve a night. Chris says he's been on a few benders, and once necked ten pills. 'But that way you end up dancing yourself into an early grave,' he adds. This idea sometimes surfaces in the music itself, in sick-humorous song titles like 'Friday Night Can Kill You', 'I Died In My Teens' and 'I Just Died In Your Arms Tonight' (which samples the soppy AOR hit of the same title by Cutting Crew). Tonight, though, Chris is accentuating the positive, telling me 'I class everybody at a rave as a friend,' with a believer's gleam in his eye.

Although Chris says that 'Rotterdam died when Elstak started to go cheesy,' Rezerection is full of testaments to the peculiar Scottish cult of all things Dutch. Everywhere there are T-shirts bearing the logos of the top Netherlands gabba labels – K. N. O. R., Ruffneck, Mokum, Dwarf, Terror Traxx, Babyboom. A few kids even sport Feynoord team-colours. The music, though, is not the kind of 'kill-your-mother' gabba played at Nightmare, but the fun-core strain that so aggravates the diehards. The big buzzwords in Scotland are 'bouncy' (one of Chris's friends says, 'I'm just off for a wee bounce') and 'cheesy' (like gabba, an insult transformed into a positive term). With its rinky-dink keyboard refrains, spine-tingly riffs and anthemic choruses, happy-core is almost disturbingly fixated. A lot of tunes recall oom-pah music or Jewish *klezmer* (in fact there's actually a gabba version of the wedding jig 'Havanagila'); others have carousel-like fairground melodies. That sense of kiddy-kartoon frolic is completed by the whirligig, funhouse hall-of-mirrors and fruit machines in the chill-out zone.

In its own senti-MENTAL way, fun-core is just as extreme as the more sadistic kinds of gabba. And the Scottish kids certainly match the Dutch for sheer mania. Stripped to the waist, tattooed and sweaty, the lads gurn like heavy metal bands posing for a photo shoot. Wee lassies twitch 'n' twirl like clockwork toys wound up too fast, their hands inscribing semaphore patterns at hyperspeed. Everywhere the trappings of UK rave's golden era circa 1991–2 are visible – gas masks, white gloves, floppy hats and jester caps, baby's dummies, fluorescent glow-sticks (which cost two quid each and last a mere six hours). And the golden age's infectious bonhomie is still alive and kickin': total strangers come up and shake my hand, sharing your soft drink or water is *de rigeur*.

By 5 a.m., though, the euphoria is giving way to battle-fatigue. And you start to notice the kids who look fed up because they can't afford another pill, or have simply caned the E so hard for so long that the chemical's lovey-dovey effect has worn off. It's then that you become alert to the dark side of E culture. In the chill-out room, there's a booth offering Lifeline's drug education leaflets, chirpy comics that try to engage the kids on their own level, with cartoons about Temazepam Tom, a cat with a wooden leg (he got gangrene from melting the sleeping pill, popularly known as 'jellies', and injecting it), and Peanut Pete comics that illustrate the dangers of paranoia and overheating. In the paramedic support room, kids suffering the effects of 'snidey E's' or over-indulgence huddle wrapped in blankets with plastic puke pots on their laps. Despite the fig-leaf of intensive drug searches on entrance, big-scale raves like Rez are highly organized spaces designed for kids to freak out, with safety nets provided if they take it too far.

As in Holland, Scotland's spate of E-related deaths gave hardcore a disreputable image and prompted a clampdown by the authorities. According to Jamie Raeburn of Scottish rave mag *Clubscene*, 'Hardcore clubbing is now almost dead.' There's the Metro in Ayr, Nosebleed in Fyfe, and in Stirling, the Fubar (it stands for 'Fucked Up Beyond All Repair'). But all the other Scottish clubs are pushing the mellow, upmarket sound of house, because they associate hardcore with 'schemie' hooligans, i.e., kids from deprived housing schemes. The big raves, like Rezerection, keep faith with the hardcore massive. 'People come to see bands like Ultra-Sonic, Q-Tex, Q-FX, 'cos they associate them with doing their first E's!' says Raeburn.

Beneath Scottish techno's bouncy, fun-core aura, there's an undercurrent of punk rage. Take 'No D. S. Allowed' by The Rhythmic State, a tirade against the Drug Squad, who have maintained an intimidating presence at raves ever since the wave of drug deaths at Hangar 13 in 1994. (A common paranoid delusion of wired-and-tired Scottish ravers is that the guy next to them is an undercover DS agent.) "No D. S." is the ultimate two-finger-salute,' says Raeburn. 'You can't blame the kids, really. Most of their clubs are being closed down, the police harass them, pull them out of clubs for having half an E on their person, really abuse them. If "they" – DJs, the media, and the authorities – are trying to take your music away, you're gonna tell 'em to fuck off.'

Only the Happiest of People Need Apply

'I'm pleased to be uncool and happy. It's like the white gloves . . . You ever seen a white glove raver start a fight? If you hate people who wear white gloves, then basically you're saying having a good time is crap.'

– Chris Howell of Kniteforce Records

Despite all the Dutch gabba T-shirts at Rez, Scottish hardcore's allegiances are shifting; several of the DJs playing tonight are from south of the border, where they're big names on the English 'happy hardcore' scene. The difference between happy hardcore and happy gabba is slight: basically, the English tracks have sped-up breakbeats running alongside the stomping four-to-the-floor kick-drum, and at 170 b.p.m., they're slightly slower than happy-gabba. But the genealogy of happy hardcore is quite different: the scene began as an offshoot of jungle.

Back in 1993, when hardcore plunged into the 'darkside', a breaka-way faction of DJ–producers like Seduction, Vibes and Slipmatt continued to make celebratory, upful tunes based around hectic breakbeats. By the end of 1994, happy hardcore had coalesced into a scene that operated in parallel with its estranged cousin, jungle, but had its own network of labels, its own hierarchy of DJs, its own circuit of clubs. Labels like Kniteforce, Impact, Remix, Hectic, Slammin', SMD, Asylum and Universal; DJ–producers like Dougal, Brisk, Sy and Unknown, Force and Styles, Hixxy, DJ Ham, Ramos and Supreme; venues like The Rhythm Station in Aldershot, Die Hard in Leicester, Club Kinetic in Stoke-On-Trent, and Labrynth in East London.

Happy hardcore takes all the elements that jungle purged as too 'cheesy quaver' – synth stab-patterns, Italo-house piano vamps, shriek-ing divas, anthemic choruses – and cubes their epileptic intensity. The euphoria of the original 1992 'ardkore was tinged with bittersweet poignancy; happy hardcore, by comparison, is relentlessly and ruth-lessly upful, with every last hint of 'darkness' or ambivalence banished from the music. The atmosphere at predominantly happy-core oriented events like Dreamscape, Hysteria, Helter Skelter and Pandemonium, is akin to a Butlin's holiday camp: a pleasure prison of enforced jollity.

Ignored by the dance press until 1997, happy hardcore developed its own media. Like their Scottish counterpart *M8*, these glossy mags – *Eternity*, *Dream* and *To The Core* – have distilled rave ideology down to its populist and democratic essence. Although they contain record reviews and interviews with artists, the bulk of the mags consists of lengthy, relentlessly positive reports on raves and clubs. As well as praising the DJs' performances, the reviewers compliment the MCs, the scantily clad girl-dancers, the lights 'n' lasers, the security staff, the toilet facilities, and above all, the crowd for being so up for it. Occasionally, the reviewer might criticize the poor parking facilities or the long queue for admission or the cloakrooms, but only in a goodnatured, apologetic way. More important than the text, though, are the photo spreads. Again, rather than the DJs, these depict the ravers: glassy-eyed and gurning boys, shirts off to expose their skinny-ribbed torsos; girls, dazed and sweaty in their unflatteringly clingy lycra leotards; huddles of friends, red-faced and grinning like maniacs, throwing mad-raver shapes for the camera and tooting their air-horns.

Where 'serious' dance mags like *Mixmag* and *Muzik* frame the DJs as auteurs and cult figures, and barely mention the crowd in their live reviews, the rave-mags treat the audience as the star.

Happy hardcore is huge pretty much anywhere the white rave audience predominates, i.e., not London, where the heavy concentration of hip hop, soul and reggae fans means jungle has more appeal. In large part, happy-core was the result of an exodus of white ravers from the jungle scene, in reaction to the influx of black youth and the attendant mood-change from bonhomie to surly attitude. Grant of Slammin' Vinyl argued that 'hardcore used to be a multiracial scene. But now jungle is mostly seen as black. A lot of people who used to be into swingbeat and ragga got into jungle in 1994, and they claim "It's our music." So the white kids are saying, "Well you can keep it then, we'll make our own music."' As well as the racial factor, the other crucial difference between jungle and happy hardcore is purely pharmacological. Junglists have mostly given up pills for ganja; happy hardcore, geared towards the perpetual crescendo of the E-rush, is for the younger kids still going through the MDMA honeymoon.

Because of its defiant cheesiness, most junglists dismiss happy hardcore as mere juvenilia for timewarp kids who haven't realized that rave's 'living dream' is over. With its rictus-like tone of relentless affirmation, its *déjà vu* piano chords and synth-stabs that all appear to be anagrams of some primordial, rush-inducing riff, happy hardcore is indeed a bit like dance music's equivalent to a rockabilly revival: nostalgia for something you never actually lived through.

In other respects, happy hardcore is closer to heavy metal. Both are scenes that just won't die, because they fulfil very basic and enduring needs for provincial youth. Like metal, happy hardcore is all about keeping the faith and unity-as-uniformity: The happy-core raver's favourite garment – the identikit black flight-jacket – is like the metalkid's denim jacket, except that logos for labels like Kniteforce and Slammin' have replaced Iron Maiden and Motorhead patches. Indeed, events like Rezerection, Dreamscape and Desire are highly reminiscent of heavy metal festivals like Castle Donnington. There's the fetish for video-nasty grotesquerie (the huge inflatable monsters hanging from the hall's ceiling at Rez), and the overpriced merchandising (T-shirts and hats kids gladly buy to testify to their tribal allegiance). There's the way hardcore's obsession with 'nosebleed' sub-bass frequencies parallels metal's love of 'earbleeding' decibellage. And the rise of the sleeping pill Temazepam recalls the mandrax and Quaaludes popular with Black Sabbath fans; combined with alcohol, these tranquillizers all induce comatose stupor or mindless violence.

Wargasm

With the English producers restoring the pounding four-beat kick-drum and playing down the breakbeat, by 1996 the stage was set for happy-core's merger with Scottish 'bouncy techno' and Dutch fun-core, to form a single rave-will-never-die sound: in effect, the re-integration of the original pan-European hardcore of 1991, only much faster. But this prospect dismayed a faction of diehard gabba fans for whom hardcore is *anti-rave* in spirit. This pan-global network of dissidents includes Nasenbluten (German for nosebleed), a terrorcore trio from Newcastle, Northern Australia, who are on a crusade to bring back 'quality gabba'.

'It serves Leah Betts right, and Anna Woods too,' sneers the band's Mark Newlands, referring to England's and Australia's famous Ecstasy fatalities. 'I never, ever saw hardcore as happy E music. I'm not a happy man, y'know. I'm always grumbling. I'm an absolute turd ... The original Rotterdam gabba, stuff by Euromasters and Sperminator, was cold and unpleasant, and it was great. We called our double-EP "100% No Soul Guaranteed" as a riposte to all those people who say gabba is monotonous, inhuman, soul-less. Of course it is! It's supposed to sound like blast furnaces! In Newcastle, all our relatives work in steel foundries. We're just trying to reflect our environment.'

Such was Nasenbluten's sense of betrayal by Paul Elstak's move towards happy-gabba that the band recorded the infamous 'Rotterdam Takes It Up The Ass'. The title phrase is sung to the 'doo-dah, doo-dah' melody of 'Camptown Races', but because the track sampled copyright material by Elstak and turns it against him, Nasenbluten decided not to release it for fear of being sued. 'We don't want our label Bloody Fist to go under,' Mark told me, ''cos other Australian hardcore bands depend on us.' Artists like Embolism, a fourteen-year-old kid with a 'real chip on his shoulder, you can tell he's probably gonna grow up to be a serial killer,' whose 'This Means Fucking War' EP was released by Bloody Fist in 1995.

Nasenbluten record their own music in mono on a crap Amiga

computer with a puny 8 bit memory. 'With the Amiga, it's impossible to get a clean, distortion-free sound,' Mark enthuses. Typical song titles include 'Feeling Shit', 'Cuntface', 'Kill More People' and 'Cocksucker' (which clocks in at a lethal 300 b.p.m.). So what exactly motivated Nasenbluten's monstrous barrage of puerile vileness, sampled belches, expletives-undeleted abuse and virulent lo-fi noise? Why have they dedicated their lives to this aural atrocity?

'I just don't like other people. I think I'm a sociopath. You get so much shit from people, but instead of burning their houses down, we let all our aggression out on the computer. Instead of killing people, we do it with sound.'

Nasenbluten's anti-rave sentiments are shared by England's DJ Loftgroover. A man on a mission, Lofty believes there's 'too much niceness in the rave scene'. Although he started out during the late eighties acid-house explosion, Loftgroover never tried E and never bought into the rave dream of love, peace and unity. 'Gabba is how I really feel – hard, angry,' he says. 'I've always had a bleak view of the world.'

Loftgroover coined a bunch of evocative terms for Nasenbluten-style extreme noise terror: 'punkcore', 'scarecore' and 'doomtrooper'. There are pockets of doomtroopers all over the UK, and when he plays at clubs like The Shire Horse in St Ives, Judgement Day in Newcastle, Steam in Rhyl, North Wales, and Death Row Techno in Bristol, Loftgroover is treated like a god. 'At The Shire Horse, the birds throw their stockings at me and I pull them right over my face like a bank robber. The kids in Cornwall go mad, giving me the finger, shouting "fuck you", and you have to do it back to them. Kids run up to me and say "Lofty, I fainted the last time you played".'

When he DJs, Loftgroover mixes in tracks by death-metal bands like Morbid Angel, Stormtroopers of Death and Slayer, and when asked about gabba's origins, he claims it's not even techno but 'probably something by Anthrax or Sepultura back in 1983 . . . The line between gabba and metal is only that thin, y'know.'

Bizarrely, given his obsession with the two most Teutonic forms of music on the planet, Loftgroover is black; if you saw a photo of him at the decks, you'd assume he was playing jungle. Clearly ambivalent about the fact that 'Seventy per cent of the people following this music are skinheads,' he stresses that he's never had any trouble even though 'some of them are giving it all that' – he mimes a frenzied Nazi salute.

'Most of the time, the look is just a fashion,' he insists, adding, 'gabba's about controlled violence. You never see people having fisticuffs at a gabba party.'

In addition to the sonic affinities between thrash and gabba, both musics share a similar audience: white working-class youth whose hopes have been crushed by the decline of heavy industry and who face unemployment or ignominious, no-security/no-future jobs in the service sector. From Rotterdam to Brooklyn, from Glasgow to Milwaukee, gabba expresses the rage and frustration of White Niggaz With Bad Attitude and No Prospects. And like metal, gabba is despised by middle-class critics who simply don't understand the mentality of those who crave music to *go mental* to.

'It's a working-class scene, there's no pseudo-intellectual element,' says Technohead's Michael Wells. 'People respond on a gut level. The apocalyptic, sci-fi and horror-movie imagery in gabba, it's all part of the trash culture these kids are into. And it's very similar to the way heavy metal uses imagery of death, destruction and anti-religion. It's a reaction against the pressure of modern life.'

It was almost inevitable that metal and gabba would join forces. Operating as Signs Ov Chaos, Wells recorded the experimental gabba album *Frankenscience* for English metal label Earache, who also put out a compilation of hardest-core gabba from Lenny Dee's Industrial Strength label. At the album's launch party at the Gardening Club in London, the T-shirts are less cuddly than at Rez – 'I'm Afraid I'm Going To Have To Kill You', 'Nightmares Are Reality', 'Where's My Money, Motherfucker?' – and the music is even harder than Arnhem: Wells and Dee unleash a remorseless onslaught of electro-convulsive riffs, sphincter-bruising bass that scores ten on my Rectal Richter Scale, and satanic synth-tones that get your goosepimples doing the goosestep.

The audience is a strange mix of shirtless skinheads and crustie types with matted dreadlocks and camouflage trousers. The anarcho-crusties belong to an underground London scene in which gabba serves as the militant sound of post-Criminal Justice Act anger. A key player in this London scene is an organization called Praxis, who put out records, throw monthly Dead By Dawn parties and publish the magazine *Alien Underground*. Praxis are part of an international network of ultra severe 'stormcore': labels like Napalm, Gangstar Toons Industry, Kotzaak, Juncalor and Fischkopf; artists like DOA,

Rage Reset, Temper Tantrum, The Speedfreak, DJ Scud, Lory D and DJ Producer.

On this circuit, gabba's perverse identification of libido with the military-industrial complex is taken even further; just check song titles like 'At War' by Leathernecks (a band named after the US Marines), Disintegrator's 'Locked On Target', and 'Wehrmacht' by Delta 9 (itself the name of a nerve gas!). Fantasies of man-machine interface and cyborg *ubermensch* abound. The ideology ranges from Underground Resistance style 'guerrilla warfare on vinyl' to full-blown techno-mysticism. In one issue of *Alien Underground*, the record reviews featured 'samples' from philosopher Paul Virilio's writings on speed and the war-machine. One review, wittily attributed to Virilio, raves about 'instantaneous explosions, the sudden flare of assassinations, the paroxysm of speed ... an internal war-machine'. Gangstar Toons Industry's 250 b.p.m. 'pure Uzi poetry' is hailed as 'exercises in the art of disappearing in pure speed to the point of vertigo and standstill'. Everything that for Virilio represents an anti-humanist cultural exterminism that must be resisted and reviled, is perversely celebrated by these speedfreak techno-junkies.

Such imagery recalls the aestheticization of war and carnage in the manifestos of the Italian Futurists and the writings of the *Freikorps* (German veterans who formed right-wing militia to beat down the Communists during the strife that followed the First World War). It also demonstrates the extent to which hardcore techno is the culmination of a feverish strain within the rock imagination. Examples include road-warriors Steppenwolf and their exhortation 'fire all of your guns at once / explode into space'; Black Sabbath's cyborg fantasy 'Iron Man', a case study in protofascist *rigor mortis*; Motorhead's iron-fisted, Hell's Angels influenced Reich 'n' roll. Greatest of all these 'rock 'n' roll soldiers' was Iggy Pop and his 'heart full of napalm', ballistic death-trip. Reflecting on this era of Stooges, when he fuelled himself with drugs like speed and LSD, Iggy declared: 'Rather than become a person singing about subjects, I sort of sublimated the person and I became, if you will, a human electronic tool creating this sort of buzzing, throbbing music ...' Similarly, PCP's The Mover told *Alien Underground*: 'Well you know I'm a machine, I'm wired up ... I'm roaming the earth and it's nice and doomy here.'

These rock and techno instances of man-machine interface fantasy have a 1957 blueprint in 'The White Negro', the essay in which

Norman Mailer imagines the building of a new nervous system by the use of intoxicants and by the conscious cultivation of the psychopath within your soul. And all find their culmination in hardcore techno's kinaesthetics of rush and crash. The rush is when your nervous-system's circuitry is plugged into the machine, supercharged with artifical energy, turned to *speed-flesh*; the crash is when the all-too-human body can't handle the pace any more. Back in 1992, the hardcore rave DJ would sometimes abruptly switch the turntable off: the nauseous, vertiginous sound of the record slowing from 150 b.p.m. to Zero was a hideously voluptuous preview of the drug comedown, the inevitable crash, only a few hours ahead. Then, woosh!, the DJ would flick the Technics' switch, and the force-field would repossess the dancer's body.

For today's digital-Dionysian, the gabbanaut, release doesn't take the form of Mailer's 'Apocalyptic Orgasm', but the orgasmic apocalypse, the Wargasm. Hence a band like Ultraviolence, who fuse thrash metal and gabba, and whose *Psycho Drama* LP is trailed with the promise: '10,000 Nagasakis in your head!' For the modern militarized libido, the equivalent of serene post-coital *tristesse* is the aftermath: post-apocalyptic wastelands, razed cities, the empty horizon, entropy-as-nirvana. Hence titles like Jack Lucifer's 'After All Wars'.

'Imagine surveying earth after nuclear destruction and enjoying what you see, that's how it feels when you listen to it,' The Mover told *Alien Underground*. PCP has been exploring such post-rave endzones for years, from The Mover's 'Frontal Sickness'/'Final Sickness' trilogy to the 'gloomcore' output of their sister label Cold Rush (a perfect phrase for the Ecstasy buzz when the empathetic warm glow has burned out). With their glacial, sorrowful synths, down-swooping drones and trudging, cavernously echoed beats, these tekno-dirges – Cypher's 'Marching Into Madness' (on the 'Doomed Bunkerloops' EP), Rave Creator's 'Thru Eternal Fog', Reign's 'Skeletons March' (from 'The Zombie-Leader Is Approaching' EP), Renegade Legion's 'Torsion' – conjure mind's eye visions of barren craterscapes or vast ice catacombs carved beneath the Arctic surface. (Cold Rush sleeves bear the legend: 'created somewhere in the lost zones'.) From burn-baby-burn to burn-out, hardcore rave's psychic economy fits Bataille's model of sacrificial violence and expenditure-without-return. The goal is to get wasted.

Slaves to the Rave

At Nightmare in Arnhem, I hear a track that seems to sum up gabba's weird fusion of will-to-power and impotence. Beneath a piteous melody that seems to waver and wilt in mid-air, a robot voice chants a fatigued, fatalistic chorus: 'We are slaves / to the rave.' Recorded by The Inferno Bros. for PCP offshoot Dance Ecstasy 2001, this withering piss take of the hardcore rave mentality had evidently become an irony-free anthem of entrapment and zombiehood.

A few days earlier Loftgroover had told me of going to a gabba club in Paris 'where they handed out straitjackets to the audience!' It's a nice joke, the perfect culmination of gabba's imagery of bedlam and psychosis, but it has a sinister undercurrent. A gabba rave *is* an asylum. It's a haven from an intolerable reality, a world that kids find at once numbingly tedious and worryingly unstable. But it's also a place of confinement where the nutters rage harmlessly; where kids vent all their anger out of their systems, instead of aiming it against the System.

TWELVE

AMERICA
THE RAVE

US RAVE CULTURE,
1990–97

'Techno is the Devil's Music! *Beware* the hypnotic voodoo rhythm, a reckless dance down the Devil's road of sin and self-destruction, leading youth to eternal damnation in the fiery depths of hell!'
— Drop Bass Network flyer for Even Furthur, May 1996.

Despite the ritual burning of a wicker man, it's hard to take Even Furthur seriously as 'an epic pagan gathering of the tribes of Evil'. The vibe is closer to a Scout retreat (which is actually what the site, Eagle Cave in rural Wisconsin, is usually hired out for). After sundown, kids sit around bonfires on the hill slope, toasting marshmallows and barbecuing burgers. The atmosphere is a peculiar blend of innocent outdoor fun and hardcore decadence. For if this is a scout camp, it's one awash with hallucinogens.

Under a disco glitterball suspended from a tree, a gaggle of amateur dealers trade illegal substances. 'Are you buying *more acid*, Craig?' asks one kid, incredulous at his buddy's intake. The vendor is offering five doses for $20. 'Weird Pyramids ain't *nuthin*' compared to these,' he boasts, then extemporizes to the tune of Johnny Nash's soul smash: 'I can see Furthur now the rain has gone / I can see all the mud and freaks at play.' Conversation turns to bad trip casualties, like the guy who went berserk, smashed in several windscreens with a log, and was carted off by the local sheriff. The LSD dealer rants about 'rich kid crybabies' who can't handle their drugs. He's also offering some G (the steroid-like GHB) and 'Sweet Tart' XTC. 'They're *mushy*,' he hard-sells, 'but there's a speed buzz, they won't smack you out — there's no heroin in them.' Later, we hear rumours of kids injecting Ecstasy — not for its putative heroin content, but 'cos of sheer impatience to feel the rush.

The scary thing is how young these kids are — hardened drug veterans before they're legally able to drink at age twenty-one. I overhear another boy enthusing about how great it is to 'hear the *old* music, like Donna Summer,' and I realize with a shock that 'I Feel

Love' came out before this kid was *even born*. In Even Furthur's main tent, Chicago DJ Boo Williams is playing a set of voluptuous, curvaceous house informed by this golden era of disco, tracks like Gusto's 'Disco's Revenge'.

Then San Francisco legend Scott Hardkiss pumps out feathery, floaty soft-core (including his awesomely eerie remix of Elton John's 'Rocket Man') sending silvery rivulets of rapture rippling down every raver's flesh. My wife points out a boy who's dancing with a folding deck chair strapped to his back, a sort of portable chill-out zone. A space-cadet girl sits cross-legged beside the DJ booth, eyes closed, rocking and writhing in X-T-C. Earlier she'd been handing out leaflets about aliens called 'the Greys', who she claims are from Zeta Riticuli in the constellation Orion and are in league with US military intelligence. Abduction stories and UFO sightings are common at American raves, doubtless because of the prodigious consumption of hallucinogens. Loads of kids wear T-shirts featuring slant-eyed ET-type humanoids.

Wisconsin belongs to America's conservative heartland. There's a certain folksy charm to its small town ways: when we tell a curious storekeeper we're in town for 'a music festival', she quaintly replies 'Cool beans!' (meaning 'Good for you!'). But there's also the unnerving underside of traditionalism, like the grotesque graveyard of tiny crosses by the roadside – a memorial to aborted foetuses put up by Pro-Life evangelists. All in all, this agrarian backwater is the last place you'd expect to find a psychedelic freak-out. But the wilds of Wisconsin is where the Furthur series of three-day raves have taken place since 1994. On the rave's flyers, the trippy typography harks back to the posters for acid rock bands in Haight-Ashbury, while the misspelled 'Furthur' originates in the destination posted on the front of the bus driven by the Merry Pranksters, Ken Kesey's troupe of acid evangelists.

During the first Furthur 'techno campout' – at Hixton, Wisconsin, 29 April–1 May 1994 – one of the promoters (David J. Prince, editor of Chicago rave-zine *Reactor*) got so blissed he danced naked on a speaker stack. On the final Sunday, several organizers were arrested by the local sheriff. At the third annual rave, there's no trouble from the law. But Even Furthur *is* a lawless zone. Although you have to pay for admission, the atmosphere is closer to England's illegal free parties than to a commercial rave. In fact, Even Furthur reminds me most of

Castlemorton, the huge 'teknival' catalysed by Spiral Tribe in 1992, which coincidentally occurred almost four years ago to the day.

The Even Furthur kids aren't crusty-traveller types, though – they're much more fashion-conscious and middle class, as American ravers tend to be. The guys sport sock hats and B-boyish silver chains that dangle in a loop from the waist to the knee. Girls have the Bjork-meets-Princess Leia space-pixie look of futuristic innocence; their shiny synthetic fabrics, bright kindergarten colours, bunched pigtails, cutesy backpacks and cuddly toys make them look even younger than they really are (mostly sixteen to twenty-two). Everyone wears absurdly baggy jeans (the hallmark of the US raver), the flared bottoms soaked in mud because continual downpour has transformed the camp site into a swamp.

Like Castlemorton, Even Furthur is a chaotic sprawl of cars, RV caravans, trailers and tents. There's no security and no lighting; you have to stumble through the mud by the fitful illumination of other people's flashlights and the glint of bonfires dotting the hill slope. All this gets to be a gas, although it's slightly perturbing that there's no on-site paramedics to deal with acid freak-outs, like the shoeless, shirtless, mud-spattered boy who keeps howling single words over and over – 'Friends! Friends!', 'Worms! Worms! Worms!', 'Dead!' – while other kids try to restrain him from fleeing into the woods. In England, the main reason to have paramedics is to help Ecstasy over-indulgers. But at Even Furthur, boiling alive in your own blood is not really a hazard. It's cold and wet, and over-exertion is difficult, because dancing is a struggle: the second tent is a puddle-strewn marsh (take a wrong step and you'll slide into a sinkhole), while the main tent's floor is slippery and sloping.

Over three days, some hundred DJs and bands perform, spanning a broad spectrum of rave music. There's a surprising amount of jungle on offer: Mixmaster Morris spins crisp 'n' mellow drum and bass in a small hillside tent, while Phantom 45 rinses out tearin' hardstep in the big marquee. Not everybody's happy about the jungle influx, though: sitting outside on a car bonnet, a gabba fan whines 'Why do breakbeats make me puke?' What really fires the pleasure centres of this mostly Mid-Western, Minneapolis/Chicago/Milwaukee crowd is the stomping four-to-the-floor kick drums of hard acid, as purveyed by Brooklyn's Frankie Bones and Minnesota's Woody McBride (whose Communiqué label co-promoted Furthur in tandem with Drop Bass Network and David Prince). Saturday's big hit, though, is French duo Daft Punk and their sinuous, sine-wavey brand of raw-but-kitschadelic house.

Unlike your regular commercial rave, Even Furthur has hardly any concessions selling food or drink. In search of liquid, we trek up the treacherously moist slope out of the camp towards the site owner's hut, where there are toilets and a soft drinks machine. It's pitch black as we trudge up the dirt road, but every so often we pass a tiny bonfire; clutches of burned-out kids huddled together on muddy ledges carved into the hillside, chatting and smoking weed. When we return down the hill, the pale roseate dawn is peeking through the trees, caressing our sore eyes. But as we get closer, our sore ears are assaulted by a 200 b.p.m. jackhammer pummel: the DJs aren't chilling-out the night's survivors but blasting ten thousand volts of gabba. At 7 a.m., gabba-phobe Mixmaster Morris retaliates with an impromptu ambient set in the second tent. At the start, he's playing quite happily to an audience of exactly zero. 'I've been here since Wednesday,' Morris tells me. 'That's why I smell so bad!' He plays on in that tent for *six hours*.

On Sunday evening, it's stopped raining at last, the mud has dried, and the slightly reduced crowd consists of the hardcore of party people who just don't wanna go home. The Drop Bass Network crew pose for a photo like end-of-year college students. I chat to their leader, Kurt Eckes, who tells me over 3000 people turned up. 'We've seen licence plates from California, Florida, Arizona, Colorado, New York, Washington DC.'

Thinking of the teenage acid-casualty the previous night, I suggest to Kurt that some of the kids here look kinda young. Do their parents know what they're up to? 'I suspect they *don't*,' he says, adding blithely that 'A couple of parents called here threatening to call the police for having fourteen-year-old, fifteen-year-old kids here without parental permission.' Eckes's nonchalance stems from Drop Bass Network's militantly underground attitude. 'There are no rules here at all,' he grins.

DBN is all about representing the rave scene's dark side. 'Within the rave scene, there's definitely some things going on which to most people seem wrong,' Eckes told *Urb* magazine. 'They seem right to us. We're just pushing those things to the limit.' DBN's version of rave might be called called *psycho*-delic rather than psychedelic.

Distancing himself from the Summer of Love idyllicism of 1988,

Eckes once declared: 'I don't see myself going to a party, taking E, hugging people, and screaming peace and love. I'm more . . . a person who'd rather go to a party, take a lot of acid, and hug speakers.' As Eckes and I chat, the nearest sound-system is pumping out Test's 'Overdub', a classic Roland 303-meets-gabba blitzkrieg unleashed in 1992 by Dance Ecstasy 2001, sister-label of Frankfurt's ultra-dark PCP. As well as a party promoter, DBN is a record label specializing in PCP-style industrial-strength hardcore and mindfucker acid; the label's third release was titled 'Bad Acid – No Such Thing'. But DBN's most punishing output is released via a sub-label called SixSixtySix. The Satanic allusion is a clue to Eckes's subcultural strategy – turning heavy metal kids on to techno (Milwaukee is a big town for thrash and 'black' metal).

As well as the Furthur events, DBN throw regular 'techno-pagan ritual parties', often timed for the solstices. One such party – Grave Rave, on Halloween Night 1992 – was treated like a modern day witches' masses by the authorities. Armed police stormed the building and arrested not just the organizers but the entire audience. After being detained in handcuffs for five hours, 973 people were issued $325 citations for 'aiding and abetting the unlicensed serving of alcohol' (in fact only a few cans of beer were found). Those under seventeen were also given tickets for violating the 'teen curfews' that Milwaukee, like many American cities, instituted to 'protect the young'. But 400 of those prosecuted pleaded not guilty, ultimately forcing the city to drop the charges because of bad publicity concerning the police's over-reaction. Undaunted, DBN threw a sequel 'Helloween 93' party called Grave Reverence, trailed with the promise: 'Demons of the darkside taking control of your soul.'

*

Even Furthur is a microcosm of American rave culture. On the positive side, Furthur wouldn't exist without the zeal of the promoters (who definitely aren't in it for the meagre profits) and the dedication of the kids, who are prepared to drive five to fifteen hours to a rave, and who sustain the geographically dispersed scene via the Internet and fanzines like *Tripp E Tymes*. On the less positive side, there's the debauched extremity of the drug use, the tender age of the participants, and the precarious relationship with the law (which is why Even Furthur took place at such a remote, non-urban location).

Despite regular outcries in regional newspapers, despite police harassment and legislative repression on the state, county and city level, rave in America has never really escalated to a national news phenomenon. Every year since 1991, current affairs TV programmes have 'discovered' rave and solemnly informed parents it's 'the latest craze', despite the fact that rave started in America as early as 1990. *20/20*'s 1997 exposé of the Florida rave scene is typical, whipping up parental fears with its references to 'blatant, brazen drug-taking' and parties situated 'anywhere that's far from adult supervision'. At these 'drug supermarkets', non-users are an 'endangered species' because 'peer pressure is profoundly strong'. Mothers of kids who've died from overdoses appear to beseech – 'We need to stop the raves!'

Yet for all its folk-devil/media-panic potential, American rave culture never hit that critical mass of public concern and outrage that really pushed British rave over the top in 1988–9. Partly that's because the subculture infiltrated the country in slow-and-steady, piecemeal fashion; partly it's because the music didn't explode into the *Billboard* charts like in the UK. But this still begs the question – why? It's even more puzzling when you consider that not only did the music originate in America (in Detroit, Chicago, New York), but that the Ecstasy/trance-dance connection was first discovered in Dallas and Austin in the early eighties.

'This was Reagan years, remember, so it was pure hedonism,' says Wade Hampton, then an upper-class Dallas teenager, later a prime mover in the California rave scene. Devoid of counter-cultural trappings, the Texas Ecstasy scene was about innocent fun – *literally* innocent, because MDMA was legal until the summer of 1985, and you could buy it over the counter in gay clubs like Stark in downtown Dallas. 'We were charging it on our parents' credit cards,' says Hampton. Despite the absence of hippy-dippy ideology, Stark and similar clubs anticipated the Balearic anything-goes ethos coined in Ibiza's Amnesia and codified by Shoom in London. The soundtrack mixed proto-techno electronic dance (Section 25's 'Looking From A Hilltop', Chris and Cosey) with Wax Trax-style industrial and indiepop like The Smiths' 'Girlfriend In A Coma'. And as XTC spread from the gay crowd to straights, a Texan equivalent to the loved-up football hooligan emerged: fratboys and jocks whose machismo melted under the influence of MDMA. 'You'd go into a bathroom and see Southern Methodist University football players wiping the mascara from their eyes. It was the first time [Dallas] men had their testosterone broken down.'

But it was these rich college kids who 'fucked it up', says Hampton. 'If you look back at the cases that were the basis for making Ecstasy illegal, it wasn't the gay crowd, it was SMU students who had enough money to buy twenty hits of Ecstasy. And they'd take *all of it*. The weird thing was that people were going *blind* – temporarily – from taking too much. Those kids' parents had enough money to raise hell – I'm talking the cover of the *Dallas Morning News* every other week, for a year.'

Outside the gay discotheques, there was also a yuppy scene of 'XTC parties' that precociously featured one of the defining aspects of rave – the eschewing of alcohol in favour of juice and mineral water. For these respectable professionals, Ecstasy didn't seem like a *drug*; it was cheap, there was no scuzzy paraphernalia like syringes or bongs, it wasn't addictive and there was no hangover. Above all, it was legal. 'It wasn't unusual to come home with a date and her parents would be higher than you guys,' Hampton laughs.

When MDMA was placed on Schedule 1, the worst category of illegal drugs, the yuppies stopped partying and the dance scene went underground. 'From the minute it was illegal, there were warehouse events, with DJs involved as organizers.' With MDMA outlawed, the drug's price soared even as its quality deteriorated; the cheaper, more dependable methamphetamine infiltrated the clubs, prefiguring the calamity that would strike rave scenes throughout America in the nineties.

Hardcore, Only 4 the Headstrong: New York Rave

In the pre-prohibition early eighties, MDMA was available in club scenes throughout America. Generally, it was used more for bonding sessions amongst friends than as a trance/dance drug. The first fully fledged rave scene was born in Brooklyn, New York, and was directly modelled on what was happening in Britain in 1989. Already a veteran DJ–producer on New York's freestyle scene, 23-year-old Frankie Bones was flown to England for an Energy rave. After the awesome buzz of playing to 25,000 people at dawn, Bones enjoyed his own personal 'Ecstasy revelation' a week later at Heaven in Charing Cross. 'I'm on my first hit of E . . . and all this shit is going through my head – "you've got to bring this back to America".'

At his first parties in Brooklyn, Bones and his crew actually played videos of English raves on screens, as a sort of training film. These first events were word-of-mouth micro-raves: 'Fifteen people in someone's room with a sound-system and a strobe.' Gradually escalating into the hundreds, the indoor jams turned into 'outlaw parties' at warehouses or beaches, advertised with handwritten flyers. After a dozen or so 'break-in' parties, Bones and Co – brother Adam X and his girlfriend Heather Heart, DJ Jimmy Crash and promoter-whizzkid Dennis The Menace – started calling the events Storm Rave.

'At first, they were just a place to hang out,' says Dennis. 'No one could get into clubs, we weren't dressed right. When I got involved, there was an outlaw party in the woods in Queens, in July 1991. You had to go to this famous Carvel [an ice cream shop] in Brooklyn, where you'd get given the map, which led you to the site in Queens. You followed this path with candles along it into the woods . . . The early parties were free, but we'd ask for donations to pay for gas for the generator. The less we asked for, the more they gave. That was back when it was *pure*.'

One of the most successful early parties took place in a brickyard, with the Storm crew building a DJ booth out of cinder blocks. 'Back then, we'd spent the whole week just scouting for buildings like that,' says Bones. 'In the fence at the back of the brickyard, we cut a hole adjacent to these freight tracks that no trains had been on in years. People parked six blocks away, walked down the tracks and climbed through the hole.' During 1992, there was a Storm Rave Allnighter every month or so, plus smaller outlaw parties with names like Tina Tripp's Magical Mystery Tour (after Frankie's girlfriend Tina). By the summer, events like Brainstorm were pulling crowds in the thousands to hear top DJs like Doc Martin, Caspar Pound, Sven Väth and Richie Hawtin.

The Brooklyn soundtrack was 'hardcore-only 4 the headstrong' (as Bones put it), music for the first flush of Ecstasy euphoria – Belgian bombast, Underground Resistance, early English breakbeat 'ardkore like The Prodigy. In typical hardcore rave fashion, Storm was part of a subcultural matrix that combined party promotion, DJ-ing, retail and making tracks. Bones, Adam X and Heather Heart ran their own Brooklyn record store Groove. This became the focus for a closeknit alliance of mostly Italian-American DJ–producers – Lennie Dee,

Mundo Muzique, Tommy Musto, Ralphie Dee, Joey Beltram, Damon Wild – who traded ideas, collaborated, and engineered each others' tracks. Frankie was at the centre of it all: sharing an apartment with Beltram, making music with Lenny Dee as Looney Tunes for England's XL label, and with Tommy Musto for Deconstruction/RCA. Then there was his solo stuff as Flowmasters and his famous 'Bonesbreaks' series of hip-house EPs, minimal breakbeat tracks designed as mixing material for DJs.

The deals with XL and RCA proved useful in an unexpected way – when the cops came to bust the parties, Bones brandished official-looking documentation with record company letterheads and claimed 'We're shooting my video inside.' Eventually, Bones got into serious trouble with the police and the fire marshals, who were cracking down on unlicensed events after a hundred people died in a fire at an overcrowded Latin Social club called Happy Land. 'They set up a police team called the Social Club Task Force to check clubs had fire exits,' says Bones. 'When they found out about the rave scene they became the Rave Task Force.'

There was also undercover intelligence work to worry about. 'On three separate occasions I had people coming to Groove Records asking me for Ecstasy. And I'm, like, "What's Ecstasy? Is it a record?" There was a track out called "Ecstasy, Don't Play Me Raw", so I'd grab a copy and say "Is that what you're looking for?" and then they'd leave. I *knew* people who had Ecstasy, but if you're the DJ and you're the one throwing parties, you don't want to [get involved in] selling pills.'

Yet, as Frankie admits, 'without Ecstasy, [the scene] would never have happened the way it did . . . That shit breaks down people's inhibitions.' Ecstasy also got rid of the troublemaker element – most of the time. 'The one time we did a party where it felt like some kids were going to start robbing people, I set an abandoned car on fire just to get everybody out of there quickly!'

As in Britain, the early 'pure' phase of rave was succeeded by a period in which entrepreneurs, legal and illegal, cottoned on to the money-making potential of the scene. In London, this involved bringing the music into West End clubs, and the MDMA-initiation of working-class non-hipsters. The key figure behind this process in New York was Michael Caruso, aka Lord Michael. 'I was friends with Michael,' says Frankie Bones. 'But he was, like, "Bones can't do these parties for ever, I'm gonna bring it into Manhattan."'

Surrounded by a thirty-strong ruffneck entourage, Lord Michael started throwing warehouse jams in the outer boroughs, then made the transition to Manhattan in 1991. His working-class following mostly consisted of Italian-American youth from the 'bridge and tunnel' boroughs (Coney Island, Bensonhurst, Staten Island) that surround Manhattan; a self-described 'new breed' who had seized on techno's futurism in a violent reaction against their parents and elder brothers' retrograde taste. By early 1992, Michael was working for Manhattan clubland mogul Peter Gatien, owner of the Limelight and the Palladium. The 'new breed' would gather at Caruso's two hardcore nights Adrenalin and Future Shock, Thursdays at the Palladium and Fridays at the Limelight respectively.

'Fifty per cent of the kids here are just into the music,' Lord Michael told me at the time. 'They get off on the aggression, 'cos New York's a very aggressive city. The other 50 per cent are taking Ecstasy or acid. Some of them smoke PCP. It's wild.' The soundtrack was full-on Belgian-British-Brooklyn brutalism, escalating from the voodoo throb of 'House Of God' by local outfit D.H.S., through djpc's speedfreak anthem 'Inssomniak' to the ungodly tintinnabulation of Incubus's awesome 'The Spirit'. With tempos peaking at a then outrageous 150 b.p.m., it seemed the only appropriate response was to headbang or pogo. Clinching the hardcore-as-thrash-or-punk analogy, the brawny boys didn't dance rave-style, they slamdanced. Young bucks with slicked-back hair barged into the fray, stripped to the waist with T-shirts hanging out of the back jean pockets like Springsteen. Others lurked at the Limelight bar and brazenly snorted cocaine through soda straws. Moby – then DJ-ing at Future Shock and making waves with tracks like 'Go' – later likened the experience of spinning for this crowd to 'playing in a penitentiary'.

As Gatien's right-hand man, Lord Michael became a major clubland power broker. 'When he met Timothy Leary in the Limelight, he really just flipped the script, he really wanted to be, like, *kingpin*,' says Bones. In a 1997 *Village Voice* exposé of Lord Michael headlined 'The King of Ecstasy', Frankie described his erstwhile buddy as 'the Al Capone of raves'. Bones also alleges that The Limelight tipped off fire marshals about a Storm Rave on 18 July 1992, because 'we were hurting the business in [Gatien's] club ... The marshal came with six fire trucks ... Conveniently, as everybody's leaving the party, there's people handing out flyers and saying "now come down the Limelight!"'

By the end of July 1992, Storm Rave had an ally in the struggle against the Limelight's commercialized version of hardcore: NASA. Located at Shelter, a club in deepest downtown Manhattan, NASA – short for Nocturnal Audio And Sensory Awakening – was the brainchild of Scotto and DB. Scotto was an in-demand lighting-director who had toured with Deee-Lite. London-born DB had moved to New York in 1989, where he DJ-ed and ran a peripatetic outlaw party called Deep with a proto-rave vibe, plus smaller events like Orange which catered to English expats with a mix of house and Madchester style indie-dance.

Kicking off at the end of July 1992, NASA was full-blown rave. The music was a different version of hardcore than either Storm or Future Shock offered – NASA's DJs favoured the breakbeat-and-piano driven tunes that were peaking in England that summer. 'The first six weeks, we lost money every week,' says DB. 'But I knew in my guts that if we stuck with it, the thing was going to pop. After six weeks, there was a line around the block, and these kids were not jaded, they didn't want to get in for free like typical Manhattan clubbers. To this day, I've never seen dance energy like it in New York.'

DB and his fellow DJs like Soulslinger and Jason Jinx were pushing the proto-jungle tunes from UK labels like Reinforced, Formation and Moving Shadow. The first time I went to NASA, I was thrilled to hear tunes I recognized from the London pirate stations. But by this point, the winter of 1992, the crowd's vibe was lagging behind the music's madness. The peak 'only lasted three or four months,' admits DB, 'it quickly became way too young, way too druggy, way too cliquey-fashion-bullshit.' Unlike the dressed-down, jeans-and-trainers Storm crowd, the NASA kids were inventing the look that became the dominant US rave style. 'It was the fusion of hip-hop culture into rave,' says DB. 'Super baggy trousers halfway down their arses, Tommy Hilfiger, Polo – preppy gear that became hip-hop clothing and then entered rave. But back in 1992, it wasn't so label oriented – lots of backpacks, lollipops, flowers in the hair, smiley faces. Very kiddy-innocent-looking – nineteen-year-olds trying to look like they were five-year-olds.'

'NASA was where that whole style of East Coast rave dancing was invented,' says Scotto. 'That dance where there's a little snakey thing going, and little bunny hop steps – that was created at NASA by this guy Philly Dave. He was an Ecstasy dealer, he wore these big white gloves, and he would come up from Philadelphia every week. One night he was fucked up and mesmerized by his own gloves, he started these moves, and that's how it started. The kids worshipped him, he was an icon. Unfortunately, he OD-ed.'

Despite being portrayed in the Gen X-sploitation movie *Kids* as a den of debauchery (chemical *and* sexual), NASA's atmosphere was initially rather fresh-faced and idealistic, thanks to the collective MDMA honeymoon. 'You could hear it in the conversations,' grins DB. 'We were going to print a T-shirt with "I really love you" on the front, and then on the back, "It's not the drugs talking".' The same was equally true of the Storm milieu. Heather Hart, then only eighteen, was putting out the fanzine *Under One Sky*, which rapidly progressed from purely musical coverage to 'a very spiritual angle', incorporating poetry, art and letter pages where kids would testify to life-changing experiences on the scene. Four years after England's 1988 rave-olution, New York was experiencing its own Second Summer of Love. The Storm-NASA axis was bolstered by the arrival of Caffeine, a rave-club in Deer Park, Long Island, where party-hard kids from NASA and Storm would end up on Sundays. Here – according to a condescending report in *The New York Times* – the universal refrain on every other teenager's lips was: 'It's just like the Sixties.'

For Dennis The Menace, the pinnacle came at a Storm rave in a trucking depot. 'At the end of the party, we were winding down, the sun was out, everyone was feeling pure and alive, in that communal unity feeling. Then someone in the middle of the floor started holding hands and putting their hands up in a circle. Kids were jumping from the back to put their hands up to touch the centre point where all the hands interlocked. People had tears in their eyes. We were just looking at each other, so happy, so open to everything. At the peak of all of it, with everyone trying to let go as much as they could, the belt drive on the turntable bust. Everyone stopped and looked at Frankie, and he kept trying to keep the record spinning with his finger at the right beats-per-minute – just to continue what everyone was feeling.' Although MDMA catalysed that communion, Dennis insists that 'The reason these kids were going out wasn't the ecstasy in the pill, but the feeling you got when everyone was together. Group energy, where one person triggers the next person who triggers the next person ... You could feel it vibrating between everyone. You can't put that in a pill.

There's kids I know that were totally straight, who never did drugs, and who were there dancing as hard as anyone 'cos they could feed off that energy.'

Live Fast, Dream Hard; San Francisco's Cyberdelic Visions

If New York's rave scene can be traced back to Frankie Bones's experiences in England during the summer of 1989, the West Coast's scene was directly catalysed, in large part, by British expatriates. In San Francisco, a remarkable number of the prime movers were from the UK: Mark Heley, the guru behind the Toon Town raves; most of the Wicked collective; Irish promoters Malachy O'Brien and Martin O'Brien (no relation); Jonah Sharp, founder of the Reflective label and music-maker as Space Time Continuum (named after his pioneering London ambient parties, Space Time); clothes designer Nick Philip.

A particular techno-pagan strand of English rave ideology was also disproportionately influential on what happened in San Francisco. The principal font of this cyberdelic philosophy was Fraser Clark, the original hippy-turned-zippy (zen-inspired pagan professional) behind *Evolution* magazine, the *Shamanarchy In The UK* compilation and London's New Agey trance club Megatripolis. Another influential figure was Psychic TV's Genesis P. Orridge, who actually ended up in SF after exiling himself from England when the authorities threatened to take his children into care. One SF party organization called Mr Floppy's was affiliated with Orridge's cult The Temple Ov Psychick Youth.

P. Orridge was actually a peripheral figure in the UK's acid house scene. But his widely disseminated ideas – psychedelia/sampladelia = the creative abuse of technology; house's 125 b.p.m. = the primordial trance-inducing, alpha-wave triggering tempo that connects Arab, Indian and aboriginal music; the manipulation of sonic frequencies to achieve 'metabolic engineering', *à la* Aleister Crowley's dictum 'our method is science, our aim is religion' – pretty much defined the San Francisco scene. In the more hyperbolic West Coast versions of rave's history, P. Orridge is credited with actually introducing acid house to the UK in the first place – a total myth-take.

At the same time, there were plenty of local sources for San

Francisco's neo-hippy version of rave: the neuroconsciousness movement's covert research into designer drugs and archaic plant psychedelics, the Internet/Virtual Reality/posthuman/'extropian'/*Mondo 2000*
scene on the fringes of Silicon Valley; New Age culture; Haight-
Ashbury's history of acid rock and psychedelic happenings ('Be Ins',
'Love Ins'). It didn't hurt that much of America's drug supply comes
from West Coast labs, making for especially strong Ecstasy in the Bay
Area.

Finally, San Francisco was a fertile area for house music because of
its indigenous disco scene, a by-product of the city's allure as a liberal,
laidback Mecca for gays from all over America. The first clubs to play
house were mixed gay/straight clubs like DV8, Doc Martin and Pete
Avila's club Recess, and its successor Osmosis. According to Jody
Radzik, a key cyberdelic ideologue who helped out at Osmosis, the
latter was 'one of the main conduits for rave ideas into San Francisco.
Then the British rave mafia took over.'

Beginning in the early summer of 1991, Mark Heley hooked up with
Diana Jacobs (who'd been involved in the gay club scene) and her
partners Preston Lytton and Craig Valentine to promote a series of
parties called Toon Town. 'The first, a collaboration with *Mondo 2000*,
didn't work out, the second one got busted,' says Radzik, 'But when
they moved it to this strange little club in South of Market – the office/
industrial area where most of the clubs are – Toon Town really took
off.' A Toon Town rave on New Year's Eve 1991 pulled a then
astonishing 8000 punters.

If Diana and Preston provided the organizational skills, Mark Heley
was the guru who articulated the vision. A Cambridge graduate who'd
written about cyberdelic culture for *iD* and *Mondo*, and had run a
'brain gym' in London, Heley is mythologized in Douglas Rushkoff's
Cyberia as a modern shaman wont to warn his acolytes that 'bliss is a
rigorous master'. 'Heley pioneered the whole cyber-rave trip, he
brought VR and brain machines into it,' says Radzik. Heley also forged
contacts with the Bay Area neuro-consciousness wizards like Timothy
Leary, Terence McKenna, Bruce Eisner and Allen Cohen, and brought
in a character called Earth Girl to set up a Smart Drinks stall. These
psychoactive cocktails – briefly popular throughout the US rave scene
– were more hype than anything else, although those containing
ephedra gave you a sort of sub-MDMA rush.

Like Heley, Radzik was a bit of a seeker. Enrolled in a Consciousness Studies degree at John F. Kennedy University and an adept of Bhakti yoga, Radzik had cobbled together a syncretic religion out of 'psychedelic, shamanic, and Hindu Bhakti practices'. Weirdly blending prophet and profit motives, Radzik marketed his knowledge of youth fashions to the sports wear company Gotcha. But this canny business sense was all part of the techno-shamanic role, fashion being a crucial medium for the dissemination of cultural viruses (or in cyber-speak, 'memes'). 'I felt I was an evolutionary agent, these ideas were channelling through me,' says Radzik. 'We thought we were setting up the morphogenetic field for rave – the idea of rave was alive, it wanted to express itself, and it was using the culture as a medium.'

Strip away the posthuman discourse, though, and the nature of the enlightenment offered by rave was actually quite straightforward. 'You go to a rave for the first time, take Ecstasy, and you're in this context of bright flashing lights, different sorts of images projected on the walls, crazily dressed people, normally dressed people,' says Radzik. 'People you don't know are smiling big at you. Everyone else is on E so there's this huge bath of acceptance. That's a tremendous experience – it changes people, turns them into ravers.'

In the UK, people had these life-changing experiences, but they didn't necessarily dress them up in cosmic significance; most people enjoyed them as relatively local transformations in their modes of self-expression and the way they related to friends and strangers. But in San Francisco, the Fraser Clarke/Genesis P. Orridge derived anarcho-mysticism went into cosmological overdrive, thanks to booster-doses of Terence McKenna's eschatological, drug-determined theory of human evolution. McKenna argues that human consciousness may have been spawned by primordial man's consumption of magic mushrooms. In this lost Edenic phase of prehistory, psylocibin's effects of 'boundary dissolution' worked to sustain an anarcho-utopian tribal society, organized around orgiastic mushroom-eating ceremonies enacted every full-moon. Plant-based hallucinogens (psylocybin, DMT, peyote) act as an innoculation against the 'tumour' that is the ego, a 'cyst' which 'keeps wanting to form in the human psyche'. Climatic changes led to to the disappearance of the mushroom cults, and thus to humanity's Fall from paradise: the ego formed in tandem with the dominator psychology of territoriality, property, sexism, class, ecocide and war. But wait, there's hope: '. . . the ego is the pathological portion of the human personality. Like any other pathology, it can be treated with pharmaceutical substances. It can be treated with plant psychedelics and it can be cured.' Rave, as a trance-dance drug-cult, is part of the 'archaic revival', helping to end our alienation from the 'Gaian matrix', the womb of Mother Nature.

This sounds reasonable enough, but McKenna has more outlandish beliefs, like the Mayan notion of End Time. Technological progress is accelerating History towards a 'bifurcation point' circa 2012, at which point human consciousness will abandon its bodily prison and merge into the Overmind. This is basically a cybertronic rewrite of the biblical notion of The Rapture. If Rushkoff's *Cyberia* can be trusted, Mark Heley seemed to believe that rave was part of this escalating evolutionary thrust towards End Time.

San Francisco rave's cyber-mystic shtick manifested itself most blatantly through fashion and flyers. Nick Philip's clothing company Anarchic Adjustment went from purveying skatepunk wear to being 'a mouthpiece for loved-up ecstasy consciousness'. T-shirts bore slogans like 'open your mind' and 'empathize'. 'We were the first to put aliens and UFO's on shirts,' claims Philip. 'One of the most popular featured a Buddha with a circuit board and the slogan "Spirituality Through Technology" . . . In San Francisco, a lot of interesting things collided together because [graphics] technology had developed a lot further than when rave started in England.' When Photoshop design software arrived in 1989, 'half the rave designers didn't know anything about design, but they had all these new tools and they were really experimenting, rather than just using old design paradigms. With the people who did rave flyers in early nineties California, the attitude was just get on the computer and make it as *mental* as you can.' Of course, the results were often cyber-kitsch, riddled with 'far out, man!' clichés. 'No one understood that we were almost spoofing ourselves for being so high,' says Wade Hampton, by this point flitting between LA and San Francisco. 'We'd put little tag lines at the bottom of flyers like "Live Fast, Dream Hard" – things the inner core of people would giggle over.'

This blend of tongue-in-cheek, retro-hippy references and genuine Ecstatic idealism also informed the first stirrings of San Francisco house music. At the fore were the Hardkiss Brothers. Their brotherhood was spiritual rather than genetic. Gavin Bieber and Scott Friedel had met at college in Philadelphia, become friends through a shared passion for Prince, then swerved from a suit-and-tie future to music, inspired by a series of revelatory experiences in Tenerife, at England's Glastonbury Festival, and at a Frankie Bones party in Long Island. The pair followed Scott's old friend Robbie Cameron to San Francisco in 1991, where they threw weekly parties like Sunny Side Up and started the Hardkiss label to put out tracks (Gavin recording as Hawke, Scott as God Within, and Robbie as Little Wing).

Their music's vibe wasn't cyberdelic techno so much as 'psychedelic funk', says Scott, 'influenced by live, traditional music as much as electronic, futuristic music. A lot of people in this scene are obsessed with the hottest and latest, but personally I have yet to hear a dance record that rivals the Beatles' singles!' One contemporary record that did deeply influence the Hardkiss aesthetic was The Future Sound Of London's sublime 1992 rave anthem 'Papua New Guinea', with its softcore breakbeats, ecstatic wordless vocals (sampled from Dead Can Dance's Lisa Gerrard) and blissed serenity.

Hardkiss's own tracks resemble Prince's psychedelic phase circa 'Raspberry Beret' filtered through Balearic house: just dig titles like The Ultraviolet Catastrophe's 'The Trip (The Remixes)' God Within's 'Raincry (Spiritual Thirst)', Hawke's '3 Nudes (Having Sax on Acid)', the latter being Hardkiss's all-time shimmerfunk classic. The halcyon imagery reflected the honeymoon period that all ravers, and rave scenes, experience with MDMA. 'It was a magical time in San Francisco,' says Robbie. 'We were going to these outdoor parties, stepping out and creating our own lives after college. We truly believed we were creating our own family – not just us three, but extending to girlfriends, wives, close friends. It was a magic burst, and you can't repeat it . . . It's like the first time you take Ecstasy, or the first time you fall in love – it never feels like that again.'

Moonstruck

For all the retro-kitsch knowingness, there was a genuine spiritual yearning behind San Francisco's positivity, expressed through imagery of Gaia and Goddess worship. Take the following pamphlet entitled 'HOUSE MUSIC & PLANETARY HEALING':

When used with positive intention, Group energy has the potential
to help restore the plan of Love on Earth ... When you open your
heart, and trust the whole group you dance with; when you feel love
with everyone, and they return it, a higher vibration can be reached.
This happens when a crowd is deep into the vibe of House ... In
the true sense of rhythmic movement, the affect is to align the
physical, mental and emotional bodies with the Oneness of All that
Is ... Help push the consciousness another level into Enlightenment
... Don't put out negative energy and feelings. Leave the old ways
behind. Throw yourself into the winds of transformation and sow
the seeds for a new world – one where the human family is together
again. When people respect and care for each other as a community-
organism. It's up to us to spread the vibe. Spread the Peace!

This leaflet was circulated by Malachy O'Brien, a British expat from
County Tyrone, Northern Ireland who was involved in the weekly club
Come-Unity and later worked with Martin O'Brien on the irregular
rave The Gathering. Strongly redolent of the Spiral Tribe's terra-
technic philosophy, the leaflet's idea of house music as biorhythmic
synchronization with Gaia was crystallized in Come-Unity's logo: a
child-like drawing of a house superimposed over Planet Earth.

The legendary Full Moon outdoor parties were where San Francisco's back-to-Mother-Nature spirit found its fullest expression. Full
Moon was the brainchild of party collective Wicked, which largely
consisted of English expatriates – Alan McQueen and his girlfriend
Trisha, DJs Jeno, Garth and Marky Mark – and had links with UK free
party sound-system Tonka. McQueen had been friends with Heley in
London and was on the same 'Terence McKenna techno-shamanism
trip', says Nick Philip. But when the increasingly spectacular and
successful Toon Town started to inspire 'copycat raves with VR and all
this shit,' people felt the scene was getting too commercial. So the
Wicked crew said 'fuck it, we're just gonna have a sound-system and
maybe a strobe.'

As in Brooklyn, most of the underground parties were warehouse
break-ins or jams thrown under bridges, beside train tracks, and (in a
nice San Francisco-specific touch) in disused tram yards. But the Full
Moon parties were held outside the city limits and under the sky.
Typical locations included disused military bunkers overlooking the
Bay and secluded sea-shore spots like Baker's Beach. 'With the high

cliffs, and if the cars were parked well away, you could escape notice and party till noon,' says Malachy. 'At one Full Moon, I was directing people across the sand dunes, and as I got near I was thinking: "What the fuck's up with the sound-system?" I reached the crest of a dune and all I could see was a sea of people, bonfires, dogs running wild, someone juggling with firesticks. Then the sound kicked in and all the people rose to their feet at the same moment. With the moon out there low over the water, it was a pretty awesome sight!'

Like Spiral Tribe's rural raves, the Full Moons were free parties. Nobody was benefiting financially, but there was still a competitive spirit of oneupmanship between San Francisco promoters, albeit on a more spiritual level. 'It was about how you could take care of people and impress them with something very psychedelic,' says Wade Hampton. 'In San Francisco, it tended to be much more natural and human-driven – hang-gliders, unicycles, anything you could possibly imagine was hauled off to the parties.' Ravers competed too – to intensify the vibe by wearing wacky clothes or by freaky dancing. 'It might be something like bringing an antique bicycle with a really big front wheel and riding it around on the beach til noon. It was a *Dali scene.*'

It was also a drug scene. 'Being San Francisco, there was a lot of psychedelics,' says Malachy. Not just Ecstasy and LSD, but 'San Pedro cactus, *ayahuasca*, Syrian Rue'. The latter is a plant-derived substance rich in a chemical called harmine, whose MAO inhibitor effect intensifies the visions caused by psychedelics. Amazonian shamans combine harmine-rich plants with the hallucinogenic tree-bark DMT to create *ayahuasca*, a potent brew that triggers 'extremely rich tapestries of visual hallucination that are particularly susceptible to being "driven" and directed by sound' (Terence McKenna).

With all these psychoactive substances circulating in the Full Moon milieu, it's hardly surprising that there were incidents of mass hallucination. At one party in late 1992, several hundred people 'saw the same spaceship come down and land,' claims Wade Hampton. 'There was this acid floating around called Purple Shield. That party is legendary in San Francisco. After that party, most people walked away *as one.*'

Take It to the Limit: the Los Angeles Rave Explosion

While San Francisco ravers talked about reaching 'higher awareness' and celebrated the DJ as a 'digital shaman', the house party scene in Los Angeles was more about fashion-conscious hedonism, rooted in the popular demand for after-hours dancing. In 1989–90, there were parties that mixed a bit of house in with hip hop and funk, like Solomon Monsieur's Dirtbox, Steve LeClair's OAP (One Almighty Party), and a series of clubs and one-offs like Alice's House, Deep Shag, and Stranger Than Fiction put together by a guy called Randy. After moving down from San Francisco, Doc Martin DJ-ed house at Flammable Liquid. There was also a long established all-night dance culture amongst Latino youth on LA's East Side.

Most clubs in Los Angeles had to close by 2 a.m. By 1990, 'you started seeing flyers for psychedelic after-parties,' says Todd C. Roberts, editor of *Urb*, LA's DJ culture magazine. 'Normal clubs started kicking people out at about 1.45 a.m., so there was lots of drunk 'n' horny guys and gals wandering around.' As in San Francisco, the key promoters who spotted the potential for all-night clubs were mostly English. Steve Levy was DJ-ing at his own Santa Monica club, West Go West. After a trip back home to London in 1989, he returned with a stack of acid house 12 inches. Following the warehouse party blueprint he'd witnessed in London – word-of-mouth, flyers, voice-mail, meet-points – Levy founded the illegal after-hours event Moonshine.

'Our first location was a building this guy had been using for an illegal casino,' remembers Levy. 'The guy was a nutcase, dodgy enough that when he kept our security deposit we didn't argue with him about it!' After a few weeks, the party moved to the Fish Factory, the basement of a fish warehouse in downtown LA. 'It stank, but you got used to it after a couple of hours. [Punters] had to go down a freight elevator. Halfway down, we'd turn all the lights out, ask everyone for the money, and search them. In LA, if you search a policeman, they have to give up the gun. Since they aren't allowed to travel without a weapon, we searched everyone to stop undercover cops from getting in.' Other locations came through contacts in the real-estate business.

After a dozen Moonshines, Levy decided to switch to legal venues. By this point – the summer of 1991 – Levy's parties were pulling thousand-strong crowds. But they weren't really raves – the party-fuel was still alcohol (hence the prohibition-era name Moonshine) rather than E, and the music was slanted towards hip hop rather than house. Levy's next venture – Truth, at the Park Plaza Hotel – was closer. Hip hop and house were in separate rooms, but the funk crowd were getting seduced by the house room's trippy projections and lasers. 'Next week they'd be rolling up in their overalls ready to *have it.*'

Promoters in suburban Orange County were already throwing ravey events; following Moonshine's lead, they started breaking into warehouses in downtown LA. If the English club organizers like Levy resembled Paul Oakenfold and Danny Rampling circa 1988, the Orange County impressarios were equivalent to Sunrise and Energy in 1989: entrepreneurs with the guts and ego to take it to the next stage. As with 1989's orbital rave explosion, the result was an escalating spiral of friendly-but-fierce competition to throw the most spectacular events in the most audaciously outlandish locations.

'For me it was all about the production, the idea of having a vision and then building it up from the ground,' says Les Borsai. From his beginnings with Steve Kool-Aid throwing parties like Double Hit Mickey and Mr Bubble, Borsai progressed to increasingly grandiose raves in downtown LA warehouses. For King Neptune's Underwater Wet Dream, 'We painted the whole warehouse fluorescent, using stencils of seahorses and fish and sharks. We put up blue lighting and bubble machines, made the whole club look fuckin' spectacular.' Suddenly helicopters and police arrived to arrest Borsai and his team. Managing to wriggle out of the law's clutches by claiming they'd only been hired to paint the place, Borsai faced the challenge of finding a replacement site within twenty-four hours. 'We found a massive underground parking structure, painted it, and brought in a huge water truck and twenty cases of shampoo. We foamed up the whole dancefloor.' But two hours after the rave kicked off, the police shut it down and arrested Borsai.

Fed up with the precarious nature of unlicensed events, Borsai hooked up with rock promotions company Avalon Attractions. The result was a series of fully legal raves that grew ever more spectacular. For a 1991 rave in a Pomona cow pasture, Borsai rented an entire carnival. Techno Flight One took place in a Disney facility which housed Howard Hughes wooden aeroplane the Spruce Goose. 'The plane sat in a moat, and Disney created dry ice effects so it looked like it was floating on clouds. This plane must have stood fifty feet off the ground, but people were so off their heads, the kids were dancing out on the wings. It was *madness*!'

When it came to rave extravaganzas, Borsai's major rival was Daven Michaels, who cultivated a larger-than-life persona – Daven the Mad Hatter – and even hired a personal publicist. Collaborating with early partners Beej and Sparky, Daven threw a rave called LSD (Love Sex Dance) which, he claims, 'changed the course of LA'. His tale illustrates the flagrant law-bending and logistical cunning required to promote raves in LA during the scene's outlaw phase. The location was 'an incredible space called the Bingo Building, which the realty management company would rent out for movie shoots. I pretended I was a location scout and kept asking them to hold it for us, saying "We're going to have a production meeting, I'll get back to you." That way, we kept the space open right up to the last minute.'

But on the day of the rave, Michaels discovered that a rival promoter was advertising a rave at the very same space. 'I hopped in my car, threw on a tie, and drove down to the building, where the kids are setting up their event. I say: "Guys, I'm John Stone from this [realty] company, you've set off a silent alarm, and you have ten minutes to get out before I call the police."' Having routed the panicked kids, Daven locked the building's entrance, then noticed that the rival promoters were still hanging around. Thinking on his feet, Michaels decided to disguise the rave as an after-concert party for Madonna, performing in LA that very night. After informing his usual security team of this ruse, Michaels hired *another* security company and fed them the Madonna after-party line, so they'd sound convincing if challenged by the police.

Pulling both their own crowd and the people who'd come for the rival rave, LSD was a huge success, spawning a series of sequels. Like Borsai, Michaels became obsessed with dazzling the kids with spectacular, 'fully themed' productions involving up to five separate installations per event. 'We worked with a performance artist on huge performance pieces that involved hydraulics. One was modelled on Ancient Rome, with this 400 pound guy called Fat Freddie wearing a toga and sitting on a throne. All of a sudden Rome crumbles, the columns crash down. Then hydraulics lift everything back together. The kids flipped for it.'

Going solo, Daven began his Paw Paw Patch series of parties. Paw Paw Ranch – 27 June 1991, in the desert city of Hemet, Riverside

County – was LA's first outdoor rave, 'the first party where the ravers saw the sun go up'. Because the idea of travelling outside the city limits was then unusual, Michaels says 'We had to trick people so they didn't realize how far they were really driving.' A year later, when desert raves were well established, Paw Paw Ranch II took place at Horse Thief Canyon Stables in Orange County; Michaels hired 'a ghost town from a company, prefab, which we transported there and erected'.

Although the British expats got the LA rave scene off the ground with their clubs ('English weeklies') and medium-scale one-offs, their following was older and relatively sophisticated. Rave ringmasters like Borsai and Daven the Mad Hatter pulled a younger, more suburban crowd who were really there to *rave*. 'To an extent we commercialized it,' admits Daven. 'The English guys never sold out ... Whereas we were always outdoing each other. And we really spent a *lot* of money outdoing each other. In the beginning, events cost between five and fifteen grand, but by the end the costs were running to well over a hundred thousand dollars.' With tickets selling from $20 to $25, and crowds between four and six thousand, 'we had to run a pretty tight ship just to keep up with each other and still make a few bucks'.

The most extravagant and over-the-top South California rave ever was probably Gilligan's Island, which took place in a Catalina casino-cum-ballroom. 1200 people were ferried over to the island on two ships. 'The budget was massive,' says Wade Hampton, 'there was never even a possibility of recouping what they spent. Eventually they took over the island, 'cos the cops wanted them to stop but they wouldn't. It was the pinnacle of Los Angeles rave – so outlawish, so brilliant, like Sunrise taking over the M25 highway in 1989. From then on, people were trying to match that vibe.'

Hampton claims that DJs were flown into the event 'on Lear Jets paid for by hot cheques' and that 'virtual crime' was rife amongst LA promoters – credit cards scams, cellular phone fraud. 'A lot of parties were boosted by doing mad things with other people's money. It was the beginning of the end.' For the honest promoters, the game was getting too risky: the huge events couldn't evade the police's notice, and a busted gig could obliterate the profits from several previous triumphs. Inevitably, LA rave began to move towards fully-licensed legitimacy. Instead of the flyers/voicemail/map-point system, promoters started to sell tickets at stores, then graduated to working through Ticketmaster. By mid-1992, LA rave was losing its outlaw edge, even as the potential profit margins were attracting fly-by-night entrepreneurs and serious criminals. But for about eighteen months, LA had the most full-on rave scene in America. It even had a techno radio station, Mars FM. Starting 24 May 1991, Mars broadcasted 'the new music invasion' all day long, interspersed with the station slogan 'we want our techno'. There was also an explosion of rave fashion on LA's streets. According to Hampton, many kids adopted the raver look first, then got into the music. 'Fresh Jive, Clobber, all these rave oriented clothing lines became very influential. If you had flyers designed by Fresh Jive, loads of kids would come to your parties. Through the desktop, computer graphics revolution, the whole culture got very visual.'

Fashion and 'balls out hedonism' (as Hampton puts it) defined Los Angeles rave, then. But there was a utopian aspect to Southern California's rave scene – the racial mixing that was going on. 'It was the first time in my lifetime I saw people from every neighbourhood – San Diego, Riverside, San Bernadino, Long Beach – coming together', says Todd Roberts. 'Every weekend you'd see a lot of people you'd never even come into contact with. It was especially nice, being African-American myself, to see [black youth] involved and not just a bunch of white kids acting weird. Rave allowed me to talk about and see LA as a better community than most people give it credit for. It *is* a very divided city. But this was the first time those walls were breaking down . . . Utopian? It was as utopian as LA could get!'

Crashing the Party: US Rave Descends into the Darkside

Ecstasy culture pivots around a utopian/dystopian axis. Any given rave scene seems to enjoy a honeymoon period of two years, tops, before problems begin to appear – the shift from Ecstasy use to abuse; MDMA burn-out and the lure of amphetamine as a cheap, dependable surrogate; polydrug experimentation. The resulting paranoia and mental confusion is aggravated by taking place in a context of drug rip-offs and criminality. First 'in' and therefore first to burn out, the scene's prime movers succumb to 'lifestyle dysfunction', even mental breakdown.

The hardcore hedonism caught up with Frankie Bones in August

1993. 'On the weekend of Labor Day, I had a seventy-two-hour thing where I was eating everything – acid, Ecstasy – and smoking angel dust ... Towards the end of my mission, my mother caught up with me, 'cos I'd wrecked my car. I was doing really weird things – the way my uncle described it to me, I didn't care if I lived or died ... My uncle had a neighbour who worked in the hospital. I was only supposed to go there for some tests, but they found so much shit in my system, they locked me up and put me on medication.'

Seven weeks later, Bones was released and went back to live with his mother for the first time in ten years. 'All I wanted to do was eat my breakfast, lunch and dinner, and watch TV. I had no interest in music.' By the end of 1993, Bones was off the medication, but his career was in tatters. It took him a year to get back into regular DJ-ing.

Bones's misadventures weren't abnormal. In Long Island, Caffeine's 'just like the sixties' vibe went from 1967 euphoria to a 1969 death-and-madness trip. 'If you exceeded your limit five times over, you were probably at Caffeine,' says Bones with a wry grin. 'Kids couldn't afford Ecstasy so they did LSD as an alternative. I remember this girl on acid just flipping out and running amok, we had to hold her down.'

By late 1993, the East Coast was 'at the bottom of the US rave scene, we went from totally the best to a bunch of bullshit ... The "poly" is what fucked everything up,' Bones says, referring to his doctors' original diagnosis of "poly-substance abuse". Finding that E alone wasn't getting them high enough any more, kids were mixing all manner of drugs into potent, unpredictable cocktails that blew their teenage minds but created an anti-dance vibe. 'Kids were combining Special K, angel dust, E's, acid, and they'd just become a ball of jelly, sitting on the floor.'

NASA was also succumbing to the darkside. 'People started taking Limelight drugs,' says DB, referring to the rampant abuse of drugs like ketamine by more cynical Manhattan club kids. 'People were lying in hallways, it wasn't so euphoric.' By 1993, says Scotto, 'the drug dealers were the heroes of the scene – you were either a promoter, a DJ or a dealer. Then the dealers were getting paranoid, having these fantasies of being a Mafia guy or a gang member.'

At one NASA night in spring 1993 – a few months before the club closed down – a girl handed me a photocopied pamphlet. Framed with smiley-faces, happy goldfish and handwritten phrases like 'group hugs', the leaflet was a heartfelt, heartbreaking plea for a return to lost innocence:

WHY ARE YOU AT THIS EVENT? THE RAVE SCENE IS NOT JUST
ABOUT TECHNO. THIS SCENE IS NOT JUST ABOUT DRUGS.
THIS SCENE IS NOT JUST ABOUT FASHION. IT IS SOMETHING
SPECIAL ABOUT UNITY AND HAPPINESS. IT IS ABOUT BEING
YOURSELF AND BEING LOVED FOR IT. IT SHOULD BE A
HARBOR FROM OUR SOCIETY. BUT OUR SCENE RIGHT NOW IS
DISINTEGRATING! OLD STYLE RAVERS — REMEMBER WHEN
EVERYBODY HUGGED ALL THE TIME — NOT JUST TO SAY
HELLO AND GOODBYE? REMEMBER WHEN PEOPLE JUST SAID
HI FOR NO REASON EXCEPT TO BE YOUR FRIEND? REMEMBER
HOW GOOD IT FELT? WHY DON'T WE DO IT ANYMORE?
NEWCOMERS — YOU ARE WANTED AND YOU SHOULD KNOW
THAT THIS SCENE IS ABOUT OPENNESS. WE ALL SHARE A
BOND — THE DESIRE TO GROOVE TO A GOOD BEAT ALL NIGHT
LONG. AND NO MAN IS AN ISLAND. EVERYONE NEEDS FRIENDS
AND THE OUTSIDE WORLD IS TOUGH ENOUGH. WE DON'T
NEED FRONTS AND ATTITUDES IN OUR SCENE. OPEN YOUR
HEARTS AND LET THE GOOD FEELINGS FLOW ... RAVERS
UNITE AND KEEP OUR SCENE ALIVE.

What's truly poignant about this leaflet is that the golden age being lamented had occurred only *nine months earlier* – an indication of just how swiftly Ecstasy burn-out and polydrug mind-rot can set in. Over in San Francisco, many of the major players in the Anglo-cyberdelic milieu were succumbing, Bones-style, to drug-induced malaise. 'There's specific people who got into serious drug trips, using speed, heroin, ketamine,' says Jody Radzik. 'Key people really fucked up.' Radzik himself began dropping out of the scene in February 1992. 'Just through getting involved in raving and Ecstasy I uncovered [personal problems] that I had to deal with. I developed a lot of insecurities, socially, and just had to remove myself.' Radzik says he 'went through a little psycho drug period too.... Maybe it *helped* in that it made things a lot worse. The Ecstasy, the speed, exposed all these huge inner flaws that I had to [deal with].'

In the spring of 1993, a tragedy occurred that cast a pall over the ailing San Francisco scene, but that also, in a weird twist, opened the way for a partial regeneration of idealism. After a Full Moon party, the

Wicked crew were driving back in their van. In the back, asleep, was
Malachy O'Brien, plus the spare sound-system he'd brought along in
case the event was busted. 'We came off the road up at Candlestick
Park, ironically near where some of the early Full Moons had
happened, and ended up in the Bay,' says Malachy. The driver may
have nodded off at the wheel after partying too hard (a common cause
of post-rave accidents); there might also have been a mechanical
failure. Whatever the crash's cause, a speaker impacted Malachy's head,
bending it so badly his neck was broken. He was left a quadraplegic.

It's a testament to Malachy's character that he's capable of talking
about the accident in terms of good fortune – 'It was a lucky escape,
there was a generator full of gasoline.' Despite his personal catastrophe,
Malachy also stresses that the tragedy reunited the divided San
Francisco scene, with promoters coming together to organize a series
of benefit raves to pay for his hospitalization and physical therapy. The
flyer for the first benefit – called Come-Unity and held in April 1993
at Richmond Civic Center auditorium – beseeched 'Music Is a Healing
Force, Dance Is a Healing Energy, Join Together and Dance For the
Healing of A Troubled World and the Healing of Malachy'. During the
rave, the DJ-ing was interrupted by a healing ceremony guided by a
shaman and a Zen monk, with Malachy appearing on a video screen
and addressing the crowd. Today, Malachy has recovered some
movement in his biceps, allowing him to operate his joystick-controlled
wheelchair and use the track-ball on a computer. After a period of
intensive physiotherapy in England, he's back in San Francisco and still
involved in the house scene, helping to run Come-Unity.

Although Malachy accentuates the positive, other scenesters
responded to the tragedy as an ill omen. 'When that happened, it was
the beginning of the end for me,' says Nick Philip. 'I don't think
everybody believed anymore that we were going to save the world. It
was just so weird that it happened to Malachy – the nicest guy, and the
person who really *lived* it. A lot of people spouted the philosophy
about saving the planet and global consciousess, but Malachy really
lived it, he gave his [proceeds] away to fuckin' charities [like Green-
peace] ... It happened to *him*, and that freaked people out ... A
number of things happened – drug related incidents, busts, someone
shot at a rave in Santa Cruz – that turned the optimism into something
different.'

Tweaked Out

Meanwhile, down the coast in Southern California, the LA rave scene was being killed by its own success. The syndrome was similar to England in 1989: media outcry, police crackdown, rivalry between promoters, gangsterism, bad drugs. The LA riots provided the *coup de grace*, destroying the precarious trans-racial alliances.

There was a symbolic death-knell in July 1992, when Mars FM dropped its techno playlist in favour of alternative rock. Protests and petitions by a group calling themselves Friends of Techno and Rave Music led to a brief restoration, but by September techno was dropped again, for good. It was probably a sound business decision, based on the realization that the record industry was backing grunge as the new youth-cultural cash-cow, not rave. The major labels had signed up a bunch of British and European rave acts; American's supremo Rick Rubin seemed briefly enthused by the idea that techno was the new punk. But grunge was a better bet. Guitar riffs, gruff vocals, a little bit of old-fashioned rebellion – this was something the record industry understood, and bands were something that could be marketed, unlike DJs and 'faceless techno bollocks'.

Mars FM's turnaround was probably also influenced by the tarnishing of rave's image in LA. The local media had discovered that the dance parties, far from being innocent extravaganzas, were bacchanals fuelled by Ecstasy. There was also a scuzzy substance seemingly unique to the West Coast scene: nitrous oxide, sold in balloons at raves for around $5. The harmless associations of 'laughing gas' were shattered in March 1992, when three young men were found dead in a pickup truck on Topanga Canyon Boulevard. The cabin's windows were rolled up; the kids, high as kites, had left the valve open on their nitrous canister and asphyxiated. As drug researcher Dr Ronald Siegel put it, 'they basically crawled inside a balloon'.

Nitrous has a surprisingly distinguished history as a psychoactive inhalant. In the nineteenth century, there was a whole discourse dedicated to 'The Anaesthetic Revelation' offered by nitrous, ether and chloroform, involving clerics, physicans and scholars like J. A. Symonds and William James. 'Sobriety diminishes, discriminates, and says no; [intoxication] expands, unites, and says yes,' enthused James in his 1902 classic *The Varieties of Religious Experience*. 'It is in fact the great exciter of the *Yes* function in man ... It makes him for the moment one with truth.' James claimed that nitrous intoxication was a thousandfold stronger than alcohol, stimulating 'the mystical consciousness to an extraordinary degree. Depth beyond depth of truth seems revealed to the inhaler. This truth fades out, however, or escapes, at the moment of coming to; and if any words remain over ... they prove to be the veriest nonsense.'

The descriptions of 'nitrous oxide trance' offered by James and other nineteenth-century inhalers sound remarkably like MDMA. Benjamin Paul Blood wrote of recovering 'the primordial Adamic surprise of Life', a gnostic realization that 'the Kingdom is within'. James described it as a sensation of 'reconciliation', in which 'the opposites of the world, whose contradictoriness and conflict make all our difficulties and troubles, [melt] into unity.' This sense of access to an ineffable enlightenment explains the addictive nature of nitrous – as Dr Siegel put it: 'just a little bit more and I'm going to get the secret of the universe'.

It's fairly safe to say, though, that for most ravers, nitrous's minute-long high was just a wicked buzz. 'You get warm and fuzzy all over and you feel like you can float – like an astronaut. Everything feels thick and soft,' is how one user put it. A slang term for nitrous is 'hippy crack': 'hippy' being a nod to its popularity with Deadheads, 'crack' evoking the way 'people keep going back for more, it becomes that futile attempt to transcend the experience,' says Todd Roberts. Taken on its own, nitrous offers a non-dancey 'head trip', he claims. 'It plays well with the strange effects and echo in the music.' Inhaled after taking Ecstasy or LSD, nitrous enhances the synaesthetic effects of those drugs, synchronizing visual hallucinations to the music.

Whether stolen from dentists or legally obtained from gas stations (it's used as a fuel additive to soup-up race-car engines), nitrous oxide became rife on the West Coast rave scene, and eventually spread throughout America. Because a $100 tank could fill 200 balloons at $5 each, the nitrous pedlar could make a 900 per cent profit. Dealers started to offer the promoters big money for the exclusive rights to sell nitrous at raves. Newspapers noted in horror the popularity of 'Just Say NO' T-shirts, which meant 'just say yes to nitrous oxide'.

Despite the freak tragedy in Chatsworth, nitrous is not harmful in itself, if used with the right mix of oxygen. Because the gas makes you pass out for a few seconds, there's a risk of injury or concussion if inhaled when standing up or in motion; morons have been known to get frostbite of the lips, tongue and throat by sucking directly from the sub-zero cylinder of liquid gas. In the rave scene, the worst side-effect of nitrous was to dampen the dance energy. 'You sit on your ass and you don't dance,' says Wade Hampton. 'People get very pale and their lips turn blue, 'cos you're depleting your oxygen supply. If you see people who've been doing it all night, it makes you want to throw up.'

Focusing on nitrous and Ecstasy, most LA newspapers missed the scoop on the real killer drug, amphetamine – lethal, if not to people's lives, then to their souls, and to the rave scene's good vibe. In the West Coast, speed and its more potent relative crystal methamphetamine (aka 'chrissie' or 'crystal meth') took over because it was both more reliable than Ecstasy and more competitively priced: $20 for a sixteenth of a gram, compared with around $28 for a pill of E. This was a false economy, however, because tolerance to the drug quickly destroys its edge over E. Users start taking huge amounts; some progress from snorting it to smoking or injecting. Because the comedown is vicious compared with Ecstasy's afterglow, the temptation is to go on 'runs' that last several days.

By the end of 1992, the burgeoning speedfreak culture in Los Angeles had coined two new slang terms, *tweaking* and *sketching*. Both mean buzzing on crystal, but 'sketching' has more of a wired-and-tired, crashing-after-a-long-run connotation. 'We called them raver-zombies,' says Todd Roberts of the tweakers. 'You'd see them stumbling across the floor, not knowing if it was Tuesday or Sunday, and not really caring. Originally, Ecstasy was the catalyst for people reaching out to you. One of the things I noticed when I first started raving was that strangers would actually say "hello" and smile.' But amphetamine closed down the open-hearted extroversion, replacing eye contact with vacant stares.

The Sketch Pad, a dark and dingy loft-space in Venice, was the raver-zombies' crash-pad. Originally running from 6 a.m. Sunday to the early evening, then later right through the small hours of Monday morning, the Sketch Pad's vibe was 'like a crack den,' says Roberts. 'It started as a rent party for the girl who ran it, then it became an excuse for people to buy more drugs or just be together if they were out of their minds.'

Crystal's effect on the rave community was to 'break down the ties of reality', as Roberts puts it. As in San Francisco, prime movers and well-known scenesters were experiencing 'lifestyle breakdowns', partying so hard they forgot about paying the bills or going to work. The crystal-fuelled runs could last for weeks. 'They weren't *awake* for weeks, but it could be a rocky road without enough sleep. Maybe work would get done one week – they'd start some projects, make some money, but then spend it on drugs. It's the addict lifestyle. Over a period of a month, if you've only spent four days working, you've got a problem.'

The shift to methamphetamine affected the sound of rave music. Roberts attributes the rise of high-tempo trance on the West Coast in 1993 to crystal. 'I think it lost its soul, the funk was gone. It had the beat and all the markings of techno, but it lost the irony, and the *fun.*' Elsewhere in America, tweakers and Ecstasy abusers followed the European trajectory of hardcore into gabba. Lenny Dee started his Industrial Strength label in Brooklyn, Drop Bass Network established their 'Midwest Hardcorps' milieu, and Southern California had its own headstrong scene led by DJ Ron D. Core and based around the record store Dr Freecloud's. The audience was younger, with little knowledge of house's roots or interest in neo-psychedelic utopianism. They hadn't grown out of the club scene; all they knew was raves, massive soundsystems, and going mental.

In reaction, the older Los Angeles DJs began a familiar retreat to house. 'One of the things that killed it here,' argues Steve Levy, 'was when several local DJs suddenly became huge fans of garage DJ Tony Humphries. They went to the Sound Factory in New York and decided to impart their new found "knowledge" to the LA crowd. The whole energy of the music, which in 1991 had been Italian piano house and Belgian techno, disappeared. It regressed from a rave thing to a club thing, and the clubs weren't fun anymore 'cos the music was fuckin' boring. It went really small, then small and dark.'

The mega-raves were dying because kids were fed up with driving long distances to desert parties that got busted. Media outcry stoked the police crackdown – not just TV news exposés, but fictionalized warnings about peer pressure and raves as 'drug supermarkets'. In an infamous episode *of Beverly Hills, 90210*, clean-cut Brandon is spiked with a drug called Euphoria by his girlfriend, and makes a right fool of himself. Next day, he's rueful about all the pseudo-profound feelings he'd thought he was experiencing, which have evaporated leaving just a ghastly hangover.

Alongside teenage drug abuse, complaints about noise and nuisance, and the danger of events without proper fire and safety measures, the police were also concerned about the arrival of gangsters and gunplay on the rave scene. At 1993's Grape Ape 3, at the Wild Rivers Water Park in Orange County, a series of incidents – fights, guns being pointed at security guards, a van set on fire – led to the rave being shut down at 3 a.m. The next summer, two fifteen-year-old boys were shot dead at a rave alongside the railroad track in San Diego's Old Town. Criminals were also applying pressure to the promoters. Daven Michaels had nitrous gangs trying to monopolize the supply at his parties, and 'mobsters from NY coming into town trying to squeeze me 'cos I had a cash business'. When he refused their offer of 'partnership', Michaels received 'death threats in the middle of the night . . . I had to call the police'.

Other Los Angeles promoters were also calling the cops – in order to snitch on their rivals. 'Originally the promoters all knew each other and made sure we weren't stepping on each others' toes,' says Steve Levy. 'What started killing it in the summer of '92 was that there'd be three different gigs on the same night. Everyone would be calling the cops. Eventually the punters got pissed off with paying $20 at the map point and rolling up to a gig that immediately got busted.' Even without the busts, several raves going off on the same night guaranteed low attendance all round, dissipating the vibe. Many original LA rave promoters dropped out of the business; Levy started his record label Moonshine, Borsai shifted to alternative rock promotion, Daven Michaels started making music. Others persisted: Ron D. Core with his Orange County hardcore scene, Kingfish Entertainment's Philip Blaine with his desert raves. Despite the downturn, Blaine's ally Gary Richards, aka DJ Destructo, pulled off America's biggest rave to date – the 17,000 strong New Year's Eve rave at Knott's Berry Farm amusement park at the end of 1992.

Trend of an Era

Knott's Berry Farm may be isolated in its immensity, but raves on the West and East coasts of America regularly draw between four and ten thousand. Herein lies the mysterious paradox of US rave culture: it's a massive subculture, but its momentum seems stalled. Since the end of 1992, it's been stuck in a peculiar holding pattern.

On the other side of the Atlantic, the situation is quite different. Despite its fragmentation into sub-scenes, European rave is essentially bigger than ever. The culture continued to escalate because new recruits arrive with each generation. In Britain, indie-rockers turned on to the new music thanks to rave 'n' roll intermediaries like Happy Mondays and Primal Scream. This never happened in America because rave is regarded as the epitome of fashion-plate Europhile trendiness; the outlandish way American ravers dress, and the goofy way they dance, tweaks the prejudices of indie-rockers and hip hoppers alike.

The fashion element really took hold in 1993, says Dennis The Menace. 'If you look at videos of the early outlaw parties, everyone's wearing jeans and T-shirts . . . Then it became whoever could wear the biggest hat, and people going out to be *seen* rather than to dance.' Especially on the East Coast, the dancing that *was* going on didn't resemble raving in the original English sense. Instead of trancing-out for hours, US teen-ravers tend to dance in spasmodic bursts – often surrounded, hip-hop style, by circles of spectators. The dancing is more stylized and ostentatious than in Europe: complex involutions of the limbs, shimmying torsions and geometric undulations that make the body ripple like computer fractals, kick-boxer skips and spinning-top twirls – all of which hark back to the breakdancing and bodypopping battles of old skool rap, but filtered through a post-E polymorphous fluidity. 'The pretzel dance', as Dennis calls it.

From NASA to his work as A & R director of Profile's techno sub-label Sm:)e, DB has been a long time crusader for rave in the USA. But even he bluntly admits that 'it's much more of a fad thing in America . . . more social and less about music. It's a place kids can meet their friends, get fucked up and stay out all night away from their parents. That may sound jaded, but most weekends I DJ around the country, and that's what I see . . . People grow into it and grow out of it very quickly. People in England burn out on the drugs too, but that doesn't mean they stop liking the music. That seems to be the way in America – once they've fucked themselves on whatever drugs they're doing, they stop liking the music and get into something else.'

In US rave, the 'whatever drugs they're doing' nowadays is a pharmacopoeia of illegal and semi-legal substances. On the West Coast, the vogue is for gamma y-hydroxybutyrate or GHB: a salty, clear liquid swigged from sports bottles and sometimes fallaciously sold as 'liquid ecstasy'. Originally favoured by bodybuilders because of its steroid-like effects, GHB developed a reputation as an aphrodisiac and a legal alternative to E (although it was actually banned by the FDA in 1990). The problem with GHB is that it affects breathing. In overdose or combined with alcohol, GHB's respiratory depression effect can lead to coma and death. Because its impact is relative to body-weight, 'a lot of women pass out,' says Todd Roberts. 'They gulp GHB like water, and you're only supposed to have a small spoonful.'

On the East Coast, another depressant drug is more popular: ketamine, a relative of PCP widely used as a veterinary anaesthetic. At raves, kids take regular 'bumps' of 'Vitamin K' to sustain a plateau state of boneless stupor. They've even started bringing blankets to parties, so they can loll around on the floor. K's popularity with ravers is mysterious: unlike E or acid, it doesn't make music sound fantastic, it's anti-social verging on autistic, and it certainly doesn't make you wanna dance. Then there's the risk of going beyond the dissociative effect of mild doses and falling into a 'K-hole', an experience that's been likened to catatonic schizophrenia. A really big dose might transport you onto truly *other* realms of consciousness wherein dwell the 'ketamine entities' aka 'machine-elves', who supervise the universe and who may tell you some interesting secrets.

When you've got sixteen-year-old kids dosing themselves with an array of substances of unknown potency and unpredictable interactions, adolescents who often aren't emotionally mature enough to surf the psychedelic maelstrom, then you have the recipe for a freak scene. 'I played at LSD in Philadelphia at New Year's Eve, and *twenty-five people* overdosed at that party,' says Heather Heart. 'There were ambulances outside all night long. The party was finally shut down 'cos some girl was unconscious and they went to wake her and she was defecating herself. These were kids overdoing it, and doing a mixture of drugs – Ecstasy, ketamine, crystal, acid. None of them were just on one thing.' Dennis The Menace argues that the polydrug culture has destroyed the synergy effect that occurs in rave scenes during the honeymoon phase of Ecstasy use: the 'rave-gasm' feedback loop of ravers, all relatively fresh to the drug, buzzing on the same pure E. Polydrug abuse shatters that synchronized rush; everyone's on different trips. 'The scene got ruined when the pills got replaced by powders,' he claims, referring to K, crystal, PCP and cocaine. 'The raves just splintered into different vibes.'

Because it was a *transplant* – literally imported by English expats, in many cases – rave has had trouble establishing roots in America. It never became a mass working-class movement, and it lacks certain key elements of the UK's self-sustaining subcultural matrix, like pirate radio. America is also a more hostile soil for rave. For rockers who still think 'disco sucks' and who hate English 'haircut' synth bands, rave is self-evidently inauthentic, a phoney fad. This prejudice is not entirely without foundation. Exempt from the picture the black house traditions in Chicago, Detroit and New York (all of which pre-date rave), and it's striking that the white rave scene in the USA has so far failed to generate a uniquely American mutation of the music. There are isolated cells of brilliance, for sure: Josh Wink and his Ovum label in Philadelphia, the Hardkiss crew, the Brooklyn milieu in the early nineties, plus a scattering of individual DJ–producers. But America has yet to spawn a creative mis-recognition of the music to rival jungle, gabba or trance. The nearest contender is the 'funky breaks' or 'breakbeat' style of house that's emerged in Southern California and Florida – a hybrid of hip hop, electro and acid house that, while great fun, is historically stuck at the level of UK rave in 1991.

According to Steven Melrose, co-founder of the City of Angels label, the West Coast breakbeat sound has little connection with house apart from its use of 'acid builds' (Roland 303 bass-riffs), and its 125–135 b.p.m. tempo. The breakbeats are popular because the four-to-the-floor house beat is just too European and disco for most American kids. 'Funky breaks stems from the first rave music from the UK that was big in the USA – the '91 breakbeat hardcore of SL2 and Prodigy.' This makes West Coast breakbeat the American equivalent of jungle, except that it's not as fast or as polyrhythmically complex; tracks usually feature just one looped break. The West Coast tracks also have a sunny, upful vibe compared with jungle, making the music 'better for that 5 a.m. in the morning, palm trees vibe.'

Formed by Scottish expat Melrose and his English partner Justin King, City of Angels is one of the leading funky breaks label. Its first release, 'Now Is The Time' by The Crystal Method (a Las Vegas outfit named after a technique for staying up all night, i.e., taking speed) defined the sound. Other West Coast pioneers include Überzone, The Bassbin Twins, Bass Kittens, DJs like John Kelley and Simply Jeff, and labels like Bassex and Mephisto. In Florida, the regional variant of funky breaks is influenced by Miami Bass – electro-descended, party-oriented rap that consists of little more than drum machine beats and booming Roland 808 bass. The leading lights of Florida breakbeat are Rabbit In The Moon and DJ Icey, whose Zone label is named in homage to UK 1991 breakbeat house labels Ozone and D-Zone.

Southern Death Cult

Florida now rivals Southern California as the USA's number one rave state. These two sunshine-states have a lot in common. Geographically and culturally, Florida is not really part of the traditional Dixie South. Just as Los Angeles was imposed on the desert, Florida is a leisure paradise carved out of an inhospitable Jurassic environment. It only really came into its own as a vacation and retirement hotspot after the invention of air conditioning. Like the So-Cal region, Florida is a sub-tropical suburban sprawl, a car culture of booming bass-speakers and rootless anomie. Ostensibly the polar inverse of the state's other big youth culture, death metal, Florida rave puts the morbid metal-kids to shame; it is infamous for taking excessive hedonism to the point of near-death experience, and sometimes taking it all the way. 'Florida, it's an active place, but the whole state's done too many E's,' says Scott Hardkiss. 'We've played a lot of parties where 3000 people are there, but no one's dancing. Everyone's off their head on [the downer] Rohypnol and E that's like heroin, sit-down E.'

Probably because of the number of wealthy old people who retire there, Florida is one of the most conservative states in America. Hardly surprising, then, that its rave scene is under siege from police departments and legislators. As with Los Angeles in 1992, the local news media used a series of rave fatalities to marshal public opposition to the deadly 'drug supermarkets'. In July 1994, eighteen-year-old Sandra Montessi died from 'cardiac dysrhythmia due to MDMA intoxication' after consuming one and half tablets at Orlando's Edge club. In the same year, Ecstasy also killed twenty-year-old Teresa Schwartz at the pioneering Orlando rave-club Dekko's. And in 1996, a young woman and her two male friends went into convulsions at a Tampa nightclub after a dealer used an eyedropper to deposit GHB on their tongues. With overdoses a regular occurrence, Orlando formed a Rave Review

Task Force in 1997, while the city legislature passed a bill to prohibit clubs from renting their spaces out for alcohol-free after-hours raves. But the ordinance only shifted the problem elsewhere – to illegal raves outside the city limits.

This kind of repression is not unique to Florida. All across America, police departments, fire marshals and city councils use teen curfews, ordinances and licence restrictions targeted at particularly notorious clubs. The anti-rave crackdown is nationwide simply because there are very few states in America that don't have a rave scene. According to the Hardkiss brothers, the entire South is kickin' – Texas, Georgia, North Carolina, Virginia, Maryland. 'In the Bible Belt, the kids go a little crazy, they need to break loose,' says Robbie. Heading up the East Coast, the Washington DC/Baltimore area is a stronghold, thanks to DJs like Scott Henry and promoters like Ultraworld. Washington/Baltimore is really part of an integrated East Coast network that connects Boston, New York, New Jersey and Philadelphia, a circuit of one-off raves to which kids travel by chartered buses as well as by cars. Another burgeoning scene, says Scott Hardkiss, is the Pacific North West: from San Francisco right up to Vancouver, via Portland and Seattle.

In the Hardkiss Brothers' hometown San Francisco, the rave scene is still going strong. Younger kids attend Martin O'Brien's The Gathering. Wicked are still active. The elders of the scene have formed 'rave communities', says Jody Radzik, tight cliques who throw small parties: the Rhythm Society of St John the Divine, Sweet, Friends and Family, Cloud Factory, Gateway Systems. The distinctive Bay Area spirituality endures, often in unusual ways – like the Planetary Masses at Grace Cathedral, modelled after the Nine O'clock Service in England and organized by Rev. Matthew Fox, who joined the Episcopalians having been defrocked as a Dominican priest after a dispute with the Vatican. On the techno-pagan tip, Dubtribe and other small outfits still throw renegade parties. The Full Moon concept migrated South to Southern California, thanks to a crew called Moon Tribe. Along with parties in the desert, many LA raves take place on Native American reservations, where the police have no jurisdiction. Like the post-Spiral Tribe sound-systems in Britain, American rave outfits exploit the local terrain, looking for 'cracks and vacancies' left by the state.

From illegal free parties through borderline events like Even Furthur to massive commercial extravaganzas, American rave survives, despite its stylistic fragmentation and regional dispersion. Whether it will benefit from the record industry's enthusiasm for 'electronica' is unclear. The major labels are trying to distance the music from drug culture by marketing techno as band music rather than a DJ culture. Where that will leave the 'real' American rave scene remains to be seen.

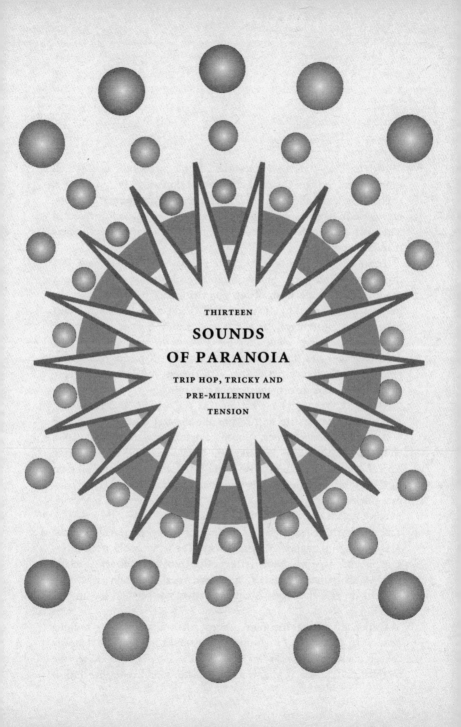

THIRTEEN

SOUNDS
OF PARANOIA

TRIP HOP, TRICKY AND
PRE-MILLENNIUM
TENSION

Musicians, bless 'em, hate categories. 'Don't pigeonhole us'; 'It's all music, man'; 'is there any kind of music we don't like? Just bad music, really' – these are the kind of platitudes regularly encountered by the journalist. In recent years, no genre designation has been more resented and rejected as a press-concocted figment by its purported practitioners than 'trip hop'.

Personally, I always thought the term was just fine. Not only does 'trip hop' sound good, but it instantly evokes what it describes: a spacey, down-tempo form of hip hop that's mostly abstract and all-instrumental. Coined by *Mixmag*'s Andy Pemberton (although others have claimed parentage), trip hop is a handy tag for a style that emerged in the early nineties (hip hop without the rap and without the rage, basically) and that, while not exclusively UK based, nonetheless remains almost totally out-of-step with current American rap, where rhymin' skills and charismatic personalities rule.

Designed for headphone-listening as opposed to parties, reverie rather than revelry, trip hop retains the musical essence of hip hop – breakbeat-based rhythms, looped samples, turntable-manipulation effects like scratching – but takes the studio wizardry of pioneering African-American producers like Hank Shocklee and Prince Paul even further. When not entirely instrumental, trip hop is as likely to feature singing as rapping. Widely regarded as the genre's inventors, Massive Attack deployed an array of divas both female (Shara Nelson, Tracey Thorn, Nicolette) and male (roots reggae legend Horace Andy) alongside rappers 3D and Tricky. The latter's solo work mixes singing and rapping, with Tricky often providing bleary 'backing raps' to his partner Martina's dulcet lead vocal. Generally, when trip hoppers do rap, their style is contemplative, low-key and low-in-the-mix.

Opponents of the 'trip hop' concept often argue that it's nothing new, citing precedents for abstract impressionist hip hop like the early collage-tracks of Steinski & Mass Media and The 45 King, the sampladelic fantasia of Mantronix, cinematic soundscapes like Erik B and Rakim's 'Follow The Leader', obscure one-offs like Red Alert's 'Hip Hop On Wax' or 'We Come To Dub' by the Imperial Brothers. True enough, but the fact remains that, with the twin rise in the late eighties of 'conscious' rap (Public Enemy, KRS1) and gangsta rap (NWA, Scarface, Dr Dre), the verbal, storytelling side of hip hop gradually came to dominate at the expense of aural atmospherics. Just as this was happening Stateside, the idea of instrumental hip hop was flourishing in Britain (perhaps because of the difficulties involved in rapping convincingly in an English accent). Some of these early collage-based 'DJ records' – M/A/R/R/S's 'Pump Up The Volume', Coldcut's 'Beats and Pieces', Bomb The Bass' 'Beat Dis' – were sufficiently uptempo to get swept up into the burgeoning house scene. But others, by the likes of Renegade Soundwave, Meat Beat Manifesto and Depthcharge, jumbled up elements of hip hop, dub reggae and film soundtracks to create a distinctly UK sound; a moody downtempo funk, high on atmospherics, low on attitude, and a precursor to today's trip hop.

In America, hip hop and rave culture are utterly separate and estranged subcultures. But in Britain, trip hop can be considered an adjunct to rave culture, just another option on the smorgasbord of sounds available to 'the chemical generation'. Like rave music, trip hop is based around samples and loops; like techno, it's the soundtrack to recreational drug use. In trip hop's case, that drug is marijuana rather than Ecstasy. Funky Porcini's James Bradell went so far as to define trip hop as 'the mixture between computers and dope'.

Living in my Headphones

Hip hop's influence in the UK blossomed in the form of jungle and trip hop, distinctly British mutants that Black Americans barely recognize as relatives of rap. Where hyperkinetic jungle is all about the tension and paranoia of London, trip hop's mellow motherlode is Bristol. Laidback verging on supine, Bristol is Slackersville UK, a town where cheap accommodation allows bohemia to ferment; members of Portishead describe it as a place where 'people take a while to get out of bed' and 'get comatosed' of an evening. Because of its history as a port in the slave trade, Bristol has a large, long-established black population. Combined with a strong student and bohemian presence, this has made the town a fertile environment for genre-blending musical activity. All these factors fostered a distinctive Bristol sound, a languid, lugubrious hybrid of soul, reggae, jazz-fusion and hip hop.

The story begins with The Wild Bunch, a mid-eighties sound-system/DJ collective renowned for its eclecticism. Members included Nellee Hooper (who later brought a Bristol-ian jazzy fluency to his production work for Soul II Soul, Neneh Cherry and Bjork) and Daddy G and Mushroom, who went on to form Massive Attack with rapper 3D. Tricky contributed raps to both Massive albums, while Portishead's soundscape-creator Geoff Barrow assisted with the programming on Massive's 1991 debut *Blue Lines*.

Blue Lines was a landmark in British club culture, a dance music equivalent to Miles Davis's *Kind of Blue*, marking a shift towards a more interior, meditational sound. The songs on *Blue Lines* run at 'spliff' tempos – from a mellow, moonwalking 90 b.p.m. (exactly mid-way between reggae and hip hop) down to a positively torpid 67 b.p.m. Massive Attack make music you nod your head to, rather than dance. 'Right from the start, we never made music in line with the tempos that were required in clubs,' Daddy G told me in 1994. 'Our music's more like something to . . . eat your food to, y'know. It's made for after clubs, when you want to chill out, learn how to breathe again.'

Distancing themselves from the party-minded functionalism of dance culture, Massive Attack cited instead conceptualist, album-oriented artists across the spectrum, from progressive rock (Pink Floyd) to post-punk experimentalism (Public Image Limited), from fusion (Herbie Hancock) to symphonic soul (Isaac Hayes). Hayes's influence came through on string-laden, mournful epics like 'Safe From Harm' and 'Unfinished Sympathy', both of which were hit singles in Britain. But Massive Attack's real originality lay in more tranquil tracks like 'One Love', with its mesmerizing clockwork rhythm and jazzy, electric piano pulsations. On 'Daydreaming', 3D and Tricky drift on a stream of consciousness, quoting from *Fiddler On Roof* and The Beatles and floating 'like helium' above the hyperactive 'trouble and strife' of everyday life. Expounding a Zen-like philosophy of sublime passivity and disengagement from the 'real', they rap of 'living in my headphones'.

Victims of 'Bristol time', Massive Attack took three years to record the sequel to *Blue Lines*. The title track of *Protection* and the album's downtempo despondency reiterated the basic Massive Attack anti-stance: the longing for refuge and sanctuary from external chaos, music as healing force and balm for the troubled soul. But in 1994, Massive were dramatically upstaged and outshone by two of their protégés, whose different takes on Bristol's 'hip hop blues' were more eerie and experimental (Tricky, about whom more later) and more seductively sepulchral (Portishead).

Throughout Portishead's debut *Dummy*, singer Beth Gibbons sounds like she's buried alive in the blues. *Dummy* is like eavesdropping on the cold-turkey torment of a love-junkie; her lyrics are riddled with imagery of bereavement, betrayal and disenchantment. 'Biscuit' is at once the album's aesthetic highpoint and emotional abyss. Through one of Geoff Barrow's dankest, most lugubrious palls of hip hop *noir*, Gibbons intones a litany of lyric-fragments, disconnected shards of anguish. 'I'm scared / got hurt a long time ago ... at last, relief / a mother's son has left me sheer.' Compounding the faltering, fragmentary quality of this abandoned lover's discourse, 'Biscuits' pivots around a lurching stuck-needle sample of Johnny Ray singing 'never fall in love again', which runs at a grotesquely lachrymose 16 r.p.m., so that it sounds like the Nabob of Sob is literally drowning in tears.

Throughout *Dummy*, Barrow expertly frames Gibbons' torched-songs with sombre soundscapes whose jaundiced desolation is steeped in the influence of film *noir* and sixties spy-movies. 'I like soundtrack music, 'cos of the kind of sounds they use to create suspense,' he says. 'Modern soundtracks, they're too digital and synthesizer-based, whereas the stuff I like involves orchestras and acoustic instruments.' Perhaps in an attempt to ward off the cliché applied to their kind of impressionistic, evocative music – 'a soundtrack to a non-existent movie' – Portishead went ahead and made an, er, existent film to accompany the single 'Sour Times'. Entitled *To Kill A Dead Man*, the ten minute short aspires to a Cold War feel, in homage to seedy espionage movies like *The Ipcress File* (starring Michael Caine). The thing about that particular cinematic genre which fits Portishead's bleaker-than-thou mood is that there's never a happy ending.

Mind-Movies

The influence of soundtrack music is a common denominator running through trip hop. Take DJ Shadow, a white B-boy from Davis, California, who's one of the very few American exponents of the genre. Shadow cites film-score composers John Williams and Jerry Goldsmith as particular favourites; his long suites of sample-woven atmospheres and spoken-word soundbites are designed to encourage people to drift off into reverie and generate their own cinematic mind's eye imagery. 'I like the music to take me places. I want people to just space out for a while,' Shadow says. Pinpointing the difference between his rap-free take on hip hop and current American hip hop, he says that he prefers to be 'the director rather than the star'.

Shadow's music offers the listener what some call 'deep time' – the kind of tranquil, spellbound immersion that you experience as a child when you're lost in a book, and which is becoming harder and harder to recover in the age of channel-surfing and blip culture. Shadow's music isn't social (he's said many times that he's not making music for the dancefloor), nor is it anti-social (as with gangsta rap), it's asocial: an aural sanctuary from the hurly-burly, music that hushes your soul.

'Ever been in a car, hanging out with people, and a song comes on, and even though everyone may be in a particular mood, really hyped up, but then the song comes on and the mood changes? Everyone starts looking out the window, staring into space, or just gets quiet. Nobody will admit that it's because of the music, but it'll affect everyone the same. There's a lot of power in that. I don't understand how it happens, but I'm trying to figure it out.'

After early efforts on his own imprint Solesides, Shadow first grabbed attention when he hooked up with London's Mo Wax label. First, there was the twelve minute epic 'In/Flux', a panoramic early seventies groovescape whose disconsolate strings, lachrymose wah-wah and fusion flute recalls both the orchestral soul of The Temptations' 'Papa Was a Rollin' Stone' and Miles Davis's elegy for Duke Ellington 'He Loved Him Madly'. These two early seventies classics captured that era's sense of 'slippin' into darkness'. With its ghostly shards of liberation rhetoric drifting by on the breeze – 'people's power', 'it's only a matter of time', 'FREEDOM!' – 'Influx' is at once an elegy for the lost ideals of the sixties and an evocation of the nineties' own gloom and millennial trepidation.

Throughout 'In/Flux' and its sequels 'Lost and Found' and 'What Does Your Soul Look Like?' Shadow's mastery of sampling makes him seem like a conductor, orchestrating a supergroup of stellar jazz and funk sidemen. Shadow's sources are far broader than the American hip hop norm: 'Lost and Found' offsets tentative dejection (a mournful keyboard figure from Fleetwood Mac's 'Brown Eyes', Christine McVie's ballad off 1979's *Tusk*) against resilient determination (a martial drumbeat plucked from U2's 'Sunday Bloody Sunday'), in order to dramatize a kind of internal battle for psychic survival in a world gone crazy.

With the release of his 1996 debut *Endtroducing*, Shadow was garlanded with acclaim by American rock critics. But he remains virtually unknown in the US rap scene. What happened to hip hop in the nineties that it has no place for a visionary like Shadow? For understandable reasons, the American rap community wanted to reaffirm the music's blackness in the face of its commercial break-through and subsequent 'vanilla' misappropriations. This back-to-black-lash took the form of an obsession with keeping it 'real'. The emphasis shifted away from production to the verbals – street-life storytelling, rhymin' skills, the rapper's larger-than-life 'Big Willie' persona. These elements increased in importance because, by pertaining to specifically African-American experience, they reinforce rap's inclusion/exclusion effect ('it's a black thing, you wouldn't understand'). Simultaneously, some hip-hop producers abandoned samples-and-loops in favour of live musicianship, because of the legal and financial hassles with sample clearance.

'What sparked me back when I was growing up was the combination of music and lyrics,' says Shadow. 'But as the lyrics started to get more important, I came to feel they were confining, too specific. I wanted to mess around with breaks, like Steinski or Curtis Mantronik did, and try to do new things with samples. Mantronix albums were about 50 per cent instrumentals, and even when they weren't, MC Tee's voice was more like texture. Sometimes I think what I do is just "sample music", an entirely different genre from hip hop. Like some people aspire to be the best at guitar, I want to be constantly doing new things with the sampler. Prince Paul, Mantronik and Steinski were doing it –

these were guys who had a stack of records behind them and just let their imaginations take over. That's my lineage, that's the tradition I want to contribute to.'

The parallel between Jimi Hendrix, who fled R & B constrictions for psychedelic London, and Shadow, a refugee from 'hip-hop pressure', is striking. In Britain, hip hop never assumed the political, counter-cultural role it did in America, but was just one of many imports (soul, jazz-funk, dub, Chicago house, Detroit techno) to take its place in the spectrum of 'street beats'. Race is rarely the crucial determinant of unity in British dance scenes (exceptions include swingbeat and dancehall reggae, both of which are based almost entirely around imported African-American and Afro-Caribbean tracks). Instead, what counts is a shared openness to technology and to drugs. And so trip hop and jungle are full of multiracial crews and black/white duos; all-white practitioners don't have to *justify* themselves like their rare American equivalents do.

From a different vantage point – that of the hip-hop 'patriot' – trip hop's racial politics look less like colour-blind utopianism and more like an evasion of tricky issues. Some have argued that trip hop simply provides white liberals a chance to experience some of hip hop's flavour without confronting any of its discomfiting aspects (ghettocen-tric rage, what KRS1 called 'niggativity'). With their veneration of old skool hip hop (Grandmaster Flash, electro, Ultramagnetic MCs) and their relative indifference towards contemporary rap, British labels like Mo Wax and Ninja Tune arguably belong to a tradition of white art school Brit-bohemians who renovate and adapt black music styles only when their cultural life is over. In the sixties and early seventies, it was blues guitar, in the nineties it's scratching and 'turntablizm'. According to this critique, trip hop is merely a form of gentrification, a case of middle-class whites moving in when the underclass blacks have moved on, or been moved out.

Rebirth of the Cool

Not 'real' rap, not proper jazz, trip hop is in some ways a nineties update of fusion. But with a crucial difference; despite its fondness for jazzy flavour and blue keys, trip hop isn't based around real-time improvisation but home-studio techniques like sampling and sequencing. DJ Krush's 'Slow Chase', for instance, is cold-sweat paranoia-funk with an implosive wah-wah trumpet solo that recalls Miles Davis's lost-in-inner-space coked-out delirium circa *On The Corner* and *Dark Magus*. With its psychedelic edge, this era of 'electric Miles' deserves the moniker 'acid jazz'. Unfortunately, that term was invented by an early nineties London scene – labels like Talkin' Loud and Dorado, bands like the Brand New Heavies and D-Note – to describe a much milder vision of fusion, inspired by the fluency of Lonnie Liston Smith rather than the fever-dreams of Miles.

Punning on acid house, acid jazz was a riposte to rave culture, signalling a Luddite retreat to live musicianship and the resurrection of the idea of clubland as a metropolitan élite (as opposed to rave's suburban populism). Trip hop has historical links with acid jazz. Mo Wax founder James Lavelle started out writing for the jazz-revival magazine *Straight No Chaser*. And much of the output of Mo Wax, Ninja Tune and similar labels like Pork and Pussyfoot, is basically acid jazz gone digital. Sampling is resorted to not for its radically anti-naturalistic potential, but as a cut-price means of making a seamless neo-fusion without actually hiring live musicians. Too often, the result is a tasteful but insipid composite of connoisseur musics like jazz-funk, rare groove and 'conscious' rap (A Tribe Called Quest, The Jungle Brothers).

The guiding ethos of this 'good music society' is *cool*. All the energies that galvanize rave music – derangement, a submission to technology, underclass desperation, emotionalism – are shunned, in the belief that 'mellow' = 'mature', that headnodding contemplation is superior to sweaty physical abandon. Accompanying this spiritually goateed (sometimes *literally* goateed) hipster ethos is a sort of drug ethic: Ecstasy is unseemly, plebeian, but marijuana is sophisticated, bohemian. The sensibility of labels like Mo Wax and Ninja Tune is what you might call *break-beatnik*.

The problem is that too little of the output of these labels lives up to the psychedelic evocations of the term 'trip hop'. Instead, what you get is muzak for pot smokers. Trip hop rhetoric promises the ultimate in fucked up, anything-goes, neo-B-boy abstraction, but too often delivers a half-assed sequencing of borrowed bits and bobs, and a mood spectrum ranging from pale blue to cheesy affability. Ninja Tune's brand of 'funkjazzticaltricknology' – as purveyed by its roster of DJ Food, Funky Porcini, The Herbaliser and Up Bustle and Out – is a prime example of such spot-the-sample whimsy. The label was founded by those late eighties DJ-record bricolage pioneers Coldcut, whose Matt Black told *The Wire* in 1996: 'I'm interested in the similarities between playing music, playing with toys and playing a game. It's the same word, so at best, we're aiming to be a synthesis of those three things.' Drawing on the conventions of E-Z listening, soundtrack themes and incidental music, the Ninja Tune artists take this kitsch and synch it up to looped grooves; the result, on tracks like Funky Porcini's 'Venus', is a densely referential melange of motifs and textures – vibes, brush-on-cymbal percussion, 'stalking' upright bass – that triggers the listener's received images of 'relaxation' and 'sophistication'.

In British record shops, Mo Wax and Ninja Tune tracks are sometimes filed in a category called 'blunted beatz'. While all music sounds more vivid when the listener is stoned (it's like instantly upgrading your hi-fi), trip hop is explicitly designed to enhance the effects of marijuana. The torpid tempos suit the way marijuana slows down time and expands the present moment. During normal consciousness, the mind is partly preoccupied by thoughts of the past and plans for the future; marijuana diminishes both memory and anticipation, thereby promoting a fully-in-the-now 'pure awareness'. In such a mind-state, the 'horizontal' development of the music (its narrative progression, the sense that it's going somewhere) is less important than the 'vertical' organization of sound. Stoned, there can be no so such thing as too many layers; perception of texture and timbre is intensified, so that the rustle and glisten of a hi-hat is endlessly absorbing. But extreme minimalism – just bass and drums, for instance – is equally satisfying, because you can focus on what normally bypasses the ear: all the different elements of the drum kit, the gooey consistency of the bass, and so forth.

With higher doses or stronger weed like 'hydroponic', other effects come into play: free association, flights of fancy, synaesthetic confusion of the senses ('seeing' the music), mild hallucinations (hearing 'voices' in the percussion, say). It's at this point that the free-floating reverie and perceptual distortions induced by the trip hop/pot combination can tip over into a darker disorientation. You can hear this crepuscular gloom in *USSR Repertoire (The Theory of Verticality)* by DJ Vadim, by far the best Ninja Tune artist. Minimal to the point of emaciation,

Vadim's locked grooves and ultra-vivid, up-close sample-textures create a feeling of entropy and dislocation. Slipping outside the schedules of normal temporal consciousness into an overwhelmingly intensified 'now' can instil foreboding rather than bliss. Paranoia is one of marijuana's under-remarked side-effects, but it's critical for any understanding of music in the nineties.

Prophets of Loss

> '"Let us sing him," said one of the fiends to the other,
> "the lullaby of Hell"'.
>
> – Fitz Hugh Ludlow, *The Hasheesh Eater: being passages*
> *from The Life of a Pythagorean*, 1857

If 'blunted' literally means without edge (and is therefore a good description for too much trip hop), in American rap slang it has come to evoke a particular kind of marijuana mind-state in which delusions of grandeur alternate with a mystical apprehension of impending doom. Weed's free-associational effect, refracted through the dark prism of paranoia, lends itself to a certain kind of conspiracy consciousness: the perception of malign patterns within the chaos, a supersititious belief that history is steered by sinister secret societies. In the nineties, Christian Right militia men and hardcore rappers found a bizarre common ground in what critic Michael Kelly dubbed 'fusion paranoia': a syncretic mish-mash of conspiracy theories, whose sources range from Nostradamus and 'The Revelation of Saint John the Divine' to science fiction like Robert Shea and Robert Anton Wilson's *The Illuminatus! Trilogy*, from black nationalist sect the Five Per Cent Nation to white supremacist tracts such as William Cooper's *Behold a Pale Horse* and Ralph Emerson's *The New World Order* and *The Unseen Hand*.

And so Busta Rhymez claims 'we got five years left' on 'Everything Remains Raw', while Onyx's 'Last Dayz' proclaims 'we all ready for these wars'. 'What's coming in the future is Armaggeddon,' Onyx's Sticky Fingaz declared in 1993. 'And we startin' an army: all the children, age one to ten. We're training them at a young age, 'cos right now the army is in jail . . . 1999, the year before the End, is going to be chaos ... People say "save the world", but it's too late for that ... You know what I wanna do, man, swear to God, I wanna rule the fucking world. That's why we're building this army of kids.'

Wu-Tang Clan and its extended family of solo artists (Method Man, Ol Dirty Bastard, Genius/GZA, Killah Priest and Raekwon) pioneered the blend of B-boy warrior stance and Doomsday vision that currently dominates East Coast rap. The Clan's 1993 debut album *Enter The Wu-Tang (36 Chambers)* begins with a sample from a martial arts movie about 'Shaolin shadow-boxing and the Wu-Tang sword'. Then there's the challenge 'En garde!' and the clashing of blades as combat commences. Wu-Tang's shaolin obsession renders explicit the latent medievalism of hip hop. In the terrordome of capitalist anarchy, the underclass can only survive by taking on the mobilization techniques and the psychology of warfare – forming blood-brotherhoods and warrior-clans (like the overtly neo-medieval Latin Kings), and individually, by transforming the self into a fortress, a one-man army on perpetual red alert. (Hence the hip-hop vogue for Machiavelli and Sun Tzu's *The Art Of War*.) The medievalism also comes through in the biblical language and superstitious imagery (ghosts, fiends, devils) employed by these rappers. What is conspiracy theory if not twentieth-century demonology, with phantasmic organizations like the Trilateral Commission, the CIA and the Masons standing in for Satan?

Listen to the Wu-Tang's raps, or those of allies like Gravediggaz, Sunz of Man and Mobb Deep, and you're swept up in a delirium of grandiose delusions and fantastical revenges, a paranoid stream-of-consciousness whose imagistic bluster seems like your classic defensive-formation against the spectre of emasculation. For the Clan, words are 'liquid swords' (as Genius's album title put it). The Wu's febrile rhyme-schemes are riddled with imagery of pre-emptive strikes, massive retaliation and deterrence-through-overkill: 'New recruits, I'm fucking up MC troops'; 'Wu-Tang's coming through with full metal jackets'; 'call me the rap assassinator'; 'merciless like a terrorist'.

Hallucinatory and cinematic, Wu-style hip hop – sometimes called 'horrorcore' or Gothic rap – is a sonic simulation of the city as combat zone, a treacherous terrain of snipers, man-traps and ambushes. In Wu-Tang producer The RZA's murky mix-scapes, it seems like 'fiends are lurking', as Raekwon and Ghostface Killer put it on 'Verbal Intercourse'. Melody is shunned in favour of a frictive mesh of unresolved motifs – a hair-raising horror-movie piano trill, a hair-trigger guitar tic – which interlock to instil suspense and foreboding. Usually, the looped breakbeats don't change, there's no bridges or tempo shifts, which increases the sense of non-narrative limbo. The self-same locked-groove repetition that works in British trip hop as a blissful disengagement from reality becomes, in American horrorcore, a metaphor for the dead ends and death-traps of ghetto life.

How is it that a very similar mixture – 'computers and dope', basically – has such radically different results on opposing sides of the Atlantic? Freed of American rap's fiercely felt duty to 'represent' the 'real' through lyrics, British trip hop can happily evade the questions – of class, race, the crisis of masculinity, the social and psychic costs of drug culture – that literally *bedevil* contemporary hip hop. Only one English trip hopper has confronted this dark matter: Tricky.

It's no coincidence that of all the trip hoppers, Tricky is the most committed to verbal expression (he described Public Enemy's Chuck D as 'my Shakespeare'). Moreover, he's made the biggest effort to build bridges between British and American B-boy culture. In 1995, he followed his debut album *Maxinquaye* with the 'Hell EP', credited to Tricky Vs The Gravediggaz and featuring two collaborations with that most Gothic of the RZA's side projects. The best is 'Psychosis', a febrile mire of mushy bass-sound which sounds like it's composed of death-rattles, groans and gasps, over which loops a sickly voice intoning the doom-struck phrase 'falling ... slowly falling'. It's an aural depiction of Dante's Inferno, a seething pit of demons. In the lyrics, Tricky notes that his given name, Adrian, is the same as the Anti-Christ's, and concludes: 'so it seems I'm the Devil's Son / Out of breath and on the run'.

The parallels between Tricky and his East Coast American brethren are striking: Jeru The Damaja recorded 'Can't Stop The Prophet'; Tricky wrote 'I Be The Prophet'. Method Man named an album after the local slang term for marijuana, 'tical'; Tricky called his sub-label Durban Poison, in homage to a particularly potent breed of weed. But where Tricky has the edge over the horrorcore rappers is that he lets himself surrender to the psychic disintegration that the American hip-hop ego so zealously fortifies itself against. American rap is all about mobilizing for battle; Tricky's music is all about entropy, dissipation. He's brave enough to stare defeat in the face.

Tricky Kid

June, 1995: I meet Tricky in his New York hotel, and learn all about the genesis of 'I Be The Prophet'. 'I had this psychic drawing done,' says Tricky, sucking greedily on the first of the four joints he's to consume in the next hour. 'See, I wanted to know where all this silver was coming from, 'cause lately I've been wearing loads of silver,' he continues. 'And the psychic woman told me it symbolizes Mercury, the messenger God. She gives you a massage and each different muscle tells different stories. She wrote that I came to this Earth too quick, I wasn't ready, but I said "Fuck it, c'mon, let's go." And she wrote "When he lands, there shall be peace." Mad, innit?'

Inspired by this psychic's analysis, Tricky wrote and recorded 'I Be The Prophet' in a New York studio during a few days off between gigs. Tricky plays it for me on his portable DAT-Walkman. It's an uncanny feeling, listening through the headphones to Tricky's eerie rasp, then glancing up and looking straight into his eyes. The music – eventually released as a single under the name Starving Souls and later as an album track on the Nearly God LP – is diffuse and denuded, reminiscent of the Raincoats' post-punk experimental classic *Odyshape* and the brittle Orientalism of David Sylvian/Ryuichi Sakamoto's 'Bamboo Music'.

Tricky as prophet? That might be going too far. Tricky himself exhibits a healthy scepticism: 'I'll believe anything! I'll pay you eighty dollars, you can tell me a story and I'll believe it. It provides me with material!' And yet there's a sense in which Tricky *is* an aerial tuned into the frequencies of anguish and dread emanating from a jilted generation. He talks of the origins of his lyrics in such terms: 'Something *passes through me*, and I don't know what it is.'

Who is Tricky? A Sly Stone for the post-rave generation (the *Maxinquaye/There's A Riot Goin' On* analogy is a critical commonplace). Public Enemy's Chuck D without the dream of a Black Nation to hold his fragile self together. The greatest poet of England's 'political unconscious' since John Lydon circa *Metal Box*. Roxy Music's Brian and Bryan compressed into one wiry body, Eno-esque soundscape gardener *and* Ferry-like lizard of love/hate. The 'black Bowie'.

The latter fits because Tricky's gender-bending imagery is reminiscent of nothing so much as the video for 'Boys Keep Swinging', where

Bowie impersonated an array of female stereotypes. On the cover of the 'Overcome' EP Tricky's wearing a wedding dress and clutching a pistol in each hand. For the sleeve of 'Black Steel' he's a diva, grotesquely caked in mascara and lipstick, mouth contorted somewhere between pucker and screwface. The song itself is Tricky's most confounding gender/genre twist of all, transforming Public Enemy's 'Black Steel in the Hour Of Chaos' into indie noise-rock, with singer Martina's frayed/'fraid voice uncaging Chuck D's suppressed 'feminine side'.

There really aren't too many black artists who cross-dress (it's hard to imagine Ice Cube in a mini-skirt, high heels and false eyelashes, for instance). This shows the extent to which Tricky belongs as much in a British art-rock tradition (Japan, Kate Bush, Bowie, early Roxy, Gary Numan) as to the more obvious hip-hop lineage. But it's also yet another indice of the compulsive, almost pathological nature of the man's creativity; like Courtney Love's kinder-whore image, Tricky's transvestitism proclaims 'something's not right here'. Especially as cross-dressing isn't a marketing gimmick or jape, but something he's done since he was a fifteen-year-old kid running around town with his ruffneck bredren in the Bristol ghetto Knowle West.

'All my mates thought I was mad anyway,' he says. 'I don't know what my grandma felt, though – she never ever said a word, even when I walked out the door with a dress on. I was really lucky, I had mates around me who said "He's mad, leave him alone . . ."'

Although his extended family was full of 'hard men', Tricky was brought up by women. After his mum died when he was only four, Tricky was brought up by his grandma; she became convinced that he was the reincarnation of his own dead mother, and would spook out the child by staring at him intensely for hours. There's a theory that the sartorial flamboyance and effeminacy of the 'dandy' constitute a form of symbolic allegiance to the mother, a perverse attempt to assume her subordinate position in the patriarchal order. In Tricky's case, it could be both a homage to the mother he barely knew, and a way of proclaiming himself an alien even amongst the B-boy band of outsiders he ran with, his surrogate family.

Can't Get No Satisfaction

'You say "what is this?" / Mind ya bizness!' So Tricky taunts the listener two thirds of the way through *Maxinquaye*. He's actually rubbing your nose in the perplexity aroused by the strange relationship described in 'Suffocated Love', but it could serve as an emblem for the entire album, a statement of malign intent. Racially, stylistically, sexually, Tricky is one slippery fellow. *Maxinquaye* is an unclassifiable hybrid of club music and bedroom music, black and white, rap and melody, song and atmospherics, sampladelic textures and real-time instrumentation. It sucks you into the poly-sexual, trans-generic, mongrelized mindspace inside Tricky's skull. How did he get into such a state? It's the drugs/ technology interface – boundary-blurring, connection-facilitating, but also fucking with stable identity, letting the id come out to play.

Throughout *Maxinquaye*, Tricky's words are as smeared and raggedly enunciated as his textures. For much of the album, he hides behind his lover Martina, either ceding the spotlight to her or literally shadowing her voice, lurking low in the mix and repeating the words in a slurred mumble, just a little out of synch. When he does take the centre stage, Tricky talks in forked-tongues, drifts, dodges definition.

When people go on about how 'sexy' *Maxinquaye* is, I sometimes wonder if their ears ever penetrate through the sensuous sonic murk and Martina's luscious mumble to the desperation and dread-of-intimacy in the lyrics. As a seduction soundtrack, 'Overcome' and 'Suffocated Love' aren't exactly amorous or arousing. The songs could be two sides of the same 'not exactly lovers' affair. Kissing, as symbol of intimacy-kept-at-arms-length, figures in both 'Overcome' and 'Suffocated', with the former's 'never been properly kissed,' and the latter's 'I keep her warm but we never kiss'. On 'Overcome', Martina's voice – which seems to crumble in her mouth like shortcake – is at its most wanly seductive even as she demarcates her boundaries: 'Emotional ties, they stay severed'. On the surface, 'Suffocated Love' sounds more upful than the clammy, baleful 'Overcome'. But Tricky's gloating, poisonous delivery, plus a love/hate lyric so conflicted and contradiction-riven you feel nauseous, place it up there with the Sex Pistols' 'Sub-Mission' and Nirvana's 'Heart-Shaped Box' as a song about the dread of female engulfment. 'Abbaon Fat Tracks' is even more unnerving. One minute, Martina's promising 'fuck you in, tuck you in, suck you in', the next she's threatening 'fuck you in the ass, just for a laugh' – and all in the same bloodless, crumpled ghost-croon, framed by hobbled guitar that's like the missing link between Isaac Hayes 'Shaft' and PiL's 'Poptones'.

Suck or be sucked: *Maxinquaye* is all about voracious, oral need, about just how far people will go to fill that void. A couplet like 'my brain thinks bomb-like / beware of our appetite' seems to testify to a limitless craving that can easily erupt into violence, just as in the middle of 'Suffocated Love' Tricky abruptly lashes from horny reverie to Cypress Hill's catchphrase 'I could just kill a man'. For the most part, though, Tricky directs his rage against himself. 'Ponderosa' is a grim tale of alcohol and the demon weed, of addiction as a descent through 'different levels of the Devil's company'. Over clanking, lurching percussion redolent of Tom Waits's *SwordfishTrombones*, Martina intones black-humorous wordplay – 'underneath the weeping willow, lies a weeping wino' – while Tricky supplies stoned grunts and bleary exhalations in the background.

'Ponderosa' and other *Maxinquaye* songs like 'Strugglin'' are based on real depression, says Tricky, 'but not through something terrible happening to you, which is what most people think causes depression. It's easy to get a depression, if you don't have a job, don't have a passion, don't exercise your brain. After working on *Blue Lines* I was getting a wage into a bank but not actually working. Massive were paying me, so I had money, and that was the worst thing, 'cause it enabled me to have weed and drink. All I did was smoke and drink, hang around in town, kill time in bars. And go to clubs, from Wednesday to Sunday.' This two year weekender-bender nearly drove Tricky round the bend. After the party, utterly wasted, he'd contemplate the waste of his life, until, in his weed-distorted paranoia, all that killed time would assume the grotesque shape of a spectre. He'd see demons in his sitting room. Out of this wasteland eventually emerged a dark magus, a sonic wizard conjuring up the paranoiascapes of *Maxinquaye*.

As with the East Coast horrorcore rappers, Tricky's blunted anxiety detaches itself from the particular and swells into cosmic, millenarian dread. Hence 'Hell Is Round The Corner', where the looped lushness of an Isaac Hayes orchestral arrangement is hollowed out by a vocal sample slowed to a languishing 16 r.p.m. basso-profundissimo, impossibly black-and-blue. And hence 'Aftermath', which trumps the morbid vision of the Gravediggaz with what Tricky described as an attempt to *see through the eyes of the dead*. Pivoting around a pained flicker of wah-wah guitar and a wraith-like flute, Tricky's post-apocalyptic panorama harks back to the orphaned drift of The Temptations' 'Papa Was A Rolling Stone'.

Where 'Aftermath' seems to find a serene, spectral beauty in the depopulated, devastated cityscape, 'Strugglin" is grimmer because it refuses the lure of entropy, won't succumb to death-wish. Sonically, 'Strugglin" sounds like Public Enemy if they'd somehow lost a grip on the 'black steel' of their ideology and hit rock bottom. Its fitful, stumbling beat – whose sampled components comprise a creaking door and the bloodcurdling click of a clip being loaded into a gun – make 'Strugglin" the most disorientating track on a relentlessly experimental record. But it's Tricky's words – confessing how he's harried by 'mystical shadows, fraught with no meaning' – and his voice, as fatigued and eroded as Sly Stone on 'Thank You For Talking To Me, Africa', that are most disturbing. 'They label me insane, but I think I'm more normal than most,' he sniggers at the end, then collapses into mirthless, wheezing laughter.

Dub Wisdom

Although there's nothing literally dub-wize on the record – no heavy echo or reggae basslines – it's clear that the influence of dub permeates *Maxinquaye*. The way Tricky works – fucking around with sounds on the sampler until his sources are ghosts of their former selves; composing music and words spontaneously in the studio; mixing tracks live as they're recorded; retaining the glitches and inspired errors, the hiss and crackle – is strikingly akin to early seventies dubmeisters like King Tubby. And of course there's also the fact that Tricky breathes sensimilla fumes like they're oxygen.

When it comes to the organization of sound, Tricky's only rivals are artcore junglists like Dillinja. More than the shared roots in hip hop and dub sound-system culture, Tricky and the junglists share a mood, a worldview even. There's a palpable aura of the demonic pervading both *Maxinquaye* and darkest drum and bass tracks like Dillinja's

'Warrior' and 'The Angels Fell': a clammy-palmed apprehension that we're living through Armagideon Time, Babylon's last days.

'Sometimes, I think everything is going to fall apart,' says Tricky. 'When I had the psychic reading, this woman was really positive, she was "No, the world isn't in trouble, we're all going to be all right." Sorry, I just don't feel that. I can't see how things are gonna get better. Sometimes I feel this is the living hell. Look at the conditions we're living in. Living in a city can't be healthy ... I think we've all got a touch of psychosis. In a city, you've got all this energy of people who ain't quite normal; that abnormal energy just reflects off everything and pushes us further down the path.'

The difference between a Rastafarian worldview and Tricky's is that for the natty dread, the evil is *out there*. Through their dress and rituals, Rastas exempt themselves from a Fallen World; being 'pure', they are destined for Zion. East Coast rappers similarly like to imagine themselves holy warriors or 'killah priests'. Hence the appeal of Oriental forms of 'spiritual combat'; hence their peculiar open-minded interest in the conspiracy theories of America's Christian Right militias (despite the fact that these white supremacists regard African-Americans, alongside Jews, Hispanics and Asians, as subhuman 'mudpeople'). Unlike all these believers, Tricky doesn't distance himself from Babylon, from the system or *shit-stem* (as some Rastafarians call it). Tricky is on intimate terms with evil. In his words and his music, Tricky opens the (l)id and lets all this contamination and corruption *speak itself*, in its own vernacular as opposed to the cut-and-dried polarities of the message-mongering 'political' songwriter (who also imagines himself 'clean'). 'I'm part of this fuckin' *psychic pollution*. I'm just as negative as the next person. I think we have to destroy everything and start again. I think everything has to end before it gets any better. And it's not going to happen in our lifetimes. Everything needs to burn and be rebuilt.'

Lines like 'we're hungry ... beware of our appetite' implicate Tricky as part of the problem, as someone convulsed by the same voracious will-to-power that's ruining the world. 'It's like, I can be as greedy as you, I want money, I want cars. I'm conditioned to want that, and the conditioned part of me says "yeah, I'm gonna go out and make money, and build an empire. I'm going to rule my own little kingdom." But part of me knows that's bullshit. But I am hungry, and you have to watch out for someone who's hungry.'

'An 'ungry man is an angry man' – so sayeth dub prophet Prince Far I. In black music, it sometimes seems that everyone's searching for the kingdom, the kingdom of heaven. Some want it now, and they will not wait: the gangsta tries to build that kingdom on earth, makes a deal with Satan (who himself decided ''tis better to rule in hell than serve in heaven'). Trouble is, there's always a bigger king out there, to make you his slave. So the smarter rude boys turn 'conscious' and dream of the lost kingdom of the righteous, calling it Zion, or the Black Nation – the pot of gold at the end of Time's Rainbow. Other black mystics – Hendrix, Sun Ra, George Clinton – dub this lost paradise Atlantis, or Saturn, or the Mothership Connection.

Tricky has come up with his own proper name for Zion – Maxinquaye. Ever the slippery trickster, he's presented two versions of the genesis of that evocative title. '"Quaye", that's this race of people in Africa, and "Maxin", that's my mum's name, Maxine, and I've just taken the E off,' he told me. Elsewhere, he's said that Quaye was his mother's surname. I prefer the first version because it makes 'Maxin-quaye' into a sort of place name: the lost Motherland.

Tricky has described 'Aftermath' as a song about 'the end of the world' and about his mother. Given her death when he was four, it's easy to see why Tricky might feel like 'sorrow's native son' (to steal a line from Morrissey), a stranger in a strange land. It's this 'primal narcissistic wound' (Julia Kristeva) that makes him morbidly sensitive to the currents of anguish and fear in the culture. Like that other mama's boy, Kurt Cobain, he seems to have no defences, no skin. And being an aerial-for-angst is taxing.

'It takes up a lot of energy, it ends up sapping me sometimes. I do soak it all up. I was in Paris doing a photo session and there was this old lady, and she looked very old and very sad. Now, that catches my eye, and it really, really hurts me. I don't like feeling like that. But it's something I can't control. It hurts me to such an extent that it confuses me. See, if some geezer comes up to me on the street and starts asking me for money, I get an instant rage. When someone comes up to me and I see this person ain't got a life, my emotions get confused. No one likes seeing that, 'cause that could be you or me. It's too scary. It's like a mirror almost.'

Cheap Thrills

'Don't Dabble In Drugs. It Is A Social Evil and Crime.'
— Signpost depicted on the CD booklet of *Maxinquaye*

Alongside everything else that it contains, *Maxinquaye* is an inventory of the psychic costs of Britain's recreational drug culture. Tricky is the conduit for the cloudy, contaminated consciousness of a smashed, blocked generation. 'Blocked', because it lacks any constructive outlet for its idealism, 'smashed' because it can find its provisional utopias only through self-poisoning/self-medication.

Where a lot of groups glamorize drugs, Tricky raps lines — 'I roll the blue bills / I snort the cheap thrills', 'brainwashed by the cheapest' — which seem to attest to a healthy quotient of shame. 'Cocaine is the cheapest thrill I've ever experienced in my life, the lowest, lowest thing. 'Cause it's totally unreal. You feel so good about yourself, but you've done nothing to deserve it. The times I've took it is with other artists, and you stand there and say loads of bullshit, how you respect them, love their lyrics, and you pat each other on the back all fucking night. E is just as bad: I like loads of nice things being said to me, and you say loads of nice things back, and you get all *deep*.'

Any old stupor will do so long as it blunts an intellect otherwise too sharply conscious of the impasses and dead-ends that constitute the present. It's the revolutionary impulse turned back against the self, imploded — just as Marianne Faithful talked of addiction as an alternative to the explosive release of terrorism, both being forms of perverted utopianism. Damp down those fires; it's better to fade away than go out in a blaze of vainglory. Like *Maxinquaye*'s cover art — metal surfaces mottled with rust, an abandoned car overgrown with brambles, flaking paint — Tricky's music makes cultural entropy picturesque. But this corrosion is costly; rust never sleeps.

'We're all fucking lost,' says Tricky, giggling. 'I can't pretend I've got all the answers. Bob Marley, he could write songs about freedom and love. I'm just telling the truth that I'm confused, I'm paranoid, I'm scared, I'm vicious, I'm fucking spiteful.'

Hollowlands, stranded limbos, aftermath zones, desertshores: Tricky's songs are the mindscapes of a generation that has lost the capacity to imagine 'a better place'. His music's nowhere-vastness externalizes the inner void left when the utopian imagination withers and dies. And yet *Maxinquaye*'s last song, the unspeakably beautiful 'Feed Me', seems to hold out a cruel glimmer of hope – a dream of the promised land, or lost motherland (Maxinquaye itself?) A place 'where we're taught to grow strong / Strongly sensitive.' The song is tentative, almost taunting – like a mirage.

'Unreal, yeah,' Tricky mutters.

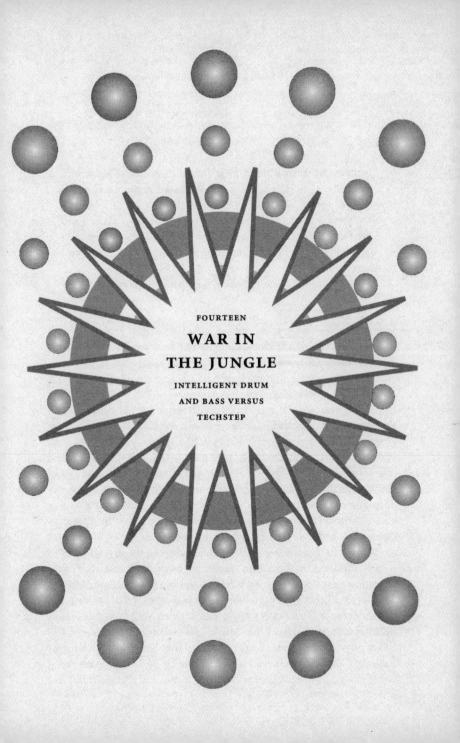

FOURTEEN

WAR IN THE JUNGLE

INTELLIGENT DRUM
AND BASS VERSUS
TECHSTEP

'The major labels are pushing ragga-jungle 'cos it's dance music with a frontperson, which is easier to sell. Whereas real drum and bass is engineer's music, all the action is behind the scenes. That's why it'll never become chart-pop. Where it will become more widely accepted is as experimental album-based music. It'll be the next century's equivalent to seventies progressive rock. None of that guitars and drums bizness!'

– Rob Playford, boss of Moving Shadow, late 1994

In the summer of 1994, the music press, the British record industry and legal dance radio stations like Kiss FM finally woke up to jungle. Initially, the focus was exclusively on the most visible side of the scene, ruffneck ragga-jungle, and coverage was often sensationalistic, alluding to unsubstantiated rumours of crack abuse.

All this infuriated the self-consciously experimental contingent of the drum and bass community – labels such as Moving Shadow, Reinforced and Good Looking; artists like Goldie, Omni Trio, Foul Play, 4 Hero, LTJ Bukem. Together, these artists had forged a sound that I dubbed, with deliberate oxymoronic intentions, 'ambient jungle' (because of the way it combined frenetic beats with a soothing overlay of multitextured atmospherics), and 'artcore'. Within the scene, vaguer and ultimately more problematic terms – 'deep' and 'intelligent' – emerged to designate the new style of drum and bass.

Starting in the summer of 1993, there had been the first glimpses of a new direction in breakbeat hardcore: away from the dark side, towards a new optimism, albeit fragile and bittersweet. From Moving Shadow and Reinforced came bliss-drenched releases like Omni Trio's 'Mystic Stepper (Feel Better)', Foul Play's 'Open Your Mind', 4 Hero's 'Journey Into The Light'. With 'Music' and 'Atlantis (I Need You)', LTJ Bukem invented oceanic jungle. 'Atlantis' was jungle's equivalent of Hendrix's '1983, A Merman I Should Turn To Be': over a susurrating sea of beats and bongos float scintillating motes and spangle-trails, and the languorous 'mmmm's' and soul-caressing sighs of a 'quiet storm' diva. If 'Atlantis' imagined utopia as a subaqua paradise, 'Music' – a near nine-minute dream-drift of nebulous texture-swirls, Milky Way synth-clusters and orgasmic exhalations – was cosmic. Radically uneventful, 'Music' and 'Atlantis' were heretically at odds with the staccato freneticism of 'ardkore. Bukem had shown it was possible to speed up the breakbeats until the body was bypassed altogether, thereby transforming hardcore into *relaxing* music. Rhythm itself became a soothing stream of ambience, a fluid medium in which you immerse yourself.

'Angel' by Metalheads (aka Goldie) sounded another death knell for darkside. Fusing Diane Charlemagne's live, jazzy vocal with 150 b.p.m. breaks, eerie samples from Byrne and Eno's *My Life In the Bush Of Ghosts*, a bedlam of sampled horns, and Beltram-style terror-riffs, 'Angel' was an astonishing soundclash of tenderness and terrorism; the song showed that hardcore could become more conventionally 'musical' without losing its edge. Timestretching – a process that allows a sample to be sped up or slowed down to fit any tempo of beat, without changing its pitch – allowed producers to make the vocal element of their track sound 'normal', as opposed to the helium-shrill, chipmunk voices in early hardcore.

As with Warp's electronic listening music initiative in 1992, ambient jungle was partly the result of an emerging generation gap within breakbeat. While younger producers still oriented their music towards DJs and dancers, the older hardcore artists were now starting to make music that worked better at home than on the dancefloor, as album tracks rather than material for the DJ's relentless cut 'n' mix. As the 'intelligent' drum and bass style took shape, its purveyors increasingly defined themselves against the populist fare that ruled the dancefloor at the big raves and clubs: on one hand, the 'cheesy' E-lation of 'happy hardcore', on the other, the rowdy, rude-boy menace of ragga-jungle. Goldie dismissed the 'booyacka' ragga tracks as unimaginative and unoriginal, immature music for immature people. Late in 1994, LTJ Bukem founded Speed, a club with an explicit 'no ragga' policy. And in 1994, the intelligent contingent had a point. Compared with the increasingly formulaic dancehall-influenced tracks, the new 'artcore' was a breath of fresh air. More than that, it was the most thrilling sound on the planet.

Shadowplay

Omni Trio is not a trio. It's actually just one guy, Rob Haigh, a mid-thirties studio wizard reared on a strictly avant-garde diet: the post-punk experimentalism of Pere Ubu, Pop Group, The Fall, the early seventies sonic sorcery of Miles Davis and dub-pioneers like King Tubby, and above all the Krautrock triumvirate of Can, Faust and Neu! 'I liked the way the German bands abandoned formal song structures and experimented with sounds and textures, the repetitive nature of the music, the shifting layers and patterns,' Haigh explains.

After starting out in an avant-funk band called The Truth Club, Haigh turned on to house in 1989 – Derrick May, early Warp, Orbital. But he was even more excited by the first hardcore tracks using hip-hop beats. When rave's great parting of the ways occurred (the anti-'ardkore media backlash of 1992), he 'couldn't abandon the breakbeats, and go back to house's Roland 909 kick and hi-hat pattern'. Sticking to his hardcore guns, Haigh avoided the cul-de-sac of trance and ambient that sucked in so many other avant-funk vets.

Bridging the gap between darkside and ambient jungle, Omni Trio's first tracks for Moving Shadow – 'Mystic Stepper (Feel Good)' and 'Stronger', from the 'Vol. 2' EP – sounded at once ecstatic and harrowed. Amidst the funerally funky clutter of stumbling, fitful breaks and tolling bells on 'Mystic Stepper', the soul-diva's exhortation 'feel good' sounds strangely wracked and uncertain, capturing the trepidation of a subculture struggling to convince itself it's having fun as Ecstasy's panic-rush kicks in. 'Stronger' is even more sorrowful and vulnerable, with its 'know I'm not strong enough' sample and heart-tremor B-line.

1994's 'Vol. 3', 'Vol. 4' and 'Vol. 5' revealed Haigh to be the John Barry of hardcore. On 'Thru The Vibe', harp-cascades and deliberate Michael LeGrand piano chords lead into a roundelay of hypergasmic female gasps and 'yeah!'s before the track lets rip with a twisting break that rattles like a rivet-gun. Despite the lack of lead vocals and conventional verse-chorus-verse structures, Haigh's hook-laden tracks feel like songs, like pop music. 'Thru The Vibe', 'Living For the Future' and 'Soul Freestyle' are epic pop-as-architecture constructions that move expertly through build-up and breakdown, orgasm and afterglow. Haigh orchestrates sampladelic symphonies out of moondust harps, mellotronic strings, seething bongos, and acappella beseechings.

But for all his brilliant arrangements, Haigh's real forte is as a virtuoso orchestrator of rhythm. Throughout his work, Haigh's beats are so nuanced, so full of varied accents, that it's like listening to a real-time, hands-on drummer who's improvising around the groove. 'Vol. 5: Soul Promenade' showcased a new development that Haigh called 'the soul step'. 'The first and third beats are emphasized, giving the illusion that the track is running at 80 b.p.m. and 160 b.p.m. at the same time. This gives the music room to breathe, and makes it easier to dance to.' Hence the ferocious elegance, the murderous panache, of Omni Trio tunes. Like the half-speed reggae bassline, the soul-step transformed jungle into smooth-grooving, sexy music.

What I really love about Omni Trio, though – as best exemplified by Haigh's all-time masterpiece 'Renegade Snares' – is the music's sentimentality; the way the tenderness of the voices and tingly, almost twee piano motifs fit the huggy, open-hearted poignancy of the Ecstasy experience. It's a quality that Kodwo Eshun captured in his plea: 'open your mind to the kindness of Omni Trio'.

Omni Trio allies and 'Renegade Snares' remixers par excellence, Foul Play were another Moving Shadow act who played a crucial role in the rise of ambient jungle. Stephen 'Brad' Bradshaw, John Morrow and Steve Gurley first weirded up the pirate radio airwaves in 1992 with the ectoplasmic textures and judderquake beats of 'Dubbing U' and 'Survival', the latter featuring perhaps the most tremulous Morse Code oscillator-riff of all time. Then Foul Play really made their mark on the hardcore scene with 'Vol. 3' and its attendant remix EPs. 'Open Your Mind (Foul Play Remix)' wafts billowing soul harmonies over viciously crisp breaks. The killer hook, though, is a diaphonous ripple of ethereal sample-stuff, a succulent squiggle-shimmer that's honey to the ear. It's the closest I've ever heard to an aural simulation of a shiver-down-the-spine, a shudder of loved-up rapture. Midway, the track veers into the twilight-zone, turns morbid and haunted, before letting rip with a veritable St Valentine's Day Massacre of rapid-fire snares. Finally the diva's voice resurges like a ghost buffeted on the breeze. Probably my favourite hardcore track ever, 'Open Your Mind' is as goosepimply as the entire works of My Bloody Valentine liquidized in a blender and injected into your spine.

'Open Your Mind' and the equally ravishing 'Finest Illusion' were like the return of 1992-style happy rave, only grown-up a bit; the callow euphoria now tinged with poignancy, a bittersweet foretaste of the comedown after the high. Like Bukem's 'Music' and 'Atlantis', 'Open' and 'Finest' shined a light at the end of the long tunnel of 'darkside'. 'Dark got silly, people trying to be the darkest of the dark,' says Brad. 'Some of it was okay, but a lot of it was definitely "rock music",' he adds, meaning music for crack heads, people who smoke rock cocaine. After Steve Gurley left the band, Foul Play lay low for a year, then in November 1994 unleashed 'Being With You', a soul-harrowing blitz of infra-red bass, cluster-bombs of phuture-jazz synth-chords and aerobatic vocal samples courtesy of swingbeat-diva Mary J. Blige. The band's own remix of 'Being', with its after-image trailing jitter-riffs, still stands as one of the most hallucinatory, positively Martian slices of artcore ever.

Ghetto Technology

As the Moving Shadow roster moved towards a sunkissed, purely affirmative sound, other artcore producers continued to insist on jungle's roots in 'darkness'. Metalheads' 'Angel' and its flipside 'You and Me' typified this meld of soothing and sinister, a style Goldie dubbed 'ghetto blues for the nineties'.

Blown away by 'Angel', I tracked Goldie down in the summer of 1993. During the phone interview, it quickly became clear that Goldie was a very angry man, who chafed against the public perception of hardcore as 'just a fun thing for fifteen-year-olds to get off their nut to'. He lambasted the West End progressive house élite, and railed against Kiss FM for their refusal to play breakbeat tracks. (Apparently, when he personally brought round an advance of 'Angel', they laughed him out of the door.) 'Maybe the only way forward for me is in film, doing soundtracks,' he wondered dejectedly. He was also deeply frustrated by his limited production resources. 'Give me Sven Vath's studio for a week,' he beseeched, almost spitting out the dismal prog-tekno guru's name, 'and I'll give you operas!'

Offspring of an English mother and an absentee Jamaican father, Goldie spent most of his childhood flitting between different foster families in the Midlands, before becoming a prime mover in the early

UK hip-hop scene. His aerosol skills took him to New York, as a participant in a BBC documentary on graffiti and B-boy culture. After a spell of flirting with Rastafarianism and reading Revelations, Goldie moved to Miami, where he worked in a flea market making customized gold teeth (hence his nickname) and got involved in the criminal underworld. Returning to Britain in the late eighties, he hung out with the Nellee Hooper/Soul II Soul/Massive Attack milieu (Massive's 3D had been one of his old graffiti buddies) and made some music with trip hopper Howie B, before getting swept up in rave culture. At hardcore haven Rage, the futuristic breakbeat techno played by resident DJs Grooverider and Fabio blew his mind. Tracking tunes by Nebula II and Manix back to their label, Goldie became part of the Reinforced crew, where he acted as a sort of producer/A & R/spokesman, and, under the name Rufige Cru, released awesome tracks like the gaseous bliss-overdose 'Menace'.

Just as aerosol-wielding B-boys transformed vandalistic I-am-SOMEBODY rage into signature and style, so Goldie's music turned the delinquent aggression of hardcore into artcore. When I first met Goldie in the flesh in February 1994, he was working on the intro of his meisterwerk, a twenty-two minute long concept track about time and the dark side of urban life. During the summer, I got a preview of the fully-formed *magnum opus*, 'Timeless'. Goldie warned me that the track would play funny tricks with my sense of time, that the twenty-two minutes would seem to pass in five, and he was right.

First came 'Inner City Life', a yearning reverie of sanctuary from 'inner city pressure', sung by Diane Charlemagne. Then the song glides into the ghetto with 'Jah', Goldie's cyber-dub riposte to ragga-jungle: pressure-drop bass, a warrior-horde of swarming breaks, and an eerie greeting-the-aliens motif *à la Close Encounters*. The track's climactic sequence is a threnody of synapse-searing strings and multi-tracked Ms Charlemagnes. Finally, a reprise of 'Inner City Life' subsides into the coda's slow resolution.

Listening to Goldie describe the track's construction, it seemed like every cobra-coiled breakbeat, every swathe of morbidly angelic strings, every haunted inflection of Charlemagne's vocal, had some autobiographical referent, some coded significance in his private mythology/demonology. 'It was time to deal with inner-city life, straight to the jugular,' he told me at his local café in Chalk Farm. 'In New York and Miami, I saw what's happening in Britain now: the first generation of rock stars' – i.e., crack-heads – 'Kids who are just going through the paradise state, who are about to become victims. "Timeless" is Revelation. It's all right taking these kids into euphoria, into a dream-state, but you have to come back to reality. What I've tried to provide is that comedown.'

'Rob and I,' he continued, referring to his engineer partner and 'perfect interface', Rob Playford of Moving Shadow, 'we're dealing with a subculture that's took a lot of drugs. Rob and I know how to tap into their heads. When you're on drugs, don't go near "Timeless", 'cos it will take your soul out, take it on a fuckin' journey, and hand it back to you, *smokin'*. We are about tapping into people's innards.'

'Technically, "Timeless" is like a Rolex,' Goldie continued, never shy to blow his own trumpet. 'Beautiful surface, but the mechanism inside is a mindfuck. The loops, they've been sculpted, they're in 4D.' Drawing parallels between the perspectival trickery of Escher and the *trompe l'oreille* effects of the duo's production, he claimed that he and Playford were so far ahead of the game that they'd had to coin their own private technical terminology for their favourite effects ('igniting a loop', 'snaking out a break', 'tubing a sound') and pet sounds ('zord', 'blade', 'twister', 'sub-stain'). 'We've learned to do magic with the bluntest of instruments,' he said, referring to the way jungle producers work with relatively low-level technology. 'It's like my graffiti paintings: give a graphic designer an aerosol and he won't be able to do shit with it. Nobody can come in and beat us at our own game.'

'Timeless' – the title track of Goldie's major label debut album – took over a year to come out. In the mean time, two other semi-conceptual jungle albums hit the racks, both created by allies of Goldie's: 4 Hero's *Parallel Universe* and A Guy Called Gerald's *Black Secret Technology*. The latter's title had a double meaning that threaded through the album's utopian/dystopian content. On one hand, it aligned Gerald Simpson with the black science fiction, Afro-Futurist tradition in pop: Sun Ra as Saturn-born ambassador for the Omniverse, Hendrix landing his 'kinky machine', George Clinton's Mothership taking the Afronauts to a lost homeland on the other side of the galaxy, Afrika Bambaataa's twin fetish for Kraftwerk's Teutonic rigour and for Nubian science, Juan Atkins and Derrick May's cybertronic mind-scapes. But Gerald originally heard the phrase 'black secret technology' on a TV talk show about government mind control via the media.

The album's title perfectly captured an ambivalence that runs through the junglist imagination, where technology figures as both orgasmatron (a pleasuredome of artificially induced sensations) and Panopticon (the terrordome in which every individual is constantly under Authority's punitive gaze). Technology promises 'total control', but there's a deadly ambiguity: does that phrase refer to empowering individuals and facilitating resistance, or to the secret agendas of corporations and government agencies? When it comes to state-of-the-art gadgetry, we're all potentially in the position of Gene Hackman's surveillance expert in *The Conversation*, who ends up fucked over by the very machinery at which he's a virtuoso.

Jungle is a subculture based around abusing technology rather than being abused by it. And so Gerald takes a boyish delight in the sheer 'deviousness' of the ever-escalating, technology-mediated struggle between Control and Anarchy. 'There's always ways around it,' he grins. 'If someone was scanning into this room with a directional microphone, we could scan them back and find out their exact location. When we were at school, we used to fiddle fruit machines. They always came back with some new trick to stop us, but we always got round it. We'd find ways to get credits on Space Invaders' machines. It was like, *ghetto technology*!'

As with a lot of post-rave producers, there's something vaguely autoerotic or even autistic about Gerald's techno-fetishism. When I ask him if he ever feels like a cyborg, in so far as his machines are extensions of his body that give him superhuman powers, he frankly admits that working in his studio, 'it's like your own world and you become like the god'. On the album, 'Cybergen' is all about an 'imaginary drug that's basically virtual reality, you're in total control of the experience. The vocal says "It's too late to turn back now," and that's making the point that it's no use saying we can't cope with this technology, that it's going to ruin society. 'Cos the technology's already here. You either cope with it or you're lost. Kids today are already totally hooked into it. Kids today are frightening! I grew up with records, and now I know how to manipulate them. When today's kids' – the Playstation generation, he means – 'grow up, they'll know how to manipulate the visual side of it.'

With its synaesthetic textures and three-dimensional, audio-maze spatiality, Gerald's music anticipates virtual reality. His music actually sounds like a datascape that's sensorily intoxicating yet teeming with threat. On tracks like 'Gloc' and 'Nazinji-Zaka', breakbeats writhe like

serpents, samples morph and dematerialize like fever-dream hallucinations, itchy 'n' scratchy blips of texture/rhythm dart and hover like
dragonflies. Like the labyrinthine, multi-tiered combat-zones in video-
games, jungle offers a drastically intensified aural allegory of the
concrete jungle; in Gerald's case, the gang-infested, post-rave Manchester where he then still lived. 'The samples of "you're gonna be a
bad motherfucker" are from *Robocop*,' Gerald says of 'Gloc', which was
named after the LA gangsta's favourite automatic weapon, then retitled
'Cyberjazz' for the album. 'It's the scene where they're rebuilding the
cop as a cyborg after he got shot up. It fits, 'cos the track's a remix,
and I rebuilt it, put it through effects, armoured it.'

Leaving behind the ghetto for the visionary ether, 4 Hero's *Parallel
Universe* cleaved more to the mystical, utopian side of the Afro-futurist
imagination. Space is the place where the race can escape terrestrial
oppression. With its astrophysical imagery (titles like 'Solar Emissions',
'Terraforming' and 'Sunspots') and jazzy cadences, *Universe* is basically
a digitized update of early seventies fusion *à la* Weather Report and
Herbie Hancock. This is drum and bass freed of the surly bonds of
gravity: quicksilver breakbeats vaporize and deliquesce, succulent
keyboards ripple and striate like globules of liquid adrift in Zero-G. On
tracks like 'Wrinkles in Time' and 'Shadow Run', the breaks seem to
fluctuate in tempo and pitch, morphing as uncannily as Salvador Dali's
melting clocks. Throughout, the percussion is so extremely and
exquisitely processed it's tactile as much as rhythmic, caressing your
skin and kissing your ears.

The Fusion Con

Parallel Universe also illustrates some of the perils of 'armchair jungle',
though. On the mellow jazz-funk glide of 'Universal Love', the creamy
'real' vocal and smarmy saxophone seem like a misguided grab for 'real
music' legitimacy. Similar problems beset Goldie's *Timeless*, finally
released in the summer of 1995 to rapturous praise. Despite the
hosannas, *Timeless* was jungle's *Sgt Pepper's Lonely Hearts' Club Band*:
50 per cent genre-bending brilliance, 50 per cent ill-advised attempts
to prove Goldie's versatility.

When he was collaborating with his drum and bass peers – engineer-
programmers like Playford, Dillinja, Dego from 4 Hero – the results

were astonishing: 'This Is A Bad', 'Jah The Seventh Seal', 'Still Life', 'Timeless' itself (a sort of nineties 'A Day In The Life', with sixties anomie replaced by nineties millenarian paranoia). But whenever Goldie roped in 'luminary' players and vocalists from the jazz-world – Steve Williamson, Cleveland Watkiss, Justina Curtis, Lorna Harris – the results were embarrassing: the jazz-rock odyssey of 'Sea of Tears', the mushy mystic quiet stormscape of 'Adrift' (which David Toop described as 'Luther Vandross on acid'). Goldie's motley array of influences – David Sylvian and Japan, Pat Metheny, Byrne and Eno, Visage, the third Stranglers' album – proved both a strength and liability. On the worst of *Timeless*, two particularly distressing sources – the slicked-out, early eighties Miles Davis of *Decoy* and *Tutu*, the clinical New Age jazz-fusion of The Yellowjackets – came to the fore, and came perilously close to fulfilling Rob Playford's fantasy of drum and bass as twenty-first-century progressive rock. Goldie's second album – 1998's *Saturnz Return* – went all the way into prog terrain with its sixty minute concept track 'Mother' which was recorded with a full string orchestra.

Why did so many artcore junglists avidly embrace the most conventional and middlebrow signifiers of 'musicality' – sax solos, over-melismatic singing? The reason was that underneath the bravado and the futurist rhetoric, a secret inferiority complex lurked. Jungle is the most digitalized and sampladelic music on the planet. No acoustic sound is involved, nothing is recorded through a microphone. Jungle is composed from data derived from recordings, video or sound-modules (Pop Tart sized encyclopedias of samples and synth-tones), and it is assembled using programs like Cubase VST (virtual studio technology), which presents loops and motifs in visual form on the computer screen. 'You feel like a conductor with an orchestra,' one producer told me. But because jungle relies so heavily on production and effects, many producers secretly believed that 'musicality' involved moving away from digital technology.

By the end of 1994, some producers in the intelligent sector of drum and bass had started to abandon samplers for old-fashioned analogue synthesizers and sequencers as used by the early Detroit techno and Chicago house pioneers; these instruments were felt to be more hands-on and 'musical' than clicking a mouse. And many began to talk wistfully of working with 'real' instruments and vocalists. Omni Trio's Rob Haigh complained to me at the time, 'There is nothing worse than seeing house artists trying to get into that live muso vibe. The live element of our music occurs on the dancefloor. House and jungle are sequenced musics, created on computers.' But few heeded the warning.

When a genre starts to think of itself as 'intelligent', this is usually a warning sign that it's on the verge of losing its edge, or at least its sense of fun. Usually, this progressivist discourse masks a class-based or generational struggle to seize control of a music's direction; look at the schism between prog rock and heavy metal, between the post-punk vanguard and Oi!, between bohemian art-rap and gangsta, between intelligent techno and 'ardkore. Often, the 'maturity' and 'intelligence' resides less in the music itself than the way it's used (reverent, sedentary contemplation as opposed to sweaty, boisterous physicality). The majority of 'intelligent jungle' tracks were no smarter in their construction than the ruff ragga-jungle anthems. 'Intelligence' merely indicated a preference for certain sounds – bongos, complicated hi-hat patterns, floaty synth-washes, neo-Detroit string sounds – over others that were harsher, more obviously artificial and digitally processed.

It had always been somewhat ironic that jungle's experimental vanguard resorted to the same rhetoric used in 1992, by evangelists for progressive house and intelligent techno, to dismiss breakbeat hardcore as juvenile and anti-musical. By early 1995, my anxieties about jungle's upwardly mobile drift towards an ill-conceived maturity became horrendous reality. In record shops, I overheard customers (ap)praising tracks in terms of how 'clean' their production was. LTJ Bukem's club Speed – initially founded on the sound premise of playing the tracks that were too experimental for the 'jump-up' junglist DJs to play out – quickly became a smug salon for the new smooth-core sound. In 1993, jungle clubs had been banished to the scuzzy margins of London. With its location just off Charing Cross Road, Speed symbolized the artcore junglists' desire to remake their once despised scene as a metropolitan élite, just another West End clique like rare groove, Balearic or acid jazz. And it worked: everyone from Deelite has-been Lady Miss Kirby Kier to ancient prog-rock bore turned techno bod Steve Hillage to acid jazz maestro Gilles Peterson to Goldie's future lover Bjork were jostling to be seen there.

Esotericism, elegance and élitism were now the watchwords. Moving Shadow caught the mood when they coined the ghastly slogan 'audio couture'; the label's output suddenly got fatally slick, with almost every release featuring their new house sound of scuttling bongos and what sounded suspiciously like a fretless jazz bass as played by some pony-tailed session man. Throughout the intelligent sector, producers studiously shunned anything that smacked of ragga boisterousness or pop catchiness; instead of hefty chunks of melody/lyric, vocal samples were reduced to the merest mood-establishing tint of abstract emotion, while keyboard motifs rarely amounted to anything as memorable as a riff, just timbral washes and jazzy cadences.

The new hegemony of tepid tastefulness coincided neatly with jungle's rehabilitation by the very people – critics, A & R people, radio programmers, techno producers – who had derided and marginalized hardcore in 1991–3. One example is the case of Pete Tong, Radio One's leading dance music DJ and A & R for London Record's dance imprint ffrr. In 1993, Tong had incurred the wrath of the hardcore scene when he remarked during an interview with a rave mag: 'To be honest the breakbeat house and hardcore just drives me to despair and I'd rather give up than play this. The couple of thousand that still exist for what I call the rave audience, I just don't want to cater for them. I'll stand in front of anyone and say it, I think hardcore is boring, uninventive and not musically going anywhere, plus I don't think it's selling records anymore ... When I say dead I mean it's no longer inventive and it's gone up its own arse. It's had a good few years but now it's time for it to give up.' In 1994, Tong signed Goldie and DJ Crystl to ffrr; the following year he clinched an exclusive licensing deal with LTJ Bukem's Good Looking/Looking Good label. At the end of 1995 Tong boasted in *Mixmag* that his proudest achievement that year was breaking Goldie internationally. Legend has it that jungle's reintegration into the spectrum of 'cool' music was symbolized when Tong and Goldie embraced on the dancefloor at Speed.

Accompanying this nauseating rehabilitation process was a subtle rewriting of history, with some intelligent junglists – Bukem, Photek, Alex Reece, Wax Doctor – citing the Detroit-aligned likes of Carl Craig and The Black Dog as formative influences, while other key ancestors, perhaps too redolent of 'ardkore's 'one dimensional' juvenilia were conveniently forgotten: Joey Beltram, Mantronix, Shut Up And Dance, the Prodigy. All this only served to reassure the recent hipster converts to drum and bass that they'd been right all along to dismiss hardcore as trashy drug-noise.

Desperate to distance themselves from ragga and to disown the ravey-ness of 'ardkore, the intelligent drum and bass contingent seized upon 'fusion' as a model of progression and maturity. Drum and bass was always a hybrid style. In the early 'ardkore days, this took the form of a collage-based, cut-up aesthetic, but 'intelligent' replaced that fissile mess-thetic with a seamless emulsion of influences. There was an explicit reinvocation of seventies jazz-fusion (samples of Lonnie Liston Smith and Roy Ayers licks, Rhodes piano trills, frilly bass parts, flute solos) and of subsequent musics influenced by that era, like jazz-funk, Detroit techno and garage. Too often, the result was a sort of twenty-first century cocktail music.

For intelligent junglists, 'jazz' signified flava, not process; there was no improv-combustion involved, just the use of a certain kind of chords. 'Jazz' also related to a specific British Black tradition, where said chord-sequences and a polished fluency connote relaxation, finesse, sophistication, upward mobility. And so on KISS FM's newly commissioned weekly jungle show, DJ Fabio would hail tracks by artists like Essence of Aura, Aquasky and Dead Calm for their 'rich, lavish production – real class!' then exhort breakbeat-fans to 'open their minds'. All this passionate advocacy on behalf of what was basically fuzak draped over unneccessarily fussy breaks!

'Intelligent' producers genuflected at the shrine of Detroit techno, seemingly oblivious to the irony that back in 1992 Derrick May, a recent and horrified visitor to Rage, had railed against breakbeat-based hardcore as 'a diabolical mutation, a Frankenstein's monster that's out of control'. Take rising producer Rupert Parkes, who – as Photek, Studio Pressure et al – built up a reputation by making jungle sound more like 'proper' techno and less like its own superbad self. At every opportunity, he would stress his Detroit 'roots', telling *iD* that he and his allies (Wax Doctor, Alex Reece, Sounds of Life) had 'more in common with Carl Craig's music than we do with the majority of jungle'. And this was true: although tracks like 'The Water Margin' had a compelling neurotic frenzy, generally Parkes's work infected drum and bass with the funkless frigidity and pseudo-conceptual portentous-ness of techno – just dig track titles like 'Resolution', 'Book of Changes', 'Form and Function'!

Alex Reece, another jazzy-jungle pioneer, was basically a house bod; in interviews, he never namechecked anyone from jungle, or God forbid, the hardcore era (which he'd detested), but would instead declare of his beloved collection of classic house tracks, 'I'd fucking cry if I lost 'em.' Like his buddies Wax Doctor and DJ Pulse, Reece's ambition was to seduce house fans into dancing to breakbeat rhythms. And so his tunes, like the Latin-tinged 'Basic Principles' and 'Feel The Sunshine', downplayed the cut-up, jagged breakbeat-science in favour of a slinky, easy-rolling flow. This disco-fication of jungle paid off massively just once, in the form of the monumental Speed anthem 'Pulp Fiction'.

Perhaps the most influential icon of jungle's gentrification was LTJ Bukem. In his music and his rhetoric, he more than anyone helped to define 'intelligence' as the repudiation of hardcore's drug-fuelled energy. In retrospect, the title of his non-anthemic anthem 'Music' seems like a poignant plea to 'take me seriously, please'. And while 'Music' and 'Atlantis' certainly warranted Bukem's status as 'the Derrick May of hardcore' (as Rob Haigh put it), the comparison began to seem less complimentary when you recall May's disdain for the 'ooligans of 'ardkore.

Despite having played at big raves like Dreamscape and Raindance, Bukem was at pains to make out he'd never really been involved in rave and had only done E a handful of times. More than most computer-in-the-bedroom producers, Bukem had the resources to enable him to break with jungle's radical sampladelia; as a child, he'd studied piano, steeped himself in fusioneers like Chick Corea, and played in a jazz-rock band. And so in his tracks, he deliberately muted the wildstyle FX of jungle's breakbeat-aesthetic in favour of more naturalistic, less chopped up rhythms. 'My sound is more realistic if you like ... you could imagine [a drummer] drumming it,' he told Mixmag in 1995. Why such a retreat – from digital anti-naturalism towards time-honoured muso values – should be regarded as an advance for jungle was never made clear.

By this point, the aqua-funk serenity of 'Atlantis' – once so startling – had become an aesthetic cul de sac. Bukem's acolytes on Good Looking/Looking Good – PFM, Aquarius, Tayla, Ils and Solo – followed their guru by expunging all of jungle's most adrenalizing and disruptive elements, in favour of a pleasant, placid formula of heart-beat basslines, smooth-rollin' breaks and watercolour synths. Bukem's own 1995 offering 'Horizons' was closer to jacuzzi than gulf-stream; its arpeggiated synths and healing chimes verged on New Age, as did the snatch of Maya Angelou wittering about how 'each new hour holds new chances for new beginnings / the horizon leans forward, offering you space to place new steps of change'.

Fusion-jungle wasn't an unmitigated calamity; tracks like E-Z Rollers' 'Rolled Into One', Hidden Agenda's 'Is It Love', PFM's 'one and only', Adam F's 'Circles' and Da Intalex's 'What Ya Gonna Do' showed it was possible to incorporate smoother textures from seventies soul and jazz-funk without forsaking jungle's polyrhythmic exuberance. But too many second division drum and bass units followed a formula. Start with an unnecessarily elongated, teasing intro; roll in the heavy-on-the-cymbals breaks; layer some wordless female vocal samples (measured, tasteful passion only, no helium-histrionics please); drag out the track, through percussive breakdowns and wafting synth-interludes, for eight minutes or longer; rinse the mix to get that airy, 'just brushed freshness' that sounds good on a really crisp hi-fi. Pursuing 'depth', but lacking the vision it took to get there, too many intelligent junglists washed up in the middlebrow shallows.

Rough Stuff

While the doyens of intelligence seemed to have forgotten what had originally made jungle more invigorating than trance or armchair techno, other producers – DJ SS, Asend/Dead Dred, Deep Blue, Aphrodite, DJ Hype, Ray Keith/Renegade – honed in on the genre's essence: breakbeat-science, bass-mutation, sampladelia. Their work proved that the true *intellect* in jungle resided in the percussive rather than the melodic. Whether they were white or black, these artists reaffirmed drum and bass's place in an African musical continuum (dub, hip hop, James Brown etc.) whose premises constitute a radical break with Western music, classical and pop.

Roni Size and sidekick DJ Die were exemplars. This duo is often regarded as pioneers of jazz-jungle, on account of their early 1994 classic 'Music Box' and its sequel 'It's A Jazz Thing'. Listen again to 'Music Box', though, and you realize that the sublime cascades of fusion-era chimes are only a brief interlude in what's basically a stripped-down percussion workout. Size's late 1994 monster 'Time-stretch' was even more austere, just escalating drums and a chiming bassline that together resemble a clockwork contraption gone mad. And the Size and Die early 1995 collaboration '11.55' was positively murderous in its minimal-is-maximal starkness. What initially registers as merciless monotony reveals itself, on repeated plays, to be an

inexhaustibly listenable forest of densely tangled breaks and multiple
basslines (the latter acting both as subliminal, ever-modulating melody
and as sustained sub-aural pressure), relieved only by the sparest
shadings of sampled jazz coloration. Forcing you to focus entirely on
what, in normal pop, is not consciously listened to – the rhythm
section – '11.55' clenches your brain until it feel like a knotted mass of
hypertense tendons. Size and Die's fiercely compressed, implosive
aesthetic recalled bebop, in so far as it's a strategy of alienation
designed to discover who's really down with the programme, by
venturing deeper into the heart of 'blackness'. Articulating this 'it's a
black thing, you wouldn't understand' subtext, and giving a gansta
twist to the music's glowering malevolence, was the soundbite at the
beginning of '11.55' – 'you could feel all the tension building up at the
convention / as the hustlers began to to arrive' – sampled from *Hustlers'
Convention*, a solo album by a member of The Last Poets.

Young producer Dillinja was, like Size and Die, renowned for
fusion-tinged masterpieces like 'Sovereign Melody' and 'Deep Love',
with their softly glowing electric piano and flickers of lachrymose wah-
wah guitar. But this tended to obscure Dillinja's real claim to genius:
the viciously disorientating properties of his beats and B-lines, which
he convoluted and contorted into grooves of ear-boggling, labyrinthine
complexity. 'Warrior' places the listener in the centre of an unfeasibly
expanded drum-kit played by an octopus-limbed cyborg; the bass
enters not as a B-line but a one-note detonation, an impacted cluster
of different bass-timbres. On these and other Dillinja classics – 'You
Don't Know', 'Deadly Deep Subs', 'Lionheart', 'Ja Know Ya Big', 'Brutal
Bass' – the jolting breaks trigger muscular reflexes and motor-impulses,
so that you find yourself shadowboxing instead of dancing, tensing and
sparring in a deadly ballet of feint, jab and parry.

If Dillinja and Size and Die were developing drum and bass as
martial art, Danny Breaks' work as Droppin' Science is more like a
virtual adventure playground, where collapsible breakbeats and tram-
poline bass trigger kinaesthetic responses, gradually hotrodding the
human nervous system in readiness for the rapid-fire reaction-time
required in the info-dense future. On tracks like 'Long Time Comin''
and 'Step Off' bass fibrillates like muscle with electric current coursing
through it, hi-hats incandesce like fireworks in slow-mo, beats seem to
run backward as uncannily as trick photography of a fallen house of
cards tumbling back together. Throughout, melody limits itself to

minimal motifs where the eerie fluorescent glow of the synth-goo is the real hook.

*

1995 – the year of jungle's mainstream breakthrough in Britain – saw jungle torn every which way in a conflict between two rival models of blackness: elegant urbanity (the opulence and finesse of fusion/garage/ jazz-funk/quiet storm) versus ruffneck tribalism (the raw, percussive minimalism of dub/ragga/hip hop/electro). Lurking beneath this smooth/ruff dialectic was a covert class struggle: upwardly mobile gentrification versus ghettocentricity, crossover versus undergroundism.

On one side were those who equated 'progression' with making drum and bass sound more like other genres (house, garage, Detroit techno), and thus more appealing to outsiders; artists like Reece, Photek and Bukem, most of whom had deals with major labels by the end of 1995. And on the other side, there were the purists who wanted jungle to advance by sounding ever more intensely *like itself*, and therefore dedicated themselves to achieving hard-won increments of polyrhythmic intricacy and sub-bass brutalism. This strategy had the beneficial side effect of fending off outsiders, because it involved plunging ever deeper into the anti-populist imperatives of the art's core (that's to say, all the stuff that happens beneath/beyond the non-initiate's perceptual thresholds). Most of these artists stuck with independent labels or put out their own tracks. Meanwhile, caught between intelligent's serenity and the ruff-stuff's moody minimalism, the idea of jungle as E'd up frisky funquake seemed to have simply dropped away altogether.

Soldiers of Darkness

By 1996, 'jungle' and 'drum and bass' were *the* words to drop. Everybody from thirtysomething jazz-pop duo Everything But The Girl to freeform improv-guitarist Derek Bailey was dabbling with sped-up breakbeats, as were techno types such as Underworld and Aphex Twin. Alex Reece's jungle-lite convinced house fans they had nothing to fear, while Bukem launched a campaign to bring breakbeat rhythms to the clubbing mainstream, playing at venues like Cream and The End. Despite having played a big role in the gentrification process with his crusade for 'jazzstep', Fabio railed against the reduction of drum and bass to mere 'wallpaper fodder' by its use in TV links and commercials. One of the most bizarre examples of this syndrome is Virgin Atlantic's use of Goldie's ghetto-blues ballad 'Inner City Life' as tranquillizing muzak to steady passengers' nerves before take-off!

Just as the commercial success of hardcore in 1992 had prompted the first wave of 'dark side' tunes, so the hipster vogue for 'intelligent' inspired a defensive, back-to-the-underground initiative on the part of the original junglists. 'Intelligent' suddenly became an embarrassing term. Even those who'd most profited from major label interest in 'intelligence', like Goldie and Bukem, renounced the word, erroneously and rather disingenuously decrying it as a 'media invention' designed to divide the scene. Meanwhile, other producers started talking about 'darkness' as a desirable attribute again.

During 1993's darkside era, when jungle was banished from the media limelight, AWOL had been *the* hardcore club. Especially after the demise of Rage, AWOL was where the scene's inner circle would gather on a Saturday Night/Sunday Morning to hear DJs like Randall push the music to new heights of ruff-cut intensity. After being dislodged from its location at Islington's murky Paradise Club, AWOL settled late in 1995 at The SW1 Club in Victoria, and re-established its former role. While some of the drum and bass élite had moved on to Goldie's Metalheadz Sunday Sessions at the Blue Note, the core jungle audience were still attending AWOL or similar nights like Club UN and Innersense at the Lazerdrome (later renamed Millennium) – havens for all those who refused the lure of 'intelligence'.

AWOL isn't an acronym for 'absent without leave', but for 'a way of life'. If you're not involved in the scene, this article of faith – that buying records at specialist shops, going to clubs at the weekend, wearing MA2 jackets and smoking a lot of spliff, constitutes a set of tribal folkways – can seem a tad overstated. But the frequency and conviction with which the claim 'jungle, it's a way of life' is restated, suggests that for the true disciple, something massive has been invested in this music. It was precisely this question – what's at stake for the fans? – that began to haunt my mind when I went to the club three times during the first months of 1996.

Ethnological research wasn't on my mind the first time; fun was. I'm not sure if I found any, at least in the conventional sense, but the visit was a reaffirmation of flagging faith; a confirmation that, despite the surfeit of pseudo-jazzy tracks, jungle was alive and kickin'.

It was also a reminder that, for all the success of album-length, home-listening drum and bass, jungle's meaning is still made on the dancefloor. At massive volume, knowledge is visceral, something your body understands as it's seduced and ensnared by the music's paradoxes: the way the breaks combine rollin' flow and disruptive instability, thereby instilling a contradictory mix of nonchalance and vigilance; the way the bass is at once wombing and menacing. AWOL is a real Temple of Boom; the low-end frequencies are so thick and all-enveloping they're swimmable. Inside the bass, you feel safe, and you feel *dangerous*. Like cruising in a car with a booming system, you're sealed by surround-sound while marauding through urban space.

This first night at AWOL, the vibe is neither celebratory nor especially moody, but neutral. In contrast to the rousing exhortations of the MC, the crowd response is subdued (not abnormal for jungle). It's not long after the tabloid and TV scare stories surrounding Ecstasy fatality Leah Betts (the teenager who died after she took Ecstasy at her own birthday party). That's initially how I account for the utter absence of any E-vibes in the area, and for the insistent verging on desperate dealer trying to offload her unusually bargain-price wares. Instead, it's champagne, Pils and ganja that appear to be everybody's intoxicants of choice. Later, I notice a gaggle of sofa-sprawled punters who do appear to be E'd up, but are struggling to conceal the fact; their flushed but impassive faces ripple and spasm as if they're trying to hold down the rising high. It's only later I realize the reason for their restraint: no one else here is loved-up, and it's as though any kind of blissed behaviour is deemed inappropriate, unseemly, a throwback.

The next time I go to AWOL, a month later, the vibe has subtly changed. The sofa-zone, which had seemed vaguely upmarket, has been moved to somewhere out of the light, and now seems seedy. Overall, the balefulness quotient has increased dramatically. This time, I'm struck by the fact that nobody seems to be having fun; or to put it another way, 'fun' doesn't seem to be the reason everyone is there. It's old news that the effervescent friendliness of 1992-era hardcore is long gone, but basic civility seems to be in short supply. Even among groups of friends or boyfriend/girlfriend couples, smiles are rarer than hen's teeth, conversation is minimal. On the dancefloor, I watch a girl expertly roll a giant spliff while her boyfriend ignores her, then hand it to him silently. With incredible rapidity, he smokes most of it, hands it back without a word or glance, and strides off. A few minutes later,

I spot a gang of super-sharp stylists, eyes masked behind sunglasses, standing erect and statuesque in the middle of the dancing throng. Their faces are frozen, their arms folded across the chest, 1986 B-boy style, but whether this intransigent posture is a salute to the DJ or disapproval, it's hard to say; their expressions are unreadable.

AWOL's resident crew of DJs – Randall, Mickey Finn, Kenny Ken, Darren Jay – sustain a mercilessly minimalist and militaristic assault, all ricocheting snares and atonal, metallic B-lines that bounce joylessly like ball-bearings in a pinball machine. The night stays at a plateau of punitive intensity, no crescendos or lulls, just steady jungalistic pressure. By about 4 a.m., the dancers are jigging about with a kind of listless mania. One girl twitches and bounces mechanically, her limp limbs inscribing the exact same patterns in the air, as if she's animated by a will other than her own. For a Saturday night out, the compensatory climax of a week's drudgery, this seems like hard work. I start to wonder if she, like me, got sucked in by 1991–2 'ardkore's explosive euphoria, its manic, fiery-eyed glee, and then got carried along by the music's logical evolution only to wind up at another place altogether. Maybe that stunned, dispirited expression on her face comes from finding herself in the midst of an entirely new cultural formation, 'a way of life' that can no longer offer release, let alone a redemptive vision.

At clubs like AWOL, the ruling sound is the gangsta hardstep and 'jump up' jungle of labels like Ganja, Frontline, Dread, Suburban Base and Dope Dragon, made by DJ–producers like Hype, Pascal, Andy C, Ray Keith, L. Double, Shy FX, Swift, Zinc and Bizzy B. By 1996, jungle had purged almost all of its obvious ragga elements; its ruffneck militancy was now expressed through a conscious alignment with US hip hop, involving the use of melancholy synth refrains from West Coast G-funk like Dr Dre, and vocal samples from East Coast rap, whether boastful ('raw like Reservoir Dogs') or threatening ('hit the deck, I got the Tek right on your neck').

With its machine-gun snares and landslide/landmine bass, this 'ruffneck soldier' style of jungle makes you feel like you're steppin' into a warzone; hence rave names likes Desert Storm or Wardance. But jungle's militaristic streak actually goes back to the early days of hardcore. 4 Hero's 1991 debut album *In Rough Territory* featured cover images of a commando unit planting a flag on enemy soil. Dego McFarlane told me Reinforced conceived their releases as 'raids' on the rave scene; they'd carpetbomb the hardcore market with multiple releases, even putting out the remix on the same day as the original, then disappear from earshot for months. Alongside the idea of urban life as a warzone, there's a fascination with the military as a sort of avant-garde of science: Goldie, one-time Reinforced A & R, talked of his protégés as 'prototypes', like they were secret weapons under R & D. 2 Bad Mice's 'Bombscare' actually employed the sound of a suspect device detonating as part of its bassline, making funky the sound of urban dread. Moving Shadow continued this idea with ultra-minimal 1994 tracks like Renegade's 'Terrorist' and Deep Blue's 'Helicopter Tune', whose roiling Latin percussion evoked the sound of the famous 'copter dawn-raid in *Apocalypse Now*.

Predator and *Predator 2* – ultra-violent movies about an extra-terrestrial hunter who goes on safari in zones of human conflict – both exerted a huge influence on early jungle. From the first movie came the sample 'she said "the jungle, it just came alive and took him"', as used in Shimon's 'The Predator'; from the sequel, the 'fucking voodoo magic' hook in Hyper-On Experience's 'Lords Of the Null Lines'. While *Predator* is set in a real jungle that's also a Central American warzone, *Predator 2* is about the urban jungle of a near-future Los Angeles, where rival drug gangs fight each other and the police. The script obsessively underlines the state of martial lawlessness, with various police officers declaring 'welcome to the war', 'you're a soldier', 'we're not winning this war'. The underlying scenario is LA as an *internal Vietnam*, with the ethnic gangs representing the Viet Cong and the LAPD losing the 'war on drugs' despite their use of military-style raids and helicopter patrols. For British junglists, though, what grabbed the imagination is *Predator 2*'s dystopian magnification of contemporary urban chaos – not to mention the clan of dreadlocked-and-ganja-puffing drug warlords called the Jamaican Voodoo Posse, and the fact that the local TV news programme documenting the carnage is called *Hardcore Report*.

By 1996, jungle's militarism had gotten ever more explicit and upfront: artist names like Soul-Jah and Military Police, track titles like 'Dark Soldier', 'The Battle Frontier' and, my favourite, 'Homage to Catatonia' by Unknown Soldier. The Terradome's 'Soldier' featured the histrionic sample 'I'm not a criminal, I'm a soldier, and I deserve to die like a soldier', crystallizing the idea of the gangsta as a one-man army, a rogue unit in capitalism's war of all against all. Some junglists seemed to be literally in training for Armageddon and the final breakdown of society. Discovering that a gaggle of top junglists had become obsessed with paintball, a war-game, *Muzik* ran a photo spread of the DJs clad in camouflage fatigues and shooting at each other. Listening to gangsta hardstep and jump up – which basically consist of James Brownian funk percussion tightened and toughened into the martial paradiddles and triplets of the parade ground – it was easy to imagine it being used as a training resource by the military; a new kind of drill (with JB barking like a sergeant!) for a new breed of soldier (more improvisatory, less regimented) that will be required for the urban conflicts of the future.

Apocalypse Noir

In 1996, a new sub-genre of jungle began to coalesce called 'techstep', a dirge-like death-funk characterized by harsh industrial timbres and bludgeoning 'butcher's block' beats. The term was coined by DJ–producers Ed Rush and Trace, who shaped the sound in tandem with engineer Nico of the No U Turn label. The 'tech' stood not for Detroit techno, dreamy and elegant, but for the brutalist Belgian hardcore of the early nineties. Paying homage to R & S classics like 'Dominator' and 'Mentasm', to artists like T99 and Frank de Wulf, Trace and Ed Rush deliberately affirmed a crucial white European element that had been written out of jungle's history.

The other important source for techstep was the first era of 'darkside', as pioneered by Reinforced artists like Doc Scott and 4 Hero. This was when the teenage DJs Trace and Ed Rush cut their production teeth with sinister classics like 'Lost Entity' and 'Bludclot Artattack'. The name 'Ed Rush' sounds like a take on the 'head rush', early rave slang for a temporary white-out of consciousness caused by taking too many E's. There was a big difference between darkside 1993 and techstep, though. The original dark-core had still oozed a sinister, sickly bliss on the border between loved-up and fucked-up. In 1996, with Ecstasy long out of favour, techstep was shaped by a different mindfuck-of-choice: hydroponically grown marijuana aka 'skunk', whose near-hallucinogenic levels of THC induce a sensory intensification without euphoria and a nerve-jangling paranoia perfect for jungle's tension-but-no-release rhythms.

The first stirrings of the return-to-darkness were heard in late 1995 with Trace's seminal remix of T. Power's 'Horny Mutant Jazz'. Working in tandem with Nico and Ed Rush, Trace tore the fusion-flavoured original to shreds, replacing its leisurely glide with slipped-gears breakbeats, spectral synths and a brooding, bruising bass sound sampled and mutated from Kevin Saunderson's Reese classic 'Just Want Another Chance'. Meanwhile, Ed Rush's No U Turn tracks 'Gangsta Hardstep' and 'Guncheck' took the explosive energy of hardcore and imploded it, transforming febrile hyperkinesis into molasses-thick malaise. The new sound made you feel like you were caged in a pressure-cooker of paroxysmic breaks and plasmic bass.

If Belgian brutalism and early breakbeat 'ardkore resembled sixties garage punk, techstep is like seventies punk rock, in so far as it's not a simple back-to-basics manoeuvre, but an isolation and intensification of the most aggressive, non-R & B elements in its precursor. All through 1996, as the No U Turn squad honed their sound-and-vision, they accentuated the self-same 'noise annoys' elements that punk exaggerated in garage rock: headbanger riffs and mid-frequency blare. Where intelligent drum and bass suffers from an obsessive-compulsive cleanliness, techstep production is deliberately dirty, all dense murk and noxious drones. The defining aspect of the No U Turn sound was its bass sound – a dense, humming miasma of low-end frequencies, as malignant as a cloud of poison gas – achieved by feeding the bass-riffs through a guitar distortion pedal and a battery of effects. Another stylistic trait was the way techstep shunned the frisky fluency of jazzy-jungle's breakbeats in favour of relative simplicity and rigour. Although the breakbeats are still running at jungle's 160-and-rising b.p.m. norm, techstep *feels* slower – fatigued, winded, like it's had the crap beaten out of it. In tracks like Doc Scott's 'Drumz 95', the emphasis is on the 80 b.p.m. half-step, making you want to *stomp*, not sashay.

Techstep is a sado-masochist sound. Ed Rush declared bluntly 'I want to hurt people with my beats,' and one No U Turn release had the phrase 'hurter's mission' scratched into the vinyl. This terrorist stance is in marked contrast to the rhetoric of intelligent drum and bass artists, with their talk of 'educating' the audience, 'opening minds' and 'easing the pressure' of urban life. Sonically, techstep's dry, clenched sound couldn't have been further from the massaging, muscle-relaxing stream of genteel sound oozed by DJs like Bukem and Fabio, all soothing synth-washes and sax loops seemingly on loan from Grover Washington Jnr and Kenny G.

While the intelligent and jazz-step producers prided themselves on their 'musicality', the techstep producers veered to the opposite extreme: a bracing 'anti-musicality'. With its incorporation of atonal, unpitched timbres, non-musical sounds and horror-movie soundtrack dissonance, the new artcore *noir* was simply far more avant-garde than the likes of Bukem. In an abiding confusion about what constitutes 'progression' for electronic music, the intelligent drum and bass producers were simply too deferential to traditional ideas about melody, arrangement, 'nice' textures, the importance of proper songs and hands-on, real-time instrumentation.

By the end of 1996, producers like Nasty Habits/Doc Scott, Dom and Roland, Boymerang, E-Sassin, Cyborgz and Optical had joined No U Turn on their 'hurter's mission'. Techstep got even more industrial and stiff-jointed, at times verging on gabba, or a syncopated, sped-up update of The Swans. Above all, the music got *colder*. The Numanoid synth-riff on Nasty Habits' awesome 'Shadowboxin'' sears the ear with its glacial grandeur, while the trudging two-step beat always makes me imagine a commando jogging under napalm skies with a rocket launcher on his hip. No U Turn themselves reached something of a pinnacle with the dark exultation of Trace/Nico's 'Squadron', whose *Carmina Burana*-gone-cyberpunk fanfares slash and scythe like the Grim Reaper.

Where did the apocalpytic glee, the morbid and perverse *jouissance*, in techstep stem from? Nico described the music-making process – all night, red-eye sessions conducted in a ganja fog – as a horrible experience that poisoned his nervous system with tension. Ed Rush talked of deliberately smokin' weed to get 'dark, evil thoughts', the kind of *skunkanoia* without which he couldn't achieve the right vibe for his tracks. Like Wu-Tang-style horrorcore rap, techstep seemed based around the active pursuit of phobia and psychosis as entertainment. Which begged the question: what exactly were the social conditions that had created such a big audience for music that fucks with your head so extensively, that appears to be 'no fun'?

Future-Shock Troops

'It's like this: some people are sharks, and some people are marks. If you can't stand the heat, get out of the kitchen. Play pussy, get fucked. Come prepared or run away scared ... You can't always count on E to shelter you from being vic'ed.'

– Breakbeat Mailing List Correspondent's riposte to other
correspondents' complaints about the loveless,
intimidating vibe at jungle events

If rave culture was a displaced form of working-class collectivity, with its 'love, peace and unity' running counter to Thatcherite social atomization, then jungle is rave music after the death of the rave ethos. Punning on the Labour history of cooperatives and friendly societies, I'd call jungle an 'unfriendly society'. Since 1993 and hardcore's slide into the twilight-zone, debates about 'where did our love go?' have convulsed the UK breakbeat community, with grim tales being related of muggings outside clubs, of fights and 'crack' vibes inside. Disenchanted ravers sloped off to form the happy hardcore scene. Others defended the demise of the euphoric vibe, arguing that jungle's atmosphere wasn't moody, it was 'serious'.

In the abscence of Ecstasy, jungle began to embrace an ideology of *real-ness* that paralleled the worldview of American hardcore rap. L. Double and Shy FX's 'The Shit', a classic 1996 roller of a jump-up tune, kicked off with a gangsta monologue: 'Yo man, there's a gang of muthafuckers out there on the dick ... Non-reality seeing, non reality feeling, non-reality-living-ass muthafuckas, man. And I don't know, man, reality, it's important to me.' In hip hop, 'real' has two meanings. First, it means authentic, uncompromised music that refuses to sell out to the music industry. 'Real' also signifies that the music reflects a 'reality' constituted by late capitalist economic instability, institutionalized racism, and increased surveillance and harassment of youth by the police. Hence tracks like T. Power's 'Police State' and Photek's neurotic 'The Hidden Camera': lyric-free critiques of a country that conducts the most intense surveillance of its own citizenry in the world (most UK city centres now have spy cameras). 'Real' means the death of the social; it means corporations who respond to increased profits not by raising pay or improving benefits but downsizing (laying off the permanent work-force in order to create a floating employment pool of part-time and freelance workers without benefits or job security).

'Real' is a neo-medieval scenario; you could compare downsizing to enclosure, where the aristocracy threw the peasants off the land and reduced them to a vagabond underclass. Like gangsta rap, jungle reflects a medieval paranoiascape of robber barons, pirate corporations, secret societies and covert operations. Hence the popularity, as a source of samples and song titles, of martial arts films and gangsta movies like *The Godfather*, *Reservoir Dogs*, *Goodfellas* and *Carlito's Way*, whose universe revolves around concepts of righteous violence and blood-honour.

Where gangsta hardstep shares the Wu-Tang Clan's neo-medieval vision of late capitalism, techstep is more influenced by dystopian sci-fi movies like *Blade Runner*, *Robocop*, *Terminator* et al, which contain a subliminally anti-capitalist message, imagining the future as a return to the Dark Ages, complete with fortress cities and bandit clans. Hence No U Turn tracks like 'The Droid' and 'Replicants', or Adam F's 'Metropolis'. 'Amtrak', another late 1996 Trace/Nico meisterwerk, pivots around the sample 'here is a group trying to accomplish one thing' – that is, '*to get into the future*'. Given the scary millennial soundscape No U Turn paint, this begs the question: why the hurry to get there? The answer: in a new Dark Age, it's the 'dark' that will come into their own. 'Dark' is where primordial energies meet digital technique, where id gets scientific. Identify with this marauding music, and you define yourself as predator not prey.

What you affiliate yourself to in techstep is the will-to-power of technology itself, the motor behind late capitalism as it rampages over human priorities and tears communities apart. The name No U Turn captures this sense that *there's no turning back*. It also has a submerged political resonance: one of Margaret Thatcher's famous boasts was 'This lady's not for turning' – her refusal to bow to pressure from liberal Tories to make a U Turn on Conservative policies like privatization and the assault on welfare. These same policies led to the catastrophic realization of another infamous Thatcher pronouncement: 'There is no such thing as society.'

The pervasive sense of slippin' into a new Dark Age, of an insidious breakdown of the social contract, generates anxieties that are repressed but resurface in unlikely ways and places. Resistance doesn't necessarily take the 'logical' form of collective activism (unions, left-wing politics); it can be so distorted and imaginatively impoverished by the conditions of capitalism itself, that it express itself as, say, the proto-fascist, anti-corporate nostalgia of America's right-wing militias, or as a sort of hyper-individualistic survivalism.

In jungle, the response is a 'realism' that accepts a socially constructed reality as 'natural'. To 'get real' is to confront a state-of-nature where dog eats dog, where you're either a winner or a loser, and where most will be losers. There's a cold rage seething in jungle, but it's expressed within the terms of an anti-capitalist yet non-socialist politics, and expressed defensively: as a determination that the underground will not be co-opted by the mainstream. 'Underground' can be understood sociologically as a metaphor for the underclass, or psychologically, as a metaphor for a fortress psyche: the survivalist self, primed and ready for combat.

Jungle's sound-world constitutes a sort of abstract social realism; when I listen to techstep, the beats sound like collapsing (new) buildings and the bass feels like the social fabric shredding. Jungle's treacherous rhythms offer its audience an education in anxiety (and anxiety, according to Freud, is an essential defence mechanism, without which you'd be vulnerable to trauma). 'It is defeat that *you* must learn to prepare for,' runs the martial arts movie sample in Source Direct's 'The Cult', a track that pioneered the post-techstep style I call 'neurofunk' (clinical and obsessively nuanced production, foreboding ambient drones, blips 'n' blurts of electronic noise, and chugging, curiously *inhibited* two-step beats that don't even sound like breakbeats anymore). Neurofunk is the fun-free culmination of jungle's strategy of 'cultural resistance': the eroticization of anxiety. Immerse yourself in the phobic, and you make dread your *element*.

The battery of sensations offered by a six hour stint at AWOL, Millennium or any 'non-intelligent' jungle club, induces a mixture of shell-shock and future-shock. Alvin Toffler defined F-shock as what happens when the human adaptive mechanism seizes up in response to an overload of stimuli, novelty, surprise. Triggering neural reflexes and fight-or-flight responses, jungle's rhythmic assault-course hypes up the listener's adaptive capability in readiness for the worst the twenty-first century has up its sleeve. If jungle is a martial artform, clubs like AWOL are church for the soul-jah and killah priest, inculcating a kind of spiritual fortitude.

All this is why going to AWOL is serious bizness, as opposed to 'fun'. Jungle is the living death of rave, the sound of living with and living through the dream's demise. Every synapse-shredding snare and cranium-cracking bass-bomb is an alarm-call saying 'Wake up, that dream is over. Time to get *real*.'

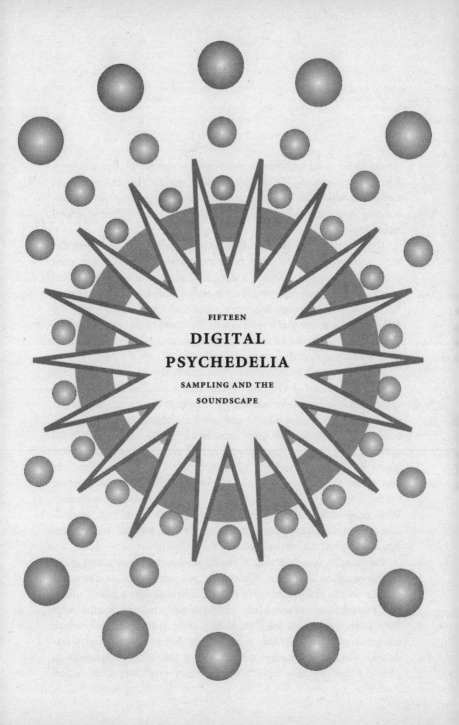

FIFTEEN

DIGITAL
PSYCHEDELIA

SAMPLING AND THE
SOUNDSCAPE

'Sampladelia' is an umbrella term covering a vast range of contemporary *hallucino-genres* – trip hop, techno, jungle, house, post-rock, swingbeat, and more. 'Sampladelic' refers to disorientating, perception-warping music created using the sampler and other forms of digital technology.

The sampler is a computer that converts sound into numbers, the zeros and ones of digital code. In its early days, the sampler was used primarily as a quote machine, a device for copying a segment of pre-recorded music and replaying it on a keyboard at any pitch or tempo. But because the sound has been converted into digital data, the information can be easily rearranged. This means the source can be disguised to the point of unrecognizability, and it opens up a near-infinite realm of sound-morphing possibilities.

At its most advanced, sampladelia drastically expands upon the recording methods developed by late sixties psychedelia. Acid rock groups departed from the 'naturalistic' model of recording (documenting the band in performance) and used multitracking, overdubbing, reversing, echo and other sonic processes to create sounds that could never be achieved by a band playing in real-time. This anti-naturalistic aspect of sampling has been intensified by recent music technology developments like 'hard disk editing', which is like having a recording studio, with a mixing desk and an array of effects, *inside* your computer. With hard disk editing (aka digital multitrack recording), sound-sources can be chopped up, stretched, treated, looped, and recombined, all within the 'virtual' space of the computer.

The sampler is not necessarily the most important instrument in the techno producer's arsenal. While some producers enthuse about the sampler as the ultimate creative tool ('the new electric guitar'), others prefer synthesizers (particularly old-fashioned analogue synths, with their knobs and dials) for their hand's on, real-time element, which requires traditional dextrous musicianship. Sampling breaks with traditional ideas of 'musicality', though, and so I'm using 'sampladelia' as general rubric for rave music's revolutionary implications: its radical break with the ideals of real-time interactive playing and natural acoustic space that still govern most music-making.

Beats + Pieces

Although the first people to use the technique – via the expensive Fairlight Computer Musical Instrument – were art rockers like Peter Gabriel and Kate Bush, the age of sampladelia really began when cheaper machines like the Emu Emulator and Ensoniq Mirage fell into the hands of rap producers. Sampling was the logical extension of the hip hop DJ's cut 'n' mix vinyl bricolage. Shifting from the block party model of the DJ-and-MC, hip hop became a studio-based art based around the producer-as-auteur and rapper-as-poet. Meanwhile, in the UK, the new cut-price samplers catalysed the 'DJ record' fad of 1987–8. Influenced by The Art of Noise, Mantronix and Steinski, artists like Coldcut, Bomb The Bass, M/A/R/R/S and S'Express created breakbeat-driven sample-collages that had hip hop's funky feel but were uptempo enough to slot into a set of house music.

Critiques of sampling focused on the regurgitative, referential nature of the practice, the gleeful disregard for conventional musical skill, and the fact that these records were brazen extravanganzas of sonic larceny. Enthusiasts promptly seized these accusations and turned them around into proof of sampling's subversiveness: its transgression of copyright, its punk-style democratization of music-making. Coldcut's 'Beats + Pieces' pre-empted and mocked the anti-sampling fogies with the sleeve slogan 'Sorry, but this just isn't music.'

By 1990, sampladelia had blossomed into a more subtle and covert aesthetic. Hip hop and rave producers increasingly eschewed blatant lifts in favour of microscopic fragments from obscure sources – partly out of a desire to be more creative, and partly because music publishers had their hawk-eyes trained on the extra royalties they could glean by prosecuting unauthorized usage of their clients' compositions. Once the sampling-as-theft notion dropped off the agenda, attitudes to the instrument split between postmodernist versus modernist. For some, the sampler is still a tool for collage, for elaborate games of Pop Art referentiality. For others, the sampler represents an easy-as-pie update of *musique concrète*'s tricky and time-consuming tape-splicing techniques. Here, digital technology functions as a crucible for sonic alchemy – the transmutation of source material into something 'new', sounds that seemingly originate from imaginary or even *unimaginable* instruments. The guiding ethos is a fierce conviction that all samples must be masked, all sources unrecognizable. Yet there's a sense in which this approach reduces the sampler to a synthesizer, and thereby misses what is truly idiomatic to the machine: taking the known and making it strange, yet still retaining an uncanny, just-recognizable trace of the original's aura.

In late nineties dance music, sampladelia mostly falls somewhere between these two poles of postmodernist referentiality and *musique concrète* re-creation. The texture of these tracks still has a touched-by-human-hand feel, but the lifts are sufficiently brief or arcane as to preclude triggering specific pop-cultural associations in the listener. The model of creativity here is seventies jazz fusion; not only is the ideology borrowed from that period, but so are most of the samples. A lot of trip hop and jungle is basically fusion on the cheap: instead of a band jamming together, the producer is like a band-leader deftly arranging the expert playing of musicians from different genres and eras.

Trip hopper Howie B, for instance, described his track 'Martian Economics' as a 'collaboration . . . like me doing a tune with [keyboard legend] Jimmy Smith, even though he wasn't there.' For Howie B and similar artists like Beck and DJ Shadow, part of the creative process is the pre-production research of going on record buying sprees, then sifting through hundreds of hours of music for suitable samples. 'I'll take anything, it can be as small as a triangle hit, and I'll spread it across a [sampling] keyboard and turn it into a tuned piano,' says Howie B. 'I'll take a Latin timbale recorded in 1932 and make it into a percussion pattern, or snatch some vocal and take it four octaves down until it's a lion's roar.'

The Body Electric

Although it can be performed live, techno is rarely *born* in real-time. Rather, electronic music is programmed and assembled sequence by sequence, layer by layer. Even the separate constituents of a track, like keyboard riffs and arpeggios, don't necessarily come into being as a discrete musical event. Step-writing, a technique whereby sequences are written on the computer screen, allows for the note-by-note construction of complicated riffs that are often beyond the real-time capababilities of even the most dextrous keyboardist. Not only does this make it easy to correct errors and add nuances, but sequences can be rearranged, run backwards and generally fucked around with on a trial-and-error basis. Furthermore, the same basic riff-pattern can be played in any 'color', with the musicians free to choose from a vast sonic palette of synthesized instruments and self-invented sampladelic timbres.

On the surface, this would appear to be a radical break with the spontaneism of rock 'n' roll. In truth, from very early on in the music's history, rock bands used studio technology to correct mistakes and overdub extra instrumental parts, if only to make the records sound as densely vibrant as the live band. In *Rhythm and Noise: An Aesthetics of Rock*, Theodore Gracyk argues that it is precisely rock's interest in phonography (the art of recording) that separates it from folk and jazz, where records are usually documents of a performance. In folk and jazz, it is respectively the song and the improvisation that count; in rock, the record is the basic unit of musical meaning. In this respect, hip hop and techno represent the apotheosis of rock's interest in sound-in-itself (timbre, effects) and virtual space (unrealistic acoustics).

Gracyk points out that even at the primal origin of rock 'n' roll – the Sun Sessions – studio artifice was involved, in the famous echo that Sam Philips slapped on Presley's voice. The brilliance of late sixties psychedelia derives from the way artists like The Beatles, Jimi Hendrix and Pink Floyd combined gritty 'feel' (live, interactive playing between a seasoned band) and the fantastical (hallucinatory effects, ultra-vivid timbres, an artificial sense of space conjured using echo and reverb). Digital music abandons all those elements of 'feel': the inflections and supple rhythmic interplay that communicate the fact that flesh-and-blood humans physically shaped this sound together in a real acoustic space. But by way of recompense, it dramatically intensifies the *trompe l'oreille* side of psychedelia: its fictitious psycho-acoustic space, its timbres and textures and sound-shapes to which no ready real-world referents attach themselves. At its most inventive, sampladelia lures the listener into a soundworld honeycombed with chambers that each have their own acoustics. This music is 'like walking through a maze whose walls rearrange themselves with every step you take' (James Gleick's description in *Chaos: Making a New Science* of fractal theory's non-linear equations).

If rock phonography uses multiple takes and overdubs to create a quasi-event, something that never 'happened', what you hear on record usually sounds *plausible* as a real-time occurrence. Sampladelia goes further: it layers and concatenates musical fragments from different eras, genres and places to create a timewarping pseudo-event, something that could never possibly have happened. Different acoustic spaces and recording 'auras' are forced into uncanny adjacence. You could call it 'deconstruction of the metaphysics of presence'; you could also call it 'magic'. It's a kind of time travel, or seance: a conference call colloquy between ghosts-in-the-sampling-machine.

Sampladelia is zombie music: dead sound reanimated like the *zombi* – a Haitian corpse brought back to robot-like half-life by a voodoo sorcerer, then used as a slave. Disembodied beats, licks, cries and riffs – born of human breath and sweat – are vivisected from their original musical context and then literally *galvanized*, in its original meaning; when electricity was first discovered, physicians would electrocute cadavers to make their limbs and facial muscles twitch, for the public's ghoulish delectation. Early hip-hop sampling was like Frankenstein's monster, funk-limbs crudely bolted together, the stitching clearly audible. With its quasi-organic seamlessness, today's sampladelia is more like the *chimera*, that mythical monster composed of the parts of different animals. Its chimerical quality parallels digital video effects like morphing, where faces blend into each other imperceptibly, and human bodies distend and mutate like Hanna-Barbera animations.

In their jeremiad *Data Trash: The Theory of the Virtual Class*, Arthur Kroker and Michael Weinstein warn that the 'archivalism' of cyber-culture is hatching 'monstrous hybrids', that 'archived body parts are disguised in the binary functionality of data and pooled into larger circulatory flows'. This could be a description of the process of converting the vinyl-encoded musical energy of flesh-and-blood musicians into the zeros-and-ones of binary code, which is then disseminated as currency throughout contemporary pop culture. 'Ours is a time of non-history that is super-charged by the spectacular flame-out of the detritus of the bounded energy of local histories': this is the *fin de millennium* sampladelic supernova, where the last eighty years of pan-global recorded sound is decontextualized, deracinated, and utterly etherealized.

Ghosts in the Machine

In *The Third Wave*, Alvin Toffler wrote of 'blip culture', where 'we are all besieged and blitzed by fragments of imagery, contradictory or unrelated, that shake up our old ideas and come shooting at us in the form of broken or disembodied "blips"'. Sampladelia can be seen as a new kind of realism that reflects the fact that the late twentieth-century mediascape has become our new Nature; it can be diagnosed as a symptom of, but also an attempt to master and reintegrate, the promiscuous chaos and babbling heteroglossia of the information society.

But sampladelia may also be prophetic, offering hints of future forms of human identity and social organization. Cyber-theorist Arthur Kroker confronts the prospect of 'digital recombinant' culture with a weird mix of manic glee and dystopian gloom. In *Spasm: Virtual Reality, Android Music, Electric Flesh*, he hails sample-based music as the cutting edge of consciousness, a preview of post-human life in the age of virtual reality. 'Just like virtual sound-objects in sampler music technology, subjectivity today is a gaseous element, expanding and contracting, time-stretched, cross-faded, and sound-accelerated.'

Kroker's belief in music as *portent* is shared by Jacques Attali, author of *Noise: The Political Economy of Music*. Attali traces a history in which each stage of music-making is a 'foretoken' of future social transformations. Music begins as sacred noise, the accompaniment to sacrificial ritual, a bacchanalian clamour in whose creation everybody participates. The next stage is the age of Representation, where music-making is the preserve of specialists (composers, professional musicians), and takes place at special events that have a symbolic, socially stabilizing function. The modern age is characterized by Repetition: the mass-mediated circulation of music-commodities (records). Reified as product, tarnished by everyday currency, and 'stockpiled' by isolated collectors, music loses its magical aura. Individuals in the twentieth century are exposed to more music in a month than someone in the seventeenth century heard in a lifetime, but its meaning is increasingly impoverished.

The fourth era of music is the age of Composition: 'a music produced by each individual for himself, for pleasure outside of meaning, usage and exchange'. Attali is vague about what this music would sound like. *Noise* was published in 1977; subsequent commentators have argued that punk's do-it-yourself creed fits Attali's criteria, while others have suggested free jazz. The Karaoke craze, where the consumer displaces the star vocalist, could be seen as industry-sponsored, top-down attempt to involve the listener; other future half-measures will involve playback equipment that allows you to remix tracks (a form of music-customization already approached by some CD-ROMs).

Lo-fi rock and electronic dance are the two contemporary genres that come closest to Attali's notion of 'composition'. Both are usually created in home-studios and are either self-released or put out by tiny independent labels, in small pressings sometimes as low as 200; both reach the public via marginal distribution networks and specialist retailers. And both are marginal scenes appealing to audiences who pride themselves on being more than 'mere' consumers. In lo-fi, a high proportion of the audience are in bands, while in dance music there's a high ratio of DJs (professional and amateur) to punters.

DJ culture represents that threshold stage at which repetition morphs into composition. DJs are chronic consumerists and collectors, who nonetheless use their stockpiling expertise as the basis for composition in its literal sense, 'putting together'. They create a metamusical flow by juxtaposition and segue. As an extension of DJ cut 'n' mix, sample-based music at its best is fully fledged composition: the creation of new music out of shards of reified sound, an alchemical liberation of the magic trapped inside dead commodities. Attali claims that the age of Composition will be characterized by a return to music's ancient sacred function. DJ cultures fit the bill; surrounded by ritualized festivity, they emphasize participation and the democratization of noise (ravers blowing their whistles and horns rhythmically).

If music *is* prophecy, as Attali contends, what kind of social organization or disorganization is heralded by dance music? The transformation of music into a mass-marketed commodity (sheet music, records) anticipated the late twentieth-century triumph of what the Situationists called 'the spectacular-commodity society' (with its alienated, passive consumer/spectators). Rave culture's decentred networks – cottage industries, micro-media, temporary one-off gatherings – may herald some post-corporate hetero-topia of the late twenty-first century. Then again, sampladelia might equally be a component of a Krokerite dystopia of 'cold seduction': 'a cool hallucinatory culture of special effects personalities moving at warp speed to nowhere,' a virtual-reality pleasuredome where the self is a will-o'-the-wisp buffeted by 'ceaseless movement in the eddies of cultural matter.'

Slaved to the Rhythm

Critiques of digital music usually focus on the fact that, despite the rhetoric of 'infinite possibilities' that surrounds it, most music made on computers sounds awful samey. Some of the acutest criticisms have come from Brian Eno. Although he pioneered many of the techniques taken up by sampladelia – loops, found sounds, the obsession with timbre, the creation of 'fictional psycho-acoustic space' – Eno is disenchanted with almost all the music currently made using computer technology. Speaking to *Wired* magazine, he complained that digital, sequenced music had merely resurrected many of the inherent limitations of classical orchestral music, with its hierarchical ranking of instruments in the mix, its rigid sense of pitch and its locked rhythms tied to the conductor/timekeeper. 'Classical music is music without Africa,' he complained, adding later, 'the problem with computers is that there is not enough Africa in them . . . A nerd is a human being without enough Africa in him or her.'

In a later interview with *Request*, Eno looked to African percussion music – which is based not just around polyrhythm, as is much rock and dance music, but around multi-tiered metres that coexist in a sort of loose interdependence – as a model of liberation. 'I like different layers to be going on simultaneously and not to necessarily be locked . . . what I like is when they sometimes lock, so there's this dramatic moment when all of those things suddenly come together, then they drift again.' Africa's poly-metric perversity has a utopian, democratic charge for Eno. By comparison, house and techno producers are 'slaves to their machines, just as most of us are slaves to [the machines we use] . . . This is a music that's particularly enslaved . . .'

This politically charged analogy – Africa versus slavery – is ironic, since it is part of the terminology of computer-based music, where instruments are 'slaved' to MIDI (Musical Instrument Digital Interface), the timekeeper machine which triggers all the different sequences and keeps them in synch. As pop culture theorist Andrew Goodwin has pointed out, this sort of critique of musical standardization echoes the notions of anti-capitalist thinkers like Theodor Adorno, who characterized the products of the pop culture industry in terms of 'part-interchangeability' and 'pseudo-individuation': superficial novelty within rigid formats (in pop terms, think 4/4 metre and verse/chorus/middle-eight structure). MIDI and other digital technologies promise infinite potential for individual expression, but only within the parameters of a rigidly structured matrix for organizing sound.

'Part-interchangeability' certainly applies to the bulk of dance music, in so far as most producers operate rather like the car-freaks who cannibalize auto parts, hot-rod their engines, and customize the vehicle's body in order to personalize the mass-produced. Similarly, dance producers build souped-up rhythm-engines using an often rather restricted repertoire of components, derived from sample CDs or sound-modules which contain hundreds of breakbeats, a cappellas, synth-patches, etc. Although the sampler does indeed offer 'infinite possibilities' for resequencing and warping these samples, most dance producers are constrained by the funktionalist criteria of their specific genre. Tracks are designed as material for the DJ to *work* into a set, and so must conform in tempo and mood. Creativity in dance music involves a balancing act between making your tracks both 'music *and* mixable' (as Goldie put it). Simon Frith points out that one of the defining qualities of digital music is the sense that this music 'is never finished and . . . never really integrated' as a composition. It is precisely this 'unfinished' aspect – the sockets, as it were – that enable the DJ to plug tracks into the mix-scape.

Reinventing the Machine

'The street tries to find its own uses for things.'
– William Gibson, *Count Zero*

More than in any other genre, electronic musicians articulate what they do in terms of their tools. Ironically, despite this technophile rhetoric, the most radical electronic dance music is often made with relatively low-level equipment and outmoded machinery; the Roland TB 303, source of the acid-house bass, and Roland's 808 and 909 drum machines are prime examples of the way in which techno musicians find new possibilities in obsolete and discontinued gear. State-of-the-art, top-of-the-range equipment is more likely to be found in expensive recording studios, where it's used in the production of conventional-sounding pop and rock. Indeed, the most widespread use of sampling is pretty prosaic: it's a means of cutting corners and costs, a way of procuring 'authentic' instrumental colours without hiring session musicians or of 'saving' a good sound without having to go through the bother of, say, repeatedly miking up the drums in a particular way. Generally, there's more space-age technology involved in the making of MOR shlock like Celine Dion than in tracks by avowed futurists like Jeff Mills.

The picture is further complicated by the fact that techno artists sometimes have a confused idea of what constitutes 'progress' for electronic music. Too often, this is conceived in terms of 'musicality'. Within the terms of genres like house or jungle, 'innovation' or 'maturity' for the genre can involve steps that, from an external avant-garde perspective, seem regressive: a move away from noise-and-rhythm minimalism towards greater harmonic/melodic complexity; 'organic', quasi-acoustic textures; highly finessed arrangements and the incorporation of 'live' vocals or 'real' musicianship.

Self-consciously 'progressive' dance music has an unfortunate tendency to repeat the mistakes of progressive rockers like ELP, Genesis, Jethro Tull et al, who sought to legitimate rock by aping the grandiosity of nineteenth-century classical music. The results, in both prog rock and prog dance, are bloated song-cycles and concept albums, ostentatious musicianship, a prissy obsession with production values. Just as the truly 'progressive' bands of the late sixties and early seventies had more in common with twentieth-century avant-classical composers (electro-acoustic, *musique concrète*, the New York school of drone-minimalism), similarly the truly radical sampladelic artists are engaged in *expanding* our notions of what 'music' can be. This involves the exploration of timbre, chromatics and 'noise-sound', the prioritizing of rhythm and repetition over melodic/harmonic development, and the elaboration of virtual space using the studio-as-instrument.

How does this project relate to technology? I believe that this music's cutting edge *is* tied to its technological underpinnings. Firstly, it's about finding out what a new piece of equipment facilitates that wasn't previously possible or even thinkable. This involves locating and exploiting potentials in the new machines that the manufacturers never intended. A frequent claim that you hear from techno producers is that the first thing they do when they've acquired a new machine is to

throw away the manual and start messing around, blithely indifferent
to the manufacturer's helpful hints. Above all, the truly progressive
edge in electronic music involves doing things that can't be physically
achieved by human beings manipulating instruments in real-time.
Rather than using techniques like step-writing to mimic traditional
ideas of musicianship (frilly arpeggios, solo-istic meanderings), it's
about inventing a new kind of posthuman virtuosity. A prime example
is the way jungle producers use sampling and sequencing software to
create fantastically complex breakbeat rhythms that are too fast and
convoluted for a human drummer to achieve, yet still retain an eerie
'feel'.

Techno-phobes often argue that electronic dance music rapidly
becomes dated because it is so tied to the state-of-the-art technology
of the day, making 'timeless art' an impossible goal. But rock and pop
are equally susceptible to being trapped in time, because of the vogues
for particular production styles and effects. These 'period sounds' are
often alluring precisely for their nostalgic charm or the way they
capture a specific pop Zeitgeist. At various points in rock history, the
leading edge of music involves a strategic retreat from the state-of-the-
art towards more limited technological set-ups. Examples include
1968's retreat from 1967's psychedelic studio excesses to a more gritty,
blues-and-country influenced sound; grunge's rejection of eighties
rock's crystal-clear production in favour of the muddy naturalism of
early seventies heavy rock; lo-fi's fetish for four track recording and
distortion. As techno has become more self-conscious about its own
history, it has staged periodic returns to period sounds, like the Roland
303, or electro's gauchely futuristic textures and stiff, geometric drum
machine beats.

Songs Versus Soundscapes

Just as they are sometimes overdeferential towards conventional
notions of musicality, techno artists often talk about what they do in
the seemingly inappropriate language of traditional humanist art –
'expression', 'soul', 'authenticity', 'depth'. This 'false consciousness' can
be attributed partly to timelag (discourse failing to keep pace with
technology), partly to the industry/media's need for singular auteur-

geniuses (as opposed to the collective creativity of scenes, with their anonymous flows of ideas), and partly as an attempt to contradict those critics who denigrate techno as cold, inhuman machine-music.

The truth lies somewhere between these two poles of expressive subjectivity and objective functionalism. Even when s/he is trying to express feelings, rather than simply make something (some *thing*) that works on the dancefloor, the techno auteur is not present in the art work in the way that the singer/songwriter can be said to be present in rock. For rock critics, the Song is a mini-novel, a story (either personal confession or character study). As instrumental music, techno is closer to the plastic arts or architecture than literature, in that it involves the creation of an imaginary environment.

The material with which the techno auteur works – timbre/texture, rhythm and space – are precisely those elements that rock criticism ignores in favour of meaning, which is extracted almost exclusively from close study of lyrics and persona. Rock critics use techniques borrowed from literary criticism or sociology to *interpret* rock in terms of the singer's biography/neurosis, or the music's social relevance. Devoid of text, dance music and ambient are better understood using metaphors from the visual arts: 'the soundscape', 'aural decor', 'a soundtrack for an imaginary movie', 'audio-sculpture'.

But these metaphors aren't really satisfactory either, since they tend towards the static (fine for ambient, but not for dance music). Dance music happens through time (it *moves*) and it's kinaesthetic (it makes *you* move). Dance tracks are less about 'communication' in the rock sense and more like engines for 'the programming of sensations' (Susan Sontag). Triggering motor/muscular reflexes and recalibrating your body, the rhythms and textures of jungle, trance, garage, etc., each make you move through the world in a different way.

Of course, rock is also rich with non-verbal elements; a hefty proportion of its pleasure and power reside in the sound, the groove, the riff. Nonetheless, critics continue to discuss rock as a series of stories or statements. Because it isn't figurative (it gets rid of both the singer and the persona/character in the song), dance music intensifies the non-referential but deeply evocative/provocative aspects at work in all forms of music – the very stuff that criticism can't *handle* (in both senses of the word). From the text-biased vantage of rock criticism, dance music is troubling precisely because it seems to be all materiality and no meaning. Entirely an appeal to the body and the senses, it offers no food for thought. Mere ear-candy, it gives you an 'empty' sugar-rush.

In this respect, techno and house exacerbate the original sins of disco, which was dissed by rock fans and crits as superficial and lyrically trite. Rave music completes the trajectory began by disco when it depersonalized the vocal mannerisms of funk and soul. In techno and house, vocals are either eliminated or survive mostly as soul-diva samples, which are diced, processed, and moulded like some ecto-plasmic substance. Rave music doesn't so much abolish 'soul' as disperse it across the entire field of sound. This is music that's all erogenous surface and no depth, 'skin' without 'heart'.

The Imagineer

Sampladelic dance music also problematizes standard notions about creativity and authorship in pop music. Not only is the Romantic figure of the Creator displaced by the less glamorous curator (the DJ-turned-producer), but the lines between art and craft, inspiration and technique, are blurred. Once, it was possible to distinguish between music and its production, between the song and the recording tricks with which it's embellished. But with dance tracks, the music *is* the production. Increasingly, the figure of the producer blurs with the engineer, traditionally regarded as a mere technician who facilitates the sonic ideas and aspirations of band and producer. In most dance music, though, it's the timbre and penetration of a bass-tone, the sensuous feel of a sample-texture, the gait of a drum-loop, that's the real hook, not the sequence of notes that constitutes 'the melody'.

All this has ignited a hotbed of fiercely contested questions about publishing credits and payment. Where do you draw the line between producer/engineer and composer? The rise of figures like Rob Playford (Goldie's partner), Howie B, Nico Sykes of No U Turn, is proof that we need to start thinking of the engineer as poet, as weaver-of-dreams. Once 'creativity' and 'composition' have been reconceptualized in this way, the history of rock suddenly looks different. Why does the law say that you can't copyright a beat or a sound? Why did Mick Jagger and Keith Richards get the publishing credit and royalties for 'Satisfaction', when it's Charlie Watts's drum part that provides the song's killer hook? We might start to rethink James Brown as simultaneously the CEO and the public trademark of a funk corporation, an early seventies polyrhythm-factory churning out breakbeats, B-lines, horn-stabs and rhythm-guitar tics – quality components of such machine-tooled durability they're still being cannabilized by engineer/producers in rap and jungle today. Instead of J. B.'s ponderous ballads and portentous Soul Statesmanship, we might consider his greatest contribution to *this* legacy to be his sex-machine repertoire of hyper-syncopated vocal grunts and gasps.

Special Effects

The problems that rock critics have with dance music are reminiscent of the hostile incomprehension with which highbrow cineastes greet certain sorts of genre movie like science fiction and horror. Cinephiles vainly search these movies for what they valourize: great acting, sparkling dialogue, character development, a non-corny plot, and meaning (insight into the human condition, social resonance). Ironically, these are values that pertain more to literary or theatrical drama, than to the cinematic *per se.*

But these elements of narrative and character are present in genre movies as mere formality, a structural framework for the purely cinematic: the *retinal intensities* of ultra-violent action, special effects, and (in sci-fi movies) futuristic *mise-en-scène* and decor. Here, the true filmic poets are set designers like H. R. Giger (*Alien*) and effects-engineers like Douglas Trumbull (*2001: A Space Odyssey, Close Encounters, Blade Runner*). With their emphasis on the sheerly spectacular and sensational, science-fiction and horror flicks simply take after their literary sources. In William Gibson's novels, what you read for are his prose-poem evocations of cyberspace as a *techno-sublime*, not the hackneyed dialogue.

If techno can be thought of in this way (the track as a framework for the display of special effects and processing), what, then, constitutes the 'sublime' in techno? The answer is *sound-in-itself*. 'If I can't create a sound that I like, I find it very hard to create a song,' Kevin Saunderson told *Music Technology* magazine in 1988. 'I get inspired by a good sound ... it gives me a feeling for a rhythm or a melody. The sound's the most important thing.' In most music, timbre and 'chromatics' are the medium, the pigment as it were, through which the important thing – the melody, the emotional meaning – is expressed. In techno, melody is merely an implement or ruse for the displaying of texture/timbre/sound-matter. This is why most rave music shuns complicated melody-lines in favour of riffs, vamps and ostinatos (short motifs repeated persistently at the same pitch throughout the composition). In the ultra-minimalist 'tech-house' of the Basic Channel and Chain Reaction labels, simple riffs serve to twist and crinkle the sound-fabric in order to best show off its properties; what you thrill to is the scintillating play of 'light' as it creases and folds, crumples and kinks.

The Now-Machine

'The richer the sensory interface, the more reduced is the function of narrative.'

– Scott Bukatman on video games, *Terminal Identity*

Basic Channel and Chain Reaction tracks have a curious quality: listening to them is sublime, but afterwards it's hard to retain anything but the faintest flavour of the experience. Bar the odd bassline, there's nothing you can hum to yourself. This is because the tracks are all percussion and timbre, the two elements of music that are hardest to memorize. In *Rhythm and Noise*, Gracyk points out that our memory of chromatics (timbre/texture in music, colour in painting) fades faster than our memory of pitch and line. Similarly, timbre and space cannot be notated on a score. Yet it's these amnesiac, ineffable, untranscribable elements in music that are the most bliss-rich.

In *The Pleasures of The Text*, Roland Barthes argues that 'criticism is always historical or prospective . . . the presentation of bliss is forbidden it: its preferred material is culture, which is everything in us except our present'. Timbre, rhythm, space: these elements in music are all related to sensuously overwhelming immediacy. They are the *now-intensive* elements in rock and in techno. Rock began the work that techno completed: accentuating rhythm, elevating timbre (distortion, effects, grain-of-the-voice), opening up dub-space. Structurally, rock and techno both fit theorist Andrew Chester's notion of *intensional* music (complexity achieved through modulation and inflection of simple melodic units, as in African music), as opposed to the *extensional* structures of Western classical music (theme and variations, crisis and resolution).

Techno and house create a subtly different form of heightened immediacy to African music – a sort of *future-now*. (This is an effect of the music's reliance on the vamp – originally a brief introductory passage repeated several times before a solo or verse in order to whip up anticipation, but in techno sometimes making up the whole body of the track.) Timbre-saturated, repetitive but tilted always to the *next now*, techno is an immediacy-machine, stretching time into a continuous present. Which is where the drug/technology interface comes into play. Not just because techno works well with substances like MDMA, marijuana, LSD, speed, etc., which all amplify the sensory intensity of the present moment. But because the music itself *drugs* the listener, looping consciousness then derailing it, stranding it in a nowhere/nowhen, where there is only sensation, '*where now lasts longer*'.

SIXTEEN

FUCK DANCE, LET'S ART

THE POST-RAVE
EXPERIMENTAL
FRINGE

'All the people I know make music in their bedrooms, and it's more personal because you're not thinking about clubs. When I go to a studio, I see people working with the specific intention to make people dance. But working in your bedroom, it's more like art.'

– Luke Vibert (Wagon Christ/Plug)

By the end of 1995, a new zone of music-making had emerged out of the ruins of 'electronic listening music': a sort of post-rave omni-genre wherein techno's purity was 'contaminated' by an influx of ideas from jungle, trip hop, all over. Not particularly danceable, yet too restlessly rhythmic and texturally startling to be ambient chill-out, this music might be dubbed art-tekno, since the only appropriate listener response is a sort of fascinated contemplation. Imagine a museum dedicated not to the past but the future, where you marvel at the bizarre audio-sculptures, let your ears wander through the sound-installations, and boggle at the noise contraptions as they go about their pointless, captivating tasks.

One of the earliest events dedicated to this new omni-genre, the Electronic Lounge, was actually situated in the bar at an art gallery, London's ICA (Institute for Contemporary Arts). Other audio-salons opened in artists' studios (New York's Soundlab), or in pub basements (London's The Rumpus Room); some evolved out of the old chill-out side-rooms at clubs and raves. Dubbed 'freestyle', 'eclectro' and, in New York, 'illbient', these events were dedicated to the astounding, near-heretical notion that you might get a series of DJs playing different styles of music during one night, or even DJs who mixed up different genres/tempos in a single set (typically, a melange of trip hop, E-Z listening, soundtrack music, mellow drum and bass and nouveau electro).

These clubs were a response to the emergence of a new post-rave/post-rap/post-rock perimeter-zone where refugees, fleeing the shackles of genre and the constraining expectations of scene, gathered to trade ideas. This circuit of home-studio, bedroom boffins includes Mike Paradinas (μ-Ziq/Jake Slazenger), Bedouin Ascent, Scanner, David Toop, Patrick Pulsinger, Matthew Herbert (Wishmountain/Dr Rockit), Mouse On Mars, Squarepusher, Luke Vibert (Wagon Christ/Plug), plus former avant-rock musicians like Kevin Martin (Techno-Animal/The Sidewinder/The Bug) and Mark Clifford (Seefeel/Disjecta). Alongside eyecatching, exquisitely packaged, collector-fetish singles and EPs – released by labels like Clear, Sahko, Cheap, Sabotage, Leaf – the prime format for art-tekno is the compilation, as with Lo Recordings' *Extreme Possibilities* and *United Mutations* series, or the Kevin Martin compiled *Macro Dub Infection* anthologies.

How is this new post-rave/post-everything music different from Warp's electronic listening music? The latter was always limited by its neo-Detroit purism (no breakbeats), plus the perennial 'progressive' anti-dance stance. As a result, 'intelligent techno was definitely rather anaemic on the rhythmic side', as Kingsuk Biswas of Bedouin Ascent put it. In 1995, jungle's polyrhythmic exuberance gave techno a hefty and sorely needed kick up the arse, forcing it to liven up its ideas about rhythm. Richard James, for instance, responded with the inspired breakbeat tomfoolery of AFX's 'Hangable Auto Bulb' EPs and Aphex Twin's 'Girl/Boy' EP.

This renewed interest in percussive complexity remains oddly cerebral in cast, though. In freestyle salons, headnodding rather than bootyshaking is the order of the day, and there's no drug factor, just beer and an occasional, discreet spliff. This is a mostly bourgeois-bohemian milieu of rootless cosmopolitans, rather than a hardcore dance scene. In the structural sense of the word, as opposed to its pejorative meaning, the post-rave experimental fringe is *parasitic* on drug-and-dance driven scenes, hijacking their ideas and giving them an avant-garde twist.

Take the mini-genre of jungle by non-junglists for non-junglists – AFX, Plug, Witchman, Squarepusher – that is sometimes jocularly referred to as 'drill and bass', because the breakbeats are so sped up they sound like Woody Woodpecker on PCP. Because these producers don't belong to the drum and bass community, they're free to take the idiomatic features of jungle – fucked-up breakbeats, mutant bass, sampladelic collage – and exacerbate them way beyond any conceivable use-value to DJ or dancer. Not only are the beats so convoluted and body-baffling they'd clear any dancefloor instantly, but the Dada absurdism of the samples creates a mood of whimsy that doesn't fit either of the two moods the jungle community demands: genteel and smooth-rollin' at 'intelligent' clubs, menacing 'n' mashed-up at hard-steppin' joints.

So AFX's 'Children Talking' pivots around daft soundbites of a little kid talking about 'mashed potatoes', while on Aphex Twin's 'Milk Man', Richard James actually sings a wistful ditty in the persona of a small boy who wishes he could get milk 'from the milkman's wife's tits'. And on Squarepusher's *Feed Me Weird Things* and *Hard Normal Daddy*, Tom Jenkinson replaces jungle's booming low-end with twiddly fretless slap-bass, played by himself *à la* fusioneer Jaco Pastorius. The most quirked-out examples from this quasi-jungle genre are Luke Vibert's first two Plug EPs *Visible Crater Funk* and *Rebuilt Kev*. Here jungle's breakbeat-science gets warped into Heath Robinson/Professor Brainstorm-style mad inventor mayhem. Plug tracks resemble cranked-up, cantankerous contraptions gone haywire; their grotesquely contorted polyrhythms will tie your limbs in knots if you're fool enough to dance. Needless to say, the reaction from the junglist community has been muted.

Twisted Science

A stylistic nomad, Luke Vibert is a prime exponent of the post-everything omni-genre. After the glacial ambience of his Wagon Christ 1994 debut *Phat Lab Nightmare*, Vibert veered off into cheesy-but-deranged trip hop with *Throbbing Pouch*. Over moonwalking mid-tempo breakbeats and bulbous bass, Vibert wafts a pungent fug of samples: keening strings, jazz-fusion woodwinds, E-Z listening orchestration, film-*noir* incidental themes, Moog synth, vibes, slap-bass, owl hoots, doowop harmonies, android vocals, etc. Vibert has an alchemist's approach to sampling. It's all about 'getting good sounds out of absolute shit. I listen to piles of cheesy records. For some reason I tend to only sample stuff I don't like!'

At times, *Throbbing Pouch*'s effect is like you're drowning and the entirety of late twentieth-century music is flashing before your ears, garbled and grotesquely intermingled. 'Phase Everyday' flits from jazz-funk nonchalance to acid-house pulserama to dubbed-up desolation within the space of a minute. Tracks like 'Down Under' and 'Scrapes' are animated audio-mazes, sonic labyrinths that mutate through time as well as elaborate through space, and whose honeycomb chambers and corridors seem alive with detail. Where most trip hop demands a prone attitude of stoned passivity from its listener, Wagon Christ music *stones you*. This is blunted music with an edge.

On the subject of drugs, Vibert once told *The Wire*: 'They're my best mate, they changed the way I heard everything.' 'Actually, I said "hash is my best mate"!', Luke told me. 'That's not true anymore, but originally it did open my mind to different sorts of music, 'cos I was a bit narrow-minded. Smoking went hand in hand with getting into dub and funk.' If marijuana is one reason Vibert's work is so disorientating, another is the queasy fluctuation of pitch he often employs, making the Wagon Christ material sound like a cross between Schoenberg and jazz-funk. Luke uses a feature on his sampler that allows him to modulate pitch and explore fractions of a tone, echoing the 'microtonality' of avant-classical composition and much non-Western musics, like Indian ragas. Hip hop often has that smeared-pitch, detuned quality too, because, Luke explained, 'when you put samples together, they're usually not going to be in tune. If you get them synched up time-wise, they're almost always off-key. And that's a wicked effect – the samples sort of gnaw at each other!'

Kinder-Tekno

Sometimes the world of post-rave electronica resembles nothing so much as a kindergarten, full of little boys daubing texture-goo on the walls and moulding sample-stuff like Play-Doh. Nobody better fits the metaphor of art-tekno as an 'adventure playground for the imagination' than German duo Mouse On Mars. Andi Toma and Jan St Werner met in a health-food store when they both got embroiled in an argument over who should get the last packet of muesli. They decided to share it. Then they discovered they both made music, and decided to share sounds, setting off an adventure that has resulted in some of the most captivating, enchanted-with-itself electronica around.

Mouse On Mars are as much a post-rock band as a post-techno outfit; they are influenced more by Can, Neu! and the Beach Boys ('Die Seele Von Brian Wilson' sampled a fragment of lunatic doo-wop from 'Wind Chimes') than by Kraftwerk. 'When we play live, sometimes people don't even realize we're an electronic band,' claimed Andi. 'We use guitars, which we put through effects and try to make fit harmonically with the sequenced and sampled elements.'

The title of Mouse On Mars's 1994 debut *Vulvaland* sounds risqué, but it couldn't be more innocent: it was inspired by an imaginary island in the German kids' TV marionette-show *Ausenberger Puppentiste*. 'It's called Lummerland,' Jan told me, 'but we adapted it to Vulvaland. That's our idea of a utopia that's here and now, not in the future where you can't reach it. Everyone has their own kind of Vulvaland where they like to go.' With the second album *Iahora Tahiti*, 'It's like we've left Vulvaland and are now ready for adventures. *Iahora Tahiti* could be a pirate cry – "We conquer Tahiti!"'

Ensconced in their studio-playpen, Andi and Jan treat their machines like playmates. 'We don't like to control them,' Andi told me. 'We trust them, let them do their own thing. If the computer goes mad because there's a thunderstorm coming and too much static in the air, and it makes a strange noise, we are very happy to use it. The machines have maximum freedom, the people have maximum freedom; they should care for each other.' Mouse On Mars music is built up from multiple layers of exquisitely naïve, music-box melodies. 'I like music-boxes a lot,' says Jan. 'It's magical – like someone smiling really strangely. I always get, how you say, a goose-skin? Goosepimples!' The duo prefer simple melodies because they don't distract from the pair's real priority, 'the melody of sound': succulent, stroke-able textures, timbres so tantalizing you want to taste or touch them, a whole palette of glow-tones and chime-colours.

Rhizomatic Renegades

In the late nineties, the German-speaking world has emerged as a bastion of post-everything experimentalism. In Austria, there's the abstract hip hop of Patrick Pulsinger and Erdum Tunakan's Cheap label, and the twisted neo-electro of Sabotage (both a label and a sort of art-terrorist collective). In Germany, Cologne and its neighbour Dusseldorf form a closeknit art-tekno/post-rock milieu that encompasses Mike Ink, Dr Walker, Pluramon, To Rococo Rot, Mouse On Mars and Jan St Werner's side project Microstoria. On a less avant-garde and more cyberpunk tip, Berlin has spawned the anti-rave scene called

Digital Hardcore. Finally there's Frankfurt, home to Mille Plateaux and its sister labels Force Inc, Riot Beats and Chrome.

Frankfurt is simultaneously Germany's financial capital and a longstanding centre of anti-capitalist theory, thanks to the famous 'Frankfurt School' (Walter Benjamin, Theodor Adorno, Max Horkheimer et al). Today, the Frankfurt School is mostly remembered for its neo-Marxist/high Modernist disdain for popular culture as the twentieth-century's opiate-of-the-people. Adorno is regularly used as an Aunt Sally figure by cultural studies academics as a prequel to their semiotic readings of 'anti-hegemonic resistance' encoded in Madonna videos. While there's no denying Adorno deserves derision for his infamously suspect comments about the 'eunuch-like sound' of jazz (whose secret message was 'give up your masculinity, let yourself be castrated'), his critique of pop culture's role as safety valve and social control is not so easily shrugged off. His verdict on the swing-jazz inspired frenzies of the jitterbug – 'merely to be carried away by anything at all, to have something of their own, compensates for their impoverished and barren existence' – could easily be transposed to nineties rave culture, which – from happy hardcore to gabba to Goa trance – is now rigidly ritualized and conservative.

Mille Plateaux shares something of the Frankfurt School's oppositional attitude to mass culture. For label boss Achim Szepanski, Germany's rave industry – which dominates the pop mainstream – is so institutionalized and regulated it verges on the totalitarian. Named after Gilles Deleuze and Felix Guattari's *A Thousand Plateaus: Capitalism and Schizophrenia* (a colossal tome that Foucault hailed as 'an introduction to the non-fascist life'), Mille Plateaux release deconstruction techno. Situating their activity both within and against the genre conventions of post-rave styles like electronica, house, jungle and trip hop, Mille Plateaux point out these musics' premature closures and seize their missed opportunities.

Szepanski got involved in student politics in the radical, post-1968 climate of the mid-seventies. He read Marx, flirted with Maoism, protested conditions in the German prison system. Later in the decade, he immersed himself in the post-punk experimentalist scene alongside the likes of D.A.F., playing in the industrial band P16D4. In the eighties he went back to college, watched the Left die and got very depressed, consoling himself with alcohol and the misanthropic philosophy of E. M. Cioran. Two late eighties breakthroughs pulled him out of the mire:

his encounter with the post-structuralist thought of Foucault, Lyotard, Derrida, et al, and his excitement about hip hop and house. While still working on a doctorate about Foucault, he started the first DJ-oriented record store in Frankfurt and founded the Blackout label.

By the early nineties, Szepanski was tripping out to *A Thousand Plateaus*. The experience was revelatory and galvanizing, because Deleuze and Guattari's theories showed him 'that you don't have to be negative or sad if you want to be militant, even if what you fight against is very bad. The Frankfurt School and Marxism has a very linear interpretation of history and a totalizing view of society, whereas Deleuze and Guattari say that society is more than just the economy and the state, it's a multitude of sub-systems, and local struggles.' From this, Achim conceived the strategy of context-based subversion which informs his labels: hard-techno and house with Force Inc, electronica with Mille Plateaux, jungle with Riot Beats, trip hop with the *Electric Ladyland* compilations, techstep with Chrome. These interventions are situated somewhere between parody and riposte, demonstrating what these genres could really be like if they lived up to or exceeded their accompanying 'progressive' rhetoric.

Founded in 1991, Force Inc was initially influenced by Detroit renegades Underground Resistance: not just sonically, but by 'their whole anti-corporate, anti-commodification of dance stance'. In its first year, Force Inc's neo-Detroit/Chicago acieed sound and 'guerrilla parties' had a lot of impact in Germany. But as trance tedium took over in 1992, Force Inc 'made a radical break,' towards an 'abstract industrial' version of breakbeat hardcore that weirdly paralleled the proto-jungle emerging in Britain. Szepanski and Co even loved the much derided sped-up squeaky-voice tracks that ruled UK rave in 1992. 'Maybe it was just our peculiar warped interpretation, but the sped-up vocals sounded like a serious attempt to deconstruct pop music. One dimension to this was using sampled voices like instruments or noise, destroying the pop ideology that says that the voice is the expression of the human subject.'

In 1993–4, Szepanski watched aghast as rave went overground in Germany, with 'the return of melody, New Age elements, insistently kitsch harmonies and timbres'. With this degeneration of the underground sound came the consolidation of a German rave establishment, centred around the party organization Mayday and its record label Low Spirit, music channel Viva TV, and Berlin's annual and massive

street rave, Love Parade. The charts were swamped with Low Spirit
pop-rave smashes like 'Somewhere Over The Rainbow' and 'Tears
Don't Lie' (based on tunes from musicals or German folk music), while
the 'intelligent' alternative was the middlebrow trance of Sven Vath
and his Harthouse label.

For Achim, what happened to German rave illustrated Deleuze and
Guattari's concepts of 'deterritorialization' and 'reterritorialization'.
Deterritorialization is when a culture gets all fluxed up – as with punk,
early rave, jungle – resulting in a breakthrough into new aesthetic,
social and cognitive spaces. Reterritorialization is the inevitable stabili-
zation of chaos into a new order: the internal emergence of style codes
and orthodoxies, the external co-optation of subcultural energy by the
leisure industry. Szepanski has a groovy German word for what rave,
once so liberating, turned into: *freizeitknast*, a pleasure-prison. Regulated experiences, punctual rapture, predictable music. Szepanski talks
of how 'techno today is stabilized and regulated by an overcoding
machine (the combination of major labels, rave organizations, mass
media)'. Rave started as anarchy (illegal parties, pirate radio, social/
racial/sexual mixing) but quickly became a form of cultural fascism.
'The techniques of mass-mobilization and crowd-consciousness have
similarities to fascism. Fascism was mobilizing people for the war-
machines, rave is mobilizing people for pleasure-machines . . .'

Just as Force Inc worked with and against the demands of the
dancefloor, Mille Plateaux began in 1994 as sort of an answer to
'electronic listening music'. For Szepanski, if not so explicitly for the
roster of Steel, Gas, Cristian Vogel, et al, Mille Plateaux output is the
musical praxis to Deleuzian theory, sonically fleshing out concepts such
as 'rhizomatic'. The rhizome – meaning a network of stems, like grass
or ferns, that are laterally connected, as opposed to 'hierarchical' root-
systems like trees – is used by Deleuze and Guattari to evoke a kind of
polymorphous perversity of the body politic. 'Rhizomatic' music might
include the fractal, flow-motion funk of Can and early seventies Miles
Davis (based around the 'nobody solos and everybody solos' principle),
dub reggae (with its dismantling of the normal ranking of instruments
in the mix), and the cut 'n' splice mixology of hip hop, house and
jungle DJs.

Rather than fusion, this is a fissile aesthetic. Achim talks of achieving
a 'synthesization of heterogenous sounds and material through a kind
of composition that holds the sound elements together without them

losing their heterogeneity'. He talks, in fluent Deleuze-speak, of 'disjunctive singularities', 'music without centre, radically fractured ... and conflicting', of opening up 'a continuum of infinite variations in which the sound material molecularizes', and of 'sound-streams' that simulate the sound of the cosmic *rauschen* (an evocative German word whose meanings include 'rustle', 'roar' and 'rush').

The music that most substantiates Szepanski's high-falutin' rhetoric can be found, appropriately enough, on *In Memoriam Gilles Deleuze*, a double CD tribute assembled by Mille Plateaux following Deleuze's suicide in 1995 at age seventy. Highlights include Alec Empire's 'Bon Voyage', a Stockhausen-meets-The Clangers electro-blip reverbscape; Christophe Charles's 'Undirections/Continuum', a *(musique) concrète* jungle of found sounds, tone-blobs and reversed *glissandi;* and Rome's 'Intermodal', a dyslexic drone-mosaic of echo/reverb effects and grievously processed bass. The most interesting Mille Plateaux artists are making a modern successor to electro-acoustic and *musique concrete*, but by using sampling and other forms of digital technology, rather than the more antiquated and tricksy methods of manual tape-splicing used by avant-classical composers. Mille Plateaux's star act, the Berlin duo Oval, recall Karlheinz Stockhausen – not just with the densely-textured disorientation of their music, but with their rarefied discourse and further-out-than-thou hauteur *vis-à-vis* their contemporaries.

Interviewing Oval is challenging. Their methods are obscure, their theory fabulously arcane, their utterances marinated in irony. Humble enquiries about backgrounds and influences are met with rolling of the eyes, sniggers, and 'next question!' Tentative characterizations of their activity are treated as a reduction or misrepresentation of the Oval project.

Perhaps all that can be safely said is that Oval's 'music' offers an uncanny, seductive beauty of treacherous surfaces and labyrinthine recesses. Their two Mille Plateaux albums *Systemich* and *94 Diskont* are the most swoon-inducing records I've heard since My Bloody Valentine's 'To Here Knows When'. The twenty minute long 'Do While' for instance, is like Spacemen 3's *Playing With Fire* pulverized into a million fluorescent splinters, then tiled into a 'musaic' grotto of impossible acoustics and refractory glints. Lovely, in an insidious, synapse-lacerating way.

Much effort clearly went into making something endlessly listenable, yet Oval have confused their admirers by insisting in interviews that music is *not* one of their interests. Turns out this isn't strictly true: 'Our effort constantly oscillates between a very conscious and affirmative use of music technology, and an often clueless, 'critical' abuse of that technology,' says Markus Popp. 'We always wanted to offensively suggest something "new" from "outside" or "before" the digital domain. "Before", in that everything we have released so far could easily have been done on a couple of reel-to-reel tape machines . . .'

Yet Oval's activity is *dependent* on nineties digital technology. According to Popp, the trio's impetus is to expose the 'conditions and constraints under which music in the nineties is created', and by extension, to interrogate the entire technology-mediated nature of today's information society. 'Experimentation in music, at least nowadays, is for most people a tame, safely "guided tour" through MIDI software and hardware,' says Popp. 'Most of the music produced by using this equipment proved to be no more than a predictable effect of the hardware or software involved.'

Oval resist this deadlock, or expose it, by having 'an audible user-interface'. In nuts and bolts terms, this involves fucking with the hardware and software that organizes and enables today's post-rave electronica. Most critical of these technologies is MIDI (Musical Instrument Digital Interface), which allows different pieces of equipment to be co-ordinated like the players in a band, or instrumental 'voices' in an orchestra. Despite, or rather because of, MIDI technology's reliance on this 'deplorably dated music-metaphor', Oval deliberately use its sonic syntax, because their real interest is in standardization. They combat the 'determinism within these programmes' by erasing the manufacturer's distinction between 'features' and 'bugs'. Just as Hendrix aestheticized feedback (a 'bug' or improper effect immanent in the electric guitar but hitherto unexploited) and hip hoppers abused the stylus and turntable, Oval fuck with digital technology: by tampering with MIDI hardware and, most famously, by deliberately damaging and painting over CDs. Taking the unhappy CD player's anguished noises – glitches, skips, and distressed cyber-muzik generated when the machine tries to calculate and compensate for missing algorhythmic information – Oval painstakingly assembled the material into the glistening audio-maze that is *Diskont*.

Typically recalcitrant, Oval reject terms like 'sabotage' or 'vandalism' to describe the CD-treatments. 'Vandalizing?' sneers Popp. 'In my perspective, the CD treatments are only a humble attempt to re-establish a decent, tangible, material basis for one of many possible musical stances in the nineties. It's our personal, tiny aesthetic margin for intervention from within software.' Oval do use the word 'disobedience', though, which also has a frisson of subversion. But perhaps the term that best describes Oval's oblique strategies is deconstruction, at least in its precise original meaning: Derrida and Co's close, rigorous reading of philosophical texts in order to unsettle the terms of post-Enlightenment thought *from within*. Deconstruction involved unravelling the rhetorical tropes and purely literary sleights that compose any text's supposedly rational argument; it meant exposing the text's blindspots, paradoxes and hidden complicities. Oval similarly talk of engaging in a kind of non-antagonistic dialogue with corporate digital culture, with Sony, IBM, Microsoft, Roland, Apple.

Blindspots and contradictions abound in Oval's own rhetoric. They speak in punk-style anyone-can-do-it terms of deliberately keeping their activity at the 'lowest entry-level', of not wanting 'to convey an image of arcane technology and years of expert study in digital signal processing and programming'. Yet their discourse is often absurdly forbidding and user-unfriendly. Then there's the way they deny any musical intentions, only to later come close to characterizing their project as an enrichment of music; they claim the invention of a 'completely new music-paradigm', or even 'a new kind of perception'. The next step for Oval is the realm of the interactive; they are working on a kind of digital authoring system. 'It's not exactly CD-ROM or hypertext,' explains Popp. 'But it will involve guiding the user through some kind of design-environment, and basically enabling people to make Oval records themselves.'

Party for Your Right to Fight

When asked about his relationship to techno, Oval's labelmate Alec Empire declares bluntly: 'Rave is dead, it's boring! House is disco and techno is progressive rock.' An engaging fellow who's constantly laughing, usually at his own utterances, Alec Empire divides his energy between fostering the Berlin-based anti-rave scene called Digital Hardcore, and recording as a solo artist for Mille Plateaux and Force Inc, where his output ranges from the edgy eclecticism of *Limited Editions 1990–94* and *Generation Star Wars* to the sombre fugue-state electronica of *Low On Ice* and the psycho-kitsch of *Hypermodern Jazz 2000.5* (a sort of twisted riposte to the E-Z listening fad).

This two-pronged campaign – rabble-rousing agit-pop versus hermetic experimentalism – reflects an interestingly jumbled background. On one hand, Empire studied music theory and, unusually for a 'techno artist', uses notation when composing his own music. On the other hand, he was a breakdancer at the age of ten and playing in a punk band by the time he was twelve. At the end of the eighties, Empire got swept up in Berlin's underground rave scene – clubs like UFO, illegal warehouse parties. Despite being a non-druggy type himself, Empire embraced acieed's cult of oblivion. 'Acid was a political movement for me, it was like stopping being a part of society . . . For a lot of people, it was about escaping from reality. At the time it made sense, politics seemed futile, with the Left dead, and even the autonomists seeming like silly kids rioting for fun.' The German scene quickly turned dark and nihilistic: 'People got into heroin and speed, there were parties in East Berlin with this very hard industrial acid sound, Underground Resistance and +8, 150 b.p.m.'

Empire dug the way this aggressive sound reflected the kids' frustration, and, influenced by UR's abstract militancy, he formed the agit-tekno band Atari Teenage Riot. Atari signed to a major label, but were dropped before they released an album. Wrecking a recording studio's amplifier and running up huge cab bills by stopping off at record stores, they were just too much trouble. By this point – the end of 1993 – Alec had already released around fifteen EPs of solo material on Force Inc and other labels, including 'Hunt Down The Nazis' and 'SuEcide', an ironic/nihilistic 'hymn to self-destruction through Ecstasy'. Meanwhile, he was experimenting with a Germanic jungle sound for Riot Beats, drawing on the influence of UK darkside tracks by Bizzy B and the Reinforced crews. Dark-core remains an influence on Digital Hardcore, which is both a scene and a label. 'Our beats are fast and distorted, but the programming is not as complex as the UK producers.'

Breakbeat appealed as an antidote to Germanic techno's Aryan funklessness, and as a multicultural statement. 'I did "Hunt Down The Nazis" at a time when skinheads were attacking immigrants. Then you'd discover, talking about the attacks to people on the rave scene, that a lot of people were quite racist. At the Omen Club, Turkish kids were turned away for no reason. There was quite a nationalistic aura to German techno, "now we are back on the map". Mark Spoon from Jam and Spoon made a comment on MTV, about how white people had techno and black people had hip hop, and that's the way it should stay. One neo-Nazi magazine even hailed trance techno as proper German music.'

Ironically, Empire now reckons that UK jungle has gotten too funky. 'The energy is missing. A whole night of jungle is just too flat. The idea of mixing, of fading tracks into each other smoothly, is over-rated. Pirate radio was better before the DJs learned to mix properly. DJ technique is just like a guitarist who knows how to make a really complicated guitar solo. A Stooges riff can mean much more, with just three notes. If the energy's not there, what's the point?'

With its speedfreak tempos and brutalist noise aesthetic, Digital Hardcore has less in common with jungle than it does with that other descendant of the original 1991 pan-European hardcore: the terrorgabba and speedcore sounds of labels like PCP, Kotzaak, Fischkopf, Cross Fade Entertainment, Praxis and Gangstar Toons Industry. Digital Hardcore Recordings' own acts, like EC80R, Moonraker, Shizuo and Sonic Subjunkies, mash up skittery 200 b.p.m. breakbeats, ultra-gabba riffs, thrash-metal guitar, Riot Grrrl shouting, and loads of midfrequency NOISE. 'In techno, in jungle, the middle frequencies are taken out, it's all bass and treble. But the middle frequencies are the rock guitar frequencies, it's where the aggression comes from.'

As well as 'boost the mid-range, cut the bass', Digital Hardcore's other key precepts are 'tempo changes keep it exciting' and 'faceless techno PAs are boring'. At their parties, DJs favour a crush-collision mess-thetic of mixed up styles and b.p.m.'s, and there are always bands playing. Instead of hypnotizing the listener into a headnodding stupor, Digital Hardcore is meant to be a wake-up call. If rave is heavy metal (rowdy, stupefying, a safety valve for adolescent aggression) and electronica is progressive rock (pseudo-spiritual, contemplative), Digital Hardcore is punk rock: angry, speedy, 'noise-annoys'-y.

In many ways, Digital Hardcore is the lo-fi underground counterpart to pop groups like The Prodigy and The Chemical Brothers, who mash together hip hop's boombastic breakbeats and techno's insurgent riffs to create a twenty-first century equivalent of rock aggression, and who've both built up a reputation as kick-ass live bands. There's a crucial difference, though. Where Prodigy's 'Firestarter' and The Chemicals' 'Loops Of Fury' are gloriously adolescent tantrums in the plastic punk tradition of The Sweet, Gary Glitter and Alice Cooper, Digital Hardcore's aural insurrection is targeted; Empire and his comrades really believe that noise can bring down the establishment's walls. Nonetheless, all this music *feels* like rock, rather than rave.

'You know, there's this foundation of musicians – German Rock Musicians Against Techno – who used to play at parties and have now been put out of business by DJs,' Alec laughs. 'We want to join it!' He adds, 'Just to take the piss,' but I think he means it, *maaaan.*

You Make Me Feel Mighty Unreal

It's a few days before New Year's Eve 1995, and downtown Manhattan's 'illbient' salon The Soundlab is paying host to Alec Empire versus DJ Spooky: an evenly matched turntable duel between the doyen of digital hardcore and local DJ-theorist Spooky. Alternating in ten minute sequences at first, then going head-to-head, the pair cut up the beats wildstyle, Spooky rockin' out in his dreads and B-boy gear, Empire impassive in an incongruously bureaucratic grey suit.

If DJ Spooky tha' Subliminal Kid – aka tha' Tactical Apparition, tha' Ontological Assassin, tha' Renegade Chronomancer, tha' Semiological Terrorist – hadn't existed, it would have been necessary to invent him. There was a gap just waiting to be filled by a figure who's not just hip to the postmodern implications of cut 'n' mix culture, but who goes out of his way to exacerbate them. That's Spooky: the DJ-as-philosopher, someone who can happily flit between the sub-cult underground of hip-hop jams, raves, ambient parties, and the highbrow overground of *Artforum*, ICA conferences, Semiotexte.

This young African-American – real name, Paul D. Miller – isn't shy of bringing the full might of his college education to bear on the humble art of spinning vinyl. And so he calls the mix-tape an 'electromagnetic canvas', celebrates ambient music as 'electroneiric otherspace', exalts the DJ as a 'mood-sculptor' and lists his occupation as 'spatial engineer of the invisible city'. The way Spooky describes it, when he's mixing he's pulling down 'ill shit' from the vast data-cloud of modern mediaculture; when he makes tracks, his approach is 'recombinant', a splicing and dicing of music's genetic code.

'My two big things,' Spooky pronounces, 'are "cultural entropy" and "post-rational art".' By cultural entropy, he means that in the age of sampladelia, cultural signifiers are becoming deracinated and ether-ealized, eventually resulting in a state in which all difference has been erased. As for 'post-rational', that's art which isn't about narrative or meaning, but a flux of sensations, 'art that's immersive'. The supreme example of both syndromes is digitalized dance music, particularly Spooky's faves, ambient, trip hop and jungle. In 'illbient' – the sound and scene that Spooky and a gaggle of downtown New York allies have conjured – the membranes between these genres have become porous. The result, depending on your allegiances, is either an exhilarating stylistic free-for-all, or a deracinated, diluted mish-mash.

In just a few years, Spooky has become both a celebrated and a highly controversial figure. For some he's a cult, a tightrope walker on the cutting edge; for others, he's a dark magus of auto-hype. Counter-culture veteran rockcrits and Marxist academics find Spooky's Baudrill-lard-meets-B-boy spiel thoroughly decadent, an elaborate pomo rationalization of political disengagement and surrender to the seduc-tions of late capitalist hyper-reality; Spooky slogans like 'seize the modes of perception' just rub salt in the wounds of these mourners for the death of History and political agency. But the fundamental difference between these sixties nostalgics and 'a child of the digital night' like Spooky is temperamental or even psychological; like many of his generation, the Subliminal Kid seems to have a more tenuous but less oppressive sense of super-ego than people who grew up before the age of McLuhan and the TV-as-glass-nipple.

In a piece in the *Village Voice* entitled 'Yet Do I Wonder' – part of a series in which African-American writers pondered questions of iden-tity and community – Spooky declared that 'every patriarchal "family value" that I have ever thought of begins to crack and fall to dust when I think about the stuff of which my everyday life is made: DJ-ing, living under almost squatlike conditions, writing.' The death of his black radical lawyer father when he was three is both biographical fact and a crucial element of the Spooky myth. Spooky knows his post-Lacanian theory: specifically, that it's the intrusion of the father that smashes the cosy mother/infant symbiosis and enforces the child's admission to the regime of language, selfhood and lack. If you don't go through this Oedipal crisis, and abandon the infant's cosmic narcissism, you don't become fully human.

The disappearance of his father from the primal scene is all part of the mythos of Spooky as anti-Oedipal prophet of the post-human aeon, wherein the self is just a 'mindscreen' for all the switching centres of influence; Spooky as polymorphously perverse psychonaut surging through and merging with the digital cosmos; Spooky adrift in the womb-like cocoon of 'bloodmusic' and liquifacient information. Or as he himself put it in the *Village Voice* piece: 'I, the Ghostface, the Ripple in the Flux, am a kid who has gotten the picture but lost the frame, and life for me is one big video-game.'

Spooky's career began in the late eighties with a college radio show called Dr Seuss's Eclectic Jungle. 'I was playing really mutated dance music – four turntables all going at the same time, turntable feedback, four CD players, two tape decks.' Then came a club called Club Retaliation, based in his hometown Washington, DC. Here Spooky enjoyed an acid revelation while DJ-ing: 'I took a ridiculous amount of liquid LSD and it radically ruptured my sense of the turntable. Most people dwell on the surface of their records, but with acid and more tactile drugs you feel like you're actually inside a moving text, the music becomes like fluid architecture . . . I started to feel very unstable, I was feeling the bass in a way I'd never done before. The immersive quality of music on acid was a revelation.'

In New York, Spooky gradually found aesthetic kinsmen in DJs and bands like Olive, Byzar, SubDub, We and Circuit Bible. Soon he had a career on his hands, playing at spaces like Chiaroscuro, Jupiter, Abstrakt and The Soundlab. Unlike the UK's marijuana-infused ambient culture, New York's 'illbient' scene is less about wombing soundbaths and vegetative bliss, more about creating audio-sculptures and environmental soundscapes. As such it harks back to a downtown bohemian tradition of multimedia events and Zen-Dada-LSD inspired happenings: Fluxus, Phil Niblock, John Cage, La Monte Young's Theater of Eternal Music, David Tudor. Illbient's reference points extend even further back (the Italian Futurists' Art of Noises, Erik Satie's 'furniture music') and further afield (Spooky cites Javanese gamelan and 'West African thumb-piano played at ceremonies').

Despite this gamut of illustrious ancestors, 'illbient' is mostly defined by its contemporary coordinates: it's a uneasy merger of post-rave ambience and abstract hip hop (freed of the figurative role of the rapper). The 'ill' indicates an allegiance to B-boy culture (it's basically a vernacular and more flava-full synonym for 'avant-garde'), but the music's non-verbal atmospherics (the 'bient) involves cutting loose from the hip hop street and all its struggles, drifting off into 'space'. The opposite of 'space' is 'compression', Spooky's great bugbear. He rails against the 'spiritual compression' of hardcore rap, which he attributes to the gangsta cult of 'realness' and psychic armature. Like the British trip hoppers and nouveau electro outfits, Spooky locates his B-boy roots in the 'old skool' era, when hip hop was oriented around the DJ-and-turntable rather than the producer-and-studio. Like Mo' Wax's DJ Shadow and Ninja Tune's DJ Vadim, Spooky belongs to a tradition of mostly instrumental collage (Steinski, Davy DMX, The 45 King, Mantronix) that disappeared when rhyming skills, storytelling and the rapper's charismatic persona took over hip hop. But whereas the old skool nostalgia of Mo' Wax and Ninja Tune is a product of British B-boys geographical and cultural distance from rap's socio-cultural context, Spooky's alienation from hardcore rap is class-based: he's black but from an upper-middle-class, highbrow background. 'Illbient' is a bohemian initiative to liberate hip hop from the thrall of the 'real'.

This explains why Spooky's own music – tracks like 'Journey (Paraspace Mix)' and 'Heterotopian Trace' on the compilation *Necropolis: The Dialogic Project*, 'Nasty Data Burst (Why Ask Why)' on the Bill Laswell organized anthology *Valis 1: Destruction of Syntax* – sound less like contemporary hip hop, more like the neo-Dada collages of British experimental units such as :zoviet*france and Nurse With Wound. 'Nasty Data Burst', for instance, is an aleatory haze of deteriorated sound-sources, featuring some eighty overlapping beats set up, says Spooky, 'to be deliberately randomized and clashing'. His debut solo album *Songs of A Dead Dreamer* is marginally more groove-oriented (trip hop with no return ticket?) but it's still hard to imagine any American B-boy recognizing this music.

Spooky's warped and warping relationship with hip hop stems from the core attitude that he shares with the rest of the international art-tekno fraternity: cultural nomadism, a reluctance to be shackled by roots, a commitment to not being committed. 'I pass through so many different scenes, each with their different uniforms and dialects. One night I'll be at a dub party, the next in an academic environment. I think people need to be comfortable with difference. Hip hop isn't, it says "You gotta be down with us," be like us.' One of Spooky's most frequent complaints is 'I'm stretched real thin at the moment'. This is partly the over-worked lament of a *fin de millennium* Renaissance man whose non-musical fronts of activity include critical journalism, science fiction, making paintings and sculptures, and participating in academic conferences. But it's also a side effect of his interest in 'schizophrenia, the idea of inhabiting all these different personae.' Stretching his self to the point of snapping, Spooky is a renegade against identity politics, an (un)real Everywhere-and-Nowhere Man.

My Funk Is Useless

The central tenets of the post-everything vanguard are: severing ties to a particular scene or community creates the freedom to drift; fusion opens up 'infinite possibilities', whereas purism is blinkered tunnel-vision. Although some remarkable music has been created under the border-crossing banner, it's also important to understand the limitations of this approach: namely, that the dissolution of the boundaries between genres tends to erode precisely what makes them distinct and distinctive, and that it disables the very functionalist elements that makes specific styles *work* for specific audiences. In that respect, Alec Empire's humorously (and accurately) titled 'My Funk Is Useless' on *Hypermodern Jazz* could serve as an art for art's sake motto for everyone from Squarepusher to Spooky.

In purist or 'hardcore' dance genres – jungle, hip hop, house, ragga, gabba, swingbeat – sparks fly from the productive friction between innovation and conservatism, between the auteur's impulse to explore and the dancefloor's requirements. These genres evolve through the pressure of the audience's apparently contradictory demands: tracks must be 'fresh', but they must also reinforce and sustain tradition. To an outsider, the soundtrack at hardcore dance events often seems 'samey'. But this predictability isn't caused by cowardice so much as a desire to create a *vibe*: a meaningful and *feeling*-full mood that materially embodies a certain kind of worldview and life-stance. As you get deeper inside a scene, the apparent homogeneity gradually reveals itself as Amiri Baraka's 'changing same'; you begin to appreciate the subtle play of sameness and difference, thrill to the small but significant permutations and divagations of the genre.

Freestyle or 'eclectro' events, by comparison, are usually devoid of vibe. Partly this is because of the absence of the drug-and-class energy that makes hardcore scenes so charged (the electricity can also be race or sexual-preference fuelled, as with the gay house scene). Partly, it's because the style-hopping freestyle menu attracts a rather uncommitted consumer: the chin-scratching connoisseur who's more likely to stand at the back headnodding than dance, who'd rather pride himself on being an 'individual' than merge with the crowd.

While hardcore underground scenes like jungle, gabba and East Coast rap are 'populist', in a global sense they seldom achieve more than 'semi-popular' status. If these subcultures constitute the classic 'margins around a collapsed centre', this makes the post-everything artists marginal even to the margins. Imagine the pop mainstream as a planet around which orbit a number of moons (the hardcore undergrounds). The post-everything perimeter is like one of Saturn's Rings: a band of pop-cultural detritus which touches the hardcore satellites but has little impact upon them. Furthermore, the perimeter-zone itself is constituted, in a very real sense, out of the dust and debris scattered by larger and ultimately more significant bodies in the musical firmament.

In this respect, the post-everything boffins belong to a time-honoured tradition. Artists like Brian Eno and Miles Davis borrowed ideas from populist genres like dub and funk, which tend to be driven by a vital blend of mercenary and spiritual motives. Sometimes, it works the other way round: Byrne and Eno's *My Life In The Bush of Ghosts* was a big influence on Public Enemy producer Hank Shocklee, for instance. But mostly the cross-town traffic is one-way. 'Parasitic' is the right word to describe this downwardly mobile dependence on 'street sounds' for stylistic rejuvenation; for instance, it's highly unlikely that the idea of accelerating and chopping up breakbeats would ever have independently occurred to Plug/Squarepusher/AFX without jungle's prior example.

If you simply equate radicalism with the ostentatious absence of use-value, then the dys-funk-tional convolutions of Squarepusher et al are conceivably more 'advanced' than most jungle. Actually, technically speaking, nothing these weirdy-beardy types have done with breaks has beaten drum and bass insiders like Dillinja and 4 Hero at their own game. What the post-rave boffins have done is hijack the metaphor of 'science' from jungle and hip hop, and transform it into a sampladelic era synonym for old-fashioned 'virtuosity'. Prog rock style, they take pride in taking dance music and rendering it undanceable. The trouble with real-world science is that for every Onco-mouse with a human ear grafted into its body or groovy new device for mass destruction, there's a myriad of non-conclusive experiments: fault-ridden machines, test-tubes full of useless precipitates and cloudy suspensions. Much the same applies to the output of sound-laboratories. In the case of breakbeat science, there's way too many examples of fiddly, funkless, up-its-own-arse programming (although to be fair, many 'real' junglists are getting as anal as the drill and bass posse).

The vogue for the word 'science' also suggests that a disembodied and dispassionate detachment is the right way to approach music. What the Squarepusher type artists have responded to and exaggerated *ad absurdum* is only one aspect of jungle: the music's complexity. They've ignored the feelings the music induces, and the subcultural reasons the sound and the scene came into being. As a result, no matter how superficially startling their form-and-norm-bending mischief sounds, their music *feels* pale and purposeless compared with music created by the jungle fundamentalists. It is vitiated by being divorced from the context that originally imbued those sounds with resonance. Worse, the whiff of stylistic oneupmanship can be offputting. Plug has been celebrated for 'fucking with sounds that say "Don't fuck with me."' Exhibiting astonishing temerity and arrogance, Squarepusher's Tom Jenkinson described his relationship with jungle in terms of the difference between 'people who pioneer and lead, and people who form groups'. But this is nothing compared with the brinksmanship of Oval, who set themselves above and against *all electronic music* (yet are dependent on its distribution network and receptive audience).

No amount of wilful eccentricity can impart the lustre of meaning to music; that comes only when a community takes a sound and makes it part of a way of life. So while I marvel at the art-tekno boffins' efforts, often I feel curiously unmoved, physically or emotionally. Fascinated but uninvolved, I find myself wondering whether anti-purism is just another ghetto, and whether 'freedom' is just another word for 'nothing much at stake'.

SEVENTEEN

IN OUR
ANGELHOOD

RAVE CULTURE AS

SPIRITUAL

REVOLUTION

By the late nineties, the British media had woken up to the fact that the nation contained two societies: the traditional leisure culture of alcohol and entertainment (spectactor sports, TV) versus the more participatory, effusive culture of all-night dancing and Ecstasy. The clash between old Britain and young Britain was dramatized to hilarious effect in an episode of *Inspector Morse* entitled 'Cherubim and Seraphim'. The plot – basically Morse versus 'ardkore – concerns a series of mysterious teenage deaths which appear to be connected to a new drug called Seraphic. Despite its overt 'just say no' slant, the episode mostly works as an exhilarating advert for Ecstasy culture. (*Literally*, in so far as Morse's remark to his detective partner – 'It's a rave, Lewis!' – was sampled and used as a soundbite by a pirate station.)

'What's the great attraction?' Morse beseeches the air, as he and Lewis join a convoy of vehicles heading to an illegal rave, their car radio tuned to a pirate station. Yet Morse perceptively notes that hardcore is 'eclectic, a collage, magpie music'; earlier, listening to a track, the fusty classical buff had been horrified to recognize samples from 'The Hallelujah Chorus – conducted by Sir Adrian Boult!' Old music, the dead wood of English culture, is vitalized by sampling, funked up by programmed rhythm.

This collision of old and new Englands reaches its peak when the detective duo arrive at the stately home where the rave, called Cherub, is taking place. Morse drones on about the noble history of the building; inside, the kids have transformed it into a future wonderland. For a TV programme, the recreation of rave's sexless bacchanalia is remarkably convincing and intoxicating. Sure, the crooked lab researcher responsible for the Seraphic drug gets his comeuppance; fleeing the rave, he crashes his car into a tree and dies. But the episode ends by allowing the sixteen-year-old girlfriend of one Seraphic casualty to utter a paean to Ecstasy: 'You love everyone in the world, you want to touch everyone and tell them you love them.' And the 'just say no' message is utterly subverted when it is revealed that the teenagers didn't kill themselves because the drug unbalanced their minds; rather, having glimpsed heaven-on-earth, they decided that returning to reality would be too much of a comedown. Who wouldn't want to give E a try after that? And who would possibly side with decrepit Morse, with his booze and classical CDs, against the shiny happy people of Generation E?

The Politics of Ecstasy

This episode of *Inspector Morse* signalled a dawning awareness in the media that recreational drug culture had become firmly installed in Britain during the early nineties, and was now omnipresent almost to the point of banality. Every weekend, anywhere from half-a-million to two million people under the age of thirty-five were using psychedelics and stimulants. This geographically dispersed but spiritually connected network of Love-Ins, Freak-Outs and All-Night Raves constituted a Woodstock every week (or rather Woodstock-and-Altamont rolled into one, given that Ecstasy's dark side was starting to reveal itself to ravers). Despite the abiding myth that E isn't as good as it used to be, anecdotal evidence suggests that Ecstasy pills are stronger than ever, while the UK price of the drug has plummeted from twenty pounds in the late eighties to around ten pounds in 1997. The question, then, is this: has rave proved itself a form of mass bohemia, or is it merely a futuristic update of traditional youth leisure, where the fun-crazed weekend redeems the drudgery of the working week? What are the politics of Ecstasy culture?

When it comes to Ecstasy's social effects, the most obvious is the way it has utterly transformed youth leisure in Britain and Europe. Because alcohol muddies the MDMA high, rave culture rapidly developed an anti-alcohol taboo. It could be argued that Ecstasy's net effect has actually been to save lives, by reducing the number of alcohol-fuelled fights and drink-driving fatalities. Some mutter darkly that it's pressure from the brewing industry, aghast at declining profits, that lurks behind the British government's anti-rave legislation.

Like alcohol, Ecstasy removes inhibitions. But because it also diminishes aggression (including sexual aggression), E has had the salutary effect of transforming the nightclub from a 'cattle market' and combat-zone to a place where women come into their own and men are too busy dancing and bonding with their mates to get into fights.

These benign side-effects have spilled outside clubland. As football fans turned on to E and house music, soccer hooliganism in Britain dropped to its lowest level in five years by 1991–2 (although some argue that improved intelligence work and tactics by the police also made a hefty contribution to eliminating violence at games). In Northern Ireland, Ecstasy encouraged fraternization across Catholic–Protestant lines, at least at non-sectarian raves and clubs; this may be one reason why the paramilitaries (who control the drug trade) have been cracking down on dealers.

Generally speaking, Ecstasy seems to promote tolerance. One of the delights of the rave scene at its loved-up height was the way it allowed for mingling across class, race and sex-preference lines. MDMA rid club culture of its clique-ishness and stylistic sectarianism; hence sociologist Sheila Henderson's phrase 'luvdup and de-élited'. Rave's explosive impact in the UK, compared with its slower dissemination in America, may have something to do with the fact that Britain remains one of the most rigidly class-stratified countries in the Western world. In many ways, MDMA is an antidote to the English disease: reserve, inhibition, emotional constipation, class consciousness. Perhaps the drug simply wasn't as *needed* in America as it was in the UK.

Yet for all the rhetoric of spiritual revolution and counter-culture, it remains a moot point whether Ecstasy's effects have spilled outside the domain of leisure. From early on, commentators noted that the controlled hedonism of the MDMA experience is much more compatible with a basically normal, conformist lifestyle than other drugs. Norman Zinberg called it 'the yuppie psychedelic'; others have compared it to a 'mini-vacation', an intense burst of 'quality time'. In his essay 'The Ecstasy of Disappearance', Antonio Melechi uses the historical origins of rave in Ibiza as the foundation for a theory of rave as a form of *internal tourism*: a holiday from everyday life and from your everyday self. At the big one-off raves, some kids spend – on drinks, drugs, souvenir merchandise, and getting there – as much as they would on a short vacation. Rejecting the idea that this is simply escapist, a safety valve for the tensions generated by capitalist work-patterns, Melechi argues that rave supersedes the old model of subcultural activity as resistance-through-rituals. Where earlier style terrorist subcultures like mod and punk were exhibitionist, a kick-in-the-eye of straight society, rave is a form of collective disappearance, an investment in pleasure that shouldn't be written off as mere retreatism or disengagement.

Melechi's theory of rave – as neither subversive nor conformist but more than both – appeals to the believer in me. From a more detached and dispassionate perspective, though, rave appears more like a new twist on a very old idea. There is actually a striking continuity in the work hard/play hard structure of working-class leisure, from the mods' 60-hour weekends and Northern Soul's speedfreak stylists, to disco's Saturday night fever-dreams and jazz-funk's All-Dayers and Soul Weekends. When I listen to The Easybeats 1967 Aussie-mod anthem 'Friday On My Mind', I'm stunned by the way the lyrics – a thrilling anatomy of the working-class weekender life-cycle of drudgery, anticipation and explosive release – still resonate. But what really grabs my ear is the poignancy of the lines, 'I know of nothing else that bugs me more than working for the rich man / Hey, I'll change that scene one day.' Thirty years on, we're no nearer to overhauling the work/leisure structures of industrial society. Instead, all that rage and frustration is vented through going mental at the weekend ('Tonight, I'll spend my bread / Tonight, I'll lose my head'), helped along by a capsule or three of instant unearned euphoria.

From the Summer of Love rhetoric of the early UK acid house evangelists to San Francisco's cyberdelic community, from the neo-paganism of Spiral Tribe to the transcendentalism of the Megatripolis/ Goa Trance scene, rave has also been home to another 'politics of Ecstasy', one much closer to the original intent behind Timothy Leary's phrase. Ecstasy has been embraced as one element of a bourgeois-bohemian version of rave, in which the music-drugs-technology nexus is fused with spirituality and vague hippy-punk anarcho-politics to form a nineties would-be counter-culture.

The fact that the same drug can be at the core of two different 'politics of ecstasy' – raving as safety-valve versus raving as opting out – can be traced back to the double nature of MDMA as a *psychedelic amphetamine*. The psychedelic component of the experience lends itself to utopianism and an at least implicit critique of the way-things-are. Amphetamine, though, does not have a reputation as a consciousness-raising chemical. While they popped as many pills as other strata of society, the hippies regarded amphetamine as a straight person's drug: after all, it was still legal and being prescribed in vast amounts to tired housewives, over-stretched businessmen, slimmers, and students cramming for exams. Amphetamine's ego-boosting and productivity-raising effects ran totally counter to the psychedelic creed of self-less surrender, indolence and Zen passivity. So when the spread of methamphetamine poisoned Haight-Ashbury's love-and-peace vibe, the counter-culture responded with the 'speed kills' campaign. The hippies' hostility towards amphetamine is one reason why the punks embraced the chemical, with journalist Julie Burchill hailing sulphate as a true working-class drug that gave you the confidence to challenge your so-called social superiors, and even boosted your IQ several points.

In their 1975 classic *The Speed Culture: Amphetamine Use and Abuse in America*, Lester Grinspoon and Peter Hedblom draw an invidious comparison between marijuana and amphetamine, arguing that pot-smoking instils values that run counter to capitalist norms, while amphetamine amplifies all the competitive, aggressive and solipsistic tendencies of Western industrial life. Grinspoon and Hedbloom call it a 'crimogenic' drug, noting the extreme social instability of speed subcultures, which are characterized by rip-offs and 'righteous' retribution, paranoia and hair-trigger explosions of violence. Terence McKenna, an evangelist for Gaia-given plant psychedelics like magic mushrooms, classes amphetamine as one of the 'dominator drugs', alongside cocaine and caffeine.

Chemically programmed into MDMA is a sort of less-is-more effect: what starts out as an empathogen degenerates, with repeated use, into little more than amphetamine (in terms of its effect). This is one explanation for a syndrome that recurs in different rave scenes: at a certain point, the subculture's self-appointed guardians (veterans of its early, golden age) start complaining that speed is killing the original spirit of the scene. Sometimes, there's a measure of truth behind this scapegoating: when MDMA's warm glow cools, punters turn to the cheaper, more reliable amphetamine. But often it's just a question of taking too many E's.

From all this we might conclude that when the amphetamine component of the MDMA experience comes to the fore, rave culture loses much of its 'progressive' edge. At one end of the class spectrum are the working-class weekender scenes, where MDMA is used in tandem with amphetamine, and the subcultural *raison d'être* is limited and ultimately conformist: stimulants are used to provide energy and delay the need for sleep, to intensify and maximize leisure time. At the other, more bohemian end of rave culture, MDMA is used in tandem with LSD and other consciousness-raising hallucinogens, as part of a subcultural project of turning on, tuning in and dropping out.

The picture is a bit more complicated than this. LSD is widely used in many working-class rave scenes, although arguably in ways that break with the Timothy Leary/Terence McKenna model of enlightenment through altered states. Hallucinogens appeal as another form of teenage kicks, a way of making the world into a cartoon or video-game. (Hence brands of acid blotter like Super Mario and Power Rangers.) And amphetamine, in high doses or with prolonged use, can have its own hallucinatory and delusory effects. Like MDMA, speed makes perceptions more vivid; its effect of hyper-acousia can escalate towards full-blown audio-hallucinations. The sensory flood can seem visionary, pregnant with portent. Serious speedfreaks often have a sense of clairvoyance and gnosis, feel plugged into occult power-sources, believe they alone can perceive secret patterns and conspiracies.

Church of Ecstasy

Nonetheless, there is a tension in rave culture between consciousness raising and consciousness razing, between middle-class techno-pagans for whom MDMA is just one chemical in the pharmacopoeia of a spiritual revolution, and weekenders for whom E is just another tool for 'obliviating' the boredom of workaday life. This class-based divide has quite a history. Witness the snobbish dismay of highbrow hallucinogen fiends like R. Gordon Wasson, who wrote about his psilocybin visions for *Life* magazine in 1957, only to be appalled when thrill-seeking 'riff-raff' promptly descended on the magic mushroom fields of Mexico, or worse, turned to its synthetic equivalent, LSD. Wasson refused to use the pop culture term 'psychedelic', preferring the more ungainly and overtly transcendentalist 'entheogen' (substances that put you in touch with the divine). Such linguistic games and terminological niceties often seem like the only way that intellectuals can distinguish their 'discriminating' use of drugs from the heedless hedonism of the masses.

The Road To Eleusis: Unveiling The Secret of the Mysteries, a book co-written by R. Gordon Wasson, is one of the sources for John Moore's brilliant 1988 monograph *Anarchy and Ecstasy: Visions of*

Halcyon Days. Using shreds of historical evidence, Moore imaginatively reconstructs prehistoric pagan rites dedicated to Gaia-worship; he argues for the contemporary revival of these 'Eversion Mysteries', insisting that a ritualized, mystical encounter with Chaos (what he calls 'bewilderness') is an essential component of any truly vital anarchistic politics. The alienation, isolation and passivity instilled by spectacular-commodity society must be 'healed through sharing in rituals of numinous synaesthesia, mutual involvement in multi-sensual actions, an ecstatic *katharsis*.'

On my first encounter with *Anarchy and Ecstasy*, I was instantly struck by the way the book, written in the mid-eighties, reads like a prophecy and programme for rave culture. Crucial preparations for the Mystery rites include fasting and sleep-deprivation, in order to break down 'inner resistances' and facilitate possession by the 'sacred wilderness'. The rites themselves consist of mass chanting, dancing ('enraptured abandonment to a syncopated musical beat' which 'flings aside rigidities, be they postural, behavioural or characterological') and the administering of hallucinogenic drugs, in order that 'each of the senses and faculties [be] sensitized to fever pitch prior to derangement into a liberatingly integrative synaesthesia'. The worshippers are led into murky, maze-like structures, like caverns, whose darkness is illuminated only by 'mandalas and visual images'.

All this sounded very like my favourite club, the Labrynth, with its multiple levels and winding staircases, its corridors decorated with psychotropic UV imagery, its convulsive, hyper-syncopated breakbeat rhythms. As for the 'hierophants' with their intoxicating poisons, this could be the nineteen-year-old dealers with their E's and trips. The Labrynth parallel appeals to me because this working-class club in East London fitted Moore's blueprint perfectly, yet its highly ritualized activities had none of the techno-pagan, neo-tribal trappings of more bohemian rave scenes.

Moore's description of the peak of Mystery rites sounds very like the effect of MDMA: '. . . the initiate becomes androgynous, uncon-cerned with the artificial distinctions of gender . . . Encountering total saturation, individuals transcend their ego boundaries and their mortality in successive waves of ecstasy.' Even the socially benign after-effects – Moore quotes R. Gordon Wasson's description of 'an indissoluble bond [that] unites you with the others who have shared with you in the sacred *agape* . . . a tie . . . with their companions of that night of nights that will last as long as they live' – is something any raver would instantly recognize. It's the reason why the rave lifestyle can become a monomania, such that 'all existence became structured around the limitless vision quests which began on the sacred nights'.

Hardly surprising, then, that organized religion has noticed the way rave culture provides 'the youth of today' with an experience of collective communion and transcendence. Just as the early Church co-opted heathen rituals, there have been attempts to literally *rejuvenate* Christianity by incorporating elements of the rave experience: dancing, lights, mass fervour, demonstrative and emotional behaviour. Most (in)famous of these was the Nine O'Clock Service in Sheffield, the brainchild of 'rave vicar' Chris Brain, whose innovations were greeted with keen interest and approval on the part of the Anglican hierarchy, until it was discovered that the reverend was loving some of his female parishioners in a rather too literal sense.

Despite this embarrassment, rave-style worship has spread to other cities in the UK like Gloucester and Bradford (where the Cathedral holds services called Eternity). There have also been a number of attempts to lure lost and confused youth into the Christian fold via drug-and-alcohol-free rave nights: Club X in Bath (organized by Billy Graham's Youth For Christ), and Bliss (a Bournemouth night started by the Pioneer Network). These evangelists are sometimes disarmingly frank about their ulterior motives: Andy Hawthorne, a techno musician and member of the Christian youth group Message To Schools, told *Muzik*: 'Dance music is the music of the kids in Manchester. The fact that we love it as much as they do is almost beside the point. We think of ourselves as missionaries. Most kids in Manchester are pagans because they don't know the basic information about the Christian faith.'

None of these quasi-rave clubs administer Ecstasy as a holy sacrament. But perhaps they should, for if any drug induces a state-of-soul that approximates to the Christian ideal – overflowing with trust and goodwill to all men – then surely it's MDMA. While rave behaviour is a little *outré* for the staid Church of England, it chimes in nicely with the more ecstatic and gesturally demonstrative strains of Christianity – from the dance-crazy Shakers to Black American gospel and Pentecostalism. Some have argued that trance-dance is a state of grace, while Moby, techno's most visible and outspoken Christian, claimed that 'The first rave was when the Ark of the Covenant was brought into

Jerusalem, and King David went out and danced like crazy, and tore off all his clothes.' But the rave experience probably has more in common with the goals and techniques of Zen Buddhism: the emptying out of meaning via mantric repetition; nirvana as the paradox of the 'full void'. Nicholas Saunders' *E For Ecstasy* quotes a Rinzai Zen monk who approves of raving as a form of active meditation that allows you to become 'truly in the moment and not in your head'. Later in Saunders's book, there's an extract from an Ecstasy memoir in which the anonymous author describes the peculiar, depthless quality of the MDMA experience: 'there's no inside', 'I was empty. I seemed to have become pure presence'. While many become garrulous on E, for others the experience is a sublime vacancy, the weightless bliss of not having a thought in your head, a dazzling, denuded clarity in which your brain feels like crisp, freshly ironed sheets. At its most intense, the Ecstasy rush resembles the kundalini energy that yoga seeks to awaken: 'liquid fire' that infuses the nervous system and leaves the consciousness 'aglow with light'.

Androgyny in the UK

What makes rave culture so ripe for religiosity is the 'spirituality' of the Ecstasy experience: its quality of gnosis, of access to a wonderful secret which can only be understood by direct, unmediated experience; the way it releases an out-flow of all-embracing but peculiarly asexual love. Clearly the most interesting and 'subversive' attributes of the MDMA experience, these aspects are also what makes rave fraught with a latent nihilism. If one word crystallizes this ambivalence at the heart of rave experience, it's 'intransitive' – in so far as the music and the culture lacks an objective or object ('rave' is literally an intransitive verb). Rave culture has no goal beyond its own propagation; it is about the celebration of celebration, about an intensity without pretext or context.

Ecstasy has been celebrated as the *flow drug*, for the way it melts bodily and psychological rigidities, enabling the dancer to move with greater fluency and 'lock' into the groove. The energy currents that MDMA releases in a flood through the nervous system could be compared to the notion of a life-force promulgated by various 'vitalist' philosophers, mystics, poets and physicians from the eighteenth century to the present: Mesmer's 'magnetic fluid, Whitman's 'body electric', Reich's *orgone*. These simultaneously spiritual and materialist theories of an *élan vital* (*élan* coming from *eslan*, an archaic French word for 'rush') may actually all be talking about the same neurological 'joy-juice' (as one Prozac expert described serotonin). The freeflowing energy without referent unleashed by MDMA also recalls Deleuze and Guattari's famous concept of 'the body-without-organs'. The opposite of the organism – which is oriented around survival and reproduction – the body-without-organs is composed out of all the potentials in the human nervous system for pleasure and sensation without purpose: the sterile bliss of perverse sexuality, drug experiences, play, dancing, and so forth. Just as a rave is made up of ravers, the human components of Deleuze and Guattari's 'desiring machine' are bodies-without-organs. Plugged into the sound-system, charged up on E, the raver's body-without-organs simply buzzes, bloated with unemployable energy: a sensation of 'arrested orgasm' expressed in pirate MC ejaculations like 'oooh gosh!'.

Described by Deleuze and Guattari as 'a continuous, self-vibrating region of intensities [that] avoids any orientation towards a culmination,' the body-without-organs is an update of Freud's notion of polymorphous perversity: a diffuse eroticism that's connected to the non-genital, non-orgasmic sensuality of the pre-Oedipal infant. The body-without-organs also echoes age-old mystical goals: Zen's Uncarved Block, a blissful, inchoate flux preceding individuation and gender; the 'translucent' or 'subtle body', angelic and androgynous, whose resurrection was sought by the Gnostics and alchemists.

In *Omens of Millennium* – a book about the contemporary resurgence of Gnostic preoccupations with angels and near-death experiences – Harold Bloom argues: 'To be drugged by the embrace of nature into what we call most natural in us, our sleepiness and our sexual desires, is at once a pleasant and an unhappy fate, since what remains immortal in us is both androgynous and sleepless.' MDMA, an 'unnatural' designer drug whose effects are anti-aphrodisiac and insomniac, might be a synthetic short cut to recovering our angelhood. My own experiences with Ecstasy substantiate these parallels. I remember one time enjoying a radical sensation of being without gender, a feeling of docility and angelic gentleness so novel and exquisite I could only express it clumsily: 'I feel really effeminate'.

Such sensations of sexual indifference have everything to do with

MDMA's removal of aggression, especially sexual aggression. E's reputation as the 'love drug' has more to do with cuddles than copulation, sentimentality rather than secretions. E is notorious for making erection difficult and male orgasm virtually impossible; women fare rather better, although one female therapist suggests that on Ecstasy 'the particular organization and particular focusing of the body and the psychic energy necessary to achieve orgasm [is] ... very difficult'. For many men, MDMA is literally a dick-shriveller; it also gets rid of the thinks-with-his-dick mentality, turning raves into a space where girls can feel free to be friendly with strange men, even kiss them, without fear of sexual consequences. Despite this, MDMA still has a reputation as an aphrodisiac – partly because it enhances touch, and partly because affection, intimacy and physical tenderness are, for many people, inextricably entangled and conflated with sexual desire.

Unaware of Ecstasy's effects, many early commentators were quick to ascribe the curiously chaste vibe at raves to a post-AIDS retreat from adult sexuality. But one of the most radically novel and arguably subversive aspects of rave culture is precisely that it's the first youth subculture that's not based on the notion that sex is transgressive. Rejecting all that tired sixties rhetoric of sexual liberation, and recoiling from our sex-saturated pop culture, rave locates *jouissance* in prepubescent childhood. Hence the garish colours and baggy clothing, the backpacks and satchels, the lollipops and dummies and teddy bears – even the fairground side-shows at raves. It's intriguing that a drug originally designed as an appetite suppressant should have this effect. Anorexia has long been diagnosed as a refusal of adult sexual maturity and all its accompanying hassles. Ecstasy doesn't negate the body, it intensifies the pleasure of physical expression while completely emptying out the sexual content of dance. For men, the drug/music interface acts to dephallicize the body and open it up to enraptured, abandoned, 'effeminate' gestures. But removing the heterosexist impulse can mean that women are rendered dispensable. As with that earlier speed-freak scene, the mods (who dressed sharp and posed to impress their mates, not to lure a mate), there's a homosocial aura to many rave and club scenes. Hence the autoerotic/autistic quality to rave dance. There's a sense in which E, by feminizing the man, allows him to access *jouissance* independently rather than seek it through women. Recent converts to raving often express the sentiment: 'it's better than sex'.

The samples that feature in much rave music – orgasmic whimpers and sighs, soul-diva beseechings – induce a feverish state of intransitive amorousness. The ecstatic female vocals don't signify a desirable/ desirous woman, but (as in gay disco) a hypergasmic rapture that the male identifies with, and aspires towards. (In that sense, rave is a culture of clitoris envy.) The 'you' in vocal samples like 'you make me feel so good' refers not to a person but a sensation. In truth, these are love-songs to the drug, or to the synergistic interaction of drug/music/ lights/people that constitutes the rave experience. With E, the full-on raver lifestyle means literally falling in love every weekend, then (with the inevitable mid-week crash) having your heart broken. Millions of kids across the globe are riding this emotional roller-coaster. Always looking ahead to their next tryst with E, addicted to love, dying to gush.

Amongst all its other effects, E incites a sort of free-floating fervour, a will-to-belief – which is why, under the influence, the most inane oscillator synth-riff can seem so numinously radiant with MEANING. But at the end of an exhilarating night out, as 'the visions we had' start to fade away (to misquote Noel Gallagher's lyrics for The Chemical Brothers' 'Setting Sun'), dawn can bring a disenchanting sense of futility: all that energy and idealism mobilized to no end. Such post-rave *tristesse* is brilliantly captured in Pulp's 1995 single 'Sorted For E's & Whizz', a flashback to Jarvis Cocker's experiences at the huge outdoor raves of 1989. 'Oh is this the way the future's meant to feel? / Or just 20,000 people standing in a field . . .' muses Cocker disconsolately – before making his way home alone, having lost his friends at the rave and been refused lifts by the very strangers with whom he'd bonded hours earlier in the throes of MDMA-induced bonhomie. In the single's sleeve note, he summarizes rave culture in four words of perfectly poised ambiguity: 'IT DIDN'T MEAN NOTHING'.

Nowhere People

In her memoir *Nobody Nowhere*, the autistic Donna Williams describes how as a child she would withdraw from a threatening reality into a private pre-verbal dream-space of ultra-vivid colour and rhythmic pulsations; she could be transfixed for hours by iridescent motes in the air that only she could perceive. With its dazzling psychotropic lights, its sonic pulses, rave culture is arguably a form of *collective autism*. The rave is utopia in its original etymological sense: a nowhere/nowhen wonderland, where time is abolished, where the self evanesces through merging with an anonymous multitude and drowning in a bliss-blitz of light and noise. It's a regressive womb-space or clandestine kindergarten; a kingdom of We 'where nobody is but everybody belongs' (Antonio Melechi).

Rave's relentlessly utopian imagery – events called Living Dream, Fantazia, Rezerection – often seems like the return of sixties psychedelia. Back then, the counter-culture was engaged in an attempt to reverse, en masse, the Oedipus Complex (the trauma that breaks the infants' paradaisical symbiosis with the mother, and teaches it to live with lack, to settle for less). While the bourgeois-bohemian strand of rave culture takes the late sixties as its model, the working-class sector is closer in spirit to disco. Rave is where psychedelia's transcendentalism meets disco's pleasure-factory: the result is what Simon Frith calls 'routinized transcendence'.

So perhaps the best classification for Ecstasy is 'utopiate', theorist R. Blum's term for LSD. The Ecstasy experience can be like heaven-on-Earth, and from there it's but a short step to the old counter-cultural slogan 'reality's a substitute for utopia'. Because it's not a hallucinogen but a sensation-intensifier, MDMA actually makes the world seem *realer*; the drug also feels like it's bringing out the 'real you', freed from all the neurosis instilled by a sick society. But 'utopiate' contains the world 'opiate', as in 'religion is the opiate of the people'. A sacrament in that secular religion called 'rave', MDMA can just as easily be a counter-revolutionary force as it can fuel a hunger for change. For it's too tempting to take the easy option: simply repeating the experience, installing yourself permanently in rave's virtual reality pleasuredome. And the longer you stay there, the more likely it is that Ecstasy will degenerate into a dead(ening) end.

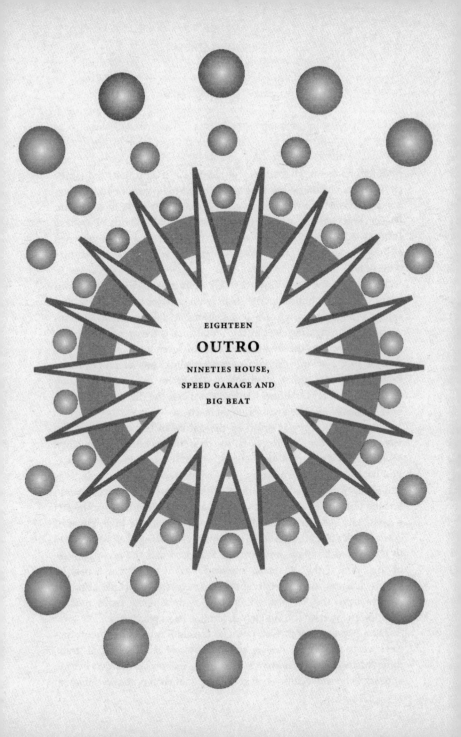

EIGHTEEN

OUTRO

NINETIES HOUSE,
SPEED GARAGE AND
BIG BEAT

Although its technophobe foes still insist that 'it all sounds the same', electronic dance music has long since ceased to be a monolith. Rather, it's a fractious confederacy of genres and sub-genres, metropolitan cliques and provincial populisms, purisms and hybrids. Post-rave culture encompasses a huge span of divergent and often opposed attitudes to aesthetics, technology, drugs, plus wildly different estimations of how much it all matters.

In a sense, you could say that rave culture is a victim of its own success. Like a political party that's won an election landslide and enjoys a huge majority, rave could afford to fall out with itself, to succumb to in-fighting. Just as the Woodstock convergence of the late sixties gave way to the fragmented drift of seventies rock, just as the class of 1977 split into factions over what punk 'was all about', rave's Ecstasy-sponsored unity inevitably re-fractured and stratified along class, race and regional lines. As early as 1991, the divisions that rave once magically dissolved reasserted themselves.

Partly this disunity is down to the nature of Ecstasy. One of the secrets of the drug's success is its context-dependent adaptability. MDMA provides a profound but curiously 'meaningless' experience. You have to supply the meaning. The overpowering feelings, sensations and idealism generated by the drug demand some kind of articulation, but the terms used are conditioned by a complex mesh of parameters – class, race, gender, nationality, ideology. Hence the huge range of 'Ecstasy talk', from the hardcore hedonism of working-class weekenders to the cyberdelic utopianism of San Francisco and the neo-paganism of the Spiral Tribe. 'Mental', 'mystical', 'avant-garde': these may be simply different ways of exalting the same experience, people using the kind of lingo they're most comfortable with. But the terms used to describe an experience ultimately determine its implications.

On a purely musical level, house and techno mutated as the musics were warped to fit the desires and purposes of different social strata, different races and regions. Once started, the process of subdivision appears to be irreversible, so that the 'we' that each post-rave fragment addresses can only get smaller and smaller. Often, the cutting-edge of each style is precisely what cuts it off from universal appeal.

For the newcomer to electronic dance music, this profusion of rave sub-genres can seem at best bewildering, at worst wilful obfuscation. Partly, this is a trick of perspective: kids who've grown up with techno feel it's *rock* that 'all sounds the same'. The urgent distinctions rockers take for granted – that Pantera, Pearl Jam, and Pavement operate in separate aesthetic universes – only make sense if you're already a participant in the ongoing rock discourse. The same applies to dance music; step inside, and the genre-itis begins to make sense. Like sections in a record store, the categories are useful. But they're also a way of talking about the music, of arguing about what it's for and where it should go. In that sense, the post-rave diaspora is a sign of health, proof that people still care enough to disagree violently about this music, that the stakes are still high.

Although I enjoy the semantic struggles over new genre terms (and have coined a few in my time – ambient jungle, artcore, post-rock, gloomcore, neurofunk) even I sometimes wonder if the endless subdivision has got out of hand. Nowhere is the turnover of new sub-styles more rapid than in house music, which is still the mainstream of Ecstasy culture in Britain, the music most clubbers dance and drug to. In 1989, 'house' was the all-encompassing general term for rave music. But in the immediately ensuing years, not only was house's primacy challenged by rival terms like 'techno' and 'hardcore', but house itself started to splinter, as an endless array of prefixes – 'tribal', 'progressive', 'handbag', and so forth – interposed themselves in front of the word in order to define precise stylistic strands.

'Handbag house' was initially a disparaging term, coined by condescending cognoscenti *vis-à-vis* the anthemic, chart-penetrating house tunes that allegedly appealed to women, and above all to the folk-mythic construct of Sharon and Tracy, stereotypes of the undiscriminating working-class party girl. Inevitably, 'handbag' – and its slightly tuffer sequel, 'hardbag' – became a rallying cry for populists not afraid of 'cheesy' emotionalism. While some of the anti-handbag hipsters affiliated themselves with American deep house and garage from New York and Chicago, another faction came up with the dubious concept of 'progressive house'. Released by labels like Hard Hands, Cowboy, Om and Guerrilla, this was homegrown English house music, trippy and trancey, and distinguished by long tracks, big riffs, mild dub-inflections and multi-tiered percussion. 'Progressive' seemed to signify not just its anti-cheese, non-girly credentials but its severing of house's roots in gay black disco. Out of the 1991–3 prog house scene emerged a number of artists who belong to a non-genre that might be dubbed 'band house': groups like Leftfield, Lionrock, Underworld, The Aloof and Faithless who sell albums in large amounts and play live.

Back in America, the equivalents to these big-sellers aren't bands but auteur producers like Masters At Work, Deep Dish, Armand Van Helden and Murk. US underground house seems to shift back and forth between songs and tracks, soft and hard, big vocals and depersonalized abstraction. Somewhere between these two poles lies the vogue for disco cut-ups: raw-yet-camp tracks, vocal-free but based around looped samples from seventies underground disco classics. Pioneering both the disco cut-up trend and the resurgence of Chicago house were the twin labels Relief and Cajual. Relief is a 'trackhead' label: its eerie, unhinged, almost psychotic output, by artists like Green Velvet, Gene Farris, DJ Sneak and DJ Rush, thrillingly revived the spirit if not the sound of acid house.

Recently, the proliferation of house sub-genres has gone into hyperdrive, with terms like nu-NRG (hard, gay, Euro house) and dream house/epic house (lushly melodic, atmospheric house influenced by trance) achieving fleeting currency. Progressive house has returned (now shorn of any pretensions to innovation and signifying no-nonsense pumping house for regular heterosexual blokes), while the purist sub-genre of tech-house boasts ultra-clean production (sounds so spangly-pristine you feel like you've already done an E) and boasts of preserving the 'lost spirit' of Chicago acid and Detroit techno. Meanwhile, a bastard form of acid emerged from London's underground milieu of squat-raves – a screeching, raucous, punk-fierce blare of overdriven 303s. The scene-and-sound's defiantly impurist attitude was emblazoned in the gloriously titled compilation *It's Not Intelligent, It's Not From Detroit, But It's Fucking 'Avin It*, mixed by crusading free party DJ-collective Liberator and released on their label Stay Up Forever.

A world away from the squalor of the squat-scene (where ketamine was increasingly the drug-of-choice,) garage – for years, the nearest thing to a static entity in the post-rave universe – spawned its own distinctively British mutant called 'speed garage'. Sometime in late 1996/early 1997, a segment of London's jungle audience began to wonder why they were listening to such dark, depressing music. Jungle had been shaped by the desperation of the recession-wracked mid-nineties; now, with 'loadsamoney' in their pockets, the junglists didn't feel desperate anymore. Increasingly alienated by the white industrial bombast of techstep, these mostly black junglists began to complain about the surfeit of distortion-drenched and melody-free tracks ('disgusting music, mad music', as V Records' Bryan Gee put it). Searching for a sound that better reflected their affluence and insousiance, the ex-junglists built a brand new scene based around the 'finer things in life' – designer-label clothes, flash cars, champagne, cocaine, and garage music.

As well as attracting upwardly mobile, 'mature' white clubbers who reviled rave culture as juvenile and lumpen, garage's mellow opulence had long appealed to junglists; where a techno chill-out room offered beat-free ambient, the second room at jungle clubs like Thunder & Joy tended to play bumpin' garage. For most of the nineties, homegrown UK garage had slavishly imitated American producers. But when the ex-junglists entered the fray, they created a distinctly British hybrid strain that merged house's slinky panache with jungle's rude-bwoy exuberance.

Like all innovations in dance music – from early eighties house to early nineties hardcore – speed garage began as a DJ-driven sound. Pirate DJs pitched up American garage imports – particularly the tuffer style of producers like Todd Edwards and Armand Van Helden – to +8 on their Technics turntables, and insinuated jungalistic elements: dub-wize effects, rewinds and ragga-MC chatter. Inevitably, DJs started to cut dubplates that sounded like their mixes; the next step was to release the tracks. And so a new genre was born. Tougher and faster than its US prototype, speed garage is a winning combination of the most crowdpleaser elements from house, jungle circa 1994, and hardcore rave: sultry divas, 'dread bass', dancehall reggae chants, 'ardkore's sped-up, helium-squeaky vocals, plus the filtering effects used by house producers like Daft Punk to make sounds shiver up your spine.

What really defines speed garage, though, is its beat: syncopated, highly textured snares with a curiously organic, wood-block timbre. Unlike house's metronomic four-to-the-floor kick-drum, speed garage is polyrhythmically perverse, riddled with itchy percussive tics, micro-breakbeats and quivery synth-stabs. And where most rave music is asexual, speed garage is lascivious – the skipping snares tug at your hips, the rumpshaker B-lines wiggle your ass. This sexiness is probably a side-effect of British clubbers's shift of allegiance from anti-aphrodis-iac Ecstasy to horny-making cocaine.

The craze for coke ties in with the way the scene resurrects the snobby exclusivity of the pre-rave club culture of the mid-eighties (the last time the economy was booming). Most speed garage clubs ban jeans and sneakers. Speed garage's ethos of 'living large' also parallels US 'playa' rap's 'we-are-the-beautiful people / we be the baddest clique' hedonism – its conspicuous consumption and luxury-commodity fetishism, its weird blend of chilled languor and latent menace. Hence the garage bootleg version of L'il Kim/ Notorious B.I.G.'s 'Crush On You' doing the rounds. If jungle was gangsta rave, speed garage is gangsta house.

Converts hail speed garage as a revolution in British dance culture. Certainly, its victory has been swift and total. In 1997, just about every jungle pirate radio station in London switched to speed garage. Jungle's populist core withered away; hitherto 'rammed' jump-up events like the Roast suddenly found their dancefloors almost deserted, with the punters defecting to speed garage clubs like Absolute Sundays, Numb Nums, Twice as Nice, Sun City, the Powerhouse and Horny. 'A lot of the dread side of jungle has gone into the garage,' says Phil Aslet from Source Direct, 'dread' referring to the dancehall reggae fans originally lured into jungle by its ragga samples back in 1994. Yet because its non-breakbeat rhythms appeal to house fans, speed garage has achieved way more popularity and commercial success than jungle ever did; genre-defining singles like Double 99's 'Ripgroove', 187 Lockdown's 'Gunman' and Fabulous Baker Boys' 'Oh Boy' (a brilliant remake of Jonny L's 'Hurt You So') were propelled into the UK Top Twenty only months after the scene's discovery by the media.

Inevitably, speed garage has inspired emnity. From house purists to drum and bass scientists, many argue that, far from being revolution-ary, speed garage is merely a crafty collage of the most cheesily effective clichés from the last seven years of UK dance. True enough – although it's hard to imagine even the sternest purist managing to resist this pleasure-principled sound's alluring obviousness. And more innovative strains of speed garage *are* emerging, like the dub-spacious, percussa-delic and succulently textured productions of artists such as A Baffled Republic and Ramsey & Fen, which recall the eighties avant-disco of

Arthur Russell. Generally, the best version of any given speed garage track is the stripped-down and weirder 'dub'.

Then there's the fierce, jungle-dominated style that's been called 'dangerous garage', tracks like Gant's 'Sound Bwoy Burial' and Strickly Dub's 'Small Step': baleful sub-bass pressure, dub-noise (sonar bleeps, sirens, gunshots, explosions of reverb) and patois dancehall shouts 'timestretched' so that the sample seems to crack apart like it's afflicted with metal fatigue. Another exciting sub-style is the spate of speed garage remakes of hardcore classics like 'Some Justice' and 'We Are I.E.'

Given that back in 1992 the garage and rave scenes were polar opposites and implacable enemies, speed garage's nostalgia for hardcore seems weird. But there's actually a continuum linking hardcore, jungle circa 1994 and speed garage – not only do the same figures crop up (Suburban Base's Dan Donelly, for instance, has now shifted his energy into his speed garage sub-label Quench), but the core attitude endures. As with all hardcore dance scenes past and present, it's the 'trackhead', FX-crazy, ruthlessly digital side of speed garage, rather than the we-wanna-move-toward-using-real-instruments, 'musical' sector, that is really shaping any kind of future sound of London.

Still, it's sheer hype(rbole) to rank speed garage alongside jungle, let alone acid house, as a sonic/subcultural revolution. Coloured by the feel-goodism of the late Major/early Blair boom, the politics of speed garage are so much less interesting than jungle's 'darkside' paradigm (temporarily outmoded in 1997–98, but probably not for long). On a strictly musical level, speed garage is a composite (house + jungle) where drum and bass was a mutant (hip hop × techno). Jungle twisted and morphed its sources; as yet, an equivalent warp factor is barely audible in speed garage.

Like most of the sub-generic turnover of the late nineties, speed garage reflects the fact that rave-and-club music seems to have reached an impasse. The extremes in every direction have been probed. The only way to advance seems to be through 'internal' hybrids (house + trance = 'epic house', for instance) or by mounting strategic, one-step-back-two-steps-forwards retreats in order to explore a path prematurely abandoned (as techstep did by reactivating elements of 1991-era Belgian hardcore). With micro-genres like harsh-step (techstep + gabba) and nu-breaks (midtempo jungle? 'intelligent Big Beat'?!) on the horizon in early 1998, rave music seems to be being torn everywhichway by linked-but-opposed processes of disintegration and reintegration. For every new subgenre that breaks off from its progenitor style, a new hybrid coalesces that reconnects parts of the shattered whole that was once 'rave'.

*

The rampant proliferation of hybrid sub-genres like speed garage may smack of hype or hairsplitting to outsiders, but it's actually a sign of house music's continued vitality, proof that it's still evolving. But I can't help feeling that in the broader cultural sense, house music and the club circuit are fundamentally conservative. At its more populist end, house has reverted back into mere disco, the soundtrack to traditional Saturday Nite fever. As for the more 'discriminating' house sub-scenes, these are simply pre-rave metropolitan clubland élitism back in full, coked-up effect.

Rave was to club culture what punk was to rock: a kind of internal revolt within the broader musical formation. Punk didn't really change the sound of rock that much, but it changed the attitude and it revived the late sixties' exorbitant expectations of what the music could do (change the world). While rave as music was initially identical to the music played in clubs, rave as a subculture inverted all the guiding principles of clubland: rave was anti-élitist, anti-cool, pro-inclusivity, pro-abandon. Eventually, that spirit, that new subcultural context, changed the music itself, resulting in hardcore, jungle, trance, gabba and all the other mongrel mutations of the Detroit/Chicago blueprints. For me, the idea and ideal of *raving* – mass communion, communal freak-out – seems crucial. When dance subcultures revert from full-on rave madness and 'go back to the clubs,' my enthusiasm begins to wane.

If Britain's house mainstream has distanced itself from the psychedelic, freakbeat element of rave – noise, aggression, riffs, juvenile dementia, hysteria – it has also reneged upon rave's counter-cultural utopianism. House clubs are now a hi-tech leisure industry, offering the paying customer the opportunity to step inside a drug-conducive, sensorily intensified environment of ultra-vivid sound-and-visuals. No sacrifices are required to participate, beyond the financial; no ramifications extend into everyday life, beyond the drug hangover. As the late Gavin Hills put it, 'Ecstasy culture is like a video-recorder: an entertainment device, something you use for a certain element of pleasure. The club structure now is like the pub structure, it has a role in our society.'

It also has a role in the economy. The dance record and nightclub industries generate huge amounts of taxable income. Big-capacity 'superclubs' like Ministry of Sound, Cream and Renaissance are closer to corporations than the traditional notion of the club promoter; these are businesses with staffs, payrolls, profit-margins and long-term expand-and-diversify strategies that encompass merchandising, club-affiliated CD compilations, sponsorship deals, even transporting their legendary vibe to other cities in the form of the 'club tour'. Along-side the corporate clubs, the other big earners in dance culture are the first-division DJs – like Sasha, Jeremy Healey, Carl Cox, Pete Tong, Judge Jules, John Digweed and Paul Oakenfold – who charge fees in the region of £2,000–£5,000 for a two or three hour set. Thanks to the 'guest DJ circuit' that links one-off commercial mega-raves and the superclubs, these DJs can play several gigs *per night* at week-ends. Factor in mid-week gigs plus all the other sources of income (mix-CDs, making tracks, radio shows, remixing pop groups), and it's clear that some of these guys must be close to becoming DJ-millionaires.

Beyond the amount of tax revenue the dance industry creates, club-and-rave culture has contributed – alongside the Britpop explosion of retro guitar bands like Oasis – to the global perception that 'England is Swinging, Again'. Despite this, the establishment attitude to rave-and-club culture is deeply conflicted. Both John Major's Conservative government and its Labour successor have maintained the war against recreational drug use. Following the media and public outcry in 1996 about Ecstasy deaths, MP Barry Legg drafted the Public Entertainment Licences (Drug Misuse) Bill. Passed just before the downfall of the Tories in May 1997, the law gives local councils and police forces the power to close down nightclubs if it is believed that drug-consumption is taking place on the premises. Given the endemic use of Ecstasy, amphetamine, acid and marijuana (a 1997 Release survey conducted in nightclubs revealed that 97 per cent of British clubbers had tried drugs, and that just under 90 per cent were planning to take some kind of illicit substance *that evening*), this law ought to mean that every dance venue in the UK should be closed down.

If the political establishment were to take a more realistic and cynical point of view, they might conclude that recreational drug use is not only an established component of British society, it's an *essential* component. Ecstasy culture is a useful way of dissipating the tensions generated by wage-slavery and under-employment; it's an agent of social homeostasis, in so far as the loved-up ambience of clubs and raves offers youth a sort of provisional utopia each and every weekend, thereby channelling idealism and discontent out of the political arena altogether. 'I reckon that if it wasn't for Ecstasy, there'd have been a revolution in this country by now,' declared The Prodigy's Maxim Reality back in 1992; although he clearly meant to praise MDMA, others might read that remark as an indictment.

Irvine Welsh, 'rave author' and icon of 'the chemical generation', confronts this idea of Ecstasy as counter-revolutionary force in his novella 'A Smart Cunt' (from *The Acid House*). A left-wing militant is attempting to recruit Brian, Welsh's most autobiographical protagonist. 'I'm thinking, what can I do, really do for the emancipation of working people in this country, shat on by the rich, tied into political inaction by servile reliance on a reactionary, moribund and yet still unelectable Labour Party?' muses Brian. 'The answer is a resounding fuck all. Getting up early to sell a couple of [political pamphlets] in a shopping centre is not my idea of the best way to chill out after raving ... I think I'll stick to drugs to get me through the long, dark night of late capitalism.' Could it be that the entire project of rave and post-rave club culture has amounted to little more than a survival strategy for the generation that grew up under Thatcher, a way of getting by? A culture of consolation, where the illusory community of the Ecstatic dancefloor compensates for the withering away of the 'social' in the outside world, ever more deeply riven by class divisions and rich–poor disparities? The explosion of pent-up social energies that occurred in the late eighties has been channelled and corralled into a highly controlled and controlling leisure system. The rave as temporary autonomous zone has become the club as pleasure-prison, a detention camp for youth.

Nineties house culture in Britain also seems utterly in tune with the apolitical, consumerist spirit of the Thatcher–Major era. House clubs offer their customers the prospect that each and every weekend can be a miniature Ibiza, a vacation from the workaday. One catchphrase seems to sum up house's 'work hard/play hard' conservatism: *having it*, or, pronounced authentically, *'avin' it*. Used as an adjective (a havin' it club, a havin' it crowd) or as a hedonist war-cry ('we're 'avin' it

LARGE, 'avin' it *major!*'), the buzzphrase captures the voracious greediness of house culture, its spirit of pleasure-principled acquisitiveness, a sort of psychedelic materialism. Neck those pills, snort some lines of charlie, puff on a big fat spliff, guzzle down those import lagers, chase the lot down with a wrap of billy whizz; let's get fucked up good and proper.

*

For me, the exhilarating thing about rave was that it was *psychedelic disco*, a mindblowing merger of rock delinquency and club culture's science of sound. At the time of writing, the most vibrant sound in dance music is the rave'n'roll hybrid called Big Beat, as purveyed by The Chemical Brothers and the Skint label's Fatboy Slim and Bentley Rhythm Ace, amongst many others. Resisting the tyranny of good taste and 'intelligence', Big Beat has brought back a sense of messy, 'mindless' fun.

Reared on the neo-psychedelic turmoil of My Bloody Valentine and that most riff-driven of rap groups Public Enemy, then radicalized by their experience of acid house during their college days in Manchester, The Chemical Brothers bring a punk-like attack to techno by accentuating the same blaring mid-frequencies supplied by distorted guitars. Take 'Loops of Fury', a black-and-white riot of stuttering beats, convulsive fuzz-riffage and floorquaking electro sub-bass; when they unleashed this monstertune at New York's Irving Plaza in 1996, I found myself pogoing for the first time in fifteen years!

The Chemicals' second album *Dig Your Own Hole* was even more rockist. In interviews, the duo – Ed Simons and Tom Rowlands – testified to the influence of sixties garage punk and freakbeat groups like Tintern Abbey, and even sampled psych-rockers Lothar and the Hand People on the awesomely monolithic mantra-stomp of 'It Doesn't Matter'. On their breakthrough single 'Setting Sun', they teamed up with the biggest rock star of the day, Oasis's Noel Gallagher, for a track that sounds like a fusion of The Beatles' 'Tomorrow Never Knows' and Public Enemy's 'Rebel Without A Pause'. Unlike those other rock/rave crossover giants Underworld, though, The Chems stay true to the most radical aspects of house and techno; they mostly shun songs and vocals, and rarely resort to melody, yet still manage to enthral through texture, noise and sheer groove-power alone.

The mentality of the milieu from which The Chems emerge – clubs like The Heavenly Social, the Big Kahuna Burger and the Big Beat Boutique, labels like Wall of Sound and Bolshi, bands like Monkey Mafia and Death In Vegas – is decidedly rockist too. It's all a bit *Loaded*-laddish and lager-loutish, a tad too close to Britpop's boy's own boorishness. Perhaps that's not so strange when you consider that The Chemicals, Fatboy Slim and Bentley Rhythm Ace all have indie-rock skeletons in their B-boy closet: Fatboy's Norman Cook played bass in jangle-pop hitmakers The Housemartins, while Bentley's Richard March was in Pop Will Eat Itself. (Indie's revenge: Norman Cook remixes Cornershop's late-Velvets pastiche 'Brimful of Asha' and it gets to Number One!)

Then again, these dodgy origins could be Big Beat's secret strength. At a time when so much electronica suffers from anal-retentive complexity, the Big Beat outfits 'regress' to those eras when rave music itself was most *rock'n'roll* in its druggy abandon: Madchester's indie-dance, breakbeat hardcore, acid house and the late eighties DJ records of Coldcut, Bomb The Bass et al. Big Beat simultaneously uses rock 'n' roll's hell-for-leather attitude to show up how too much of today's electronic music is po-faced, while deploying club culture's arsenal of drug-tech effects to make trad guitar bands look terribly dated. Of course, this hasn't stopped dance purists dissing Big Beat as rock 'n' roll tarted up with ideas ripped off techno and house, or trad-rockers dismissing it as inane party music without the redemptive resonance of your Verves and Radioheads.

Guilty as charged on both counts, for sure – but so what? Big Beat's sole *raison d'être* is to generate excitement and intensity: what could be more rock 'n' roll, more rave, than that? Big Beat tracks are crammed with crescendos, drops, builds, explosions, crowd-inciting drum rolls and wooshing sounds that pan across the stereo-field. These roller-coaster thrills 'n' spills carry over to Big Beat DJing, a style-hopping frenzy closer to a jukebox than to the house/techno DJs seamless mixing. Where the latter is designed for MDMA's sustained plateau of bliss, Big Beat's jagged, epileptic-eclectism reflects the polydrug norms of the late nineties. Where once the E in 'Generation E' stood for Ecstasy, now it stands for *everything*.

And yet Big Beat could not have emerged without Ecstasy culture's prior existence; most of its pilfered repertoire of licks and kicks originally evolved specifically in order to tantalize the Ecstatic body. Big Beat represents the latest stage in British rave's abiding musical narrative: the attempt to fuse house and hip hop, a compulsion that runs from the late eighties DJ records through bleep-and-bass, 'ardkore and jungle, to who knows what future (per)mutations. And so tracks like Fatboy's 'Everybody Loves A Filter', Dr Bone's 'I Came Here To Get Ripped' and Environmental Science's 'The Day The Zak Stood Still' marry rush-activating riffs, stabs and tingle-textures with boombastic breaks 'n' sub-bass; DJing, Norman Cook has been known to mix Public Enemy's 'Bring The Noise' over the acid-tweekin' 303-driven funk of Josh Wink's 'Higher State of Consciousness'.

Now that The Chemical Brothers fancy themselves as 'mature' album artists, Norman Cook has usurped their role as rave-saviour. Truer to Big Beat's immediacy-is-all-that-counts attitude, the debut Fatboy Slim LP *Better Living Through Chemistry* is more like a 'greatest hits' singles collection than an album. It's also a compendium of tried-and-tested devices for triggering the rave 'n' roll rush. 'Song For Lindy' features an oscillating piano-vamp melody-riff that flashes back to Brit-rave's euphoric peak circa 1991; 'Everybody *Needs* A 303' rubs seventies slap-bass up against Roland acieed bass-drone, topped with a psychedelic soul chorus courtesy of Edwin Starr; 'Going Out Of My Head' has the nerve to nick the powerchord-riff from The Who's 'Can't Explain' and the nous to make it feel modern rather than mod (none of Britpop's sepia-tinted retro-referentiality). Bentley Rhythm Ace's own killer tune 'Return of the Hardcore Jumble Carbootechnodisco Roadshow' pivots around a frenetic chickenscratch-guitar riff that draws a white line between 1966 mod's amphetamine-frenzy freakbeats and 1998 Big Beat's pills-and-Pils fuelled pandemonium.

Above all, what I hear in the Skint sound and similar labels like Bolshi is the partial return of 1992's breakbeat 'ardkore. Take Bolshi producer Rasmus. His exhilarating EP 'Mass Hysteria' recalls the scratchadelic mayhem of DJ Hype and Danny Breaks's 'I Can't Understand It'; tracks like 'Afro (Blowing In The Wind)' feature old skool rap sliced 'n' diced into locked-groove blurts of glossolalia, 78 r.p.m. squeaky voices, incongruous eighties pop samples. Unwittingly resurrecting 'ardkore, Big Beat is a bit like jungle's retarded cousin – it occasionally steals the odd jittery rhythm-programming trick from the breakbeat scientists, but generally favours much more simplistic looped breaks.

Compared with the sophistication of drum and bass, Big Beat may seem like a step backwards. But at this point in techno's history, 'how experimental is it?' is not really the most helpful question to ask of a new music. 'Does it work? Does it get me worked up?' may be more telling. (After all, *most* scientific experiments lead to inconclusive results or abject failure; similarly, *most* experimental dance music is seriously dysfunktional when it comes to working as a desiring machine). Big Beat's back-to-1992 tendency parallels the way seventies punk reactivated the adrenalizing minimalism of mid-sixties garage punk. But maybe pub rock is a better analogy, with beery Big Beat as the necessary back-to-basics initiative before the real revolution, a techno-punk that's hopefully just round the corner.

Such a punk-style revolt is sorely needed. Too many post-rave genres bear an uncanny resemblance to progressive rock: conceptualism, auteur-geniuses, producers making music to impress other producers, muso virtuosity reborn as the 'science' of programming finesse. Purist genres like Jeff Mills-style minimalist techno initially defined themselves against the 'cheesy'-ness of hardcore rave and happy house ('cheese' meaning the corny-but-effective elements in music) by dedicating themselves to the pursuit of endless subtleties. The thing about cheese, though, is that it creates flava and increases the phat content of any given music. When it comes to cheese, I'll choose a pungent cliché over an insipid subtlety any day. In fact, I'd argue that the entire history of dance music is about the creation of potent clichés – sounds and effects so good that other people couldn't resist copying them. Clichés like disco's snare-crash, acid house's 303 bass-squeal, hardcore's Morse-Code pianos and 'Mentasm' noises, jungle's 'Amen' breaks, gabba's distorted kick-drum, and house's skin-tingling EQ/filter effects.

To invent a cliché from scratch is a great feat. The Chemicals, Fatboy Slim and the other Big Beat acts may not have actually invented any *new* clichés, but by inventively crushing together all of the golden oldies from rave, house, rap, disco, ad infinitum, they've reminded us that dance music is supposed to be about fun, about *freaky dancing* as opposed to headnodding and trainspotting.

*

The rock-like qualities in The Chemical Brothers, Underworld and The Prodigy are precisely what has enabled them to cross over into the American mainstream. Although the 'Electronica Revolution' has been trailed in the US media as the long-overdue arrival of techno to

America, it's readily apparent that the British invaders have met the post-grunge audience halfway.

The Prodigy's story is the most bizarre example of this 'market repositioning' syndrome. Back in late 1992 The Prodigy seemed, for all their hit singles and healthy album sales, like a band without a future: their destiny was surely to go down the plughole along with the rave scene *Mixmag* gloatingly accused them of destroying with a single song, 'Charly'. But over the next two years, The Prodigy sidestepped the decline of the mega-rave circuit and pulled off an astounding feat of self-reinvention. By 1994, the band were playing rock festivals, selling to *NME* and *Melody Maker* readers, and wowing the crits with *Music For the Jilted Generation*: a vaguely conceptual album that protested the crackdown on rave culture, from local councils refusing licences for commercial events to the Criminal Justice Act's assault on illicit raves.

After a slew of hits – the rock-guitar propelled 'Voodoo People', the awesome slow-mo break-and-bassquake 'Poison' – The Prodigy scored their greatest triumph in early 1996 with 'Firestarter', a metal-riffin' hymn-to-destruction that sampled grunge grrls The Breeders and The Art of Noise. Transforming dancer/MC Keith Flint into star vocalist and videogenic focal point, 'Firestarter' went straight to Number One in the UK. Appearing at the MTV Europe Awards to pick up a trophy for Best Dance Video, The Prodigy greeted the youth of the EC with a matey 'hold it down! – a vintage 1992 rave buzzphrase – as if to confirm 'ardkore's historical vindication. It had become what it always secretly had been, for those with ears to hear it: the new rock 'n' roll.

Several months later, 'Firestarter' became a heavy-rotation buzz-video in America, igniting a major label bidding war (amazingly, The Prodigy had already been signed and then let go after just one album by two substantial American labels, Elektra and Mute). Madonna's Maverick – a Warner Bros. sub-label – won the war, at considerable expense. With corporate heft behind it, The Prodigy's third album *The Fat Of The Land* went straight to Number One in America (and in another twenty or so countries as well). But by this point – with almost every *Fat* track featuring vocals and guitar-riffs where once there had only been samples and breaks, and the hectic rave tempos slowed to a Big Beat pummel – The Prodigy *were* a rock band, to all intents and purposes. Liam Howlett even declared in interviews that he'd never

liked house or Kraftwerk (Detroit techno's sacred source). The Oi!-
meets-jungle menace of 'Breathe' and a cover of L7's 'Fuel My Fire'
defined The Prodigy's new sales shtick: an apolitical update of punk
offering post-grunge kids an aerobic work-out for their frustration and
aggression. On-stage and in video, mohican-sporting maniac and self-
proclaimed 'youth corrupter' Keith Flint pulled grotesque faces and
threw twisted shapes like some cartoon cross between Alice Cooper
and Vivian from *The Young Ones*.

For underground techno and house fiends, the American music-
industry sponsored buzzword 'electronica' – the rubric under which
The Chemical Brothers and The Prodigy have been hyped – is already
a dirty word. Like 'rave' – the milieu in which The Prodigy originally
honed its crowd-pleasing stagecraft – the term 'electronica' holds out
the threat of the music's corruption, as it makes the transition from
intimate clubs to stadiums, from discriminating cognoscenti to a mass
audience. The house and techno purists want to keep the music
contained at the level of the pre-rave, club-oriented scenes in Detroit,
Chicago and New York.

And yet the myth and the reality of rave still haunts this music, even
the sub-scenes that explicitly define themselves against its populism.
However much 'we' might disagree over the future course of the music,
'rave' is what keeps us talking to each other. This can be seen in the
success of Tribal Gathering, the UK dance festival. Its very name
acknowledges the Balkanization of post-rave culture, even as it seeks to
resurrect the lost unity by shepherding the scattered tribes together.

In 1996, Tribal Gathering was touted as the successor to the
Glastonbury rock festival, which didn't happen that year. But at
Glastonbury, the side-shows and bazaars are strictly supplementary to
the main arena, where fifty thousand plus convene to watch the
headlining bands. For the thirty thousand who attend Tribal Gathering,
the experience is far more disparate. In 1996, TG offered seven circus-
size tents catering for different tastes: Nexus for jungle and happy
hardcore, Planet Cyberpunk for bangin' techno, Astral Nuts for Euro
trance, Tribal Temple for Goa Trance, Planet Erotica for house and
garage, Planet Phunk for trip hop. Each of these tents was approximately the same size. Even the biggest, Starship Universe (at 6500
capacity) was nowhere close to being the focal point of Tribal
Gathering, despite its line-up of crowdpleasers, crossover acts and
genre-blenders, like Leftfield, Black Grape, Carl Cox and Josh Wink.

Tribal Gathering's decentred structure is the only sensible way to reconcile the mega-rave ideal of thirty-thousand-people-in-a-field grooving to the same beat, with the post-rave reality of shattered consensus, uncommon aims and different strokes. In years to come, there will doubtless be more and more tents, as sub-genres sub-divide. (Indeed in 1997, happy hardcore got its own tent, separate from jungle; how long before the happy hardcore sub-style 'trancecore' gets its own marquee?)

What I wondered as I wandered from tent to tent on that May night in 1996 was whether the gathered tribes were fraternizing, or simply co-existing in adjacence. There were a lot of non-aligned types drifting about, but it seemed equally possible that most people gravitated towards their own kind and fixated on their particular drug/technology fix. It was hard to imagine any of the hardcore massive in Nexus stepping out of their particular locked groove in order to check out what was Goa-ing on in Astral Nuts, or vice versa. What was really odd about the event was the Goa-heads could have enjoyed a similar line-up of DJs at regular Goa events like Return To The Source, for about half the price, and without having to trek forty miles to the event; the junglists and happy-core kids could equally have heard a similarly stellar selection of DJs at events like World Dance. The extra £15 everyone had paid was basically their homage to the myth of rave, the living dream of unity-in-diversity. They were subsidizing a ritual re-enactment of something that was long lost but that still mattered in some obscure way.

In Britain, on the eve of acid house's tenth anniversary, there's a sense of legacy and achievement, a feeling of 'what a long strange trip it's been'. Nostalgia abounds (although there's disagreement over when exactly the lost golden age was: 1988–9, or 1991–2, or even 1994, the year jungle broke through), a nostalgia expressed in double and triple CD compilations of house classics and hardcore anthems, in 'Back to 92' raves and 'Old Skool' events. Genealogies, canons, and counter-canons are being drawn up, historical knowledge and narratives accumulated.

In America, the feeling is rather different. The rave scene grows steadily but seems stuck in a holding pattern; the much-vaunted 'electronica revolution' may be that scene's long-deferred explosion into mass consciousness, but will more likely be a top-down, corporate-imposed phenomenon, oriented around bands rather than DJs, and slyly distanced from the taint of drugs.

I have a pet theory that the vitality of a pop genre is in inverse ratio to the number of books written about it. Compared with the thousands of biographies, essay collections and critical overviews that clog up rock's arteries, only a handful of tomes (academic efforts included) have addressed the dance-and-drug culture – despite the fact that in Europe it's been the dominant form of pop music for nearly a decade. I guess this inverse-ratio theory makes my own effort here one of the first nails in the coffin. But we've a long, long way to go before this music is dead and buried, mummified as a museum culture like rock 'n' roll. The Rave Hall of Fame is a couple of decades away from being built. Ten years on, this culture – call it rave, or techno, or electronic dance music, whatever – still feels incredibly vital. It's only just hitting its prime; internal revolutions and reconfigurations like punk surely lie ahead. If this precise moment feels like a pause for breath, it's only because there's so much still ahead.

NINETEEN

TRANCE
MISSION

THE LATE-NINETIES
RESURGENCE OF
TRANCE

A girl daubs her face and arms with fluorescent paint, then turns to admire her handiwork in the luminescent beams of an ultraviolet lamp. Her boyfriend, dancing nearby, has a samurai-style topknot, a shaved skull dotted with phosphorescent green spots, and a satanist's beard. Behind the couple's heads, on the cliffs that loom above the grassy dance floor, you can see what looks like two gigantic fireflies doing a mating dance. Squint through the darkness, and the courtship choreography resolves into the semaphore-like movements of a pair of green extra-large glow-sticks, waved by a long-haired hippie lurking in the jungle canopy.

The location is a remote farm deep in the densely forested hills of Puerto Rico, and the event is El Cuco, a three-day festival for psychedelic trance music organized by New York promoter Tsunami. Psy-trance represents the hardcore underground end of trance's vast spectrum. From the next-generation ravers packing superclubs like Gatecrasher in Sheffield, to the full-moon raves in the deserts of Southern California, trance resurged in the last few years of the nineties to reign supreme as the world's most popular and pervasive form of electronic dance music. In Germany, trance soundtracked Berlin's annual Love Parade, a million-strong street carnival so accepted by the mainstream that leading politicians turned a blind eye to the blatant Ecstasy use and competed to associate themselves with the event. In Israel, trance was even bigger but inspired the opposite response – a media panic about a counterculture of youth too druggy and decadent to defend the country against its hostile neighbours. Many Israeli tranceheads were kids who freaked out after three years' compulsory military service, grew their hair long, and went to Goa, the mother lode for psy-trance culture. Some of these AWOL youth never came back, inspiring an Israeli mothers' movement concerned about the music's corrupting effect.

If you remapped the globe to reflect the influence and prestige of nations when it comes to electronic dance music in general, Britain would swell to the size of the Pacific Ocean, Germany would absorb all of Eurasia, the USA would equal North and South America combined, and France would be Australasia. But if you adjusted the atlas in ratio to the global distribution of *trance*, especially the underground form of psy-trance, the globe would actually resemble how the world really looks. See, there're scenes for psy-trance in countries you never hear from when it comes to the other, hipper sorts of techno: Macedonia, Colombia, Poland, Switzerland, Bolivia, Croatia, Portugal. In August 1999, the Solipse festival in Ozora, Hungary, drew 30,000 nomadic hippie ravers from across the world to celebrate the solar eclipse and dance to a line-up of bands and DJs that was non-stop psy-trance. In Russia, there's an annual trance festival called Orbita, while the Ukraine boasts massive trance raves on the beaches of the Black Sea, Finland has a thriving scene of forest raves, and there are Japanese trance parties in Mount Fuji national park. Even within the Big Four nations, psy-trance thrives in cities that don't have the lustre of perceived cool, such as Hamburg, Germany, where the annual Voov Experience festival takes place.

Psy-trance is an 'equal opportunity' genre when it comes to making the music too: there are leading exponents of psychedelic trance operating in Israel, Australia, Sweden, Greece, Denmark. It's a truly pan-global style, with no real origin or primary location. Despite being initially associated with the techno traveller's dance-and-drug paradise Goa, it draws nothing from the environment or local culture. Really, it's a sonic virus that hatched in the early nineties amongst the nomadic bohemians who gather every winter during Goa's party season, and was then brought back to European clubs. Apart from the music itself, the defining Goa trait was the deployment of 'black light' (aka ultraviolet) in tandem with fluorescent clothes, body paint and decor (the latter typically involving brightly coloured tapestries hand painted in luminous ink and using fantastical imagery that blends Hindu goddesses and cosmic science fiction). Goa's 'fluoro' tradition started because ultraviolet lamps were more portable in the jungle environment than other rave staples like lasers and strobes.

After a couple of years of faddish popularity in the early nineties, Goa trance returned underground, changed its name (to psychedelic trance) and continued its virulent transglobal diffusion. Goa itself became increasingly despoiled, inspiring a quest for 'the next Goa', an exotic place not yet overrun with tourists or ruined by a police crackdown on drugs. A circuit of alternative destinations opened up for 'trancepackers', trance-loving backpackers. Thailand became a prime location for full-moon 'frenzies' at Koh Phangan and Haad Rin village, but that country soon became too popular, so the serious 'heads' moved further afield, to Bali and to Nepal's mountains and lakes. With its prime season occurring at the same time as Goa's (January/February), Australia emerged as the next serious contender. Thousands of trancepackers descended upon the long established hippie resort of Byron Bay, the easternmost point on Australia's coast. Here, and elsewhere in Australia, there were huge raves in the bush, like the Rainbow Serpent Festival and the Summer Dreaming. Then came South Africa, with its Rustlers Valley raves, followed by Vene-zuela, Mexico, Brazil, Madagascar, Morocco . . .

If you heard Goa trance in 1994 and dismissed its frilly curlicues of arpeggiated synth and mandala-Mandelbrot texture-swirls as comically kosmik hippie shit, you might be surprised by the way it subsequently mutated. True, the early Goa sound of Juno Reactor and Green Nuns of the Revolution was maximalist to a fault, writhing with polytendril-led patterns. But in the late nineties, psy-trance plunged into a dark phase of minimalism and abstraction. Hamburg-based psy-trance gods X-Dream pioneered this harsh new psy-sound. Squatting on a grubby mattress at the abandoned orphanage that serves as living quarters for El Cuco's DJs and bands, X-Dream's Markus Maichel explains how he shifted from using his synthesizer keyboard 'as a musical instrument that plays notes' to a 'controller that triggers noises and drum loops'. Psy-trance is still a busy, event-full music, but instead of Goa's fractal density of melody-lines, you get a bedlam of mad effects and sonic surprises ambushing your ears – jabbering bionic parakeets, scuttling bursts of ricocheting drums, single guitar riffs that leap out of the mix to smack you round the chops, verminously wriggling noises like soundworms infesting your brain. Denmark's Kox Box and UK pro-ducer Hallucinogen (real name Simon Posford, he's widely regarded as the best in the genre) are especially inventive, favouring grotesquely distorted and distended snippets of voice that sound like a human being literally being stretched on a rack, harsh delay effects that create the aural equivalent of the drunk man seeing double or triple images, and moments when it sounds like the groove's clockwork mechanism has exploded and is scattering coils and cogs every which way.

'Twisted' is one of the scene's buzz terms. 'Psy-trance is all about tweaking the sounds,' says Opher Yisraeli, an Israeli-American who DJs as India Drop. 'A house producer will use sounds that are more "flat" – that is, like real acoustic instruments, without any effects on top. But a psy-trance producer will "twist" the sounds using every effect and filter available – the crazier, the better!' Psy-trance's abstraction means that the style of music it has most in common with is, bizarrely, drum and bass. Rhythmically, they couldn't be further apart: psy-trance's textured freak-out is layered on top of a pounding four-to-the-floor kick and implacably chugging Moroder bass. But psy-trance and drum and bass are all about sound-engineering as a way of transforming your obsessive-compulsive disorder into an aesthetic and a career. Like drum-and-bass producers, psy-trance artists are obsessed with stereo-spatial trickery: they love to make sounds leap and veer across the speakers.

The other thing shared with drum and bass is a fetish for the darkside, signposted with unnerving samples like 'I'm sure there's gonna be more than one unpleasant surprise before we're done' or 'LSD hints that there is an area of the mind that could be labelled *unsane* – not insane but not sane'. X-Dream's Jan Mueller explains that the psy-trance raves are actually structured to include a 'dark music' phase, before shifting to uplifting 'morning music' at sunrise. 'A crucial part of the party is when the heavy sound is played in the middle of the night, so that the people can freak.' Just as drum and bass's warped sounds dovetail with the skunkanoiac effects of super-strong weed, psy-trance plays off the aural hallucinations triggered by LSD and psilocybin mushrooms. Explains Kara Walker from Philadelphia psy-trance party organizers Gaian Mind, 'some of the sounds used from synths like the Roland 303 and the Juno 6 are connected to that constant buzz or hum in the back of your brain when you're on magic mushrooms. And those crazily echoed samples, with intense delays and heavy filters creating a sort of after-image effect, that goes well with psilocybin and DMT, because those drugs can cause a weird delay effect in your hearing.'

Heard at its best over a big, crisp sound system, psy-trance is fierce, aggressive music, full of shredding and ripping sounds. Sometimes, the music seems to *sizzle*, making real the American anti-drug advert that shows an egg in a frying pan and the slogan 'this is your brain on drugs'. There's the same ultra-clinical digital precision you get in melodic trance, but it's a kind of abrasive cleanliness – sounds so squeaky and rubbery they make your ears itch. That crisp attack of sound has a lot to do with the fact that DJs mostly play DATS (Digital Audio Tape) rather than vinyl. The tradition started in Goa because vinyl is heavier to transport into remote areas. DATs have helped the music to propagate far and wide like an exotic disease. Mingling on the international party circuit, DJs swap DATs of their own tunes with each other – similar to the dubplate system in drum and bass, except that DATs are easily copied, which means a track can proliferate across the world in a few weeks.

*

Paralleling the global reach of psy-trance are 'progressive' and 'Euro', two more mainstream styles of trance. Progressive is a sort of tasteful adult form of trance, slow-burning and subtle, as purveyed by globe-trotting DJ superstars like Sasha, John Digweed and Seb Fontaine, and created by producers like Breeder and Hybrid. Progressive's roots go back to the English 'progressive house' sound of 1992–3, as pioneered by Leftfield and Spooky (whose Charlie May now collaborates with Sasha in the recording studio) and pushed by labels like Guerrilla, Hard Hands and Cowboy. Trance without the cheesy E-motionalism, house purged of its gay disco roots, techno stripped of black feel or jazzy tinges – progressive seems mostly defined by its inhibitions and checked tendencies. So what makes it 'progressive', precisely? Perhaps because, unlike deep house, none of the sounds used in the style really resemble 'real' acoustic instruments. The music seldom 'moves' like a conventional instrument does (the basslines, for instance, couldn't really be imagined as played on a bass guitar). With its abstract whooshing sounds, blurry pulses and stereo-panning effects, progressive has evolved into the ultimate 'big room' music, the sheer spectacular size of its sound perfect for the main dance floor at super-clubs.

In addition to size, progressive is into length: long tracks, long sets, the long mix. DJs like Sasha and Digweed deliberately select character-less tracks rather than orgasmic anthems because those 'run of the mix' sort of tracks can sit together for a protracted period. You can't really tell when the transition between records starts or is completed. The result is a level, peak-less experience (Sasha and Digweed ration out three climaxes per nine-hour set). Progressive's sonic featurelessness carries over to the DJs (an endless roll call of Nicks, Johns, Daves), and the blankness of the track titles ('Force 51', 'Overactive', 'Emotion

Surfer', 'Rhythm Reigns', 'Gyromancer', 'Supertransonic') which avoid conjuring up images or outside-world evocations in favour of a vague spirituality/futurity. Purging all the aspects of rave that harked back to earlier youth movements like hippie and punk (or for that matter, disco or hip hop or reggae), progressive has achieved a perfect non-referential purity.

Even more popular than progressive is the more melodic Euro-trance style as purveyed by Paul Van Dyk, Ferry Corsten, Tiesto, Energy 52, Three Drives On a Vinyl, et al. This style is packed with precisely the cheesy elements that the Sasha-type progressives shun: anthemic choruses, crescendos, drum-rolling builds and beat-free breakdowns, heart-tugging refrains. Imagine the enchanted flutter of a lobotomized Philip Glass, or the cuddly-and-cosmic feeling you'd get if you tripped with the Teletubbies. Listening to the kind of music called 'trance' in the late nineties, it was a jolt to recall that the original 1993 wave of trance from Frankfurt and Berlin was hard, cold music. That phase of trance was massively cool for a good few years, then got eclipsed by drum and bass as the hipster's favourite. Yet trance secretly remained the people's choice on many rave floors across the world. In 1998 it began to resurge dramatically, dominating clubland again thanks partly to a massive increase in Ecstasy use caused by the return of high-quality E in the form of the famous 'Mitsubishi' brand of pills. You could see the vibe change in clubs – scenes of blissed-out abandon the like of which had not been witnessed since the 1988–92 golden age: people caressing their own necks and chests, stroking each other's faces and arms, swept up in a gentle frenzy of touchy-feely tenderness, orgiastic yet chaste.

This renewed enthusiasm for Ecstasy, after years in which its reputation had suffered because of its unreliability, coincided with a dearth of music congenial to taking E. Trance rushed back in to fill the vacuum. Compared with the emotional dryness of late-nineties techno and drum and bass, trance was accessible – highly melodious, euphoric, with emotions that corresponded to 'normal' human feelings (long-ing, poignancy, tenderness, etc.). Where techno and drum and bass producers titled their tracks using terminology from astrophysics or biogenetics, Van Dyk's most famous anthem 'For An Angel' was inspired by meeting his girlfriend! Sensuous and uplifting like house, but with the banging rave energy that house lacks, trance rode the Mitsubishi wave and by 1999 it had achieved an almost tyrannical popularity.

The Esperanto of electronic dance, trance became the world's most beloved form of techno. But it was also the most hated and despised – connoisseurs dismiss it as cheesy trash, not serious or 'deep' like minimal techno and drum and bass. People with an emotional and intellectual investment in concepts like 'subculture', 'underground', 'hardcore' etc. typically characterize trance's spirit as meek and mild, lacking in edge. And there's certainly some element of truth to the stereotype of the trance fan as white, middle class and apolitical, unwillingly to deal with the 'urban' (code for 'black') elements of dance culture. Consciously or not, trance producers had refined out both the black gay disco elements of house and the hip-hop/reggae-derived ruffage of hardcore.

This musical blanding out seemed to parallel the corporatization of dance culture. The chaos of the early nineties rave scene, which was anarcho-capitalist and borderline criminal, had been gradually replaced by a professionalized and hugely profitable clubbing industry. Going to raves in 1988–92 was often edgy, equally likely to result in unforeseen adventures or some kind of disaster. But the UK superclubs like Cream and Gatecrasher where progressive and trance held sway were efficient and well-organized spaces designed for dependable enjoyment. The result was that you got what you paid for – but nothing more. The 'surplus value' that came from participating in the rave underground disappeared. What's weird is that for the new generation of clubbers, the 'quality night out' consumerist ethos of the superclubs inspired huge loyalty. They identified with these mini-corporations so intensely that they marked their bodies with brand-name logos – tattoos of Cream's symbol or Gatecrasher's heraldic British lion logo.

Based in Sheffield, Gatecrasher became the symbol of the new trance culture in all its ambivalence. The club's slogan 'Market Leaders In Having-It-Right-Off Leisure Ware' played up their corporate image. 'Having it' means full-on, pill-gobbling, getting-messy-on-the-dance-floor hedonism; the 'Having-It-Right-Off Leisure Ware' slogan, while a cute joke, showed how an underground drug culture had been transformed into an almost legitimate mainstream leisure industry. Yet some commentators hailed the new generation of crazily dressed ravers filling Gatecrasher and similar trance-oriented UK nightclubs like Sundissential and God's Kitchen as a massive rejuvenation for British dance culture, even a 'revolution'. Dance journalist Bethan Cole visited Gatecrasher as a sceptic but was blown away by the fervour and madcap creativity of the crowd, who called themselves 'the Gatecrasher kidz', 'mentalists' or 'nutbags', and developed their own look blending elements of rave, eighties New Romanticism, cyberpunk and Ibiza's carnivalesque fancy-dress vibe. Gatecrasher kids are into hi-tech gadgets, flashing Cyberdog T-shirts, toy robots, Teletubbies – anything that's futuristic, shiny and pleasing to the tripping eye. 'Lots of the kids paint their faces bright blue or orange in this really primitive childlike way,' recalled Cole. 'Boys spike their hair up in blue and green. And the kids are very interactive with the DJs, holding up gigantic banners or writing notes.' Walking through the club, she added, 'there's this eerie sense of things moving around you – kids with glove puppets and glow-sticks, light guns and those laser pens that write stuff in the air. There's an eerie intensity about the whole place – childlike and innocent but also very druggy. You could smell that suburban odour of Pantene hair conditioner mingled with the chemical tang of drugs being sweated through the skin.'

The Gatecrasher name is also synonymous with the Mitsubishi pill. With high-MDMA-content pills in plentiful supply again, Crasher kids and others at similar clubs across Europe seized the chance to gorge themselves on quality E. 'A lot of these Crasher kids were *really* fucked up,' Cole observed. Indeed common slogans on banners held by the kids are 'Fucked Again!' and 'Never Too Many!' Some nutbags shave the Mitsubishi logo onto the back of their heads, daub it on their bodies in body paint, even get it as a tattoo. Others spell out the word 'Mitzis' with kindergarten-style brightly coloured plastic letters attached to their scalps!

Because E generates a surfeit of love and will-to-belief, a lot of that energy ends up focused on the DJ. This syndrome of Ecstasy-induced worship elevated the first-wave-of-rave DJ godstars like Sasha and Oakenfold, and now it created a new pantheon of crowd-pleasers like Tall Paul, Judge Jules and Paul Van Dyk. 'When Paul was playing the encore to one of his six-hour sets, me and my friends held up a sign saying "Van Dyk Is God", with each word on a piece of A4 paper,' a Gatecrasher regular who travelled 124 miles from his home town Preston to get to the club told me. Although Van Dyk himself rejected the linkage of his popularity to the Mitsubishi upsurge and claimed to have never tried Ecstasy, the dewy-eyed melodic refrains and twinkling textures of tunes like his glorious remix of Binary Finary's '1998' fit the MDMA sensation like a glove.

The first Ecstasy explosion was messy and chaotic, its dazed participants creating a new culture as they went along, improvisational and ad hoc. What's different about the Mitsubishi-driven trance resurgence – and the reason why it couldn't be a revolution – is that the social and economic mechanisms were in place to channel and exploit its energy. The 'big room' sounds of progressive and trance, with their audio-visual pyrotechnics and punctual climaxes, illustrate how rave's explosive energies have been corralled by the clubbing industry. Sound becomes spectacle; dancers become pseudo-participants. The fact that even the illegal substructure to European club culture – the drug labs and big-time dealers – realized that the only way to salvage Ecstasy's fading prestige was to put out 'quality' pills, a dependable product competitive against other drugs like cocaine, only reinforced the sense that rave had become a big business.

*

People who hate trance often accuse of it of lacking 'funk' or 'soul' – for basically being too white. The 'funkless' accusation is pretty undeniable. Rooted in Giorgio Moroder's Eurodisco with its rhythmic grid of evenly emphasized four-to-the-floor beats and regular-as-clockwork sequenced pulsations, trance creates a sensation of surging through a frictionless soundscape. The 'soulless' critique is a bit unfair, though.

Mild-mannered Van Dyk let slip a hint of anger when I put the 'soul' accusation to him: 'When people talk about "soul", they mean black people, music that comes out of the blues. But we Europeans have soul – I have a heart, I have feelings. They don't have a monopoly on that.' And it's true, there is a European soulfulness to trance, a quality that descends from Kraftwerk's *Autobahn*, *Trans-Europe Express* and most of all *The Man-Machine*'s 'Neon Lights', with its serenely gliding monorail-like motion. Listen to trance and you think of the glistening, hygienic beauty of a modern unified Europe where parochial differences are slowly fading, the Europe of high-speed trains, autobahns, the pedestrian-only and pristine boulevards of city centre shopping districts, the noiseless moving walkways of airports. (It seems somehow appropriate that seminal trance club Dorian Gray was actually located *inside* Frankfurt's airport.)

This is why trance and progressive flourish wherever the romance of streamlined, sterile modernity holds sway, from Hong Kong to Sao

Paolo (the most European and modern of Brazil's cities). Part of the point of progressive and trance is that they're everywhere-and-nowhere sounds, completely post-geographical. With the *Global Underground* series of progressive superstar DJ mix-CDs, the sleeve notes always point out that the hip, 'educated' crowd in whatever city that mix-CD is notionally based around – Buenos Aires, Shanghai, Cape Town – *always already* know the tunes that Sasha/Trevor Seaman/whoever is spinning. Progressive/trance is music whose 'locale' is the Globe – an abstraction. A big part of the music's allure is its aura of streamlined pleasure-tech, where the tracks are components to be assembled into seamless mixscapes by ultra-skilled technicians, who whizz back and forth across the global superclub circuit. The matt silver-grey fabric of progressive's sound seems like it's made from the same shiny synthetic material as the DJ bags and vaguely space-age-looking clothes these jet-setting jocks favour.

*

A world away from progressive's global quasi-underground, psy-trance is a genuine subculture. The Mitsubishi wave didn't have much impact in these quarters, because psy-trance fans tend to look down on E as a 'fluffy' drug strictly for lightweights. 'You'll find a lot of people at psy-trance parties who are only on mushrooms or acid,' a psy-trance fan called Gordon told me in Puerto Rico. 'They're much more honest hallucinogens, because they let you go where your mind chooses to – you're not locked into one emotion like with Ecstasy.' Gaia-given 'organic' substances like peyote, DMT and psilocybin are preferred over synthetic designer drugs. Mushrooms and DMT evangelist Terence McKenna is something of a godfather figure to the psy scene, his voice frequently sampled on tracks.

Like the original counterculture and its offshoots from the Grateful Dead to Popol Vuh, psy-trance combines the shamanic use of hallucinogens with the gamut of Eastern spiritualities and polytheistic paganisms. The result is a syncretic spirituality mishmashed from chunks of Tao, Hinduism, Zen Buddhism, hatha yoga, Mayan cosmology and Wicca, then spiced with alien abduction theories and other renegade forms of parascience. At psy-trance parties, you frequently spot signs of overt transcendentalism: a guy meditating in yoga's lotus position, a conga of people sitting on the floor massaging the neck of the person in front.

Chai shops selling a very strong Indian-style tea laced with honey, cream and cardamom spices (ideal for replenishing energy after all-night dancing) are a big part of the scene. There's also a bazaar marketplace element, with people selling self-designed T-shirts, jewellery, handcrafted objects and food. And psy-trance has developed a whole fashion look that mixes sixties hippie garments (loon pants, bell-bottoms, ponchos, shawls, tie-dye and paisley leggings, op art bikinis, knee-high boots in shaggy white mohair), Third World ethnic kitsch (batik fabric, mesh sarongs, cowrie-shell necklaces, fluorescent Hindu-style bindis between the eyebrows) and cyberdelic rave gear (luminous tongue piercings, flashing light contraptions wrapped around your wrist, 'No Speak Alien' T-shirts). A lot of the ethnic garments come from Bali, while the intricate, fractal-patterned T-shirts done in glowing inks are made by a UK company called Space Tribe.

To an unkind eye, your average psy-trance party resembles a detention camp for fashion criminals. The scene puts a premium on looking like a freak: absolutely anything goes. At El Cuco, I see a plump chap wearing one-strap dungarees decorated with astrological moons and planets and a boy wearing an outsize papier mâché monster-head. Other popular looks for the male psy-trancer are the '*Jesus Christ Superstar*/Khao San Road in Bangkok' backpacker look (straggly-bearded, lank-haired, body odour optional) and the 'Israeli hunk/Milli Vanilli' look (mocha skin, long mane of oily curls, hairy muscled chest on display). Psy-trance women look a whole lot better, for some reason. Combining ultra-feminine flamboyance and tomboy practicality, the female trancepacker blends hippie chick, Tank Girl, and beach babe (white halter-tops, hair swept away from the face using white plastic sunglasses, suntans). Another micro-trend is for girls to wear headscarves and kerchiefs, making them look like peasant milk-maids on a Soviet collective farm or kibbutz women picking oranges. Indeed this trend actually stems from the huge Israeli influence on the scene. Even the characteristic psy-trance style of dancing – bouncing on the balls of their feet, shoulders braced as if dancing in a wind tunnel – is nicknamed 'the Israeli stomp'.

For psy-trance fans, Goa and all the other far-flung destinations that have superseded it, represent a fantasy of taking a permanent vacation from Western industrial reality in the mystic Orient. It's psychedelic tourism, basically. And this is the subculture's major ideological blind spot. Despite the Gaia-awareness and the fluoro imagery of Hindu gods like Shiva and Ganesh, places like Bali, Nepal and Thailand really serve as exotic backdrops to hi-tech raving, with the added attraction of being places you can live very cheaply and where drugs are inexpensive and readily available. There is also some truth to the widespread 'trustafarian' stereotype that identifies psy-trance with the upper middle class. Possibly it's the sheer cost factor of taking plane trips across the globe that makes it a sport of the well off, or perhaps it's a class-inflected generational rebellion: the children of money taking trips outside the parental culture of ambition and acquisition, looking for something both spiritual and earthy. Despite all this, there remains something inspiring about the willingness of psy-trance devotees to travel long distances and deal with the absence of Western comforts and conveniences. It's this dedication to adventure that makes psychedelic trance a true underground, whereas its mainstream counterpart is ultimately an anti-culture.

I start to understand this in the last hours of the El Cuco festival. The grey predawn light is demystifying, stripping the site of its silvered full-moon enchantment and revealing what looks disconcertingly like a bulldozed clearing in the deforested Amazonian jungle. But it's eerie, too, like that 7 a.m. moment in nightclubs when the lights come up and you can see the hardcore survivors – spent, zombie-eyed, yet still manic. There's a man in fluorescent warpaint and black loon pants, stomping back and forth across the dance floor in a lurching frenzy, his eyes black and lost. There's a Dalai Lama lookalike kneeling in the lotus position and beseeching the heavens with outstretched arms, and a dainty Japanese waif frozen still, lost in the music, utterly freaked. Dawn is peeking through the treetops, but X-Dream are still in full-on darkside mode, grinding out the harshest sounds of the entire weekend, barely more than a vast blare of distorted kick drum and pummelling bass. A willowy girl with waist-length blonde hair, cobwebby lace shawl and bell-bottoms starts to rock out dementedly, stamping her feet and flailing her arms – her eyes narrowed to burning slits of intensity, her mouth a snarl of joy. She grabs her headscarf-wearing friend by the hand and the two hippie chicks caper and prance in a full circuit around the dance floor, like Greek maenads celebrating the rites of Pan. The look on the blonde's face explains everything, a strange mix of fiery-eyed glee, defiance and triumph. It's the 'we-made-it' look – not just 'we made it through the night', but 'we made this adventure, this scene, for ourselves.'

TWENTY

TWO STEPS
BEYOND

UK GARAGE AND
2STEP

London: late summer, 2000. Step into Twice As Nice, a Sunday-night club in the dead centre of the city and it's like the 'in da club' sequence of an R & B video. Everywhere you look there's Brandys from Brixton, Beyonces from Bethnal Green, Sisquos from Stepney. And look, there's Aaliyah – the real one, cavorting on the gigantic video screen that shows non-stop R & B videos. Make your way through the sharply dressed press of flesh, and you find the main dance floor bumping 'n' flexing to the sound called 2step garage. The name distantly originates from the legendary Manhattan club the Paradise Garage and the tradition of soulful house music it (posthumously) inspired. But sonically 2step is a bastard child rather than a purist descendant. It's a mongrel mishmash of influences – Timbaland-style R & B's twitchy beats, jungle's booming bass, house's slinky synth-riffs, dancehall's raucous MC jabber, and still more. After two years hatching in London's dance underground, 2step has the UK pop charts locked down, with artists like Artful Dodger and Sweet Female Attitude busting into the Top Five all through the year 2000. Yet the sound has paradoxically remained an underground pirate radio-driven sound even as it dominates the mainstream.

Like every Sunday, Twice As Nice is 'a roadblock, off the hook', as the MC boasts. People flock there to be seen as much as to wind down after a weekend's clubbing at other UK garage hot spots. Look, there's drum-and-bass icon Goldie in the DJ booth ostentatiously hugging Spoony from The Dreem Teem, a trio of leading garage DJs. Goldie's no fool, he knows that jungle is no longer runnin' t'ings on the streets of London town. The producer's trademark teeth aren't the only glittering things at Twice As Nice. Everybody's rolling with gold – bracelets, rings, necklaces, hoop earrings. Women sport ice-encrusted chokers and diamond-twinkling cheek studs. Bad boys stride through brandishing Moët bottles, little towers of plastic champagne flutes stuck on the bottle neck. Twice As Nice is *incandescent* with money. The dry-cleaning bills alone must run into thousands. 'We bubblin' criss,' chants the MC, using a Jamaican patois term that means shiny/

slick/sharp-dressed to simultaneously praise Spoony's mixing and celebrate the ghetto fabulous crowd.

Like most UK garage clubs, Twice As Nice bans trainers, jeans,
baseball caps. Scene outsiders often criticize the dress code as elitist.
Defenders of the policy argue that it's good to encourage people to
make an effort, and that the dress code keeps trouble out. Actually, the
only people deterred by the garage veto on trainers and jeans are
scruffy but harmless white college kids. And everybody knows that
gangstas like to dress expensive – which is why there are metal detectors
on Twice As Nice's doors.

Compared with the early days of the scene, when the soundtrack
was 'speed garage', the designer-label flaunting is more subtle – discreet
Versace logos on the back of the collar, rather than pants covered with
the word Moschino or 'Dolce & Gabbana Is Life' T-shirts. The bodies
underneath the costly clothes have been hard-earned too – one muscle
boy sports a condom-tight pink vinyl T-shirt that looks like it's been
sprayed on. Everybody is immaculately groomed and sweatlessly cool;
some guys even carry handkerchiefs to dab away any perspiration.
Then there're the real stylists – Jamaican rude boys in bowler hats or
even dove-grey morning dress, like they've come straight from a
wedding; dancehall queens in diamond-brimmed Stetsons and glitter-
ball-like frocks made entirely from dazzling decals. The men purse
their lips disdainfully into a scowl-sneer, as if some appalling affront
to taste and decorum has been perpetrated (could it be my trousers?).
The women have perfected a blank gaze of hauteur, occasionally
shattered by sunburst smiles when the DJ drops a 'ladies tune' like B15
Project's 'Girls Like This'.

According to London folklore, the garage scene spawned itself from
the jungle scene when the women left the dance floor en masse, bored
by the harsh, tuneless dead end that drum and bass had driven itself
down with the techstep sound of No U Turn et al. The girls sought
refuge in the smaller garage room that most jungle raves offered, where
the music was soulful, sensual and more manageably groovy at 130
b.p.m. rather than jungle's frantic 170 b.p.m. It was like a giant light
bulb clicked on above the collective head of London's jungle massive:
no women on the floor = no vibe. In 1997, virtually every pirate radio
station in the city switched from jungle to speed garage. Since then the
refrain 'the girls love this tune' – typically uttered by record-store
assistants as a recommendation, not a diss – has functioned as a self-

policing mechanism, keeping the scene on track. Garage's deference to the 'ladies massive', to the female demand for singalong choruses, diva vocals, and wind-your-waist rhythms suitable for close dancing with your partner (or somebody else's partner), has kept the music deliciously poppy even in its most underground form. In 1998–9, as the stop-start, push-me/pull-you 2step style evolved out of pumping four-to-the-floor speed garage, it really felt like garage was a new form of chartpop in exile, just biding its time until the inevitable mainstream breakthrough.

*

Although there are lots of inputs in the 2step mix, the style really achieved self-definition as a London-specific spin on the stuttering kick-drums template built by R & B producer Timbaland on tracks for Missy Elliott, Aaliyah, Jay-Z and many more. Timbaland's innovations opened up a whole new 'BeatGeist' for American R & B and hip hop, as his ideas were creatively plagiarized by producers like She'kspere (TLC, Destiny's Child) and became hegemonic across urban radio in America. 2step was UK rave culture recognizing and assimilating the cyborg funk of this nu-R & B, saying 'yeah, we'll 'ave this, ta very much.'

In America, there was a famous advertising campaign for pork that disingenuously described it as 'the Other White Meat'. Someone could, much more honestly, do the exact same for Aaliyah, Missy and the rest of the Timbaland stable: sell it as the Other Electronic Music, to experimental techno connoisseurs who reckon weirdy-beardy types like Squarepusher are actually doing anything original rhythmically. At its utmost, R & B can be as denatured and borderline dysfunctional as the most abstract, arty electronica from Cologne. It figures that UK garage – a scene largely composed of ex-junglists – would dig the Timbaland sound, as both his style of R & B and jungle uses rhythmic patterns as melodic hooks. Jungle, Timbaland-style R & B and 2step all have a breakbeat aesthetic: they break up the even flow of four-to-the-floor rhythm (as in pumping house and traditional garage, including speed garage), riddling the groove with hesitations, erotically teasing and tantalizing gaps. Drum and bass slowed to a languorous frenzy, 2step is lovers' jungle. But the style is rapaciously omnivorous, stealing ideas from all over the genrescape: nu-R & B's clusters of rapid-fire kicks, jungle-style micro-breakbeats, house-influenced hi-hats and synth-

vamps, electro's Roland 808 bass-boom, reggae's slinky skank. Hearing
these intricately programmed tracks is like moving through a mesh of
pointillistic percussion, your body buffeted and flexed every which way
by cross-rhythms and hyper-syncopations. On tracks like Leee John's
'Your Mind, Your Body, Your Soul', the drums are so digitally
texturized it's as if the whole track's made from glossy fabric that
crackles, crinkles and kinks with each percussive impact.

After Timbaland's rhythmatic influence kicked in, the next stage of
interface between UK rave culture and US urban music took the form
of a massive spate of bootleg 'garage' versions of R & B hits, like
Architechs's helium-vocalled revamp of Brandy & Monica's 'The Boy
Is Mine', a tune that ruled London through most of 1999. Using
timestretching to speed up the vocals so that they fit 2step's brisker
tempo, Architechs made the duetting divas sound like ghosts of
themselves, wavery and mirage-like. They also added crowd noises 'to
make it feel like a contest between Brandy & Monica', Architechs's
City told me. 'We wanted it to sound like a real soundclash with the
crowd dividing its support between the two girls.' Having failed to
interest Brandy's UK record company EastWest in the idea of releasing
the remix officially, Architechs put it out as a white-label bootleg.
Played incessantly on the pirates, 'B & M Remix' eventually sold 20,000
copies – a staggering feat, given that regular record stores won't stock
bootlegs and the record was only available via London specialist stores.
This craze for illegal remixes even transformed Whitney Houston into
a London underground star – there were around ten different garage
bootlegs of 'It Ain't Right, But It's Okay'. Producer Zed Bias released a
number of illicit remixes at the height of the bootleg mania, and says
that he has it 'on good authority' from major label people that, far
from being annoyed by the illegal bootlegs, 'they *want us* to do
unofficial remixes' – partly because street buzz is a form of promotion
and partly 'on the off chance that a slamming bootleg comes out which
they can pick up cheap. See, if they didn't want us to do the bootlegs,
they wouldn't put the a cappellas on the 12-inches.'

Another R & B influence on 2step is the obsession with 'vocal science'. Coined by dance pundit Anindya 'Bat' Bhattacharyya, vocal
science refers to the techniques of processing vocal samples that 2step
producers deploy to such intoxicating results. Going back to the
harmony group SWV in the early nineties, R & B producers have long
used technology to make the voice sound unnaturally bright, sweet and

'perfect' – mostly recently with the pitch-correcting device known as Autotuner, which can be misused to make a voice momentarily glisten with an angelic perfection that is eerily posthuman. 2step producers similarly use effects such as phasing to create a kind of cyborg-melisma, making the voice scintillate, twinkle or tremble. Updating the diva-sampling techniques of jungle, 2step producers micro-edit vocals into staccato riffs, treating 'human soul' as plasmatic material to vivisect and rhythmatize. In a weird way, it's the more subtle deployments of these techniques that are most disconcerting (like the ecstatic shiver-stutter woven electronically into the word 're-e-e-mix' on Artful Dodger's remix of Craig David's already ultra-warbly vocal on 'Fill Me In'). It's unnerving because the line between the human and the artificial isn't so clearly defined and because the biomechanical bliss it incarnates is so seductive.

Although R & B remixes continue to stream out (reworking a current R & B chart hit = fast-money-music for 2step trackmasters on the rise and on the make), by 2000 the scene plunged into Phase Two of its merger of R & B with house: generating its own good songs and fine vocalists. After three years developing outside the limelight, UK garage shimmered like a galaxy of talent, from the pop garage of Artful Dodger and Shanks & Bigfoot, to the 'musical' option of Wookie and MJ Cole (guaranteed to please acid-jazz fans, Mercury Prize judges and owners of coffee tables worldwide), to the more experimental auteur-producers like Zed Bias, Dem 2, Groove Chronicles and Steve Gurley. Then there's the entire subgenre of reggae-influenced garage outfits like Master Stepz and M-Dubs, who often work in tandem with charismatic MCs like Creed, PSG, Sparks & Kie and Richie Dan.

MCs are a crucial part of UK garage. Most started out in the jungle scene, but some come from a UK dancehall or home-grown hip-hop background. 'Rappers and ragga MCs had a hard time in this country,' says Ras Kwame of M-Dubs. 'But now thanks to 2step, 'nuff man get a chance to come through and express themselves 'pon the mic.' Building on the UK reggae sound-system tradition of 'fast chatting' and jungle MCs, rapid-fire flow, garage MCs have developed a distinctively English style of sinuous and sibilant speed-rapping, riddled with stuttering effects and switching seamlessly between Jamaican patois and Cockney patter. Garage MCs also retain some of their original role as 'host of the party'. It's the MC who mediates between the dance floor and the DJ in the 'rewind' ritual, when the crowd shouts 'Bo!' if they love a record that's just been dropped into the mix, whereupon the MC instructs the DJ to immediately stop the tune, manually 'wheel' the disc back to the start and 'come again'. This audience participation ritual is so crucial in 2step that Craig David and Artful Dodger harnessed it for their breakthrough hit 'Rewind (When the Crowd Say "Bo! Selector!")'. When drum and bass gradually fell into the orbit of techno, the MC – both as sample-source taken from dancehall or rap records and as a live partner to the DJ in the club – began to disappear from the music. But the jungle MC reappeared in UK garage, effectively Jamaican-izing house music – a striking mutation, given the homophobia of dancehall reggae and the gay disco roots of house. Indeed, the rude-boy factor of the ragga patois voice in speed garage anthems like Gant's 'Sound Bwoy Burial' probably acted to 'inoculate' against the 'effeminate' sensuality of house (in the tune the MC talks about 'ruffhouse', as if christening the new genre the track is birthing in front of our ears and sharply distinguishing it from regular house music). In 2step, the gruff, chest-puffed-out boom of garage MCs like Creed provides the yang to the high-pitched divas' yin.

It's not just dancehall, though: seventies dub and roots reggae also have a vital presence in UK garage. New Horizons, for instance, picked up on the latent Jamaican element in New York house (with its B-side dub remixes) and developed a strange and wondrous micro-genre of reggaematic house – from their 1997 classic 'Find The Path', with its churchy organ vamps, Gregory-Isaacs-on-helium falsetto, and skanking dips and afterbeats woven into the four-to-the-floor pump, to 1999's 'Scrap Iron Dubs EP', with its bassbin-busting low-end frequencies and lewd 'slam down ya body gal' chants. Even stranger mix-and-blend came with R & B bootlegs like Large Joints' 'Dubplate' and the anonymous illegal version of KP and Envyi's 'Swing My Way'. Both bootlegs set the divas' gaseously processed vocal adrift in a dubby echo chamber, over a groove built from a flickering reggae keyboard lick and a chugging house beat. Abducting unsuspecting R & B goddesses into a Jamaican soundworld, these tracks offer typical only-in-London recontextualizations of non-UK sources.

All these Jamaican inputs show that 2step garage's amalgam of 'Black Atlantic' sounds (house, dancehall, electro, R & B, jungle, roots 'n' dub) is at once the latest chapter in the hardcore/jungle/drum and bass continuum and that tradition's self-deconstruction: the point where the music reaches out to genres beyond the borders of the rave and pirate radio narrative, such as R & B and dancehall (which is the *other* Other Electronic Music). 2step is paradoxical proof of two opposed syndromes. More than ever, music in the digital era is post-geographical, drifting across the 'Black Atlantic' and the world, intersecting with the desire of communities and populations remote from the music's original context. At the same time, and perhaps as a semiconscious form of resistance against globalization and digital deracination, there's a stubborn persistence of the local, the tribal. You can see this in hip hop, with its intense regionalism, its city-based sounds and 'hood mythologies. And you can see it in UK garage, which – like jungle before it – is full of references to place, from the early speed-garage anthem 'It's A London Thing' by Scott Garcia and MC Styles to Middlerow's 2000 tune 'Millennium Twist' with its Dickens-inspired lyrics and chorus 'L.O.N.D.O.N., London / That's where we're coming from'. 2step's musical sources are actually 'coming from' everywhere *but* London, but the final composite is indelibly stamped with a fierce sense of geographical identity.

*

Like jungle before it, UK garage represents itself as more than just music: it's A Way of Life, the urban folkways of a vibe-tribe. Friday, after work, it's down to record stores like Uptown or Rhythm Division, to check out the latest tunes on white label. Later, getting dressed up before heading out to Liberty or the Gass Club, garageheads tune into pirate stations like Freek or Mack to hear even more upfront tunes on dubplate. Saturday, clothes shopping at Proibito or Zee & Co., and then maybe one of the big monthly raves like Exposure. Sunday, chilling out, in the sun if you're lucky, and then onto Twice As Nice. Completing this sense of UK garage as a world unto itself, the scene even has its own summer resort, Ayia Napa in Cyprus, to rival the traditional clubbers, destination of Ibiza.

Underneath the flash, monied surface, UK garage has a less glam-orous but utterly crucial side which is its solid economic infrastructure. This is what enabled the scene to thrive as a self-sufficient entity for three years before the mainstream got interested: a network of small independent labels, rave promoters and club managers, DJ and MC agencies, and pirate radio stations. It's almost impossible to overstate the importance of pirate radio. Locked On, the garage scene's leading indie label, is named after the slang term for being tuned into a station's signal, while its uniform 12-inch-single sleeves depict a transistor radio's FM frequency dial. Zed Bias, who compiled the mix-CD *Sound of the Pirates* for Locked On, explains: 'Pirate radio is really the kids' link to the scene – 'cos if you're a teenager, you can't get into clubs yet. A lot of pirates are actually run by kids, so that's where you'll hear the future of the music. The pirates break new tunes.' MJ Cole's debut album *Sincere* includes 'MJ FM', an immaculate pastiche of a pirate radio show that's intended as tribute not parody. 'I should really dedicate the album to the pirates,' says Cole. 'Without them I wouldn't even have started making garage. The weird thing is how this music is still so underground, even after it's gone Top Ten. And that's down to the pirates. They're still pumping it out.'

In the late nineties, London plunged into a new golden age of radio piracy not seen since the first explosive wave of jungle in the 1992–4 period. DJ Luck, owner of Lush FM, estimates 'there're over a hundred stations in London, and around sixty per cent play garage. At the moment the FM band is so rammed, there's no space left.' Most are local and sporadic in their broadcast, but Lush belongs to the premier league of roughly twenty pirates with the financial and organizational muscle to withstand the raids mounted by the authorities.

The HQ of Flex FM, another leading pirate, is a third-storey room in a dilapidated house in the dowdy semi-suburbs of South London. The walls are covered in graffiti – 'ALL DA RAGGAMUFFIN BOOM-LICK SELECTOR', 'DJ Felix D, Harry Barefoot, Lady Cheryl, Pixie, MC Warma'. Joint-rolling detritus is strewn over the mantelpiece. Empty lager cans and Bacardi Breezer bottles choke the Victorian fireplace. It looks like the kind of soiled and sordid squat where you'd find nodded-out junkies, but this Sunday afternoon the house is a hive of energy. Flex FM is a power station generating currents of cultural electricity that transfixes an audience scattered across London.

The trio responsible for the excitement – station owner DJ Dee Kline plus MCs Sharkie P and Hyperactive – make a perfect picture of UK garage's multiculturalism. Dee Kline is lanky, white and scruffy; Hyperactive is Asian and neat in his white Nike baseball cap and Dolce & Gabbana T-shirt; Sharkie is Jamaican and buff in pink fishnet vest. The two MCs take turns chatting 'pon the mic while the other holds the mobile phone and relays big shouts texted in by the kids out there in listener land. 'Bigging up the Man like Richard . . . Hold it down, the Lady Emma . . . Anthony in Balham, wass' happenin' bro?'

Hyperactive does a rap about his grooming rituals: 'Colgate attack/ My plaque.' Then Sharkie P consults his dog-eared exercise book full of rhymes and goes into a toast using the melody of Suzanne Vega's 'Tom's Diner'. Scratching deftly on top of his own remix of Ol' Dirty Bastard's 'Got Ya Money', Dee Kline cuts to a bass-heavy garage remake of Soft Cell's synthpop hit 'Tainted Love' from 1981 (a time before most of Flex FM's teenage audience were born). UK garage's not scared of cheese. Like Puff Daddy, producers take 'hits from the eighties' and reinvent them. There's a garage anthem based on the melody from UB40's cod-reggae hit 'One In Ten', DJ Luck & MC Neat remade Stevie Wonder's 'Masterblaster', and artists as unlikely as Tracy Chapman, Carly Simon and Sade have had songs covered or sampled.

This cheeky hip hop collage approach is what Dee Kline is all about. Based around samples of a TV comedian imitating a Rasta, Dee Kline's ganja-themed 'I Don't Smoke' was a pirate anthem and then reached Number Eleven in the pop charts after being licensed by major label EastWest. The canny Warners subsidiary also picked up the sample-laced 'Bound 4 Da Reload' by Oxide & Neutrino, which did even better: straight in at Number One. Hanging out at EastWest, this eighteen-year-old duo look like archetypal garage kids: Caesar haircuts, flash mobiles, gold bracelets, spaceship Nikes. Together with their clique So Solid Crew, a thirty-strong MC/producer/vocalist collective, Oxide & Neutrino also run a pirate station, Delight FM. It was while DJing on a pirate show that Oxide got the idea for 'Reload', his very first track. Someone phoned in a request and when his voice went on the air, you could hear *Casualty*, the TV show about a hospital emergency room, on in the background. When DJ Oxide faded up the track on his deck, *Casualty*'s theme fitted perfectly over the beat.

Tunes like 'Reload' and 'I Don't Smoke' are polarizing the UK garage scene, creating an instant generation gap. The old-guard axis of garage DJs like Tuff Jam and The Dreem Teem regard these sample-based tracks as 'novelty tunes' devoid of the sexy swing that the scene was originally founded on. 'There's a committee being set up by all the UK garage dons, just like the top jungle DJs and producers did back in '94 when the music was crossing over,' says Zed Bias. These scene elders are blocking the new music – a futile and pre-doomed attempt to arrest the very mutational process that spawned UK garage in the first place. 'They're trying to control things, but they haven't kept their finger on the pulse. All they've done is shut themselves up in this

exclusive little room.' Meanwhile, the younger audience who grew up
on jungle and pirate radio love the new, rough-hewn style of garage –
what Dee Kline calls 'future rave'.

Neutrino attributes the snide comments made by established DJs
about 'Bound 4 Da Reload' to sheer jealousy at its astounding success.
But it's probably as much because the track sounds less like garage and
more like a new-millennium renovation of electro topped with nagging
and nasal rapping from Neutrino. All it really has in common with the
garage played at swanky clubs like Twice As Nice is the 130 b.p.m.
tempo. 'Reload' doesn't actually sound like a cheesy novelty song at
all. It's bleak and ominous, from the doom-booming sub-bass palpitations to the morgue-chilly echo swathing the track and the ice-stab
pizzicato violins. The latter are 'Strings of Death', maybe, given the
samples of gunshots and an agonized voice pleading 'Will everybody
please stop getting shot!?!' – a black humorous allusion to the rising
blood-tide on London's streets. Taken from the UK gangsta movie
Lock, Stock and Two Smoking Barrels, the sample in 'Reload' plugs into
the grim realities of a Britain where crime is soaring, despite or maybe
because of the boom-time prosperity. Wealth remains unevenly distributed through society, and kids are under enormous peer pressure to
own status commodities like mobile phones, expensive clothes and
jewellery.

Propped against the counter of Uptown Records in D'Arblay Street
just a few minutes' stroll from Oxford Street, a black girl complains
bitterly: 'S'like I was sayin', garage is all commercial now. Nobody's
keepin' it real.' The real-ness is coming. Just like drum and bass when
it reacted against LTJ Bukem-style coffee table jungle, the next wave of
garage producers are stripping the music down to bass and beats.
You're even starting to hear the kind of caustic industrial noises that
originally drove the girls dem out of the techsteppin' main arena and
into the garage side room in the first place. It smacks of cutting your
nose off to spite your face, but it's an inevitable cycle. UK garage's
sublime equilibrium between yin and yang, treble and bass, light and
dark, has been maintained for an improbably long time. 2000 is UK
garage's *fourth fabulous summer in a row* – an eternity in the high-
turnover world of British dance culture. Now the scene looks set to
plunge into wintry darkside mode, as if girding itself for the next
recession.

At the club Liberty, you can hear this taking effect. 'Here come da basslick,' shouts the MC, and when the B-lines drop, the girls shimmy downwards to a crouch, ragga-style. Thing is, there actually aren't many ladies on the dance floor, probably because the music's nothing but sandworm-wriggly low-end frequencies. 'As soon as the treble and the big vocals disappear, suddenly it's all blokes,' says garage scenester and vocal scientist Bat. 'Usually, it's like this all-girl moshpit up in front of the DJ booth.'

Liberty's atmosphere is a strange mix of swanky and skanky – it's the kind of place you stumble on champagne bottles left treacherously underfoot. An alarmingly skinny blonde, Uma Thurman on a hunger strike, grinds her jaws (a telltale sign of cocaine abuse) as she 'bogles' with her black boyfriend, grinding her scrawny butt against his crotch. Everywhere eyes are cold, faces barred like shop windows in a run-down area. Garage fans still call themselves ravers, but Ecstasy's loved-up vibe is an ancient memory. It's not that people don't do E, it's just not a special thing anymore. People take it along with whatever else is around – drink, spliff, cocaine. In the chill-out room, Luke, a pasty nineteen-year-old, chews furiously on a lollypop and confides that he's dropped 'three Mitsubishis'. Most people would be a melting blob of love on just one, but Luke's totally impassive. Garage's behavioural codes enforce restraint and deem abandon unseemly.

*

Somewhere between Liberty's unsmiling gloom and Twice As Nice's collective superiority complex, Cream of Da Crop is UK garage perfectly poised midway between ruffneck moodiness and pop effervescence. You'll hear baleful B-line dubplates next to Posh Spice promising 'this tune's gonna punish you' as guest vocalist on Truestepper's chart smash 'Out Of Your Mind'. The club's vibe is pleasant, too, thanks partly to a sizeable contingent of Asian youth, who tend not to project as much attitude as their white and black counterparts. It's the latest stage in the long-running infatuation between Indian kids and Caribbean culture, from bhangramuffin MC Apache Indian to Talvin Singh's tabla-laced drum and bass. Cream of Da Crop's dance floor is like backstage at Miss Asian Subcontinent. Small and dapper, the boyfriends weave bhangra moves into their dancing, bringing a sinuous fluency to garage's characteristic taut sashay.

This slice of 2step heaven is sandwiched between nasty slices of reality, though. On the way to the club, I witness the aftermath of a racial attack: sheltering in the entrance of a 7/11, an Asian boy clutches a tissue to the back of his head to staunch the blood while his friend tells their story to a policeman. Leaving Cream of Da Crop at 6 a.m., I'm stalked by a junkie beggar who eventually threatens to jab me with an AIDS-infected syringe – this, after I've already given him a pound coin and a cigarette!

UK garage's good times are hard won, precarious. Underneath the positivity veneer of songs like Brasstooth's 'Celebrate Life', there's a premonition that global capitalism, aka Babylon Inc., is gonna knock the ground from under you again, real soon – so grab the high life while you can. There's an image that crystallizes the scene for me: a black guy, supersharp in an ankle-length leather overcoat, shadow-boxing with a bottle of Moët clenched in one fist. The soundtrack is a chart-bound anthem that's played at least once an hour at every club I visit: Wookie's 'Battle'. Its staccato, one-note melody is tense and militaristic; the lyrics warn about wearing masks and the struggle to survive. The radio mix goes into full-on uplifting Brit-soul, promising 'we will overcome'. But the mix that rules the clubs is darker – a roiling, ominous bassline and just that first, white-knuckle verse, the one that starts 'Every day is like a battle' and ends 'Your soul it will be lost'. The redemption, the release, never comes.

TWENTY-ONE

IN THE MIX

DJ CULTURE AND
REMIXOLOGY

What is a DJ? Someone who plays other people's records – for a living, for love, ideally for both. The majority of DJs – at weddings, parties, bars, rock clubs, discotheques – 'play' records in the rudimentary sense of the word: slap them on the turntable one after the other. But in hip hop and house, and in all the rave and club-based hybrids of those two black American musics, the DJ *plays* records in a different sense – one that's closer to playing an instrument, or playing with a plastic, mutable substance. As this element of 'play' got ever more re-creative, the DJ came to be considered an artist.

The ascent of the DJ-auteur began as early as the mid-seventies. The wind beneath his wings (then and now, it's too often a 'he') was technological: the invention of the 12-inch single, and the development of turntables and mixers specially designed for the DJ's needs. The first 12-inch singles started to appear in 1975 as DJ-only promos. Not long after came the first commercially available 12-inch, Double Exposure's 'Ten Per Cent', on the New York disco label Salsoul. With its deeper grooves spread over a broader span of vinyl than the 45 r.p.m. 7-inch single, the 12-inch offered better sound quality and made it easier for DJs to locate precise points in the track, thereby enabling accurate mixing. The extended versions of tracks on the 12-inch offered a plethora of stripped down, non-vocal passages and percussion-only breakdowns, which in turn provided entry points for mixing into the next record.

If the 12-inch was the software element of the DJ revolution, its hardware equivalent were the DJ-oriented turntables developed by companies like Technics, whose SL-1200Mk2, launched in 1979, rapidly became the professional jock's deck of choice. With the SL-1200Mk2, the key DJ-friendly innovation was 'pitch adjust' (a slider that allowed the DJ to slow down or speed up the r.p.m. of a disc by a factor of plus or minus eight) and a high-torque direct-drive motor which could take a record from standstill to full speed in less than a second. Pitch adjust facilitated the synchronizing of records of different tempo. The quick-start function is useful when bringing in the new track on beat, and is used in tandem with 'back-cueing' – rewinding the track in slow motion and listening through headphones until you find the precise drum hit from which you want to kick off.

Synchronizing and seamlessly segueing tracks of different b.p.m. is called 'beat-mixing', and it's the basic DJ skill. Beat-mixing is comparable to driving a car: with enough practice, most people can learn to do it. 'It's not that hard,' says DB, one of America's top drum-and-bass DJs. 'But it is hard to be good at it, to hold a mix for a minute or more without wavering, without the kick drum and the snare drum falling out of synch and sounding like a drunk guy falling down the stairs.'

There are basically two different kinds of mixing: smooth and rough. House and trance, styles based around the pump and pound of the four-to-the-floor kick drum, are oriented around 'the long mix', says DB. 'The records are constructed so that they fit together very well. As one track is ending, the bassline will drop out, just as the bassline on the next record is about to drop in. The drums will naturally break down – the middle chunk of the record will be the full drum kit, but then gradually the percussion and the hi-hats will stop, and you'll end up with just a kick drum. And the other track will usually start with just a kick drum.'

The other major style of mixing is the choppy, cut-up mode associated with the hip-hop tradition of breakbeats and syncopated basslines, as extended by jungle. Here the cross-fader on the mixer (the machine that allows the DJ to fade or cut between two turntables) is used to hurl into the mix brief snatches of the coming track, teasing ear-glimpses that whip up anticipation, or to oscillate violently back and forth between the two tracks. With jungle, the duration of the mix – the period when both tracks overlap – is usually much shorter than with house or trance.

If beat-mixing is the basic skill that most can master, there's a whole dimension of turntable trickery that's perhaps comparable to stunt driving. Using two copies of the same record, DJs can set the second disc running a beat behind the first and cross-fade back and forth to create stutter effects, where a beat, lick or vocal is doubled or even tripled. Keep the fader dead centre, and the two copies of the same record running out of synch creates a woozy effect called 'phasing', 'flanging' or 'swirling'. Then there's the array of hands-on tricks that involve the direct manipulation of the disc's speed of rotation. 'That's my trademark,' says techno DJ Richie Hawtin. 'I do a lot of spinning things up faster and then slowing them back down. I'll slow records down to about half their original speed, 'cos when you slow rhythms down, other rhythms start to emerge out of them. In some ways, you're bringing the energy down, but in other ways, at half speed, more notes and sounds become apparent, and it becomes *more* intense.' Then there are DJs like Carl Cox and Jeff Mills who use three turntables rather than the standard pair; and whose strenuous slam-jam sets involve the lightning-fast concatenation and cross-hatching of the most explosively exciting sections of a huge number of tracks.

Virtuoso DJs like Hawtin, Cox and Mills are quite scarce, though. Most of the time, what separates top DJs from the rest of the pack isn't so much their technical skills as their sensibility. If DJing is like driving a car, what counts is the DJ's ability to 'take you on a journey' (which is how DJs tend to describe their art). And that comes down to taste, combined with an intuitive sense of what the 'passengers' (the audience) want to experience. The DJ constructs the raw material of sundry tracks into a meta-track, an abstract emotional narrative with peaks and lows (alongside 'journey', the other metaphor favoured by DJs is 'telling a story').

'There's a lot more to DJing than just mixing two records together on beat,' says Paul Oakenfold, one of the most successful DJs in the world. 'Anyone can learn that, like you can learn to play guitar. You've got to know keys and arrangements, structure and depth. That's what makes a good DJ stand out.' Like a lot of veteran DJs, Oakenfold waxes nostalgic for a bygone golden age of DJ artistry, before the business became so lucrative that soulless artisans entered the field looking for glory and big bucks. Derrick May, a veritable DJ-philosopher, has a similarly mournful take on the 'lost art' of set-building and mixing. 'Most of that philosophy has been lost. There's very few guys who really follow the art of mixing, the art of *blending*. Anybody can slash, cut and do all that fun stuff with the cross-fader. But not many people really know how to blend records and make records *speak* to each other. Make music *out of* music . . . You can elevate people just from the power of a mix, you can make people truly *believe* in you. Nowadays, most people go to a club and the DJ is like a jukebox. Even if he's playing the best records, he's not playing them with any sort of emotion or any sort of personality.'

What can it possibly mean to say that a DJ playing someone else's records – music in whose creation he had no part whatsoever – can exhibit a *personality* that makes all the difference? For DJs, the expressive element of what they do resides in the juxtaposition of these already finished artworks, the connections made between different tracks, the transitions and contrasts between moods, the up-and-down dynamics of a set. With their juxtaposition of classics, obscure tracks, unjustly neglected oldies and new tunes, the best DJs are constructing a sort of argument about the historical roots of the music and where it should head in the future. In this respect, DJs are closer to critics than the traditional conception of the artist. Indeed, DJs love to talk of what they do in terms of 'educating the listener'. This means exposing the audience to music they might not have encountered, pushing the envelope of a particular scene's collective sensibility, and hipping newcomers to the roots of that scene's sound.

The etymological root of 'educate' is 'lead'. The 'good' DJ is shepherd to an audience that is implicitly posited as a flock of dangerously impressionable and easily impressed sheep. The 'bad DJ' is, paradoxically, the crowd-pleaser, the mercenary who leads the flock astray by only giving them what they already love (anthems). In his suggestive essay 'The Booth, the Floor and the Wall: Dance Music and the Fear of Falling', Will Straw pinpoints a tension in DJ culture between populism and connoisseurship. Pander to the crowd's will too much and you'll get the reputation of being a 'cheesy' DJ. But play only 'deep' music and you'll find yourself playing to a semi-deserted dance floor, sparsely populated by cognoscenti – the sort of people too cool to emit the kind of fervour that creates a killer vibe. Noting that DJs are notorious for never dancing, Straw argues that being 'hip' is cerebral, about being in possession of disembodied knowledge, and has nothing to do with the conventional connotations of the word 'hip' (hip-shaking, sexuality). The DJ in his booth and his head-nodding acolytes clinging to the club walls are contrasted with the implicitly feminine abandon and hysteria of the dance floor proper. The DJ labours to elicit uncontrolled physical responses that he, as a member of the connoisseur class, disdains and denies himself. He is the maestro, seducing and arousing the 'female' crowd, guiding it through a multi-orgasmic frenzy.

Although female DJs like Mrs Wood, DJ Rap, Lisa Lashes and Sandra Collins achieved high profiles in their respective scenes, DJ culture remains distinctly masculine. The presence of women on the dance floor is not reflected by the proportion of women in the DJ booth. The gender imbalance is, if anything, even worse when it comes to the production of techno, despite the 'white collar' nature of electronic music (its reliance on computing skills that aren't physically taxing, and that are transferable from information-based professions in which women are strongly represented). Partly this can be attributed to the homosocial nature of techno: tricks of the trade get passed down from mentors to male acolytes. Partly it's because DJing and sample-based music go hand in hand with an obsessive 'trainspotter' mentality: the amassing of huge collections of records, the accumulation of exhaustive and arcane information about labels, producers and auteurs, the fetishization of particular models of music-making technology. Collecting goes hand in hand with the music-critical discourses that construct canons and genealogies.

Like criticism itself, DJing depends on a certain arrogance, a propensity for characterizing oneself as an *authority* (in both the knowledge and leadership senses). As well as seeing themselves as educators, DJs often style themselves as soldiers crusading for a cause. Certain DJs become identified with a particular sound or subgenre – Jeff Mills and minimal techno, Grooverider for the dark, techy strain within drum and bass – and function as the ambassadors and public figureheads for a whole community of producers. Known as the Godfather, Grooverider has a stable of 'boys' who make tracks with his vibe in mind and offer them to the DJ in DAT form. For a long period, Groove has the exclusive right to play these prerelease tunes, which he will get pressed up at his own expense as 'dubplates' (10-inch metal acetates that last for about thirty plays before wearing out). Sometimes producers talk of being inspired by a particular DJ's sensibility or technical style (Randall's 'double impact' mixing at AWOL, for instance) and rushing home from a gig to make a track.

This peculiar deferential attitude and the displacement of creativity from the artist to the turntable selector can sometimes be hard to fathom. Far from dismantling the rock-star system in favour of a radically democratic anonymity, dance culture has shifted the impulse to worship onto the DJ-as-virtuoso. The DJ-as-godstar phenomenon has a lot to do with Ecstasy. The drug generates overwhelming emotions and sensations, plus a peculiar will-to-believe, that must be given a focus. Just as it's possible to fall in love with someone you've only just met while under the influence of E, similarly that hyperemotional charge rubs off on the DJ, who seems to have a lot to do with the feelings coursing through your nervous system. This is not to deny the importance of the intuitive sense of what an audience wants to feel, where it wants to go, that experienced DJs develop. But in the throes of Ecstasy, it can feel like the DJ is actually reading the crowd-mind, playing the dancers' *bodies*.

Legendary DJs owe their godlike status in part to being at the right place at the right time. Most of Britain's ruling DJs – Oakenfold, Sasha, Carl Cox, Fabio and Grooverider – began their career in the thick of the 1988–90 acid house/Madchester explosion. By the early nineties, the network of commercial raves and rave-style big-room clubs had created a 'guest DJ circuit' with the leading DJs travelling up and down the country. In pre-rave days, DJs tended to have residencies, regular club nights. But now they became nomadic guns for hire, earning fat fees for performing short sets on bills crammed with other stellar DJs. Smaller clubs maintained loyal followings purely through their vibe, but the big-capacity 'superclubs' needed the drawing power of big-name jocks and were prepared to cough up the money. By the mid- to late-nineties, Britain's first-division DJs – Sasha, Jeremy Healey, Pete Tong, Judge Jules, Tall Paul – could charge fees in the region of £2,000 to £5,000 for a two- or three-hour set. These celebrity DJs could afford to keep a driver on salary to shuttle them between gigs and maybe even another assistant just to lug the record boxes. Factor in half a dozen lucrative gigs over the course of a three-day weekend, plus midweek sets, excursions to Europe or America, the rise of dance-music festivals like Tribal Gathering, and the tripling of fees at New Year's Eve, and you're talking about certain DJs getting close to being millionaires, just for playing other people's records. In 1999, the *Guinness Book of Records* identified Paul Oakenfold as the world's most successful DJ, earning £728,000 purely from his record spinning.

Successful DJs get extra income from mix-CDs, remixing singles by pop stars and rock bands, playing shows on radio stations, endorsing products and producing their own tracks. With all the dosh, adulation and fringe benefits (first-class flights and hotel suites, top-brand booze from promoters, free drugs from hangers-on, even DJ groupies), little wonder that the DJ became the new rock star, what EveryBoy dreamt of becoming. 'Turntables are outselling guitars,' crowed Oakenfold.

As early as 1996, though, there were stirrings of a backlash against the guest DJ circuit. DJs were getting sick of the travel-induced stress, the burnout caused by sleep deprivation and jet lag. Many were frustrated by having to play brief sets and started to talk wistfully of the old days when they could take audiences on five-hour journeys through peaks and lows. Clubbers, meanwhile, increasingly resented the inflated ticket prices for name DJs who turned up five minutes before they were due on, and who played with no idea of the club's vibe or what music had been played earlier in the evening, leading to the same handful of current 'big tunes' getting played again. Promoters were struggling with the huge fees and expenses demanded by celebrity DJs and their booking agencies. The result was a return to the idea of the residency, albeit in modified form: instead of the resident DJ as someone actually resident in the town in question, these were guest residencies, superstar DJs contractually bound to play a particular club on a regular basis. The most famous example was London-based Paul Oakenfold's 42-week stint in 1997 at Cream in Liverpool. For Oakenfold, the Saturday-night residency provided both the comfort of routine and the opportunity to take risks: longer sets offered more space for breaking new tunes, while the residency meant a faithful audience prepared to go with the DJ's flow.

*

The iconic focus of rave culture, DJs increasingly became a marketing tool for the dance music industry. The phenomenon of the DJ mix-CD evolved out of the trade in mix-tapes. Sold in street markets, specialist record stores and by mail order, the mix-tape is usually of dubious legality, in so far as the producers of the tracks that the DJ mixes together don't get a penny. The demand for mix-tapes is highest in anonymous hardcore dance scenes where the artists' profiles are much lower than the DJs'. In early jungle, for instance, mix-tapes were popular because they contained a high proportion of dubplates: tracks to which only certain DJs had access, and which wouldn't be commercially available for several months. You bought the mix-tape because you knew that you'd get a certain sound from a particular DJ, and the tape would provide all the current hot tunes in that style. The mix-CD simply took this idea and made it legal, by paying royalties to the track's original producers and record company (paid per minute of usage in the long continuous mix). Most of these mix-CDs, however, are not documents of live mixing using turntables, but digitally woven together in the studio, achieving a pristine perfection but inevitably being somewhat sterile compared to the live DJ experience.

Alongside the mix-CD, the other big earner for the DJ is doing remixes. In the pre-rave eighties, a remix meant an extended, marginally more dance-friendly version of a pop song. Remixing involved hiring a well-known DJ to apply his specialized knowledge to the task of adjusting a song to fit dance-floor requirements, given that records originally mixed for radio or the domestic hi-fi sound tinny compared to records tailored to club sound systems. In the nineties, remixing evolved way beyond its early modest premises. Partly this was as a result of a business strategy of maximum market penetration: instead of just one remix on the flip, dance tracks began to come with a slew of reinterpretations in tow, each designed to appeal to a specific dance scene. These remixes, performed by DJs and producers renowned in those scenes, became increasingly remote from the original in terms of tempo, rhythm and instrumentation, so that only the key riffs or vocal hooks of the original track might be retained. Gradually, remixing became a creative activity in itself; the original track became the pretext and springboard for the remixer to create an almost entirely new piece of music which might contain only tiny shards and ghostly traces of its source. Indeed, when a remixer is hired they are typically provided with only a few sound-files – certain key hooks, riffs, samples – as opposed to the entire original track, because it's assumed they will construct an entirely new groove. This is basically re-*production* rather than re-*mixing*.

In the more experimental zones of electronic dance culture especially, it became the norm for remixers to operate with an almost contemptuous disregard for the material. Yet this is sanctioned by the clients, who delight in the unrecognizability of the end product. This quasi-adversarial attitude of remixer towards remixee was encapsulated in one of the nineties dance scene's biggest buzzwords: 'versus'. One of the first examples occurred in 1990 when Mancunian techno crew 808 State transformed avant-garde trumpeter Jon Hassell's 'Voiceprint' into a Latin-tinged house track; the credit ran Jon Hassell vs 808 State. There were sporadic sightings of the term in years to come, but the 'versus' trend really blew up in 1995 with Massive Attack vs Mad Professor's *No Protection* and *The Auteurs vs μ-Ziq*. On the former, UK reggae producer Mad Professor created a dub version of Massive's

Protection that many fans and critics considered superior to the original album. Since Massive's languid trip hop is deeply informed by reggae and sound-system culture, it wasn't such a huge leap for the band to invite their hero to rework the album. But art-techno boffin Mike Paradinas of µ-Ziq and wordy songsmith Luke Haines of The Auteurs came from utterly opposed aesthetic universes, and Paradinas wasn't shy about revealing his contempt for the material he was dealing with. The result was the merciless mutilation of Haines's finely honed rock-lit. After this came a deluge of 'versus' records, which ranged hugely in the degree of devastation wrought upon the remixee. In some cases – *Tricky vs The Gravediggaz, David Holmes vs Alter Ego* – they weren't remixes but artistic collaborations, or even (*Freaky Chakra vs Single Cell Orchestra*) split albums.

The idea of 'versus' comes from the reggae tradition of the sound-clash, an event where sound systems competed to attract the majority of the audience to its end of the hall or enclosure. 'In the early days of reggae, you might have *Kilimanjaro vs Jah Love Music,*' says reggae historian Steve Barrow. The nineties vogue for 'versus' chimes in with the widely held belief that dub pioneers like King Tubby, Joe Gibbs and Lee Perry are the founding fathers of today's science of 'remixology'. Tubby and Errol Thompson (Joe Gibbs's engineer) were the first remixers, claims Barrow. 'At first dubs were just called "instrumentals", then they started calling them "versions". Gradually, more effects were added – echo, thunderclap, etc. – and dubs got closer to what we now think of as a remix. By 1982 dub had run its course in Jamaica, it had become a formula.' But this was just the moment at which dub techniques were being used by New York electrofunk and disco producers, in remixes and vocal-free B-side instrumental versions.

Dub's repertoire of tricks – dropping out the voice and certain instruments, extreme use of echo and reverb in order to create an illusory spatiality, mixing board treatments like phasing, the use of sound effects – still permeate dance music. They've also become part of the arsenal of post-rock, the genre of experimental guitar bands who've abandoned the model of recording as a document of live performance and embraced the studio-as-instrument aesthetic of hip hop and techno. On 'remix albums' like God's *Appeal To Human Greed*, the subtext is always 'versus': the remixer, usually a kinsman from the world of post-rock, is given licence to deface and dismember the track to the point where there's no discernible relationship between the original and the new version. When Kevin Martin from God and Techno-Animal hired arty junglists Spring Heel Jack to rework 'Heavy Water' he told the remixers 'they could leave *nothing* of the original if they wanted. They were astounded!'

Post-rock's passion for remixology is more than just a knock-on effect of their interest in club-based and post-rave musics. 'People have lost respect for the heart of the song,' Martin claims. Instead of a finite entity, he argues, the song is treated as a set of resources that can be endlessly adapted and rearranged. This notion of music as process rather than object underlies two of Martin's most successful projects. The compilation series *Macro Dub Infection* tracks dub's spread as a 'subcultural virus' throughout nineties music culture, contaminating everything from hip hop and house to jungle and post-rock. *Techno-Animal versus Reality* is a sort of post-geographical, virtual jam session. Five guest artists (Porter Ricks, Alec Empire, Wordsound, Ui and Tortoise) supplied Techno-Animal with 'minimal material', to which Martin and his partner Justin Broadrick added rhythm tracks. The results were then handed back to the guest artist, who transformed it into a finished piece of music; Techno-Animal also produced their own version of each track. The subtext of both *Macro Dub* and *Versus Reality*, says Martin, is 'just how important the processing and treatments have become in modern music – it's almost like musicians are accessories to the process now.'

*

While remixology has rejuvenated left-field rock, there are times when you have to wonder if the fad hasn't gone too far. Is there perhaps a case for a neoconservative stance – the idea that it's time to bring back remixes that *enhance* the original or bring out hidden possibilities, rather than dispense with the blueprint altogether?

You also have to wonder if remixology isn't often just a giant scam. There's a story, possibly apocryphal, concerning Richard 'Aphex Twin' James – a highly sought-after remixer, even though he's infamous for obliterative revamps that bear scant resemblance to the original. Hired by a famous band's record company to do an overhaul, James agreed, then promptly forget all about the assignment. On the appointed day, a courier arrived chez Aphex to pick up the DAT of the remix. Initially taken aback, James quickly recovered his composure and scuttled upstairs, rifled through his massive collection of demos and unfinished tracks, picked one at random and handed it to the messenger. Band and record label both professed themselves highly pleased with his reinterpretation! True or not, most of James's remixes might as well be all-new compositions. The scale of devastation is in ratio to his estimation of the band. Curve and Jesus Jones got absolutely decimated. But post-rockers Seefeel received loving, respectful treatment, with Aphex's gorgeous remixes of 'Time To Find Me' retaining most of the original track.

In genres like trip hop, house and jungle, the simultaneous release of a bunch of barely recognizable remakes by several different remixers (four, six, sometimes more!) is a common occurrence. Dance music has its own 'remix albums' – DJ Food's *Refried Food*, Bjork's *Telegram* – where one artist's album is reworked by a stellar cast of guest producers. The Shamen's CD-worth of remakes of the same song 'Move Any Mountain' also included a disassembled version that isolated the components of the song, so that listeners could construct their own remix. Another variation is the 'remix tribute' album, where instead of covers of songs by the original artist (as with the rock tribute album), illustrious ancestors like Chris & Cosey, Yellow Magic Orchestra and Can get their classic remodelled by their aesthetic progeny. (The Can remix record second-guessed the diehard's knee-jerk response, with the title *Sacrilege*.) And increasingly there are auteurist collections that corral all the remixes done by a renowned producer and present them as just another crucial facet of their artistic output, such as Aphex Twins' cheekily titled 2003 remix anthology *26 Mixes for Cash*.

Of all the genres of nineties dance, jungle took remix-mania the furthest. As a result, the genre had a fluid, hazy-round-the-edges notion of authorship. Often, a track will be popularly attributed to its remixer; generally, remixes are so dramatically different from the originals that this seems only just and proper. For instance, Omni Trio's 'Renegade Snares' is often regarded as a Foul Play track, owing to their remix and subsequent 'VIP' re-remix. Jungle has introduced some new twists to remixology. There's the 'VIP Remix' (basically a marketing buzzword), and there's the sequel, on which the original artist reinterprets his own work. For instance, Goldie followed his Metalheads darkside classic 'Terminator' with 'Terminator II', but on a different label (Reinforced) and under a different name (Rufige Cru).

Posing questions about authorship and attribution, remixing also problematizes the notion of copyright. If, in the age of 'versus', the remix is tantamount to an all-new track, why should the original artist get all the royalties? At the moment, copyright still generally remains with the original artist, and the remixer gets a flat fee. (In more underground or esoteric scenes, no money changes hands – instead artists do 'swaps', taking turns to remix each other's work.) But there are cases where remixers have gotten percentage points in the contract, earning royalties, and even occasionally getting a publishing credit in the new version of the song. 'Then again,' suggests Kevin Martin, 'with so much of this music being sample-based, you could argue that neither the artist nor the remixer are "creators" in the traditional sense. It's more the case that both the artist and the remixer act as "filters" for a sort of cultural flow.' This metaphor of filtering fits Brian Eno's notion of the modern artist as no longer a creator but a *curator*. In the age of information overload and artistic overproduction, Eno has argued, 'it is perhaps the connection maker who is the new storyteller.' This is exactly the role that DJs fulfil. As archivists who trawl the stacked past and tastemakers who sift through the present deluge, they possess the skills required both to re-present other people's work in an aesthetically coherent context (the DJ set) and to re-produce another's work altogether (the remix).

The gap between remixing and DJing is narrowing; recreating other people's tracks in the studio and recombining them in the DJ booth are gradually merging into a single continuum of mixology. Most mixers come with 'kill switches' and EQing, functions that allow the DJ to alter the frequency levels on records, thereby enabling the DJ to engage in live remixing. Used during the transition between two tracks when both records overlap, kill switches cut out entire frequency bands. The DJ can combine, say, the bass of the first track with the treble and mid-range of the incoming track; the resultant mesh is basically a new track that lasts the duration of the mix. EQing (boosting or lowering the frequency levels) can also be used to add extra dynamics to the experience, in the mix or at any point in the record. DJs are also increasingly using effects processors with functions like echo, phasing and reverb, or deploying drum machines to add an extra tier of polyrhythm, or programming mini-samplers to throw simple beat loops or riffs into the mix.

Turntable manufacturers are continually coming up with new DJ-friendly functions, like a button that makes the turntable go backwards.

'If you were just playing records backwards once in a while, that wouldn't be so interesting,' says Richie Hawtin. 'But as soon as you add the element of EQing and effects on backwards records, you're getting into really uncharted territory.' Then there's the CD mixer – long resisted by DJs, because of their attachment to vinyl. The latest high-end CD mixers can mimic most of the hands-on techniques DJs use to manipulate vinyl discs, such as scratching, and have a number of advantages, like looping functions and the ability to adjust a track's speed by a factor of plus or minus sixteen without altering the music's pitch, thanks to a time-stretching/time-compression chip. CDs have another advantage – they are much lighter and more capacious than vinyl records, and it's far cheaper to burn prerelease tracks onto a CD than to press up a dubplate.

With the range of possibilities open to the DJ ever-expanding, and the cult of the utterly transformative remix showing little signs of waning, the idea of the dance track as a finished product has been obliterated. Not only is the moment of completion deferred, but the creative process slips back and forth between DJ booth and studio. For his Purpose Maker label, Jeff Mills makes ultra-minimal tracks that he describes as 'DJ tools'. Essentially unfinished work, this music is only fully 'com-posed' (put together) when it is meshed with other minimal tracks. Here Mills has only self-consciously highlighted what is the general rule in rave music: the vast majority of the tracks don't make sense when heard in isolation, because really they are raw ingredients for the DJ-chef to turn into a meal. The DJ tests the material for its latent capabilities and applications, but in a sense, the material also tests the DJ, challenging his skills and spurring him on to new performance heights. This peculiar feedback loop between studio and booth characterizes all forms of techno, from house to jungle. There's no definitive version, no moment of completion; everything remains *in the mix*, always and forever.

*

In the ten years since *Energy Flash* came out, music sequencing software that basically places a virtual recording studio inside your computer has become ever more affordable and widely used. In addition to dramatically expanding the options in terms of arranging and process-ing sounds available to your average producer, these technical advances have also spilled over into the realm of DJing. First came 'virtual

DJing' programmes such as Traktor, which features graphic representations of turntables on the computer screen, but involves clicking and dragging the mouse to activate the onscreen controls like pitch-adjust. Then more tactile and physically engaging programmes arrived like FinalScratch and Serato Scratch Live. These work through the use of quasi-records placed on real turntables and manipulated by DJs using their traditional repertoire of skills.

Invented by the DJing technology company Stanton, FinalScratch led the way, but Serato Scratch Live, launched in 2004, seems to be catching on with the DJ cognoscenti on account of its greater stability (its relatively compact software programme means it's less likely to crash your computer). The basic set-up is the Serato programme, a pair of 'control records' (the same size as a 12-inch single), and a mysterious box connected by cables to the mixer, turntables and laptop. On the latter, the DJ archives thousands of MP3s (downloads, promos from other producers, or digitized versions of her old vinyl collection – which can now remain at home, safe from wear and tear or the risk of damage or loss). During the DJ performance, tracks are selected and 'placed' on two turntables graphically represented on the computer screen interface. And then . . . well, how *does* it work, exactly?

DJ Ripley, a San Francisco-based breakcore DJ and early Serato adopter, explains: 'There is a click track on the control record telling the computer, via the stylus, "You've come this far along the track."' Her partner Kid Kameleon explains that no sound passes through the stylus, just this time code. 'The platter tells the MP3 in the computer exactly where the stylus is to such a degree of accuracy, you can scratch. Move the control record back and forth in real time and it simulates the sound of the music going back and forth. So it's *like* the sound is actually inside the platter but there's not actually any music inside it at all.'

Like FinalScratch, Serato enables DJs to transfer their hard-learned physical skills – cueing, mixing, scratching – to a new digital format that's vastly more convenient in terms of storage capacity and portability. It also has a few extra computer-enhanced DJing powers. 'You can have a track run backwards,' says Ripley. 'There's a pitch adjuster within the programme, so you can adjust the b.p.m. within the computer as well as on the turntable, and that could give you a wider range in terms of speeding up or slowing down the music.' The main 'superpower', though, is simply 'the ability to have at your disposal

2,000 songs' – the equivalent of twenty crates of vinyl. All that choice might create its own problems, of course, but with some 'data management skills', conscientious track labelling, and the advance creation of playlists to narrow one's focus, it's fairly easy to navigate the mire of options. 'I don't just turn up to a gig unprepared, but the beauty is I can abandon my set list if I want to,' notes Ripley. 'All my other music is there.'

Although the primary appeal of Serato is to DJs who have come up through spinning vinyl, Ripley reckons it will appeal to first-time DJs too. 'It is just a really fun interface for playing electronic music, whereas Traktor or other purely digital interactions, you're sitting there clicking a mouse or poking buttons. There is a learning curve with all of these systems, and if it's not that physically enjoyable, people won't persevere.' Analogue-fetishizing sentimentalists continue to insist that vinyl not only sounds better in terms of its frequency spectrum (especially the sub-bass) but also has a mystical aura, a 'soul' or 'warmth' that digital lacks. But on most sound systems, the difference between analogue and digital is imperceptible, and it seems likely that the sheer convenience (no more lugging crates, no more apartment space-devouring record collections) and flexibility of Serato and similar programmes will triumph.

The other format increasingly adopted by DJs, especially those operating in the left-field electronic field of glitchy dance music and experimental 'sound art', is Ableton Live. Developed by Robert Henke and Gerhard Behles of the brilliant 'heroin house' outfit Monolake and launched commercially in 2001, Ableton is loop-based sequencer software designed for performance and allowing for such intense degrees of improvisation it verges on live composition. The programme enables producers to build an arrangement from an arsenal of beats, patterns, samples, and other components, synch them up rhythmically and then tweak every element using the full studio repertoire of signal processing, panning effects, etc. – *all in real time*. There's a caveat, though. As Kameleon puts it, 'You have to *do* the work.' Ripley elaborates, 'It requires that you preload, set it all up in advance, cut things up and identify them and assign them.' There's an awful lot of preparation before you get to the spontaneous part.

Although Ableton has been heralded as the future of DJing by superstars like Sasha, it seems to lend itself more to producers looking to perform their own electronic music. It's especially useful for people who want to integrate their own productions with other people's tracks. 'There're people doing hybrid sets, half their own material and half other people's, all meshed together,' says Kameleon. 'And you get people doing re-edits on the fly, taking a track and chopping it up. That can be fun.' Not limited to live Ableton use, but also released on vinyl, the mid-noughties fad for 're-edits' is basically the neoconservative backlash against remixology imagined earlier in this chapter: a return to the original idea of remixing, where all or most of the original track is retained, but it's chopped up and rearranged sequentially. It's an irony that one of the uses of the absolutely latest, super-advanced leap forward in technology is enabling people to get back to how things were done in the eighties.

TWENTY-TWO

BACK TO
THE FUTURE

RETRO-ELECTRO, NU-WAVE
AND THE EIGHTIES
REVIVAL

New York: spring, 2002. Go to Berliniamsburg, the Brooklyn club at the epicentre of New York's eighties-inspired 'electroclash' scene, and you feel a peculiar sensation: it's not exactly like time travel, more like you've stepped into a parallel universe, an alternative history scenario where *rave never happened*. The audience recycle and recombine elements of eighties New Wave and New Romantic fashion: asymmetric haircuts, ruffs, skinny ties worn over collarless T-shirts, punky-looking studded belts and wristbands, little cloth caps. But nobody really looks like they're from 1981 – in fact, they look much sharper and, on the whole, not nearly as silly. The same applies to the music: for all the analogue synth-tones and one-finger melody refrains, the vocoderized robot-singing and 'Blue Monday'-like sixteenth-note basslines, the soundtrack isn't exactly a period-precise revival. There's a textured intricacy to the rhythm programming and production that testifies to the technical advances of the last fifteen years of digitized dance music, to lessons that can't be unlearned.

'A season ago, the scene was more overtly eighties retro than it is now,' says Larry Tee, the promoter and resident DJ behind Berliniamsburg. 'Starting out, we had to play a lot more original eighties tunes because there weren't enough contemporary releases. But now there're almost too many new records to pick from and we don't need to pad out our DJ sets with old stuff. And the fashion has kind of reflected that shift. A season ago, it was that whole New Wave early-eighties look of skinny ties, stripes, polka dots. Now there're still eighties flourishes but it's much more subtle.'

Maybe the key 'what if' in this alternative history scenario is 'what if Ecstasy had never been invented?' Bored by the entire gamut of post-rave club music on offer – from filter house to trance and progressive – a new generation of trendy club kids have rejected the ease of release offered by house music's warm pump 'n' flow. Essentially, they've taken the E out of house, and rolled back history to the cold, stilted, neuro-Euro sounds that originally inspired the guys in Chicago and Detroit.

This new generation have abandoned the very ethos of Ecstasy culture: the principles of egalitarian unity and 'only connect', the notion of submerging your ego in the oceanic hypno-flow of the rhythm and merging with the crowd. The dance floor is reconfigured not as a space of unity but as a stage for poseurs and coke-spiked narcissistic display. Nu-wave electro also breaks with the 'in the mix' aesthetic where tracks are anonymous elements for the DJ's seamless montage. Instead, nu-wave songs compete to stand out, through domineering vocals, larger-than-life singers (as opposed to the depersonalized diva-as-raw-material approach in most modern dance), witty lyrics and extravagant amounts of obscenity and trash talk.

Berliniamsburg scene-anthem 'It's Over' by Hungry Wives proclaims: 'The scene is dead ... Twilo got sold on eBay' (a reference to the late unlamented Manhattan superclub where tranceheads flocked for Sasha and Digweed). Rave's once-transgressive ecstasy had become routinized rapture. Having never witnessed rave in its early explosively anarchic form, having only known E-culture as a fixture, predictable and plebeian, these very young nu-wave kids are rejecting the notion of trance-dance itself – as narcotic, lulling, null. Instead, they're grasping for some kind of edge: a different kind of tension.

*

The prototype for Berliniamsburg was Club Badd, a night started by Larry Tee and partner Spencer Product in New York's East Village, and catering to a disenfranchised audience, 'people who were bored with the abused dance formats available' (Tee is referring here to house/techno/trance/drum and bass). Badd drew a crowd of 'drag queens, disaffected gays, fashion straights, As Fours [a reference to the As Four series of art/fashion loft happenings], alterna-rockers, and electro freaks.' The club arose in response to a widespread sense of lack, a feeling that New York nightlife was moribund, locked in a stale and interminable groove of filter disco and Eurotrance. At the same time, the traditional NYC enclave for gay dance culture – the deep-house scene centred on Body & Soul – was self-stifled by its own reverence for the lost golden age of disco. As Hungry Wives' 'It's Over' puts it: 'The tranny minions have no place to go / They are homeless ... It's the same song, honey / Over and over and over and over / The scene is dead, sweetie.'

Many of the international (rising) stars of nu-wave performed at

Club Badd – Fischerspooner, WIT, Tiga, DJ Hell, Crossover – but the night never really took off. But when Tee and Product shifted their activities to Brooklyn's Williamsburg neighbourhood – the area that took over the bohemian role that Manhattan's East Village used to have, as a home for struggling artists and rock bands – the fledgling electroclash scene suddenly became the place to be. In terms of media attention and subcultural momentum, the turning point came in the autumn of 2001, when Tee staged the two-day Electroclash festival in Manhattan, featuring acts like Peaches, Adult. and Chicks On Speed. But Electroclash the Festival became marred by controversy, because – until the two sides fell out – it had been originally conceived as a collaboration between Larry Tee and DJ Hell, the founder of German label International Deejay Gigolos, the leading international force behind the retro-eighties electro sound. What promised to be a potent and all-conquering alliance – a transatlantic axis of nu-wave – rapidly disintegrated for reasons that remain unclear. DJ Hell alleged in *Village Voice* that Larry Tee 'stole the whole concept and even the name of the Electroclash festival.' Tee denied this and attributed the breakdown of relations to Hell demanding 'total creative control'. But he acknowledged that Hell had been doing nu-wave style music for a good while before he leapt into the scene.

Then again, the notion that any single person invented and 'owns' the concept of eighties-revisionist dance music seems daft. It's an idea that occurred more or less simultaneously to different people across the globe. It's also an upshot that had a certain inevitability, given that the entertainment industries, on both the mainstream and underground level, increasingly operate through reworking the massive archive of pop-cult material that's been amassed over the decades. International Deejay Gigolos and Berliniamsburg are crucial nodes in a global rhizome of neo-electro and nu-wave synthpop, a network with outposts in Canada (Tiga, Solvent), Germany (labels like B-Pitch Control, Lasergun, Muller), Holland (Viewlexx, Legowelt), Britain (Ladytron, DMX Crew, Les Rhythmes Digitales), Chicago (Tommi Sunshine's club Electro-Sweat, Felix Da Housecatt's Glamorama project) and Detroit/Ann Arbor (the mighty triumvirate of labels Ersatz Audio, Interdimensional Transmissions and Ghostly International, plus outfits like Dopplereffekt, Ectomorph and Adult.). In New York itself, in addition to Berliniamsburg and Tee's label Mogul Electro, there're operators like John Selway, Khan, Daniel Wang and Metro Area.

Back-to-the-eighties is the trend that's been coming and coming for the longest time. What originally looked like just the briefest of trendlets intended to bring a frisson to jaded clubland palates has turned out to be the fad that refuses to fade. Electro? That's so 1998, surely! Earlier, actually. The original, ahead-of-everybody electro reactivators were Drexciya, an Underground Resistance-affiliated unit of Detroit techno guerrillas who created a potent mystique through their stringent policy of faceless anonymity. Starting in the early nineties, their tracks often had a 'bumpy' electro feel that broke with the steady-stomping four-to-the-floor of most techno. One member of Drexciya broke off from the group, briefly collaborated with Ectomorph's Brendan M. Gillen, then formed Dopplereffekt. The latter's increasingly dodgy Teutonic-parodic releases – 1995's *Fascist State*, 1997's *Sterilization (Racial Hygiene And Selective Breeding)* – played a key role in reintroducing electro rhythms into the techno sound-stream.

A scholar of electronic music history, Ectomorph's Gillen diagnoses the revival of interest in electro as the return of techno's repressed: funk, sub-bass, melody, vocals. Electro's syncopation appealed at a point in the mid-nineties when techno was tied to the thumping metronome of the four-to-the-floor kick. Where jungle producers responded to techno's increasing stiffness by funking things up with vintage, hand-played breakbeats, the new electro artists programmed their drum machines to create brand new quasi-breakbeats. These were riddled with syncopations but sounded 'dry', lacking both the fuzzy warmth of acoustically miked drums and those barely perceptible inconsistencies and micro-accents that give human drumming its 'feel'. The electro beat can be funky as hell, but listen closely and it's the acoustic equivalent of pixel-vision.

Electro's funk is dependent on the same drum machine that underpinned early hip hop, the Roland 808. Alongside its distinctive snare, hi-hat, clave and rimshot sounds, the 808 is most famous for the sub-bass rumble produced by detuning the kick drum – a smudged, redzone undertow that still quakes beneath contemporary regional rap styles like Miami Bass and New Orleans Bounce. The nouveau electro artists of the late nineties used the 808 to create stabbing, percussive basslines (BOOM! Bup-bup ba-BOOM!) which syncopated with the intricate drum patterns and made the dancer bump 'n' grind rather than stomp in strict time, techno-style. These 808 B-lines also connected the new electro with the sleazy underworld of ghetto tech, the

booty-shaking soundtrack for dancers at strip bars. Hugely popular
with Michigan's black working class, ghetto tech's lewd bump 'n' grind
is a world away from the refined atmosphere of Detroit techno and its
satellite scenes from Berlin to London. Yet in Detroit itself, the bangin'
porno-electro of ghetto tech like DJ Assault vastly outsells the likes of
Stacy Pullen. Where Detroit techno seeks to transcend the earth(l)y
plane, ghetto tech prefers base materialism (at degree zero, all the
tracks are about the female posterior) to spirituality, profanity to
profundity.

Alongside syncopation and bass, the third aspect to electro's appeal
to fatigued techno-heads was its melodic content. As Gillen puts it, by
the mid-nineties techno was more about *tones* than *tunes*: minimal
techno, especially, was an anorectic style that stripped itself down to
'just rhythm and texture'. Bored by its austerity, producers started
harking back to the pocket-calculator jingles of electro and the aching
romanticism of eighties synthpop, with its soaring tunes and 'intricate
interlocking keyboard lines'. The decisive turning point that pointed
ahead to the eighties-inspired resurgence of nu-wave, though, was the
return of vocals. The first neo-electro had been almost entirely instrumental (give or take the odd terse one- or two-word vocoderized robot
chant), and thus still compatible with a minimal techno vibe. The real
break with techno came with the blatant pop appeal (and pop
ambition) of 1998's 'Space Invaders Are Smoking Grass' by I-f, an
artist from Den Haag in Holland. This track featured a vocoderized
voice singing an actual honest-to-goodness tune. Ersatz Audio – home
base for neo-electro pioneers Le Car and Adult. – signposted this
major shift in techno sensibility with their EP 'Oral-Alio: A History of
Tomorrow'. This medley of voice-based, eighties-flavoured synthpop
songs was intended as a mini-manifesto, a critique of techno's
'language barrier – [its] fear, or reluctance, to incorporate vocals'.
But this rediscovery of vocals, melody and lyrics, was actually going
on across the dance-culture spectrum, from Green Velvet's black-
humorous monologues to The Horrorist's folk tales for ravers and
2step's vocal science.

What the nu-wave contingent of I-f and Adult. specifically were
doing was rolling the history of techno back all the way to its very
dawn: its bizarre, still not quite fathomable origins as a Black American
imitation of English synthpop. 'I always get a kick when people say
the first "techno" record was Cybotron's "Alleys Of Your Mind",' says

Adam Lee Miller of Adult. 'That 7-inch single was 1981. To me, it was just a New Wave record. It sounds particularly close to "Mr X" by Ultravox. I think people called it techno simply because Juan Atkins was black.'

This seems a good point at which to ponder: when we listen to something and identify it as 'eighties', what exactly are we responding to? What is the 'eighties'-ness in this music? It's an aggregate of attributes (coldness and cleanness of synth-sound, squareness and stiffness of groove and rhythm) and absences (obvious example: the absence of R & B influences, jazziness, 'blackness' of feel, makes the music sound European). There are specific hallmarks that seem to evoke the early eighties: the arpeggiated sixteenth-note basslines (endemic in eighties music from New Order to Italo-Disco to industrial groups like Nitzer Ebb), the dispassionate sung-spoken monologues on records like Miss Kittin's 'Frank Sinatra', and the android-like vocoderized vocals.

Vocoder-mania is a curious quirk of today's electropop vogue: it's become the privileged signifier of 'eighties', but it wasn't actually *that* popular in the real eighties, give or take the odd Telex or Kraftwerk record or Giorgio Moroder solo album. In fact, from Divine and Depeche Mode to The Human League and Orchestral Manoeuvres, the hallmark of first-wave synthpop was the deeply human and often distinctly fallible singing on the records – Marc Almond's torrid, pitch-erratic vocals in Soft Cell being a classic example, not forgetting the slightly unwieldy baritones of Dave Gahan and Phil Oakey, and the gauche 'n' gawky singing of the girls in The Human League. It's also hard to work out what the Miss Kittin-style bored-rich-girl monotone is referencing (Grace Jones circa 'Warm Leatherette' and 'Private Life'? Forgotten electronic ice-queens like Gina X or Regine Fetet of Hardcorps?). Both the deadpan vocal and vocoder trends show the way that retro movements always reinvent and fictionalize the past. Even when they try hard to be meticulously faithful and purist, they inevitably amplify certain aspects and suppress others.

The keyword crystallizing everything simultaneously appealing and problematic about the nu-wave explosion is 'retro-futurist', that seemingly self-contradictory concept. Producers are reaching back to recover that lost sense of electronic music as bracingly new, startling, alien (as opposed to what electronic sounds had become by the late nineties – an omnipresent but barely noticeable thread in pop's fabric). That lost futurity is signposted by stiff mechanistic rhythms and synth-sounds that are cold (meaning deliberately artificial-sounding, not corresponding to traditional acoustic instruments like horns, strings, piano). This 'machine-music and proud of it' stance is a dissident gesture in a context where a lot of temporary electronic producers strive for 'warmth' and 'musicality', prizing organic textures like the Rhodes electric piano and using digital technology to simulate hands-on human feel and jazzy swing by programming slight rhythmic imprecisions. Renouncing that played-not-programmed feel of suppleness and subtlety, nu-wave electro 'flaunts its synthetic nature', as Warren Fischer of Fischerspooner put it.

The nu-wave's coldness isn't just sonic, though: it relates to the emotional spectrum of the music, which encompasses numbness, alienation, neurosis, isolation. Lyrically, songs echo the man-machine imagery and fears about technology's dehumanizing and controlling effects that pervaded the first wave of electropop: early John Foxx-fronted Ultravox, Gary Numan, The Normal (aka Daniel Miller of Mute Records). The Normal's 1978 single 'Warm Leatherette' is a particularly seminal reference point and was covered by Chicks On Speed in the early years of the electro revival. Inspired by J. G. Ballard's novel *Crash*, it's a catchy ditty about the eroticism of car accidents: 'The handbrake penetrates your thigh/Quick, let's make love before you die.' Its flip side 'TV OD', about a cathode-ray junkie who sticks the aerial into his veins, anticipated David Cronenberg movies like *Videodrome* with their grisly meshing of the organic and machinic.

Of all the nu-wavers, Adult. have most zealously pursued the themes of anomie and modernity. On songs like 'Human Wreck', 'Lack of Comfort', 'Silent Property' and 'Dispassionate Furniture' the sonic textures – sterile yet abject – conjure a mood of desolate decadence: lost souls stranded in sleek luxury, with commodity fetishes and kinky machines as their only companions. Dopplereffekt were also pioneers here, with songs like 'Porno Actress' and 'Plastiphilia' evoking voyeurism and perversion, deflections of desire from its 'natural' course. The frigid pulsations of 'Porno Actress' suggest love action so emotionally numb, the protagonists get freezer-burn when they fuck.

Dopplereffekt play it dead straight, but with most of the nu-wave groups, the hollow-inside pose is sluiced through a fair amount of campy humour. A key reference point for the Berliniamsburg milieu is the 1982 cult movie *Liquid Sky*, a bizarre, low budget science-fiction

film set in downtown New York, where nihilistic death-tripping drug
fiends and fashion freaks are preyed on by aliens. Adult. covered 'Me
And My Rhythm Box', a song sung in a *Liquid Sky* nightclub scene by
a performance artist. 'If there's one movie that really identifies this
whole new look that you get at Berliniamsburg and the As Four parties,
it's *Liquid Sky*,' says Larry Tee. 'Because the fashion in that film is so
wrong. It wasn't even eighties style, it was their idea of futuristic
fashion. That film is the bad mistake of the eighties, so horrible, yet so
weirdly watchable now.'

What *Liquid Sky* tapped into, and what the whole electroclash/
nu-wave sensibility reactivates, is a futuristic update of late nineteenth-
century decadence à la Oscar Wilde and *Against Nature*, J. K.
Huysmans's late nineteenth century novel about a dandy aristocrat
who dedicates himself to artifice and monstrosity. Wilde declared that
sincerity was the enemy of art, and in this spirit electroclash rejects
wholesome authenticity in favour of all things synthetic and fake. The
motto: 'Keep it *un*real.' The Electroclash Festival celebrated self-
reinvention and artifice – from the porno-punk theatrics of Peaches to
the performance art spectacle staged by Fischerspooner, with their
costume changes, choreographed routines, props and backdrops, and
cast of more than ten performers. Fischerspooner pitched themselves
as the vanguard of a New Pretentiousness movement. 'Our goal is to
indulge and embrace the superficial and not to get too wrapped up in
issues of integrity,' frontman Casey Spooner said. 'We're completely,
unabashedly and absolutely prepared to say that we're pretentious and
superficial.' Or as My Robot Friend sing it on 'The Fake', another
Berliniamsburg anthem, 'We are the fake / No hearts for you to
break / The fake machines / Pretend to live on TV screens.'

If post-rave club culture is organized around Ecstasy-emotions –
empathy, cuddly sentimentality, mass fervour – nu-wave is predicated
on removing the Ecstasy vibe (by definition, uncool – all about warmth
and flow). Initially, it's refreshing to enter a club like Berliniamsburg,
where the whole night isn't organized around a monolithic mood-
sensation (Ecstasy). Not that it's necessarily a temple to clean living
or anything like that. The venue Luxx is round the corner from
a notorious spot for copping cocaine. Larry Tee says that if there's a
drug vector to the scene, 'It's circled back to the old disco drugs of the
seventies, minus the Quaaludes.' The shift to ego-burnishing powders
is signposted by tunes like Vitalic's 'You Prefer Cocaine' or Kittin &

Hacker's 'Frank Sinatra' with its allusion to 'sniffing in the VIP area'. Australian dance critic Tim Finney described DJ Hell as 'a cocaine producer. It's all treble sounds and big personalities. International Deejay Gigolos are trying to engage with a certain experience of dancing as a culture that was all about elitism and snootiness and music-as-fashion versus music-as-music.'

Nu-wave rewinds to the pre-E era when clubbing was all about clique-ishness and 'the beautiful people': an aristocracy of larger than life characters dedicated to standing out from the faceless herd of nonentities. 'I am legendary / You are not' declaims the chorus of Hungry Wives' 'It's Over'. Kittin & Hacker's 'Frank Sinatra' is half satire, half celebration of the velvet-rope superiority complex of the rich and famous. Nu-wave is all about the cold glitter of glamour's impenetrable surfaces. Its aura of hierarchical hauteur connects back to the gay New York tradition of vogueing, with its fashion-magazine-derived imagery and rampant Europhilia. Larry Tee's many exploits include co-writing the hit song 'Supermodel' for transvestite star RuPaul. In the early nineties, he was also involved in the superfreaky New York clubland milieu centred around the notorious Michael Alig, America's answer to Leigh Bowery. From early eighties New Romantics at Blitz to the grotesques and poseurs at Bowery's Taboo, from Alig's decadent Limelight scene to the cross-dressing queens of vogueing, there's a common ethos that is pure glam rock: intensely hierarchical, fiercely competitive, bitchy as hell. The Berliniamsburg scene is just the latest iteration of this tradition. Tee's stable of protégés includes performers with movie-star names like Tobell Von Cartier and Sophia La Marr, whose Berliniamsburg favourite 'Useless' starts with the regal and deliciously preposterous proclamation: 'I'm Catherine Deneuve!!!'. Elsewhere in nu-wave, you get imagery of executive lifestyles and jet-set glamour – Kittin & Hacker's 'Stock Exchange', the formal business-wear look and sterile office environments used by Adult. and Ersatz Audio in their artwork. This echoes the imagery of early eighties groups like Heaven 17, whose sleeve for 1981's *Penthouse and Pavement* depicted the group as corporate executives discussing business plans and negotiating deals on the telephone.

In reaching back to the early eighties, nu-wave is also looking to a time when rock and club culture were closer and had a lively conversation with each other. This explains why Larry Tee will praise Adult.'s version of 'Me And My Rhythm Box' as 'just so *shattered* and so rock

'n' roll' and why he stresses how he'll throw some rock 'n' roll into the
mix during his Berliniamsburg DJ sets, tunes like Andrew W. K.'s
'Party 'Til You Puke'. It's why My Robot Friend's 'Fake' wields the
promise / threat 'our rock 'n' roll will kill you dead.' And it's why
International Deejay Gigolos use the famous photograph of Sid Vicious
ironically flexing his puny arm muscles and wearing McLaren and
Westwood's outrageous 'two cowboys with their cocks hanging out'
T-shirt. Groups like Le Tigre and Peaches, who come from a more
punky riot grrl background, are big on the scene. Fronted by grrl icon
Kathleen Hanna, Le Tigre is New Wavey dance-pop with a lo-tech
garage punk aesthetic, all spiky riffs and feminist sloganeering, while
for all her brain-bashing techno beats Peaches has more in common
with Joan Jett, Billy Idol, or Suicide singer Alan Vega than anyone
in dance culture. In an echo of punk, attitude and charisma are
considered more important than production finesse or beat-science.
There's a nostalgia for a time when pop was full of freaks and weirdos,
people like Prince or Boy George.

*

Within the context of a fatigued dance culture, nu-wave is refreshing,
irreverent, a reason to go out again. It is already the Next Big Thing in
this corner of the world (electronic music). But there are doubts
whether it has what it takes to go all the way and become the next big
thing in mainstream pop. Nu-wave is catchy enough to seem poppy in
in the melody-deficient world of tracky techno and semi-songful house.
But it's alarming how so many of the genres most memorable tunes
are covers: Fischerspooner's version of Wire's 'The 15th', Tiga's reinvention of 'Sunglasses At Night' (originally by Canadian eighties pop
star Corey Hart), WIT's nu-wave take on New Wave hit 'Just What I
Needed' by The Cars. On the whole, nu-wave producers seem superior
at beats and textures, and rarely as good at songwriting and pop
arrangement as their inspirations. It's not clear if anyone has the sheer
pop genius flowing through their veins to write a song like The Human
League's 'Love Action' or Numan's 'Cars'. The scene's roots in techno
come through in the fact that some of the biggest and best tunes are
instrumentals: Legowelt's impossibly stirring and portentous 'Disco
Rout', the magnesium majesty of Vitalic's 'Poney Part 1' (as if glamour
somehow abandoned its human husks and became a free-floating
ectoplasmic incandescence, a brilliantine trembling and aching of the

air itself), the cold glimmering beauty of Der Zyklus II's 'Elektronisches Zeitech'. Then there's the question of stellar singers, and whether the scene really has any. Beyond its rather overused and distinctly tired robot-chic, the excessive deployment of vocoder and similar electronic distortion effects suggests this is a convenient ruse for masking the absence of really top-quality vocalists. One exception is Linda Lamb on 'Hot Room', whose haggard and baleful grandeur suggests some unholy hybrid of Marianne Faithfull, Nina Hagen and Kim Carnes. Then there's Solvent's amazing 'My Radio', which uses vocoder not as a robo-gimmick but to communicate an unearthly and angelic sense of awe and devotion.

If these tracks achieve a sonic gloriousness that propels them beyond the 'retro' trap, too much nu-wave seems trapped by its tongue-in-chic irony. It feels like there's some indefinable line that's yet to be crossed before this genre transcends period pastiche and tackles the challenge of somehow being more about *now* than *then*. Because if it is about then . . . well, the eighties classics remain impossible to beat.

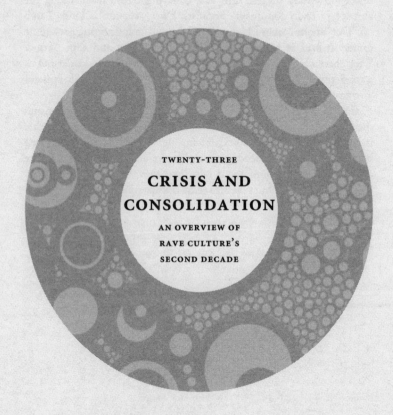

TWENTY-THREE

CRISIS AND CONSOLIDATION

AN OVERVIEW OF
RAVE CULTURE'S
SECOND DECADE

Signing off on *Energy Flash* the first time round, I used the idea of 'a pause for breath' to describe the feeling in 1998. *You've Come A Long Way Baby* is how Fatboy Slim titled his album of that year, and there was a palpable feeling that rave, having travelled so far so fast, was now stopping to take stock, looking back at the journey to date. But, I argued, the forward surge would resume soon, there were still new frontiers to conquer.

This turned out to be wishful thinking. What happened next is that the scene got even bigger, yet the music stayed stuck, its development arrested. Then the boom turned to bust, while the music underwent a kind of implosion. Replacing revolution with involution, it plunged deep into its own vast accumulated history, working through the sprawling sonic legacy through a series of internal hybrids and subtle renovations.

Dance culture reached its absolute peak in popularity and mass cultural hegemony during the three-year period 1998–2000. The reigning genres – big beat, filter disco, fluffy trance – were unabashedly poppy. Tracks by leading artists in those genres – Fatboy Slim and Chemical Brothers with big beat; Stardust, DJ Spiller and Modjo with filter; Paul Van Dyk and ATB in trance – hit the toppermost reaches of the charts across Europe and many other territories in the world. Electronic dance was so hot, Madonna leapt on two successive techno bandwagons, assimilating trance with 1998's *Ray of Light* and aping Daft Punk-style French house on 2000's *Music*.

These were the years when superDJs charged obscene amounts for remixing singles by pop groups and for a few hours spinning records in a club. The years of massive dance festivals and superclubs with grandiose plans of turning themselves into shopping-mall-like leisure complexes. A time of hubris and complacency, stoked by a blizzard of cocaine. The culture kept on swelling: in the boom's swansong phase, Fatboy Slim drew 250,000 people to a free outdoor party on Brighton's seafront, with disastrous – and for Norman Cook – bloody expensive consequences. But the music no longer hurtled forward.

In a literal sense, it had stopped hurtling – the exponential escalation of b.p.m. had halted when drum and bass and gabba reached the outer limits of speed circa 1997. While small tribes of headstrong maniacs pushed the tempos even faster (deep into the Zone of Fruitless Intensification) dance culture as a whole took a step sideways. What's striking about the late nineties is the across-the-board rediscovery of house music, a strategic downshift in tempo and embrace of a warmer, more organic palette of sounds. Oh, house in its crasser and tamer forms (handbag, tribal, funky) had stayed popular throughout the nineties; it was clubland's default option. What I'm talking about is the adoption of the house template by artists who'd hitherto been in the vanguard of innovation, and by consumers who were the leading edge of hip taste.

The London hardcore continuum was one of the first places the shift registered: in 1997 the bulk of the scene abandoned drum and bass for speed garage, a drop of approximately 30 b.p.m and a switch from chopped-up breakbeats to the pump-and-pound of four-to-the-floor house. But a similar let's-go-back impulse surfaced in other areas of the late nineties dance culture. Robert Hood and Dan Bell, for instance, talked about wanting to restore an 'original "jack" element' – meaning a Chicago house feel – that had been expunged from minimal techno (a genre they'd helped to instigate) in its remorseless pursuit of reduction and rigour. Another example is electronic experimentalist Matthew Herbert (aka Dr Rockit, Radio Boy, et al), who we last glimpsed in the 'Fuck Dance Let's Art' chapter. In 1996 he decided to fuck the art and dance, opening up a new house-oriented alter ego, Herbert, for the album *100 Lbs*. Actually, what he really did was *fold* the artiness into house's groove matrix. 1998's *Around the House* showcased Herbert's newly subtle approach to avant-gardism. Topped with exquisite jazzy vocals from Dani Siciliano, the album sounded like a voluptuous condensation of the textural/rhythmatic innovations of American deep-house producers like Mood II Swing and Masters At Work. But the lush 'musicality' was really *musique concrete* disguised, because many of the spongy textures and glitch-riffs were derived from the sampled sounds of household objects being used (*Around the House*, geddit?).

It wasn't just producers who fell in love with house, it was punters too. Hipsters who'd never had much direct experience of house as a clubbing culture, whose point of entry into rave had been hardcore/

drum and bass, or Aphex Twin/art-techno/Intelligent Dance Music aka IDM, suddenly discovered the delights of house, the amazing richness of its legacy and diversity of its sound-spectrum. This shift in allegiance was partly a response to the way that drum and bass and techno had driven themselves down anorectic, self-desiccating dead ends of punitive purism and hair-shirt minimalism. House signified a return to pleasure and pleasantness.

But the new blood entering house in the late nineties weren't content to be humble neophytes, listening respectfully to the sage advice of deep-house connoisseurs. Many of them wanted to reform and expand the genre, bringing back an earlier ideal of house as a catholic and aesthetically flexible genre (hence the term 'house-not-house' that circulated for a while). In this view of house history, the true spirit of the genre was fundamentally opposed to fundamentalism of any sort, including that of the deep-house custodians (a curmudgeonly and snobbish lot, on the whole) who tried to freeze the style and keep it 'pure' (i.e. changeless). The opposing view held that house's true anti-essence was *im*purist, a pragmatic openness to outside influence. Rather than getting paranoid about stylistic contamination like, say, the nineties Detroit techno cultists did, these new school house producers of the late nineties slyly assimilated rhythmic and texturological tricks from the overtly experimental forms of electronica, then craftily resituated them within house's pleasure-principled context. Producers like Daft Punk, Armand Van Helden, Green Velvet and Basement Jaxx revitalized house by working in elements of hardcore rave aggression, industrial techno bombast, jungle's marauding bass-science, and art-techno's twitchy glitcherie.

Leaders of a French scene that included Bob Sinclar, I:Cube and Alan Braxe, Daft Punk pioneered a monstrously popular yet hipster-credible style of disco-flavoured house. Their 1996 debut album *Homework* ranged from kitschy retro-tinged hits like 'Around The World' and 'Da Funk' to gratingly raw drug-noise like 'Rollin' & Scratchin'' and 'Rock 'n' Roll'. Falling somewhere in between those extremes was the classic 'Musique', a loop-da-looping disco cut-up that precociously featured a technique known as the 'low-pass filter sweep', an effect that makes riffs or vocal samples seem like they're receding tantalizingly into the background before surging back in full ecstatic force. Sounding like a cross between panning and phasing, the low-pass filter sweep combines a spangly, spectral unearthliness with a teasing, suppressed-sounding quality. A fabulously effective trigger for the E-rush, filter FX soon became the basis of an entire genre. Thomas Bangalter, one half of Daft Punk, collaborated with Alan Braxe to create the defining filter-disco anthem, Stardust's 1998 'Music Sounds Better With You', a two-million-selling smash built from an astonishing woozy-oozy male vocal (sung by Benjamin Diamond), cocaine-crisp Chic-style rhythm guitar, and a snatch of strings. The audio equivalent of a glitterball, 'Music Sounds Better With You' was widely interpreted as a love song to the Mitsubishi brand of E.

Another UK Number One filter smash was Armand Van Helden's 'U Don't Know Me'. Featuring Duane Harden's imploring falsetto, this orchestral disco stampede was an unusually 'deep' outing for Van Helden, better known as sole inheritor of New York's rough and ready hip-house tradition. Like Todd Terry's proto-hardcore anthems of the late eighties, Van Helden's tunes were huge in the UK. All wooshing dark-diva vocals and jungle-style wah-wah bass, his ominously erotic revamp of Sneaker Pimps's 'Spin Spin Sugar' was a formative influence on speed garage. Collaborating with underground rappers like Company Flow's MC Ren, throwing in gunshot sounds and generally flexing his ruffneck credentials, Van Helden sometimes seemed to be overcompensating for the fact that his genre was one that most hip hoppers still regarded as 'gay'. Ironically, his biggest and best tunes have been the least macho – like the languorous, lovesick 'Flowerz' and 'U Don't Know Me' itself, whose don't-judge-me lyrics slot into a gay disco-house tradition of anthems that defiantly demand respect from a hostile world. Still, if he wasn't so conflicted, Armand 'I Am A Raw Individual' Van Helden wouldn't make such compelling records.

Just as ferociously impurist, Basement Jaxx probably did more than anyone to awaken outside interest in house at the close of the nineties. Their 1999 debut *Remedy*, full of audacious hybrids like the ragga-driven thug-house of 'Jump 'N' Shout', drew a huge amount of attention towards a genre that the Jaxx, ironically, had every intention of leaving behind. Having started out in the UK purist house scene alongside Idjut Boys and Faze Action, Simon Ratcliffe and Felix Buxton quickly tired of that milieu's smug piety and decided that the best way to honour house's spirit was by vandalizing its forms.

Early Jaxx tracks like 'Fly Life' and 'Set Yo Body Free' took what Ratcliffe called 'the untouchable sexiness and polish of American deep house' and roughed it up with English aggression, attitude and noise.

The duo incubated their style, which they punningly dubbed 'punk garage', in the cramped and rowdy basement of a Brixton pub called George IV. 'That's where our chaos came from,' Ratcliffe recalled. 'There was always feedback, records jumping, things going wrong. But people cheered because there was a real vibe – it wasn't clinical.' The duo became obsessed with colliding musicality and anti-musicality (the 'ugliness' and 'wrongness' of early Chicago house, hardcore rave and so forth). The punk aspect came to the fore on *Remedy*'s stand-out tune 'Same Old Show', which pivoted around a baleful sample from New Wave ska band The Selecter, then blossomed on *Rooty* with the headbanger house of 'Get Me Off' and 'Where's Your Head At', the latter sampling a doomy Gary Numan riff and featuring an Oi!-like jeering hooligan chorus. But there was a whole other vein of Jaxx tracks that recalled Prince circa *Sign O' the Times* – insanely detailed production, warped vocal multitrackings, maximalist-not-minimalist extravagance (ideas that other producers might spin out for entire tracks occurring as sonic singularities, gratuitous one-offs). A good rubric for the Jaxx sound would be the Prince-echoing moniker 'The Genre Formerly Known As House'.

Ironically, given their attempts to move beyond house, artists like Van Helden and Basement Jaxx served as a gateway drug that turned disillusioned drum and bass and techno heads onto the glories of the disco-house tradition. One New York club defined the mood at the cusp of the new millennium: Body & Soul. Founded in 1996 by two veterans of the seventies, Francois Kevorkian and Danny Krivit, plus their younger comrade Joe Claussell, the club was conceived as a restoration of the open-minded, eclectic ethos of the gay dance underground of the mid-seventies, before disco had even been codified as a defined style, let alone commercialized as mainstream pop. Emulating David Mancuso's party The Loft, Body & Soul had an alcohol-free juice bar and a fabulously crisp sound system. Many of the audience turning up at B & S when the club opened early on Sunday afternoons were middle-aged veterans of The Loft and Paradise Garage.

Harking back to Mancuso's approach, Kevorkian, Krivit and Claussell almost always played tunes from start to finish, rather than mixing them. In opposition to the cult of DJ virtuosity (jocks like Sasha showing off their seamless mixing by picking compatible samey-sounding tracks), the B & S crew believed in the sacrosanct integrity of the Song. DJing, they felt, was the art of 'programming', the selection and sequencing of songs to tell a story. Soul classics by Stevie Wonder and Curtis Mayfield got dropped next to seventies disco obscurities and nineties Afro-house full of Fela Kuti-like percussion and dubby FX. It wasn't all spiritually healing vibes and organic earthy textures – sometimes the DJs would play thrillingly chilly electrodisco like Donna Summer's 'I Feel Love', while they were fond (some would say, overfond) of a technique called 'crossover' which cuts whole frequency bands out of the music and creates violently lurching, staccato dynamics. Applied by the B & S DJs to, say, a hoary old slice of rock disco like the Stones's 'Miss You', crossover transformed the original into something jaggedly futuristic, as though a latent house track was fighting its way out of the song's body, *Alien*-style.

B & S was very much a response to the divide in New York club culture between rave-style superclubs like Twilo and the more intimate 'vibe' or 'soul' clubs playing deep house. On one side, white glow-stick warriors from the bridge-and-tunnel zones of New Jersey, Queens, Long Island, got stoked on E and rallied to superstar DJs from Europe. On the other, visiting Europeans and jaded hipsters flocked to worship at the shrine of all things authentically old school – the largely gay and black dance underground, where the DJs are local boys. By 1999, Body & Soul was getting hailed as the best club in the world, and tourists were arriving from all over the world – purist house scholars from the UK, party-hard Eurotrash, immaculately retro-styled Japanese waifs – in search of a time-travel simulacrum of back-in-the-day. Body & Soul and similar clubs like Bang the Party effectively transformed the New York prehistory of house into a veritable heritage industry similar to jazz in New Orleans.

*

That 'the best club in the world' was based on the idea of *restoration* – a return not just to the golden age of early house, but to the 'original principles' of the pre-disco underground – seemed to symbolize the closing of a circle. Rave had gone all the way out to the farthest extremes in every conceivable direction, and then all the way back to the start. And now it was stalled. In the first few years of the twenty-first century, dance culture seemed to be struggling to come up with a great leap forward. Instead of a Next Big Thing, all it could generate was Next Medium-Sized Things, newish hybrid genres like broken beats and nu-skool breaks. These micro-scenes flashed up briefly on the specialist dance media screen but were of minimal interest to the outside world. To stake its claim on the wider world's attention, dance music needed to smack listeners upside the head with mind-blowingly unfamiliar new sounds. That's what it had done repeatedly from the late eighties to the late nineties, surging into unknown territory so rapidly you had to scramble to keep up with its constant mutations. Even those who couldn't stand a genre like jungle, couldn't deny its radicalism, the fact that it sounded like nothing they'd ever heard before. In contrast, the new substyles in twenty-first-century dance had a kind of 'plausible deniability', such that sceptics or lapsed believers could dismiss them as mere tweaks to established forms.

While the cool undergrounds bustled with medium- or smaller-sized activity, the mainstream of clubbing 'n' drugging had driven the music into nullifying dead ends like the bang-bang-bang-bang-you're-brain-dead style known as hard house. The combination of corporatization, complacency and crappy music proved lethal. You started to hear murmurings of disquiet at the end of 2001, when the normally booster-ish dance-mag *Muzik* claimed that the industry was in total denial about the oncoming crisis: attendance at clubs was declining, record sales were sliding, the only real growth area was chill-out compilations. The stores and the charts were awash with the latter, suggesting that clubbers were choosing to save their money and take their drugs at home to a soundtrack of stoner muzak, rather than pay a small fortune to attend megaclubs with their sterile, shopping-mall-like atmospheres, bouncers carrying walkie-talkies, and extortionate drinks prices.

Another factor was that the original audience for dance was tiring of going out because it was getting older, while the tidal waves of fresh recruits that had repeatedly restocked the movement during the forward-surging nineties were no longer materializing. Next Medium-Sized Things aren't compelling enough to make converts. Electronic dance music had also simply been around for such a long time (in 2002 it was *fifteen years* since acid house) that familiarity bred, if not outright contempt, certainly ennui. The next generation of cool kids were turning away from 'faceless techno bollocks' towards more face-full music: garage-punk revivalists like the Hives and White Stripes, neo-post-punkers like the Strokes and the Libertines, the freak folk of Devendra Banhart and Joanna Newsom. In their different ways, all these artists were stylish-looking and intensely tuneful, charismatic and literate. More often than not, they put on an entertaining show, as opposed to fiddling with laptops or turntables like the sallow-faced technicians of electronica. Paul Oakenfold once bragged that turntables were outselling guitars. By 2002, the situation was reversed: guitars outstripped decks as more kids wanted to be rock stars than DJs. There was also competition from rap and R & B. Spurred by a turn-of-millennium burst of adventurous beat-making and futuristic production by figures like Timbaland and the Neptunes, hip hop increasingly beat electronica at its own game on club dance floors, even as its mad-catchy tunes made it into the globally dominant form of chart pop.

The decline in dance's fortunes was precipitous. Record sales dropped from thirteen per cent of the total UK market in 2000 to a measly seven per cent in 2004 – almost *halved*. A series of dramatically ominous landmark events heralded the industry's contraction. In 2003, Cream, one of the world's biggest superclubs, closed; Gatecrasher drastically scaled back from a weekly club to a monthly event. Other clubs tried an image makeover, distancing themselves from the gurning pill-monster market and adopting a more glammy aura of velvet ropes and bottle-service tables, where music was a cosmetic backdrop rather than the central experience. The 'music head' clubs that prospered in the new reduced conditions were ones like London's Fabric, which wasn't locked into a particular sound and didn't cater to the caner community. Switching between genres on a weekly basis and booking DJs who weren't superjocks but tastemakers in their respective specialist sounds, Fabric appealed to a compact but enduring constituency: dance fans whose sensibility was discerning but non-purist.

Dance music's mainstream was imploding, leaving an array of micro-scenes and little undergrounds orbiting a collapsed centre. One major consequence was the near-extinction of the dance media, as the general readership withered away and genre fanatics found their information through other sources (increasingly the web). At their late nineties peak, all the UK dance magazines collectively sold around 250,000. But then three of the big five closed within eighteen months of each other – first *Ministry* in early 2003, then *Muzik* and *Jockey Slut*. This left just the long-established specialist publication *DJmagazine* and the market leader *Mixmag*, whose circulation slid from well over 100,000 at its height to its current humiliating figure of under 40,000. It would be lovely to think that *Ministry* and *Mixmag* were punished for their relentlessly lowest-common-denominator approach – the endless pix of clubbers off their tits and club babes in furry bras and micro-skirts and teak-toned fake tans; the fawning and content-free profiles of celeb DJs. But the demise of the more trainspottery *Muzik* suggests the problem was simply a dearth of people interested in reading about dance as it devolved into unconvincing sub-flavas like 'smash house', 'tribal tech' and 'funky-chunky twisted house'.

Part of the dance mags' lowbrow approach to boosting circulation was endless rehashed articles about drug use, all those 'What drugs are YOU on?' reader surveys and 'Are drugs driving you mad?' scare stories, which resembled nothing so much as the 'new' angles on sex that women's mags like *Cosmo* dredge up every month. Even earnest *Muzik* tried to latch onto the 'chemical generation' trend, launching a column in which readers related their excruciatingly embarrassing tales of crazy, undignified or plain dumb things they'd done when off their heads (few of which contained sufficient narrative structure to qualify as anecdotes). As club culture became sanitized, practically the only edge factor left was the continued illegality of Ecstasy and other dance drugs. Yet by the early noughties, most young people were utterly blasé about E – the 'magic pill' had become safe, passé, naff. The declining allure of the drug/dance combo as leisure option and marker of youth cool was symbolized by the plummeting price of E. By 2002, its dealer-to-punter unit cost had dropped to as low as £1 in certain parts of the UK – making it even more lowly and commonplace than a pint of lager, perhaps just a notch above inhaling lighter fluid.

In America, where rave culture in its full-on form never got deeply entrenched in the mainstream of society, electronic dance music's eclipse came swifter. The late nineties had looked promising: OK, the much-vaunted Electronica Revolution turned out to be a false dawn, but the serious end of the music (drum and bass, home-listening techno) continued to make inroads with American ex-indie types. Matador, home of lo-fi outfits like Pavement, went all Warp-y, licensing records by the likes of Boards of Canada, while Daft Punk and Basement Jaxx were as hip as could be. Big beat and trance DJs played to increasingly massive crowds in particular parts of the country. Paul Oakenfold, bullish as ever, was confident that America was the next commercial frontier for dance.

The big obstacle to crossover was access to the airwaves. MTV had been enthused by electronica's 'Next Big Thing' candidacy – the channel programmed videos by The Prodigy, Chemical Brothers, Orbital and Underworld, and launched Amp, a late-night show

dedicated to more experimental electronic music. But by the end of
1997, it became clear that electronica was being eclipsed by the craze
for ska and swing: in an almost pointed repudiation of machine music,
American kids wanted to dance but weren't prepared to dance to
actual, y'know, dance music. So MTV shunted electronica back into
the ghetto (Amp ended up in the graveyard slot of Sunday night
between 2 a.m. and 4 a.m.). As for US radio, it had only ever been
open to electronica at its most song-ful and rock-like – Prodigy's
digital simulacrum of punk, Chemical Brothers' Britpop-with-break-
beats – and wasn't prepared to playlist the purer forms of instrumental
electronica for fear of alienating listeners. Nor did it get behind groups
like Basement Jaxx and Daft Punk when they made rock-friendly
moves. Daft Punk's inspired merger of disco and FM soft-rock on
2001's *Discovery* alchemized its schlocky sources (ELO, Supertramp,
Frampton, Van Halen) to achieve a splendour of sound that felt
almost religious. But this fantastique-plastique sound was out of step
with the rock trends of the day (nu-metal, the new garage punk) and
without serious radio support or MTV hit videos, *Discovery* sold only
500,000 in America – a decent result but way out of proportion to its
monstrous success in Europe. Basement Jaxx's *Rooty* likewise shifted
less than 250,000 in America, putting this heavy-hitter of Anglotronica
on a *Billboard* par with the runt of Roc-A-Fella's litter or a side project
by Tool's drum technician.

In a cruel irony, electronica reached the American mainstream not
as crossover pop music that grabbed your attention full-on, but as
background music, the soundtrack to TV commercials or 'interstitial'
music as used on channels like Bravo and ABC News. Massively touted
as a star for 1998, Fatboy Slim never really had a proper hit in America,
but his tunes were heard in countless commercials and dozens of
Hollywood movies, with Moby and the Crystal Method close behind
him. Sped-up breakbeats, acid riffs and other Ecstasy-associated sounds
were plastered as a glaze of 'cool' and 'contemporary' over products as
square as Mastercard, BMW, Smint breath fresheners and even the US
Army. Big beat briefly became the signifier of 'youth today', even
though far more actual American youth were listening to nu-metal and
rap. There were technical reasons why it worked well in commercials:
big beat's high-energy style suited the frantic fast-cut pace of advertising. It also just happens that the advertising industry is based
in hipster-dense cities like New York, Los Angeles and London, where

electronica at that point was the music of choice for information-technology-wielding young professionals.

Music usually becomes Muzak only after it has been chartpop for a good while, but in America electronica skipped the radio hegemony stage and went straight to ubiquity. The combination of overexposure and lack of real success left American dance culture in an unhappy limbo – neither underground nor mainstream. As if that wasn't bad enough, the ailing rave scene then started to get a battering from the authorities – a non-coordinated but virtually nationwide campaign of anti-rave legislation at the state or city level, local police forces cracking down on promoters and club owners for drug use at their events, and, in New York, overzealous enforcement of the 'cabaret law', which forbade dancing in bars unless the proprietor had purchased an expense licence. Continuing the 'quality of life crimes' campaign of his predecessor Rudy Giuliani, this was Mayor Bloomberg appealing to property owners concerned about nocturnal noise in their neighbourhoods.

Hang on a minute, why were people *dancing in bars* anyway? The rise of the DJ bar wasn't just an American trend, but happened on both sides of the Atlantic. As the formerly packed superclubs closed, moved to smaller venues or went irregular, club nights increasingly moved into pubs and bars. These could be vibey (especially if the bar was an illegal after-hours drinking den) and the intimacy was cool compared to the impersonal megaclubs. But small-is-beautiful had serious downsides. Through its evolution at raves and big clubs, this music had reached the point where it was made for large sound systems; the music didn't achieve the right degree of scale and sensory overload on a bar's titchy audio set-up. The reduction in the size of events was also a knock to the scene's self-image. When the massive is no longer *massive*, the vibe diminishes significantly. Dance had contracted to the hardcore believers and the cognoscenti, but the fly by night fashionista types actually play an important role in creating a sense of 'this is the place to be'. And that floating hipster vote had simply drifted off elsewhere.

*

You knew things were ailing in America's post-rave dance culture when DJs started emigrating to Europe. In the USA (and in the UK too), smaller crowds and the decreasing number of clubs meant fewer gig opportunities and smaller fees. The superstar jocks clung onto their position at the top (albeit often having to journey much further afield, to territories that were only just entering their dance culture boom-phase, like Latin America). It was the mid-level DJs, the ones who had been making a solid living or were on the verge of going full-time professional, who really felt the crunch. Noticing that the vibe was still alive in Europe, DJs started moving to cities like Barcelona and Berlin because the work prospects were better, the cost of living cheaper and the cultural climate more supportive. The most high-profile émigré was Richie Hawtin. His move to Berlin in 2003 confirmed that Germany was now the spiritual homeland for electronic culture.

Germany was setting the tone musically too. Most of the decade's leading record labels – Kompakt, B-Pitch Control, Perlon, Playhouse, Get Physical – are based there. And for the greater part of the noughties, the connoisseur consensus sound has been a German invention, microhouse – nowadays an unsatisfactory umbrella term for an increasingly diverging array of sub-styles, but originally a useful and era-defining concept coined by techno writer Philip Sherburne in 2001. As the term suggests, microhouse basically entails the transposition of the minimal techno aesthetic onto the warmer sound-palette and more relaxed, inviting tempo of house.

The groundwork for the genre's emergence had been laid down in the mid to late nineties by the cluster of producers surrounding Berlin's twinned labels Basic Channel and Chain Reaction, artists like Porter Ricks, Various Artists, Monolake and Vainqueur. Drawing on dub's spatiality and subtractive aesthetic, they distilled house down to its barest essence – no songs, no vocals, barely any melodies, sometimes not even a drum track. The result was a music made entirely of texture, pulse-rhythm and space. Initially monotonous, Basic Channel/Chain Reaction's often ten-minute-long tracks gradually revealed themselves to be endlessly inflected, fractal mosaics of flicker-riffs and shimmer-pulses. The musician/critic Kevin Martin coined the term 'heroin house' to describe the amniotic/narcotic aura of this sound, as warmly cocooning and spongy as the womb's velvety lining. The BC/CR minimalist impulse involved seeing just how reduced – in terms of notes – you could make a pulse without it becoming purely percussive, just another beat. On tracks like Maurizio's 'M6' and Resilient's '1.2', riffs were miniaturized to the point where they became two-note sub-vamps, texture-ripples and tectonic sound-shudders so contourless they were at the lowest threshold of memorability. Yet for all the sound's abstraction, the BC/CR heart-pulse connected back to Chicago and its primordial 'jack' rhythm.

Another key figure who paved the way for microhouse was producer Wolfgang Voigt aka Mike Ink, who, like Basic Channel, gathered around him a coterie of like-minded musicians to record for his labels Profan and Studio 1. Voigt made some 'heroin house' himself under the appropriately amorphous moniker Gas, most notably 1998's awesome *Konigsforst*. Here he sampled refrains and sonorities from German classical music, weaving them into a subtly shifting tapestry over a muffled, changeless four-to-the-floor beat, the reverberance and majesty of the original orchestral recordings creating an atmosphere of airy vastness and altitude that felt positively alpine. In terms of being a midwife to microhouse, though, Voigt's crucial contribution was founding the record label Kompakt. Just as Basic Channel/Chain Reaction was based around the Berlin techno store Hard Wax, Kompakt took its name from Voigt's record shop in Cologne, where he worked alongside his partner Michael Mayer, soon to become the most renowned and popular DJ in the microhouse genre.

There's a subtle but crucial semantic difference between 'minimal' and 'micro'. Minimal evokes modernist austerity and severity – stark lines, clarity of form, absence of ornament. 'Micro' suggests the miniaturization of detail. Where minimal techno records were so reduced they were almost empty, just pure body-battering percussive insistence, microhouse could often be relatively busy, teeming with tiny sonic events. This aesthetic drifted into dance music from the post-Oval realm of glitchtronica, music made out of the hums, tics and crackles generated by vandalized CDs, traumatized hardware and daydreaming machinery. Initially known as 'clickhouse' before Sherburne's neologism caught on, the genre's brain-tickling intricacy was also influenced by the latest developments in computer software – sequencing and virtual studio programmes like Reason and Fruity Loops, digital signal processing and plug-ins, and Ableton Live. A quantum leap in home studio production, these 'digital audio workstations' altered the entire aesthetic of dance music from the late nineties onward. Their dramatic expansion of artists' ability to fine-tune and fiddle encouraged producers to make tracks full of densely layered detail and to programme rhythms where changes occurred in every single bar. The result was an aesthetic of 'audio trickle', as critic

Matthew Ingram terms it – music that kept the listening ear diverted with its constant peripheral fluctuations but which often lacked a strong central core.

Mille Plateaux's *Clicks & Cuts* compilations of 2000 and 2001 corralled a bunch of left-field electronica figures like Curd Duca and Kit Clayton but also a number of key figures who would take the 'sound dust' aesthetic onto the dance floor: Jan Jelinek (aka Farben), Vladislav Delay, Thomas Brinkmann, Hakan Libdo, Geez 'n' Gosh. At this emergent point, microhouse had an eerie but compelling blend of ascetism and sensuality. Listening to artists like Pantytec and Isolee, it was as though house's song-flesh had been stripped to reveal the music's inner organs, the grotesque gurgles and base bubblings gener-ated by its gastro-intestinal plumbing. Grooves were constructed out of *musique-concrete*-like timbres, an onomatopoeic cornucopia of ploots, crickles, schlaaps, grunks. But even at their most tic-riddled and Tourettic these were definitely grooves, with an unmistakable wiggle to their walk. Although the rhythmic feel was house, micro's sensibility still bore the hefty imprint of minimal techno and IDM. But Vladislav Delay made a key shift that pushed the emerging genre closer to deep house. Under the name Luomo, he introduced elements of songfulness and the human voice on the album *Vocal City*. For the sequel, *The Present Lover*, he pushed even further, creating an eighties-tinged quasi-pop even more prominently daubed with female air-freshener vocals, music that had all the dazzling gloss and prissy delicacy of Prefab Sprout and Scritti Politti but little of the melodic memorability.

A curious but productive tension bubbled inside microhouse, a conflicted relationship to the Black American traditions it drew on. On the face of it, this was house music distanced from its black and gay roots, a European abstraction and distillation that felt ethereal and disembodied even as it worked your body in the club. Yet there was also a pronounced vein of homage to the traditions of blues, gospel and soul that nourished disco and house, from the Playhouse label-affiliated club called Robert Johnson, to artist names like Losoul, to Thomas Brinkmann's Soul Center records (woven from snippets of raspy R & B vocal and snatches of call-and-response) and Geez 'n' Gosh's gospel-sampling albums *My Life With Jesus* and *Nobody Knows*. At the same time there was an equally strong impulse towards Ger-manic identity. Wolfgang Voigt talked presciently in the late nineties of his fervent desire to create 'something like a "genuinely German pop music"' and throw off the influence of Anglo-American pop (largely based on black American music). This interest in nationality (as opposed to nationalism) led him to investigate Wagner, schlager, Alban Berg, volksmusik, brass bands playing polkas, marches and so forth, all in the quest to locate some kind of German audio-cultural DNA. Hence the Gas records: attempts 'to 'bring the German forest to the disco' that were informed by childhood memories of Voigt family expeditions to the Konigsforst near Cologne and to the Alps.

This push-and-pull between Afro-America and Mittel Europa reflected German youth's mixed feelings about its own culture and history. In a weird way, the German techno community's obsession with Detroit (Tresor's talk of a Berlin-Detroit alliance, the 313 phone code T-shirts on sale in Hardwax) was a form of displaced patriotism. Worshipping Detroit became a way back to embracing their own Germanness, which could be comfortably affirmed because Kraftwerk and Moroder were mediated through black people (Detroit's own Germanophilia). As microhouse evolved, though, the Euro aspect came into the ascendant. Listening to the genre's leading figures in 2002–3, DJs like Michael Mayer and Superpitcher, you started to hear more elements of a strictly nineties and Nordic provenance: sounds that flashed back to Jam & Spoon circa 'Stella' and 'Age of Love', tunes that bordered on fluffy trance, even tracks that were like a midtempo and tasteful version of gabba. In 2003, Mayer talked of the Kompakt sound as 'a German sound . . . which is not rooted in black music, but maybe German folk music and polka.'

But instead of tapping into the kind of cultural legacy Wolfgang Voigt had sought to reclaim, microhouse was much more a reflection of contemporary Germany, the modern, forward-looking centre of a unified Europe. The pounding, punishing techno that ruled E-Werk and Tresor in the early nineties had fit the old clichés of Prussian discipline and severity; microhouse, in contrast, was far more sensual, representing a hedonism tempered by taste. Again, the contrast between 'minimal' and 'micro' was telling. 'Micro' has none of 'minimal's intimations of renunciation and ascetic spirituality. Micro is suggestive more of exquisitely finessed design features that only the connoisseur appreciates, or even *notices*. Microhouse is music for the generation that grew up with mobile phones and iPods and the gamut of chic portable pleasure-tech (the label name Kompakt is perfectly attuned to this sensibility). You could see this minimal-to-micro shift in men's hairstyles: the slaphead look of the early nineties techno soldier was replaced by short-but-not-severe hairstyles suggestive of a kind of restrained dandyism, often with a Neu Romantique ironic-retro eighties quality.

Metrohaus, I call it: DJs like Superpitcher and Mayer are well groomed, willowy, epicene types, and the places they play tend to be designer bars with glitzy-but-arty decor. Microhouse appeals to European middle-class youth, kids who are bohemian in their drug taking and sexual freedom but bourgeois in their love of designer commodities and careerism (typically working in media, the arts, design, computing). The music found a similarly urban but ninety-nine per cent white (and Europhile) audience in America.

Microhouse is a post-rave sound: you can get fucked up to it, drugs definitely enhance the rich detail in the sound, but it's not essential, because the energy level of the house tempo doesn't demand cranking up your nervous system artificially. The music appeals to the mind and the body in equal measure, works as well at home as in the club. Personally, I found it the default option for when you had people round for dinner, perfect audio decor (how metrosexual is that!). Artists like Isolee and Koze hit just the right median point between stimulating and unobtrusive: the music wasn't bland, but it didn't impose itself either.

Because the model was house rather than rave, though, the slow builds and the plateau-like chug-chug-chug of it all make for a bit of a *level* experience in the club. And the detail-oriented aesthetic, with its minute, occasionally verging-on-imperceptible fluctuations of texture, resulted in an oddly centreless music that left people who'd been through the rave heyday like myself crying out for some full throttle, for-the-jugular energy. Avoiding the 'rude 'n' cheesy' side of rave, microhouse is a connoisseur sound, made by and for people who've been immersed in the culture for some while and who simply don't want crass riffs and anthemic hooks. Earlier I mentioned the concept of the Zone of Fruitless Intensification, the numbing death trap that every style of music seems to drive itself into eventually. In micro's case, that was reached circa 2003–4 when the music got too nouvelle-cuisiney.

Perhaps that explains why there was a sudden self-generated shift within Eurodance towards the MONSTER RIFF. The biggest European dance-floor anthem of 2004 was 'Rocker' by German techno veterans Alter Ego, its crude chugging rhythm and squealing riff blatantly modelled on heavy metal. Rising producers like Black Strobe, Tiefschwarz and Kiki released tracks steeped in the influence of industrial and Goth. Kiki even parodied Andrew Eldritch's hollow-chested doom-drone baritone on 'The End Of The World'. Then came a post-Daft Punk wave of French rifftronica spearheaded by the distortion-obsessed duo Justice and the former thrash-metal fans behind the label Ed Banger.

The most peculiar aspect of Eurotronica's sudden penchant for rocking out was the fad for schaffel. In its simplest form, this meant replacing house's evenly emphasized four-to-the-floor beat with a 6/8 time signature. If that doesn't conjure any associations, think 'Spirit In The Sky' by Norman Greenbaum. The swing and stomp of early seventies glam rock and glitterbeat was the main inspiration, but another source, authentic to Mittel Europa, was the polka. Wolfgang Voigt can claim to have pioneered the idea of schaffel back in the mid-nineties with his T. Rex sampling Love Inc. track 'Hot Love'. And it was Kompakt that really pushed the fad in 2004 with schaffel tracks galore and the compilation series *Schaffelfieber* (which translates as *Shuffle Fever*). Titillating as the craze was, schaffel seemed a sure sign that dance had lost its way and had entered a midlife crisis of aesthetic rudderlessness. Through its own evolutionary path, techno had often hit upon rock-like riff structures and blaring noises. But this was something altogether different and really rather lame: the wholesale importation of a rhythmic structure from a thirty-year-old rock fad.

Constant innovation had been a central aspect of rave music's self-conception from the start. But by the mid-noughties, the movement seemed to be going through the uncomfortable process of shedding that part of its identity and coming to terms with the idea that its own future would no longer involve futurism. If you look at the historical arc of dance music, there's a striking resemblance with rock's evolution, except that instead of moving forward in decade phases, the metabolically accelerated rave scene proceeded through five-year units. Dance's equivalent to the sixties would be 1988–92: the era of the first raves, when the music glowed with the starry-eyed euphoria of a culture's extreme youth and the flow of immortal anthems seemed endless. Next came the seventies, the half-decade from 1993–7: a darker, more troubled, but still incomparably rich period of genre fragmentation, drug-malaise-induced darkness, increasing musical complexity (concept albums!) countered by punk-like strategies of renewal-through-reduction. From 1998–2002, dance moved into a self-referential and auto-cannibalizing phase akin to the rock eighties: revivalisms galore, fads for electro and synthpop, acid house and early jungle.

How to characterize the muddled period from 2002–7? I would argue that this actually resembles the nineties in rock, a *post*-postmodernist phase, rich in invention but lacking a clear direction forward. Grunge, for instance, didn't dramatically expand the boundaries of the rock form, but neither was it a straightforward revival or retro-eclectic pastiche. Likewise, in recent years the sharpest operators in dance music – Tiefschwarz, LCD Soundsystem, Recloose, Maurice Fulton, Booka Shade – are roughly equivalent to PJ Harvey or Pavement, artists working within an established form but finding new possibilities. Today's producers have a scholarly knowledge of the history of dance music. They are skilled at getting period-evocative sounds and take delight in hunting down little crevices of obscure, out-of-the-way music (like the early eighties disco-meets-Krautrock-based Cosmic scene in northernmost Italy, inspiration for the 'space disco' sound pioneered by Lindstrom). But although the source material they work with is totally precedented and sometimes predates rave itself, these producers cleverly weld disparate elements into composites that feel fresh. It's the distinction between innovation and originality. We rarely get the shock of the new that the acid-house bass or mentasm noise or jungle breakbeats offered. Instead we get the milder thrills of the subtle twist or artful permutation. Oh, there are still a handful of artists pushing the music into unknown spaces, like the brilliant Chilean-exiled-to-Berlin DJ-producer Ricardo Villalobos, creator of mind-bending tracks like 'Dexter', whose pendulously gloopy textures make it feel like Time itself is slowing down, or 'Fizheuer Zieheuer', a 37-minute-long, emaciated dub-house groove whose sole melodic content consists of horn refrains sampled from a Serbian brass band. But overall, dance music today is recombinant, the soundtrack of an era of consolidation.

*

And what about the legacy of hardcore rave, the burning heartcore of *Energy Flash*? Anyone who actually experienced that nineties surge is going to be spiritually scarred for life. The folk memory of that moment – when future-fucking innovation was massively popular rather than confined to the academic ghetto – has also affected many who came afterwards and didn't witness it with their own ears. So it's not surprising that the populist vanguard sounds of hardcore, gabba and jungle still reverberate through the contemporary soundscape. That period serves as the touchstone and prime resource for two of the major genres that emerged in the last ten years, breakcore and dubstep.

Breakcore could almost be conceived as a riposte to microhouse. The style is patched together from all the rude 'n' cheesy street sounds that could never be part of the Kompakt universe: jungle, gabba, dancehall, Miami bass, gangsta rap, etc. Ironically, the scene started as an offshoot of IDM, aka 'intelligent dance music'. The connective bridge was the 'drill 'n' bass' sound, the fad for parody-jungle spearheaded by IDM gods Squarepusher, Luke Vibert and Aphex Twin. Although the drill 'n' bassheads often seemed to be smirking, many actually had genuine affection and admiration for breakbeat hardcore. For some, 1992-and-all-that had been their entry point into electronic music in the first place. One such true fan was Mike Paradinas, aka μ-Ziq. Along with the abstract electronica you'd expect, his Planet Mu label became a home for breakcore whippersnappers like Venetian Snares and Shitmat, as well as new music by real-deal hardcore veterans like Producer, Hellfish and Bizzy B. Planet Mu also released an anthology of archival jungle by Remarc entitled *Soundmurderer*.

Remarc-style 'rinse out' junglizm – the 1994 sound of shredded Amen breaks and ragga samples – is the cornerstone of the breakcore genre. Producers like Venetian Snares made the style even more frenetic and fractured, mashing the Amens until the music became mosh-able rather than danceable. Many breakcore folk had been into hardcore punk before getting into electronic music. The Tigerbeat 6 label in San Francisco became a focus for this emergent breakcore sensibility. Here indie rock's aesthetic (and *ethic*) of lo-fi and DIY meshed with the obsessive-compulsive geek science of electronica. The result was music perfect for the generation raised on video games, a cartoon-crazy romp riddled with audio pratfalls and sonic japes, an insanely event-*full* sound created by producers seemingly scared witless of losing the listener's attention.

Kid 606, the founder of Tigerbeat, was a classic exponent of breakcore's attention-deficit-disorder style. His records collided IDM mannerisms (post-Oval glitches and hiccups, wisps of Aphex-like melody, graunchy Autechre noise) with lumpen rumpus nicked from a host of 'Stupid Dance Musics' – gabba, jungle, ragga et al. Real name Manuel Depredo, the Kid had an almost Tourette's-level compulsion to be the thorn in IDM's side, puncturing the scene's po-faced pomposity. One gambit involved tweaking American IDM fans' chronic Anglophilia: their worship of first-wave electronic listening music luminaries like Richard D. James, their endless online discussions about Autechre's 'granular synthesis' techniques or the huge sums they'd paid for rare early EPs by Boards of Canada. The Tigerbeat 6 stance was defiantly patriotic and iconoclastic: Depredo's buddy J. Lesser wrote a track called 'Markus Popp Can Kiss My Redneck Ass', followed shortly by Kid 606's 'Luke Vibert Can Kiss My Indie-Punk Whiteboy Ass'. In both cases, of course, the sacrilege masked anxiety of influence vis-à-vis the pioneers of – respectively – glitch and drill 'n' bass. Along with the spiky, sarcastic attitude, another punk-rock trait was Tigerbeat's emphasis on live performance, which broke with the IDM norm of static laptop twiddlers. Lesser often stage-dived mid-set, while Blectum from Blechdom, a female duo whose music collided abstract-expressionist electronics with potty-mouthed grrl humour and *Ubu Roi*-like scatological grotesquerie, brought a performance-art element to their shows, sometimes playing encased inside a gigantic two-person body suit.

Tigerbeat 6 were just one node in an international network of breakcore – labels like Broklyn Beats, Irritant, Mashit, Cock Rock Disco, producers like Speedranch Janksy, Hrvatski, V/Vm, knifehand-chop, Donna Summer. It's an incestuous little rhizome, endlessly inbreeding through split singles, one-off collaborations, remix swaps. With records released in editions of 500 or less, breakcore was the fulfilment of DIY-punk's ideal of a culture where there's no gap between engaged artist and passive spectator, if only because almost everyone on its fervent but distinctly compact dance floors is either a DJ or producer themselves. For those who remember nineties rave as a lived experience, breakcore induces a cognitive dissonance, a sort of temporal rupture where you're neither in the present nor back in the day but caught in the eerie limbo of retro. Because it's so referential (and reverential) towards jungle and gabba, breakcore can't help but remind you of a time when these sounds were popular on a mass level. The material this music is built from carries the memory-afterimages of huge crowds flailing their limbs to abstract noises and convulsive beats – a poignant aural mirage of a massive that's simply absconded.

As for London itself, the city-state heartland of the hardcore continuum ... well, at the cusp of the noughties, the scene started to split into three distinct directions. First, there was UK garage: after 2step's 1999–2001 pop crossover boom collapsed, the sound went back into the underground. Four-to-the-floor garage and 2step were now static styles, their evolutionary potential exhausted. But they remained popular fare both as golden oldies and as new tracks in the vintage style, on the pirates and in clubs, where UKG continued to supply the perennial demand on the part of adult clubbers for a classy soundtrack for getting expensively drunk and copping off. Speed garage in its purest form thrived as the North of England style known as 'bassline house', pure 1997 timewarp bizznizz. But in London itself, garage actually regressed a bit, reverting to what the music sounded like before the prefix 'speed' got added to it: a de-junglized sound known as 'urban house' and then simply 'funky house'. Timmi Magic, one of the veteran garage DJs pushing this sound, talked about getting rid of the MC and the rewinds (the dancehall/jungle elements) and filling the resulting vibe deficit with ... a live percussionist. Oooh gosh.

'Urban/funky' was a literally reactionary development: it expelled the MC as a reaction against grime. Long before the term 'grime' took hold, the genre was emerging in the form of 2step tracks featuring rapping instead of singing, and where the MC had equal billing with the track's DJ-producer. Soon this style became a genre in its own right, a movement dominated by teenage boys rather than mixed-gender adults (2step's constituency). In some ways, grime really lies beyond this book's remit, as it's barely dance music. Aggressive and high-energy, the physical responses it inspires are closer to pogoing or moshing than winding your waist. That, or people at grime raves just stand stock still, nodding heads intently to the word-flow. Grime DJs don't mix, they slap track after track on the decks in the style of dancehall DJs, dropping quick adrenalin-jolt bursts – rowdy chorus plus hottest verse – sometimes as short as one minute. Yet in another sense grime is totally a product of the rave continuum: it represents the true and final flowering of the artistic potential I detected earlier in *Energy Flash*, all those hardcore MCs spouting ephemeral but sublime nonsense over the pirate airwaves.

The MCs' status had grown steadily through the jungle and garage years, but their role still remained supportive to the DJ. Even when they appeared on records, their careers were largely based around a few trademark catchphrases or signature vocal licks. Then MCs started to write actual verses, extended takes on traditional boasts about their own mic skills, gradually getting into narrative and soliloquy. Suddenly, circa 2001, the scene was swarming with MC collectives – So Solid Crew, K2 Family, Genius Crew, Pay As U Go Kartel, Heartless Crew, Roll Deep. It was as if only by ganging up for sheer strength of numbers could they shove the DJ out of the spotlight. Grime's torrential wordiness reversed the aesthetic priorities of rave music. Rave had always been about the non-verbal sublime, but now verbose and swollen egos trampled over the loss of self that was originally house music's premise. Grime inverted rave in other ways. Aggression and cynicism replaced loved-up bonhomie. Lyrics teemed with imagery of 'slewing' and 'merking', slang for killing and maiming that mostly signified the destruction of rival MCs in verbal combat, but sometimes spilled out into real-world violence. In one ghastly case, the rising young MC Crazy Titch was sentenced to life for his role in the murder of *the friend* of a rival MC who had insulted Titch's cousin Durrty Goodz (another top grime MC).

Anti-rave in spirit, grime's sonic substance is nonetheless an extension of the rave continuum. The beats that MCs spit over are full of sounds that hark back to particular phases of the techno-rave tradition – snaking miasmas of mentasmic noise, gabba-like stabs, bruising bass-blows in the jump-up jungle style. Grime beat-makers like Wonder, Wiley, Terror Danjah and Dizzee Rascal have produced some of this decade's most inventive electronic music. On Terror Danjah tracks like 'Juggling' and 'Sneak Attack', the intricate syncopations, texturized beats, hyper-spatial production and 'abstracty sounds' (Danjah's own phrase) reveal the producer's roots in drum and bass. Other tunes like 'Creep Crawler' and 'Frontline' – all bass-blare fanfares and ominous horn-like stabs pummelling in the lower mid-range while high-pitched off-key synths wince like the onset of migraine – constitute a sophisticated response to the bombastic club bangers built by American street rap producers such as Swizz Beatz and Lil Jon.

In its early, protozoan stage, grime recalled the 1993 era of darkcore. The music retreated from the glossy poppiness of commercial 2step into a murky underworld of gritty, lo-fi tracks in many cases bashed

out, legend has it, on PlayStations. Much early grime was submusic –
unfinished experiments, prototypes thrown onto a rapidly shrinking
marketplace just for the hell of it – but it nonetheless possessed a
compelling ugliness that was inadvertently avant-garde. The scene was
flooded with 'eight bar' tunes: skeletal instrumentals similar to the
'tracky' aesthetic in minimal techno except that these weren't DJ tools,
they were MC tools, designed to simultaneously enable and test the
rapper. The rhythm switched every eight bars, allowing MCs to take
turns dropping sixteen bars of rhymes using both beat-patterns.
Musical Mobb's gabba-like 'Pulse X' was the original eight-bar classic.
Then came Wiley's endless series of low-key, skeletal instrumentals
themed around ice or snow ('Igloo', 'Frostbite', 'Eskimo', 'Ice Rink').
These asymmetrically structured grooves, with sidewinder B-lines that
'slinky downstairs' (as DJ Paul Kennedy puts it) and glinting melody-
splinters, were peculiar enough to work as stand-alone aesthetic objects.
But most grimestrumentals were strictly functional fare that only came
alive with a great MC riding them.

Like the electro-influenced Dirty South rap it resembled, grime's
sound-palette was cheap and nasty, sourced in the digital synthesizer
timbres of pulp-movie soundtracks, video-game music, and mobile-
phone ringtones. The genre's deliberately clunky and lurching rhythms
represented a pendulum swing away from the lithe, nubile swing of
UK garage to a hypermasculine stiffness. The one thing that survived
from the 2step era was the belief that grime belonged at the top of the
charts. A peculiar byproduct of this blazing ambition was the scene's
craze for DVD releases like *Risky Roadz* and *Lord of the Mic*, which
contained documentary material, shoddily filmed single promos and
live footage. It was as though the scene was DIY-ing the sort of TV
coverage it felt it deserved but wasn't getting. Yet while some leading
MCs got signed to major labels and the scene scored a few hits, the
reality of grime is that it's a micro-culture, oriented around small-run
vinyl-only pressings and CD mix-tapes sold directly to specialist stores.
Just like breakcore, it is an 'engaged' culture with a high ratio of
performers (aspiring MCs, DJs, producers) to punters.

Dubstep, the third offshoot of UK garage, is something like grime's
taciturn elder brother. It carried on the darker, more experimental
side of 2step represented by producers like Groove Chronicles, Dem 2
and Steve Gurley. The dubstep style in its early days was a moody and
minimal garage mutation that dropped the songs and the pop-fizzy

euphoria in favour of . . . empty space. The swing was still there, but everything else was stripped back to concentrate on 2step's tense, textured snares and warm, sinuous bass. Key figures at this emergent point were Horsepower Productions and the Ghost label, founded by ex-Groove Chronicler El-B. As Philip Sherburne noted, there were plenty of parallels between what these early dubsteppers were doing and the microhouse producers – the minimalist aesthetic, the neurotically intricate production full of tiny details – to the point where an alternative moniker to dubstep could be microstep.

Just as microhouse began to sprawl stylistically – 'not just one sound . . . 1,000 micro-trends,' observed Mayer in 2003 – to the point of becoming meaningless as a term, dubstep evolved into a coalition of subgenres: the clinical technoid tracks of Plasticman (a name revealingly close to Richie Hawtin's alter ego), the No U Turn-like caustic bombast of Vex'd, the digital dub of Skream and Kode 9, the jazzy drum-and-bass echoes of Boxcutter. What united them as a genre was that certain DJs played all these flavas in a single set, while most producers had at least one stab at each style. Once again the parallel was with microhouse. Dubstep bore the same relation to the hardcore continuum that microhouse did to the Eurotechno tradition. A consolidation sound rather than a great leap forward, the constituents of dubstep came from different points in the 1989–99 UK lineage: bleep 'n' bass, jungle, techstep, Photek-style neurofunk, speed garage, 2step. These traces worked through their intrinsic sonic effects but also as *signifiers*, tokenings-back addressed to 'those who know'.

You could see microhouse and dubstep as two parallel homeostatic systems, where the music keeps shifting internally but the entity as a whole isn't really moving forward. In microhouse, elements of techno and disco, electro and house, acid and trance, get shuffled; in dubstep, the repertoire mostly consists of the stuff that microhouse would never touch: reggae, jungle, speed garage. The genres are homeostatic systems because it's as though an internal pendulum seems to pull the music back if it goes too far in one direction – a self-correction mechanism motored by the popular demand for variety and by the impulse of producers to do something different (both for creative satisfaction and to make a name for themselves). These internal flavour-shifts are compelling if you're deeply immersed in the scene, but the further out you get from total involvement, the more inconsequential they seem.

With my personal history I really ought to belong to dubstep's prime constituency but I've never quite succumbed to that totally immersed state of involvement. My stumbling block is that for all the reams of discourse that have surrounded dubstep, I've yet to read anyone pinpoint precisely what dubstep's One Big New Idea is. The closest contender is the style known as 'half-step', which for a couple of years back there became oppressively hegemonic to the point where fans started complaining about the overload of torpid tempo tunes with tremolo basslines (the subgenre is also nicknamed 'wobblestep). Pioneered by the crew Digital Mystikz, the half-step style is, as its name suggests, ponderously slow and bass-heavy. An early landmark was 'Bombay Squad' by Loefah, the most talented of the Digital Mystikz trio. The track's groove feels half finished or partially erased: massive echo-laden snare-cracks, a liquid pitter of tablas situated in a corner of the mix, and that's it, apart from the track's sole melodic coloration, the plaintive ululation of a sampled Bollywood diva. Oh, and not forgetting the dark river of sub-bass, which is what really gives the tune any propulsive power, given the weirdly lateral, rim-of-a-crater feel of the drum track.

Dubstep's fetish for 'bass weight' plugs it into the Jamaican sound-system tradition – as with roots 'n' dub, this is music that's only really heard properly through a massive sound system (or in dubstep's case, at temples of booms like FWD and Digital Mystikz's own club DMZ). At its least, the rolling rootical B-lines and clanking skank drums make dubstep merely a marginal update of On U Sound and digidub, that despiritualized British version of reggae that amplified the head-fuck element of FX and sub-bass while stripping out the songs and the vocal yearning. There are also parallels with (and in some cases direct influences from) the German style of dub-house pioneered by Basic Channel and artists like Pole.

Apart from its somewhat fatigued theology of bass, the other defining aspect of dubstep is its self-mythos as a London sound. Where grime defines itself as an East London thing, dubstep presents itself as a product of its South London environment – specifically that dowdy interzone stretching from Brixton (where the Victoria Line halts) down to Croydon on the edge of the Greater London area. In the early days of dubstep, activity was clustered around the Croydon record shop Big Apple, which in time-honoured hardcore tradition was also a record label that put out tracks by local boys Skream and Benga. Like the E3, E15 et al postcodes that spawned grime, this area of South London is only reachable by car, bus or the old Victorian railway system, which has slowed gentrification and meant that the area remains an internal suburb secreted within the city, lacking the leafy semi-rural attractiveness of classic suburbia but equally devoid of the glamour and excitement of central London.

That area of South London is where I lived when I first moved to the city after university, places like West Norwood and Streatham. So when I heard early dubstep tunes like Mark One versus Plasticman's 'Hard Graft' and heard the talk of Croydon as the New Detroit, it was easy to project sense memories of that area onto the music – to hear the slabs of dismal sound and the leaden beats as depictions of the psychogeography of shopping schemes and deck-access low-rise housing blocks, concrete walkways and underpasses. Dubstep's emptiness definitely evokes urban desolation rather than pastoral isolation: the music's timbral palette of cement-grey tones and the production's cold, dead echoes conjure the vibe of built-up areas that are normally bustling but are now eerily deserted, creepily quiet.

J. G. Ballard pops up regularly as a reference point in discussions of dubstep, with people comparing that area of South London to the Shepperton/Heathrow interzone of semi-suburbia where *Crash* takes place. Critically acclaimed dubstep producer Burial invited the comparison with his debut album's concept (South London flooded New Orleans-style, due to global warming, a scenario which recalls Ballard's *The Drowned World*) and the way he tests his tracks by driving through South London at night, making sure the tunes have the right atmosphere, 'the distance' he's looking for. Burial localizes his music with titles like 'South London Boroughs' and 'Southern Comfort', whose rippling canopies of amorphous sorrow-sound do for SE19 what Gas's *Konigsforst* did for the woodlands near Cologne. 'Night Bus' alludes to the arduous public transport options available to Londoners who've gone out clubbing but don't have the resources to afford a cab back to Zones 3, 4, 5 or 6, the low-rent areas where they live. A beat-free Gorecki-like waft of mournful strings, the track captures the poignancy of these small hours treks across the slumbering metropolis, the gloom of a bus full of disappointed revellers coming down from the high or entering the sour stage of drunkenness, offset by the majesty and romance of London seen from the top deck, neon twinkling like a recumbent Milky Way.

From tracks like 'Pirates' to the artist alias itself (an almost scholarly allusion to the reggae soundclash and the 'burial tunes' that slay the rival sound system), Burial's album could almost be an audio essay about the London hardcore continuum. Yet in another sense Burial's music, and dubstep in general, could equally be about any city anywhere. The tension and dread, the sensations of grandeur and possibility battling with desolation and entrapment, would be familiar to any metropolis dweller across the globe. Which must surely explain dubstep's success in spreading across the world, helped through blog buzz and uploaded DJ sets. It's managed to proliferate more effectively than grime, which is so bound up with local character (and characters). Grime is about mouthy MCs spitting in thick accents and impenetrable slang; more often than not, their subject matter is parochial business, feuds with other MCs and such like. Instrumental music goes international so much easier. Dubstep has a far better fit than grime with all those old nineties notions of techno as a post-geographical sound, a musical force that is actively deterritorializing and border-crossing.

Grime attempted to turn the Londoncentric hardcore tradition into an authentic UK hip hop, burning up rave's sonic residues as rocket fuel to propel MCs into the starry firmament of global pop. Dubstep seems much more tied to the past. Where grime adapted to the facialized pop culture of rap and R & B, dubstep sticks with the 'faceless techno bollocks' principle. Burial, the artist who has garnered more outside-world attention than anyone else in his scene, is also the most opposed to celebrity: Underground Resistance-style, he refuses to be photographed or reveal his real name. Burial has also made explicit the keep-the-faith conservatism in dubstep through the elegiac tone of his album, which, as Mark Fisher argues, is almost a requiem or funeral eulogy for rave culture. In the song 'Gutted', there's a low-key sample, a faltering but stoic male voice declaring, 'me and him, we're from different, ancient tribes ... now we're both almost extinct ... sometimes ... you gotta stick with the ancient ways ... old school ways.' Kode 9, whose Hyperdub label releases Burial's records, has described dubstep as 'the ghost of jungle', referring to a rhythmic quality of half-step where the low-end reminds you of the half-speed basslines in jungle and your brain supplies the missing hyperspeed breakbeats. But the other sense – dubstep as rave's afterlife, or even a form of mourning without letting go – seems just as applicable.

The ghost of rave stalked UK pop culture in 2006, with the *NME-*

pushed phantasm of 'nu-rave'. The coiners of the term, The Klaxons, covered Kicks Like A Mule's hardcore hit 'The Bouncer', peppered their tunes with rave-alarm siren noises, and talked of their high-energy guitar/bass/drums sound as being an attempt to get 'that early nineties euphoric feeling'. But they quickly disowned nu-rave as a gimmick to get attention, barely more than a joke. Nonetheless, the fact that there was a flurry of indie bands throwing gigs in illegal spaces to audiences waving glow-sticks, while rave-era style enjoyed a vogue in the fashion world, suggests that the *idea* of rave – blurrily grasped, based on pre-teen memories of N-Joi and Altern-8 on *TOTP* – still signified something in the collective unconscious. The last full-blown youth culture *movement* with its own fashion, slang, dance moves, rituals; an eruption of madness on a mass scale ... rave's Dionysian daftness was bound to seem appealing compared with the pall of cool that ruled UK music since at least The Strokes. If nu-rave was a false start, rave's uptake by retro culture at some point in the fairly near future seems inevitable.

Of course, dance culture has been having its own internal revivals since the late nineties (acid has come back so many times now I've lost count). And what happened to electronic dance music in the ten years following *Energy Flash*'s publication – not so much the retro-moves, which were mostly amusing, but the general loss of forward momentum – did cause me quite a bit of dismay and distress. Things were pretty bustling at first, but by circa 2002, it started to feel like things were grinding to a halt. Like any embittered believer, I did a fair amount of lashing out. My attitude was probably similar to people who lived through the sixties adventure and then were disillusioned by what happened in the seventies, the fragmentation and entropy.

Now the dust has settled, I have a more clear-eyed appreciation of things. New musical and subcultural formations can never maintain their momentum indefinitely: at some point they settle into a steady-state pattern. It happened with jazz, with rock, with hip hop, so how could it not happen with techno-rave? This decade's major genres of electronic music – microhouse, dubstep, breakcore – are essentially extensions of the ideas and ideals of the previous decade, the nineties. And there is a certain honour to that – knowing your era, keeping faith with its principles. Given the deadlock and outright retreat that characterizes the rest of pop culture in the noughties – rap stuck in a locked groove of gangsta bling, rock regressing in several backwards directions simultaneously, pop prettily vacant – there are worse things than sticking with and sticking by the decade that represents the last blast of full-tilt futurism in mainstream pop culture. 'We are nineties people' . . . Yeah, I can live with that.

TWENTY-FOUR

FLASHBACKS

A DIALOGUE WITH
THE AUTHOR

Some people call *Energy Flash* **'rockist' – a rock fan's version of techno. You do make loads of parallels with rock history and with specific rock bands. Yet many people involved in club culture think dance music has** *nothing* **to do with rock and they often actively hate guitar music . . .**

Rock was what I grew up with. I bought dance records from almost the git-go – funk and disco were highly esteemed in post-punk culture – but it's fair to say that rock was my primary listening for the dozen years before I got into raving in 1991. So inevitably that's going to inform my take on techno. One reason I made these rock comparisons, though, was as a rhetorical strategy to win people over, to make things understandable to people who know rock history but are pretty unfamiliar with techno. Comparing Joey Beltram to Black Sabbath is a good aural correlate. It transmits an idea of the sound, and the cluster of attitudes associated with heavy-metal parallels a certain hardcore rave mentality. The other thing is that it's always nice to find patterns in your own taste. In '91, when I started going to raves, I found a lot of what I loved about rock music super-intensified in hardcore techno. But it was a new context – different technology, a whole new set of crowd rituals and behaviour – so that made it fresh, 'the rock of the future'.

These rock/rave parallels are objectively real, I think. There is a certain kind of slamming energy, fusing aggression and euphoria, that you get in rock from garage punk through The Stooges to hardcore punk, and it's very similar to what's pulsing inside the more banging kinds of techno. The fact that expressions to do with 'rock' – rocking the crowd, 'let's rock' – occur in rave suggests that the energy-essence is really close. Also, rave and rock are riff-based, whereas house music is more pulse-oriented. The riff is one of those things that critics never write about, but it's central to the power of rock *and* rave. Riffs are hooks that are simultaneously melodic and rhythmic. A riff is a mnemonic motif, but also a rhythmic motive, something that engages your locomotor system, works your body, revs you up.

I totally disagree with the notion of a 'pure' dance culture allegedly uncontaminated by rock attitudes. True, house music in the original American form follows this straight line back to disco. But in the UK, whatever its sonic ancestry from house, rave's *ideological* sources were psychedelia (ideas of the second summer of love, counterculture, an underground of drugged freaks) and punk (do-it-yourself, this brutalist, bring-the-noise aesthetic). So many of the original UK rave participants were punk or post-punk veterans. The same applies to the US rave scene, which is a separate entity from house music over there. I've met loads of Americans who were into industrial music or hardcore punk *immediately* before converting to rave. So there's definitely a migration of attitudes. Then, when rave evolved into IDM, electronic dance culture became the inheritor of rock's seriousness, all those ideas of musical progress and challenging the listener.

The main area of convergence between rock and rave is the opposition between underground versus mainstream. Most dance scenes have an anti-pop sensibility. True, they are populist, but their populism takes the form of tribal unity against what they perceive as a homogeneous and blandly uninvolving corporate pop mainstream. So it's the massive versus mass culture. Tribal initiates are felt to have a more committed, participatory relationship with music than the desultory, passive pop consumer.

What does a concept like 'underground' really mean, though?

In dance, 'underground' doesn't have a political meaning beyond a vague militancy (being a soldier for a certain sound) and an equally vague opposition to all things corporate. The mainstream pop industry is seen as a purveyor of a diluted, compromised version of 'the real thing,' which in its true vital form is music of the streets.

'Underground' doesn't equate particularly with the counterculture or the political left. Like hip hop, rave is a post-socialist culture. Entrepreneurial activity is a medium of expression: throwing warehouse parties and promoting raves, running small labels, DJing, operating specialist retail stores, producers selling their own tracks. All these people want to make money but they want to generate 'cultural capital' too, through doing something cool and edgy. So underground versus mainstream, that is a split within capitalism – it's micro-capitalism versus macro-capitalism. The latter is the enemy not because it's corrupt or interested in profit, but because it's bureaucratic, clueless, slow-moving, it can't respond nimbly to the massive's rapidly evolving taste.

What happened by the mid-nineties was that some micro-capitalist units were getting businesslike and became more like small corporations (Warp, Cream), while elements within the corporate music industry were moving in to co-opt dance culture (big record labels starting boutique labels, licensing big club tracks). The hallmark of the macro-capitalist mindset is the long-term view and trying to achieve economies of scale (the blockbuster mentality). Micro-capitalism is short-term, it's oriented to the quick killing – say, a hot white-label bootleg of an R & B tune with uncleared samples that will net several thousand quid in a few weeks, a record that sells itself through word of mouth. Whereas the macro way is to establish artist careers oriented around albums and marketing campaigns.

Does the opposition 'underground versus pop' really hold? Surely one of the things about rave – especially UK hardcore 1990–2 – is that it's chartpop?

True. And even the stuff that didn't smash into the charts was pretty poptastic. I suppose one of the things that runs through all the stuff I like most in music, it's either art-into-pop or street-into-pop. I don't tend to have that much interest in stuff that stays ghettoized, whether that means totally street/underground, or the art ghetto of ivory-tower experimentalism. Oh, I like some stuff that is stuck in those ghettos, but what's most exciting to me is when art ideas or street ideas invade the mainstream, or at least seem to have this pop potential that suggests they could do that, whether it actually happens or not.

The word 'hardcore' disguises this poppy side to all that UK rave music of the early nineties. Hardcore makes you think of the opposite of softness, of easily consumable music. Hardcore also suggests 'not for the general public', something too raw to be accessible or acceptable to most consumers. Hardcore sounds a bit initiates-only. With hardcore rave, that wasn't the case: this was populist music and incredibly instant in its appeal, to the point of being philistine. The 'hardcore' relates more to the idea of the music getting faster and more intense in parallel with the audience's escalating drug intake.

'Hardcore' as a concept is the intellectual spine of *Energy Flash*. In the first edition of the book it refers not just to breakbeat rave but a continuum of stuff that makes dance-floor crowds go mental,

everything from jack tracks and acid tracks through Todd Terry to
Northern bleep, Belgian techno and gabba. More often than not, these
are tracks that weren't made with artistic intent or any preciousness,
tracks knocked out quickly, sometimes made with mercenary motives,
to fit into the ruling sound that month on the rave floor. Tracks that
pander to the will of the crowd, its hunger for manic drug-noise. And
that cater to the DJs' need for mixable material, a plethora of hot-off-
the-press tracks that sound texturally homogeneous and operate within
the same b.p.m. range. So copyists cloning the reigning sound means
more grist for the DJ mill.

In the ten years since *Energy Flash* first came out, I have tended to
use the term 'hardcore continuum' to refer to a specifically Londoncentric tradition going from breakbeat rave through jungle to speed garage
and grime. This continuum is based around an enduring infrastructure:
pirate radio stations, places like Music House where people get dubplates pressed up, specialist record stores, dingy clubs. And despite all
the mutations in the music, there's a sonic continuum too, the core
musical principles from 1990 to now are the same: beat science seeking
the intersection between 'fucked up' and 'groovy', dark bass pressure,
MCs chatting fast, samples and arrangement ideas inspired by pulp
soundtracks. The b.p.m. have oscillated wildly, particular elements in
the mix wax and wane, but in a larger sense *this is the same music*. You
could even see it as a conservative culture, except that its credo is 'keep
moving forward'.

**Your allegiance to 'hardcore' isn't just sonic, though, it has a class
dimension, right? The bourgeois intellectual, attracted to the lumpen
energy of dance culture. Isn't this a form of slumming?**
A tiny bit maybe. Then again, the whole landscape of popular
culture is criss-crossed by relationships of longing, fantasy, projection.
White people wanting to be more like blacks is the classic one, and the
British wanting to become American is another (and vice versa, sometimes). No one wants to be what, or be where, they are. I think the
essence of pop – maybe of music – is 'be reasonable, demand the
impossible'. So pop culture is full of these strivings to heal the wounds
caused by class and race, doomed fantasy attempts to achieve wholeness.

There's definitely a certain romanticization of the lumpen in my
hardcore obsession, but it's not based in a desire to actually live that
life in all its desperation – more that I'm impressed by the sheer

rapacity of proletarian pleasure-taking. It's like that Pulp lyric in 'Common People', 'they burn so bright and you can only wonder why'. Yet that is chastened by the knowledge that many burn bright, then burn out.

I'd always been suspicious of rock writing that romanticized the noble workers as the salt of the earth. Partly because the music I loved and supported as a critic up to that point had been more art-into-pop than street-into-pop: psychedelia, post-punk, indie rock. What really changed was encountering, in rave, a working-class culture that was avant-garde and bohemian in its excessive hedonism: a psychedelic proletariat. So really I became infatuated with this working-class music only when it crossed into 'my' terrain. It's not like class tourism, taking a trip into some exotic, other place. 'They' had come nearer me. But that happened through rave's own drug-fuelled dynamic rather than conscious attempts to be arty or avant-garde. Suddenly, this music that had seemed a bit lightweight back in 1989, with all those piano-vamping Italo-house tracks, it got 'heavy'. It was like an upsurge of the Dionysian in pop music, and as such on the same wavelength as the late-eighties rock I'd celebrated in *Blissed Out*.

But there was definitely a fascination and a weird sort of admiration for the headstrong pill-popper mentality ... That E-monster vocabulary embedded itself in me. It almost became my own personal 'new lad' cult. Hardcore's way of talking about drugs was way more appealing than all that transcendentalist, techno-pagan prattle you got in other sectors of the rave culture. Hardcore slang, all about rushes and buzzing hard, made it much less lofty. It wasn't about changing the world, like in the more high-minded bohemian scenes, but about altering the energy in a room *right here, right now*. It was juvenile and present tense, a glimpse of how intensely life could be lived that maybe would inspire you in other contexts, but it wasn't too freighted with political or philosophical significance.

This 'slumming' critique ... This idea that I should 'stick to my own kind' goes against the spirit of boundary-crossing, mutagenic energy that is the essence of this music. The energy can't be contained, it will infect people it wasn't intended for. Take jungle in 1994 – I still cannot understand how anybody could hear that music and not respond to it as an energy signal, a *summons*. So rather than 'slumming', I'd represent it in a better light: a refusal of class destiny. But ultimately, it's purely selfish: I just associate better vibes and better nights with the hardcore clubs. Whereas the scenes full of people 'just like me', like those early nineties chill-out parties or the later 'eclectronica'/illbient events ... there's no real spark, no energy in the air. So it's all about the kind of room you want to be in.

You're talking about 'vibe' here – a word that crops up a lot. What do you mean exactly? In what circumstances does 'vibe' emerge?

'Vibe' is one of those vague terms that can mean lots of things. It tends to signify blackness, as in *Vibe* magazine, which is all about 'urban' music – rap and R & B. Vibe got used in UK garage in a similar way, code for black. So when I talk about the vibe disappearing from drum and bass, I'm talking about the blackness going as the ragga samples get phased out, the bass loses its reggae feel and becomes more linear and propulsive, rather than moving around the beat with a syncopated relation to the drums.

More generally, though, vibe at a basic level means a good atmosphere, and more than that a *coherent* atmosphere. Not necessarily rowdy or euphoric, it could be a downtempo, moody atmosphere. But it's about when you enter a club and there's a palpable feeling of energy or emotion that everyone's tuned into and, more than that, everybody is helping to create. That's not necessarily a black thing: it can be any place organized around a monolithic mood-sensation. Gay clubs, especially the more hardcore kind – banging NRG music, boys with their shirts off – are totally vibe-full. You get drug-inflected crowd dynamics in trance clubs, gabba raves, metal gigs – all sorts of subcultures work through vibe. Vibe is about *collective single-mindedness*.

That often entails a degree of homogeneity, as when a dancehall bashment is ninety-eight per cent Jamaican. I attended a conference where an African-American guy in the audience argued that black music scenes got ruined when too many white people started turning up to them, because the bodies of white folk vibrated differently. Everybody laughed, but he kinda meant it. If there is an element of truth there, it's because different ethnic groups or classes have different codes of behaviour and expression, which sets up different rates of energy transmission, thresholds of disinhibition. There's a lot we don't understand about crowd dynamics, pheromones and so forth. For instance, there's been research that suggests that Ecstasy is more toxic at a rave than taken at home. You hardly ever hear of people dying of

E unless it's at a rave. It's not just because it's hotter – these particular experiments controlled the temperature parameter – but because being in a collective environment of hyperactivity and overstimulated nervous systems somehow aggravates the drug effects. The stereotyped actions, the repetitive gestures, the frenzied atmosphere, all add up to create a kind of *social toxicity*. Which is the same as *social intoxication* if you think about it – that ancient concept of the contact high.

'Vibe' is also related to secret knowledge, being an initiate, the idea that the music is only understood by an exclusive sect. You can see it in those knowing smiles and the electric glances that pass around when a certain drop happens in a track, or a particular sound or riff comes in that creates synergy with the drugs that everyone's on. It's a little initiates-only, but the crucial distinction here is that it's not elitist so much as *tribal*. Subcultures are vibe-tribes, and with tribalism there's always a small 'we' that get it and a larger 'them' who don't. There is a certain tribe-vibe you get when the participants are all committed to the music as a subcultural project and they've made an effort. With outdoor raves, there's the whole element of the physical journey, putting up with a certain degree of discomfort – the lack of proper toilets and other club facilities. There's also the collective buzz of doing something illegal, being a co-conspirator in carving out a little zone of outlaw space in our over-controlled world. But equally the tribal commitment could involve going to a legal club or warehouse that's in a shady part of town, with similarly bare-bones facilities. There's an element of a rave as a collective construction project, people building something temporary but special, an EVENT. Especially at American raves, where the punters are part of the entertainment, part of the decor – what with their spectacularly over-the-top clothes, the 'liquid' dancing and complicated glow-stick-as-majorette's-baton twirling they do.

Homogeneity – whether it's racial as with dancehall, or sexual with gay-club music – facilitates a strong vibe-tribe effect. But mostly it's an elective tribalism, people of all sorts of backgrounds and types coming together and merging around a particular vibe. With real tribes, you're born into them and its world view is the total horizon of reality for you. With elective tribes, it's a role you step into and then step out of when you go back to your 'civilian' existence of work and family. Social homogeneity isn't essential to creating vibe, but musical homogeneity is. Clubs based around eclecticism, it's very hard for them to have a vibe. It takes a really inspired DJ to take a load of disparate styles and thread a vibe through it. Another thing that's key to vibe is a visceral element of people letting loose, that collective thing of releasing the pressure. IDM performances, people standing around and watching a guy whose face is glowing from their open laptop, that's not gonna generate much vibe, and nor are sound-art installations at museums. The word 'curated' – that's the death of vibe right there! That sort of music is better served as home-listening, even as a headphone thing – it's about the individual lost in a sound-world. Vibe is totally about a shared experience, the collectivization of sound sensations. It's no coincidence that vibe-full musics often derive their names from social spaces, like 'house' coming from the Warehouse in Chicago or 'dancehall' coming from the place where people come together to get down.

One of the things that techno people certainly used to talk about a lot was the idea of electronic music as placeless and global. What you're saying about the importance of location goes against that . . .

There's this big tension in dance culture between music as a post-geographical phenomenon, a force of deterritorialization, and on the other hand, the tremendous mystique and mythology to do with specific cities that spawned the sound, like Detroit, or legendary clubs where the music is heard at its utmost. It's like both syndromes are going on simultaneously. The music drifts around the world, as import records or nowadays through the web as MP3s and downloadable DJ sets, and the music also *absorbs* influences from everywhere. Most scenes have some kind of global presence, outposts in the major cities throughout the developed world. Yet equally, these subcultures totally go in for fetishizing origins and roots, they have this intensely territorialized sense of ancestry. They're all about the tribe coming together in a particular temple of sound, a club – Cream, Twilo, AWOL, FWD. You get tracks being made specifically for one club and its sound system, like the tune 'Twilo Thunder'.

The idea of techno as placeless gets overstated, there's that equation of the post-geographical and the utopian – utopia literally meaning 'no place'. The culmination of that line of thought was when the Future Sound of London staged a 'virtual club' through the internet, the idea being that in the future no one would go to clubs, they'd just tune in from across the globe. But the idea didn't catch on because the screen is no substitute for the sensory overload of a club, the physical experience of being a body in a crowd of other bodies all tuned into the same sonic force field. The heat, the *smell* of it.

There's another aspect to this idea of dance music as site-specific and it's that the music is designed for huge sound systems, for the DJ's mix, and most of all for dancing. It's site-specific and rite-specific – the tracks contain behavioural cues, the breakdowns and drops are designed to trigger collective responses. Any given track is a component in a subcultural engine, and in isolation it could easily seem as perplexing and functionless as an engine part separated from the car. There's a certain surreal appeal to having a carburettor lying on your coffee table, but you'd not be getting much use out of that component. The vast majority of dance tracks are functional and context-depend-ent. They're like the soundtrack to a movie.

How does all this relate to the concept of 'scenius' that crops up regularly?

Brian Eno's 'scenius' definitely fits the idea that it's not about a record and a listener in isolation, it's about music that's activated and potentiated when it's part of a subcultural matrix. The main appeal of the scenius-versus-genius dichotomy, though, is that it provides a way of understanding how rave music evolved without the traditional music historian's reflex of fixating on specific individuals who changed the course of the music and precise places and moments where turning points occurred. The development of breakbeat science is a case in point, people will tend to fixate on key DJs like Fabio and Grooverider, producers like Goldie and 4 Hero, the club Rage. But the idea of speeding and chopping up breakbeats occurred independently and simultaneously across the UK and other countries too all through the early nineties. Breakbeat science evolved in tiny increments on a month-by-month basis. It was driven by consumer demand in a sense: the crowd will respond to some micro-innovations as opposed to others, so the music gets pushed along in a certain evolutionary path as much by popular desire as by producer intent. Producers are often DJs or in close contact with the DJs, so they get a sense of what is working on the dance floor. The name DJ will sift through the tracks offered by his stable of producers and only press up as dubplates the ones he knows will work.

Scenius doesn't exactly get rid of auteurism so much as it collectivizes it. Instead of art as this quasi-autonomous realm separate from the social, art that's 'timeless' and 'placeless', this music is 'dated' and 'placed' – but in a good way. Some tracks are only good for a dance-floor season, and only speak to a particular population. Perhaps the most interesting line to follow is the diagonal where there's a tension between the experimental impulses of the auteur-producer and the demands of the dance floor. Labels like Reinforced in jungle or PCP in gabba are particularly compelling to me for the way they walk that line between experimental and populist. Stuff that's either side of the diagonal can be either too homogeneous (pure scenius) or too quirkily non-functional (pure genius).

You're quite dismissive of dance music that isn't functional – that's your bone of contention with IDM, right?

Well I love a lot of purely experimental electronica. But it's the idea that this is more intelligent than pure dance-floor fodder that is annoying. I'm fascinated by the mystery of groove, what makes one set of relations between textured percussion elements so compelling, and another just ordinary; all the ways that a drum track can dovetail with the bass and the other melodic-percussive cogs in a song. Creating something that works on the dance floor is no mean feat – it involves its own kind of intellect. The idea that leaving behind the groove, or complicating it to the point of dysfunction, is smarter than building dance-floor killers is ridiculous. The slippage there is this idea that something that fails to work your body must therefore be cerebral! Actually, making a track that doesn't function probably requires less brain power, because it's easier to break the rules than it is to bend them. You can break the rules of jungle easily, by making a track that's 40 b.p.m. too slow or too fast. But to make a track that brings a new flavour but still works as jungle is quite hard.

The anti-groove thing you get with so much IDM, where they take rhythmic ideas from dance genres but mess them up, is related to another assumption in experimental music generally which is: absence of structure = freedom. Not only is this both pat and old hat, but genuinely startling surprises are relatively scarce in the experimental field. In their own way, all these subgenres of abstract whatnot are quite conventionalized. The innovations become clichés really rapidly, something you saw with the whole post-Oval glitch area. A lot of the signifiers of supposed intelligence or experimentalism are actually conventions constructed at particular moments by labels, fans, artists and critics together. Overall, I think the ratio of maverick inspiration to herd mentality is about the same in dance and non-dance.

Another genre you don't seem to rate that highly is Detroit techno. What gives?

Actually, I have total respect and love for the original music. Well, I can remember being slightly underwhelmed by that first Detroit compilation in 1988, it didn't seem as out-there as the acid-house tracks. But as music, all the original stuff is undeniable. That said, at the time, Detroit seemed more like an adjunct to Chicago house. You only really started to get people going on about Detroit as this lost origin and foundational set of principles that had been betrayed when hardcore took over in 1991–2. It was a reactive and reactionary myth. The rave explosion had really been fuelled by acid house, Todd Terry and Italian piano house. 'Strings Of Life' was a rave anthem, sure, but if there had only ever been Detroit techno ... there'd simply *be* no rave culture. There'd just be this network of small, hipster scenes in various cities around the world. This idea of Detroit as the alpha and omega of electronic dance music seems historically inaccurate because it's not like electronic dance music didn't exist before Juan Atkins and Kevin Saunderson and May started making tracks. They were largely responding to music from Europe. It's more realistic to see Detroit as a crucial node in a network, a way station, somewhere the music stopped for a while before moving on. Detroit's big innovation was stripping out the voices and the song element. That was an important shift.

When those guys decided – quite late in the day, almost a last-minute thing – to settle on the word 'techno' as the name for their music, that in itself was something that set off a lot of reverberations. What do you think of the role of technology in all this music?

It's complicated. Techno and its sister genres identify themselves as machine music, there's a cult of various sound or rhythm-making equipment, bands taking names like 808 State or House of 909 after Roland drum machines. And sonically there's a cult of the machinic, whether it's a mechanistic rhythm feel that isn't swinging but inhumanly regular, or it's square-wave synth-sounds that don't resemble acoustic tonalities, or hard-angled riffs. But the idea that techno music is about cutting-edge technology obscures the fact that the culture is largely based on outmoded machinery and media! Vinyl, by the time rave took off, was already meant to be obsolete. If you think of pirate radio ... the idea of broadcasting through the air, rather than cable, was pretty quaint: it's something that's been around since the early twentieth century. A lot of the most fetishized drum machines and synths weren't the latest gear, they were often outmoded or discontinued models, as with the Roland 303. The latest top-of-the-line equipment is more likely to be in the recording studio used by Beyoncé or some modern rock band than in Jeff Mills's studio. Even MDMA had been around for years. Somehow all these *old things* that had been hanging around for ages came together in this amazing cultural synergy, like the parts of a jigsaw puzzle.

Clearly, though, the idea of new technology, or finding the new thing to do with technology, is at the heart of electronica's self-conception. What happens is that a new piece of technology becomes available, and at first it's so expensive that only established, wealthy musicians and producers have access to it, and they use it to do things that are old-fashioned, in line with the music that made them wealthy in the first place. Then the equipment drops in price dramatically and everybody has access to it, and in those circumstances it tends to be culturally astute non-musician types (some in the Eno mould, others street-smart teenagers) who find all the unexpected applications of the new machinery. You get a bunch of startling innovations, and then things level out again as everyone assimilates the new technology and the old hierarchies of talent over non-musicality reassert themselves again. Being a post-punk veteran I tend to valorize the surge moments when the sharp-witted DIY barbarians seize the new tools or think up new ways of bending existing tools, e.g. hardcore, with the sped-up breakbeats and sine-wave basslines and squeaky voices. I really like those moments when people who break the rules because they don't *know* the rules seize the initiative, and you get all kinds of interestingly wrong-sounding music, improperly integrated fusions. When 'musicality' comes back, as it inevitably does, it's less interesting ... because 'music' has been done really hasn't it? There's an awful lot of good, musical stuff on the planet already!

People often find the 'genre thing' in dance music annoying. Why are there so *many* subgenres? Isn't a lot of it just hair-splitting or hype, generated by journalists and scene boosters?

I've always been slightly amazed by how rock critics get in a lather about dance's genre-mania. Their genre-phobia often presents itself as virtuous scepticism, this 'I'm not easily fooled' immunity to hype. But it's less about not being credulous as it is incredulity – sheer stubborn disbelief that this dance-music thing could be big enough or *deserving* enough to have all these internal divisions. But the electronic dance culture is massive, it involves millions all across the globe, and it's been going on for twenty years at least. Something that big is bound to fragment and many of the fractures are going to be meaningful. Ninety per cent of the genre terms originate from the subcultures themselves. Rather than journalist inventions imposed from above, they're semantic condensations of popular desire. Mostly they arose for practical reasons. In the earliest days, people just talked about 'house'. Then differentiations within house gradually crept in: deep house, hard house, tribal house. At a certain point, the word 'house' alone wasn't useful as an umbrella term for everything. So many records were being made, in different territories, that the stylistic parameters were drifting apart. When DJs or punters went to record stores and asked the salesperson about the new records that had come in, the assistant would ask 'What you looking for?' and as a result a degree of ter-minological precision emerged to characterize these different flavours of house. Some terms would gain currency and spread through the culture, often materializing first in flyers for raves or clubs. Promoters found it expedient to give some indication of the range of sounds you could expect at the event. You want people who are into the sound to come to the club, otherwise it's neither viable nor vibey.

The first major split was between house and techno, the latter indicating a harder, harsher sound, more overtly futuristic and instru-mental rather than songful. Then as the music mutated and splintered further, talking of all these new flavours as subcategories of house or techno made less and less sense. Hence hardcore, jungle, trance, gabba. Usually the split-off was preceded by an intermediary phase – I remember people talking of 'jungle house' or 'jungle techno', 'gabba house'. Then the new genre breaks off as an independent entity.

There is one major downside of the style-fragmentation syndrome in dance music, and this is that it's made clubbing less unpredictable. Since sonic styles are often linked to different groups of people, this increasing genre-precision went hand in hand with social stratification. The original ethos of rave – social mixing, sonic mishmash – has faded, although there have been periodic attempts to resurrect the original notion of 'house' as a more diffuse and catholic category, and also anti-genre revolts into pure eclecticism.

If you're plunging in at the deep end as a dance-music neophyte, the genre-mania can be confusing and off-putting. But the definitions and distinctions get more urgent the more steeped you are in the culture. It's a way of talking about the music, about where it should go next. One of the reasons dance culture keeps generating all these new genre terms is because the participants have this urgent feeling that they're moving into new territory and they want to signpost that. So it's an expression of the culture's neophiliac and future-minded orientation. Rock has loads of subgenres too, but generally speaking hype-energy condenses more around individual buzz-bands or artists. In dance, where auteurism is not such a force, it coheres around new genres or scene formations. The genre is the level at which it makes most sense to talk about the music, its future *and* its past.

What are the specific challenges in writing about dance music?
'Rhythm Is A Mystery', as K-Klass put it. It is hard to write about why one groove or beat is more compelling than another. Even if you get into drummer talk of triplets and so forth, or into programming technicalities, the 'it' – that edge of distinction, of excellence and difference that sets one track or producer apart – just endlessly recedes from your grasp. It's relatively easy to write generalities about 'break-beat science' but almost infinitely harder to convey the signature that makes, say, a Dillinja track instantly recognizable to the trained ear. The same applies to any genre of dance music – it's really hard to explicate precisely what makes a producer superior to another. That said, you could say the same about a songwriter's melodic gift in pop music, or the ineffable quality of a certain guitar player's way with riff or solo. But with these other genres there tend to be more ways you can avoid the music, and talk instead about lyrics, persona, biography. Dance music, by diminishing or stripping away altogether the other elements that you might critically latch onto as a bulwark against the mystical materiality of music, does shove you head first into the realm

of pure sound. Writing about dance music confronts you in a very direct way with the old 'dancing about architecture' futility/absurdity dilemma – because it is so purely musical, functional ... I suspect a lot of the people who might have made good dance critics, who have real taste and knowledge of its history, become DJs instead – because you can actually support the music and evangelize in a very direct way: playing it to people. Why bother to write about it, then? As my old fanzine comrade Paul Oldfield put it, because there's 'the possibility that words might fail interestingly or suggestively.'

Most dance reviews, when you boil them down, all they're saying is 'this is a funky record'. One odd thing about dance journalism as a whole is that it almost never discusses dancing itself – the specific physical responses triggered by whatever genre they're writing about. I do go in for that a bit in *Energy Flash* – discussing how the music demands or enforces certain kinds of movement – but I'd like to have taken it further.

So what would you change about this book, or add to it, if you were doing it again?

I'd have more about the experiential side of clubbing and raving. The structure of a night, the journey you go on. The adventures, the ephemeral encounters, the fleeting perceptions. Scoring drugs, the anticipation and nervousness involved in that. The crowd reactions and the relations between intimate strangers on the floor – those pursed, knowing smiles of people on E. A big part of what dance culture is about as an experience is hard to capture and convey.

In a lot of ways, poetry is more effective. There's a book called *Cyber Positive* by an outfit called o[rphan] d[rift] that contains a lot of prose poetry evocations of the more extreme experiences you can have with techno and drugs. The one good bit in the club-culture Britmovie *Human Traffic* is where the annoying storyline finally reaches the rave floor and the white hole of Ecstatic experience in which narrative incandesces: the voice-over from the lead character Jip intoning about how 'we're thinking clearly yet not thinking at all ... We flow in unison ... I wish this was real ...' Some of the 'talking head' commentaries in Maja Classen's *Feiern: Don't Forget to Go Home*, a documentary about the Berlin techno scene, have this quality, with the interviewees slipping into a phenomenological or spiritual register: 'it was the wordless time ... it was our poem of bliss', 'time feels like a space that's expanding and finally disappearing'. What's great about that documentary is that it sidelines the whole trainspotter side of dance culture in favour of what the music makes possible: certain sorts of spaces and relations, a loss of self that feels like finding your true self, an intense if transitory sensation of contact and communion.

There's a massive contradiction running through *Energy Flash*. As a critical history, it's necessarily 'recollected in tranquility'; there's an impulse to collect and contain, contextualize and interpret. Genre genealogies are traced, auteuristic arcs delineated. Yet the energy centre of the book, what fuels it, is anti-historical and against interpretation. It's my memories, blurred and fragmentary, of this period of my life organized around convulsive bliss. Throughout most of my really intense raving experiences, I never really cared who the DJs were or what the tracks playing were called. I can't name a single DJ that I went to check out in that first year and a half, and although I would really have liked to know what the tracks were on all the pirate tapes I was recording off the radio, I wasn't making any effort to find out. I was just going with the flow of it all. At that time raving was primarily about the experience of going out with my friends as a gang and bonding: you had a rough idea of what the music would be depending on the choice of club, but that was it really. It was only later on that I became a discriminating consumer, started to develop a knowledge of labels and producers.

That seems the next stage in the process for a lot of people, going from being a mad-for-it raver to an informed fan. But initially you're just infatuated with the scene and the weird adventures you're having. It's like a love affair, you fall in love with the culture and also with your crew, but it's a kind of pure, sexless love, like being a child-gang almost. Most of my UK crew were girls, but I was married. It's precisely the asexualizing aspect of Ecstasy that enabled new forms of collectivity to emerge. In a sense E breaks up the couple dyad, while simultaneously making coupling much less of a priority. You're there for the scene.

Talking of rave and gender ... it seems like rave in its purest form was a liberating space for women and they're strongly represented on most dance floors. Yet the ratio of female to male when it comes to DJing or producing the music is poor – significantly worse than rock.

That contradiction is puzzling. Obviously there are a fair number of female DJs, more so than there are producers, but it's a long way from fifty-fifty and, kinda like the corporate world, the top-paid DJs are overwhelmingly male. Yet it's true that rave did free things up for women, the absence of an oppressively predatorial sexual vibe made a big difference. You could see it in the clothes raver girls wore – often there'd be tomboy, techno-warrior, tank-girl-type clothes, or a sort of cybernaut look that's not explicitly sexualized. You'd get quite a lot of short hair, androgynous, sometimes a faintly lesbian-like look. Or that candy-raver, girly-girl look redolent of the C86 look that's been big in indie rock culture since the mid-eighties – cute but innocent, desexualized. But then, gradually, as rave turned into a superclub thing, you started to get a reversion to the pre-rave idea of dancing as display and sexual theatre. And with that came the glammed-up 'club babe' phenomenon, furry bras and lots of exposed tanned skin. You'd get this cheesy imagery on dance-magazine covers and club flyers and worst of all on CD sleeves, especially funky house compilations and all those awful chill-out comps. For some reason these are as likely to be *paintings* of some non-existent perfect glamour babe as they are a photo of a model. Really bad paintings of semi-naked women – that's become a house-music signifier! It's as though Woman became the symbol of Pleasure itself, this state of paradisiacal perfection. Either that, or Woman becomes a symbol of abandon and rapture, at once object of the male gaze and a self-pleasuring subject. You can see it in the way the Chemical Brothers' videos almost all feature an athletic and physically graceful girl as the focal figure.

To auto-critique myself a bit here, in some of the chapters in *Energy Flash* there're places where I focus on a particular girl or pair of girls dancing, making them into emblems of the Dionysian, the ecstasy and surrender that's the essence of the music. It's a slippage that's easy to do, especially as girls often are dressed better, look cooler and dance better than the boys. But there's more than that going on, it's like a slippage between 'Rhythm is a Mystery' and 'Woman as Mystery'. There're various respectable arguments you can make that dance music is innately feminine in its structure, that it avoids the phallic orientation of rock (I'm not sure about that, a lot of rave music is really riffy and aggressively thrusting). But what's interesting, and depressing, is that the feminization aspect to the music and culture co-exists with an indifference verging on aversion to feminism. Instead of sexual politics, you get sexual apolitics.

That brings up the question of what exactly are the politics of Ecstasy + electronic music + dancing?

Rave is weird, because for the most part any political edge it had was largely imposed on it by outside forces, who literally made dancing (in certain contexts) a crime against the state. My general feeling is that whatever ravers' political commitments or lack of them in their outside-world lives, the raving space in itself serves as a haven from the struggles of the real world. There was an element of impudence and insubordination in taking over abandoned buildings or staging unlicensed outdoor events, but with a few exceptions it was non-ideological disobedience, closer to criminality than to anarchism. Through provoking hostile responses from authority, rave got reluctantly politicized to some degree. Just by turning up, the raver was in some senses insisting on the right to peaceful assembly. And by taking illegal drugs, there was an assertion of the right to use one's own body in the pursuit of pleasure in any fashion you wish, so long as it doesn't harm anybody else. Michel Foucault might possibly have regarded these activities as anti-fascist, untheorized strategies of resistance against the police, against medical and psychoanalytical institutions, all these disciplinary regimes that supervise and control the flow of populations and the proper uses of the citizen's body. In fact, Foucault, towards the end of his life, got involved in the American gay disco subculture in San Francisco and had all these hardcore sex-and-drugs experiences. In one interview from that era, he talked about the need to bring drugs 'into culture', arguing that there were good and bad drugs, and the real question was discriminating between them.

The other aspect of rave that is proto-political is its collectivism. In the UK, rave emerged at the end of a period in which the idea of collectivity had undergone a violently imposed erosion. The trade unions (which were incredibly powerful during the seventies such that as a child I knew all the names of the union leaders from TV and they were so famous that TV comedians would do impersonations of them) were pretty much crushed. Thatcher's ideology was that there was no such thing as society, just collections of individuals involved in the exchange of commodities; things like public transport were being systematically run down in favour of private car ownership. So rave was answering social needs, and also spiritual ones, for places where you communed with large numbers of fellow humans. Hence the enduring analogies between rave and church, between rave and the football match. Governments have always had a problem with the people assembling, have always feared the mob and popular disorder. And a rave is like a *constructive riot*.

Constructive, in the sense of being positive energy, yes. But these temples of sound are temporary. They don't leave anything behind. Aren't they just a waste of energy, in the end?

Years ago I ran into the writer Steve Beard at a jungle event. He'd read this early, rabidly enthused and hyper-theoretical piece on rave I'd done for *Artforum*, and his gloss on it was that I was describing 'a sacrificial cult of base materialism'. The terms are from Georges Bataille, who believed there was this innate, aristocratic drive in human beings towards extravagance, a will to expenditure-without-return. In other words, the opposite of the Protestant bourgeois ethics of prudence, thrift, investment for the future. Bataille and others like the Situationists would see this potlatch spirit as anti-capitalist in the sense that the Gift or the totally Gratuitous Act break with relations of exchange. One of the most striking things about rave is how wasteful it is – financially, but also in terms of energy and emotion (all that squandered-in-advance serotonin). The sheer amount of money people waste on getting wasted is staggering – the number of pills and other substances. All those overpriced soft drinks. In rave, there's a literally ecstatic aspect to this expenditure without return. (The word 'spend' incidentally was Victorian slang for having an orgasm, the male ejaculation.) Raving is totally unproductive activity, it's about wasting your time, your energy, your youth – all the things that bourgeois society believes should be productively invested in activities that produce some kind of return: career, family, politics, education, social or charity work . . . That's the glory of rave. It's about orgiastic festivity, splendour for its own sake. Who's to say these fleeting intensities aren't as valid a pursuit as building something that 'lasts'? All things must pass, and you can't take it – your life-force – with you, after all.

In *Energy Flash* I wanted to convey that delirium, but also examine the sociohistorical reasons why a whole culture grew up based *around* delirium. So the book flits back and forth between the historical mode of past tense and the tense present of the drug/music interface. The urge to escape History occurs *within* History, it's conditioned by its context. So there's a split impulse there and it comes back to this contradiction at the heart of the book: I suppose you could say with this chunky tome I'm trying to salvage something from all this wasted energy, my own but also millions of people. *This is what we did with our time; **this** is how we made it Our Time.*

Index